Urban Politics

NEW YORK STYLE

Urban
Politics
NEW
YORK
STYLE

Editors

Jewel Bellush & Dick Netzer

M.E. Sharpe, Inc.
Armonk, N.Y.   London, England

Available in the United Kingdom and Europe from M. E. Sharpe, Publishers,
3 Henrietta Street, London WC2E 8LU.

Library of Congress Cataloging-in-Publication Data

Urban politics, New York style / edited by Jewel Bellush and Dick Netzer.
    p. cm.
   ISBN 0-87332-602-4—ISBN 0-87332-603-2 (pbk.)
    1. New York (N.Y.)—Politics and government—1951–   I. Bellush,
Jewel, 1924– . II. Netzer, Dick, 1928–
JS1228.U73   1990
320.97471—dc20   89-77913
                                                 CIP

Printed in the United States of America

∞

MV   10 9 8 7 6 5 4 3 2 1

To our grandchildren: Noah, Rebecca, David, Daniel, and Max
Enjoy the city!

Contents

Figure and Tables

Acknowledgments

Many people and organizations have given time, money, and their creative energies towards the work involved in producing a book of this genre. Judge Ted Diamond of Magistrates Court, who earlier in his career served as a researcher for the classic *Governing New York* (by Wallace Sayre and Herbert Kaufman), sparked the idea that a book of this kind was needed. We began with a series of seminars with the authors of the various chapters in which Robert F. Wagner, Jr., helped forge the framework for our work. Many officials in public life and the civic community of New York, too long to list, cooperated with us in our research. Drs. Susan Tenenbaum, of Baruch College and Bernard Bellush, through their discussions with one of the editors, proved invaluable critics.

Special bouquets to the Urban Research Center staff at New York University—dedicated and hard-working. Jeannie McCloskey served as coordinator of the project, overseeing the preparation of the chapters, organizing our seminars and skillfully discovering the appropriate institutions for fund-raising. Linda Wheeler Reiss did an exceptional job tracking missing footnotes in between the big task of transcribing materials to disk; she proved to be our key player in insuring that we met our final deadline. Jean Gordon did much of the inputting of the manuscripts, and was very helpful in the final phase of the project. Fellow researchers at the Urban Research Center, two of whom are authors of chapters, provided a daily sounding board for ideas, notably Roy Sparrow, Mitchell Moss (Director of the Center), Joseph Viteritti and David Eichenthal.

We would also like to gratefully acknowledge the financial support of The First Boston Corporation, Morgan Guaranty Trust Company of New York, Dillon, Read & Company, Inc., Ehrlich-Bober & Company, Inc., and Brown & Wood, without whose support this project would never have gotten off the ground.

At M. E. Sharpe, we thank our former editor, Barbara Leffel, whose enthusiasm we appreciated, the present editor, Michael Weber, and the skillful Rebecca Gross.

This book was made possible in part by funds granted by the Charles H. Revson Foundation. The statements made and views expressed, however, are solely the responsibility of the authors.

I

Overview

1

New York Confronts Urban Theory

Jewel Bellush and Dick Netzer

In many respects, New York City is an unnatural wonder, quite unlike any other American city and also unlike megacities in other industrial countries. Its government and politics, its physical attributes—like the celebrated skyline and high population density—and many of its social characteristics—like the extraordinarily high percentage of the city's population that is foreign-born—are different. But New York City at the same time shares with other American cities an array of political and governmental institutions, practices, traditions, and pressures, ranging from the long dominance and then long decline in the role of party organizations in local government to the city's ultimate dependence on outside actors and forces to shape its political destiny.

New York City "Exceptionalism"

Historians and social commentators have written about the notion of "American exceptionalism," the idea that American conditions are so distinctive that the historical experiences of other countries have no relevance to them. Parochial New Yorkers and unfriendly outsiders often feel the same about New York City: it seems so different from other American cities and the American experience in so many ways, particularly in ways significant for government and politics.

First of all, while New York City is smaller geographically than Tokyo and numerous Third-World megacities and not much larger than London and Paris, other factors give it an order of magnitude larger than all other American cities. Its population is larger than that of forty of the fifty states and about two and a half times that of the second- and third-ranking cities. A large population alone makes for differences in political and governmental processes: its disadvantages include the fact that the public organizations are harder to control, and local and individual voices are less easily heard, while its advantages include being able to afford specialization, expertise, and advanced technology.

Second, large size is combined with amazing diversity of population and of economic activities. There are no insignificant sectors or groups: all are numerous enough to attract attention to their needs and demands.[1] Third, all those demands are addressed to a single local government entity, the municipal government itself, rather than to wholly separate city, county, school district, and other local government entities, the typical case in the rest of the United States. Moreover, that single local government unit is responsible for important functions that are handled elsewhere by the state governments, a product of a distinctive political and economic history: New York City, throughout this century, has contained a larger share of statewide population and economic activity than is true of the biggest city of any other state (except Hawaii).

Fourth, government in New York has a tradition of activism. For good or ill, it does things that are not done at all by state or local governments in most other places in this country, or it does things on a grand scale that are peripheral and small-scale elsewhere. Or at least New York City's government did these things before the traumatic fiscal crisis of the 1970s; in those earlier days, New York was sometimes accused of trying to "build socialism in one city," paraphrasing a slogan dating from the early years of the Soviet Union.

The combination of the city's size and complexity, concentration of governmental responsibilities in the municipal government itself, and the activist tradition make for a huge city government apparatus (with more than 300,000 employees) and budget, the fourth largest governmental budget in the United States.[2] A huge, activist government located in the country's media capital naturally gains intense media attention: anything that is colorful in New York City public life is likely to be in the most intense spotlight, however briefly.

Finally, for most of the two hundred years from about 1750 to about 1950, New York was the locus of innovation, not emulation, in so many areas—technological, organizational, social, and cultural—that New Yorkers became highly resistant to learning from other Americans, and their political institutions and processes became parochial in important respects. To study New York City government and politics is to study something that, at first blush, seems sui generis.

"How Many More New Yorks?"

But although New Yorkers may be slow to learn from other Americans, there is much in the New York City experience during the past three decades, since the publication of *Governing New York*, by Wallace Sayre and Herbert Kaufman (New York: Russell Sage, 1960)—the intellectual point of departure for this book—that is relevant for urban government and politics elsewhere. Indeed, the relevance of New York was worrisome to many in the 1970s, in the wake of the fiscal crisis, when a widely asked question was the one in the subheading—how many other cities will go through terrible fiscal crises?[3]

In reality, most of the structures, processes, actors, and pressures that are central to an understanding of New York City government have counterparts in other cities. The subjects of most of the chapters of this book will have a familiar ring outside New York. For example, the decline of party political organizations and the emergence of new institutional arrangements to fill the vacuum occurred at different rates and times in different cities, but are common to the experience of most large, old cities. The themes of "reform," or nonparty, local politics, such as strengthening executive power, changes in the role of legislative bodies as checks on the executive and centers of decision making, bureaucratic reorganizations such as decentralization, and professionalizing municipal personnel, personnel management, and relations, occur again and again in most cities. The impact of the media and of technological change on electoral politics and on how city governments communicate with citizens is an issue everywhere and, indeed, for state and federal, as well as city, governments.

The city government is increasingly buffeted by outside actors and forces— more federal and state requirements and interventions, more powers transferred to "governments outside government" in the form of public authorities, more exposure to the vicissitudes of global economic developments—while increasingly dependent on its own fiscal resources and wits, as federal fiscal assistance recedes and state governments live within self- and voter-imposed fiscal straitjackets. This too is a familiar theme across America in 1990, not only a New York scenario. Many issues may be carried to extremes, or reduced to absurdity, in New York politics, but there are lessons to be learned in those extreme manifestations.

Theories of Urban Politics

Early in this century, scholars began to develop, from their own empirical observations and the work of journalists and other contemporaries, theories about how social and political decisions were made in American cities. By the 1920s, the most eminent of these scholars, mostly sociologists, had propounded what became known as the elitist model of power and influence. The leading figures were Helen Lynd, Robert Lynd, William Lloyd Warner, and Robert Schulze, and the best-known work was Floyd Hunter's, *Community Power Structure* (Chapel Hill: University of North Carolina Press, 1953).

The elitists contend that the city's decision-making process constitutes a hierarchical structure, with a centralized power arrangement based on economic interest. Urban society, they claim, divides itself into distinct social classes with those at the top sharing similar social and political concerns, largely shaped by their economic interests. Major resources are concentrated in this economic elite, enabling it to exercise dominant influence in the governmental process, resulting in policies that benefit it. Party and governmental officials, bureaucrats, and civic leaders, among others, are subordinate to this upper elite. While elites may, at times, reach out for other sectors of society, sensitive to their own interests, they influence, indeed often manipulate, these elements for their own purpose. Some elite theorists, however, do allow for a less monolithic view and have suggested that multiple pyramids of power may also be found in American cities.

By the 1950s, a number of political scientists analyzing the governance of American cities had concluded that the elitist model was, quite simply, inconsistent with the reality that they observed. They proposed an alternative, which has become known as the pluralist model. The leading pluralist writers included Edward Banfield, Nelson Polsby, and Norton Long; the most influential work was Robert Dahl's *Who Governs?* (New Haven, CT: Yale University Press, 1961). Wallace Sayre and Herbert Kaufman's *Governing New York City* is perhaps one of the most powerful statements of the pluralist school of urban politics and government.

Responding to the elitists' analysis, the pluralists reject the predominance of class, arguing that a variety of influences shape individual and group behavior, for example, ethnicity, religion, political ideology, and cultural background, among others. For them, urban America is seen as a complex mosaic of autonomous groups, competing in myriad ways for control of the policy-making process. Elitist theorists, they complain, sought to fit their findings into tight ideological frameworks. In the real world, diverse groups pursue their own goals and purposes, often conflicting with each other and making competing claims on the system. Through a protracted process of bargaining and compromise, public policies evolve with various participants constrained or held in check by other actors, in a "natural" kind of balancing. For example, the business interest is checked by a labor union, the landlords must confront tenants, Catholics face Protestants, and on it goes.

Governed by fair rules (democracy reigns), there is a sensible order and stability to the system that ensures compromise and accommodation among the groups—no one can have it all. While pluralists acknowledge the elitist claim that the active, interested, and affected groups are relatively small in number and often dominate the policy process, these groups generally share power.

Each group specializes in one or a few functional areas, for example, teachers focus on education, hospital administrators on health, and builders on zoning rules. No one group can be said to dominate the whole process.

Multiple centers of decision making comprise the fundamental fabric of the political process. These centers constitute discrete islands of decision making, in which different actors participate and are influenced by different interest groups. Central to their argument is that each consists of a complex of decision-making "islands." From each such island emanates a flow of decisions and actions embodying the stakes and prizes of politics. The flow from any given island is only loosely related to the flow from all the others; all are, by the same token, relatively autonomous. Every island is composed of a cluster of participants especially concerned with the types of decision that issue from it.[4]

While pluralists admit that resources are limited, they are optimistic, claiming that all groups have some resources with which to play the game. Because the political process is open and competitive, Sayre and Kaufman write that "anyone who feels strongly enough about any governmental decision need not feel, or be, entirely alienated." If a group is determined, patient, and works hard, it has a chance to be heard and even win something. Further, the system is structured to provide multiple points of access to groups, ensuring that the game provides for a wide range of opportunities for participation and governmental responsiveness.

Some inhabitants of the city have been slower than others to make use of the weapons the political system places within their grasp, but most—even immigrants from lands with altogether different traditions—have learned quickly, and there are not many who accept passively whatever the system deals out. They have learned that governmental decisions of every kind in the city are responsive to the demands upon the decision centers.[5]

Although pluralism can be described in other ways, Sayre and Kaufman give expression to the central core of ideas concerning group influence and policy formation. Their model can be categorized into three major propositions, which are not entirely consistent with recent New York experience and need modification: (1) the inevitability of group political activation; (2) the decision-making process as providing multiple points of access to groups; and (3) the responsiveness of the city's political system.

Group Activation

Sayre and Kaufman believe in the "inevitability" of group formation whenever individuals come to share certain attitudes and needs. "Anyone who feels strongly enough," the authors suggest, can organize a group and play the city's political game. But group formation is in itself a complex and difficult process. Participation in group politics necessitates overcoming certain obstacles in what has been described as "the prerequisites for participation."[6] Minimally, these include the capacity for organizational behavior, leadership, knowledge, and awareness.

Polsby and others note that pluralists, including Sayre and Kaufman, misread the relative "quiet" inside the growing black and Latino communities and the lack of group formation, as a sign of satisfaction with the system.[7] The lack of minority mobilization of group activity, they concluded, was evidence that the system was operating effectively. Within a few years of publication of their book, however, the agitation generated by the civil rights revolution, the student protests on campus, the peace demonstrations and widespread community turmoil challenged this basic proposition of the pluralist model.

Points of Access

Admittedly, the playing field is an extensive one for group participants since the multiple cracks in the system provide for large numbers of actors whom activists can contact: a host of elected officials and an abundance of bureaucrats. However, pluralists imply that these public players operate as neutral performers, serving as impartial arbiters in response to group conflicts. But there are no neutral players in the political process—officials, whether elected or appointed, have their own ideological outlooks and political affiliations and are affected by a myriad of factors that influence their response to different group pressures, identifying with some and unfriendly to others. Along these lines, Clarence Stone pointedly observes that "a city's governmental machinery may be influenced to operate *consistently* in favor of some interests at the expense of others—even if the other interests are a sizable and active political force."[8] This will be illustrated at various points in the book; for example, as city administrations changed, different groups won access to the major and his top aides.

There is an important academic criticism of the pluralist approach that is relevant at this point. Sayre and Kaufman, like other pluralist writers, looked at actual decisions that had been made and found that they had been made in open and accessible ways. Bachrach and Baratz pointed out in 1962 that the openness of the process often did not extend to the formation of the decision-making agenda: politicians and agency heads could choose not to address some issues at all and effectively narrow participation, while being very open in their handling of the smaller number of decisions that were on the public agenda.[9]

Pluralism as Fluid and Accommodating

Pluralists perceive influence as dispersed, noncumulative, and highly specialized. Different groups win and lose in a system that is active and changing.[10] The evidence in this book reveals that neither this fluid interpretation nor the view of the elitists of a single dominant interest in control holds. Distinct sets of players come together to shape public policy. Public officials are by no means neutral bystanders or servants of outside interest groups. During the antipoverty politics of the 1960s, a patron-client relationship emerged as dominant; during the fiscal crisis in the mid-seventies, the governor, key city bankers, and a coalition of public service unions shaped key decisions; and in the 1980s, Manhattan developers, with support from the city's chief executive, literally etched a new skyline for the borough. In each of these situations, there were winners and losers from the decisions who were out of the action, unable to affect the results. Policy was evolved and power exercised within a particular, structured set of relationships, with significant interest groups having little or no impact.

A final aspect of the pluralist model to which we take exception is the optimistic anticipation that the process is one of accommodation, marked by a bargaining and negotiating style. Essentially, pluralism is a calmly played, tame game. The turmoil during the 1960s, particularly the interracial tensions that surfaced, proved the inadequacy of the pluralist political style. Indeed, the full impact of the conflicts and the anger those tensions engendered are still apparent in the city, making the pluralist accommodating, give-and-take ambience one that is seldom encountered in some policy areas. Group hostility and distrust are still with us. Conceivably, increased formal participation in political life by blacks and Latinos, especially in the highly symbolic form of becoming electable candidates for the top offices—like David Dinkins's successful run for the mayoralty in 1989—may give a new lease on life to the accommodating aspects of the pluralist model in time. At least one would hope so.

Officials as Survivors

Most journalists and some scholars subscribe to a theory of urban politics that is, in a sense, consistent with either the elitist or pluralist construct, but has a different focus, the behavior of those who actually wield governmental power, the elected and appointed office holders. In this model, officials are motivated almost entirely by the desire to stay in office and advance, either by election or appointment. That is, officials may have their own beliefs and aspirations for society, but in their public roles they behave in a neutral way, doing what is necessary to survive and advance.

The most abstract of the scholars who propose this model are the "public choice" theorists, mainly economists. Their version is an economic theory of politics, similar to the way economists view the markets for ordinary goods and services provided through the private sector. Under the theory of public choice, each of the participants in the public arena tries to maximize his or her "utility," the gains in terms of net benefits from government actions and policies to that individual, as he or she defines and perceives those benefits—which may be in material terms (like a new road or a job in the public sector or better Medicare coverage) or may be in the form of other kinds of satisfaction (such as pride in redevelopment of the city's waterfront). In deciding how to vote, either in referenda or when choosing officials, citizens seek to maximize their own self-interest—in the sense just described. Politicians seek to get and keep office by maximizing votes. And the managers and public employees who actually deliver services try to behave in ways that maximize their own job security and job satisfaction. In this theory, there is no generalized social good about which interests contend. Instead, the social good emerges from the processes of public choice. If voting and other public sector decision-making mechanisms permit all the self-interested individual preferences to be expressed smoothly and accurately, the outcome is socially optimal.

It is, of course, a caricature to picture voters as utterly self-centered and officials as largely indifferent to the policies they adopt and implement, concerned only with their careers as office holders. Public choice theory says not that officials are uncaring or unprincipled but that, when push comes to shove, political survival will be the most important consideration. The theory clearly is, like many theories, an enormous oversimplification. While there are only a few heroes who "would rather be right than be president," most would rather be right *and* be president; the theory suggests that nearly all politicians would rather be president than be right. Moreover, voting results more often than not, even in referenda, have obscure meaning for the decisions on particular public issues. Candidates take—or fudge—positions on a whole catalog of issues, and referenda results at a single election often are contradictory. Thus, it is often hard to determine what the actual preferences of voters are on issues, and it is impossible for elected officials to be no more than mirrors of those preferences. Similarly, public employees may be very much concerned with survival and promotion, but their everyday actions are also swayed by their individual convictions and the beliefs they share with coworkers, like professional ethics and biases.

But to the extent that survival *is* a primary motivation, the results of politics— the policies that are adopted and how those policies are applied in practice—will be explained in the first instance by what it takes to put together coalitions that win at the polls: raising money from economic interest groups; gaining favorable media attention; attracting campaign workers, endorsements and other forms of support; appealing to ethnic and other group concerns; and mastering the mechanics of the electoral process. Outcomes also will be explained by what happens *within* the bureaucracy: policies that are conducive to internal success will be implemented vigorously, while policies that appear to entail considerable hazards—media criticism, union opposition, heel-dragging by the ordinary public employees doing the work—will be quietly, or even noisily, sabotaged. Thus, policies and practices may be adopted and implemented that conflict sharply with the views of majorities of the population as reflected in polls on single issues: large majorities may support the death penalty in a state that has none or may call for police officers to patrol on foot rather than in cars—without affecting police practices—to note only two conspicuous and frequent cases.

Much that has happened in New York City government since 1960 has been explained on the basis of what it takes to win elections and win the bureaucratic struggles between elections.

In one of the most serious and careful studies along these lines, Professor Martin Shefter (in *Political Crisis/Fiscal Crisis*, New York: Basic Books, 1985) has formulated an account of New York City's political history—and policy outcomes—since the 1850s in which there are long recurring cycles: elected officials seek to win and gain power and stay in power by generous public spending; this is successful at first, but eventually leads to a fiscal crisis. The fiscal crisis makes fiscal rectitude the election-winning platform for a few years, until the memory of the previous crisis has receded (to oversimplify Shefter's treatment). In Shefter's account, the elected officials do not survive the cyclical upheavals, but the policies that do are those that can win elections; neither elitism nor pluralism has much to do with the results, but rather it is the stage of the budgetary extravagance/retrenchment cycle that predicts the election outcome.

Making Simple Theories More Complicated

We think that the bare bones of "public choice" theory tells us little that is illuminating about urban politics and government, and that models of electoral behavior like Shefter's, like the theories of elitism and pluralism, do not do justice to the complex reality that is urban government, New York style. Each of the theories and models has contributed to thinking about urban government and politics, in the form of penetrating concepts and terms that provide short-hand explanations. Readers will find these concepts and terms used time and again in this book. But the models blur at the edges when applied: the theory found in this book is an inelegant amalgam of the several approaches. Some of the elements of our synthesis are these:

Elitism, old and new style

Neither New York City nor the rest of the country ever was a particularly deferential society, in which the political views of people who were eminent by reason of birth or achievement outside politics were treated with respect by ordinary people and voters. Thus, the elitist theory had a ring of implausibility about it from the day it was first propounded. If anything, we have become less deferential. Individuals and organizations that are powerful, respected, or even celebrated in one arena—business, the arts, religion, education, and so on—find it ever more difficult to translate their eminence into decisive influence in politics and government, despite the occasional election of a celebrity from outside the arena of public affairs to high political office.

But the power of money in politics is now so great that there *is* a sense in which the elitist theory holds. In New York City politics, as in some other cities, contributions from people connected with real estate development have constituted a large share of campaign funds. The money may not have been decisive in elections: the candidate of the "moneyed interests" has often lost in watershed elections. However, the money has bought access, and at times the policies congenial to the contributors have prevailed, even when the favored candidate lost. Conceivably, new campaign finance laws effective at the city level in 1989—like the federal laws, they provide public financing to match small contributions and limits on total spending—may reduce the influence of money over time, as they are intended.

In the nineteenth century, when elites did have considerable political influence in cities, the rise of strong party organizations made this influence tolerable in our democracy. The elites had to come to terms with the claims of ordinary people that were channeled through party machines. The parties were the face of pluralism. However, the parties are a shadow of their former selves. They have been replaced by other types of groups and interests, but their role in the electoral process has been replaced by money and the media, which can be seen as forms of elite dominance.

New influences and constraints

The idea of pluralism usually has a positive connotation—groups emerge and gain access in order to present their claims on the city government for services and facilities, protection, and simple recognition and status. If pluralism is redefined to comprehend not only groups and interests within the political entity—the city itself—but also all the forces that constrain as well as positively influence urban government decision making, then the theory includes the roles of the federal government, the state government, and the public authorities—in New York, often arms of the state government—and even extends to the constraints and influences of the world economy. While American cities have never been autonomous, New York City in the past had a good deal of freedom of action, which has been reduced by its much greater dependence on state and federal funds, by an increased array of state and federal controls on how the city uses its own money, by the transfer of functions to the public authorities, and by the vulnerability to external economic forces.

"Street-fighting pluralism" and populism

Theodore Lowi, writing late in the 1960s, held that the pluralism celebrated by the theorists had to produce results that were inimical to effective and truly representative government: as the 1960s were unfolding, pluralism seemed to be making it impossible for government to plan and manage, while giving power and authority to private groups without any real legitimating processes.[11] Douglas Yates wrote about the urban politics of the late 1960s and early 1970s as "street-fighting pluralism," with bitter contention, violent language, and sometimes even violent acts as neighborhoods and groups competed for pieces of an expanding pie of public sector goodies—grants, jobs, and services.[12] This pluralism was very different from the accommodating mode about which Sayre and Kaufman wrote. Yates correctly forecast in 1979 that this type of conflict would subside in an era of fiscal scarcity, in which there were few incremental goodies to be distributed. However, street-fighting pluralism seems to have been succeeded by a new political disease, the virulent form of populism known as single-issue politics. The disease infects both national and local politics.

Single-issue politics refers to the mobilization of angry citizens around an issue that becomes so emotionally charged that those mobilized treat that one issue as a litmus test for elected officials: "We will vote for you *only* if you agree with us on this issue: it is immaterial that we agree (or disagree) with you on a hundred or thousand other issues." Across the nation during the past twenty years, such emotive questions as abortion, gun controls, prayer in schools, the flag, and questions with heavy racial connotations—like school busing—have become the single issues on which political careers were made or broken. In New York City, the first notable such issue in modern times was the Forest Hills housing controversy around 1970, centering on a proposal to build a public housing project that almost certainly would be occupied largely by low-income blacks on the edge of an upper-middle class white community. For the white organizers of the protesters and the protesters themselves, that became the litmus-test single issue.[13]

To some extent, the focus on symbolic single issues was a natural response to the change in the economic context and the swing from the optimism of the 1960s to the pessimism of the late 1970s and 1980s, nationally as well as in New York. It became more difficult for politicians to win support by responding favorably to claims for additional funding. Most of the symbolic issues have no price tags attached—either not at all, as in the case of veneration of the flag, or not in the form of explicit appropriations of public funds.

However, the single-issue crusades in New York City after the fiscal crisis often involved questions that, unlike those involving race and belief, are usually—in New York and elsewhere—the stuff of ordinary political compromise and trade-offs, rather than fights to the political death—such as environmental, transportation, and taxation questions. For example, during much of the 1980s, extending into the 1989 elections, the city's plan to cope with the impending loss of its last landfill site for disposal of solid waste by building waste-to-energy incinerators became such a litmus-test issue: for many, how a candidate voted on the plan became the sole relevant question.[14] In the mid-1980s, the existence of long lines of vehicles waiting to pay tolls on the Staten Island approach to the Verrazano-Narrows Bridge and a proposal to eliminate the lines by changing the toll collection method (at a very high cost in lost toll revenue) became the single life-or-death issue in Staten Island politics.[15] In the late 1970s, a threatened reform in property taxation, required by court rulings, that would make taxes more uniform generated considerable hysteria in working-class homeowner neighborhoods in Brooklyn and Queens. These homeowners feared substantial increases in their tax liabilities. Several members of the state legislature from those districts encouraged the anxiety, sensing that this would become the single issue that could guarantee their reelection for life, in seats that had been marginal.[16]

It is not clear just why questions that are, on the face of things, not especially emotionally charged should have been transformed into no-compromise, no-quarter-given contests during the 1970s and 1980s, especially in New York, where the use of the referendum to decide public issues is very limited. Whatever the reason, New York politicians in the 1980s often seemed to cower in the face of single-issue populism. There always have been circumstances in which politicians followed, rather than led, their constituents, but it is difficult to think of many significant political decisions that were made in the 1980s that were not on the side of what was immediately popular.[17]

The politics of limits and scarcity

It may be that, as Douglas Yates suggests (see above), there is no one right model for analyzing urban politics. Instead, there are several models, each appropriate at different stages of long cycles in local economic and fiscal conditions and the national political environment. The Sayre and Kaufman model of a fluid, accommodating pluralism with virtually all groups receiving some rewards describes urban politics when the resources available to city government are expanding gradually and are expected to continue expanding at a reasonably steady rate. That was the situation in New York City from the bottom of the Great Depression in 1933 until the mid-1960s.

In the mid-1960s, the rewards at the disposal of urban governments abruptly increased sharply and seemed likely to continue to do so. Meanwhile, national politics became very confrontational, first in the civil rights revolution and then over the war in Vietnam. So, pluralism became less accommodating and the "street-fighting" mode emerged. In the fiscal crisis of 1975, pluralism of any type proved unworkable, and the decision making was done by a new cluster of power, in effect a new grouping of elites. The street-fighting ended because there were no spoils over which to contend, but the new power wielders found their decision-making authority bounded in particular cases by single-issue populism.

As of 1990, it is unclear whether there really are cyclical patterns and cyclically appropriate models, rather than irreversible changes in both real-world circumstances and the models that depict, in simplified form, those circumstances. If New Yorkers and their counterparts in other large American cities see scarcity and limits as a more or less permanent condition, then the pluralism models, with or without street-fighting, may not be relevant for a long time to come. Instead, urban politics may turn, as the 1989 city elections did in New York, on national ''social'' issues, like crime and drugs, and on which politicians engender the least personal hostility among the diverse parts of the electorate. On the other hand, if there is a new wave of liberalism nationally, as historian Arthur Schlesinger predicts will come in the 1990s, a variant of the pluralism model will come into its own, as the appropriate way of looking at urban politics.

Mayoral leadership styles

The mayor of New York has so much power and is so central a figure in the everyday life of the city in this media age, that his or her[18] leadership style is an independent factor in the way the city is governed and how city politics are played out. Mayors can and do shape, to some extent, the ways in which groups compete and they can affect, at the margin, the nature of the clusters of power that are, for a time, the real decision makers.

It was not just the conditions of the times, but also Mayor Wagner's personal style, that made New York politics inclusionary and accommodating in his day. John Lindsay's style—charismatic and dramatic, with the theme of the drama a familiar one in democracies, the leader of aristocratic background reaching out to the downtrodden for his constituency—had to result in the contentious exclusion of some groups, notably white middle-class ethnics, as the price for the inclusion of blacks and Latinos. But, for the most part, Lindsay retained, because of his background and manner as well as his policies, the allegiance of the establishment of business interests and civic reformers. Ed Koch had no such natural constituency and could gain the support of that establishment only over time, on the basis of policies that went further in those directions (favoring economic development and strong management) than his predecessors adopted. Koch was quick to use his personality—his quick tongue, short temper and blunt manner—to develop a strong appeal to the white middle class and Latinos who vote. But those traits also made him enemies quickly, notably in the black population.

Race and politics in New York

When Sayre and Kaufman wrote in 1960, race was not a central focal point for New York politics. Indeed, it seemed to many observers that blacks and Puerto Ricans—there were few Latinos in New York who were not Puerto Rican—were just other ethnic groups, like white ethnics, in political, economic, and social terms, with rather more severe obstacles to their progress due to racial prejudice and barriers. As a major study concluded in 1959:

> In historical perspective, the Negroes and Puerto Ricans in the New York Metropolitan Region do not present the radically new problem they seem to pose in the columns of the daily newspaper. Rather, their adjustment, difficult as it is, is but the most recent of a long series. . . . These newest arrivals have thus . . . assumed the role formerly played by European immigrants.[19]

This may well be true in economic terms, allowing for the fact that it took some of the most prominent white ethnic groups several generations to work their way to middle-class prosperity. In important ways, the city government and the city as a society continue to function as a social mobility machine, providing avenues for advancement—if not for the immigrants themselves, then for their children and grandchildren—for most of those who arrive here at the bottom of the social and economic heap. In the prosperous periods of the 1960s and 1980s, the private sector of the city economy provided more and better jobs for blacks and Latinos, substantial numbers of those jobs with decent status, pay, and chances for advancement. The public sector did much better in this respect, in terms of both the relative numbers of jobs held by minority people and the status of those jobs. The City University, which had been a main component of the social mobility machine by opening higher education to the children of immigrants in an age when, nationally, only a small fraction of the college-age population went to college, has been a much larger institution since the 1960s, reaching large fractions of the city's black and Latino high school graduates.

The social mobility machine has worked unevenly and imperfectly, with thousands left behind. But thousands have moved upward on the social and economic ladder. The pluralist writers of the 1960 vintage would have predicted that this upward mobility would be accompanied by changes in political behavior and identification and a blurring of the sharp lines between the minorities and the white majority, much in the way many Italian-Americans have become conservative Republicans who have little hesitation in voting for noncountrymen, even when there is an Italian-American candidate. No doubt, there has been some movement along these lines among middle-class blacks and Latinos. But race is even more sharp a dividing line in New York politics today than it was in the early 1960s, and blacks and Latinos are not—and do not see themselves as—just another group of immigrant newcomers. Nor are they seen that way by whites. The alleged favoritism toward blacks, as Lindsay's reaching out to them was seen by many whites, and Koch's seeming indifference to blacks in his years as mayor, have accentuated race as a divider, and made bargaining, coalitions, and accommodation more difficult. Whether this is a permanent condition is not clear. As the minorities become voting majorities and win the top offices, political behavior may alter substantially in the direction of the accommodating mode.[20] The victory of David Dinkins in the 1989 Democratic mayoral primary, in which he won not only nearly all the black votes cast, but a majority of the

Latino vote—for the first time for a black candidate for citywide office in New York—and nearly 30 percent of the white vote is a hopeful sign.

How to Study Cities, Including New York

The eclectic, even disorganized, theoretical edifice for the analysis of urban politics, New York style, just outlined was not the starting point of this book. Instead, this theory seems consistent with the findings of the authors of the chapters. There was no common ideological or theoretical point of departure for the studies. The authors employed three conventional methods in their review of political developments in New York since 1960—historical, comparative, and analytical. Usually, the reader will find a mix of these methods within a single chapter.

Historical

The coverage here spans some thirty years, dating from Sayre and Kaufman's book, which effectively ended with the 1950s. In that long period, there were dramatic changes in politics, and even more, in the external conditions that shape government and politics, such as:

- the transformation of the city's economy, including the very rapid shift from manufacturing to advanced services, especially finance, internationalization, and the swings from boom to bust to boom;
- demographic changes, notably, the sharp increase in the proportion of the population that is black, Latino and Asian, many of them recent migrants from abroad, making the city's population as foreign-born as ever in its history;
- changes in the political climate that reflected both the city's own economic and social changes, such as the swing from the optimism of the 1960s to a more pessimistic outlook during and subsequent to the fiscal crisis in 1975, and national political changes, such as the conservatism of the 1980s; and
- a communication revolution that changed the dominant source of information on government and politics, from newspapers to television, and also revolutionized the technology of political campaigns.

Virtually all the chapters incorporate the consequences of these major historic changes into the analysis, but some review the changes themselves at greater length. Dick Netzer's chapter deals explicitly with the changing city economy, how those changes influenced the political climate, and the trauma of the 1975 fiscal crisis. Shirley Jenkins shows how the ethnic factor has been indigenous to New York, as the major port of entry to the country, requiring the political system and governmental process to respond to each wave of newcomers.

Charles Hamilton looks back to a Harlem political sage, J. Raymond Jones, who urged his constituents to become activists in the city's political life as the key to developing their own power base. Against this backdrop, Hamilton concludes that President Lyndon Johnson's strategy in the war on poverty in the 1960s did not incorporate Jones's advice and thus left blacks in their traditional patron-client relationship. Edwin Diamond contends that, over the last thirty years, the media have not been independent voices that challenged and criticized the political side of life in New York, but rather uncritical reflecting mirrors, dealing with the same issues in the same ways, in particular the pathology of crime, crisis, and corruption. Richard C. Wade traces the history of the political parties and their important role and functions. He shows their steady decline throughout the twentieth century, hastened by events since 1960, and poses critical questions: if there are no party politics, what replaces them and with what consequences?

Comparative

The span of the book's coverage also enables our writers to examine important aspects of the city's decision-making processes through comparing different actors, groups, and other factors, for example:

- the electoral coalitions of the four mayors who held office between 1960 and 1990;
- the different styles of executive leadership of Robert Wagner, John Lindsay, Abraham Beame, and Edward Koch;
- how the swings in political climate impacted city government;
- how different groups of newcomers adjusted to the city and became part of the city's politics—the old Europeans, blacks, Latinos, and Asians; and
- changes in political participation and influence, such as the opening of the political system to the minorities in the early 1960s and the dominance of developers in key decisions by the end of the 1970s.

A comparative analysis of the pluralist and elitist models is used by Jewel Bellush in her overview of the pressure groups that appeared dominant during these past thirty years. She shows that, on one hand, the pluralist model is defective in not allowing for the emergence of "clusters of power," which actually dominated the political scene: first, the groups that constituted the "community revolution" of the 1960s; second, the coalition that emerged during the 1970s fiscal crisis; and third, in the 1980s, the interests in the city's physical development. On the other hand, the elitist model would not have predicted the nonelitist composition of the first two of these clusters of power. Only the third, the extensive Manhattan office development by the city's powerful real estate interests, fits the model. The author shows that while power does congeal and produces winners and losers of the city's prizes, these clusters have limits to their life expectancy. For example, the community revolution, and its opening of the political process to new groups at the bottom, was displaced by the change in climate—from optimism and hope to a more pessimistic, conservative era.

Jenkins underscores the importance of understanding the differences among ethnic groups that have sought the dream of success in New York City: where they come from, their cultural backgrounds, socioeconomic status, and whether their skills match the needs of the city. It is this author's contention that these differences require particular responses from the city government, e.g., Spanish-speaking patients in a hospital emergency room require translators if the medical attendant does not speak their language; in mental health, the availability of therapists and aides conversant with the clients' cultural backgrounds is essential.

Author David R. Eichenthal shows how the changes in ethnic politics impacted on the city's chief executive. In the early 1960s Mayor Robert F. Wagner, Sr., reached out to the city's voters in the New Deal tradition: a broad coalition of different classes, the older ethnic groups, and union people, among others. Sparked by the civil rights revolution and in an effort to broaden his own constituency, Mayor John V. Lindsay reached out to the city's blacks through his strategy to decentralize the schools and involve them in education. This evoked tension and confrontation among other ethnic groups, influencing the 1977 coalition of Mayor Edward I. Koch, in which he presented himself as the candidate responsive to the needs of the city's white, middle-class ethnics.

The decades of the 1960s and 1970s, as reflected in David Rogers's chapter on decentralization, were filled with innovative and exciting experiments in bringing city government closer to its citizens. New forms of citizen participation and involvement in decision making were invented—in the delivery of everyday services, ranging from schools to sanitation, and in the process for approving proposed physical changes in local communities. In comparing the different approaches to improving citizen input and government output (service delivery), Rogers provides both students and scholars with criteria for evaluating new instruments that have been designed to extend the channels for democracy in big cities.

Analytical

Some chapters focus on the New York experience with regard to changes that were common to American cities during the 1960–90 period and analyze the causal factors and the consequences of these changes:

- the steady decline of political parties and the disappearing political machine;
- the increase in state government intervention in city affairs;
- the changing role of the federal government in urban affairs; and
- the interplay of racial and class factors in city politics.

New York has often served as a laboratory for political innovation. Among the reforms discussed and evaluated are:

- political decentralization (of schools);
- administrative decentralization (to community boards);
- enhancement of executive authority;
- public authorities: the government outside government;
- charter reform, especially the enhancement of the city council's authority; and
- bureaucratic reforms, which expand the reach of civil service, aim to improve the budget process, and encourage productivity.

Parties, Wade contends, "once provided continuity between mayoral administrations; they no longer do." While the party system has atrophied, this does not mean the end of politics, but rather the emergence of a new kind of politics. The more independent electorate routinely splits tickets, responds to factional appeals centering on personalities and dispersed neighborhoods, and has only weak affiliations to labor union alliances. This electorate is, on balance, better educated than that of previous generations, but the increased education levels among voters has not prevented declining election turnouts, especially among younger voters, and the voters do not seem better informed than in bygone years. As both Wade and Diamond underscore, television is now the dominant source of political information, and it is not good at delivering complex political messages or encouraging actual participation, whether in elections or anything else.

In desperate need of money, New York and other cities have sought assistance from state and federal coffers, with a concomitant shift of decision-making power, write Gerald Benjamin and H.V. Savitch. The erosion of New York City's once-considerable home rule has not been entirely benign, but it has been persistent, not only in regard to the city's power over education, health, and welfare, but also in many other areas. Resolution of the fiscal crisis exposed, in dramatic ways, how the city literally lost control, during 1975 and 1976, over its decision-making apparatus, explored in the Dick Netzer and Annmarie Hauck Walsh chapters, but touched on throughout the book. The city regained many, but not all, of its powers as it recovered from the crisis.

In 1989, the U.S. Supreme Court decision that the Board of Estimate violated the principle of one-person, one-vote led to a complete revamping of the city's governmental structure. Will the proposed structural changes make a difference as to who wins and who loses in the city political game; and more particularly, will the minority population gain more influence? These questions are addressed by David R. Eichenthal in his chapter on the pre-1990 structure and by Joseph P. Viteritti in his chapter on the new structure.

Eichenthal details the roles of the various elected bodies and officers, some of which—like the Board of Estimate and the borough presidents—are peculiar to New York and have mixed administrative and legislative functions. There were many elected players in the city's affairs, with a fragmentation of responsibility that precluded effective checking and balancing of the mayor's power. The city council in particular—the logical counter-balance to the mayor—has not changed its form for some fifty years during which, the author writes, "no one ever praised it." Yet the new charter places great hopes in the council by eliminating the Board of Estimate and assigning many of its powers to the council. Will this body thus be converted into a more effective one by adding formal responsibilities? Indeed, what part do the formal organization and structure of the city government play in determining its effectiveness and its impact on its citizens' quality of life? Does charter change promise too much, or are we, the editors, unfair in raising the question?

Often neglected in the city's policy-making process are the state representatives from the city to Albany, the state capital. According to Eichenthal and Benjamin, the city delegation plays an important role at the statehouse and city members of the legislature also are important actors in municipal and neighborhood politics and governance. This is especially the case for the substantial group of black and Latino members, who have been effective in pressing the needs of their constituencies through their own caucus in Albany and within the city and the neighborhoods.

Democratic values at times conflict with "good" administrative principles, suggests Blank, thus causing hard-to-resolve conflicts about the management of city government. An obvious example is the principle of good government first adopted in this country a century ago and vigorously advocated by progressive reformers, the selection and promotion of administrative personnel by merit. The marked increase of sensitivity concerning discrimination due to class, race, and ethnicity has created pressure to modify this principle of classical professionalism.

Traditionally, the focus of urban government scholarship has been on structure, process, and problems with little to no attention accorded the emergence of a powerful organizational arrangement that has radically changed the system of city governance in many ways—the public authority, which (in its American form) was born in the New York area in the 1920s. Walsh traces the development of authorities, analyzing the factors causing their extensive increase. Governor Nelson Rockefeller was a prolific creator of new authorities, extending them into wholly new fields, both statewide and within the downstate metropolitan area. But mayors, notably Mayors Lindsay and Koch, also have advocated the use of authorities to help in solving problems they confronted—even, in some cases, where the result was some loss in the mayor's own powers.

Organization of the Book

The book is divided into six sections: I. Overview; II. Governance; III. The Dependent City; IV. Politics; V. Demography as Politics; and VI. Epilogue.

I. Overview

Chapter 2. *"The Economy and the Governing of the City."* Historically, the political decision makers viewed the city's economy as essentially invulnerable; New York's preeminence would continue, whatever else happened, and anyone asserting otherwise was a false Cassandra. The chapter examines not only the economy as such, but also, the perceptions of the economy by the political actors, and how that has changed and affected the outcomes.

II. Governance

Chapter 3. *"Changing Styles and Strategies of the Mayor."* New York is a strong-mayor city and therefore much about the governing of New York is a function of the ways in which the mayor approaches the job and how he or she performs. There have been major differences among the mayors since 1960 in personal style, ideology, outreach, and response to constraints and opportunities.

Chapter 4. *"The Other Elected Officials."* The mayor's dominance makes the share of the power pie that the other elected officials divide a relatively small one, and this has been fragmented between the Board of Estimate and council and between New York's members in the state legislature functioning as policy makers, providers of constituency services, and as movers and shakers in the local party organizations and the members of the council and the borough presidents who aspire to the same roles. (Changes under the newly proposed charter will be considered in Chapter 15.)

Chapter 5. *"Bureaucracy: Power in Details."* Bureaucratic systems constitute one of the most pervasive and persistent elements in the city's decision-making process—often resilient and generally resistant to change. The thrust of reforms for better management, increased productivity, improved personnel, and better budget-making promised an improvement in the delivery of services. The author questions the results.

Chapter 6. "Community Control and Decentralization." During the decade of the 1960s, such terms as "decentralization of power," "community control," and "power to the people," were among the most popular. In its heyday there were fairly radical proposals for decentralizing power linked to extravagant claims for the new approach. The city's schools, neighborhoods, and community boards became channels for various innovative arrangements, which the author cautiously evaluates over the subsequent decades of their implementation.

Chapter 7. "Public Authorities and the Shape of Decision Making." Nominally, public authorities are more important now than in 1960, if one considers the authorities' share of the financial aggregates—MAC's share of the total city debt and the MTA's share of total public capital spending in the city—and the even wider range of functions they perform in economic development, housing, and water and sewer finance. The author analyzes the functions and influence of these authorities and particularly their relationships to the power of city public officials.

III. The Dependent City

Chapter 8. "The State/City Relationship." The state's role in the affairs of the city has grown considerably: it provides a larger share of the city's budget; it performs as direct provider of services that were previously controlled by the city; and it controls and regulates the city government more closely than in most of this century. The play of party politics at the statehouse is detailed both for the legislative arena and the office of the governor.

Chapter 9. "The Federal Impact on City Politics." Since the 1960s, the federal government and the city were allies in the expansion of public services. There were adversarial episodes and some elements of federal control that were resented, but the main role of the federal government was to provide additional money to expand services and introduce new programs. Beginning with the Ronald Reagan presidency, things were quite different, but even so, the federal role continues to be more important than it was in 1960.

IV. Politics

Chapter 10. "The Withering Away of the Party System." By 1960, F. D. Roosevelt, the welfare state, Fiorello LaGuardia and Robert F. Wagner, Sr., among others, had drastically transformed the role of the parties in governing

New York. There has been considerable atrophy since then. The discussion includes whether parties still have a role and what other institutions or mechanisms have emerged to take their place.

Chapter 11. "Clusters of Power: Interest Groups." Both the size and influence of a city like New York spark the participation of a wide variety of contestants for the rewards of political activity. The major economic, social, and political interest groups are identified, as well as the roles they performed and the strategies they pursued.

Chapter 12. "The Media in the Game of Politics." Sayre and Kaufman briefly described the press as contestants in the city's political games and as a channel for other contestants. Television was not the influence it is today. The authors analyze the major changes which have taken place—the decline in city-wide press, the rise in the number of very local, community-oriented newspapers, and the major new thrust of television as the dominant force.

V. Demography as Politics

Chapter 13. "Needed, More Foxes: The Black Experience." The one factor least understood in the Sayre and Kaufman book was race. Within a few years the civil rights revolution was underway and although there was a new challenging role for blacks in city politics, the author contends that a patron-client relationship continued to be maintained. A somewhat different interpretation can be found in Rogers (Chapter 6) and Bellush (Chapter 11).

Chapter 14. "New Immigrants: Ethnic Factors in Governance and Politics." This chapter deals with the white ethnics, the various Latino immigrants, and the Asian newcomers—comparing them to both the older European migration and the black experience. Ethnic politics is viewed as an old phenomenon in city government, affecting the prospects of candidates, the electoral process, and the responsiveness of government to their special needs.

VI. Epilogue

Chapter 15. "The New Charter: Will It Make a Difference?" The Supreme Court declared the Board of Estimate unconstitutional, a violation of the principle of one-person, one-vote. In response, the Charter Commission, appointed by the mayor, quickly set to work preparing a brand new government structure, in a new city charter, which was approved by New York voters in the November 1989 election. The key issue remaining, will the new charter make a difference? Will it make government more effective? Will it increase minority representation in the decision making of city government, as intended and, indeed, required by the Federal Voting Rights Act?

Notes

1. Sometimes, the New York tradition of noisily clamoring for attention can be a mixed blessing for those clamoring. Until a few years ago, most members of New York's large Haitian minority preferred a low profile, to avoid the attentions of the Immigration and Naturalization Service. But, being New Yorkers, some Haitians couldn't resist placarding the subway stations with posters demanding, in French (a language understood by fewer than one in a hundred non-Haitian New Yorkers), an end to the deportations of illegal immigrants, thus calling attention to themselves most dramatically.

2. After the federal government and the state governments of California and New York, comes New York City.

3. The wording of the question is that of Terry Nichols Clark, who wrote a number of papers on the topic, for example, in *New York Affairs* 3:4 (1976). The answer to the question is, not many: there were a number of other large cities in the Northeast and Midwest that had serious fiscal difficulties in the 1970s and early 1980s, but by no means all of them did. The cities that avoided crises did so by cutting back in the face of economic adversity at early stages; the cities that had full-blown crises did not cut back until forced to do so.

4. Herbert Kaufman, *Politics and Policies in State and Local Governments*. Englewood, NJ: Prentice-Hall, 1963, p. 110.

5. Sayre and Kaufman, *Governing New York*. New York: Russell Sage, 1960, p. 721.

6. Jewel Bellush and Murray Hausknecht, *Urban Renewal: People, Politics and Planning*. Garden City, NY: Doubleday Anchor Books, 1967, 278ff.

7. Nelson Polsby, *Community Power and Political Theory*. New Haven, CT: Yale University Press, 1967.

8. Clarence Stone, *Economic Growth and Neighborhood Discontent*. Chapel Hill, NC: University of North Carolina Press, 1976, p. 18.

9. Peter Bachrach and Morton Baratz, "Two Faces of Power," *American Political Science Review* 56 (December 1962).

10. Critics of the pluralists agree that the system tended, at least into the 1960s, to "disperse inequalities," but argued that the mere fact of dispersal does not make a political system either open or democratic. Peter Bachrach, *The Theory of Democratic Elitism*. Boston: Little, Brown, 1967.

11. Theodore Lowi, *The End of Liberalism*. New York: Norton, 1969.

12. See *The Ungovernable City*. Cambridge, MA: The MIT Press, 1977 and "The Mayor's Eight-Ring Circus," *New York Affairs* 5:3 (Spring 1979): 10–28.

13. The protesters won: a small public housing project for the elderly, mostly white, was built instead. The mediator in the controversy was lawyer Mario Cuomo, subsequently Governor of New York. See Mario M. Cuomo, *Forest Hills Diary: The Crisis of Low-Income Housing*. New York: Random House, 1974.

14. The first phase of the plan, providing for the construction of the first plant at the former Brooklyn Navy Yard, had been narrowly approved by the Board of Estimate. In the 1989 elections, at least one environmental group, the New York Sierra Club, conducted a vigorous telephone campaign on behalf of candidates for contested offices who had opposed the plan—even after the plan's approval. For some residents of one of the adjacent neighborhoods, this became the sole factor in the contest for the local city council seat.

15. The Staten Island congressman persuaded his colleagues in Congress to amend the Federal highway-aid law to require the Metropolitan Transportation Authority to collect the toll only in the westbound direction, so that whatever backup there was occurred in Brooklyn, not Staten Island.

16. In 1981, the legislature passed a reform bill, over the governor's veto, that in effect froze the previous practices. The legislators who had made it their single issue won. The irony is that the houses in those neighborhoods were and are considerably over-assessed relative to other small homeowner properties; over the long term, these home-owners probably will pay higher taxes than they would have under the system of uniform assessment proposed by the governor.

17. The Brooklyn Navy Yard incinerator was one of the exceptions—the plan *was* enacted; another example is the vetoes by Governors Carey and Cuomo of bills reinstitut-ing the death penalty.

18. There have been no women mayors as yet, although there was a woman—Carol Bellamy—next in the line of succession, as city council president, between 1978 and 1985.

19. Oscar Handlin, *The Newcomers*. Cambridge, MA: Harvard University Press, 1959, p. 118.

20. Because of the very high rates of Asian and non-Puerto Rican Latino immigration, it is unlikely that the traditional minorities, non-Latino blacks and Puerto Ricans, will ever become a majority of voters; whether the traditional minorities gain substantial political power will depend on the political behavior of the "new minorities."

2

The Economy and the Governing of the City

Dick Netzer

The condition of the local economy is among the most important considerations—often *the* most important one—in the minds of the political actors in nearly all American cities today. Elected executives and legislators, appointed agency heads, the varied interest groups ranging from taxpayer associations to unions of municipal workers to supporters of more public spending for particular causes, and the media see the vulnerability of the local economy as a constraint on policy decisions and hoped-for economic development as a priority objective of policy. This is true in New York City, as it is in all regions of the country, for cities of all sizes.

However, economic conditions and trends were barely mentioned in the Sayre and Kaufman book, published in 1960. Sayre and Kaufman did not misrepresent the politics of New York in their day: quite the contrary. They correctly reflected the perceptions of the times. In the late 1950s, there was a real sense among all the important actors in New York politics—inside government and among the outsiders like the media, business and financial leaders, and civic groups—that the New York economy was rich and strong, indeed for all practical purposes invulnerable. To be sure, if there were serious nationwide economic problems—depressions, recessions, inflation—New York City would not escape unscathed. Individual industries and sectors would fail, as well as flourish, as they had over the years—but new activities would develop to replace the old ones, and the city would remain the country's unchallenged economic capital, by a wide margin.

The economic goose not only laid many golden eggs, but seemed to be immortal. There seemed to be no reason to worry whether the economy would be hurt by the kinds of political decisions that had been in the New York tradition since the early part of the nineteenth century: taxes that were far higher than in most other places, regulations that made for high costs of doing business and living in the city, land use controls that foreclosed some types of economic activity, and other manifestations of an activist, at times overbearing, municipal government. New York's economic magnetism was so strong—in the view that overwhelmingly dominated public life—that the higher costs would be ignored by all those enterprises that considered expanding in New York, planned to move from elsewhere, or most importantly, would be born in New York from the fertile brows of local and immigrant innovators.

Moreover, there was a widely held belief, shared by progressive reformers, social democrats, and many in the business community, that activism on the part of the municipal government was good for the economy. This was obviously true in the provision of transportation facilities and other infrastructure that were directly essential to economic growth, but often very expensive in New York conditions—for example, the need to bridge wide rivers. But many also were convinced that the creation of a municipal higher education system open to all bright students without charge, the development of a network of municipal hospitals and clinics, city and state government steps to improve and increase the housing supply, public efforts to provide day care for children, the creation of public markets and other such programmatic efforts undertaken decades before any other American city, were important to New York's economic dynamism—and could be easily afforded.

This is not to say that money issues were absent from New York politics. Controversy about the level and distribution of municipal taxation and spending always has been at the center of political discourse at all levels of government in this country. If anything, such controversy was more intense in New York than elsewhere in bygone years. As Martin Shefter tells us in *Political Crisis/Fiscal Crisis* (New York: Basic Books, 1985), during the century before 1960, New York politics often seemed to center on a conflict between high spenders and fiscal conservatives, with five cycles of extravagance leading to fiscal crises and drastic retrenchment. These controversies were about who paid and who benefited. There were real differences among the political actors about the distribution of costs and benefits, unwillingness on the part of those who were not benefiting to pay taxes for the benefit of others, and eagerness to put off paying for municipal pleasures which led to heavy borrowing and then fiscal crisis. But in those days, few doubted that the economy had the capacity to support whatever level of spending emerged from the political process. Fiscal crises were not a sign of economic weakness, but a method of resolving political conflicts.

The Invincible Economic Machine

The complacency was warranted during the first half of the twentieth century. Despite the spread of the population and industrialization away from the Northeast, New York City's economy appears to have grown moderately as a share of the national economy during the thirty-odd years from the end of World War I in 1918 until the early 1950s, as the 1929–50 data in Table 2.1 and Figure 2.1 show. In the 1920s, office activities grew rapidly in all the big cities; New York

Table 2.1a

Changes in Total Employment, 1929–88, New York
City Compared to the United States
(employment in thousands)

Period	New York City	United States
1929–50	1,130	14,352
1950–60	−54	8,489
1960–69	299	18,607
1969–77	−616	13,804
1977–88	503	28,686
Within 1977–88 period:		
1977–81	166	9,989
1981–85	180	9,854
1985–88	157	8,843

Table 2.1b

Employment in New York City as Percent of the United States, 1929–88

Year	New York City as percent of United States
1929	6.0%
1950	6.5
1960	5.6
1969	4.8
1977	3.5
1981	3.4
1985	3.3
1988	3.2

Sources: Except for 1929, data are from June 1989 tabulations made by the Regional Plan Association for the Metropolitan Transportation Authority. The coverage is comprehensive, and includes the self-employed, as well as wage and salary employment. The 1988 data are preliminary. The 1929 New York City figure is estimated by the author on the basis of data in various volumes of the New York Metropolitan Region Study, published by the Harvard University Press between 1959 and 1961. The 1929 U.S. figure is from U.S. Department of Commerce, Bureau of Economic Analysis, *National Income and Product Accounts for the United States, 1929–82, Statistical Tables* (1982), Tables 6.6A and 6.9A.

was the focus of the boom in the securities and financial markets; New York was the birthplace of a number of new manufacturing industries, notably electronics, while holding onto its dominance of the apparel industry; and the port continued to be, by a wide margin, number one in the country.

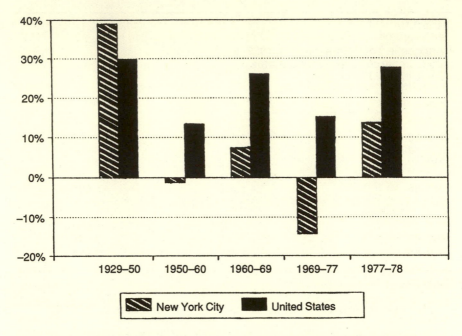

Figure 2.1. **Percent Changes in Employment, New York City and United States**

During the Great Depression of the 1930s, New York City's economy declined in absolute terms, but the decline was far smaller proportionately than in the rest of the country in the first part of Depression, and the recovery in the late 1930s was swifter in New York City.[1] During World War II, the city economy did well in all its traditional activities—from manufacturing uniforms for the armed forces to serving as the main port of trans-Atlantic embarkation for both troops and war materials—and the city fully shared in the immediate postwar boom, which was extended by the Korean War in the 1950–53 period.

The 1950s as a whole were not years of rapid economic growth for the country, and it turns out that they marked the beginning of New York City's relative economic decline. As Table 2.1a shows, total employment in the city changed little during the decade. A pattern that has become familiar emerged: employment in goods-handling activities (manufacturing, wholesale trade, freight transportation) declined as jobs moved out from the city to the surrounding metropolitan region, as well as to other parts of the country and world, while office and service jobs increased, particularly in Manhattan. It was not evident that this was occurring during the decade, still less that this was the start of a new long-term trend, for the economic data were neither complete nor timely—and there were few experts who devoted themselves to tracking the local economy.[2]

So, it was easy to deny that the New York economy was showing signs of vulnerability, even when one's attention was called to some of the signs. Denial, with vigorous condemnation of the messengers bearing bad news, was in fact the usual response. For example, the city government commissioned the U.S. Census Bureau to conduct a special census of the city in 1957, with the expected results a population that was larger than in 1950, to serve as the basis for larger grants of state government fiscal aid that was distributed on a per capita basis.[3] The census reported a small decline in population, rather than the expected increase. The results were denounced by leading figures in the city as inaccurate and unprofessional.[4]

Two years later, in 1959, the first book in what was to be a series of ten volumes of the New York Metropolitan Region Study, conducted for the Regional Plan Association by a Harvard team directed by Raymond Vernon, was published. In *Anatomy of a Metropolis*, Edgar M. Hoover and Vernon analyzed the economic evolution of the New York region and the structure of its economy in the 1950s, as a background for projections in subsequent volumes.[5] Hoover and Vernon developed theories of urban and regional economic development, synthesized from pioneering work done by the handful of economists who had been active in the new field and from their own sharp insights. The intellectual structure that they and their coworkers forged quickly became the definitive point of departure for thinking about the economies of cities. But their thinking had a hostile reaction in the public life of New York City, for they did *not* see the local economy as invincible.

Feet of Clay

In *Anatomy of a Metropolis* and in Vernon's final volume, *Metropolis 1985*,[6] New York is seen as an unparalleled incubator of new economic activities. New products, services, industries, and types of organizations are nurtured in New York (if not actually born in the city) by an environment that offers a host of supporting services; quick responses and flexibility with respect to space, labor supply, internal movement, and contact with markets; and most of all, access to information for decision making. As the economic activity matures and becomes more standardized, it requires more space and needs less in the way of improvisation: the best location is likely to be outside the crowded center of the largest city.[7] Thus, from the time it became the dominant American city around 1825, New York has repeatedly lost important industries or pieces of industries—it's hard to believe, for example, that New York once was the major American center for copper refining—but developed new replacement industries faster than the old ones were lost.

Centers of innovation very likely will be specializing in growing, rather than declining, economic activities, because, while not all new services and products are successful, some are and become the basis for growing firms. New York thus tends to have a very favorable "mix" of activities, which is important because—in one of the generalizations that emerged from the Vernon study—the rate of growth of a city is a product of how favorable to growth its *mix* of industries is, and how large a *share* of each industry that city can capture. And New York, because of its high costs and other disadvantages for mature activities, tends to do badly in retaining its share of any given industry.

The Hoover and Vernon analysis indicates that New York City is likely to do worse in maintaining its shares over time, so unless its mix is spectacularly good, the city economy must decline relative to the rest of the country and world. The inevitability of loss of shares has a simple and obvious explanation: with population increase and technological change, more and more places become feasible sites for producing things that once could be done only in the central parts of the largest cities. So the large old central cities lose shares to their own suburbs, to newer and smaller cities in other regions, and to producers in Third-World countries.

In retrospect, the projections in *Metropolis 1985* for both the city and region seem quite optimistic: both city and region were projected to have more people and economic activity in 1985 than they actually did. But in 1960, the projections for the city were not seen as optimistic at all. The city's population was projected to decline slightly, and employment in the city was projected to be about 12 percent higher than in the mid-1950s, with a substantial decline in manufacturing employment. To true believers in the glorious past and future of the New York economy, a group that included most public figures, these were unacceptable prophecies of doom and gloom.

The Soaring Sixties

The years between 1961 and 1969 were prosperous ones for the country and New York City as well, so the gloomy forecasts seemed irrelevant. Employment in New York City increased from just under 4 million in 1960 to just under 4.3 million in 1969, while nationally employment increased by 26 percent. Although the national growth was more than three times as fast as New York City's, New York's economic performance was impressive, for few of the nation's large cities in the Frostbelt showed any job growth at all. It seemed that, while other old central cities might well be doomed to economic decline, New York was not.

The city government found it increasingly difficult to balance its annual budget in the first half of the 1960s, and there was occasional sharp debate about tax policy measures. But the fiscal difficulties were blamed—correctly, for those years—not on the weakness of the economy but rather on structural, institutional, and political factors, like inadequate state government aid and state constitutional and statutory restrictions on the city's freedom to act. For example, in the economic section of Mayor Robert F. Wagner's *Annual Report for 1962* (the issuance of these annual reports was unique to the Wagner mayoralty), the strength of the city economy is celebrated by pointing out how resistant the city had been to the national recession of 1960–61, as it had been to earlier national recessions after World War II; attention is then focused on how both the economy and the city government are hobbled by state restrictions on the city's power to borrow to finance its public works program.

As Chapter 12, by Edwin Diamond and Piera Paine, on the role of the media, recounts, the stage was set for the 1965 mayoral campaign by a dramatic series in the *New York Herald-Tribune* on "The City in Crisis," which received widespread attention. The series focused on the social problems of the city, and how the city government was failing to deal with them—or even making them worse. John Lindsay campaigned, and won election, as a reformer who would deal with these problems and also with the budgetary difficulties that the city had been finessing over the previous decade. Lindsay promised fiscal rectitude: no more lightly disguised unbalanced operating budgets, a comprehensive reform of the city tax system, a new deal in aid from the state and federal governments, and an honest capital budget for public works.[8] Lindsay's fiscal reform platform was provided by a Temporary Commission on City Finances that had been created by the city council and appointed by Mayor Wagner in 1964; the commission's second interim report, published just after Lindsay's election, included many of the key features of the Lindsay platform.[9]

Thus, the Lindsay administration and the second half of the 1960s began in a setting of widespread alarm about the city's finances. Officials, civic groups, and the media were not concerned (with a very few exceptions—see below) about whether the city economy was strong enough to provide the needed funds or whether the deficiencies in the city's finances undermined the economy. Instead, they were concerned about the city's apparent inability to tap the economy sufficiently to finance growing expenditures and about the expedients that had been developed to circumvent that inability including operating deficits, the exhaustion of reserve funds, and increasing short-term debt. The problem was defined as an inadequate and inequitable revenue structure, combined with poor management practices.

Within a few weeks of taking office, the new mayor announced a "fiscal reorganization" program that would have provided a 20 percent increase in total revenue from city sources, mainly from the approval by the state legislature of a new city personal income tax. The Lindsay tax program received wide support across the political and pressure group spectrum. The tenor of the support is shown in this language from a report to the president of the city council—a newly elected Democrat who might have been expected to score points off the Republican mayor:

> It is apparent that New York City has no choice but to tap its own revenue resources much more heavily than it does now. The services it renders to those who live and work here are extensive and costly. They must be maintained and

improved if the City is to preserve its preeminence and prosperity as a business, financial and cultural center and be a sufficiently attractive place to make millions of people want to continue to live and work here. New York, like all cities, is vulnerable to migration of business if tax costs become excessive. However, there is a far greater danger of people and businesses leaving New York because they do not find essential services and attractive living and working conditions than because of unwillingness to pay the necessary costs.

The report then recognizes the need, and justification, for more federal and state aid, but concludes, "Nevertheless, the immediate problem remains to increase taxes and revenues from its own sources in the best and least harmful way."[10]

The Lindsay tax program was enacted, with some modifications that sharply reduced the net increase in revenues. The immediate "fiscal crisis" of the mid-1960s was over, and the city's operating budget was in overall balance for most of the first Lindsay administration. That balance was achieved despite very rapid increases in city spending: it was the result of the enactment of the Lindsay tax program combined with the buoyancy of the city economy that generated additional revenues from a given tax structure, *plus* something new: large increases in federal and state aid.

Fiscal Aid from Outside

Fiscal relations among the levels of government tend to change in discrete waves. This is especially true of relations between the federal government, on the one hand, and the state and local governments, on the other, but the political and social forces that encourage the federal government to expand or contract its aid to state and local governments also work on state government policies toward their local subdivisions. During the Great Depression of the 1930s, the acceptance by the federal government of a major role in combating the depression and in relieving distress, combined with the collapse of local property tax bases across the nation, led to a massive shift in the relative roles of the levels of government in providing and financing public services. There was substantial new federal help in financing state and local spending for relief to the unemployed and destitute, for highways and other public works, for health services and for housing; also, the federal government had its own programs in these areas. Mirroring the federal initiative, the states substantially increased aid to the localities for schools, welfare, health, and highways.

Prior to the Depression, in 1927, local governments accounted for more than two-thirds of civilian public spending in the United States, with the federal and state levels each responsible for about one-sixth of the total. Aid from the higher levels financed less than 10 percent of local spending, and almost all of it was from the states. By 1940, local governments accounted for only about one-half of total civilian public spending, and about one-third of their spending was financed from federal and state aid. Those relationships changed little during the 1940s and 1950s, despite rapid increases in state and local spending after World War II, and despite considerable political pressure for expansion of the federal role. By the mid-1960s, local governments were still making 45 percent of total civilian public expenditures and financing two-thirds of that amount from their own revenues.[11]

Then there was a new wave of federal expansion in the form of the Great Society programs of the Johnson administration and their expansion in subsequent administrations until the end of the 1970s. Much of the additional federal spending was done through the medium of state and local governments. Meanwhile, the state governments were becoming more active in areas that for them had not been traditional, in particular, in dealing with environmental and urban problems, and they also were responding to widespread hostility to the local property tax by providing greater aid to local governments for traditionally local functions, notably schools. By 1980, local governments made only 36 percent of civilian public expenditure, compared to 45 percent in the mid-1960s; local governments financed from their own funds only 20 percent of civilian public expenditure, compared to 30 percent fifteen years earlier. The peak in federal assistance to state and local governments was reached in 1979. With the advent of the Reagan administration, there was a new wave in intergovernmental fiscal relations, this one a substantial reduction in federal aid to state and local governments. In some important states, the severe recession of the early 1980s, voter-imposed limitations on state taxation, and other factors produced retrenchment at the state level, including reductions in state aid to local governments. During the 1980s, the percentage of total civilian public spending financed from local revenues rose slightly; the striking thing was not the magnitude of the increase, but the fact that there was any increase at all, for the first time in the twentieth century.[12]

For New York City, federal and state aid grew very rapidly in the second half of the 1960s. As Table 2.2 shows, such aid financed 21 percent of the city's operating budget in 1959–60, but 41 percent of a budget that was two and one-half times as large ten years later, in 1969–70. The dollar amount of aid increased fivefold over the decade. In the 1965–70 period, the average annual growth in aid was an astounding 27 percent.

Thus, without crises, the city financed a rapidly expanding budget. The rate of growth over the decade (which was much faster in the second half than it had been in the first), at an annual average of 11.5 percent, was almost four times as great as the increase in consumer prices locally, and far above the 4.4 percent average annual increase in the prices paid for goods and services by U.S. state and local governments in general. The city adopted new programs, greatly expanded old ones, hired more staff, increased staff compensation, and generally acted as if it had no limits.

Table 2.2

Revenues for New York City's Expense Budget in the 1960s

Source of revenue	Percent distribution		Average annual increase, 1959–60 to 1969–70
	1959–60	1969–70	
State and federal aid	21.2%	40.7%	19.0%
All city revenues	78.8	59.3	8.4
Property tax	44.0	28.9	6.9
Other city taxes	25.7	22.9	10.2
User charges	6.2	4.1	6.9
Miscellaneous	3.0	3.4	12.9
All revenue sources	100.0	100.0	11.5

Exhibit:	Price level increases, 1960–70
Consumer prices, U.S.	2.7
Consumer prices, New York area	3.1
Prices paid by state and local governments	4.4

Sources: New York City budget data from Dick Netzer, "The Budget: Trends and Prospects," in Fitch and Walsh, editors, *Agenda for a City: Issues Confronting New York* (Beverly Hills, CA: Sage Publications, 1970), Table 1, p. 652. Consumer price data from *Statistical Abstract of the United States, 1980*. Fixed-weight price index for purchases of goods and services by state and local governments from *National Income and Product Accounts of the United States, 1929–82: Statistical Tables* (1986), Table 7.1.

In a political sense, there really were none. In other American cities, claims and demands for increased public spending have to be addressed to diverse bodies and officials, each usually having some reason to say no, despite the immediate political attractions of saying yes. Outside of New England and some states in the South, schools are operated by independent school districts rather than by the municipal government. There are separate county governments serving most cities. In many cases, special districts provide services that are the responsibility of the city government in New York. And in nearly all cases, the state government's role as a service provider is larger than it is in New York today, and even more, than it was in the 1960s.[13] In New York City, the city government is where one turns for more public spending, and this was even more true in the 1960s.

Moreover, there are not multiple centers of decision making within the municipal government.[14] The mayor is *the* decision maker. This was especially true of budgetary matters in the years between the charter revisions of 1961 and

1975, when there was no practical way for the legislative bodies to overrule the mayor in the process of adopting the annual budget and the mayor had extensive powers to modify the adopted budget on his own during the fiscal year. So, in the 1960s, all pressures for more spending focused on one person, the mayor. Even if the mayor had been ideologically inclined to say no (and neither Robert Wagner nor John Lindsay were conservatives), it would have been hard to do so, unless there were the countervailing pressures of fiscal stringency. By the late 1960s, both the mayor and the groups pressuring him for more spending were fully aware that, one way or another, the money *was* available, for almost any conceivable increase in spending. For the mayor to say no on the grounds that the budget would not permit the spending would have been transparently untruthful, as well as being perceived as hard-hearted.

The growth in spending was fostered not only by the actual flow of aid and tax revenues, but also by the renewed sense of economic invincibility. For example, two politically powerful members of the 1966 Temporary Commission on City Finances dissented from the very first sentence of the commission's critical second interim report (the one that formed the basis of the Lindsay fiscal program), objecting to the use of the term "financial crisis"; they considered that "this characterization belies the City's basic economic strength."[15]

Intimations of Mortality

In retrospect, it is obvious that the environment and the city policies of the late 1960s carried the seeds of fiscal disaster. City spending could not continue to increase indefinitely at such rapid rates but, in that climate, it seemed virtually impossible to be frugal in small or large ways: there was no way to get off the up escalator. Moreover, although the fiscal resources were ultimately available in the form of aid and local revenues, the politically easy way to resolve the annual tussles about the budget typically was to resort to a combination of small tax increases and fiscal sleight-of-hand, like using the capital budget, financed by borrowing, to finance various types of operating expenditures.[16] Such practice in the use of this "fiscal gimmickry" came in handy when the economic tide turned, in 1969.

The late 1960s were a period of economic optimism generally. Most economists making long-term projections at that time forecast high rates of national economic growth, and this was true of those making projections for the New York region as well. For example, the Regional Plan Association projected that employment in the region would grow between 1964 and 1985 at more than twice the rate it grew between 1950 and 1964, and only slightly slower than the nation; personal income per capita would continue to be well above the national levels, although the gap would diminish. Office employment would grow especially rapidly, within New York City as well as in the rest of the region, with the office employment growth rate for the city between 1967 and 1985 well above the rate between 1959 and 1967.[17]

A number of forecasters who shared the general optimism nonetheless worried about whether the city economy was not being undermined by the very high levels of city and state taxes: while tax levels had always been well above the national averages in New York, the adverse disparity had grown during the 1960s. State and local taxes in relation to personal income had been about one-tenth above the national average in New York State at the beginning of the decade, but were 25 percent higher by the end of the decade.[18] The trend seemed as important as the actual levels, in particular the sense that there was no resistance to ever-increasing levels of expenditure and taxation.

In *Financing Government in New York City*, the 1966 NYU report to the Temporary Commission on City Finances, there had been considerable emphasis on the need to consider economic competition with other areas in determining both the level and nature of city taxes. One of the staff studies had documented the heavy economic costs of the city sales tax during the decades when the city was surrounded by territory in which there was no sales tax at all.[19] The commission's own reports had echoed that theme, and also stressed the need for expenditure restraint. The commission and its supporting staff were dismissed as Cassandras for these cautionary notes. In fact, the Lindsay administration's tax reforms followed those recommended by the commission in important respects and departed only in matters where the issue was the economic harm that might be done, for example, with regard to the structure of the business taxes the city employed.[20]

By 1969, a number of observers were warning that both the economy and the city's policies were shakier than they seemed. In that election year, the Ford Foundation financed a study of where New York City was and where it should be going, to serve as an analytical tool for a new city administration. In the study, organized by the Institute of Public Administration,[21] most of the authors of chapters dealing with specific functions advanced programs that required large increases in spending, and most were optimistic about the outlook. But the authors whose focus was economic were decidedly guarded.[22] The budget chapter was the gloomiest, suggesting that the city faced a choice between sharp retrenchment in expenditures and huge, economically destructive local tax increases, year after year, with retrenchment the obviously preferable strategy.[23]

The Economic and Fiscal Slide

Even as these warnings were being dismissed, the national and city economies had turned: the long boom of the 1960s ended in 1969. For the country, the end of the decade ushered in a period of alternating recessions and recoveries, with employment and income significantly higher after each full cycle than it had been previously. There were national recessions in 1969–71, 1974–75, 1980, and 1982–84, with recoveries in between. But in New York City, there was a long slide from 1969 to 1977, uninterrupted by any recovery, and then a fairly continuous recovery through the 1970s and 1980s. The employment data in Table 2.1a and 2.1b and Figure 2.1 document these divergent trends over the long term; the year-by-year trends in the 1969–78 period are shown in these employment indexes:

Year (1969=100)	New York City	U.S.
1969	100.0	100.0
1970	98.9	100.3
1971	95.3	100.6
1972	94.0	103.6
1973	93.5	108.2
1974	91.2	110.1
1975	87.7	108.6
1976	86.0	111.6
1977	85.6	115.4
1978	86.5	120.7

For decades before 1969, the New York economy had suffered less severely than the rest of the country from recessions and depressions: why were things reversed after 1969, when the country caught a cold and New York nearly died from pneumonia? In part, the answer is found in the special nature of the 1961–69 boom in New York, which was heavily dependent on expansion in the financial services industries, particularly the securities industry, which doubled its employment in the city during the period as it struggled to keep up with the 1962–69 bull market, a boom in office building construction, high rates of construction of apartment houses until about 1967, and expansion in public-sector employment, especially city government employment.

The first three of these four props for expansion were knocked away by 1970. The securities markets flattened and, as firms and the exchanges installed long-overdue new technology that reduced back-office labor requirements substantially, employment in the industry was reduced by half within a few years. The office building boom ended in the early 1970s with high vacancy rates in new and old office buildings and bankruptcies of developers, as such building booms almost always end. The apartment house construction boom in part had been stimulated by efforts to beat the deadline set in a revised zoning ordinance; its end was guaranteed by the extension of rent regulation in 1969 to new buildings.[24] As the national economic downturn became visible, there were reductions in corporate headquarters staffs and in the demand for a variety of business services that also were felt particularly sharply in New York City.[25]

Meanwhile, the losses in the goods-handling activities, especially manufacturing, that had been going on since the early 1950s accelerated. This was a regional phenomenon, not just one confined to New York City. Throughout the metropolitan areas of the Northeast, jobs in traditional goods-handling activities were disappearing. There were a number of factors that aggravated the long-term trend. By 1972, all the railroads serving the Northeast were in bankruptcy and seriously threatening to discontinue all service.[26] In late 1973, there was the first international oil crisis and a huge increase in oil prices, which had an especially severe impact on the costs of doing business in the Northeast, which was very dependent on imported oil for power generation, as well as in industrial uses. The competitive position of the Northeast was further weakened by fiscal difficulties in a number of cities and states in the early 1970s (well in advance of the 1975 fiscal crisis in New York), often temporarily resolved by large tax increases.

Although the national economy revived in 1972, the Northeast in general and New York City in particular continued to decline. At first, the reaction of public officials and most other observers was that the local recession had to be temporary: it was prolonged despite the national upturn because of the weakness in securities industry employment and in office building construction, and those adverse influences would soon dissipate. The optimism about the basic strength of the New York economy continued into the early 1970s.

This was not mere boosterism, but the predominant view of the experts. For example, a volume completed in early 1972 by Eli Ginzberg and the staff of the Conservation of Human Resources Project at Columbia University virtually ignored the then current recession and minimized most of the deep-seated problems it recognized, focusing on "the feedback mechanisms that have begun to operate—and that we believe will accelerate—that augur well for the city's future."[27] A second 1972 book, prepared by the economics department of the First National City Bank (now Citibank), also ignored the recession and addressed longer-term policies that would help realize the great potentials it saw; the conclusions of a briefer study by the same group published in early 1974 (this study focused on the New York region, rather than the city) are typified by this quotation:

> The region's economy is structurally strong, concentrated in the service and financial job sectors that are expected to continue to expand rapidly on a nationwide basis. Although it was slow to rebound from the national recession of 1969–70, the region's economy can be expected to expand significantly in the 1970s, though not as rapidly as the national economy.[28]

As late as May 1974, when the Port Authority of New York and New Jersey published another of its economists' occasional long-term analyses of the region's future, the current troubles were viewed as reflecting "the depth of the impact of the 1969–70 recession on regional employment," that is, there was not a severe structural New York problem but only "the extended effects" of the 1969–70 recession.[29]

There were dissenters, but they were in the minority. The Maxwell School of Syracuse University conducted a major study of the relation between the economics changes that had been occurring and the city's finances, for a State Study Commission for New York City that had been established by Governor Nelson Rockefeller. The study, completed in April 1973, was not only less optimistic for the long run than other analyses, but also viewed the post-1969 events as important and indicative of a "clear reversal" in the favorable trends of the 1960s.[30] These findings were dismissed not only as unwelcome news, but also as another set of criticisms of the Lindsay administration by a commission that was seen as an instrument of the hostility between the governor and mayor. A December 1973 report by a Twentieth Century Fund task force that expressed great concern about the city's economy, the city government's finances, and the service delivery performance of the city government was treated as irrelevant by the incoming Beame administration.[31]

Squaring the Budget Circles, 1969–74

However unwarranted the prevalent optimism may have been by 1973 and 1974, at the outset of slide in 1969 and 1970 it was reasonable for city officials to act on the assumption that the budgetary problems caused by the recession, in the form of lower revenues than had been expected, would be temporary.[32] In the spring of 1970, when it had become clear that revenues were well below expectations, the decision to resort to short-term borrowing as an expedient solution was plausible. As Table 2.3 shows, there was a large increase in the level of short-term debt outstanding at the end of the 1969–70 fiscal year, and an even larger increase during the 1970–71 fiscal year. In that year, too, the temporizing was plausible: the economic recovery was slow, it was true, but was bound to occur in New York as it had in the nation by the next fiscal year, when some of that added short-term debt could be paid down.

Let us turn to early 1971, with the 1971–72 budget in preparation. Economic recovery is still delayed, and there is a new adverse development: the rapid growth in state aid is about to end. In an early sign of the conservative reaction against the liberalism of the 1960s, the New York State Legislature rejected a large tax increase package proposed by Governor Rockefeller, for the first time since Rockefeller took office in 1959, thus precluding any large increases in state aid.[33] In fact, state aid to New York City—aside from welfare and Medicaid—was virtually unchanged between 1970–71 and 1971–72 and increased only slightly in the following fiscal year. However, the initial political response in the city was, once more, to hope for the best and assume that the governor would return to the fray in the following year and this time prevail; Rockefeller had

Table 2.3

**Annual Changes in New York City Short-term Debt,
End of Fiscal Year, 1960–75**
(in millions of dollars)

June 30	Change from preceding year	Cumulative changes	
		Period	Amount
1961	31		
1962	−3		
1963	157		
1964	85		
1965	183	1960–65	453
1966	−201		
1967	164		
1968	14		
1969	6	1965–69	−16
1970	564		
1971	1,088		
1972	343		
1973	(113)	1969–73	1,881
1974	939		
1975	1,184	1973–75	2,122

Source: Based on data in U.S. Census Bureau, annual report on *City Government Finances*. The census reports incorporate certain authorities with the city government, notably (from the standpoint of short-term debt) the New York City Housing Authority. However, the authorities' short-term debt has not been very volatile on a year-end to year-end basis, so these data do not distort trends in the short-term debt of the city government more narrowly defined, especially during the 1970s. There is a more serious problem, however: census data are based on data given to the census people by city officials. There were a number of serious errors in those reports in the years just before the fiscal crisis, especially in the data for fiscal 1975 (truly reliable city financial data for fiscal 1975 have never been developed). It is clear that the short-term debt figure was one of those in error; most errors were understatements of expenditures and debt.

always prevailed before this. The assumption was that the flow of state aid would increase after a year's pause. More short-term borrowing to cover the operating deficit seemed reasonable.

Nevertheless, by mid-1971, Mayor Lindsay and his aides no longer were confident that procrastination was a sufficient response. The mayor announced a serious retrenchment program that called for actual reductions in staffing—including, if necessary to meet targets for individual agencies, actual layoffs (for the first time since the 1930s), as well as not filling vacant positions. Implementation of the program began that summer. The retrenchment program did not succeed in reducing the size of the city work force, but it did stop the increase. Between October 1965 and October 1970, the number of full-time equivalent city employees, broadly defined, had risen by nearly 90,000, more than 30 percent. Between October 1970 and October 1973, the number remained virtually constant.[34]

Conceivably, the Lindsay administration might have pursued retrenchment so vigorously that the eventual fiscal collapse could have been avoided. However, by the end of 1971, Lindsay decided to run for the 1972 Democratic nomination for president. The political pain of drastic retrenchment is so great that the mayor must be on the job full time (or the cutbacks must be ordered by someone outside the city government, as happened in 1975). Moreover, it was impossible for a mayor running for national office as an advocate for expansive urban policies— Lindsay's posture in the 1972 campaign—to be an advocate of layoffs and cutbacks at home. The retrenchment campaign became a low-key one and was not enough to offset the large increases in spending at constant staffing levels, in the form of increases in compensation of staff and spending for contracted health, social, and other services provided by private (mostly nonprofit) organizations.

The deficit for the 1971–72 fiscal year was a good deal smaller than in the previous year, as the data in Table 2.3 suggest, in part because of the retrenchment and in part because of national economic trends, in particular inflation. In the short run, inflation is a good thing for New York City budget makers. A large part of the city's revenue are very sensitive to price increases, in particular sales and income taxes, and most of its spending responds to inflation only after some lags. In 1972 and 1973, inflation accelerated throughout the nation (in fact, worldwide), and the city's revenues in current dollars climbed considerably, despite the continued weakness of the city's economy.

In the fiscal year 1972–73, the operating budget was in such good shape that short-term debt was reduced. Inflation helped, but another external event helped even more: federal revenue sharing began in that year. The revenue-sharing bill was passed just before the 1972 elections, and Congress directed that the treasury pay an initial eighteen-months' allocation to state and local governments immediately. So New York City, like other governments, received a sudden infusion of new money that was substantial; in subsequent years, the revenue-sharing payments covered only a twelve-month period, and the annual allocations grew little, so that revenue sharing was no longer a source of new funds to meet growing expenditures, after that first installment.

By early 1973, when the 1973–74 budget was being prepared, the Lindsay administration was a lame duck one: Lindsay had announced that he would not seek reelection for a third term. Comptroller Abraham Beame, who had run for mayor back in 1965, became the probable Democratic nominee and next mayor, and dominated the budget-making process in 1973. At Beame's instance, the

Lindsay administration's very generous revenue estimates for fiscal 1974 were further inflated in order to nominally balance the budget, and Beame advanced a complex plan to keep the transit fare from rising, that entailed large amounts of additional short-term borrowing. With the city's economy continuing to slide, virtually no increase in state and federal aid, and substantial increases in city spending, an operating deficit of roughly $1 billion for 1973–74 was the result.

The Beame administration was fully and formally responsible for the budget for 1974–75, having taken office at the beginning of 1974. Federal and state aid did increase in the new fiscal year, but a severe national recession began in 1974 and the city's economic slide worsened. Once again, the "solution" was to grossly exaggerate expected revenues, providing paper balance of the operating budget, but making another huge deficit, this time well over $1 billion, inevitable. In addition, the Beame administration carried the practice, begun years earlier, of using the capital budget—which was intended for land, buildings, and long-lived equipment, financed from bond issues—for current operating expenses to its logical extreme. The great bulk of spending in the 1974–75 capital budget was for operating purposes, with the largest single item what was called "transit fare stabilization," that is, operating subsidies to the Transit Authority financed by bond issues.[35]

The temporizing and myopia of the Lindsay and Beame administrations in the face of what, in retrospect, seems a blindingly obvious need to cut back in the 1970–75 period, were not as irresponsible as hindsight suggests. All those experts were saying that the city economy was basically sound and bound to turn up soon and other experts were saying that rescue *had* to come from greatly increased state and federal aid (as federal revenue sharing did in 1972–73). The city's deputy mayor, one of the ablest of the new breed of public policy analysts and public managers, postulated that it was virtually a natural law that city expenditures increased by 15 percent annually, while revenues from existing taxes and tax rates rose by only 5 percent annually (these were figures for New York, but the notion was said to be true of all large cities). If that was an inevitable condition for America's cities, then state and federal governments surely would have to act to provide the missing annual percentages. In addition, there was real concern about cutting back on city staffing and spending at a time when the private economy was declining. Officials were aware that retrenchment under such conditions would cause distress. There was no explicit policy to increase city spending to combat the decline, but rather a reluctance to make things worse.

That, however, does not explain the most conspicuous element of the 1970–75 rise in city spending, the increase in employee compensation levels at rates far in excess of the increase in the price level. The most impressive increases in both pay and fringes benefits were for the uniformed services, at that time very heavily white ethnic, with very few blacks or Latinos. The racial and other ethnic conflicts of the late 1960s had left a residue of anger and political disaffection among white ethnics in general and the city's uniformed work force in particular. The generous labor settlements were one way of buying off this disaffection and demoralization.[36]

The passivity of the actors who were not city officials, in the face of the deepening troubles, is striking. The city had an ample supply of good-government interest groups, some of which paid special attention to fiscal matters (see Chapter 11, by Jewel Bellush, "Clusters of Power: Interest Groups"), but their responses to the economic and fiscal slide of the first half of the 1970s ranged from the muted to the irrelevant. New York's business leadership never has been united, but is very much divided along sectoral and professional lines (real estate, commercial banks, securities firms, insurance companies, major law firms, publishing, and so on), so it was too much to expect concerted intervention by business leaders. The fact is that business leaders seemed no more aware of the depth of the economic and fiscal problems than anyone else, until 1974.[37] As Edwin Diamond and Piera Paine document in Chapter 12, "The Media in the Game of Politics," the media were slow to awaken. In 1974, after Beame took office, editorials in the *Times* began to show real concern, but less alarm than the facts in the front-page and Metropolitan Section stories by *Times* reporters warranted.

The state government in effect washed its hands of the city, by granting to the city virtually any powers that the city government requested. This largesse was in part a substitute for providing more aid from higher state taxes or from funds diverted from other state spending, including aid to suburban local governments. But the main reason for the hands-off posture of state-level political leaders was the avoidance of the obvious hazards of almost any state intervention. The only state government action that contributed to the solution rather than the problem was a freezing of the provisions of state and local employee retirement systems in 1973, preventing any further liberalization and permitting cutbacks for new employees, if those could be negotiated with the unions.

The Bubble Bursts

The dramatic events of the year or so beginning in the fall of 1974—the fisca crisis itself—have been the subject of numerous accounts, and most of the facts are recounted in other chapters of this book, from a variety of standpoints: how the crisis affected and was affected by the different clusters of power, the roles of the elected officials, the part played by the state, and the federal role in the crisis. The details need not be spelled out again in this chapter. What does need emphasis are the ways in which the different participants in the city's governing and politics became aware of the dire reality of the fiscal and economic situation, and how narrow the policy choices were.

The year 1974 was a difficult one for the country, politically, because of the Watergate investigation that led, in August, to President Richard Nixon's resignation and, from the standpoint of the economy, because of rapidly rising prices and interest rates in the early part of the year and the onset of what proved to be a very sharp recession later in the year. Any businesses or units of government that borrowed heavily found the market conditions for new debt unfavorable, and New York City was a heavy borrower indeed. During the fiscal year ended June 30, 1974, it borrowed just over $5 billion and in the next fiscal year nearly $6 billion, in each case close to 40 percent of the total for all municipal governments in the United States.[38] By late 1974, new city debt issues carried what were seen by investors of that day as extremely high interest rates—around 7 percent—for tax-exempt securities, and small investors eagerly snapped up the new issues. The major banks, which had been important purchasers of city securities up to that time, did not purchase in late 1974, but continued to act as underwriters of the new issues.

In November 1974, a new governor was elected, Brooklyn Congressman Hugh Carey, the first Democrat to be elected since 1954. Because of recession and inflation, as well as the long slide in the New York economy, the state's own fiscal position looked ominous. Moreover, several of the authorities created in the expansive days of Nelson Rockefeller's governorship to finance and develop housing seemed to be overextended and one—the Urban Development Corporation (UDC)—was on the edge of defaulting on its short-term debt; it did default in December. Carey and his friends and advisers thus were confronted with the signs of impending fiscal and economic crisis for the state government within days of the election. But they also were well aware of the even more serious coming crisis for the city government at that time.[39] The incoming state administration thus became the first of the major players to recognize that a crisis was at hand.

The UDC default appears to have persuaded even the optimists in the financial community that the city's financial position was grave. By the early spring, the major banks and securities firms were unwilling to underwrite, as well as to buy, new issues of New York City debt. If anything, those decisions were overdue. By early 1975, it should have been clear that, sooner rather than later, the city's short-term debt would become so large that there would be no hope of ever repaying it: at that time, the outstanding short-term debt was equal to a full year's revenue from the city's taxes. Properly speaking, the fiscal crisis dates from the refusal to underwrite new borrowing. With a large operating deficit and billions of dollars in maturing short-term notes, the city *had* to borrow large sums, in order to meet day-to-day expenses and pay off the maturing notes. If the city could no longer borrow, then it would quickly default on its obligations.

At this point, it might have been expected that the mayor and other city officials would sound the alarm and treat this crisis as something new, different, and far more grave than the annual game of budget balancing that had gone on since 1969. They did not, and the media also continued to see this as a somewhat more difficult version of the old game. Meanwhile, the Carey administration provided an $800 million advance to the city in May to cover the most immediate cash needs, and the governor asked a small group of advisers and experts to devise a longer-lasting solution. The plan, translated into law by the legislature in early June, provided for the creation of a new state agency, a Municipal Assistance Corporation for the City of New York with a board of directors of nine: five designated by the governor and four by the mayor.

MAC (as it came to be known) had two main functions. The main one was to replace the short-term debt that had been incurred to finance operating deficits (then thought to be about $3 billion) with long-term bonds. The funds for interest and repayment of these bonds would come from certain revenue streams that previously had come into the city's own coffers, but which now would be diverted to MAC, to use for debt service (with any excess over debt service needs paid to the city), notably the city sales tax. Because the revenues pledged for MAC debt service were so much larger than the amounts needed, it was assumed that there would be no problem in marketing the $3 billion in bonds.

MAC's second function bolstered this assumption. The law required the city to correct the financial practices that had led to the crisis—running operating deficits, using the capital budget for operating purposes, and engaging in a variety of questionable accounting and budgetary practices—with MAC monitoring the city's performance in these respects. So, by early June, the expectation was that the immediate fiscal crisis would be resolved by fiscal reforms and MAC borrowing, an expectation that was widespread in the media and among the experts in and out of government.[40] They were, of course, very wrong, for two reasons. The first is that once confidence in the safety of a type of financial asset has been shattered, it is very difficult to restore. By June, the financial community, institutional investors, and a good many individual investors had been spooked: New York City debt was seen as unsafe, to be avoided, and the MAC bonds that were about to be issued were new and untried, perhaps just as dangerous as New York City debt.

Second, the sense that the immediate crisis had passed encouraged the kind of posturing that had become par for the course during the previous decade, as the June 30 budget-making deadline approached each year. In this round, the mayor had proposed two budgets, an "austerity budget," with a somewhat slower rate of growth in spending than had been the norm, and a lower "crisis budget," that called for some layoffs. The one to be adopted would depend upon the extent of state authorization for a range of new city taxes and increased state aid; thus, the two-budget approach was a tactic designed to put pressure on the state. The state government, being both hard pressed itself and aware that the situation was not one of business as normal (given the economic situation, it was clear to the

Carey administration that new city taxes were a very bad idea), did not respond to the threats.

The city administration's response in late June was to increase the pressure by mailing layoff notices to large numbers of city employees, especially in the uniformed services. As hoped, the unions responded vigorously, with a brief sanitation workers' strike and demonstrations by the police union.[41] So, just as the first MAC $1 billion bond issue came to market, there was noisy discord about the city's budget; investors had to believe that the city's finances *and* management were entirely out of control—which was an accurate perception. There was a marked unwillingness to purchase the bonds, and the issue failed: that is, the underwriters ended up owning, unwillingly, much of the bond issue and selling the rest at heavy losses.

Thus, in early July, the city's financial situation seemed desperate. The operating budget for the fiscal year that was just beginning was likely to be in deficit by close to $2 billion—in the absence of massive retrenchment. There was a $1 billion capital budget to be financed with borrowed money. And there was $6 billion in short-term debt that would have to be repaid. Bankruptcy in the form of default on the short-term debt seemed likely, but there was also the real question concerning how to meet payrolls, if no money could be borrowed.

By late July, the state government assumed responsibility for the day-to-day financial management of the city government, with state budget officials overseeing retrenchment steps, as well as finally obtaining accurate data on the tangled state of the city's finances. The leadership of the MAC board was reconstituted, with investment banker Felix Rohatyn emerging as the key player and MAC acting not only as the immediate fund raiser for the city but also as the deviser of longer-term solutions. MAC improvised during the summer and early fall, raising money to keep the city government going by selling its securities to some financial institutions and to public employee pension funds. By late summer, the public employee union leadership not only was well aware of the truly bad state of affairs, but also had become active players in devising solutions, a role that was to continue throughout the 1970s.

Although the crisis was making headlines daily and although layoffs of city employees had begun, few people in the city government—aside from those who actually had received layoff notices—shared the awareness of the union leadership, the state administration, the financial community, and the media. Disbelief, inertia, and self-interest combined to produce considerable resistance to retrenchment steps.[42] At the very top of the city government, the quest for traditional fiscal gimmicks, rather than serious revision of city policies and practices, continued. By the end of the summer, it was clear that the state's supervision of the city's finances had to be formalized and made much tighter, if there was to be any hope of ever restoring confidence and regaining the ability to borrow money.

As more of the actors became aware of the extent of the problem, they also became aware that there were few choices of action available to resolve the crisis. Formal bankruptcy was no solution, but was a threat to all parties, since that course would place all the decision making in the hands of federal judges.[43] More assistance from state funds was necessary, but neither the governor nor the legislative leaders were willing to provide more aid without some assurance that there would be a permanent solution. Federal assistance, in the form of loans or loan guarantees, surely would be essential, but the federal government was even more unlikely to help without drastic reforms of the city's finances. And, eventually, the city would need access to the regular credit markets, without external props, which was only possible if investors believed that the city was a good risk. Together, these considerations dictated that outside monitors would have to closely supervise the city for some period, that its accounting and budgetary practices would have to become examples of the best—rather than the worst—practices, and that retrenchment and fiscal conservatism would have to be the rule for some years to come. As former Mayor Wagner repeatedly pointed out, quietly, to the main participants, "That is what the people expect."

The Recovery and Its Aftermath

At the end of August, Governor Carey called a special session of the legislature and proposed passage of what became, a few days later, the Financial Emergency Act of 1975. The act created an Emergency Financial Control Board dominated by the governor, which was given extensive power to control the city's finances. The board's approval was required for the city's annual budgets, its multiyear financial plan, all contracts, and most of the city's financial management procedures (like revenue estimating and accounting systems). The city was required to balance its operating budget within three years and to remove expense items from its capital budget immediately; it was also required to move rapidly to what is known as "GAAP accounting," that is, accounting based on "Generally Accepted Accounting Principles." The act established a structure of internal funds that provided effective and immediate control over the flow of money, something that did not exist previously and had hampered the retrenchment efforts earlier in the summer; it also spelled out what would happen in the event of the city's defaulting on its debt, another gap that had been exposed by the crisis.[44] In addition, the act provided for a moratorium on the repayment of the city's short-term debt, to buy time to devise a comprehensive solution to the debt problem.[45]

The new control mechanism and rules by themselves (including the appointment of new financial managers within the city government itself to operate the new systems) began to turn things around. In the New York area, both institutional investors and the directors of the public employee pension funds found it more feasible to buy MAC bonds in substantial amounts, now that a stable financial management structure, with the prospect of balanced budgets, was in place. That structure was important in securing, after considerable struggle, federal intervention in the form of the New York City Seasonal Financing Act of 1975, under which direct U.S. Treasury short-term loans were made to New York City, to be repaid within the same fiscal year, over the next three years.

There were a number of conditions to the federal intervention, including imposing temporary city tax increases, which were strongly opposed by state and city officials as harmful to the city's economy—the first time ever for concerted opposition to tax increases on such grounds. Another condition was assumption by the state of some financial responsibilities that, in the rest of the country, are usually state rather than local government responsibilities. The senior colleges of the City University became parts of the state government; the state defrayed state court and corrections costs that previously had been met by the city itself; and over several years the state increased its share of Medicaid costs. To a considerable extent, the argument was not one of equity, but rather the recognition that the state government can tap a geographically broader, and thus stronger, economic base than the city government, once again indicating a major shift in political perceptions about the local economy.

By the end of 1975, the recovery was underway, although the retrenchment in city government spending continued. By early 1978, when a new mayor took office, the operating budget was close to balanced and MAC was borrowing with little difficulty. Although the crisis was really over, the Carter administration supported a new three-year federal loan guarantee act, which served more as a backup for MAC and later direct borrowing by the city government than as an actual source of funds; by 1981, there obviously was no need for yet another federal program to support city borrowing. In the new city administration of Edward I. Koch, the operating budget was quickly balanced and annual budget surpluses—sometimes of as much as $500 million—became the rule; the temporary tax increases of 1975 were allowed to expire, and a number of small city tax cuts, as well as large tax incentives for specific economic development projects, were instituted (along with a succession of very large reductions in the rates of the state personal income tax, this done entirely on the grounds of making the state more competitive economically).

The recovery owes much to what was happening in both the national and local economies. Nationally, the late 1970s were years of high inflation, which was good for the city's tax revenues. Locally, the city's economic slide ended in 1977 and growth resumed, slowly at first but then fairly rapidly in the 1980s. But the fiscal recovery was far from being an accidental byproduct of economic conditions. Policies changed radically. The key contributors, as the previous discussion indicates, were:

> The state government, in taking control of the city's financial management and in assuming a larger share of the costs of public expenditures;

- The federal government, in providing short-term financing, especially in the 1975–78 period;
- Municipal employees and their unions, in accepting postponement of salary increases, some reductions in fringe benefits, and large-scale layoffs and in investing pension fund assets in MAC and city bonds—and later on, recognizing that new collective bargaining agreements could not involve the extravagant terms that were typical of the early 1970s;
- The public at large, in accepting that some service reductions were inescapable in the crisis and in voting for politicians who were advocates of fiscal prudence;
- The leaders of the New York financial community, who organized important elements of the financial rescue and who committed substantial funds of their own firms at crucial moments (generally turning a profit in the end, but that was by no means certain at the time); and
- The new group of top-level city officials, who implemented the new rules beginning in late 1975.

Table 2.4 shows how sharp was the break in policy between precrisis and postcrisis, in expenditure and revenue terms. Between the fiscal year 1969 and fiscal 1976, city spending rose by 30 percent, after adjusting for inflation. In the next seven years, city spending declined by one-third, after a similar adjustment. In the first period, as the private sector of the local economy was collapsing, the city hired more staff, paid them more in salaries and fringe benefits (even in relation to inflation), increased welfare rolls and payment levels, as well as payments for contractual services and subsidies. In the second period, as the private sector began to recover, the city laid off staff, kept increases in compensation levels below the inflation rate and cut back, in real-dollar terms, in most other types of spending.

In the 1969–76 period, revenue increased in real terms by 14 percent, with a much larger increase in outside aid than in the city's own revenues. But, in view of the decline in employment of roughly 14 percent during these years, an increase of 10 percent in the city's own revenues after adjusting for inflation is an extraordinary result: it means that the burden the city was putting on the weak local economy had increased sharply. In contrast, between 1977 and 1983, the city's own revenues declined by about one-eighth in real terms, in the face of economic expansion: the economic burden was declining, and this was announced policy.[46]

The table shows that revenue and expenditure increased once more in real terms between fiscal 1983 and 1988, by about 15 percent over the five years, with the city's own revenues increasing by 23 percent in real terms. Although there were some tax and user charge increases during the period, the great bulk of the increase came from expansion of the local economy—an increase of

Table 2.4

New York City General Fund Expenditure and Revenue, Fiscal Years 1969–76, 1976–83, and 1983–88

	Percent change in real terms[a]			Absolute numbers (in millions of current dollars)			
	1969–76	1976–83[b]	1983–88	1969	1976	1983	1988
Expenditure	29.5%	−33.2%	15.7%	6,253	13,713	15,699	22,416
Revenue	13.8	−22.5	15.5	6,145	11,843	15,733	22,426
Source of revenue:							
City taxes and user charges	9.7	−12.7	22.7	3,569	6,629	9,919	15,017
State and federal aid	19.5	−35.0	3.3	2,576	5,214	5,814	7,409
Surplus or deficit[c]	—	—	—	−108	−1,870	34	10

Source: Based on data in the New York City Comptroller's Annual Reports for the year indicated, with reorganization of the data from the 1969 report to match the more recent definition of the General Fund.

a. Data are deflated from current dollars to real terms (constant dollars) by use of the U.S. price index for state and local government purchases of goods and services.

b. The decline in expenditures between 1976 and 1983 does not represent a pure cut in the costs of government, because of the transfer of certain expenditures to the state. Excluding the transfers to the state, the decline was about 29 percent in real terms. The other two time-period comparisons are not affected by any similar large shifts in responsibility.

c. In the 1980s, the city generally had large actual surpluses, which were then transferred to cover the following year's spending. The figures here are after such transfers.

nearly 10 percent in the employment level and an even more rapid increase in incomes, business profits, and property values, even after adjusting for inflation. During these years, in contrast to the 1969–76 period, the increased expenditure went mainly to expand the number of employees, rather than for increased compensation (in real terms) of the same corps of workers or for increased subsidies.

A Permanent Change in Outlook?

The 1975 fiscal crisis was a profound consciousness-raising experience with regard to perceptions about the vulnerability of the local economy. Before the crisis, most decision makers in and out of government, both at the city and the state levels, saw the economy as a neutral backdrop—a provider of revenues, but not a limiting consideration. After 1975, there was a radical change, and virtually every important decision was viewed as subject to constraints imposed by the vulnerability of the local economy. The large increases in revenue and expenditure after 1983 shown in Table 2.4 suggest that, perhaps, this change in perceptions was a temporary one, that would fade quickly as memories of the fiscal crisis receded. An obvious question, fifteen years after 1975, is whether the sense of economic and fiscal vulnerability remains a central feature of New York City politics and government.

The answer is that the political consciousness of economic vulnerability remains strong, although it has been argued that city policies on spending, taxation, and regulation should have been more conservative, in the interests of the economy. During the late 1980s, city budget expansion was halted quickly when adverse economic signs appeared, as in the wake of the 1987 stock market crash, and resumed only when the immediate economic outlook appeared more promising. The city's debt management policies have been cautious, for example, the city resumed seasonal borrowing (within a single fiscal year) in 1979 and has limited the amount of such borrowing to 5 percent of the total operating budget, about one-tenth of the ratio that existed in 1975.[47] While some changes in the city's tax system were populist measures that were adverse to economic development, other changes were explicitly designed to be helpful to sectors of the local economy.[48]

Actual and proposed increases in spending for city services frequently were justified as necessary for economic development (although the connection typically was, at best, a very long-range one). Notable examples include the arguments that improved schools were essential to provide a better work force to attract business, and that large outlays for housing programs were necessary if housing availability would not deter businesses from locating in New York. For example, Felix Rohatyn, the single most important figure in the fiscal recovery from the crisis who was still chairman of MAC in 1989, wrote that major reform of the school system was necessary not only because "a decent public education should be considered a basic civil right," but also because

New York City's economy will rapidly deteriorate without a supply of skilled employees for tomorrow's predominately service economy. Furthermore, the cost of unemployment and crime resulting from the high dropout rate will drive more people and businesses out of the city.[49]

Moreover, although there were complaints that the Koch administration was unnecessarily generous in its overt financial incentives and bending of land-use controls to encourage development, none of the political actors really have been critical of the high priority given to economic development. This was evident in the 1989 mayoral campaign, in which there was little mention of such issues, despite the superficially attractive position of attacking "giveaways." Shortly before the primary election, in responding to the specific question from an interviewer, "Would you continue the city's tax abatement program for developers?" all five opponents of the incumbent mayor answered evasively, rather than seize the opportunity to denounce Mayor Koch's policy of aggressively assisting developers.[50] To readers in other American cities, where growth and economic development have been winning issues in local politics for decades, it may not seem startling that this is now the case in New York as well. But, to long-time New Yorkers, the transformation is a major one.

Notes

1. In part, New York City did better than the nonfarm economy as a whole because New York was less dependent on heavy manufacturing, which suffered grievously. Another contributing factor was that New York's financial institutions were relatively less devastated by the 1929–33 financial collapse (for example, none of the city's savings banks folded and by the mid-1930s they were making mortgage loans aggressively). But perhaps the most important factor was the massive public works program going forth under city and state government auspices, mostly directed by Robert Moses, using all available city, state and—especially—federal funds. Although the federal government financed public works projects all across the country as a means of job creation, New York officials were far more aggressive in securing and using the available funds. New York had one special advantage: when the Depression struck, there was a blueprint for the massive public works program in hand, in the form of the 1929 Regional Plan of New York and Its Environs, prepared over seven years under the auspices of an influential citizens committee that became the Regional Plan Association.
2. For example, prior to the 1960s, there was no regular collection or publication of employment data by borough within New York City. Urban economics, as a field of specialization for economists, was invented, for all practical purposes, in the middle and late 1950s. By 1960, there were fewer than one hundred American academics whose research focused on urban economic questions and probably only half as many economists with that focus in government and in banks and other private-sector organizations— in the entire United States.
3. Such special censuses became common practice, as more states adopted aid programs tied to population statistics. The New York City 1957 special census was an early example.
4. Attacks on the accuracy of Census Bureau results for the city have become a habit with New York political figures. Mostly, the criticism is that minorities and immigrants are "under-counted" by census takers.

5. Edgar M. Hoover and Raymond Vernon, *Anatomy of a Metropolis*. Cambridge, MA: Harvard University Press, 1959.

6. Raymond Vernon, *Metropolis 1985*. Cambridge, MA: Harvard University Press, 1960.

7. Of course, some economic activities never mature in the sense of becoming so standardized that they can do without face-to-face communications and superb flows of information—some types of financial and other business services are the prime examples, and they continue to flourish in central locations. But even in these cases, some parts of the operations can be split off and relocated to less expensive places as, for example, the credit card operations of the largest New York banks were moved first to the suburbs and then to distant states.

8. The capital budget was supposed to provide for long-lived assets—land, buildings, equipment, highways, bridges, sewers, etc.—as it was financed mainly by bond issues. In the first half of the 1960s, as much as 25 percent of expenditures listed in the annual capital budget were for current operating purposes (like salaries of the staff of the Department of City Planning). The city was so slow in actually committing the funds for true capital purposes that projects included in one year's capital budget might not have been started for four or five years, and often were canceled or drastically revised after the capital budget was adopted.

9. The commission was chaired by Earl B. Schwulst, chairman of the board of the Bowery Savings Bank; its vice-chairman was Professor Wallace Sayre. It had a research staff that operated under the guidance of the commission's secretary, Joseph D. McGoldrick (a professor of political science who had been city comptroller in the administration of Fiorello LaGuardia) and also contracted with New York University for a substantial portion of its research work. The commission published three reports, *Meeting New York City's Urgent Fiscal Problems* (November 30, 1964), *Toward Fiscal Strength* (November 30, 1965), and *Blueprint for Fiscal Improvement* (June 15, 1966), which were bound together in a final report, *Better Financing for New York City* (August 1966), and a number of staff reports. The NYU work, directed by the author of this chapter, was published in a book, *Financing Government in New York City* (New York University Graduate School of Public Administration, June 1966).

10. Report of the Advisory Group on City Taxation to the President of the City Council, released by the President of the City Council (May 5, 1966).

11. See the data and discussion in Dick Netzer, "State-Local Finance and Intergovernmental Relations," in Blinder, Solow, Break, Steiner and Netzer, *The Economics of Public Finance*. Washington, DC: The Brookings Institution, 1974, pp. 374–86.

12. Percentages calculated by the author from U.S. Census Bureau annual reports on governmental finances in the United States, using the methods developed for the mid-1960s analysis cited above.

13. New York City's role in the provision of public assistance and social services—elsewhere the province of state agencies in nearly all cases—remains unique. New York City also is alone, among American cities, in incarcerating criminals for long terms and in operating large parts of the state court system; much of the costs of these functions is now paid by the state (which was not true in the 1960s). In the 1960s, the city also had a much larger role in higher education and in transit than it does today.

14. See Chapter 3, "Changing Styles and Strategies of the Mayor," and Chapter 4, "The Other Elected Officials," both by David R. Eichenthal.

15. *Toward Fiscal Strength*, p. 1. One of the two dissenters was appointed to the initial board of directors of the Municipal Assistance Corporation at the height of the 1975 fiscal crisis and had no doubt that *that* was a true crisis. Although he was one of the mayor's designees, he was one of the "hard-liners" on the MAC board and supported drastic action to limit the city's fiscal discretion.

16. For example, at the mayor's request, the state legislature authorized the city to treat operating expenses of the vocational high schools as a capital budget item, on the specious grounds that this was an investment in human capital.

17. Calculated from data in Regional Plan Association, *The Region's Growth*. New York: Regional Plan Association, 1967, and Regina Belz Armstrong, *The Office Industry*, A Report of the Regional Plan Association. Cambridge, MA: The MIT Press, 1972. Both the national and regional employment projections were too optimistic. The actual gap between national and regional personal income per capita in 1985 was larger than RPA had projected; there was considerable shrinkage in the gap for the city, but less for the rest of the region.

18. U.S. Census Bureau, *1982 Census of Governments* 6:4; *Historical Statistics on Governmental Finances and Employment* (1985), Table 28; and annual Census Bureau reports on governmental finances.

19. Henry M. Levin, "An Analysis of the Economic Effects of the New York City Sales Tax," in *Financing Government in New York City*, pp. 635–92.

20. Among other things, the commission had recommended taxing utilities, banks, and insurance companies like other businesses, rather than on distinctive bases at much higher effective rates. The Lindsay administration ignored that advice; in the 1980s, under the Koch administration, substantial changes in those taxes were made, after demonstrable economic harm had occurred.

21. Lyle C. Fitch and Annmarie Hauck Walsh, editors, *Agenda for a City: Issues Confronting New York*. Beverly Hills, CA: Sage Publications, 1970.

22. They included Emanuel Tobier on the economy, Frank S. Kristof on the economics of housing in New York, and Dick Netzer on the budget.

23. See the editors' interpretation of the budget chapter, pages 20–21, Fitch and Walsh, *Agenda for a City: Issues Confronting New York*.

24. Rent control in New York had survived from World War II, under state law and either state or city administration, but applied only to buildings constructed before 1947, in order *not* to deter construction of new buildings. In 1969, a new system of rent regulation, called "rent stabilization," with somewhat less severe provisions, was applied to post-1947 buildings. In 1974, state legislation provided than when an apartment in a building under the old rent control system was vacated, that apartment would be placed under the newer rent stabilization system. The 1974 structure continues to this day. There are only a few units left under the old rent control system, but there have been declines in the number of units under rent stabilization because of condominium and cooperative conversions.

25. One consequence in New York was a decline in the hotel and restaurant business that had been extremely prosperous during the 1960s. A substantial number of prominent expensive restaurants closed between 1969 and 1972.

26. In 1973, Congress enacted legislation, in response to this threat, that resulted in the creation of Conrail, which was initially a government corporation with heavy subsidies. Conrail provides freight service along the routes of the bankrupt private carriers. Subsequently, Conrail became profitable (after drastic pruning) and was sold to private investors.

27. Eli Ginzberg et al., *New York Is Very Much Alive*. New York: McGraw-Hill, 1973, p. xv.

28. First National City Bank, *Portrait of a City*. New York: McGraw-Hill, 1972; First National City Bank, *Metro New York: An Economic Perspective*. New York: First National City Bank, March 1974. The quotation is from p. 10 of the latter.

29. The Port Authority of New York and New Jersey, *People & Jobs*, A Forecast of Population, Households, Labor Force and Jobs in the New York-New Jersey-Connecticut

Metropolitan Region: 1975–1990. New York: The Port Authority of New York and New Jersey, May 1974, p. 5.

30. Maxwell School, Syracuse University, Roy W. Bahl, Alan K. Campbell, and David Greytak, *New York City: Economic Base and Fiscal Capacity*, a study sponsored by the Temporary State Commission to Make a Study of the Governmental Operation of the City of New York, April 1973. The commission's chairman was Stuart N. Scott and the Commission is often known as the Scott Commission. Its executive director was Stephen Berger.

31. Twentieth Century Fund Task Force on Prospects and Priorities of New York City, . . . A Nice Place to Live. New York: The Twentieth Century Fund, 1973. My own even more pessimistic perspective on the city economy in early 1974, reported in quotations in the *New York Times* and "The Cloudy Prospects for the City's Economy," *New York Affairs* 1:4 (Spring 1974), was viewed by the Beame administration in the way that the Lindsay administration had viewed the Scott Commission's report, as an attack by a political enemy. The *New York Affairs* article was dead wrong in its appraisal of the fiscal situation: it assumed that the city would be retrenching and thus defusing the fiscal dangers.

32. New York City's tax structure had become relatively sensitive to economic fluctuations, with the adoption of the personal and corporate income taxes in 1966.

33. In the 1970 elections, the Conservative party nominee, James Buckley, won election as U.S. Senator over the liberal Republican incumbent and the Democratic nominee. Candidates for the legislature running with the Conservative party nomination did very well, and the Conservative party supplanted the Liberal party as New York's third-ranking party.

34. The data are from annual U.S. Census Bureau reports on public employment. City employment is broadly defined to include the Transit Authority, the Housing Authority, the Triborough Bridge and Tunnel Authority, the Health and Hospitals Corporation, and certain smaller quasi-independent agencies, as well as the agencies that fall within the city's budget formally. The broader definition is appropriate, because the city did have important financial obligations for most of these agencies at that time.

35. Such unsound use of bond issues had ample precedent in New York City's history. During the Civil War, the city issued bonds in order to pay the "bounties" that bought young men exemption from the draft, and later that century issued long-term bonds to install soon-rotted wooden sidewalks in the Bronx.

36. Some of the material in this section is based on the contents of a presentation that the author made several times in late 1975 and 1976, recounting the origins of the fiscal crisis and what happened during the height of the crisis. That presentation appears in print in several forms. See, for example, Dick Netzer, "The New York City Fiscal Crisis," in Benjamin Chinitz, editor, *The Decline of New York in the 1970's*, proceedings of a conference held in November 1976, State University of New York at Binghamton (1977), pp. 156–66.

37. During Mayor Lindsay's second term, there was a Mayor's Fiscal Advisory Committee, consisting of city officials, financial leaders, and a few independent policy advisers. Comptroller Beame had a similarly constituted Technical Advisory Committee on Debt Management. The two groups met together in the last year or so of the Lindsay administration. The mayor and a few of the outside members repeatedly expressed alarm at the deteriorating situation, but most of the financial leaders were reassuring. One, perhaps the most conservative of those present in ideological terms, was given to denouncing the pessimists as ignorant alarmists.

38. Again, these data are from U.S. Census Bureau annual releases. They comprise long-term debt issued plus short-term debt outstanding at year's end, excluding (in the New York City case) authority debt.

39. Carey's most senior adviser was former Mayor Wagner. Other advisers included Stephen Berger, who had been executive director of the Scott Commission, Manhattan City Councilman Robert F. Wagner, Jr., and housing developer Richard Ravitch. At the first meeting of Carey's budget transition task force, in November, Carey agreed with one task force member's argument that dealing with the coming New York City fiscal crisis was far and away the most serious of the many fiscal problems with which Carey would have to deal. In fact, Carey interrupted that member's presentation to complete the argument.

40. The back cover of the Summer 1975 issue of *New York Affairs* 2:4, which was sent to the printer at the beginning of June, headlined the issue as containing "Dick Netzer on the Aftermath of the Fiscal Crisis." The article in question begins, "By the time this is being read, the immediate fiscal crisis of New York's city government that was in the headlines when this piece was written (in late May), will have been dealt with. . . ." The article went on to discuss the need for more fundamental reforms in the substance of what the city government does and how it operates—scaled-down aspirations and more frugal provision of services—in the light of the city's economic vulnerability. The article was of course wrong about the fiscal crisis being over—that took many more months—and called for budget retrenchment in ways quite different from most of those that actually took place over the next two years. However, the hope that the city government "under the lash of financial hardship" would retreat from its overbearing posture of the late 1960s and early 1970s—its overt hostility to private business, the nonprofit sector, voluntarism, and anything like sacrifice within government itself—was realized to a considerable extent over the next decade.

41. The police union went so far as to distribute leaflets at airports and rail terminals warning visitors that it was now unsafe to visit "Fear City," because of the prospective reduction in the size of the police force, by June 1975 considerably larger than it had ever been.

42. For example, employees who were laid off were not removed from payrolls for some weeks after the effective date of the terminations and, despite explicit orders to slow work on construction projects in order to save cash, this was generally not done. The most dramatic examples of heel-dragging were found in the City University: the Board of Higher Education announced a list of totally bogus cuts in spending (like terminating degree programs that had been authorized, but never started) and, with two exceptions, the individual colleges continued to fill vacant positions for the coming academic year. The result of the latter actions was a near-collapse of the system at the end of the fiscal year as the money ran out and much deeper staffing cuts than should have been necessary.

43. The city government's chief lawyer, the corporation counsel, and his political sponsor, the city council president, were the only advocates of municipal bankruptcy in high places. They expressed confidence that a federal bankruptcy judge would direct that no debt service payments be made, while authorizing continued operating expenditure at the precrisis level. Virtually all the other actors could imagine a federal judge ordering layoffs, wage and pension cuts, and service reductions, as well as deferment of debt service payments. In the 1977 elections, the council president was defeated in the Democratic primary by a state senator who was not well known, in part because the incumbent was seen as having behaved irresponsibly during the fiscal crisis.

44. The act included a variety of other requirements and sanctions, notably making it a misdemeanor to obligate the expenditure of city funds without authorization. Such a provision had been in effect in the federal government since 1933 but, in the absence of this sanction, city officials frequently committed the city to unauthorized spending.

45. The moratorium was later declared unconstitutional by New York's highest court, but by that time there was considerable market acceptance of MAC bonds. Much of the

short-term debt was exchanged for MAC bonds, and MAC was able to borrow money to pay off the rest.

46. During these years, state aid to the city declined even more in real terms, but this was fully offset by the transfers of responsibility to the state (see note b, Table 2.4). Federal aid, however, declined by more than 40 percent in real terms and another 19 percent by 1988; in absolute dollars, federal aid was virtually unchanged from 1976 through 1988, although the price level more than doubled.

47. City of New York, *Comptroller's Report* 15:2 (August 1989).

48. The major populist trend was a substantial and continuing shift in the distribution of the property tax burden, away from homeowner properties toward business property. Operating in the other direction, there were reductions in a number of business taxes, on commercial rents, small unincorporated businesses, financial corporations, and energy use.

49. *New York Times*, September 2, 1989, p. 23.

50. *New York Times*, September 2, 1989, p. 26.

II

Governance

3

Changing Styles and Strategies of the Mayor

David R. Eichenthal

The period between 1960 and 1989 was a time of historic change for New York City: as in many other urban centers throughout the United States, it was a time of economic, social, cultural, and political transformation and upheaval. These changes were reflected in the styles and leadership strategies of New York's mayors.

National changes in policy and politics had a special impact on the nation's largest city. The transformation of New York from a city dominated by white ethnic groups to one dominated by persons of color is perhaps the greatest change of the period. The demographic shift and an accompanying shift in political power can be attributed, in part, to a series of federal policies. Suburbanization, encouraged by national housing and transportation policies of the 1950s and 1960s, led to the exodus of the white middle class from urban centers.

As blacks and Latinos increased in the population, there was a need for increased political representation as well. Federal antipoverty programs and civil rights legislation increased minority representation opportunities. Community-based antipoverty programs became training grounds for a new generation of black and Latino political leaders.[1] The federal Voting Rights Act provided unique protection for minority participation in the electoral process.[2]

Changes in politics at the national level have also affected New York and the institution of the mayoralty. During the 1960s and 1970s, political scientists proclaimed the death of the urban political machine. Local politics, following the trend in national politics, became less dominated by party leaders who were replaced by the media.

There were also changes unique to New York City. Federal attention to urban issues, particularly the antipoverty initiatives of the Great Society (the social programs launched during the administration of Lyndon B. Johnson in the 1960s and for the most part continued through the 1970s), led to a shift in the city's role in addressing basic policy issues. Historically, New York had been a leader in social policy programs. The federalization of these efforts led to a reduction in municipal autonomy.

Sweeping economic changes also affected New York politics. New York's economic fate became more dependent on the fate of the nation and the world than ever before. New York's fiscal crisis of the mid-1970s led to federal intervention mainly because of the risk of damage to the nation's financial system from a New York City bankruptcy. During the 1980s, New York became increasingly sensitive to a global economy where the United States was no longer the sole dominant power.

These new forces have all had an impact on the role of the mayor. Changes in population and power and shifts in government authority to Washington and Albany have resulted in changes in mayoral style and strategies of governance. In addition, the media have revolutionized the ways in which the mayor's powers are exercised: the mayor now simultaneously persuades and acts as chief executive. The decline of political party organizations has resulted in changes in the mayor's ability to govern at the community level. And combined, all of these changes have radically transformed the way in which we elect mayors.

This chapter discusses how these changes have affected the role and functioning of the mayors between 1960 and 1989. Not everything has changed. While New York is comprised of five boroughs containing diverse people with diverse interests, it continues to be one city, with the mayor as the key and most visible political player. As Sayre and Kaufman wrote some thirty years ago, "The office of Mayor is first and fundamentally a symbol of unity for the city."[3]

Mayoral Style and Mayoral Strategies

There is no single model of urban government in the United States. Some cities have mayors, but many do not: instead, these cities are governed under a "professionalized" system of city managers selected by the city's elected governing body. Many cities have both mayors and city managers, with the mayor functioning as little more than a figurehead. Other cities do not have a city manager system, but their local legislature, usually called the city council, exercises considerable power over the municipal budget and mayoral appointees.

Political scientists have categorized these different government structures as strong-mayor and weak-mayor systems. Since consolidation of the five boroughs, New York has had a strong mayor. Charter revisions throughout the twentieth century have incrementally shifted power between the mayor, the Board of Estimate,[4] and the city council (or in its earlier incarnation, the Board of Aldermen). However, the mayor has always held the central role in New York City's policy-making process. The effect of dividing the power of "counterbalance" to the mayor between the council and the Board of Estimate has had the effect of weakening both legislative bodies.

Closely associated with the contrasting weak-mayor and strong-mayor model of urban government is the distinction between municipal governments dominated by reformers and those dominated by political machines. "Weak" mayor systems of urban government grew out of the progressive movement of the early 1900s: city manager governments, along with civil service reforms, were seen as a means of "professionalizing" and making municipal government more efficient, while ridding urban government of the corrupt influences of machine politics. New York City during the last thirty years was hardly the classic machine model, but elements of machine politics persisted along with antimachine reforms. New York politics remained fiercely partisan and, at times, political patronage appointments were an important aspect of city government. Indeed, the patronage system during the Koch administration was responsible for scandals in city government that were the worst in nearly forty years.[5]

At the same time, New York City government grew more professional: the selection of appointees for the critical commissioner positions became less a function of politics and more of merit.[6] Even if mayors had wanted to revert to the machine patronage model, the mid-1970s fiscal crisis would have precluded that. Thus, both the willingness and the ability to provide the "fat" of patronage declined, hastening the decline of the machine.

The gross distinctions that both the strong/weak mayor model and machine/reform model seek to draw are inapplicable to New York. For New York during the past thirty years has been subject to constant change and stress. The mayors—Wagner, Lindsay, Beame, and Koch—were forced to adopt different styles and strategies to cope with these changes. Rather than seeking a single model of the mayoralty, it is more helpful to look at mayoral leadership strategies in the context of different models. Here the works of Sayre and Kaufman and Douglas Yates provide useful starting points.

Sayre and Kaufman set out three types of mayoral strategy to address public policy issues: *innovation, arbitration,* and *mediation.* These strategies are often a function of the personal styles of individual mayors. Active mayors are more likely to use a strategy of innovation, in which they both set the public policy agenda and vigorously pursue a problem-solving strategy. Where outside pressure groups have set the public policy agenda, arbitration allows mayors to decisively act upon the preset policy options. More passive mayors are more likely to employ a strategy of mediation in attempting to arrive at consensus public policy.

Douglas Yates, in *The Ungovernable City,*[7] suggests four different models of mayoral leadership: *crusader, entrepreneur, boss,* and *broker.* Crusaders rely extensively on symbolism: they lack resources and political clout and can only exercise leadership through dramatic example. Entrepreneurs are the "strongest" mayors: they have sufficient political and financial resources to allow them to act decisively on substantive policy issues. Yates notes that entrepreneur mayors are particularly active in economic development policy where they can exercise political power on behalf of and within the business community. Like entrepreneur mayors, boss mayors have substantial financial and political resources: however, boss mayors exercise their power primarily to maintain control, rather than to set new policy agendas. Finally, broker mayors lack political and fiscal resources and seek only to mediate conflicts between various interest groups.

The Yates models are particularly applicable to New York mayors since 1960. According to Yates, financial resources and political power, more so than style, are critical to the type of leadership strategies that a mayor can employ. During much of the time since 1960, financial constraints have been severe and the mayor's political power has declined in the face of greater dependence on state and federal governments and the lack of support by effective political machines. Thus, Yates's models seem very relevant for analysis of the Wagner, Lindsay, Beame, and Koch mayoralties.

A full assessment of mayoral leadership over the last thirty years warrants a book, rather than a section of a chapter. Instead, we can only look briefly at a single policy area and how it has been addressed by different mayors. Labor relations is an area where mayors enjoy unique executive autonomy: while state law now dictates many of the terms of the negotiation process, neither the city council nor the Board of Estimate have had much say in the actual negotiation of municipal labor contracts. Since labor relations have played an important role in the administration of each of the four mayors in office between 1960 and 1990, it is a good topic for a case study of mayoral leadership.

Mayors as Crusaders and Innovators: Symbolic Politics

Lindsay's First Term

In 1965, John Lindsay was elected as an "outsider," without much formal organizational support and over the opposition of the city's Democratic machine, pledged to drastically change the ways in which the city government functioned. Lindsay had to rely on public image and rhetoric, at the outset, rather than the conventional instruments of political power. Moreover, it was a time of social and political tensions, particularly about civil rights and the Vietnam War, and of rapid political and social changes nationally. Urban problems were the focus of a degree of political attention never before, or since, seen. Thus it was inevitable that Lindsay's first term would be characterized by symbolic politics. According to Yates, Lindsay's strategy was "to dramatize urban problems through moralistic rhetoric and force of personality."[8]

Simultaneously, Lindsay had to build his own political links to the bureaucracy, for he had neither the ties to the upper ranks of the bureaucracy that old hands like Wagner and Beame had, nor the links that come with regular political organizations. He also had to build links to the neighborhoods, to develop channels through which to deal with rising community tensions. A first step was to centralize the policy-making process: administrative agencies were limited in their discretion and placed under the direction of City Hall–based mayoral assistants. Lindsay was able to achieve his organizational goals to a considerable extent: city agencies were restructured under the umbrella of a small number of "superagencies" on the federal government model, "neighborhood city halls" were created, and Lindsay's outreach to black and Latino neighborhoods was rewarded with relative calm while other urban ghettos burned. These moves were not wholly successful. The superagencies were ultimately dismantled. And Lindsay's outreach to minority communities was viewed as a form of appeasement by the white middle class and as a neglect of their concerns.

Lindsay's application of the crusader strategy to labor relations was very dramatic, but largely unsuccessful. Lindsay "dramatized the fight between the public interest (which he represented) and selfish greed (represented by the unnamed power brokers),"[9] labor leaders being prominent among the "power brokers." During Lindsay's first term, there were two major teacher strikes, a sanitation strike, a transit strike, a strike by welfare caseworkers, and a strike by municipal hospital doctors and nurses. By 1968, New York was described as "strike city."[10]

Lindsay's confrontational style was dictated by both the political environment and the strategy of innovation. Lindsay acted as a crusader because he interpreted his election in 1965 as a mandate for innovation. His predecessor, Mayor Wagner, had been criticized for his informal style of labor negotiation. But it must be noted that collective bargaining in the public sector, and in New York City, was relatively new in the 1960s. Neither the legal framework nor the administrative machinery was well developed. Mayor Wagner was able to rely on his close relationship with the union leaders and the few precedents in contract negotiations of long standing, notably in transit. But Lindsay had no such experience and his initial relations with the union leaders were hostile, not friendly. In addition, municipal labor unions were undergoing considerable internal stress and change, in part because they too were just learning how to bargain collectively (they had a long history of political action, however) and in part because of the changing ethnic composition of the municipal work force. Lindsay's role as a crusader was thus dictated by both his political situation and that of the municipal labor unions.

Koch's First Term

Edward Koch's candidacy was similar to Lindsay's first candidacy in 1965: both were "outsider" candidates who had pledged to radically alter the status quo. Lindsay was constrained by his lack of political power. Koch was constrained by the severe financial controls that had been implemented in the aftermath of the 1975 fiscal crisis. Initially, Koch could make few substantive policy changes and thus he utilized a good deal of symbolism. Koch sought to reassure the city's shrinking middle class by initiating a series of neighborhood town meetings in the outer boroughs; he repeatedly proclaimed a New York City renaissance and in 1978 he was conspicuous in the campaign for a renewal of the federal backing for the city's borrowing that had been provided initially in late 1975. Koch's crusading style was successful in two important respects. The middle class felt assured that it had a champion in City Hall and, for both New Yorkers and the rest of the world, the fiscal crisis faded quickly into an unpleasant memory.

During his 1977 campaign, Koch had urged reforms of the civil service law, evoking the opposition of many of the municipal labor unions. The Koch administration's first municipal bargaining session was confrontational. However, the fiscal crisis and the city's effort to win federal loan guarantees effectively prevented labor from striking to enforce its demands. As part of the resolution of the fiscal crisis in 1975, unions had invested pension funds in city securities. Their "co-ownership" of the city created a conflict of interest between the demand for higher wages and the need to maintain fiscal stability. In addition, labor peace was a necessary component of the city's effort to win federal assistance.

Koch's role as a crusader in labor relations was demonstrated in the 1980 transit strike. By 1980, city-union labor negotiations had returned to normal. Although the city of New York had no formal role in transit negotiations (transit workers are employed by the Metropolitan Transportation Authority, a state agency), transit settlements had traditionally set the terms for other municipal labor contracts. The Koch administration make a decision to "take" a transit strike.[11] Koch skillfully used symbolism throughout the strike, attacking the "wackos" in the transport union (as Lindsay had attacked the power brokers), while greeting commuters walking to work. Ultimately, Koch failed to achieve his ultimate goal, as the strike settlement was considered by labor experts to be "significantly higher . . . than the previous round of negotiations."[12] However, Koch's style appealed to the public and attracted wide media coverage and support, as he marched—defiantly and with much fanfare—with displaced subway riders across the Brooklyn Bridge.

Mayors as Entrepreneurs: Economic Development

In Yates's model, an entrepreneur mayor uses economic development to maintain and strengthen executive power. Assuming that a mayor is free of fiscal constraint, he can select from among different projects and use his political power and financial resources to push development projects to completion. The entrepreneur mayor is likely to try to avoid the obstructions and delays of the established bureaucracy by relying on new or strengthened separate agencies and authorities to advance development projects.[13]

Koch's Late First Term and Early Second Term

By 1981, the economic revival of the city was more than a mayor's rhetoric. Private sector employment was rising, new building projects were being launched and the Koch administration was actively implementing economic development policies. The economic success contributed to Koch's political popularity. In 1981, he won reelection easily and, by early 1982, Koch was the favorite to become the next governor.

The Koch administration's economic development strategy relied heavily on indirect incentives to private developers, such as tax abatements and favorable zoning changes. In addition, the city initiated a rapidly expanding capital spending program to renew infrastructure;[14] Koch vigorously supported large new public works programs launched by state authorities and the state government itself, typified by Koch's support for Westway, a proposed major new highway for the city's West Side.[15] Koch was able to take economic development policy out of the bureaucracy by becoming the first mayor to designate a deputy mayor for economic development and making the mayor-dominated Public Development Corporation the directing force in economic development policy.

Although the economic recovery was evidence of the success of the entrepreneurial strategy, some critics—most of them opponents of Koch on other grounds, as well—considered the strategy a bad one. They charged that tax abatements and zoning changes were unneeded gifts to the rich and powerful because most of the new construction was in the form of Manhattan office buildings or very expensive Manhattan housing. The critics alleged that increases in employment benefited mostly commuters.[16]

During 1981 and 1982, the Koch administration's labor relations strategy changed, as had Lindsay's, to a less confrontational style. There are a number of explanations for this change. First, the confrontational style may have gained media support, but had not been particularly effective in reducing union power, as was the case in Lindsay's early years. Second, the mayor's labor negotiators were more experienced. Third, by 1982 Koch was seeking friends, as he entered the contest for governor. A final explanation, in keeping with the Yates models, is that Mayor Koch's real political power increased greatly between his taking office at the beginning of 1978 and 1982, enabling him to depart from the confrontational style of a crusader.

Mayors as Brokers and Bosses: Mediation and Consensus

Wagner's Third Term

Yates argues that under Mayor Wagner, the broker style was "practiced consum-mately."[17] Wagner sought to carefully balance the divergent interest groups in New York City by employing a quiet, personal, nonconfrontational style. Wagner's mediation strategy was necessary after the 1961 mayoral campaign. After facing a primary challenge from the Democratic organization throughout the city and a strong general election challenge, Wagner won with coalition support from within the city bureaucracy: "Before the end of the election most of the larger city bureaucracies had political representation in the inner core of the new administration."[18]

Wagner applied the mediation strategy to labor relations more than any other policy area. In 1958, Wagner, through an executive order, had established the city's collective bargaining process. While Wagner could not always provide generous contracts to labor, he always took "pains to give the union hierarchy a feeling of importance."[19] No city initiative in labor policy was ever undertaken without first clearing it with organized labor.

Lindsay's Second Term

By 1969, John Lindsay was paying the price for his crusading first term. Lind-say, defeated in the Republican primary, shifted his strategy from confrontation and innovation to mediation. Basic municipal service delivery became a priority. Lindsay won accommodations with the unions and the support of many Demo-cratic elected officials in the general election. Lindsay's limited political re-sources, left unconsolidated and shaped by a desire for higher office, produced a broker mayor.

Applied to labor relations, Lindsay's mediation strategy ended the confronta-tional style of the first term. Indeed, the settlements after 1968 that avoided strikes were criticized by some, including Koch's labor negotiator, as "total capitulation."[20] Mediation also became the rule in dealing with neighborhoods. As in the case of labor relations, the initial crusader strategy had produced painful consequences in the form of middle-class backlash. Lindsay's appeal to minority neighborhoods by support of school decentralization, antipoverty com-munity organizations, and scattered-site public housing had generated enormous hostility.[21] So Lindsay reached out to middle-class communities through a series of low-key meetings and by developing "neighborhood city halls," that is, ad-ministrative decentralization of city government explicitly designed to improve service delivery in middle-class sections.[22]

Whether the mediation strategy would have been successful enough to help Lindsay gain a third term is unclear. Nearly all the initiatives of Lindsay's second term were halted by Lindsay's bid for the Democratic nomination for president in 1972. The presidential campaign diverted the attention of the mayor and his top aides. His defeat in the early primaries led to a loss of political prestige and probably made his retirement from office at the end of 1973 inevitable.

Beame Administration

Beame's leadership strategy in the first year or so of his term was defined by his relationship with the Democratic organization and the bureaucracy. His 1973 candidacy pledged a return to normalcy in city government, normalcy meaning the tone and style that had been characteristic of mayors between LaGuardia and Lindsay, that is, from 1945 to 1965. Group representation, rather than crusading leadership, was the hallmark of the new administration. By 1975, Beame's three deputy mayors represented the alliance: the bureaucracy (James Cavanagh, a long-time city budget official), the machine (Stanley Friedman from the Bronx Democratic organization), and minorities (Paul Gibson). Beame's broker policies extended to labor relations as well. During the early years of the Beame administration, Beame's nonconfrontational style led to relatively amicable collective bargaining settlements, with terms similar to those of the contracts negotiated during Lindsay's second term.

After 1974, Beame's power was limited by the fiscal crisis. The state, through Governor Hugh Carey, acted as the broker of the interest groups that brought the city through the crisis. There was labor peace, for the unions were partners in the coalition that Carey put together.

Koch after 1982

Edward Koch's bid for governor in 1982 had an impact on city government similar to John Lindsay's bid for president ten years earlier. Koch needed a secure political base before he could run statewide: as a result, Koch had to make concessions to what remained of the city's Democratic machines. Some concessions had been made as early as 1977 when Koch won the support of the organization in the Democratic runoff, but it was Koch's bid for governor that allowed party leaders to take over parts of the bureaucracy.

After the mayor's defeat in the gubernatorial primary, the tone of city government was markedly less activist than the tone that had marked Koch's first five years in office. Following his landslide reelection in 1985, Koch should have been able to reassert his political power and act like the Koch of his first term. But corruption scandals gripped city government beginning shortly after Koch's

January inaugural. The scandals did not involve the mayor himself, or indeed, most agencies, but only those parts of the city government that had been ceded as "turf" to party leaders earlier. A number of top-level officials were forced to resign, and most of those who resigned were later convicted of crimes related to scandals in the city's Transportation Department. Three of the Democratic party leaders who were allied with Koch during his gubernatorial bid were implicated in the scandals.

During the last years of the Koch administration, the mayor appeared to be far more averse to taking political risks than had been true earlier. The city government seldom launched new policy initiatives. However, Koch's new posture as a broker mayor did not have a significant impact on his labor relations policy. Prior to 1982, Koch had already adopted a less confrontational strategy.

Differences in mayoral leadership strategies reflect a combination of the mayor's personality and the political environment. Given the divergent interests in New York City and the complex policy issues which the mayor must confront, Sayre and Kaufman wrote, "Most mayors find themselves compelled by the nature of the office, their political posture, and their personalities to be mediators more often than arbitrators, and to be arbitrators more often than innovators,"[23] and "the most likely leadership style to emerge is that of the cautious political broker."[24]

The record of the early years of the administrations of John Lindsay and Edward Koch indicates that innovative leadership is possible in New York. But innovative leadership is often limited by the very ingredients that inspire it—political and financial constraints. The potential for crusader mayors to overcome this problem is largely unknown since both Lindsay and Koch gave in to aspirations for higher office. In each case, the failure to gain the higher office caused a loss of their innovativeness in their subsequent years as mayor. The experience of the mayors with regard to labor relations suggests that leadership strategies are inextricably woven into the political and financial assets of the mayor, which in turn suggests that no mayor is likely to be an innovator for very long.

Changes in Mayoral Function and the Exercise of Mayoral Power

If mayors are destined to act as mediators and brokers, in what capacities are these strategies applied? In 1960, Sayre and Kaufman listed four mayoral functions: chief of state, chief executive, chief legislator, and chief of party. Mayoral power has always been the result of the interplay of all four of these functions. But in the past thirty years, these functions have changed, and with these changes in function have come changes in power as well.

The mayor's roles as chief of state and chief executive have merged, in large part due to the growing importance of television. Prior to television, the mayor's exercise of his chief of state role had the greatest influence over his public persona: nonsubstantive duties (that is, ribbon cuttings and greeting foreign dignitaries) attracted press and public attention, projected the mayor's image, identified the mayor with the city and thus helped to give the mayor the advantage of favorable public opinion in controversies with other political actors. But television has directed attention to the mayor's exercise of executive power, rather than his ceremonial role, and mayors have sought to "package" their executive function for the media.

The executive power is vested in the mayor by the City Charter. The mayor has substantial control over the day-to-day operations of city government. Agency heads at federal and state levels will often cultivate independent support within the legislative branch but, by and large, this has not been the case in New York. Commissioners are solely dependent on the mayor in part because, with few exceptions, their appointments are not subject to confirmation by a legislative body.

In addition, over time mayors have developed increasingly elaborate mayoral staffs. During the Lindsay administration, the practice of appointing special mayoral assistants to oversee substantive agencies was begun. Since then a number of mayoral staff agencies, including the Mayor's Office of Operations and the Criminal Justice Coordinator's office, have been created to effectively oversee mayoral agencies.

One indicator of the growth in mayoral staff power is the greater use of the institution of the deputy mayor. In the Wagner era, there was a single deputy mayor, who also was designated "City Administrator," who combined the role of trouble-shooter, overseer of administrative matters that cut across a number of departments, and operations planner. Subsequent mayors created additional deputy mayors and often gave them substantial authority. The deputy mayors were persons close to the mayor who had oversight responsibilities for broad policy areas, each of which involves a number of agencies. Throughout his term of office, Mayor Lindsay had two deputy mayors. Upon taking office, Mayor Beame appointed three deputies and gradually increased the number to six. When Mayor Koch assumed office in 1978, he appointed seven deputy mayors. However, in a major staff shakeup, Koch reduced the number of deputy mayors to three in 1979. Koch undoubtedly recognized that it was possible to expand the mayoral staff without continually creating a new deputy mayor position.

As a member of the Board of Estimate, the mayor was able to block actions by the board that would have challenged mayoral power. Most legislative initiatives within the city council have been at the prompting of the mayor, and mayors have made extensive use of their power, conferred by the charter, to issue executive orders that can make substantial changes in policy and administrative practice.

The interaction of the media and the mayor's executive power has helped build the public image of the mayor over the past thirty years—especially the image of management of the city at times of crisis. Both John Lindsay and Edward Koch were particularly effective at this media packaging process.[25] At a time of urban unrest, Lindsay packaged his executive actions in the context of being a healer. Thus, the most memorable image of the Lindsay administration was that of the mayor walking the streets in New York's black and Latino communities. Contrast Lindsay's image with that of Edward Koch. Koch sought to portray himself as the leader of the city's middle class. The media symbol of the Koch administration is again, the active mayor, at the Brooklyn Bridge encouraging commuters to walk across the span while deriding strikers during the 1980 transit strike.

Lindsay and Koch were able to create these images because they understood the media and their power to dominate its coverage of city government. Both Lindsay and Koch owed their success at the polls in large part to the media. Lindsay's campaign for mayor was born at the old *Herald-Tribune* and Koch's first campaign was strongly aided by a front page endorsement from the *New York Post*. Both Lindsay and Koch dominated local news coverage during their years as mayor.[26]

Mayor Abraham Beame failed to cultivate an executive image through the media. He was ill-equipped to do so. Unlike the charismatic/photogenic/urbane Lindsay or the quintessential New Yorker Koch, Beame was viewed as a colorless party functionary in the media, although the media were friendly to him during the 1973 campaign and in his first year in office. That benign attitude changed to scorn in 1975, with the onset of the fiscal crisis. Thus, during Beame's greatest test as an executive, he was unable to manage the media, nor could he control the policy agenda. During the fiscal crisis and in the aftermath of the 1977 blackout,[27] the press portrayed Beame as a mayor unable to manage the city.

The mayor does retain certain aspects of the chief of state role described by Sayre and Kaufman. New York remains the largest city in the United States and has increasingly become the center of a global economy. In addition, New York's immigrant communities continue to be large, and affect local politics. For example, the State of Israel has played an important role in New York City politics due to the strength of the Jewish vote. Finally, both John Lindsay and Edward Koch had served as members of Congress and had been particularly active on foreign policy issues.

All of these factors explain the degree of attention that mayors devote to foreign policy. Of recent mayors, Edward Koch clearly relished the mayor's foreign policy role and was outspoken on a wide range of foreign policy issues including Israel, Soviet Jewry, Soviet-American relations, democracy in China, and the international drug trade. New York City has also played a leadership role in attacking South African apartheid. The city was one of the first U.S. governments to apply sanctions against companies with operations in South Africa.

As the chief of state role has merged with chief executive responsibilities, and mayors have come to be defined by their media image as an executive, the mayor's role as chief of party has declined. The media, particularly television, allow the modern mayor to directly persuade voters. As a result, the mayor is no longer dependent on the machinery of a political party to govern. But without the party base, the mayor must be a skillful coalition builder among those interests that are key to a successful candidacy—especially when the mayor seeks higher office. The decline in the mayor's role as chief of party is a dramatic change from the mayor described by Sayre and Kaufman. They suggested that a mayor who is ineffective as chief of his party will be perceived as weak, and thus be incapable of governing. John Lindsay proved them wrong. Lindsay, elected as a Republican/Liberal in 1965, was denied the Republican nomination in 1969, losing in the primary to State Senator John Marchi. Yet, despite rejection by his own party, Lindsay won reelection running only on the Liberal line.

The decline in the mayor's role as chief of party is also the result of the growing independence of candidates seeking other elective offices, who have become less dependent upon the mayor for support. Because of the increased cost of campaigns and the ineffectiveness of the party organizations, all candidates are pretty much on their own. Traditionally, support of the mayor was critical for statewide candidates: yet, during his three terms as mayor, Edward Koch failed to support a single winner in a seriously contested Democratic primary for statewide office.[28]

Finally, the mayor's role as chief of party has undoubtedly been blurred by the fusion candidacies and party changes during the past thirty years. John Lindsay started his mayoralty as a Republican/Liberal, was reelected as a Liberal, and ended his term as a Democrat. In 1981, Edward Koch became the only candidate for mayor to win both the Democratic and Republican nominations.

Reliance on media image for mayoral power has left mayors vulnerable to challenges from both localized power bases and outside political forces. Unlike political parties, the media do not give the mayor an adequate means of reaching out into local neighborhoods. The links between City Hall and the average New Yorker, once provided by the political machine and their block and precinct captains, no longer exist. As a result, mayors have often faced strong community-based opposition to their exercise of power. During the Forest Hills housing crisis, Mayor Lindsay had no means of leveraging community support through party loyalty. Similarly, opponents of Westway and other economic development projects have defied mayoral support for these projects and attempted to defeat them through both the legislative and judicial process.

The absence of a strong link between the mayor and neighborhoods has also contributed to the NIMBY, or "not in my backyard" phenomenon. During the 1980s, communities have been unwilling to accept unpopular city facilities, such as jails, community-based mental health facilities, and housing for low-income or homeless New Yorkers. Community advocates argue that their resistance to these projects is in large part due to the failure of City Hall to work with communities during the planning stages of the project. When mayors controlled party organizations, they could more easily impose plans on communities without risking community-based opposition. However, some of the limits on the mayor's ability to deal with neighborhoods are a result of the changing demography and the increasing racial and ethnic stresses; even old-style party machines probably could not have overcome these tensions.

Mayoral power has also been subject to challenges from outside political forces in the federal and state governments. This vulnerability is attributable to the increase in New York City's dependency on outside funds. In the fiscal year 1961, state and federal aid accounted for just under 20 percent of New York City's operating budget and under 5 percent of the capital budget. By fiscal year 1985, federal and state aid accounted for over 36 percent of operating revenues and almost 30 percent of capital budget revenues. At the height of federal aid to the city during the late 1960s, intergovernmental assistance totaled over 40 percent of operating budget revenues.

As is often the case, with money comes power. As New York grew more and more dependent on outside funds, the state and federal governments were able to exercise greater authority over New York City. With federal and state aid often come set terms of program implementation, and New York's policy agenda became driven less by the mayor and more by eligibility for outside funding.[29]

Federal and state authority reached its peak during the fiscal crisis. Congress set a number of highly restrictive conditions for its financing assistance in 1975 and again in 1978, and the U.S. Treasury Department established an office that closely scrutinized New York City fiscal matters during this period. The state legislature authorized the governor to virtually take over New York City's budget process in return for providing financial assistance as part of the bailout of New York City. The result was that the mayor was largely stripped of his executive authority.

The lack of mayoral control over the party allowed the city's congressional and state legislative delegations to act as independent political power brokers. These legislators were no longer the "ambassadors" of the mayor in Washington and Albany, but independent players in the policy-making process. Thus, while the changed role of the media encouraged mayors to act independently in the exercise of their executive power, without the benefit of party support, the lack of party leadership has led to challenges to mayoral power from both the community level and from Washington and Albany.

Electing Mayors: Primaries and Third Party Fusion Candidacies

Since 1960, primaries and fusion candidacies have produced a process of electing mayors that is in some ways more open, but the side effects are not entirely benevolent. Like the mayoralty itself, mayoral campaigns have come to be dominated by the media. The media focus for campaigning has made elections very costly, so the process is really fully open only to those who can raise very large amounts of money. Also, the changes in the electoral process themselves have further weakened the party organizations. The openness of the process to "outsiders" who can raise money has encouraged inexperienced candidates—like the two Republicans in 1989—who conceivably would have been very inept mayors if elected.

In 1961, Mayor Robert Wagner faced strong primary and general election challenges from Arthur Levitt, New York State comptroller, and Louis Lefkowitz, New York State attorney general, respectively. Although Wagner prevailed, and subsequently took control of the party machinery from Democratic leaders who supported his primary opponent, challenges to incumbent mayors have since become the rule. In 1965, Wagner declined to seek a fourth term as mayor in part because of a potential primary challenge and the predicted fusion candidacy of Congressman John Lindsay. Lindsay, a liberal Republican, had the support of the Liberal party, which had historically supported Democratic candidates. Throughout the next twenty-four years, the Liberal party continued to play a significant role in the election of mayors, although it generated declining numbers of actual votes on election days. After 1965, the Liberal party's main electoral role was to offer one of the Democrats or Republicans a chance to run in November as an independent if denied the major party nomination in the primary election. In return, mayors and governors gave the small band of long-time party officials some patronage jobs to dispense.

In 1969, Mayor Lindsay was defeated in a rare Republican primary by State Senator John Marchi. The Democratic candidate, Mario Proccacino, emerged from a crowded Democratic primary field. Lindsay, winning the support of liberal Democrats and Republicans, was reelected on the Liberal line, after having broadened his base of support to include some of the most important municipal workers' unions. In 1973, the threat of a crowded Democratic primary field was a factor in Lindsay's decision not to seek a third term. Two-time Comptroller Abraham Beame emerged from the primary field, having defeated Congressman Herman Badillo in a runoff.[30] Beame defeated Republican John Marchi in the general election.

In 1977, Mayor Beame was challenged in his own Democratic party primary by a field of six candidates and failed to even reach the runoff. Congressman Edward Koch defeated Mario Cuomo, who was then a member of Governor Hugh Carey's cabinet (as secretary of state) in the runoff, and survived a stiff challenge from Cuomo on the Liberal line in the general election. In 1981 and 1985, Koch, despite his popularity, was challenged in Democratic primaries by Brooklyn Assemblyman Frank Barbaro in 1981 and City Council President Carol Bellamy and Assemblyman and Manhattan Democratic Party Leader Herman Farrell in 1985. In 1989, Edward Koch faced a primary field of three other candidates and was defeated by Manhattan Borough President David Dinkins. Dinkins went on to defeat former federal prosecutor Rudolph Giuliani running as a Republican/Liberal fusion candidate.

Since 1960, in six elections where incumbent mayors sought reelection, they faced primary challenges in all six and lost the primary on half of those occasions. Primary challenges for the mayoral nomination have become the rule, rather than the exception.

Who Runs for Mayor?

Despite having a smaller population than Brooklyn and Queens, Manhattan has continued to produce most mayoral candidates. Of the four mayors since 1960, only Abraham Beame of Brooklyn was not a Manhattan resident. In 1989, all six of the candidates for the Republican and Democratic nomination were Manhattan residents.

Before 1960, only three members of Congress had ever run for mayor: however, since 1960, the mayor has become an attractive "off-year" option for members of Congress.[31] Six members have run for mayor in the past thirty years, with two—Lindsay and Koch—being successful.

Diversity in candidate ethnicity, gender, and race has also increased since 1960. Jews and Italians continue to dominate the candidate field, with Jewish candidates—Beame and Koch—enjoying more success in general elections than Italians—Procaccino, Congressman Mario Biaggi (in 1973), Cuomo, and Barbaro. However, the most significant change has been the increase in candidacies by Latinos and blacks. Herman Badillo's candidacies in 1973 and 1977, and the candidacies of Manhattan Borough President Percy Sutton (1977) and Herman Farrell (1985), set the stage for the eventual election of David Dinkins in 1989.

Women candidates also have started to play a role in mayoral elections. In 1977, former Congresswoman Bella Abzug was initially thought to be a favorite in the Democratic primary. In 1985, City Council President Carol Bellamy was a serious primary challenger to Mayor Koch. In addition, both the Liberal and Republican Parties have nominated women (Mary Codd and Dianne McGrath respectively).

The New Power Brokers: Money and the Media

Since 1961, campaign spending has taken on new importance in New York City mayoral campaigns. The growth of television advertising and the decline of political party organizations had increased the power of campaign contributors and media consultants. Candidates who once had to rely on district leaders to produce votes now must take their case directly to the public. To do so, they need the resources that can only be provided by large contributors and the "packaging" of media consultants.

In 1961, campaign spending in a mayoral campaign surpassed $2 million for the first time. Seeking reelection without the support of the Democratic county leaders, Mayor Robert Wagner spent in excess of $1 million in the primary and general elections; Wagner's Republican opponent, Louis Lefkowitz, also spent close to $1 million in a losing effort.[32] Significantly, television was not yet a major means of campaigning in 1961. Wagner and Lefkowitz probably invested most of their campaign funds in building field organizations. Ordinarily, Wagner, as the Democratic nominee, would have been able to rely on the support of the party organization: however, Wagner's primary victory was a defeat for the regular organization. Thus, he had to invest in building an organizational alternative to the party.

By 1965, spending in the mayoral campaign had doubled: the two major party nominees spent more than $4.1 million. John Lindsay spent more than $2.5 million, outspending his opponent Abraham Beame by almost $1 million.[33] In part, increased use of media explained the spending increase. Lindsay had used television to increase his citywide name recognition. Yet, field organization still played an important role in the campaign: the Lindsay campaign created an independent club organization throughout the city.

John Lindsay won the 1969 mayoral election on the basis of his television advertising. Lindsay had lost the Republican primary and had only the Liberal line. His "crusader" first term had alienated much of the New York middle class. Lindsay hired David Garth to direct his media campaign. Garth fashioned a media campaign that sought to convert Lindsay's weaknesses into strength. His commercials portrayed the mayor's position as "the second toughest job in America" and had Lindsay conceding that mistakes had been made during the first term. The commercials were effective enough for Lindsay to run successfully to the left of both his conservative Republican and Democratic opponents. In focusing resources on television advertising, Lindsay again spent more than $2 million on the campaign, outspending both of his opponents by approximately $1.5 million.[34]

The 1973 mayoral campaign appeared to signal a reduction in campaign spending, despite the growing importance of television advertising. Total spending by candidates who reached the general election dropped to slightly over $2 million, close to the 1961 spending level. All four candidates for the Democratic nomination used television extensively. Assemblyman Albert Blumenthal spent more than half of his total primary campaign budget on advertising, approximately $150,000. Congressman Herman Badillo spent $70,000 for television ads in the final week of the campaign alone.[35] But no candidate was able to spend enough on television to overcome the party support of Abraham Beame.

By 1977, spending in mayoral campaigns returned to the pre-1973 trend. Mario Cuomo and Edward Koch spent more than $3.4 million. The seven candidates for the Democratic nomination spent close to $5.3 million in the primary alone, and Edward Koch's total expenditures of $1.8 million represented the most ever by any Democratic candidate for mayor.[36] Television advertising became the primary means of voter contact in 1977 and, based on the results, the most successful. Two of the candidates for the Democratic nomination, Mayor Abraham Beame and former Representative Bella Abzug, had strong organizational support from the Democratic machine and the liberal community, respectively. Both invested funds in field organization.

Both Mario Cuomo and Edward Koch were relative unknowns. Cuomo had failed in his one prior bid for elective office and held a low-profile state government office. Koch, though an effective congressman from Manhattan, started the campaign in single digits in the polls. Both turned to experienced media consultants to direct their campaigns. Cuomo selected Gerald Rafshoon, who one year earlier had directed the successful media campaign for President Jimmy Carter. Koch turned to David Garth, who, after successfully guiding John Lindsay's media campaign, had also done television advertising for Hugh Carey's winning campaign for governor in 1974.

With a small field organization, Koch relied extensively on Garth. Garth created two images for Koch. One was highly personal: Koch was linked to Bess Myerson, the first Jewish Miss America, and a heroine to the Jewish community, to combat rumors that Koch was gay. The other was strategic: Garth perceived that voters were looking for a mayor who was capable of managing New York. The result was a series of ads based on the theme, "After eight years of charisma, and four years of the clubhouse, why not competence?" With Koch and Cuomo spending over $1 million on television time during the primary election and runoff, television dominated the 1977 mayoral election, and became a permanent part of the process of electing mayors.

While overall campaign spending decreased during the 1981 mayoral election, Mayor Koch still spent close to $1.7 million on his reelection, outspending his closest opponent by almost $1.5 million dollars. Although Koch had the support of all five of the county Democratic leaders, his campaign still emphasized television advertising. Finally, in 1985, Koch spent $7 million in his reelection effort, breaking all previous records for campaign spending. Again, Koch spent substantially on a media campaign, but also conducted an extensive direct mail campaign.

The trend since 1961 suggests that media campaigns have replaced the party organization as the key to electing mayors. The "antiorganization" candidacies of Wagner, Lindsay, and Koch all coincided with increases in campaign spending. Successful reform candidates needed to spend more to overcome the opposition of the Democratic party leadership. But the 1981 and 1985 reelection campaigns of Edward Koch suggest that increased campaign spending and extensive use of television advertising have become institutionalized in the electoral process.

Media consultants see this as a positive development, arguing that they have taken the power away from the party bosses. According to one media consultant, ''Anybody can run for office if they can get enough backing to get on the tube. They don't have to pay party dues any more; they don't have to come up through the ranks; they don't have to kiss the butts of party bosses. . . .''[37] While party organization power is diminished by the emphasis on the media, there are still power brokers in the process. Media consultants who are successful become valued commodities and can demand input in shaping candidate views and agendas. Large campaign donors can do the same and, often, the appearance that they do suggests relationships as dangerous as the relationship between the old political machine and officeholders.

The linkage between contributions and influence is a relatively old one in American political history. It certainly predates the heavy use of television advertising. For example, Mayor Wagner's 1961 campaign was embroiled in a scandal when a member of Wagner's City Planning Commission solicited contributions from developers and real estate interests.[38] But the cost of television advertising in the expensive New York media market has increased the size of donations, and not surprisingly, many of those donors have important business relationships with the City of New York. Between 1982 and 1985, Edward Koch's campaign committee received over $250,000 in contributions from underwriters of New York City bonds and close to $1 million in large contributions from real estate interests.[39]

It was this linkage between campaign contributions and the appearance of impropriety that prompted the city council to adopt a system of public financing for municipal campaigns for the 1989 election. Contributions for mayoral candidates were limited to $5,000 per donor, and total spending was capped at $3.6 million per candidate for the general and primary elections combined. Once candidates reached a threshold of contributions, they received public matching funds so that the actual amount that candidates could raise was limited to a figure below $3.6 million.

The 1989 election was the first under the new system of public finance and may not be typical of future elections. However, at least one expected result did not occur in 1989. Some proponents of campaign finance reform had suggested that by limiting expenditures, candidates might be forced to reduce their spending on television advertising and instead invest in field organization. This was not the case in 1989. Instead, most of the mayoral campaigns invested their limited resources almost exclusively in media. To the degree that field organization played a role in the campaign, as it did for David Dinkins, it was because of an existing field organization that had remained from Jesse Jackson's primary win in New York City one year earlier. Thus, while the power of large campaign contributors may be limited by campaign finance reform, the experience of one election suggests that media consultants will have a growing influence over the mayoral election process.

Conclusion

The ways in which the mayor functions and is seen are very different from 1960—as depicted by Sayre and Kaufman—in at least three respects. First, the mayor is no longer the head of his party, and the party itself matters very little. Second, the politics of the mayoralty now depend mainly on how the mayor is depicted by the media, and how effectively he or she can use the media in support of policy, administration, and reelection. Third, the election process has changed considerably. It is much less structured, even a free-for-all, tied to media presentation and dependent upon media consultants.

One thing that has *not* changed is the value of incumbency. Even if the mayor no longer has political power as party head and no longer can count on the party organization in the quest for reelection and in communicating with the neighborhoods, the mayor retains substantial executive power and easily commands media attention. The mayor is a formidable figure, vulnerable to defeat over specific policies or for reelection only in the event of extraordinary circumstances, like the fiscal crisis for Mayor Beame in 1977 and the scandals and racial tensions of his third term for Mayor Koch in 1989. It is the mayor, and no one else, who sets the tone and policies of city government.

Since the spectacular initiatives that New York's city government took under the leadership of Fiorello LaGuardia in 1934–45—vast public works programs, reforms in virtually all the operations of city government and new social policy efforts in health, welfare, and housing—New Yorkers have expected their city government to be an activist one, responding to virtually every perceived public problem. Mayors, until the fiscal crisis of 1975, accepted that it was their duty to do so, and so pressed to expand the scope of city government even more. In the 1980s, with the recovery from the fiscal crisis, New Yorkers again began to expect a lot from city government, and thus from mayors.

But changes in conditions since the 1960s actually have reduced the ability of mayors to respond effectively to perceived public problems, even the ability to effectively deliver ordinary municipal services. Racial tensions and poverty have aggravated some of the social problems, making them far more complex and less responsive to conventional policy interventions. And any city government response that is efficacious is likely to be very costly. Meanwhile, the various external constraints on the city government's freedom of action, principally stemming from federal and state government rules and from awareness of the city's economic vulnerability, limit the city government's capacity to do more, or even as much, as it has done in the past. Being mayor of New York may not have been "the second toughest job in America," as alleged by David Garth on behalf of John Lindsay in 1969; it may be just that in 1990.

Notes

1. See generally J. David Greenstone and Paul E. Peterson, *Race and Authority in Urban Politics: Community Participation and the War on Poverty*. Chicago: University of Chicago Press, 1976. For a different point of view, see Chapter 13, by Charles Hamilton.

2. The Voting Rights Act contains a special provision requiring preclearance of any changes in the electoral process in certain jurisdictions where minority voting has been low, relative to population, in the past. The preclearance provision applies to three of New York City's five boroughs.

3. Wallace Sayre and Herbert Kaufman, *Governing New York*. New York: Russell Sage, 1960, p. 657.

4. The Board of Estimate consisted of the mayor, the city council president, the comptroller, and the five borough presidents. In 1989, the Supreme Court ruled that the distribution of votes on the board violated the representational principle of "one person, one vote." See Chapters 4 and 15 on elected officials and on the new charter, by David Eichenthal and Joseph Viteritti, respectively, for more on the Board of Estimate. The new charter approved by the voters in November 1989 eliminates the Board of Estimate and assigns many of its functions to the city council. Whether the changes strengthen or weaken the mayor remains to be seen; both results were foreseen by opponents of the proposed charter.

5. The scandals centered on patronage appointees to the city's Department of Transportation, and eventually extended to Democratic county leaders in Queens and the Bronx, the Bronx borough president, a former county leader in Brooklyn, and members of Congress. During the Lindsay administration, there had been major scandals in the Police Department, involving traditional police corrupt practices but not patronage. Previously, in the O'Dwyer administration in the late 1940s, there had been a major patronage-related scandal that led to the mayor's resignation.

6. In fact, only a very few of the important commissionerships have been held by patronage appointees of the traditional type since 1960. Most were selected because of their demonstrated managerial skills, in private industry or in government, or because of their professional expertise, in health, social welfare, housing, finance, engineering, etc. See also, Theodore Lowi, *At the Pleasure of the Mayor*. Glencoe, IL: The Free Press, 1967.

7. Douglas Yates, *The Ungovernable City: The Politics of Urban Problems and Policy Making*. Cambridge: The MIT Press, 1977.

8. Ibid., 148–149.

9. Ibid., 150.

10. A.H. Raskin, "Why New York Is 'Strike City,'" *New York Times Magazine*, December 22, 1968, p. 7.

11. Interview with Robert Linn, responsible for negotiating with the unions on behalf of the city during much of the Koch administration, August 13, 1987.

12. Mary McCormick, "Labor Relations," in *Setting Municipal Priorities: American Cities and the New York Experience*, Charles Brecher and Raymond Horton, editors. New York: New York University Press, 1984, p. 303.

13. See Chapters 11 and 7 by Jewel Bellush and Annemarie Hauck Walsh for more on these processes.

14. The city had been underspending on the maintenance of city buildings and infrastructure for years, and there had been almost no capital spending in the mid-1970s, at first because the capital budget was used to defray operating deficits and then, after the fiscal crisis hit, because of restrictions on city spending.

15. Westway was hotly opposed by most environmental groups, liberal Democratic politicians in Manhattan, and much of the intellectual establishment concerned with public affairs, but strongly supported by the business community, the unions, and most politicians from the other boroughs of the city. Thus, most of the elements of the Koch coalition were for Westway, while some of his most strident enemies were opposed to the project.

16. The latter charge was based on comparison of two inconsistent sets of statistics for the years between 1977 and 1982. It is not clear whether the point was a valid one for those years, but all the data showed that, after 1982, city residents fully shared in the growth of jobs within the city.

17. Yates, *The Ungovernable City*, p. 153.

18. Theodore Lowi, *The End of Liberalism: The Second Republic of the United States*, 2nd Edition. New York: W.W. Norton, 1979, p. 184.

19. Raskin, "Why New York is 'Strike City,' " p. 7.

20. Interview with Robert Linn. Some of the most substantial gains by the unions occurred not through collective bargaining but as a result of action by the state legislature and court decisions, over the continued opposition of the Lindsay administration.

21. See Chapter 11 by Jewel Bellush for an account of the main controversies, notably the Forest Hills scattered-site housing controversy that brought Mario Cuomo to prominence, as the mediator.

22. See Chapter 6 by David Rogers for discussion of the two types of decentralization of the Lindsay years.

23. Sayre and Kaufman, *Governing New York*, p. 685.

24. Yates, *The Ungovernable City*, p. 152.

25. John Lindsay and Edward Koch had the advice of the same media consultant, David Garth. Garth's influence on mayoral politics is discussed in the next section.

26. See Chapter 12, by Edwin Diamond and Piera Paine, on the media.

27. During the summer of 1977, a lightning storm destroyed some high-capacity transmission lines in Westchester County; appallingly incompetent responses by controllers for the New York State Power Pool and the Consolidated Edison Company resulted in a blackout that lasted for more than twenty-four hours in most of the city. There was extensive looting in some sections of the city and no coherent response by city authorities. Twelve years earlier, in November 1965, there had been a much more extensive blackout that affected the entire Northeast, but there had been virtually no civil disorder in New York City at that time.

28. In 1980, Koch supported Bess Myerson, who later served as his commissioner of cultural affairs, for the U.S. Senate. She lost the primary to then-Representative Elizabeth Holtzman. In 1982, Koch challenged Mario Cuomo for the Democratic nomination for governor and lost. In 1986, Koch supported John Dyson for the Democratic nomination for U.S. Senate. Dyson lost to public interest lawyer Mark Green. Finally, in 1988, Koch's candidate for president, U.S. Senator Albert Gore, was trounced in the New York Democratic primary.

29. See Chapters 8 and 9 on the city's relations with the state government and with Washington, by Gerald Benjamin and H. V. Savitch, respectively.

30. New York State law provides for a runoff between the two top vote-getters in a primary for citywide office where no candidate receives 40 percent of the vote. This provision was added after the 1969 Democratic primary resulted in the nomination of

Mario Procaccino. Procaccino's victory was seen by professional politicians as an example of how, with no runoff, a very weak candidate could be nominated, with little chance of winning the general election.

31. Members of Congress do not risk their seats in Congress because mayors are elected in the odd years following a presidential election, while congressional elections are in even years.

32. Leo Egan, "Campaigns in City Cost 2.2 Million," *New York Times*, November 29, 1961, p. 30.

33. Sydney Schanberg, "Lindsay Campaign Costs of $2.5 Million Reported," *New York Times*, November 24, 1965, p. 1.

34. Clayton Knowles, "Lindsay Outspent Both His Opponents," *New York Times*, November 26, 1969, p. 32.

35. Frank Lynn, "Mayoral Candidates Seek To Thwart Voter Apathy," *New York Times*, May 29, 1973, p. 1.

36. Frank Lynn, "Seven in Democratic Race Mount Final Drive With Heavy Spending," *New York Times*, September 1, 1977, p. 1; Maurice Carroll, "Cuomo Top Candidate in Debt for Campaign," *New York Times*, December 11, 1977, p. 71.

37. Diamond and Bates, *The Spot: The Rise of Political Advertising on Television*. Cambridge: The MIT Press, 1984, p. 373.

38. Clayton Knowles, "$25,000 Dessert Pleases Wagner," *New York Times*, September 28, 1981, p. 34.

39. Study of Campaign Contributions by State Senator Franz Leichter, November 26, 1985.

4

The Other Elected Officials

David R. Eichenthal

Broadly speaking, local governments perform two functions: they *implement* policy, that is, they administer laws and programs enacted by local, state, and federal legislatures and they *develop* policy, a process involving legislative enactment, oversight, and reform. The obvious structure that matches its function is a strong executive branch, capable of flexible day-to-day administration and an equally powerful legislative branch to both set policy and oversee executive performance, with the two branches operating under rules that provide checks and balances.

At no time between the formation of the city with its present boundaries in 1898 and the publication of this book has New York City had this ideal local government structure. Instead, in recent decades, executive power over long-range policy has been unchallenged, with the mayor having quasi-legislative powers through the use of executive orders. But the mayor's administrative powers were hampered by the presence of a quasi-legislative body, the Board of Estimate, that could reject various administrative initiatives. Legislative power was divided between the board and city council. However, in many areas, neither had effective policy-making powers: given the split in legislative authority, neither was an aggressive overseer of executive power.

There has been dissatisfaction with the structure of New York City government for decades. Six charter revision commissions functioned between 1936 and 1989, with City Charter changes that significantly reallocated powers effective in 1938, 1962, and 1977, prior to the fundamental changes of 1989. As if the structure of New York's municipal government were not sufficiently complex, during the past three decades, state legislators also have come to play an increasing role in the municipal policy-making process.

Editor's note: This chapter deals with the structure of city government as of 1989. The U.S. Supreme Court decision that held the Board of Estimate to be in violation of the one-person, one-vote rule required drastic changes in that structure. The changes are discussed in Chapter 15 on the new city charter by Joseph Viteritti.

The remainder of this chapter will examine the power beyond the mayor from three different perspectives: the institutional history of the Board of Estimate, city council, and state legislature in the policy-making process; the exercise of institutional power in the context of government functions—legislative, budgetary, and oversight; and the nature of nonmayoral elected officials' political power.

Who the Actors Are

Every four years, New Yorkers elect a mayor, comptroller, and city council president. At the same time, voters in each borough elect a borough president, and voters in each of the city's councilmanic districts elect their representative to the city council. New Yorkers also elect (every two years, not coinciding with the municipal elections) members of the state senate and state assembly: in 1989, 25 of the state's 61 senators and 60 of the 150 members of the assembly were from New York City.

The mayor, the comptroller, the council president, and the five borough presidents comprised the membership of the city's Board of Estimate between 1938 and 1989. The board had extensive powers over land use policy and city contracts and had the power to revise or reject the mayor's proposed annual budget.[1] Citywide officials (the mayor, comptroller, and council president) each had two votes, while each of the borough presidents had one vote. The nonmayoral members of the board had other duties under the charter, but membership on the board constituted their most important and powerful base of power.

The city council is the city's legislative body. It has the power to enact local laws and a broad mandate to oversee the performance of city agencies. The council also has limited advice and consent powers over certain mayoral appointees and shared authority over the city's annual budget with the Board of Estimate.

The state legislature exercises considerable power over city affairs. Under the state's home rule and preemption doctrines, once the state gains authority over an area of local law, all future revisions of law must come from the state legislature, rather than the city council. The legislature's power is balanced by the requirement that when legislation specifically addresses an issue in one jurisdiction, that jurisdiction must enact a home rule message before the legislature can act. However, control over the process, once it shifts, continues to remain in the hands of state, rather than local, legislators. In addition, state legislators exercise control over state-created agencies that are major actors within the city, such as the Metropolitan Transportation Authority and the Urban Development Corporation, and city agencies created by state law, such as the Board of Education and the city's courts.[2]

Political Institutions at Work

The Board of Estimate

Sayre and Kaufman described the Board of Estimate as "the queen" on "the chessboard of the city's politics."[3] Three decades later, the Board of Estimate was eliminated from the chessboard altogether, in response to a successful federal court challenge to the equal voting power of borough presidents representing boroughs whose population varied, at the extremes, in a ratio of six to one.[4]

Earlier, changes in the city's governmental structure were designed to allow the Board of Estimate to check more effectively the power of the mayor. In 1901, the board's composition was changed to remove mayoral appointees. In the 1930s, the Thatcher Charter Commission sought board *control* over the mayor; by enhancing the board's powers, the backers of Republican Fusion Mayor Fiorello H. LaGuardia sought to prevent Tammany Hall from regaining total control of city government when the Democrats recaptured the mayoralty. As a result, the board received the mandate "to direct the business affairs of the City," an administrative role more suitable for an executive than a committee.[5]

The 1961 Charter Revision removed the bulk of the board's legislative powers, but the board members used their budgetary and land use powers to challenge the mayor on both administrative and legislative issues. In the early 1970s, the board substantially affected the final budgets of Mayor John V. Lindsay.[6] More recently, Mayor Edward I. Koch and the members of the Board of Estimate engaged in bitter disputes over the location and nature of sites for homeless shelters, jails, incinerators, and other unappealing facilities.

The Board of Estimate's initiatives were affected by its peculiar structure and its mixture of powers and functions. Conceptually, the board was both an administrative and legislative body; it exercised power over city contracts and played a major role in the budgetary process. Because these functions were combined, neither was performed well. As elected officials, board members were ill-suited to collectively "manage" the city. As quasi administrators, they nonetheless took legislative actions.[7] The board also frustrated real separation of power; the board's challenges to mayoral authority often failed because of the mayor's presence on it.

The comptroller was the "potential giant of the Board . . . a magnet to draw around him the rivalries toward the mayor felt by the other members."[8] Because the comptroller is the city's chief fiscal officer, there often has been an unclear line between his roles as an independent auditor and as a rival to the mayor. Ideally, the comptroller should have used his political power to enforce his findings as an auditor and his seat on the board as a voice for fiscal responsibility. Too often, the comptroller's power has not been so used.

The borough presidents have been a tangible expression of the city's past: its origins in separate cities and counties.[9] In many urban counties across the country, the chief elected county official is the county executive; in New York City, the functional equivalents of county executives are borough presidents. Unlike county executives, borough presidents have extremely limited executive powers. Structurally, borough presidents represent decentralized city government; they supposedly voted on the board as their borough's representative. In reality, "The origin of borough government had nothing to do with genuine local government. . . . [It was] purely political."[10]

Historically, the city council president had been the weakest member of the Board of Estimate. Unlike the mayor, comptroller, and borough presidents, the city council president did not have any substantive powers aside from his or her membership on the board. The lack of an independent source of power, combined with the lack of support from the staff that would exist if the council president had other functions, hobbled the council president in the policy-making process.

The council president does technically preside over the city council. However, like the vice-president's role in the U.S. Senate, the council president does not have voting rights, except in the case of a tie and generally plays a limited role in council deliberations.

The primary power of the city council president is the right of succession in the event of the death, removal, or resignation of the mayor. Sayre and Kaufman referred to the city council presidency as an office "of ambiguity and inhibited anticipation";[11] John Nance Garner and John Adams's comments on the vice-presidency are equally applicable to the city council presidency.[12]

The City Council

By 1989, the city council had existed in the same form for fifty years: no one ever praised it. The council replaced the Board of Aldermen under the 1938 charter revision, and was initially structured to strengthen legislative power over the mayor. Almost twenty-five years later, the Cahill Commission again sought to strengthen the city council, by reducing the powers of the Board of Estimate, making the council the city's sole legislative body. In 1975, the charter was amended again to mandate that the council regularly review city agency performance. Despite these efforts to enhance its power, the council has never emerged as a potent legislative body.

The State Legislative Delegation

In 1961, Sayre and Kaufman dismissed the role of state legislators in the city's policy-making process. The New York City state legislative delegation was seen as claimants, participants, and instruments for the city's influence. Lacking the

political power of the mayor, legislators—no less than any other official dependent on the party machinery—were subservient to the mayor.

Since 1961, New York City's state legislators have become an independent force
in the policy-making process. This change has largely been a function of the growing overall state role in the city's governance. The basic constitutional provisions
with respect to home rule have not changed. However, more and more legislation
involving city policy must emanate from Albany rather than City Hall. In addition,
New York City Democrats have come to control the state assembly: Democrats have
been in the majority in the assembly in all but six of the years between 1964 and
1991, and New York City members dominated the Democratic caucus.

Exercising Power: Legislative, Budgetary, and Oversight

Legislative Power

The City Charter provides that the city council shall be "the local legislative
body of the city." During the past twenty-five years, the council has initiated
some important legislation, for example, in regard to pollution abatement and
gun control. In recent years, the council has enacted landmark gay rights, anti-
smoking, and campaign finance legislation; however, all of these major initiatives have come only with the support of the mayor. By and large, the council
has failed to act independently, in part because its power has almost always been
limited by powers exercised by other actors in the policy-making process. Until
the 1961 charter revision, the Board of Estimate had acted as "the upper chamber in a bicameral city legislature."[13] Most local laws were subject to Board of
Estimate approval. Although the 1961 revision was intended to enhance the
power of the council, it instead increased the power of the mayor by reducing the
power of the board, while leaving the legislative power still divided.

Although after 1961, the board no longer had the power to enact local law, it
retained broad quasi-legislative authority over land use, contracting, and franchise issues until 1989. Under the charter's uniform land use review procedure
(ULURP), the board had ultimate authority over virtually all economic development projects. The board also had the power to approve certain contracts that are
not the subject of competitive bidding. In addition, the Bureau of Franchises, an
agency of the board, administered grants of operating authority for industries as
diverse as bus service and telecommunications. The board's continuing role in
these quasi-legislative areas reduced the importance of the council.

The council's powers also are limited by the intervention of the state legislature in New York City affairs. The legislature does so in one of three ways: first,
the legislature can enact New York City legislation after the city council passes a
home-rule request; second, the legislature can enact laws applicable only to
jurisdictions "with more than one million inhabitants"; third, the legislature can

create a regional authority to perform functions previously the responsibility of the city government itself. Thus, interest groups, the governor, or even the mayor can use the legislature for "end runs" around city council resistance, even on questions that are of no concern to the rest of the state.

Some city issues have long been subject to intervention by the state. The state has always exercised authority over criminal justice policy, although local governments control their own police forces and the council has authority to define certain acts as misdemeanors. Prosecutors and criminal court judges are state officers, governed by state law rather than municipal ordinance.

But in the late 1960s, a wave of state policy takeovers occurred. As a result of state legislative initiatives, the city government's power over educational policy was reduced; school decentralization and the reorganization of the Board of Education made it more difficult for the mayor to affect school policy and operations. The board's structure and operations are matters of state, not city, law. Efforts to change the system must be directed at the state legislature, not the city council.

New York City's labor relations policy also became a matter of state law, rather than locally adopted policy. The New York City Collective Bargaining Law, which first went into effect in 1967, mandated the creation of a citywide bargaining unit to negotiate labor contracts for employees in mayoral agencies and created the Office of Collective Bargaining to administer the law and resolve labor-management disputes. Nonmayoral agency employees' contracts are governed by the state Taylor Law. While much of the Collective Bargaining Law reflected local policy adopted during the previous decade, these initiatives had largely been those of the mayor. Thus, the council has been virtually shut out from the city's labor relations policy.

The 1960s also marked the end of the city's legislative authority over the service responsible for the consolidation that created the present city in 1898, the transit system. In 1953, the state legislature created the New York City Transit Authority. While transit policy was no longer under the direct control of the City of New York, the mayor still exercised power through his appointment of a majority of members to the board of the Transit Authority. However in 1968, the city's power over its own transit system became subordinate to the state. As the price for regionalization of transportation and the resulting increase in funding resources, the chair of the newly created Metropolitan Transportation Authority (MTA), which was designated a state agency, was appointed by the governor, not the mayor, and the Transit Authority became a subsidiary of the MTA. Now, most issues involving New York City mass transit policy are controlled by the governor and the state legislature, rather than the mayor and city council.

The fiscal crisis during the 1970s marked the next wave of state policy takeovers. Arguably, the state legislature was as responsible for the crisis as the city council: like the council, it had sanctioned much of the financial gimmickry of the 1960s and early 1970s and had granted the city the authority to continue its policy of deficit financing. However, the legislature, unlike the council, did not lose power as a result of its fiscal irresponsibility. Instead, the state legislature played a critical role in approving the restructuring of the city's debt and setting many of the emergency fiscal policies in place. Although Governor Hugh Carey provided much of the leadership during the fiscal crisis, the elevation of the issue to the state level again gave rise to increased state legislative power over the city.

The fiscal crisis also shifted control over more of the city's services to the state government. Perhaps the most significant example of this shift was the state's takeover of the City University of New York. As a result, all city education policy—elementary, secondary, and higher—is now subject to state, rather than local, legislative control.

Since the fiscal crisis, the shift of major city functions to state control has continued. Rent regulation, which became a state government function in 1947 as federal rent control was being phased out, was turned over to city administration and policy making in 1962 and a new program, rent stabilization, was added to the city government's housing powers in 1969. For more than twenty years, rent regulation was the most controversial and perhaps the most important of the municipal housing policies. Historically, the council had played an active role in these issues, ranging from direct legislation to overseeing the city agency that administered the programs. However, in the 1980s, administration of rent control and rent stabilization was shifted from the city Department of Housing Preservation and Development to the State Division of Housing and Community Renewal.

Thus, the city has substantially reduced power to act in four of the most critical policy areas—transit, rent regulation, education, and labor relations. The city's elected officials have ceded power to the state (usually involuntarily), and thereby to the city's state legislative delegation. Legislative initiatives in these spheres by the city council (or, before 1990, the Board of Estimate) is now almost totally preempted by the state's role.

The council's legislative powers have also been challenged by the mayor, through the promulgation of executive orders. Under the City Charter, all powers not specifically delegated to other bodies are vested in the mayor. The mayor also has the power to act by executive order. Over the years, the mayor has used the executive order to promote civil rights, define the powers of deputy mayors, and, frequently, to create new city agencies: the Auditor General, Bureau of Labor Services, Office of Labor Relations, Office of Operations, New York City Youth Bureau, Department of Employment, and Human Resources Administration are all entities governed by executive order rather than statute. In addition, the Public Development Corporation, which has become the city's lead agency for economic development, operates without statutory authority under a twenty-year-old executive order.[14]

In recent years, the courts have narrowed the mayor's "legislative" powers. In 1980, Mayor Koch issued an executive order banning employment discrimination by city contractors on the basis of sexual orientation. The New York Court of Appeals held that the mayor did not have the authority to issue such an order; the court went on to hold that the executive order was "an enactment of policy which the City Charter leaves to the City Council."[15] However, to date, the court's ruling has neither effectively curtailed executive power in other areas nor encouraged the council, or others, to challenge other existing executive orders.

The city council's powers are delimited in the City Charter. The council has the power to revise most provisions of the City Charter, subject to mayoral veto. Those provisions that the council cannot revise can be changed by citizen referendum. But every major charter revision, including the most recent effort in 1989, has been the result of an independent commission, appointed either by the mayor, the state legislature, or the governor. Instead of dictating the terms of the legislative process, the Council has been content to leave this chore to others, often to its detriment.

Budgetary Power

Under the pre-1990 charter, the mayor proposed the city's expense and capital budgets for adoption by both the Board of Estimate and the city council. But the board had historically played a more important role than the council in the budgetary process. More recently, other actors have weakened the fiscal powers of the local legislative bodies: as a result of the fiscal crisis, the city's state legislative delegation has had an increasing influence over budgetary matters.

Prior to the 1960s, the board, under the leadership of the comptroller, had been a force for fiscal conservatism.[16] Lawrence Gerosa was the last comptroller before the 1961 charter revision and the last to be a consistent voice for fiscal conservatism, opposing additional city taxes and new debt. As a member of the board and as the city's chief fiscal officer, Gerosa successfully opposed much of the spending and fiscal gimmickry which, when later implemented, contributed to the city's fiscal crisis.

Under the 1961 charter revision, borough presidents lost control over borough agencies, thereby greatly limiting their power to dispense patronage. Their budget-making powers became the primary means of winning political power, by bargaining for spending proposals for their boroughs. Gerosa's successor, Abraham Beame, was an ally of his fellow board members rather than a fiscally conservative opponent of budgetary logrolling. Although Beame had served as the city's budget director, he was also a product of, and dependent on, the support of the Brooklyn Democratic organization. As a result, Beame did not have the political independence to effectively curb the Board of Estimate's excesses, had he wished to do so.

How did the city finance the increased spending throughout the early 1960s? The spending was financed through new taxes, increased rates of old ones, and increased borrowing. As early as 1961, the Moore Commission noted that "the only consistent area of important Council action . . . has been that of taxation.''[17] Between 1957 and 1960, the council had enacted twenty-three increases in municipal taxes. With state legislative authorization, the council continued to enact new taxes, extend old taxes, and increase tax rates into the early 1970s.

The tax increases imposed by the council did not solve the fiscal problems, which increasingly were temporarily dealt with by such stratagems as consistently overestimating revenues and underestimating expenses.[18] As a result, the city balanced its budget on paper but never in reality, with the deficits covered by increased indebtedness. The comptrollers were not voices of fiscal restraint; neither Beame, who was again elected as comptroller in 1969 and became the leader of the opposition to the high-spending Lindsay administration—but not to its spending policies—nor his successor when he was elected mayor, Harrison Goldin. No doubt Goldin was on the scene too late to prevent the fiscal crisis that struck in 1975, but his failure to sound alarms or urge radical shifts in policy earned him a fair share of the blame for the crisis in the landmark 1977 Securities and Exchange Commission report on the crisis.

Ultimately, the state government was forced to temporarily take over the city's budgetary powers. In 1975, the legislature, responding to the leadership of Governor Carey, declared the city to be in a state of financial emergency and enacted legislation imposing a freeze on city employee salaries, creating a moratorium on the repayment of the city's short-term debt, and establishing the Municipal Assistance Corporation as a means of borrowing on behalf of the city government. The legislature also created the position of special deputy state comptroller for the city of New York to monitor city finances. Finally, the Emergency Financial Control Board was established and empowered to approve or reject the city's annual budget and all contracts (including collective bargaining agreements). Of the seven board members, only two, the mayor and city comptroller, were city officials.

In the 1980s, the council and the board again assumed their places in the budgetary process. However, the mayor retained effective control of the budget, with the board and the council usually contesting marginal items, rather than pressing for fiscal responsibility or new budgetary policy directions.[19] The state legislature continues to play a powerful role in the budgetary process. State aid finances close to one-fifth of the city expense budget, a proportion that has fluctuated in a narrow range during the last twenty-five years, while the state's financing of capital outlays within the city has increased enormously. The state has also taken over all costs related to two federal programs, Supplemental Security Income and Medicaid.

The legislature provides considerable funding to government programs in the city outside the normal state budget process. Through the member-item budget, individual members can allocate funds in the state budget for specific projects in their districts. This practice has come under considerable attack; some legislators have grossly abused the process, using appropriations to fund, among other things, a cheese museum and parochial schools. However, member-item funds have also gone to innovative programs in housing, senior citizen assistance, and education. Legislators argue that the member-item budget process allows them to circumvent the state and city bureaucracies and provide necessary programs for their constituents. These types of programs, which traditionally would have been funded by the city, yield tremendous political benefits for the legislators who can take direct credit for new aid to a local school or for funding a community organization.

Oversight

City council

The council has the power under the charter to serve as the primary oversight body in city government. In 1971, the Scott Charter Revision Commission recommended that the council be authorized to conduct investigations of city agencies. The 1975 charter revision enhanced the council's investigative powers by clarifying the powers of standing committees to conduct investigations, creating a Legislative Office of Budget Review, granting specific subpoena powers to standing committees, and creating a broad charter mandate to investigate and assess the performance of city agencies. In addition, the charter directs the city Department of Investigation to conduct investigations upon the instruction of the council. But the council has made little use of these broad investigative powers.

With the election of John Lindsay in 1965, the first Republican mayor in two decades, the Democratic city council appeared to be the natural counterbalance to the mayor. Within a month of Lindsay's election, Council Majority Leader David Ross and City Council President-elect Frank O'Connor pledged that council investigations would be stepped up during the coming four years. To support these efforts, the council amended the charter to give itself greater power over the spending of its own budget; budgetary freedom allowed the council to hire new staff to conduct its investigations.

One year later, there had been few successful oversight efforts. However, the council did increase its staff, adding twelve new staff positions. The new council staff was justified as a means of providing the council with improved investigative capacity. Instead, new staff positions became "a patronage trough for hungry Democrats" who were shut out of the new Lindsay administration.[20]

In 1969, Thomas Cuite succeeded David Ross as majority leader. One year later, Cuite created eight council subcommittees to provide regular oversight over the city's administrative agencies. In 1971, the Citizens Union issued a report critical of the city council's failure to provide effective oversight; it criticized the "absolute domination" of the council by Majority Leader Cuite, as well as the increase in the council's payroll over the past six years.[21]

In 1986, Peter Vallone replaced the retiring Thomas Cuite as city council majority leader. Vallone hired more than forty new city council staff members in his first seven months in office. In announcing the creation of a special team of council investigators, Vallone proclaimed, "With our expanded and expanding staff, no longer can agencies over which we have little or no control deceive us." Staff investigators have the mandate to "probe the operations of every agency funded in whole or in part by the city with an eye to insuring that every dollar paid by every taxpayer is accounted for and well spent."[22]

During the past quarter century, every new council majority leader has entered office proclaiming the need for the city council to become an equal partner in city government by providing more effective oversight. Simultaneously, every majority leader has determined that the way to achieve this increased power is by increasing the council's payroll. In 1959, the council staff numbered eight; in 1987, the council central staff exceeded 120.

By and large, the increase in staff has not resulted in more effective city council oversight. Efforts to oversee the creation of the superagencies during the Lindsay administration did not yield positive reforms. The council's much-heralded investigation of the Human Resources Administration in 1968 produced heated rhetoric, but few results. Under Peter Vallone's leadership, only a few of the committee chairs carried out constructive oversight efforts. Councilwoman Ruth Messinger, the council's leading reformer, challenged city tax abatement policies in her role as the chair of the Subcommittee on Revenue Enhancement. Councilman Abraham Gerges produced several thoughtful reports on the city's failed policies on the homeless as chair of the council's Select Committee on the Homeless. However, these efforts are notable as exceptions, and even they have not been translated into positive legislation.

Comptroller

The charter also provides broad investigative and oversight powers to the comptroller. The comptroller's power to audit the expenditure of city funds is at the core of his or her role as the city's chief fiscal officer. The audit power extends beyond examination of fiscal issues and allows for review of programmatic and policy initiatives as well. By exercising this audit authority, the comptroller can comment on and criticize the executive's capacity to implement virtually every city policy. This power is unique to the comptroller under the structure of city government. Since there is a generally weak legislative oversight, some have argued that the comptroller must serve as "the principal check on the mayor."[23]

Like auditors generally, the comptroller does not have the authority to implement the findings and recommendations of most audit reports. Instead, the comptroller must generate sufficient public outrage and press coverage to force the mayor to act or—prior to 1990—convince the other members of the Board of Estimate to vote to change city policy. Even if the comptroller succeeds at changing mayoral policy per se, there are no guarantees that the policy changes will continue unless the comptroller remains vigilant.

Since 1961, comptrollers have often either underutilized or abused their oversight power. In 1961, Abraham Beame was Mayor Wagner's hand-picked candidate for comptroller; he had served as city budget director and was part of Wagner's "anti-bossism" slate. With Wagner effectively controlling the Board of Estimate and Beame politically tied to Wagner, the comptroller's oversight role was limited.

In 1965, Beame, like his predecessor Gerosa, ran unsuccessfully for mayor. His successor, Mario Procaccino, did not have sufficient influence over the board to force the mayor to respond to comptroller audits. As a result, Procaccino became the first comptroller to rely on public outrage as a means of implementing his audit findings. Procaccino publicly criticized Mayor Lindsay's administration of municipal programs, in particular targeting mismanagement in the city's public hospitals. Although Procaccino's audits did little to effect changes in city policy, they provided him with the platform that enabled him to win the Democratic nomination for mayor in 1969. However, Procaccino, the second consecutive single-term comptroller, became the third consecutive comptroller to unsuccessfully seek the mayoralty.

The 1969 election marked the return of Abe Beame to the office of comptroller and the beginning of the four-year period that marked the zenith in the comptroller's oversight power. Beame adopted Procaccino's approach of using public outrage to enforce the audit power. Unlike Procaccino, Beame was also able to successfully lead the Board of Estimate in revolts against the mayor.

Beame's most successful challenge was on the issue of consultant contracts. As part of its effort to reform city government, the Lindsay administration had brought in numerous outside consultants to conduct reviews of city agencies; between 1968 and 1971, the city spent $10 million on consultant contracts. Under the city charter, the comptroller has the power to refuse to pay illegal claims. Beame argued that the consultant contracts were illegal; they were the result of neither competitive bidding nor Board of Estimate approval. Lindsay challenged Beame's decision in court, but the comptroller prevailed.[24]

Beame's successor, Harrison Goldin, was perhaps the most successful comptroller in the use of audits to generate public outrage. Goldin, who served as comptroller longer than any of his predecessors (sixteen years), used the audit power to criticize both mayoral and nonmayoral agencies. Mayoral agencies often quietly agreed to implement the smaller changes suggested, in advance of publication of the audit reports, so Goldin's oversight efforts were often effective in substantive detail, if not politically. However, Goldin's inability to lead the

Board of Estimate made many of his more controversial interventions—those not quietly accepted by the mayor's appointees—ineffective.

The state legislature

The legislature also has played an aggressive role in conducting oversight investigations of city agencies. During the mid-1970s, the assembly Office of Legislative Oversight and Analysis conducted an investigation of the city's fiscal crisis. In 1977, the assembly created a Subcommittee on City Management, and during the next three years, the subcommittee conducted investigations of the city's Addiction Services Agency, the Summer Youth Employment Program, the city's real estate auction process, and mismanagement at the Health and Hospitals Corporation. It was often a more aggressive watchdog of city policy than any of the city council's standing committees. In addition, the subcommittee's efforts produced tangible results. Following the subcommittee investigation of price fixing in the asphalt industry, the city agreed to build its own asphalt facility to ensure competitive prices.[25]

Political Power: Where It Comes From, Who Gets It, and What They Do with It

Where It Comes From

Political power in New York is a function of popular support and money, and is driven by ambition. The Board of Estimate before 1990, the council, and the state legislative delegation have had the resources, through use of their discretionary powers, to attain political power. The members of each of these institutions have used their powers to different degrees and with different outcomes.

Money

The members of the Board of Estimate (especially the mayor, of course) had the greatest access to the dominant factor in New York politics—money. The board's powers allowed its members to participate in decisions on zoning, mapping, and other land use controls; tax abatements; the awarding of noncompetitive contracts, leases, and franchises; and a variety of other economic development and urban renewal matters. Conflicts of interest are endemic, though in most cases, the conflict is ethical, not legal.[26]

Borough presidents

Borough presidents became, in the 1980s, major players in the trading of economic development incentives for political support. Their involvement in economic development can be divided into three areas: land use, tax abatements, and coordinated subsidization. Borough presidents influenced both the beginning and end of the Uniform Land Use Review Procedure (ULURP); they appointed community board members and voted on ULURP applications before the Board of Estimate. As members of the Industrial and Commercial Incentives Board, they have considerable say over which developers receive tax abatements. Finally, as members of the Board of Estimate, borough presidents nominated five members to the New York City Public Development Corporation, the primary coordinating agency of city-sponsored economic development. PDC also works closely with boroughwide economic development corporations, whose staff is often closely aligned with the borough president.

The borough presidents have used these powers to gain political support. Throughout the 1980s, developers contributed heavily to the campaign funds of the borough presidents in recognition of their power over economic development issues. Between 1982 and 1986, developers with applications before the Board of Estimate contributed in excess of a quarter of a million dollars to the borough presidents. Comptrollers and council presidents also benefited from their roles on the board and participated in the implicit tradeoff of economic development policy for campaign contributions. The comptroller has another set of powers that affects the generosity of contributors: the comptroller determines where city funds will be invested and which brokerage houses will float New York's municipal bonds. Not surprisingly, comptrollers have been able to attract sizeable campaign contributions from the city's financial community.

Constituent service and patronage

Political power depends on more than money; there must be an element of popular support as well. While the exceptional elected official can maintain popular support on the basis of personality or ideology alone, continued political survival usually requires constituent service and/or patronage.

Borough presidents have pursued a combination of patronage and constituent service as a means of maintaining their popular support. Borough presidents have maintained strong ties with their county political organizations, and in the cases of Donald Manes and Howard Golden, borough presidents served simultaneously as county leaders. As a result, they have had access to nonborough presidential patronage positions in the executive branch and in the court system where judges are often products of the Democratic party organization.

Borough presidents also have retained popular support through constituent services by local community boards. Historically, community planning board members have been appointed by the borough president. However, their role was reduced during the Lindsay administration, when the mayor sought to impose an executive system of decentralized government. The mayor's little city halls were linked directly to Lindsay, and thus, possessed more power than the community planning boards. The elimination of little city halls under the Beame administration, combined with the 1975 charter revision, made community boards the primary city service liaison agency in the community. Although 50 percent of community board members are nominated by council members, the borough president retains the ultimate power of appointment. In addition, every borough president now has a staff member devoted to community board liaison. Finally, community boards look to the borough presidents for their ability to translate community board priorities into city budgetary appropriations.[27]

Like the borough presidents, state legislators are able to win popular support through a combination of constituent service and patronage. State legislators have moved beyond the tradition of providing community services through the political clubhouse. Virtually all New York City members of the state legislature maintain offices in their communities, with regular office hours and staff. In many ways, state legislators are able to overwhelm the community outreach capabilities of their councilmanic and borough president colleagues. In 1989, there were sixty assembly members and twenty-five state senators from New York City; between 1938 and 1989, there were thirty-five or fewer council members elected from districts. State assembly members represented districts that were only about half the size of council districts during those five decades, allowing them to focus more attention on individual constituents. In addition, state legislators now have direct responsibility over traditionally municipal functions. For example, constituent complaints about education and transportation are now appropriately addressed to state, not city, legislators.

Politically, state legislators have become among the most powerful local officials in the city. Legislators now frequently control their district leaders, enabling them to provide local patronage positions. The member-item budget has been used to solidify ties between community groups and the local assembly member and state senator.

The growth in state legislative political power has been the result of the development of an alternative political power structure for New York City Democrats in Albany and the simultaneous reduction in mayoral control over party machinery. A New York City Democrat has held the Speaker's chair in the assembly continuously since 1974. This gives New York City assembly members their own voice in state politics, independent of the mayor's. It has also given them extraordinary access to new sources of patronage; members no longer have to rely on City Hall for political jobs when political plums are now directly available in legislative staff positions. There has been abuse. Shortly after the 1986 revelations of serious corruption in New York City government, a major scandal broke involving the existence of no-show and exclusively political jobs in the legislature.

As the state legislative delegation's political power was growing, mayors increasingly lost control over party machinery. Media coverage, rather than patronage and community service, had become the key to mayoral popular support.

The council president also had access to popular support through constituent service. The 1975 charter revision provided for the council president to perform a "super-constituent service" role; the council president had the duty to oversee, coordinate and facilitate responses to citywide service complaints. This ombudsman role allowed the council president to increase his or her staff, thereby increasing links to the electorate.

Members of the city council heretofore have derived the limited political power they wielded from their provision of constituent services. Unlike members of the state legislature, council members have only recently opened district offices and started to communicate with constituents through regular newsletters. By 1989, virtually every council member had a district office staff. However, as latecomers to constituent service provision, council members are at a significant disadvantage in the constituent service competition with community boards and state legislators.

Who Gets It

Who runs for the second-tier (second to the mayor, that is) elected offices? Between 1961 and 1990, there were only three comptrollers: Abraham Beame, a former budget director; Mario Procaccino, a former judge; and Harrison Goldin, a former state senator. By contrast, there were seven city council presidents during the same period, including two former mayoral appointees (Paul Screvane and Sanford Garelik), one former borough president (Andrew Stein), and one former state senator (Carol Bellamy).

There have been twenty-three borough presidents. The officeholders have been the most diverse group, by race and gender, in city government. In twenty-five years, there were five black borough presidents—Hulan Jack, Edward Dudley, Constance Baker Motley, Percy Sutton, and David Dinkins—all of Manhattan, two Latinos—Herman Badillo and Fernando Ferrer—both of the Bronx, and two women—Constance Motley and Claire Shulman of Queens. Of the fourteen other Board of Estimate members to serve during the same period, none were black or Hispanic, and only one was a woman, Bellamy. Prior to serving as borough presidents, eight members had served as council members, seven as state legislators, three as judges, and three as deputy borough presidents. In addition, two served as administrators in city government. Aside from those borough presidents who also achieved power as party leaders—Donald Manes and Howard Golden—only three nonmayoral members of the board served for more than eight years between 1961 and 1990—Robert Abrams (Bronx borough president), Percy Sutton, and Goldin.

What They Do with It

Of the thirty-two members of the Board of Estimate to hold office between 1961 and 1989, only four were elected to higher office: Abraham Beame was elected mayor; Herman Badillo was elected to Congress; Robert Abrams was elected state attorney general in 1978 and reelected in 1982 and 1986; and Andrew Stein was elected council president.

Until the 1950s, service as city council president or president of the Board of Aldermen had been a stepping stone to the mayoralty. Mayors McClellan, Mitchell, LaGuardia, and Impellitteri had all held the position prior to becoming mayor.

Since the 1950s, no city council president has successfully sought any higher political office. In the middle of his one term as council president, Frank O'Connor received the Democratic nomination for governor, but was trounced in the general election by Nelson Rockefeller. Paul O'Dwyer was an unsuccessful candidate for the U.S. Senate in 1976. During Carol Bellamy's two terms as council president (1978–85), there was widespread speculation that she would seek any one of a number of statewide offices.[28] Finally, in 1985, Bellamy challenged Ed Koch in the Democratic primary for mayor and was soundly defeated.

Comptrollers have been slightly more successful. Abraham Beame won his party's nomination for mayor twice while serving as comptroller, and was elected once; Mario Procaccino received the Democratic nomination for mayor, but lost; and Harrison Goldin was the Democratic nominee for state comptroller in 1978, but lost as well. Goldin also sought the Democratic nomination for mayor in 1989, unsuccessfully.

City council membership has changed considerably over the past twenty-six years. In 1960, Sayre and Kaufman described the members of the council as "a gathering of party wheelhorses";[29] the council was composed of twenty-four Democrats and one liberal Republican; there were no women or Latinos on the council and only two blacks. By 1987, the representative nature of the council had improved dramatically. Women held ten seats in the council, blacks held six seats, and Latinos held three seats.

In an effort to enhance representation of the minority Republican party, the 1961 charter revision created ten at-large seats on the council, with each borough having two at-large members. At-large council representation helped produce some of the council's better members during the 1970s. Henry Stern, Robert Wagner, Jr., and Robert Steingut were all elected as at-large council members. However, in 1981, a federal court declared that the at-large seats represented a violation of the equal representation principle and council at-large representation ended in 1982.[30]

Between 1938 and 1957, no council member had ever been elected to state-wide or citywide office and no former member had ever been elected mayor. Until the late 1960s, service on the city council was often followed by judicial appointment; two of the council majority leaders during the 1960s, Eric Treulich and David Ross, both left the majority leadership for the security of the judiciary.

Since the 1960s, council members have enjoyed greater upward political mobility. Ed Koch progressed from the city council to Congress to the mayoralty and Ted Weiss, after fifteen years as a member of the council, was finally elevated to Congress in 1976.

Five council members have moved on to serve on the Board of Estimate, and, in 1987, two of the seven members of the New York City Board of Education were council alumni.

Finally, like other elected bodies, the membership of New York City's state legislative delegation has become more diverse. By 1988, the assembly delegation contained twelve blacks, twelve women, and three Latinos; the senate delegation included four blacks, two women, and two Latinos. Perhaps the best indication of the growth in power and prestige of state legislators is their ability to successfully seek higher office. Of the three citywide elected officials holding office at the end of the 1980s, two, Harrison Goldin and Andrew Stein, were former state legislators; eight of the city's fourteen congressmen were also former state legislators.

Is This Any Way to Run a City?

Over one hundred years ago, one of the nation's first scholars of public administration, Woodrow Wilson, wrote that "power and strict accountability for its use are the essential constituents of good government."[31] If we judge the structure of New York City government during the 1960s, 1970s, and 1980s by this standard, it clearly failed.

New York did not have a single institution devoted to assuring strict accountability for the exercise of executive power. The mayor's powers often went unchecked due to the absence of a single powerful counterbalance. The problem was not an absence of counterbalancing institutions, but an abundance. In theory, the presence of the city council and the Board of Estimate should have maximized mayoral accountability. In practice, we have seen that the division of power between the council and the board have left the mayor's policy discretion and executive abuse of power largely undeterred.

Neither institution had the power necessary to curb the executive. The council, the city's sole legislative body by charter mandate, had to compete with the board, the state legislature, and the mayor, in the formulation of role. The board, though it had a preeminent role in the budgetary process, shared its power with the council and the state; its power was compromised by the mayor's membership. Oversight powers were divided between the council and the comptroller, with one having the power to affect change but not the will, while the other had the will but not the power.

Unable to perform the traditional functions of a legislature, both the board and the council have been of limited service to the citizens of New York over the past two and a half decades. The council has developed an institutional inferiority complex; although its leadership regularly proclaims new beginnings, little action results from the rhetoric. Its members often satisfy themselves by winning battles for new power, new staff, or higher salaries, then retreat from the promised performance which justified the new power. The Board of Estimate has provided some legitimate challenges to mayoral power. However, its efforts were all too often preempted by the concerns of individual members seeking political power.

It is probably inevitable that elected comptrollers see themselves as future mayors; since the LaGuardia administration, comptrollers have been open rivals of the mayor. Each of the three comptrollers in office between 1961 and 1989 became candidates for mayor, and the comptroller's primary function, the oversight audit power, has been exercised largely as a weapon in the mayor/comptroller rivalry. Only Abraham Beame was able to use his position as comptroller to lead the Board of Estimate, but the price for leadership of the board was high; although Beame could effectively attack the mayor, the fiscal policies and practices he espoused in the course of the rivalry contributed greatly to the fiscal crisis that struck in 1975, after he had become mayor.

The city council president presides over an office with little power, or point, aside from providing an elected successor to the mayor. The job of successor at the federal and state levels—the vice-president and lieutenant governor—is equally powerless, but federal and state constitution makers have refrained from trying to embellish the offices with formal duties that can do no more than complicate the functioning of government.

The council and the borough presidents compete for grassroots political power. Both seek to provide constituent service as a means of gaining public support. Here, competition may have more salutary effects. At least in theory, the more elected officials seeking to provide constituent service, the more constituents will be satisfied with government. It is unclear whether the additional actors in constituent service improve its quality, or lead to wasteful duplication of effort.

The major new actor in the municipal policy-making process has been the state legislature. More than board of estimate members or council members, state legislators are able to effectively challenge mayoral power due to their independent base of power in Albany. In the absence of effective checks at the local level, the state legislative role has been positive. In the case of the fiscal crisis, the state's role was critical to the very survival of the city.

In more normal times, the city needs a local government that effectively and responsibly governs municipal affairs. The criteria for the appropriate structure for municipal government in New York are those set by Woodrow Wilson over a century ago.

Notes

1. When the board considered the budget, the mayor could not participate in the board's vote.
2. See Chapter 8 by Gerald Benjamin, on the state/city relationship and Chapter 7 by Annmarie Hauck Walsh, on public authorities, for a fuller treatment of these relationships.
3. Wallace Sayre and Herbert Kaufman, *Governing New York City*. New York: Norton, 1965, p. 652.
4. For further discussion of the decision and its consequences, see Chapter 15 by Joseph Viteritti.
5. Laurance Tanzer, *New York City Charter*. New York: Clark Boardman Co., 1937, p. 480.
6. In addition, the board, led by the then-comptroller Abraham Beame, waged a major fight against the mayor on the issue of consultant contracts. This will be discussed in detail in the section on the comptroller.
7. For example, because of the interaction between land use provisions of the charter and the construction of shelters for the homeless, the Board of Estimate, rather than the city council, set the city's policy on housing the homeless.
8. Sayre and Kaufman, *Governing New York City*, p. 633.
9. In 1898, the then-city of Brooklyn and the counties of Queens and Richmond (Staten Island) were consolidated with the city of New York. Even after consolidation, the city's structure was altered when, in 1914, the Bronx became a separate county.
10. Governor Al Smith quoted in Moore Commission, *Staff Report 20,* (1961), p. 77.
11. Sayre and Kaufman, *Governing New York City*, p. 632.
12. John Nance Garner said that the vice-presidency "isn't worth a bucket of spit." However, John Adams remarked that as vice-president, he was "nothing, but he could be everything."
13. Sayre and Kaufman, *Governing New York City*, p. 627.
14. Although the Public Development Corporation is not authorized by the city council, the majority does appoint five members of the corporation's twenty-member board.
15. The court held that "an executive may not usurp the legislative function by enacting social policies not adopted by the legislature." *Under 21* v. *City of New York*, 65 N.Y.2d 344 (1985).
16. According to Sayre and Kaufman, *Governing New York City*, p. 630, "The Board . . . has an affinity for the status quo. Its dominant characteristic is its capacity to absorb, as if it were a great sponge, the constant stream of proposals for change."
17. Moore Commission, *Staff Report 31* (1961), p. 14.
18. Charles Morris, *The Cost of Good Intentions*. New York: Norton, 1980, p. 216.
19. See Chapter 11 by Jewel Bellush on the increases in mayoral authority that resulted from the fiscal crisis.
20. Charles Bennett, "Council Called Patronage Haven," *New York Times*, January 19, 1966, p. 30.
21. Maurice Carroll, "Report Criticizes Council Make Up," *New York Times*, February 27, 1971, p. 28.

22. "Vallone Reshuffles City Council Staff to Press Inquiries," *New York Times*, July 27, 1986.

23. Steven Clifford, *Office of the Comptroller of the City of New York*, City of New York (1973), pp. 28, 30.

24. See *City of New York* v. *Beame*, unpublished opinion (42768/70, J. Grumet), af'd 37 A.D.2d 89 (2d Dept. 1971).

25. See Daniel Feldman, *Reforming Government*. New York: Wm. Morrow, 1981.

26. For details, see Jewel Bellush's Chapter 11 on interest groups.

27. See Chapter 6 by David Rogers for more extensive treatment of neighborhood government during the past thirty years.

28. In 1982, Bellamy was actively preparing for a race for state comptroller, but decided against running when Mayor Koch announced his candidacy for governor.

29. Sayre and Kaufman, *Governing New York City*, p. 81.

30. *Andrews* v. *Koch*, 528 F. Supp. 246 (1981).

31. Woodrow Wilson, *Congressional Government*. New York: Meridian Books, 1956, p. 189.

5

Bureaucracy: Power in Details

Blanche Blank

In the generation that has passed since Sayre and Kaufman wrote about New York's civil service there have been dramatic changes in America in general and in New York City in particular.

The city's civil service (meaning by that its 300,000-plus public employees and its elaborate labyrinth of rules) has responded to these changes slowly. Its bureaucratic byways would still seem familiar to a traveler who had passed though a generation ago. Although the ethnic and racial mix of the people working in most agencies has changed visibly, the structures and procedures of an overall "civil service culture" cast a shadow that has been hard to dispel. Individual agencies, each with its own special departmental penumbra, have moved at varying paces and with individual styles to face new problems and recurring ones. They have adapted in different ways to old and new clientele groups. And they have also responded in special ways to changes in leadership. Yet over and above noticeable agency changes, the corporate culture of the civil service is still palpable.

It may be the very essence of any bureaucracy to move cautiously, even ponderously. This natural tendency is exacerbated by our American dedication to a check and balance system and a desire to keep our civil service "independent" of the partisan pulls of electoral politics. We are also a people very prone to ambivalence in regard to our public affairs. Our responses to critical questions of public policy frequently run in equal and opposite directions. We are prone to giving mixed signals. We admire "productivity"; but not any more than we admire "democracy." We insist on "equal opportunity" and "minority rights"; but not at the cost of our attachment to "achievement and merit." We abhor corruption, but a clever outlaw can still be a hero. Since we are unwilling to make up our minds, unable, perhaps, to offer a neat and logical "order of priorities," we may ourselves be causing some of the special problems about which we later complain.

It is, after all, our civil service—in New York and all the nation's cities—that repairs streets, tunnels, and bridges, puts out fires, collects garbage, fills potholes, maintains parks and playgrounds, runs schools, libraries, prisons, and hospitals, issues licenses, and operates public housing projects. It also provides a long list of services for the aged, the handicapped, the poor, the homeless, the mentally distressed, the victims of emergencies, the unemployed, and those on welfare. In New York City, all these are the business of a single municipal government.[1] The city's annual budget—the cost of delivering those services— passed the $25 billion mark by the late 1980s.

A Critical Paradox: Productivity versus Democracy

New York's civil service is expected to be both productive and democratic, and therein lies the essential paradox that accounts for much of the public's displeasure. Each goal is necessary and proper, yet they are often incongruent. Productivity refers to efficient and effective practices: the greatest number of outputs for each unit of input. Democracy, on the other hand, is more complex; some measure of equal opportunity, representativeness, freedom, public accountability, limitations on unrestrained power, fair procedures, and access to the secret ballot to express the popular will. Thus, democracy in America is a tall order, and it brings in its wake certain well accepted principles of doing public business: "separation of powers," "checks and balances," "federalism," "proceduralism," "elections," "party politics," and a large role for "public opinion." Each is a constraint on the "efficient" delivery of public services.

Though business too adheres to democratic standards of civil rights, worker safety, and corporate democracy, it does so at its own pace and in its own way. The civil service, on the other hand, systematically violates the principles of good management not by choice, but as a matter of law. It is mandated to do so in order to be democratic. Consider the following hoary recommendations from our nation's most widely accepted management theorists—and note the manner in which the city's democratic imperatives frustrate them.

Virtually all management theorists agree that authority must be commensurate with responsibility, that there should be unity of command and a strict scalar process. This means that an officer should not be held accountable for tasks and outputs that he or she cannot properly and sufficiently control; that there should be one boss in an enterprise, and that all persons in an organization should be arrayed in a hierarchy in which each one knows exactly to whom he or she gives orders and from whom he or she takes them. But in New York City, authority is demonstrably in no way commensurate with responsibility, and there are many bosses and breaks in the chain of command.

Authority is limited by many levels of law and many decades of tradition. Responsibility is limited only by an ill-informed public opinion. The public, for example, routinely holds the mayor responsible for the city's educational deficits; but the mayor does not even control the Board of Education, to say nothing of the vast educational bureaucracy that spreads beneath it. That is, he or she has little authority over the matter. The mayor is also popularly held responsible for the "welfare mess," the "homeless," and the "drug problem." Each of these, is in turn, enmeshed in policies over which the mayor has no control such as nationally determined immigration and drug traffic programs as well as federally mandated definitions and dollars that determine welfare entitlements.

Commissioners, too, face this dilemma. They may be held responsible for large budgets and billion-dollar contracts, but their authority to award bids or to adjust salaries in their departments is curtailed by civil service rules and state laws. They are not free to exercise their own judgment. Contracts must go to the lowest bidders and promotions and raises are routines, not rewards.

The related idea that there should be only one boss is also the victim of our national tradition of "separated powers" and "divided powers." The mayor shares the reins of the city with a Board of Estimate (before 1990), a city council, a set of "independent" boards and commissions, and occasionally even the borough presidents. He also shares power with the governor and with the Washington bureaucracy, all of whom can and do frustrate and even contradict him. This has happened in regard to city policy on gay rights, on housing the homeless, and on various projects connected with the city's redevelopment plans. Line commissioners share their power with various staff officers such as the budget director.

There are many weak links in the New York City civil service system "chain of command." Legislation of both the city and state protecting civil servants and the considerable contract coverage that has evolved from city union negotiations violate this canon in many ways. Rank-and-file workers not only have protection against a supervisor's disciplining and considerable independence from him or her in matters of promotion, but under union regulations, many workers are free to report to union stewards matters that in the private sector would be thought to be under the "chain of command." For example, a park department supervisor complained that when he called a worker's attention to the fact that his nameplate was askew (and he did this very politely), the worker reported him to the union, called it harassment, and complained further that the supervisor's very appearance at the playground was an "inappropriate unannounced visit."

There are a number of other conventional precepts about hiring and promoting solely on the basis of merit that are systematically undermined by city realities. The merit tradition abjures nepotism and race, yet the politics of New York City consists of election games played out precisely in class, race, and ethnic terms. The entire civil service has long been viewed as a reservoir of jobs for various ethnic groups. Indeed, one of the adages of increasing "Americanization" has been a niche in the civil service. In earlier decades, for example, the Police Department was, in line with this tradition, an entirely

Irish fiefdom. In later years, the Sanitation Department fell to the Italians along with the Irish. The finance offices of the city were frequently Jewish ghettos, and quite recently the Human Resources Administration has become predominantly black. Moreover, the racial-ethnic "percentage" is still the acceptable measure of our city bureaucracy's "representativeness" and is so regarded by our citizens. In recent years, national legislation and court decisions have interpreted "affirmative action" to mean that minority "representativeness" is not only an acceptable criteria for hiring and promotion, but a legally mandated one. Thus newer goals have replaced the classical "professionalism."

Clubhouse politics, moreover, is not yet dead at the level of the state legislature, which controls many of the city's resources. Therefore, those city departments that do a lot of business upstate find that it makes sense to "play politics" and they support administrative appointments that have the imprimatur of key legislative "pols." Practical politics decides management theory here.

Another well-established rule of sound management that must bow to the "real politics" of the New York City civil service is the requirement that decisions be made at the lowest level consistent with the availability of information and expertise, and be made on the basis of a rational cost/benefit analysis, and that they be kept as simple as possible. All of these common sense caveats are violated in New York City out of legal necessity. The city is enjoined to be more concerned with procedural fairness than with substantive results. This is true in terms of decisions made in procuring personnel as well as the decisions made in procuring goods and contractual services. The centralized rules dictating city procedures produce curious effects: exams that do not relate to needed talents and supplies and services that do not relate to safe and sound production. The rules made at the national and state levels that dictate welfare payments, for example, are part of the reason why the city's homeless live in hotels that cost over $1,000 a month for a single room.

Finally, there is what Donald M. Kendall, chairman of the board and CEO of Pepsico called the "most important job of top management, . . . to create a vision of the organization, a sense of purpose," so that everyone in the organization can be enlisted in making the mission a success.[2] But New York's mayor and his department heads are faced with multimission agencies and a political system that in truth does not offer much help in determining just what it is that represents the "mission." The task of sorting out priorities both among and within the city's agencies is a very inexact science.

Our normal democratic legitimatizing device, elections, does not help here. Our elections are simply a method for selecting personnel. The party platforms that routinely accompany our candidates are vague, ambiguous, and often contradictory. It is usually impossible to know which official stands for which program, and, certainly, one cannot know the order of priority that any partic-

ular program has in the grand scheme of things. An elected mayor is, therefore, at the mercy of quick-changing public opinion polls that may offer some
guidance in terms of electoral success, but no substantive help in setting up an
orderly agenda for the Police, Health, Parks, or any other city department.

There is one even more basic impediment to the pursuit of productivity. It
is the array of human motivations that the noted psychologist Abraham
Maslow has called the "hierarchy of needs"—survival, security, sociability,
status, and self-actualization. In general, these personal needs tend to eclipse
any concern for broad institutional goals. This problem is well put by Michael
Lipsky in his *Street Level Bureaucracy*: street bureaucrats, he says, "have
different job priorities than managers." The street-level workers are "interested in processing work consistent with their own preferences."[3] They usually have little interest in an agency's overall commitments and even less
interest in the finer points of efficiency. Moreover, an intelligent worker generally suspects that any newly minted "efficiency" programs usually mean a
cut in the agency's labor force.

Other psychologists have conducted experiments that further illuminate the
world of the street-level worker. The force of peer pressure and the strong pull of
the "sociability" needs of workers, for example, take precedence over productivity. Potential "Stakhanovites"[4] are anathema to most workers. There is an
unstated but well-understood modest norm for every operation, and woe betide
the maverick who tries to upset these norms. Peers are more important to the
rank and file than productivity.

But since these drives and inhibitions are operative in the business world as
well as in the public arena, why are they especially counterproductive in the civil
service? The answer is that business has a far larger number of carrots and sticks
available to mitigate the usual effects of "human nature" than does the public
sector. Business can usually generate more and faster promotional opportunities
than the civil service, and its potential for punishment is also far greater. Firing—even demoting or transferring or reprimanding—is an onerous chore in the
public sector. Rare is the bureau chief who has the time or the courage to live
through the complicated procedures and professional risks imposed by civil service regulations. And where the statutes and rules do not foil a conscientious
manager, the unions probably will.

Indeed, the negative effects of unions (from the perspective of management
prerogatives) may be more keenly felt in public agencies than in private corporations. In government enterprises, the top executives and managers who are
traditionally expected to be the countervailing force against the rank and file's
expected and understandable push for "more" are actually beholden to that
same rank and file. It is, after all, the unions who can and do deliver the
campaign funds and votes that put these executives in (and out) of office.

Moreover, New York City, in dealing with a multiplicity of unions, must always face the "citywide" implications of management initiatives. While there are analogies in the private sector, this concern is somewhat heightened in the public domain. It was very difficult, for example, for the Sanitation Department to introduce productivity incentives around 1980 by awarding extra money saved through work efficiencies because the city labor relations negotiators were fearful of the implications this might have had on other union contract bargaining. The plan almost foundered on this consideration, but was adopted—and confined to Sanitation—in the end.

The Persistence of Productivity

Despite all the logic and evidence one can produce in defense of the proposition that productivity is only a "sometime" thing for the public service, its allure persists. It has permeated the management reports of Mayor Koch and has had a long history of attraction for some of his predecessors. The pursuit of productivity has been around since the early years of this century when Luther Gulick's "efficiency and economy" movement and Ridley and Nolting's passion for "measuring municipal outputs" were in full swing. The Lindsay administration, however, may be credited with popularizing the notion of productivity in city government. Lindsay brought with him from Washington the excitement about management improvement that permeated the federal government in the late 1950s and early 1960s, some of the specific tools that had been adopted there, such as a new planning and budgeting tool called a "Program, Planning, Budgeting System" (PPBS), and officials who had worked on such systems in Washington, like his budget directors.

Mayor Beame and his deputy mayor, John Zuccotti, also worked on productivity. They established a Productivity Council and experimented with "Management Information Systems" (MIS) and "Management by Objectives" (MBO), which were then among the newer management improvement techniques of the corporate world. They also introduced the Management Plan and Reporting System, the precursor of today's Mayor's Management Report, which has been required by the city charter since 1977.

During the Koch administration, the measures used in the productivity game became more numerous and somewhat more sophisticated. The claims of productivity gains and budgetary savings made in the Koch management reports, although modest relative to the overall size of the city budget, were frequently challenged. However real or exaggerated the achievement of productivity goals, the Koch administration could claim credit for advances in measuring them.

In sum, then, "efficiency and economy" are not the only appropriate standards to apply to government agencies. The citizens of New York demand a democratic city. And this means electoral politics, affirmative action, checks and balances, and a heavy regard for procedural fairness, which typically impair, rather than advance, productivity.

A Bird's Eye View of the Civil Service

At the end of the 1980s, New York City's public bureaucracies were organized in 34 departments, over 2,500 job titles, and more than 300,000 incumbents. The common aspects of the civil service are the standards (and practices and traditions surrounding the literal standards) promulgated by state law, the state Civil Service Commission, city laws, and the city Civil Service Commission that define the personnel procedures, financial procedures, benefit structures, and regulations concerning union negotiations, contract arrangements, conflict of interest, and other ethical and political injunctions.

There are, however, decided differences among the departments in both substance and style, relating to a number of variables. In the remainder of this section of the chapter, six variables making for differentiation among agencies are analyzed: (1) the size of the agency; (2) the basic nature and complexity of its mission; (3) the number and nature of clientele and pressure groups surrounding the agency; (4) the number and type of unions involved; (5) the agency's relationship to the mayor; and (6) the character of the agency's leadership.

Size

Table 5.1 offers an alphabetical listing of the city's agencies. The total number of full-time employees, approximately 300,000, is 3 times larger than the combined work force of the 10 largest corporations in the city. It is greater than the 1980 populations of 119 out of the 169 cities in the United States with populations over 100,000.

Table 5.2 classifies the agencies by employment size. More than half of the city's agencies have fewer than 1,000 full-time employees: 12 have fewer than 500 and 9 fewer than 300. According to the celebrated writer on management, Peter Drucker, only this last category comprises "small" enterprise. All the others are "large" in the sense of requiring, in Drucker's view, "professional management." This need for professional management does indeed make a big difference in how agencies are run. In New York City government, however, the trappings of professional management, in the form of Department of Personnel controls and services, are applied more or less uniformly to *all* agencies, regardless of size.

Some of the small departments chafe at the unnecessary formality. Some of the larger ones complain of the inadequacies. One commissioner, whose department has close to 5,000 employees, said:

No overall program for middle managers exists. No rational method of recruit-ment or training exists. No systematic rotation plan like they have in the private sector. There is nobody in the city you can approach for a filing system or the techniques that have proved useful and compatible elsewhere.[5]

Table 5.1

New York City's "Administrative" Branch of Government, 1986

Line agencies	Number of full-time employees
Department for the Aging	290
Department of Buildings	737
Department of Consumer Affairs	263
Department of Corrections	7,737
Department of Cultural Affairs	41
Office for Economic Development	163
Department of Environmental Protection	4,732
Fire Department	13,525
Department of General Services	3,204
Department of Health	3,722
Health and Hospitals Corporation	49,009
NYC Housing Authority	9,124
Department of Housing Preservation and Development	3,473
Human Resources Administration/Department of Social Services	24,957
Department of Juvenile Justice	557
Landmarks Preservation Commission	50
Department of Mental Health, Retardation, and Alcoholic Services	286
Department of Parks and Recreation	4,373
Police Department	32,731
Department of Ports and Terminals	238
Department of Probation	1,293
Department of Sanitation	12,045
Taxi and Limousine Commission	459
Department of Transportation	5,939
Department of Employment	413
Board of Education	70,640

Overhead agencies	
City Planning Commission	395
Department of Finance	1,861
Department of Investigation	112
Law Department	1,005
Office of the Mayor	1,643
Department of Personnel	500
Department of Records and Information Services	38

Sources: Most data from the *Mayor's Management Report*, January 30, 1986. For the departments visited individually in the course of preparing this chapter, the figures were taken from internal documents and apply to different dates, but the lack of precision is minimal.

Table 5.2

Employment Size Distribution of New York Agencies

Category	Full-time employees	Agency
Very large	More than 30,000	Board of Education Health and Hospitals Corporation Police Department
	20,000–29,999	Human Resources Administration/ Department of Social Services
Large	10,000–19,999	Fire Department Department of Sanitation
	5,000–9,999	Department of Corrections Department of Transportation NYC Housing Authority
	2,000–4,999	Department of Environmental Protection Department of General Services Department of Parks and Recreation Department of Housing Preservation and Development Department of Health
Moderately sized	1,000–1,999	Department of Probation Law Department Department of Finance Office of the Mayor
	500–999	Department of Juvenile Justice Department of Buildings Department of Personnel
	300–499	City Planning Commission Department of Mental Health, Retardation, and Alcoholic Services Department of Employment
Small	Under 300	Department for the Aging Department of Investigation Department of Consumer Affairs Office for Economic Development Department of Ports and Terminals Commission on Human Rights *Taxi and Limousine Commission *Department of Cultural Affairs *Landmarks Preservation Commission *Department of Records and Information Services

* Fewer than 100 full-time employees

The very largest departments probably fare better. They are usually able to "end run" unwanted centralization and they can often do their own training and executive development.

In any event, size is doubtless a factor in each agency's relationship to the centralized machinery, to the mayor, and ultimately to the public.

Nature and Complexity of Mission

Another distinguishing element is the basic nature and the complexity of the missions that agencies are assigned. One fundamental distinction is recognized in the literature of organization theory: "line" organizations versus "staff" organizations. The line agencies actually produce or deliver some product or service. Staff agencies offer the top executives information and advice and may perform housekeeping activities like purchasing and personnel. Some authors use the term "auxiliary" to describe the housekeeping type of operation.

Most staff and/or auxiliary departments have reasonably simple missions. But line departments can vary considerably. There are: (a) departments with relatively simple missions, an overriding single focus that is clear and for which the necessary division of labor does not produce too many conflicting subdivisions; (b) a middle group where the mission may have two or three prominently discrete subdivisions and some amount of internal tension; and (c) a group where there are not only more numerous subtasks, but where these individual missions are very likely to generate cross-currents and ambivalence within the department itself.

Any department, even those with apparently simple and singular missions, may harbor considerable tension. But there are certain departments where internal tensions are virtually inevitable. These are ones with complex missions. What is suggested in Table 5.3 is that there are some departments whose missions are intrinsically more susceptible to ambiguity and to ideologically oriented leadership (about which more later) than others.

The Police Department is an excellent example of a "complex mission" department. The mission may be the preservation of "law and order," but "law" and "order" are two different things, more often than not. Order can often be restored or attained most efficiently by ignoring the law, rather than the reverse. Moreover, the Police Department (as will be discussed later) has a long array of subsidiary missions, most of which are actually of a "social service" character rather than a "law enforcement" character.

Health, to take another example, contains both preventative and palliative missions, making it ripe for internal ruptures along ideological lines. In contrast, the Sanitation Department seems less strangled from within by potential controversies over what it should be and do.

Table 5.3

New York City Agencies Grouped by Nature of Mission

Agencies with relatively few and less complicated missions	Taxi and Limousine Commission, Transportation, Ports and Terminals, Sanitation, Landmarks Preservation, Juvenile Justice, Environmental Protection, Fire, Buildings, Consumer Affairs, Cultural Affairs, Economic Development, Employment, all of the overhead agencies
Agencies with a middle range of missions and ambiguities	Departments of Aging, Probation, Housing Authority, Housing Preservation, Health and Hospital Corporation, Correction, Parks and Recreation
Agencies with complex and contradictory missions	Departments of Police and Health, Human Resources Administration, and Board of Education

The Nature of a Department's Clientele and Other Surrounding Pressure Groups

For some departments, every citizen is a client: the Police, Sanitation, and Fire departments are probably the best examples. Not only is everyone a consumer, but almost everyone is aware of being so. The Department of Environmental Protection has this same ubiquitous character—but is less recognized as such and therefore sometimes appears to have a more specialized clientele—the businesses that pollute and the environmental activists. Then there are agencies where almost everyone on one day or another will be a consumer, but the degree of daily concern with the department may be somewhat mitigated because usage is seen as only potential. This group includes the Department of Health, the Health and Hospitals Corporation and even the Parks and Recreation Department.

The remainder of the city's departments have special clienteles, that is, special categories of people who use their services while other citizens—though they are affected by these services and even more, by the consumers of the services—do not. These include the Probation Department, the Human Resources Administration, the Department of the Aging, and a number of others. In a class by itself are the overhead agencies whose clients are the other twenty-seven departments.

In a similar vein, departments may be characterized by the number and power of pressure groups other than the clients in their orbit. These groups include civic associations, unions, professional associations, neighborhood associations, and other special interest groups. Once again, some departments attract only a few relatively low key and ineffectual groups while others attract some powerful voices. Some departments attract mainly supportive groups, others magnetize adverse as well as supportive voices. The Parks Department has in tow, for example, a few relatively small and quiet pressure groups that are mainly supportive. The Landmarks Preservation Commission, on the other hand, attracts relatively few groups, but they are powerful and usually hostile. The Police Department draws many competing interest groups: civil libertarian, victims' rights, ethnic association of every hue, unions (their own and others), citizen action committees, community boards, and more. Human Resources and the Health Department contend with varied professional associations and neighborhood groups often at odds with one another, conflicting clienteles, conflicting unions, and neighborhood associations.

What is ultimately significant in the formation of public policy and in determining the style of the different departments is the nature, the strength, the persistence, and the continuity of the pressure groups in the departmental orbits. Quite clearly, such departments as Correction, Juvenile Justice, Probation and the Department of Mental Health and Retardation enjoy less sustained support than the Police Department or the Sanitation Department. It is often a case of help coming in inverse ratio to the need for it. The groups with greatest clout often surround the departments least in need of it.

Number and Types of Unions

Approximately sixty different unions represent the members of New York City's civil service. There are some managers, provisionals and part-timers who are not union members, but the collective bargaining agreements that determine basic agency policies, prescribe (although by indirection) conditions that determine their life-style as well. Most of the large unions work through particularized and numbered locals. Thus, District Council 37, of the American Federation of State, County and Municipal Employees (AFSCME), with over 100,000 members, includes 61 such units, such as: No. 299, Recreational Workers; No. 371, Social Service Workers; No. 372, Schools Division; No. 420, Hospital Employees; No. 768, Health & Welfare Employees; No. 1508, Uniformed Park Employees; No. 1062, Supervisors of Automatic Plant and Equipment; and No. 983, Motor Vehicle Operators. The International Union of Operating Engineers, similarly, has about a dozen units.

By 1967, New York State had passed the Taylor Law, which provided the basic ground rules for union representation and bargaining for all public employees at all levels throughout the state. The administration of this law is in the hands of the Public Employment Relations Board (PERB). However, New York City was authorized to cover this field through its own special agency—the Office of Collective Bargaining (OCB). The OCB covers all departments under the direct control of the mayor and a few other agencies that have elected to come under its jurisdiction. The only city employees who are under the auspices of PERB are the teachers and the transit workers. The OCB and PERB interpret the regulations of the Taylor Law in regard to the certification of unions, the organization of employees into unions, and the arbitration of disputes between unions, between unions and agency heads, and between employees and agencies. The OCB also wrestles with the definition of "unfair practices" and, of course, the never-ending supervision of collective bargaining agreements.

In general, collective bargaining in New York City covers such conventional matters as wages, hours, pensions, benefits, shifts, safety, and working conditions. It also covers, perhaps less traditionally, disciplinary actions, efficiency methods, use of technology, transfers, job classifications, and employers' orders and prerogatives. The unions are represented in the bargaining sessions by their individual leaders. These leaders come in an interesting variety of shapes and flavors. Their particular styles, their personal relationships with each other and with the mayor, as well as the size and cohesiveness of their rank-and-file cohorts, are all important ingredients in the game of who gets what. Among the most successful, powerful, and colorful of such leaders was Victor Gotbaum. The special (and friendly) working relationship that he had developed with former Mayor John V. Lindsay was an important factor in city public service in those years, as was his close personal friendship with Felix Rohatyn during the fiscal crisis years. His disdain and enmity for Koch proved equally significant. So too, the role of Albert Shanker, until recently the articulate and urbane head of the American Federation of Teachers (AFT) or the feisty and cantankerous Mike Quill of the Teamsters Union or the persistent and persuasive Philip Caruso of the Patrolmen's Benevolent Association (PBA)—all have played important roles in the city's collective bargaining.

The city, on the other hand, is represented by the Office of Municipal Labor Relations (OMLR). The profile of the people in this bureau is invariably lower than those of the union leaders. There are approximately eighty persons employed full time in collective bargaining work in New York City, including the administration of the city's health plan. For a few years, Koch appeared to have accomplished a simplification in which the city's bargaining was conducted with a single team of labor leaders, who were to represent all the important unions. By 1985, this arrangement had, as was probably inevitable, fallen apart. But there does remain far greater consolidation than had been traditional. Many commissioners, however, try to work out day-to-day operating problems and grievances directly with their departmental union officers.

In general, there are perhaps ten models of agreements working within two basic frameworks: one for the uniformed personnel of the city and the other for the civilian employees. An intricate minuet of "parities" is danced to produce this dual mode that maintains the subtle—but nonetheless significant—differentials among police, fire, transit and sanitation workers and the far more substantial difference between all of these uniformed troops and the other rank and filers.

The collective bargaining arrangements put managers and supervisors in ambiguous positions. Take, for example, police sergeants, lieutenants, and captains. They are certainly managerial in type—yet they are also unionized and are represented by a series of special unions: the Captains Endowment Association, the Lieutenants Benevolent Association, and so forth. Other professionals and administrative personnel also have their special unions. There is, for example, the Committee of Interns and Residents, the Association of Supervisors and Chief Managers (in the New York City Housing Authority), and the Council of Supervisors and Administrators of the City of New York (Board of Education).

Relationship to the Mayor

It is a well-accepted axiom of policy analysts that public outputs are a result of the workings of what is called the "iron triangle." That is, policy results from the compromises made by key bureaucrats in an agency, the critical pressure group protagonists, and the chairs of relevant legislative committees. But in New York City, the last named "angle" in the triangle can be eliminated since there was no genuinely independent and effective legislative body before 1990.[6] What must be substituted in this tripod is the mayor (or a very close representative of his). In other words, a key variable in understanding agency operations and outputs is the relationship between an agency and the mayor.

The fact that Mayor Koch was a long-standing and very special friend of Bess Meyerson's, for example, had a great deal to do with the relative success of the Department of Cultural Affairs during the years that she was the commissioner. Her department enjoyed ever-larger budgets during her tenure, always a good indicator of departmental strength. The same thing is often said about the Department of Parks—where Mayor Koch had a long and close association with Commissioner Henry Stern. Of course, any commissioner can be thought of as having the support of the mayor since it is the mayor who appointed him or her. But there are constraints on the mayor's discretion in making appointments: strong unions, professional associations, campaign payoffs, and a few legal mandates (for example, the head of the Law Department must be a lawyer). Nonetheless, there is still ample room for the mayor to push some of his own circle of friends and advisers into the realm of commissionerships, deputy commissioners, and special advisers. Some commissioners are therefore more equal than others. Nor is this in anyway inappropriate. They may be highly qualified and, more than that, they provide one of the few vehicles available for the mayor to push for the programs he may have advocated during his election campaigns. Those commissioners who have easy and continuous access to the mayor are in a better position to move public policy than others. Thus, this relationship is a key variable.

Character of Agency Leadership

The actual character of an agency's leader (and the character of the chief deputies) may well be the most significant single factor determining what makes an agency tick. Commissioners generally determine their departments' priorities since the mayor speaks only in broad generalities and responds only to immediate brushfires.

It is also the commissioners who generally deal with the multiple pressure groups who are always offering advice or demands, which are frequently mutually contradictory and narrowly self-serving. Even the community boards that are supposed to be the voice of the people are only effective in calling attention to individual grievances, sporadic crises, and the parochial problems of each individual neighborhood. The "independent watchdog groups," such as the Citizens Budget Commission and the New York City Partnership, are voices that generally confine themselves to procedural and managerial reforms. Thus, service prioritization is left to the agency heads.

The commissioners also have the singularly significant job of culling good deputies—either from outside the agency or from among the merit appointees. One commissioner said that the success of his 5,000-person department rested on his 150 managers—particularly the top dozen. Probably this selection, and the ability to get enthusiastic support from first-line supervisors, are the most important tasks of a commissioner, as was noted by Sayre and Kaufman a generation ago. It is, as Victor Gotbaum always said, "up to management to manage. The worker will go along."[7]

The agency head may be the key to the agency's performance, but leadership is impeded by the "role ambiguity" involved in a New York City commissionership. Although all the commissioners (and the top deputies) are appointed by the mayor and serve only at his pleasure, there is usually less "pleasure" involved than may be assumed. This may be due partly to the incompatibility that results from the role that outside pressures may have played in the original appointment. There is also a line-staff ambiguity: that is, a commissioner is a staff officer for the mayor—expected to give advice and act in concord with peers in a cabinet setting. On the other hand, the commissioner is also a line officer expected to lead and control his or her troops and to bear ultimate responsibility for the delivery and quality of an important public service. Thus the commissioner may as often as not be a competitor, even an adversary, of other commissioners vying for scarce resources—rather than a helpful teammate.

Moreover, while the commissioner may be expected to be a professional seeking purely professional goals, he or she must remain forever mindful that his or her appointment and tenure are owed to the mayor. This often boils down to meaning that partisan electoral politics must outweigh professional or administrative criteria. This too creates ambivalence. There is also ambiguity in the pull a commissioner feels between leading the troops and heeding the troops. They must be behind him—but not too far behind. In order to win loyalty and cooperation, a commissioner may bend too far and find himself co-opted. In such cases, public goals are displaced by the personal needs of the civil servants (their "Maslovian mission," page 111 above). And it is here that the relative strength of unions and pressure groups plays an important role. A strong commissioner knows how to keep his unions in line with his sense of mission. Commissioners must also face the heterogeneity, mobility, and gargantuan size of the city, their somewhat constrained salary structure, the high degree of uncertainty in their tenure of office, the lack of privacy, and the relatively modest executive "fringes" available.

The literature of organizational leadership devotes much attention to classifying leadership styles and types. The labels are snappy, even intriguing, and have some application to New York City government. But not much. One commissioner has suggested that there are essentially four types of commissioners: the celebrities, the ethnics, the business tycoons, and the civil servants. But perhaps the most realistic classification is the dichotomy between "idealogues" and careerists. The former are people who come to a department with a zeal to accomplish some overriding public agenda. The latter come to a department to ride out the inevitable storms and survive, indeed, to prosper.

Certain city departments attract ideological commitments. There is room in a Police or Law Department, for example, for a "crack-down on crime" ideology, as against a "civil libertarian, bill of rights" type of ideology. A Human Resources Administration might harbor either a "strict constructionist," "work ethic" type, or a "social justice," "redistribution of wealth" type. A Parks Department leaves room for the sort of person who may be committed to an ideology of the park as a wilderness oasis (the quiet nurturing of leaves and trees), as against another sort who might view our parks as places to entertain as many citizens as possible with as large a variety of events as possible. In a department for the aging, there may be an ideology that leans more to community services as against strategies of individual care. And clearly in the world of health there is room for many competing medical and social ideologies.

These departments often attract ideologues. And the nature of their ideology can be important in the department's administration. Thus one can note a profound difference between the Human Resources Administration under Commissioner Mitchell Ginzburg as against that department under Commissioner Blanche Bernstein. The former was committed to a welfare ideology that centered on serving welfare clients. Client entitlements were in the foreground. The latter commissioner was committed to an ideology of returning welfare clients to the mainstream. Rules concerning ineligibility became the focus.

On the other hand, there are probably a far greater number of civil service leaders (both commissioners and those in middle management) who might be called "careerists" in that they are intensely and primarily concerned with the necessities of making pragmatic decisions in the light of their own (and their chosen subordinates') tenure, future promotions, or successes. This type of leader is not necessarily any less capable or productive than the former. Indeed, it could well be the reverse. These are people who know that there are complex forces to be balanced in any given agency, and that the survival of the agency, along with their own self-improvement, are the core of any possible achievement. The successful commissioner is the one, whether ideologue or not, who is seen as fighting for his or her department. Even if he or she loses some battles, his or her troops are likely to rally and are more apt to look for ways to solve their problems.

Minority Representation in the Civil Service

The city government is recurrently charged with being prejudiced against (or at least unsympathetic to) its minorities. In the New York of the 1990s, the "minorities" in focus are blacks and Latinos.

The civil service is at the core of this concern because it has been the traditional way out of poverty in New York. It has been generally regarded as the first rung on the "success" escalator that is so important to the American Dream. Indeed, Sayre and Kaufman referred to this a generation ago in regard to earlier minorities. They wrote:

> Immigrants who have felt the whiplash of contempt, minorities encountering occupational and other barriers and groups denied status in other ways, find in the city's political system an escalator out of the social cellar. They use it. They use it to state their aspirations and their discontents, to win recognition as spokesmen for a constituency, to win office for themselves or those they endorse, to win career opportunities in a bureaucracy for their groups, and to secure public policies which meet their needs as they see them.[8]

Here, of course, Sayre and Kaufman spoke of the whole political process, but they noted that "the governmental bureaucracy in this city represents another kind of political state." Thus civil service was viewed as one of the most important "prizes" in their game orientation of New York City government and it is still playing the same role.

Not only do the city's agencies represent job opportunities (and reasonably prestigious and secure ones at that), but they also represent a chance to affect policy. It is the city's bureaucrats who actually deliver the city's services. It is they, after all, who truly decide whether a policy is carried out.

How representative is the civil service of minorities? How responsive is it to them? The ability of the civil service to be "representative" and "responsive" is constrained by recruitment methods that have the force of both law and tradition behind them. The early twentieth-century municipal reform movement, the depression of the 1930s, and the large wave of Jewish immigration all contributed to producing a merit system civil service almost entirely recruited and promoted through written examinations. The early reformers were primarily concerned with keeping the rascals out; and the examination system was indeed a sufficient barrier against many of the old "clubhouse" types. The expansion of municipal employment amidst the dire unemployment of the 1930s required that there be a job allocation system that looked fair: written competitive exams filled the bill. And finally, the large cohort of new immigrants, heavily Jewish in origin for whom reading and writing are part of their religious rites, rallied to exams.

Once established, traditions die hard. Thus, even after some examinations were proven irrelevant for the jobs to which they applied, there was a reluctance to give them up. Moreover, the substitute procedures for such exams occasionally went awry and dampened the pursuit of alternative measures. The blacks and Latinos for whom many of the tests as well as the companion seniority system were unfair, have been pressing their cases in both the political and judicial arenas and have met with some success.

Not surprisingly, incumbent mayors since 1960 have pointed to increases in minority civil service employment during their terms as evidence that minorities are fairly represented in New York's civil service, while critics have pointed to data that show how far there is to go yet. Thus, an official report in 1985 showed sharp improvements during the Koch administration: in that year, blacks comprised 32 percent of the total work force in the mayoral agencies of the city while Latinos held about 10 percent of the city's jobs.[9] A 1987 study that was critical of the city's performance reported substantially the same percentages.[10] Koch argued that his achievements in minority employment were far better than those of his predecessors: Koch administration figures showed minorities comprised only 7.4 percent, 14.3 percent, and 19.4 percent of all civil servants during the administrations of Mayors Wagner, Lindsay, and Beame, respectively. Koch claimed that he improved on that because over 50 percent of all "new hires" during the 1980s were minorities. According to another 1985 report, the minority percentage of "professionals" in the civil service had more than doubled between 1971 and 1985, from 17 percent to 36 percent; minority "top administrators" had risen from 24 percent to 35 percent.[11]

However, during these years, the minority percentage of the total population of the city was rising sharply. Indeed, the minority percentage of the civil service was higher than the minority population of the city in 1963 and 1971, but well below the minority percentage of the population in 1985.[12] How progress is appraised also is affected by the particular time periods chosen (for example, Puerto Rican employment in the city's services doubled during the 1960–71 period, on a very small 1961 base, but grew more modestly in percentage terms from 1971–81), and by whether the focus is on new hires or the overall position.[13] Thus, a different picture can be derived from superficially honest data.

Agencies differ considerably in their employment of minorities. Some services are predominantly white: Finance, Sanitation, Fire, Parks and Recreation, Planning, Environmental Protection, and Transportation. On the other hand, there are domains that have been over 40 percent (and in some instances over 50 percent) black since the early sixties: Welfare, Hospitals, and—since its inception—Human Services. Health, Housing, and Corrections have been close to or over 33 percent black across these decades. In the late 1980s, New York City still had a municipal work force that was segregated in important dimensions.

How do minorities stand with respect to salaries? Here are two different perspectives: a January 2, 1986, press release from the Office of the Mayor stated that "in 1985, 95 percent of all minority workers earned $13,000 or more per year compared to just 50 percent who earned that well in 1981. By 1985, 67 percent of all minority workers earned more than $16,000 a year, up from 20 percent in 1978." The figures indicate progress, but note that there is no allowance for inflation and that two different base years are chosen for comparison. In contrast, an April 4, 1985, internal memo from the Department of Research of District 37 of the American Federation of State, County and Municipal Employees (AFSCME) showed that 46 percent of all minority workers earned less than $16,000, while only 11 percent of white workers fell into that category. Moreover, 52 percent of all white workers earned over $25,000, while only 18 percent of all minority workers did so. The mayor's picture suggests optimistic progress, the union's emphasizes how far is still to be travelled. Both are right.

Although it is now traditional to include women in any discussion of minorities, the practice is misleading. Women are the majority group in our society, and sexual discrimination has far different roots than racial and ethnic prejudice. But hiring in the New York City civil service has been anything but sex-blind. There are occupations that are (and traditionally have been) heavily female: teachers, nurses, and social workers. There are areas where women have been traditionally taboo: Fire, Police, Correction, and Transportation—among others. In 1987, there were only forty-one female firefighters and four female sanitation collectors.

In 1971, women constituted over half (sometimes over 60 percent) of the work force in the departments of Welfare, Hospitals, Health, Education, and Human Services. They were between one-third and one-half of the departments of Finance and Planning. At that time, women constituted 42 percent of the total city work force and 53 percent of the overall city population.[14]

As to female rank and salary: in 1971, 36 percent of the occupational category listed as "officials and administrators" in city government were women as were 55 percent of the "professional" category. These figures include education and health agencies.[15] The previously cited mayor's press release reported that, in 1985, 64 percent of all female civil servants earned more than $16,000; 94 percent earned more than $13,000. But District 37 data for 1983 showed that the percentage of female workers earning less than $16,000 was four times that for males. Moreover, 90 percent of all females earned less than $25,000, in contrast to only 51 percent of the male workers at that time. As of 1987, only 8 percent of the female workers in mayoral jobs earned $28,000 or more, while 26 percent of the males did. A 1987 report card on this whole matter concludes that "occupational segregation by sex and race in the New York City work force is extreme" and that promotional opportunities are lacking for those municipal employees who work in female and/or minority dominated jobs.[16]

So up to this point, the picture is one of progress in achieving "representativeness" in the civil service, but a very long way yet to go. There is the far more difficult question of its "responsiveness," whether the services delivered meet the special needs of minority residents, a question examined in more detail in Chapter 14 by Shirley Jenkins.

Managing the Civil Service: The Department of Personnel

The Department of Personnel is an overhead agency that services, supervises, and sustains the entire civil service. Its mission is to classify, recruit, examine, select, place, promote, train, transfer, develop, retire, and discipline the city's army of workers. Under Mayor Koch, as well as in earlier administrations, one of the department's goals was to decentralize many of these operations.

In a typical year (1984), the department administered 236 open, competitive promotional and license exams to 171,437 people. Over 69,000 people took over 100 technical tests for positions ranging from engineer to maintenance worker— 15 different job titles. Over 11,000 took management qualifying exams. The department also conducted background checks and investigations. Between July and October of 1985, the Investigation Division had been assigned 17,974 cases. Some of these investigations required police and FBI cooperation. Each year leaves in its wake a huge backlog. There are also hundreds of training workshops, special absence control programs, alternate work scheduling programs, and internships for the department to mount.

The department operates within the strict parameters of a set of complex laws and rules. Some emanate from the state government; others from the city government itself. Indeed, the department sees its chief mission as safeguarding these rules: a decided priority of procedure over substance. At times, the rules appear to hamper rather than help in the recruitment, development, and retention of able people.

It is a department that does not have many friends. A number of the line executives with whom it deals have said, "They've never been able to give us any real help." Others have been particularly upset over one or another specific failing—whether the timing of exams or the inadequacy of a training program. Still others have said, "We just try to avoid it." As for the department's rank and file, the state of their morale was described as "low" by the executive director of District Council 37 of AFSCME, Stanley Hill—lower indeed than that of the civil service as a whole, which is itself not known for particularly high morale.

Why should this be so? Perhaps because the Personnel Department is at the very vortex of conflicting imperatives. Bureaucratic efficiency, democratic myths, and human nature pull it in opposing directions. More than most agencies, it has undergone repeated internal reorganizations and has been the focus of numerous outside investigations and reports, some with vitriolic messages. Yet it seems as though "the more things change, the more they stay the same." Every reform in the agency seems to breed the seeds of its own inevitable deterioration. There are always unintended consequences.

The merit system itself, for example, was meant to replace the old-style political party patronage system used earlier in this century to fill public service posts. But, in recent years, the system has become so rigid that merit has become meretricious. The original structure for that reform, the Civil Service Commission, was itself "reformed" in 1954, that is, replaced, by the creation of the Department of Personnel. By the end of the 1980s, the circle may have become full. The Personnel Department has fallen short of reform expectations and the aforementioned Stanley Hill has called for the reestablishment of the Civil Service Commission to its former full-time status as a necessary antidote to what he sees as inadequacies in the Personnel Department. It has failed, in the eyes of some, to reduce rigidities and, for others, it has failed to retain rigidities. Hill, on a number of occasions, felt that civil service rules and practices once considered inviolate were being steadily eroded. Others complain that those very rules and practices are what make the system unworkable. In any event, time and again, the particular reforms the department has initiated have backfired and produced this curious cycle in which today's reform becomes tomorrow's fatal flaw.

Another example is the persistent concern about the use of "provisionals," "exempt" positions, and "non-competitive" ones. These are titles for which no examinations need be given. The "provisional" posts are designed to allow temporary appointments where it is impossible or impractical to wait for an exam. "Exempt" posts are a category designed for high-level and confidential positions for which educational records and job experience are deemed sufficient: lawyers, doctors, and architects, for example. The "non-competitive" title is for jobs where simple standards, perhaps a driver's license, are adequate. The latter are sometimes called "unassembled" exams. The "laborer" category— used for unskilled workers—generally does not have any type of test or standards procedure. Finally, the term "unclassified" is the term used for agency heads. These titles have often been manipulated to achieve some necessary flexibility and rationality in the appointment process.

In 1987, for example, it was charged that over 30,000 city employees in mayoral agencies had been excluded from competitive examinations by clever title rearrangements, and that the rule that "provisionals" must be terminated after nine months was also being flouted. The normal exam and appointment procedures (as will be explained later) are rigid and time consuming. They may exclude the rascals, but they have also kept out minorities. Thus, department executives must use loopholes. Many have given up trying to rationalize the system—so from time to time they may be guilty of subverting it.

The formal method of entrance into the New York City civil service is by examination, consisting of written short-answer, knowledge-based questions. The tests have appeared increasingly less job related. They have often been accused of containing racially biased materials and have occasionally produced racially skewed and, in some instances, bizarre outcomes. Absurd technical questions are used where street wisdom would suffice. On the other hand, a City Hall reporter told of a test so simple and irrelevant for the uniformed department for whom it was intended, that a third-grade class passed it. Promotion also is ordinarily via examinations of the same character as the entrance exams, with the results often racially skewed. Moreover, the promotion system is a serious deterrent to the lateral entrance of college-bred recruits, a frequent priority target for recruitment for middle-level positions, along with minority persons.

The Personnel Department's efforts to modify the tests to respond to these complaints have not been very successful. For example, strenuous efforts were made to develop bias-free exams in Police and Sanitation in the mid-1980s. Over $100,000 was spent in 1985 to achieve an appropriate test for a promotional police exam that would not be racially prejudicial. The new exam did not yield the expected minority candidates, and so the department resorted to a quota system. A Sanitation Department entrance exam designed to permit female success yielded so many passing candidates that a system of random selection had to be instituted.

The department has had no dearth of advice over the years. During the 1960s and 1970s, six commissions and study groups examined the agency's practices. These included a 1961 Brookings Institution study directed by David Stanley, the 1966 report of the Mayor's (Lindsay) Task Force on City Personnel, the Personnel Council study in 1972, the findings on personnel questions of the 1975 Charter Revision Commission, a 1975 report by the consulting firm of Griffenhagen-Kroeger Report to the Department of Personnel, and the 1976 report of the group chaired by Richard Shinn, CEO of Metropolitan Life Insurance.

These reports recorded largely identical complaints and offered very similar proposals as remedies. For the most part, they read as if equally applicable to 1990. Consider what the 1966 Task Force had to say:

> Instruments for identifying and rewarding merit are frequently turned into rigid irrelevant procedural rituals. Probationary periods are generally treated in a perfunctory manner with employees almost automatically and without serious scrutiny being moved into tenured positions. Performance ratings are not now used as an effective tool for evaluating employees performance and consequently merit increases are not systematically tied to pertinent measure of evaluation. The written tests now heavily relied on, are not always the best method of screening and selecting employees for promotion.[17]

During the years since 1966, the department's own annual reports and the utterances of a series of able personnel directors have given the impression that the problems were understood and the necessary changes had been initiated. The needed changes were specified: more flexible hiring, broader and more effective recruitment, better training, special attention to supervisory posts, management development programs, more sophisticated types of exams, and more reliance on actual performance in promotions, for acceleration in hiring and placement, better performance evaluation systems, merit pay, decentralizing many operations, and extending probationary periods. That some of these reforms would require civil service rule changes, and some even new state legislation, was duly noted. But the problems remain.

The agency appears to be "in the wrong place, at the wrong time, with the wrong mission." It has tried to fulfill the role of being the mayor's right hand in charge of personnel, but the department has been severely handicapped by the historic strength of its sibling, the Office of Management and Budget (OMB). The OMB is comfortably tucked inside the Mayor's Office and is obviously not only physically closer, but also closer to the mayor's heart. This is an office with real power. It has many carrots and many sticks and everybody knows it. For decades it has been the bane of the Department of Personnel. It is OMB that controls the actual "lines" available (that is, the positions). Merit increases, promotional vacancies, training funds, money for compensatory time off, indeed every item with a dollar sign (which is everything), goes through OMB. For decades, Personnel has been the second team and everyone knows that.

Personnel is also caught up in an adversarial relationship with the unions. More often than not, the unions line up behind the status quo. They protest the use of provisionals, and they have ritually rallied against new initiatives in examination procedures and content. Moreover the unions, the Mayor's Office, and other urban analysts see an element of redundancy between the role of Personnel and the Office of Collective Bargaining. The union leaders often feel they can afford to ignore Personnel and concentrate on the latter. The real arena is the world of union contracts and they are right. Today these contracts cover many of the conditions of work and benefits that in another era might have been the sole prerogative of the Personnel Department. Almost every commissioner concurs in this evaluation.

But at the core of the department's historic difficulties is the mission itself. It is "Mission Impossible." The legal mandates begin with the erroneous assumption that everyone wants a civil service job. Thus, the overriding statutory task is the avoidance of favoritism and the promotion of fairness in initial appointments, promotions, and all of what the Founding Fathers called the "emoluments" of office.[18] It is not possible to operate under this erroneous assumption, pursue this statutory task, and, at the same time, attract and retain the brightest and the best and help develop latent talents.

Even if the department's mission were sensibly specified, it is doubtful that one central agency can effectively serve so great a variety of agencies. The city needs ferry pilots and physicians, clerks and comptrollers, social workers and street cleaners. Usually, the most effective recruitment and training is done at the department level. Centralized efforts are either irrelevant or redundant. Thus the department has been frequently asked by its guardians, clients, and critics to devolve as many of its functions as possible to the line departments. It is generally believed that the operating agencies themselves are probably better equipped to recruit, train, and place their own personnel. The logical endpoint of such decentralization would be the virtual elimination of the Personnel Department, and some critics have been quite forthright in suggesting just this.

Two Close-ups of the Civil Service

The Police Department

Police work is the quintessential local government function in America. It has grown from the days of village "night watchmen" to the current complexities of "police science." In New York, as in most, if not all, cities, the Police Department is the most visible and most closely watched of all public agencies. It is a department organized along military lines: a bastion of hierarchy, specialization, rules, professionalism, and records. It is a classical bureaucracy, but it is subject to an extraordinary array of centripetal forces. It provides an excellent example of the tensions that arise when an agency has ambiguous and often conflicting goals and a host of conflicting clients. "Be productive" but "be democratic." "Administer the law" but "be practical." "Be a friend to the community" but "keep your distance." It is also a department where leadership is particularly important but where it is especially bedeviled.

At the close of 1986, the Police Department had approximately 28,000 uniformed personnel and 5,000 civilians filling the 7 divisional commands, 19 zones, and 75 precincts into which the city is divided for police purposes. This made it the city's third largest department. The operating head of the uniformed service is the commissioner, assisted by a number of deputy commissioners, inspectors and deputy inspectors, chiefs, assistant chiefs, and deputy chiefs. Almost all of these people, save the deputy commissioners, are usually selected from the pool of available captains. The latter, along with some 1,000 lieutenants, 2,200 sergeants, and the rank-and-file patrolmen are selected as they have been for many decades, through a system of civil service entrance and promotional examinations. Promotions above the rank of captain are "discretionary." Candidates at this level are recommended by top executives from among the ranks immediately below. These candidates are then reviewed by a series of advisory panels and two candidates are finally forwarded for final selection by the police commissioner.

While most selection procedures have remained relatively static, except for exam content and physical requirements, today's typical police officer is a far different person than the officer of the 1960s and 1970s. In the police department of the 1980s, more than 10 percent of the force was female, a fourfold increase over the 1970s' percentage. Minority groups constitute almost 21 percent of the force—up from 12 percent in 1974.[19]

What is more, the newer class rosters in the Police Academy show an even more pronounced trend in these directions. Among the 1987 recruits, approximately 30 percent were women, 22 percent were black, and over 30 percent were Latino.[20] And since more than 12,000 new people have been recruited for the Police Department between 1982 and 1987 in order to compensate for reductions in the force due to retrenchments and retirements, this "new image" police officer will have considerable impact on the city's police profile and police personality. Recruitment for this department is aided by the use of special cadet programs aimed at college sophomores and by the promise of an opening job that in 1987 paid $28,000 after a six-month probation period.

The traditional police recruit of a generation ago almost instantly became an "insider," initiated into a cynical, authoritarian, tough-guy police culture best described by Arthur Neiderhoffer in his well regarded portrait of the police, *Behind the Shield*. Today's police recruits are carefully screened and trained to make certain that they both represent and are sensitive to the culture of their precincts. Entry-level training for recruits takes place at the Police Academy and centers on social science, law, police science, and physical education. It takes about five months. They also receive other units of training outside the academy. Later training occurs on a part-time basis and includes human relations, executive development, and ethical awareness programs.

Despite the substantial changes in both recruitment and training, there is still a strong undercurrent of "we" versus "they" among the city's police. And the typical officer relishes a more macho image than is warranted by an objective analysis of what it is that the police actually do day-to-day on the streets of New York. This gap between rhetoric and reality; the greater heterogeneity of the force; the facts that today's officers are younger, less likely to come from a police family tradition, and are very much stamped by the permissive culture in which they were nurtured—all of these factors present the department with both critical problems and great opportunities.

The Police Department is expected to protect the lives and property of all the people within the city (residents, transients, foreign visitors, among others). It is therefore engaged in both crime prevention, crime protection, and to some degree crime punishment. The department also plays a regulatory role in connection with taxi service, cabarets, pawnbrokers, and certain other businesses that require licenses. Beyond that, there are community services performed routinely by the police: store checks, auto accident investigations, traffic control, intervention in cases of family disputes and school violence, and referring people in distress (including vagrants, alcoholics, and the homeless) to appropriate social service agencies.

The police are also expected to cope with ensuring order at large public events and to be prepared to respond to a variety of possible disasters. They are often called on to administer emergency first aid, comfort lost children, and give help to travelers. They also offer special instruction in the public schools on crime prevention and the dangers of drug abuse. Indeed, the Personnel Department identified some 400 police functions.[21] Eighty to ninety percent of what the police now do is social service—a far cry from their role in earlier generations, an even further cry from the public's image of what police do. While these are the formal missions of the department, other agenda have also dominated the scene. In the 1970s for example, the major issue in the department (as in the nation) was "race." The recruitment of minorities became one of the department's highest priorities. There was a cost here, however, in terms of internal police morale. Some of the traditional ethnics, the Irish and Italians, who used to constitute 40 and 25 percent of the force, respectively, resented what they saw as special privileges and inroads on the merit system and seniority.

Starting in the early 1960s, still another "democratic" mission pressed against a somewhat resistant police force. The police were year by year given more and more instructions concerning how to protect citizens' rights. As the U.S. Supreme Court fleshed out the meaning of our civil liberties under the Bill of Rights and the Fourteenth Amendment, the Police Department had to temper the traditional zeal for "fighting crime." It was no longer enough to make as many "collars" (arrests) as possible and to rack up a good record of convictions. Now there was a greater concern for the propriety of their methods. Much time, energy, and money have been spent (and are still being spent) on police training to assure that every officer is well acquainted with the Supreme Court rules on proper police behavior in arresting and questioning suspects.

While all students of police affairs agree that these rules are absolutely necessary to ensure the fair administration of justice, to most police officers they are seen as real threats to effective and efficient law enforcement. Many police officers claim that most of their effective "leads" must be pried out of unwilling suspects almost immediately upon apprehension. Thus the typical police officer is made to play with what he or she regards as naive "Marquess of Queensbury Rules" against adversaries bound by no rules and is also forced to endure what he or she sees as judicial "leniency" and "revolving door" probationary procedures; for such officers there is bound to be, as Neiderhoffer suggests, a strong "reinforcement of cynicism."[22]

But the voices of reformers—whether minority groups protesting police racism or civil rights groups decrying police evasion of citizens' privileges—will not be stilled. Most of these groups have had actual experiences that generate their hostility to the police. They frequently see the police as "the enemy," and it is true that there are many ethnic ghettos where the police cannot count on any community cooperation. Indeed, they can and do count on almost general hostility. This, in turn, gives rise to a vicious cycle of police resentment and fear that often finds its outlet in unnecessary and inappropriate uses of force.

Indeed, brutality and corruption are the twin problems that are endemic to this department. Sayre and Kaufman a generation ago were ready to concede that a New York City police commissioner could do little more than prevent these sicknesses from "reaching epidemic proportions."[23] No era has been immune, certainly not the decades since Sayre and Kaufman wrote: charges of police brutality and corruption dogged the Lindsay administration in the late 1960s and early 1970s and the Koch administration in the late 1980s. During the Lindsay administration, the now famous allegations of Sergeant David Durk and Patrolman Frank Serpico led to the establishment of the Knapp Commission, which reported in 1972 that it had found "widespread corruption." A large ring of plainclothesmen were then "on the pad," taking bribes from gambling houses and other illegal operations. The disease spread from top to bottom and, before the episode was concluded, police morale had been badly shattered and public confidence badly shaken.

In 1986, the corruption problem was more confined. About a dozen police officers in one precinct were alleged to be stealing narcotics from the sources that they arrested. In this 1986–87 episode, however, the Police Department employed its own internal mechanisms for uncovering the corruption in its ranks and the commissioner himself investigated the matter. During the late 1980s, a special prosecutor at the state level was instituted to routinely investigate police matters. This office was created in order to forestall any "cozy arrangements" between city district attorneys and the police, such as had been discovered earlier. This special effort to eliminate corruption, however, has taken its toll on "productivity." Most police officers avoid arresting "druggies." They leave this to the Narcotics Division, which was given this special monopoly by the Knapp Commission in an effort to reduce corruption. It also reduces arrests.

The charges of brutality were so severe during Lindsay's administration that the mayor attempted to initiate an independent civilian police complaint board. The PBA successfully campaigned to review this in a referendum, where the voters rejected it decisively. At a later time, such a board was created within the Police Department itself, but had limited credibility in the black community because it was not an independent entity. The existence of the board did little to mitigate the complaints of brutality that arose in a succession of cases during the Koch administration.

Other complaints from the black community about the police may be less dramatic, but more significant. "The reason black people feel the police are the enemy is because of the service they get. You go to a place like 124th and Lenox or 118th and 8th and you see prostitutes and junkies hanging around. You don't get that on Park Avenue or in Riverdale. And there's no way you can tell me the police can't get those people off the street."[24] This is the estimate of Detective Roger Abel, president of the Guardians Association, an organization of 2,000 black police officers in New York City.

The police commissioner, no matter who he has been, insider or outsider, has had to fight vigorously to keep control of his department in the face of these problems. And in this fight for control, he always encounters an entrenched bureaucracy whose recruitment is largely outside his grasp, whose tenure usually far outlives his own, and whose outlook is that of the "street bureaucrat." There is also a powerful police union—the PBA—to articulate that outlook and concern with salary, working conditions, benefits, procedural traditions, and, most particularly, safety. The rank and file, however, are themselves often divided along ethnic lines and these ethnic groups are another of the pressures a commissioner must parry. There are the Guardians, noted above, the Emerald Society (Irish), the Pulaski Society (Polish), the Steuben Society (German), the Shomrin (Jewish), the Columbia Society (Italian), and the Hispanic Association. Some of these groups have, on occasion, been at loggerheads with the PBA. In 1986 the Guardians, for example, upbraided the PBA for scuttling Commissioner Ward's rotation plan for combating corruption. Commissioner Ward was New York City's first black police commissioner and was regarded as "their man." They therefore felt the PBA was undermining the commissioner's status and authority.

The control problems of the commissioner are also exacerbated by the unusual amount of discretion that of necessity resides in the rank and file. Instead of the classical mode in which discretion broadens as you move up the hierarchy, in the world of police there is an inverse order. A patrolman has more latitude in decision making than the commissioner. What is more, the cop on the beat must act without much time for reflection. The amount of discretion directly allocated to every patrolman is also enlarged by the ambiguities found in many laws and in the ambivalence of citizens about just how strictly they want these laws enforced. What, for example, is the meaning of "disorderly conduct," "loitering," "causing a crowd to collect," "consorting with persons of evil reputation," or "using vulgar, profane and indecent language"? What is required to "get permission to enter a premise or a vehicle"? And just how vigorously does the community really want the police to enforce the law? How about tickets for speeding? Arrests for soliciting? Proffering a bribe? Gambling?

For almost all of these varied (and often opposing) views, there are organized spokesmen. The clienteles and pressure groups that are in the orbit of the Police Department other than the unions and ethnic societies run the gamut from the local National Association for the Advancement of Colored People and the American Civil Liberties Union, to the conservative National Rifle Association and Knights of Columbus, and hundreds of church, neighborhood, and business associations. Every one of these has access to the department either directly or indirectly through the media. Thus, the pulls and pushes on this department are relentless. And while the diverse cross-pressures may be self-canceling in the long run, in the short run they can often damage the department.

The commissioner's control is also vitiated by the difficulty of combining functional expertise with geographically dispersed service delivery. He must disperse highly centralized data systems and other technological functions into a network of neighborhood precincts. He is further hampered by a severe lack of accepted output measures and a dearth of scientific evidence concerning effective measures of crime prevention and control. All of this makes it very hard to run a tight ship.

Indeed, many of the internal yardsticks used by the police to satisfy the perennial search for productivity are pathetically inadequate for measuring genuine public satisfaction. It is hard to obtain either professional or public agreement as to proper indices of police efficiency. Is a department more efficient when it gives out a greater number of traffic tickets, or is this simply a spurious campaign to "make the numbers"? Is an increase in the use of various resources (foot patrols, vehicles, information systems) a proper measure of anything, or do we stick to outputs? If outputs are the name of the game (reduced felonies, fewer drug sales in Washington Square Park), are they attributable to the police?

There never has been agreement on whether something as obvious as an increase in the number of felony arrests should be viewed as a plus or a minus for the department. Should it be taken to mean more police are on the ball; or that they are simply foregoing some other activity; or that there has been a failure in their crime prevention mission? At times, the productivity games can get really out of hand and charges have been made on occasion that the police are actually encouraged to engage in "enticements" to crime (virtually seducing a potential victim) or to make reckless arrests, solely in order to achieve a "good record."

Thus any police commissioner in New York City faces terrible dilemmas. Even a commissioner with the racial and professional credentials held by Benjamin Ward may not be able to defuse the ethnic tensions that keep arising and keep draining police energies. Indeed, Ward was frequently assaulted by the black community as being the pawn of a white mayor who was himself accused of racial insensitivity. Moreover, Ward had personal weaknesses (wine and women), which were exploited and tarnished his image. Though the mayor always publicly supported him, theirs was not a close personal relationship. Benjamin Ward had to walk a careful line, as did most of his predecessors. Perhaps the wonder of it all is that the department has not been more seriously crippled by its recurring scandals—both at the top and at the bottom—and by its complex mission. Most commissioners have, whatever their basic attributes and styles, essentially managed to "keep the peace" in an extremely volatile and glaringly spotlighted arena. Maybe that is all that can be expected.

There is, however, always hope for more. The 1987 report of a Special Advisory Committee on Police Management and Personnel Policy, appointed by Mayor Koch in 1985, is a case in point. This emphasized the *systemic* problems that beset the department and offered remedies that transcended the persona of commissioners. The chair of this panel, John E. Zuccotti, a former deputy mayor, advised the mayor that the department suffered routinely from serious management problems and urged changes in the way its officers are recruited, trained, and promoted. The problems, he said, "are the inherent results of a Civil Service system that is archaic, rule bound, uninformed and unimaginative."[25] The committee talked of a "severe supervisory crisis" because of sergeant vacancies, an ineffective system of evaluating officers, and inadequate supervisory training. The problem was exacerbated because the police force in the late 1980s constituted the youngest and most inexperienced in over a generation, due to the cuts made during the fiscal crises of the 1970s, normal attrition, and considerable turnover among the top leadership.

For at least two decades, reformers have suggested that a share of the department's difficulties stems from its rigid reliance on written exams as well as its short probationary period of eighteen months. Despite persistent expert advice, the PBA continued to insist that promotions should come only through traditional civil service examinations and that the probation period should remain as is. The 1986 advisory committee again pointed out that the "problem of irrelevance and unfairness in testing are systemic" and that the use of racial quotas to remedy this situation has been demoralizing. Quotas have led to the implication that the qualifications of those minorities appointed were not up to par. Such accusations, though unfounded, have been demoralizing.

The Zuccotti report therefore underlined the need for achieving needed racial diversity (a department "representative of the community it serves") by "putting more resources into recruiting, by removing unfair barriers to access, and by utilizing more sophisticated techniques of selection and promotion."[26] The committee recommended, more specifically, an intensive recruitment campaign at the City University (where over 50 percent of the student population is "minority"). They also proposed creating a special high school for students interested in criminal justice careers, eliminating application fees, giving New York City residents preference, and confining written exams to job-related knowledge documented in concise reading lists.

Permitting the Police Department to take full charge of its own personnel needs might also simplify and improve service delivery. There are actually few functions here for the Personnel Department, such as the selection and administration of the initial written entry exams. Increasingly, the de facto situation is that the police are left to run matters their own way. It is probably time to let the de jure arrangements catch up.

Almost inevitably, the Police Department is an agency that is in a state of virtually continuous crisis management. Complex and conflicting missions, plus ambivalence and ambiguity over outcome measures, ensure that the police will continue to fall short of citizens' hopes and their own professional goals. There is an irreducible tension between the demands of democratic design and the equally compelling need for public safety and order. This tension will inevitably prevent the police from fully satisfying themselves or the community.

The Sanitation Department

The Sanitation Department is widely regarded as among the city's best-managed agencies. This was true throughout the 1980s and in earlier periods as well, for example, in the late 1950s and early 1960s. The major reason—aside from the department's good fortune in its commissioners in both periods—is that the department has been able to demonstrate substantial productivity improvements, more so than any other large city agency: a 50 percent productivity increase between 1981 and 1986, for example.

Why should the productivity goal be more appropriate here than elsewhere? The department's operations are highly amenable to technological improvements in the form of new and more productive equipment, but that is the case for a good many other city agencies that have shown much smaller productivity gains, such as the Fire Department. The major reason is that the Sanitation Department, in a good many respects, does resemble a business operation more than other agencies.

To begin with, the department does have actual private-sector counterparts, and this is appreciated both within and outside the department. The department does not pick up refuse from business premises, which are served by private refuse collectors. Like the private companies, the outputs and costs of the department are measurable. Its products (or at least a good part of its output) are well understood by the public at large. Piles of garbage and dirty streets are clear and unambiguous and are easily identified with the efforts of this single department. The Department of Sanitation can no more easily pass the buck for poor performance than can the telephone company or the corner dry cleaner.

Like most private businesses, the Sanitation Department is not much of a magnet for the media. The TV crews and the press melt away quickly after the first big snowstorm of the year. Citizens and communities are less emotionally involved with sanitation than with, say, police or fire services. There are far fewer "images," whether benign or malevolent, to interfere with daily rounds. Sanitation men are neither heroes nor devils: they are just out there to get the work done. Nor is sanitation much more prone to corruption than most private businesses. There are simply fewer opportunities for graft, and most of them are pale stuff compared to what can happen in other agencies. Also, the department has not been a focal point for racial conflict. The pressures for more minority recruitment and advancement that are kept at a high-decibel level in other departments are more muted here, probably because the job of sanitation worker does not have the glamour or status associated with the police and fire services.

Other conditions conducive to success in the pursuit of the productivity goal include the department's moderate size; the occasional (rather than constant) presence of its pressure groups, usually of the "civic reform" type; a cooperative, albeit powerful, union; and a history of commissioners who usually have been highly professional and enjoyed a positive (though not personal) relationship with the mayor.

But the single most significant factor conducive to the department's productivity success is probably the clarity and relative simplicity of its mission—like the usual private business. The department offers four basic services: garbage collection, waste disposal, snow removal, and an enforcement program to deter littering, illegal dumping, and other violations of the city's Health and Administrative Code. These are unambiguous goals, and they are mutually reinforcing, not contradictory. The department has not been asked to take on any special programs that have other worthy but not necessarily consistent goals. Thus the department's entire energy is focused on "sanitation." This helps.

Recently, the agency has employed roughly 12,500 people—all but 5,000 in the uniformed forces. Most of these troops are white Irish or Italian males but, by 1987, 18 percent were blacks. Latinos and women, however, were in very short supply. The department has been aware of this problem. It has had trouble with some of the "merit" examinations it has been using (as was discussed earlier), but it has not had to face the sustained and highly visible fights that other departments have endured.

The uniformed service is essentially composed of teamster-type jobs requiring considerable brawn and the ability to handle heavy equipment: hydraulic trucks, plows, salt spreaders, and so forth. All that is needed on entrance is a driver's license. But after three months of departmental training, a recruit must successfully earn a chauffeur's license and finally a Class Three chauffeur's license. This permits a person to drive just about anything that moves. It usually takes about a year to qualify for this.

After probation, the job pays $23,000 per year (1987) and after two or three years, a sanitation worker is usually eligible for a "two-team truck," which operates with a daily incentive program. This reduction from the traditional three-man truck to only two men has been a major part of the department's productivity achievement in the 1980s. To gain employee acceptance, the commissioner and his predecessors not only avoided any layoffs, but they also had one-third of the savings that occurred redistributed as cash incentives to the teams. This typically netted a worker between $70 and $90 a week, which put sanitation salaries very close to police salaries.

At a later stage in a worker's career, there is a one-in-eight chance to be promoted to a supervisory post. But even without promotion the top-scale workers averaged about $40,000 annually in 1987. Virtually all promotions are made from internal civil service exam lists. Appointments to borough and general superintendent titles (each with several grades) also are made from within the service. The relatively high earnings, the usual generous civil service fringe benefits, and the promotional opportunities make the department attractive to a large labor pool and helps inspire the rank and file to make productivity a priority. In fact, in 1986 more than 45,000 applicants filed to take the department's entrance exam.

One of the department's proudest achievements has been the development of a "profit center" at its Bureau of Motor Equipment. Sanitation uses about 1,000 people to fix motor vehicles. At one time, as many as 60 percent of its vehicles were out of service for repairs and maintenance. "Down time" of that proportion meant over 1,500 sanitation workers immobilized on any given day. Using a collaborative labor-management process, the bureau has managed to reduce the out-of-service rate to about 15 percent. Moreover, costs of standard types of vehicle repairs and servicing are below those bid by private garages and the bureau has bid successfully for the vehicle servicing business of other city agencies. To some extent, the economies are attributable to technological fixes, including better equipment, but for the most part the savings have come from changes in methods of work, most often suggested by the workers themselves.

Another success of the department is in measuring effectively. It gauges its street cleaning, for example, through the use of a well-validated psychometric "cleanliness" rating instrument. Every month, a professionally procured sample population has been shown photographs of actual streets and been asked to rate them. The standards for "acceptably clean" have been set very high, and no words have been minced at the bottom of the scale. "Filthy" is one of the choices. Most of those involved in this exercise were very confident of its usefulness and reliability. The city began measuring street cleanliness in 1974. By 1985, with a total cleaning work force of 2,221, the city could boast that 74.3 percent of its streets were rated "acceptably clean."

Although the department has been sensitive to the productivity goal for a long time, the more explicit use of private-sector approaches dates from the beginning of the Koch administration in 1978, with the advent of Commissioner Norman Steisel. Steisel, for example, initiated a number of "competitions" as devices for improving productivity, rewarding winning crews of one competition with Super Bowl tickets and another with luncheons that included spouses.[27] Other such measures included campaigns to raise morale, an improved uniform, better heavy equipment, a public relations effort, a career development program, better internal communication, an office rehabilitation effort, better training, broadbanding, cleaner lines of authority, and department handbooks. Finally, there were detailed designs for measuring inputs and outputs so that the department could do a fair evaluation of all of these strategies.

The Sanitation Department has managed its own operations well, but has had less success in dealing with what are likely to be the most serious types of problems of the future, problems the solutions to which depend on the behavior or regulations of others. For example, the citizen must separate garbage for recycling and reduce the generation of waste products in response to disposal difficulties,[28] and the task of finding new disposal sites and methods must satisfy federal and state requirements. It may be that productivity gains will lag as the department's mission becomes more complicated, but, so far, this is a department that has been able both to measure and to measure up.

Conclusion

All large organizations (including those in the private sector) suffer from a long list of common pathologies: red tape, impersonality, rigidity, waste, apathy, and goal-transference. In late twentieth century America, add racism and sexism. It is no surprise that New York City's civil service shares these disabilities. But problems in New York City tend to be magnified—by size, heterogeneity, and the intensity of media coverage. There is no day without complaints about service delivery, without heartbreaking stories about the failures of the system, without outrage over some new case of corruption, and without titillation over some personal peccadilloes inside the city's agencies. But, as everyone concedes, good news is not fit to print.

The city's departments are performing as might be expected, routinely. They are peopled with neither saints nor devils. The average civil servant has as many personas as an average corporate worker. There are those who are merely "doing time"—waiting for the pension at the end of the tunnel. Others are fired up with enthusiasm for one or another mission. Their leaders, too, reflect almost the same range of reactions.

Mayors can and do influence the overall tilt of the system through the commissioners they appoint and through the general policies that they espouse. A mayor whose bottom line is a carefully balanced budget will produce different service results than one whose major mission is to mend the "safety nets" for the ill, the homeless, and the unemployed, but the differences are marginal. As in all the public arenas of America, the system does not permit wild policy swings. Change is always incremental as it is too in New York City government.

The most significant changes likely in the near future are ones that will flow from an acceleration in the trend toward privatization. Although the precise cost-benefits of the movement toward permitting private enterprise to undertake the public's business have not yet been explored fully, it is a "reform" that has caught on. We can also expect further tinkering with the civil service system itself. It may well be that the Personnel Department will disappear. It has already shed many of its functions. The overall setting of standards for examinations and for other operations will probably be left with a central agency, but they could be made more flexible so that a civil service career will become more attractive to a larger audience and so that people will be more likely to move in and out of the service as the public's needs, as well as their own, demand. This means more job-related exams, greater reliance on performance during a probationary period, swifter methods of screening, placement, and disciplining, flexible pensions, better training, and elimination of the waste and confusion now caused by overly centralized personnel operations and duplication of a number of personnel functions among the line departments, the Personnel Department, the Office of Municipal Labor Relations, and the Office of Management and Budget.

Notes

1. In other cities, the provision of some of the most costly public services that fall under the municipal government in New York is handled in part by other units of government—the state itself, county governments, or special districts—and some of the services are simply not provided to the extent they are in New York.

2. *New York Times*, November 18, 1987, p. 7.

3. Michael Lipsky, *Street Level Bureaucracy*. New York: Russell Sage, 1980, p. 18.

4. That is, individuals whose output is far above what had been considered the norm for the unit, and thereby induce supervisors to establish higher norms. The word derives from the Stalin era in the Soviet Union, in the 1930s, when a worker named Stakhanov was held out as the ideal, for doing just that.

5. The commissioner asked not to be quoted on this point.

6. See Chapter 4 by David Eichenthal on the weakness of the city council, the designated legislature, and the quasi-legislative Board of Estimate.

7. This statement was made very often during his years as executive director of District Council 37. See also Jewel Bellush and Bernard Bellush, *Union Power and New York*. New York: Praeger, 1984.

8. Wallace Sayre and Herbert Kaufman, *Governing New York City*. New York: Russell Sage, 1960, pp. 42, 44.

9. Edgardo Vasquez (Chair), *Report of the Mayor's Commission on Hispanic Concerns*, City of New York, December 10, 1986 (offset), p. 91. These figures excluded the Education Department and the Health and Hospitals Corporation. The inclusion of these two agencies would have enlarged the minority percentages significantly.

10. The Urban Research Center of New York University, *Wage Discrimination and Occupational Segregation in New York City's Municipal Work Force: Time for a Change*, August 1987 (mimeograph), p. 3.

11. Office of the Mayor, *Report on Minorities*, January 2, 1986 (mimeograph), pp. 1, 2.

12. New York City Commission on Human Rights, *The Ethnic Survey*, 1964 (offset). This report was not paginated. New York City Commission on Human Rights, *The Employment of Minorities, Women, and the Handicapped in City Government*, a Report of a 1971 Survey, undated (mimeograph), p. 17.

13. The conclusions reported in this paragraph along with those in the remainder of this section are based on a comparative analysis of the reports on race and sex in city government cited above and below.

14. New York City Commission on Human Rights, *Analysis of Employment in New York City Work Force by Sex and Race*, Director, David Preston, undated (probably 1973) (mimeograph), pp. 6, 16.

15. New York City Commission on Human Rights, *Analysis of New York City Work Force*, p. 36.

16. Urban Research Center of New York University, *Wage Discrimination and Occupational Segregation*, Executive Summary.

17. *Report of the Mayor's Task Force on City Personnel*, Chair, Harold Riegelman, Director, B.D. Blank, May 3, 1966 (offset), p. 4.

18. *Federalist Paper #46*.

19. *New York Times*, November 24, 1986, p. B9.

20. *Mayor's Advisory Committee on Police Management and Personnel Policy, Final Report*, Vol. II, February 24, 1987 (offset), pp. 10, 11. The recent recruit figures updated in an interview with report's director, Joseph P. Viteritti, February 16, 1988.

21. Edith F. Lynton, *Hiring Policies in the New York City Uniformed Services*, Center for Women in Government, Albany, June 1986 (offset), p. 6.

22. Arthur Neiderhoffer, *Behind the Shield*, Garden City, NY: Doubleday, 1967, p. 45, Chapter 4 and Appendix. The entire book is suffused with material on police cynicism.

23. Sayre and Kaufman, *Governing New York City*, p. 289.

24. *New York Times*, January 2, 1987, p. B2.

25. Joseph P. Viteritti, *Police Professionalism in New York City: The Zuccotti Committee in Historical Context*, Center for Research in Crime and Justice, New York University Law School, Occasional paper, 1988, p. 11.

26. Mayor's Advisory Committee, *Police Management and Personnel Policy, Final Report*, Vol. I, February 24, 1987, pp. 27–52.

27. Both rewards were attacked as a misuse of public funds, which indicates how difficult it is for a public agency to emulate successful private-sector methods.

28. An example of the latter is the abandonment of cars on the city's streets—more than 65,000 vehicles a year.

6

Community Control and Decentralization

David Rogers

Decentralization has been a time-honored concept in American communities since the early New England colonies and the Mayflower compact. It was typified in the town meetings and notions of self-rule of that time. It has only been tried in any significant way in America's cities, however, since the 1960s, and that has certainly been the case in New York, which was, as usual, ahead of the rest of the country in major reforms.[1]

The 1960s was the time for a major upsurge in decentralization efforts, for fairly obvious reasons. It was the decade of the so-called "community revolution" in which concern was expressed in many circles—among leaders of various political movements, in civic organizations, and among elected officials—about the lack of responsiveness and accountability of the government in dealing with local service delivery problems.[2] John Lindsay, the mayor of New York City during much of that period (1965–73), was a leading figure among big city mayors not only in highlighting as big issues the alienation of the citizenry from local government and their powerlessness, but also in implementing a series of decentralization and other management reforms to deal with these problems.[3]

This chapter places the New York City experience with decentralization in broad historical context by tracing what happened as various forms were developed and implemented, that is, (1) what the main *forms* were; (2) the *diagnosis* (of what was wrong with city government) on which they were based; (3) the *process of their implementation*, particularly the politics; (4) the *results*, in terms of changes, if any, in service delivery and in the service delivery system; and (5) finally, *lessons* that may be learned, both as to organizational forms and the kinds of political strategies necessary to get appropriate forms implemented (i.e., what to do and what *not* to do). In brief, the chapter constitutes an analytical history of how New York City fared in its various attempts to decentralize city government.

A few general observations are useful in helping orient the reader to the complexities of what the chapter will cover. First, it is important to have a broad historical perspective on decentralization. Decentralization as well as centralization tend to go in cycles, both in the public sector and in business. Each is often seen as an answer to the excesses of the other, a major problem being that neither can function without the other. The general point that decentralization needs a strong center and that centralized functions can only work effectively with strong grass roots delivery capabilities may seem almost too obvious to mention. But it has often been lost in the many debates on the subject.

Second, decentralization, like any other reform, can only be analyzed in a political context. Indeed, much of the historical analysis to follow is an analysis of the politics of various decentralization programs in New York City, which ultimately determined the extent of their implementation and how effective they would be in improving service delivery.[4]

Finally, there has been a strongly ideological bent to much of the research, as well as the public debate, on decentralization. I want to indicate at the beginning my own biases. Having done many field studies indicating what I regarded as severe bureaucratic pathologies in the city's centralized service delivery agencies, and having seen the ways in which these pathologies had contributed to poor service delivery and to many other forms of social harm—increasing the alienation of citizens, particularly poor minorities, and at times escalating racial and ethnic tensions, as minority areas were not well served—I have supported decentralization as one reform strategy. Others who judge decentralization sometimes fail to be explicit about their biases.

More specifically, the chapter will cover the following: (1) Sayre and Kaufman's image of New York City and its governance and of how decentralization might affect that governance; (2) developments of the 1950s and 1960s, both in New York City and nationally, that led to increasing pressure for decentralization; and (3) an assessment of the city's three most significant decentralization initiatives: *the community school district system in the public schools*, emanating from the struggle over community control and resulting in the 1969 School Decentralization Law; the almost diametrically opposite *Office of Neighborhood Government (ONG) strategy* of Mayor Lindsay, a city hall mayoral-initiated administrative decentralization and district service cabinet program; and the still very different *community board system*, resulting from the New York State Charter Commission recommendations and established in 1977, after a voter referendum of November 1975.

The community school district system began in 1970 and is still in operation. The Lindsay administration's Office of Neighborhood Government program began implementation in early 1972 and operated for only two years before being largely eliminated by Mayor Beame, Lindsay's successor. The community boards, which began (with substantially their present powers) in January 1977, are still in operation.

These are not just three discrete and unrelated decentralization programs, and it is important to see the evolutionary process that took place. The first of the three, the decentralization of the public schools, came closest to political decentralization, giving new powers to elected community school boards. The fallout from the divisive racial and ethnic controversy that that reform spawned, or at least its political management (or, perhaps in this case its mismanagement) brought on, led the mayor and his top staff to a new and potentially much less divisive administrative decentralization program of district manager–district service cabinets. The most recent community board system represents a watered down form of each of its two predecessors. It has elements of political decentralization through community boards, but they are appointed rather than elected, and they have advisory powers only. It also has elements of administrative decentralization, but the district managers, appointed by the borough presidents and local councilpersons rather than the mayor, have even less power than they had under the Lindsay ONG system. And the district cabinets' role as service delivery and planning bodies, orchestrated in large part by the district manager, is also much more limited than before.

The chapter ends with an attempt to make some broader sense of this historical experience, including some discussion of the lessons from the experience—on matters of organizational design, agency management, and political strategy. It also suggests some directions that future reforms might take to improve the governance of the city.

Sayre and Kaufman's Image of New York City, Its Governance, and Decentralization

Sayre and Kaufman's analysis of New York City government presented a positive view of how the city was governed, both in the publication of the first edition in 1959 and in the preface to the second edition in 1965. By 1970, however, in Sayre's chapter on the mayor in Lyle Fitch and Annmarie Walsh's *Agenda for a City*, there is a much more negative view of how the city's government works, this change having much relevance for understanding the context for decentralization.[5]

In the earlier, more positive view, they argued that despite problems associated with the city's size, diversity, and complexity, it was managed democratically and in a reasonably efficient manner. They saw it as open and responsive to new group interests, with issues getting addressed and resolved in expeditious fashion, primarily through negotiation. They attributed this in large part to what they saw as the balance between two forces—what they called centrifugal ones, which referred to the continued emergence of new participants (interest groups, governmental agencies, programs) with new demands, and centripetal ones, which refer to processes of coalition formation and aggregating interests. In brief, they viewed the political process in the city as a kind of benign balance between the forces of differentiation and integration.[6]

In Sayre's 1970 piece on the mayor, he highlights more recent developments: an increasing political fragmentation, correspondingly weakening the power of the mayor and making the city much less governable. His main point is that during the 1960s there had been a significant shift in the role of the main constituencies the mayor had to deal with. One was the bureaucracies, which had increased in power, having become more autonomous and more insulated from outside review and demands for accountability (with bureau chiefs and unions having gained considerable power). A second was new interest groups, particularly those representing minority (black and hispanic) populations. In the 1960s, a period of rising expectations, these groups often engaged in confrontation politics, making strong and volatile demands, particularly on human service agencies (schools, welfare, antipoverty programs), reflecting in part their unstable leadership and fluctuating membership and, as newcomers not knowing how the system worked, their utopian demands on it. Third, all the while that these developments were taking place, political party organizations, one of the main mechanisms of representing citizen service needs to city government, were declining in power under the onslaught of the reformers. The city was seen from this perspective as having become more difficult to manage, with the mayor increasingly unable to handle the new, more recalcitrant constituencies.

The point of summarizing the Sayre and Kaufman and the later Sayre perspective is not just historical curiosity. Rather, it helps in understanding the context for decentralization and in interpreting what it may mean to the city and what its long run prospects may be. Sayre and Kaufman, as centralists, argued in their book, as did Sayre in his later piece, that there had to be consolidation at the top (in the mayor's office and in the agencies) for the city to be governed better. They omit mention of decentralization as part of any possible consolidation strategy, and one might speculate that they probably regarded it as contributing to further fragmentation—that is, to adding more layers of middle-management bureaucracy and more negative veto groups among local citizens, blocking needed borough and citywide projects. One of the only direct hints of how at least Sayre felt about decentralization came from an article he wrote for the *New York Times* in 1972, entitled "Smaller Does Not Mean Better Necessarily," in which he argued that a recent neighborhood government proposal of Governor Rockefeller was a Republican Party strategy to cut into Democratic power in the city.[7]

Part of the reason Sayre and Kaufman omitted any mention of decentralization was that it didn't exist in any significant way through the late 1950s when they completed their book. There were, however, early experiments with community planning boards, initiated by Robert Wagner, Sr., when he was borough president of Manhattan, to give citizens more voice in land use decisions and service delivery in their neighborhoods. The fact that there was no discussion of these boards suggests that Sayre and Kaufman did not see them as part of any solution to the city's governance and management problems.

Developments of the 1950s and 1960s, Leading to Decentralization

Several developments of the 1950s and 1960s, some highlighted by Sayre and Kaufman, led to increasing support for decentralization and culminated in the community struggle over the public schools.[8] One was the city's accelerating demographic changes, that is, the exodus of the white, middle class and the influx of new minority populations, mainly blacks and hispanics. These new groups, often from rural areas, placed big demands on city services, particularly those in human service agencies.

At the same time, the agencies, staffed mainly by whites, were becoming stronger and more autonomous, since municipal unions and the civil service had grown in power and the reformers had helped diminish the power of political parties to make the bureaucracy more responsive to citizens' service needs. Elected officials, particularly the mayor, seemed to have increasingly lost control of the bureaucracies, at just that time in history when new minority groups were making strong demands for services. These groups constituted a sizeable, needy population that the city, with its long-time traditions of liberalism and social justice, had always tried to serve.

Meanwhile, there were the city's many white ethnic groups, mainly in the outer boroughs and predominantly lower-middle class, who claimed that they also had serious service needs and resented the many funded programs for poor minorities and the special attention the mayor seemed to be giving to them.

Another critical element in the situation was that the new minorities as of the early 1960s had not shared in the rewards municipal government could distribute to nearly the same degree as had other waves of newly arriving ethnic groups. Each of several previous waves had received jobs in large numbers in city agencies in return for their votes. By the times that blacks and Latinos had arrived, however, an overt ethnic patronage strategy had been ruled out by civil service reforms. One exception was the antipoverty program that provided many jobs to blacks and Latinos, but it started experiencing severe cutbacks after 1967.

Then there was the experience with urban renewal and highway construction projects. These projects were usually accompanied by the removal of large numbers of poor minority populations, and one political aftermath was to build up increasing resentment toward City Hall and other levels of government responsible for the displacement.

A series of developments, then, had escalated in the 1950s and early 1960s, setting the stage for an upsurge of decentralization proposals. Various surveys at the time indicated that many residents of New York and other big cities, not just minorities, felt alienated from city government, which they perceived as generally unresponsive and as lacking in even minimal standards of productivity and accountability.[9]

As indicated above, Mayor Lindsay was particularly sympathetic to these concerns of New York City residents, and he placed the issue of trying to increase the responsiveness of local government to citizen needs very high on his agenda. He and his staff initiated a series of reforms in that direction, and several decentralization programs were among them. The programs took different forms at different times, depending on the political climate. They constituted a major element in Lindsay's many attempts to improve the performance of city government.

Three Decentralization Strategies

The Public Schools: Community Control and Political Decentralization

The first major effort at decentralization in New York City was in the public schools. This decentralization turns out to have been an example of political rather than administrative decentralization, at least in intent. The push for decentralization came out of the community control movement, which was, in turn, a product of the 1960s. The agenda of the leaders in the movement was to transfer political power, not just from the staff at headquarters to those in the local district office, but rather from the professional staff to elected lay or citizen boards at the local level.[10]

Background

It was particularly appropriate that the schools were the site of this initial decentralization reform. In New York, as in other big cities, they had been the focus of considerable controversy since the Brown decision of 1954, mandating desegregation. Blacks, in particular, resented the fact that the public schools had failed to improve their quality of education, either through compensatory programs or through desegregation. Other groups, including but not limited to Latinos, had also become alienated from an agency that was increasingly seen as insulated, mismanaged, and dominated by professional educators who had successfully deflected and absorbed all past efforts at reform, which had no significant impact on the schools' performance.

The larger context of community control included more than just the limited success of compensatory education programs and then the limited implementation of desegregation. There were, in addition, many other developments of the 1960s that fed into this—the black power movement, the student protests, and New Left attacks on bureaucratic institutions in general (business, government, universities), federally funded community action organizations that pressed for more grass roots power over traditional service delivery agencies, and, finally, the ethnic succession politics of the city. Indeed, in regard to the latter, an item very high on the agenda of community control advocates was the transfer of power to run and staff the school system to blacks and Latinos: jobs as teachers, supervisors, and district and headquarters staff; contracts as education consultants; and membership on community school boards to set district policy.

Diagnosis

As David Seeley has pointed out, community control was an ambiguous concept with different strands, some of them potentially contradictory.[11] One was political—emphasizing the power of minority and other community groups to control their schools, making professional educators accountable and responsive to them. Another was more institutional, emphasizing the need to reconnect the schools to their communities through partnerships with community organizations, other agencies, and families.

Two common targets for attack, notwithstanding these differences, were professional power and the central bureaucracy. The professionals were seen as having become increasingly insulated and unresponsive to legitimate demands of citizen groups for improved education, as having a monopoly over definitions of professionalism, and as having externalized the blame for the failure of the public schools to educate most of the city's poor, minority populations.

The central bureaucracy, in turn, was seen as having failed to adapt to change by undermining the implementation of innovative programs, and by being grossly mismanaged in its day-to-day support services—budget, personnel, school construction, zoning, curriculum, and business services. The insulation and lack of responsiveness of headquarters were a particular source of frustration. And parents and civic groups throughout the city shared horror stories about their futile attempts to deal with headquarters staff on such matters as zoning, appointments of teachers and principals, and school construction. Moreover, other groups, including business, universities, and other government agencies joined in with accounts of their disappointments, as they tried to develop collaborative programs with the schools or simply to secure information on the schools that should have been part of the public record.

The goals of community control advocates were wide ranging, reflecting the many potential benefits that were assumed to result from its effective implementation. Those benefits included: (1) more accountability of the educators to their school and district constituencies; (2) more parent and community participation in educational decision making; (3) increasing educational innovations; (4) a more organic relation of schools to communities in curriculum, staffing, and program linkages to outside agencies; (5) more jobs within the school system for district residents; (6) political training and the development of more local-level leadership; (7) improved legitimacy of the schools; and, ultimately, (8) improved student performance.

This was quite a formidable agenda, but community control advocates, at least taken collectively, clearly had all these things in mind. They had invested a lot in the movement and were soon to be disappointed as implementation proceeded. The fact that the movement took on all these dimensions undoubtedly contributed to the strong resistance that soon arose, particularly from educators who felt that their jobs and their autonomy as professionals were being threatened. There were clearly several sets of goals—economic, political, community development, as well as education. And the threat that their pursuit by community control advocates posed to groups already holding jobs and bureaucratic power soon helped to escalate the conflict over the issue that became citywide and tore the city apart.

The opposition to community control was quite formidable, and it came mainly from New York City educators through their teachers' union and professional associations that argued that community control would have devastating effects on the schools. Local groups—political clubs, church groups, and so on—without much interest in improving the schools, would solidify their power base, they argued. Doing this would also increase segregation, the use of racial and ethnic criteria in staff appointments, parochialism in curriculum (e.g., black culture programs), nepotism, and local corruption. In addition, they argued, breaking up the system into many small districts would be inefficient, leading to much duplication of administrative and curriculum services, abandoning the important economies of scale that the centralized system provided. And the net result of such a politicized, racist, parochial, and inefficient system, they concluded, would be deteriorating schools, heightened ethnic and racial conflict, and declining student performance.

This is the context in which community control became a strategy for redesigning the New York City school system. Viewed in such a context, the movement made sense. Given the political power of the educators, however, and a larger coalition of municipal employees who supported them, prospects for implementation of such a strategy were not as great as its advocates had hoped.

Highlights of implementation: political history

In retrospect, this push for political decentralization was supported by what turned out to be an insufficient coalition, reflecting a short-lived movement for community control.[12] The goals of community control advocates to have elected lay boards make major policy decisions on staffing, curriculum, and a variety of ancillary support services were very threatening to the educators and activated strong opposition from them. The push for community control was so threatening, in fact, that it took two legislative sessions in Albany (1968 and 1969) before a compromise law was pieced together at the last moment, a law that many community control advocates regarded as a patchwork reform at best. They were so angry and disappointed that many urged local residents not to vote in the first community school board elections, as a gesture of protest.

The decentralization coalition at its peak included leaders and parents in poor minority communities, particularly black areas, with episodic support from some establishment organizations, mainly Mayor Lindsay and his administration, the Ford Foundation, the New York Urban Coalition, and some independent Reform Democratic groups from Manhattan. All these establishment participants, however, backed off early in the fray, after being subjected to enormous pressure. Lindsay faced an increasingly irate group, not only of New York City educators, but of other municipal employees as well, who saw community control as a threat to hard earned job rights, gained through years of collective bargaining. They saw community control as giving elected citizen boards the power to hire and fire city employees and to dictate agency policies and programs. For these city employees, the schools' struggle looked like the "entering wedge" for similar reforms in their agencies.

The community control controversy soon became a racial and religious as well as labor conflict, in which Mayor Lindsay was seen as inappropriately taking an advocacy position for one side only. More specifically, the educators, particularly through the teacher's union's outspoken president, Albert Shanker, chastised the mayor for supporting the demands of militant blacks against the school professionals. At this point in history, the school staff was predominantly white and Jewish, and the controversy became defined publicly as in large part a Jewish-black confrontation. Lindsay's political support was so eroded as a result of how the educators, other city employees, and Jewish groups defined his role in the school struggle that he was forced to back off considerably from his early support.

The same political backlash affected other establishment members of the coalition. The Ford Foundation's support for community control led New York City educators to lobby in Washington for new legislation forbidding foundations from supporting such advocacy groups, and the legislation passed.[13]

The New York Urban Coalition, as well, was forced to abandon the advocacy programs of its early years (1967–69) and work instead on programs that would not alter the basic power structure of the school system. Its labor members, reflecting the concerns of their municipal employee constituencies, simply forced the coalition to water down its positions on community control.[14]

Despite the coalition's coming apart, a decentralization law was in fact enacted in 1969 in Albany, establishing a community school district system of first thirty-one and later thirty-two boards. As discussed above, from the perspective of community control advocates, the legislation did not give community boards broad enough powers to make much difference in how the schools would be run. Nevertheless, a compromise community school district system was set up with some powers in the hands of community boards and their professional staff—curriculum, staffing (e.g., boards could select their own superintendent and also principals and teachers from certified lists of the Board of Examiners, the group who administered all tests for professional and administrative positions), repairs and maintenance, and food programs—but with many checks and balances in the form of concurrent powers in the chancellor's office at headquarters.

In order for decentralization to work, several other changes were necessary: the central board had to willingly comply with the law and bestow on the community boards the powers that were now theirs, and headquarters had to convert much more into a standard setting, monitoring, and technical assistance agency than before. These changes did not take place to any significant degree, as documented in three reports done at various intervals since decentralization was first implemented, including one by the author.[15] The following themes stand out in regard to the first several years of implementation:

1. There was no significant planning or preparation for the change. The central board and headquarters moved slowly in training staff and board members in the districts and at headquarters to assume the new roles required under decentralization. Part of the problem lay in the adversarial relationship between the districts and headquarters and each side's lack of trust in the other. One central board member reported his disappointment at the low attendance by community board members at training sessions he had set up for them through a management consulting firm. The community school board members, on their side, argued that the trainers knew little about education, the New York City schools, or the communities: their politics, ethnic traditions, and educational concerns. Consider the following observations from a State Charter Revision Commission report of 1974:

> The transition from centralization to a decentralized system was very awkward. No clear plan guided the changeover. [p. 14]
> Initial training for community school board members was inadequate. It was given at inappropriate times and did not stress the kinds of problems the boards would encounter. Nor did the interim board adequately instruct community school boards in the provisions of the Decentralization Act. . . . Central staff to provide technical assistance was either lacking or poorly trained. [p. 90]

2. *Part of the problem was the legislature's failure to specify how implementation would be carried out and evaluated.* The legislature not only enacted what was widely regarded as an ambiguous law, but it was then reluctant to impose on the Board of Education any more specific implementation requirements or evaluation procedures. While such reluctance was not unique to this legislation, it enabled the Board of Education to implement the law in a limited way.

3. *Perhaps more significant in its impacts than legislative inadequacies was the Interim Board's lack of commitment to giving the districts powers that the legislation provided and its tendency to consolidate and expand its own power.* When decentralization began in September 1970, the school system had an interim board of five members, appointed by each of the borough presidents, and established in May 1969. Its main role was to manage the transition to decentralization, in addition to having day-to-day oversight for the entire school system. The chancellor's office was left vacant, while the board searched for a qualified person, and it remained vacant during the entire transitional period (May 1969 to September 1970). Those who temporarily filled the position were on an "acting" basis. One result was that this interim board tended to absorb more and more authority. Moreover, its interpretation of the Decentralization Law restricted the powers of the districts far beyond what the law ever intended, notwithstanding its ambiguities and notions of concurrent powers.

Later, when the Interim Board did hire a chancellor, Dr. Harvey Scribner, the commissioner of Vermont's education system and a strong supporter of decentralization, it allowed him limited discretion to run the school system and implement the law. Indeed, the board forced him out after two years, at least partly because he was such a strong advocate of decentralization and because it had become used to trying to run the system itself.

The net result was that decentralization got off to a slow start in terms of headquarters support. Little systematic effort was made to train either headquarters staff to assume needed monitoring and service roles of district staff or community school board members to take on the new responsibilities in management and policy making that decentralization supposedly gave them. One of the more dramatic instances of the Interim Board's limited compliance with the law was its refusal to allow districts to run their own lunch programs. One district (District 2 in Manhattan) sued the central board to have this right.[16] While the district finally won the case, it reluctantly decided that the continued conflicts and red tape it would encounter in dealing with the central bureau in charge of food programs would not make it worth the effort. The commission report summarized the problems the districts faced in trying to secure headquarters support:

> Responsibility for assistance to districts was highly fragmented at central headquarters. Central staff to supply technical assistance was either lacking or poorly trained. . . . The districts could hardly assume the burdens of such

complicated systems as lunch services and repairs without technical assistance. First the Interim Board did nothing to provide or train the required personnel, then it refused to transfer powers (given by law to the boards partly on the ground that the districts lacked the requisite technical capability). [pp. 90–91]

The Board of Education's policies have prevented the local boards from exercising their statutory grant of power. Specifically, the pattern that emerges is that of a central authority which has constrained, sometimes illegally, the power of the community school boards. [p. 122]

A further example of this pattern of noncompliance by the Interim Board is that while the Decentralization Law allowed up to $250,000 to each district for maintenance and repairs of school buildings, in actual fact, the central board kept those funds.

In brief, in order for decentralization to work, it needed much more headquarters leadership and support than it received, at least in its first three to four years of operation. Not only did the Interim Board and its staff at headquarters fail to provide the technical assistance and powers to community school boards that were necessary for them to function effectively, but the monitoring and standard-setting roles of headquarters were also not performed well. A task force of executives on loan, for example, working with several districts in 1973 and 1974 to help improve their management capability, pointed out to top headquarters officials how in at least one case, a district had overspent its budget for the entire fiscal year several months before the year's end. These officials not only claimed not to know about this on their own, but they then denied that it could happen.[17]

One way of looking at most of these implementation problems is that they were simply start-up, transitional ones that would work themselves out over time. To some extent that has been the case. As headquarters evolved in the mid-1970s, it became somewhat more rationalized. A new deputy chancellor position was created to manage and modernize many of the business and support services. Several overlapping and duplicating functions were consolidated at headquarters. A community school district affairs office was established to provide more monitoring and technical assistance from headquarters and representation of community school board and district interests. And districts did begin to establish collaborative relations with personnel, budget, curriculum, funded programs, and other central offices whose staff provided more monitoring and assistance than had been the case earlier.[18] Moreover, a strong, new reform chancellor came in from outside in 1977, Dr. Frank Macchiarola, a former community school board chairman in the Flatbush area of Brooklyn; he made further improvements in headquarters and its relationship with the districts.

Yet, a major report, *Governing The New York City Schools* (February 27, 1987), by the staff of the Public Education Association and based on over seventy interviews and years of direct experience, covering in particular the last few years, pointed to many of the same shortcomings at headquarters, contributing to the ineffective implementation of decentralization and hampering the schools' performance. Acknowledging, as well, serious shortcomings of community school boards—for example, some had become inappropriately politicized in staff appointments, parent participation was often minimal, both in elections and on boards; school employees, people from local political clubs, and religious, parochial school interests often dominated many boards—they highlighted as well many headquarters shortcomings that continued to drag the schools down. They concluded the following:

First of all, headquarters had never really dedicated itself to implementing the law and supporting the districts.[19] Its staff had instead competed for power and resources. Headquarters staff in a wide range of functions (curriculum, staff training, and business bureaus) were often concerned more with their own departmental agendas than with facilitating local priorities. It mismanaged business and managerial support functions (maintenance and repairs, school construction, and supplies), so that districts and schools were not well served. It showed limited commitment to training and technical assistance for community school board members and district staff. It often failed to consult with the districts through mechanisms that had been set up for that purpose—for example, a consultative council of community school boards and a negotiating council for citywide collective bargaining. It continued to operate with a Board of Examiners that inhibited the recruitment of non–New Yorkers, that perpetuated informal networks of insiders, and that had been recommended for extinction in studies and reports dating back to the 1940s. And it maintained confusion and conflict in relations between the central board and chancellor, with the board continuing to function cumbersomely as a management committee.

Second, they reinforced the finding of earlier reports, including the author's *110 Livingston Street*, that headquarters continued to overregulate the districts and schools, limiting their flexibility, while at the same time failing to set standards for performance and monitor compliance. Most importantly, it had failed to reorient the headquarters staff to assume new support and monitoring roles more consistent with decentralization.

The fact that the same bureaucratic pathologies existed at headquarters after more than four decades of reports and studies and after decentralization was enacted to overcome these pathologies indicates how entrenched the bureaucracy has become. A larger lesson emerges from the school experience, namely, that before one can decentralize effectively, if that is seen as a solution to some of the organization's problems, one has to have a coherent and reasonably well-functioning center. That has never been the case with the headquarters bureaucracy of the New York City school system. Stated more bluntly, it is difficult to effectively decentralize chaos.

For the schools and districts to work effectively under a decentralized system, headquarters must be converted into an effective monitoring and service agency, and that has not happened in the nearly twenty years of decentralization. Moreover, ambiguities in the law and its granting of concurrent powers to the chancellor as well as the districts helped perpetuate the central bureaucracy. In brief, effective decentralization can never exist without a strong center, and that has yet to develop.

Impacts, results of decentralization

Looking back at seventeen years of decentralization, various scenarios have been constructed as to its impacts. It may be seen as having had mainly positive effects, mainly negative ones, or, for some people, having been largely irrelevant to the performance of the schools. What is the evidence?

First, while results of reading tests are imperfect measures of school performance, reading scores have not gone down and in fact have risen considerably since decentralization. Thus, 33.9 percent of students in grades 2–9 were reading above grade level in 1971, compared with 65 percent in 1986.[20] And this has taken place despite developments that should have pushed them down—the continued exodus of middle-class students, the increase of poor minority students, and the city's severe fiscal problems that led to the big cutbacks in the 1970s.

Many factors other than decentralization obviously affect reading scores, including the tests themselves that have changed at least five times since 1971. But clearly, while decentralization has been in existence, things have improved on this indicator.

Second, the city has had much more social peace around the public schools since 1971 than before.[21] Again, while many factors affect that, including the general political climate, decentralization has allowed many districts to pay more attention to educational issues than before. Having the city quieter politically may have its costs, given the importance of some level of protest to encourage needed change. But beyond a certain level, and New York City was certainly at that point in the late 1960s, too much of the school's limited resources can be spent trying to manage the protest, rather than carrying on educational programs.

Third, looking at the backgrounds of school staff and community school board members, there is increased representation of minority groups and professionally qualified and competent people. Much of the decentralization struggle reflected a politics of ethnic succession, and that has been taking place. Thus, the number of minority superintendents increased from none in 1970 to fourteen in 1987. The proportion of black teachers increased from 12 percent in 1980 to 17.6 percent in 1986, with a predicted growth to 20.2 percent in 1990. The corresponding figures for Latino teachers are 5.3 percent in 1980 to 8.1 percent in 1986, with an anticipated growth to 9.4 percent in 1990. There were 194 black principals in 1986 and 75 Latinos, compared with 68 black and 8 Latino principals in 1970.[22] Moreover, membership on community school boards increased for blacks from 16.3 to 25.7 percent under decentralization and for Latinos from 10.1 to 17.7 percent.[23]

Many New York City educators claim that ethnic succession has nothing to do with education and some claim that the quality of staff has actually deteriorated with decentralization. While there have been some professionally competent whites who have been pushed out under decentralization, and some not so competent minorities who have been hired, on balance, my judgment is that there has been no decline in quality. Many superintendents and principals were unable to function effectively in a more community-oriented school system, where they were accountable to a locally elected board and parents' association. Moreover, some of the new minority superintendents are among the best in the city, and there has been much professional leadership from minority educators at all levels, as teachers, supervisors, and administrators.

One significant change under decentralization leading to increased minority representation has been a broadening of definitions of professionalism. An understanding of the culture of minorities and the ability to relate effectively to minority students, parents, board members, and community organizations have become criteria used to recruit staff to schools and district offices, complementing the use of traditional educational criteria.

Fourth, many able superintendents have been appointed in community school districts, both minority and white.[24] There were good ones before decentralization, but in the aggregate, those under decentralization are at least as good as their predecessors. They are much more oriented toward their district and its community, just by the conditions of their appointment, than were their predecessors, many of whom were marking time until they could get downtown to 110 Livingston Street, the headquarters offices of the New York City schools.

In addition, districts and schools developed many effective programs under decentralization: collaborative programs with community agencies, alternative schools, magnet schools, experimental schools, districtwide programs to improve math, reading, and other basic skills, and staff training and development programs.[25] Some minority districts, for example, District 4 in East Harlem, District 1 on the Lower East Side, District 13 in Downtown Brooklyn, Brooklyn Heights, and Park Slope, produced dramatic gains in school performance for minority students. District 4, for example, developed a network of some twenty-five alternative, magnet schools that were established and run by teachers. The teachers and students are there by choice, and teachers have a big voice in running those schools. Those schools are seen as so attractive that several hundred white middle-class students attend from outside the district. That same district created the equivalent of a local voucher system, where students may choose to go to a regular school, a bilingual school, or one of these alternative schools. District 13, with a markedly different style, raised learning standards, developed a more coherent curriculum, and established many programs to evaluate teachers and provide assistance to those who need help.

Contrary to the fears of many opponents of decentralization, several districts have more ethnically integrated administrative and supervisory staffs. One district implemented a big desegregation program. District 22 in the Flatbush area of Brooklyn experienced an increase in the early 1970s from 20 to 50 percent poor minority students. Its community school board and superintendent then implemented a program involving the busing of roughly 2,000 black students from overcrowded schools in the north to underutilized ones in the south. This was done with much community participation and district initiative in securing outside federal funding. And the reading scores in the receiving schools went up both for the students bused in and those already there.

The downside of decentralization is also important to note, however. Parent participation has been low, and many district elections and boards reflect that. Voter turnout in community school board elections has declined from 14 percent in 1970 to 6 percent in 1989 (despite a vigorous campaign in 1989 to increase turnout).[26] This has allowed other interests to dominate the boards, particularly people from local political clubs, religious groups, and Board of Education employees. The percentage of community school board members from the latter group, for example, increased from 8.3 percent in 1970 to 24.3 percent in 1987. In some cases, principals deemed incompetent or unfit would be fired from one school, only to be hired at another, largely because of their political networks among community school board members. And some boards became involved in ethnic and other forms of patronage, thereby downgrading educational quality.

In addition, some districts tended to follow ethnically exclusionist personnel policies. Also, some districts were the subjects of grand jury investigations, as a result of charges of corruption in district management. More generally, local school staff sometimes voice the same frustrations with their districts that have traditionally been expressed about school headquarters—that the district office is too removed, that it is mismanaged, and that it controls and constrains individual schools rather than acting as a facilitator and source of support.

In the late 1980s, reflecting these concerns, the central board, under the leadership of its president, Robert F. Wagner, Jr., urged, along with some state legislators, an overall evaluation of how decentralization has worked and possible changes in the decentralization law. The issue remains politically charged, even though the climate is not nearly as volatile as it was in the 1960s.

Some areas of consensus have emerged, however.[27] One is that there should be reforms preventing Board of Education employees and people associated with local political clubs from serving on community school boards.[28] This might help to facilitate more parent participation. Another may be that individual schools rather than districts should be the focus of management and control. Still another is that election reforms are urgently needed. The system of proportional representation in school boards is almost impossible for the average citizen to comprehend and has put off many voters. It has allowed special interest groups, rather than parents, to dominate boards. Also, there is much concern about illegal electioneering.

There remain many areas of disagreement, and eventually policy decisions and perhaps legislative changes will have to be made. Perhaps the biggest needed change relates to personnel matters; Board President Wagner, concerned about local patronage and a possible decline of professionalism, has suggested that perhaps the appointment of principals and community superintendents be made by headquarters rather than by community boards. Some black leaders argue that these appointments are among the most important powers the boards have and should never be taken away from them.

There are other governance and management issues as well. Some observers argue, the author among them, that coterminality—the alignment of various local or community districts having different functions within a single boundary—should extend to the schools and that these school districts should be integrated into district service cabinets to facilitate more needed collaboration with other city agencies.[29] Some argue that the central board should be eliminated, to be replaced by a commissioner who would be appointed by the mayor and function as a member of the mayor's cabinet. This might enhance further the needed collaboration of the public schools with other agencies. In 1988, the legislature assigned the responsibility for school construction to a new quasi-independent authority; conceivably, other functions, especially housekeeping functions of one kind or another, might be contracted out to other city or state agencies or even to private firms.

There are different points of view regarding the relevance of school decentralization. For some, decentralization has been and always will be largely irrelevant to improving education.[30] It is seen instead as an attempt to deal with a political issue—the powerlessness and alienation of minorities. For others, decentralization has been harmful, for reasons cited above.[31] And finally, for still others, it is a strategy with much potential that has already brought some benefits, including improved education, and might bring others if designed well.

It is clear that community school boards and districts need reform and that some have become politicized in ways that have not enhanced education and probably have hurt it. It is also clear, however, that headquarters needs a major overhaul as well and that its politics and mismanagement have continued to obstruct the effective delivery of educational services in the city. A central question that emerges is what roles should appropriately be played by different levels in the system—headquarters, the district offices, and the schools—and with what kinds of collaborative relations with outside agencies and groups.

Administrative Decentralization through District Managers and Service Cabinets

Despite the near political disaster for Mayor Lindsay resulting from the public schools struggle over community control, New Yorkers retained a strong interest in citizen participation. And one of the mayor's key staff on education matters, Lewis Feldstein, was still working in 1969 and early 1970 to deal with that concern. The Office of Neighborhood Government (ONG) was established at City Hall in 1970—declared in the city administration as "the year of the neighborhoods"—with Feldstein as its director, to develop a strategy.

ONG's first plan of June 1970 included elements of political decentralization, calling for the strengthening of community planning boards that had been in existence since 1963.[32] This plan was shelved, after hearings throughout the city indicated much disagreement about how to select community boards and what their role might be. Since the city had already been severely polarized in the schools controversy, and the mayor badly hurt politically, another approach seemed called for. The city administration certainly wanted to avoid any more shattering confrontations between the unions of municipal employees and community militants.

Other developments also helped shape the new directions the proposal took. One was the possibility of an HEW federal grant for a program in services integration.[33] The other was the advice of two outside consultants to develop a new format that deemphasized political decentralization and pushed instead for administrative decentralization. The latter, it was argued, would help to rationalize the delivery systems of city government at the local level as a precondition to increased citizen participation that might be pursued only as a long-term goal. After all, the argument went, until the city had set up the machinery to enable it to respond well to citizen concerns for more and better services, it made little sense to expect much improvement just by encouraging citizen access to government. This became defined, then, as an administrative reform strategy, rather than as a devolution of power to give citizens more voice, and was initiated primarily by City Hall to improve service delivery at the local level.

Diagnosis

The diagnosis on which the ultimate design was based was that city government had at least two major shortcomings that some form of administrative decentralization might reverse: (1) its lack of coordination across agencies; and (2) its unresponsiveness to the service needs of neighborhoods at the delivery sites. The notion was that many local service issues transcend agency boundaries and require the coordination of staff across a wide range of agencies. Moreover, many service delivery decisions—for example, regarding the deployment of staff and the scheduling and location of services—were seen as made better by local service chiefs at the point of delivery, familiar with neighborhood conditions, implementation problems, and program impacts, rather than by some staff downtown or even in a borough office who were often too removed. These ideas weren't that new; the Model Cities and multiservice center programs of the 1960s embodied them.

The shift from political to administrative decentralization led to a new program design in June 1971 that included the following components:[34]

- effecting the administrative decentralization of city agencies, giving local service chiefs in various districts more authority to make resource allocation decisions and fine tune programs;

- establishing district service cabinets of the service chiefs to plan and coordinate service delivery;

- having a district manager as the key local official, functioning as an integrator, to orchestrate this new service delivery mechanism, and appointed by the mayor through ONG;

- converting the crazy quilt patchwork of overlapping agency service districts into coterminal ones, having common district boundaries;

- developing district management information and budget systems to further support local administration; and

- expanding ONG to the field to manage a series of new, experimental districts set up to embody these design ideas and further develop them.

This was a program, then, for what students of public administration have labelled areal administration, designed to facilitate more local planning and coordinated service delivery than are likely in a governmental structure composed of centralized and functionally specialized agencies. An analogue to organizational design changes in business is when large corporations change their structures from centralized functional departments to more decentralized product divisions, so that they can be more consumer and market oriented.

It was apparent to many of the mayor's top staff that the consumers, in this case, city residents, were not happy with the quality and level of services local government was providing. Several surveys at that time indicated high levels of citizen dissatisfaction and a low sense of political efficacy or hope that they could change things.[35]

Several developments contributed to the city government's poor inter-agency coordination and responsiveness: (1) agency and program specialization; (2) attempts at centralizing executive authority downtown and in the mayor's office (for example by creating "superagencies"), but not at the point of delivery; and (3) the decline of territorial political party organizations and the absence of any other institutions to articulate local needs and adapt citywide agency programs to particular local service concerns.

Based on that kind of thinking and armed with some lessons from the school decentralization struggle, the Lindsay administration, through ONG, set up eight demonstration districts to develop and test this new decentralization concept. The program was implemented through existing community planning board districts, of which there were sixty-two in the city at that time; that had the advantage of being of manageable size (the average population of these districts being roughly 125,000), with many city agencies having field districts serving that size population. Seven of the eight districts were in the outer boroughs and included three middle-income, white ethnic areas (Bay Ridge, Maspeth-Ridgewood, and Wakefield-Edenwald), three transitional ones (the Rockaways, Washington Heights, and Crown Heights), and two poverty areas (Bushwick and the South Bronx). While portrayed as a nonpolitical, managerial reform, this selection of districts was made in a political context and served the mayor's constituency concerns. Having been labelled in the 1969 mayoral campaign and in many other settings as a Manhattan-based, limousine liberal, with stronger ties to minority constituencies than to others, the mayor had begun paying increasing attention to white ethnic populations in the outer boroughs.

Political history

The mayor did not give the program high priority initially, reportedly not wanting to risk his reputation on it. Then, Feldstein obtained a federal grant, which helped build support. There was one critical cabinet meeting of superagency administrators and agency commissioners at which two powerful city administration officials, Edward Hamilton (then budget director) and Jay Kriegel (mayoral adviser), supported the program.[36]

The first four districts were established with district managers and cabinets in January 1972. The managers, chosen by the mayor, through ONG, were given a salary and status equivalent to those of a deputy commissioner. However, they had no formal authority to issue orders to local service chiefs or to the chiefs' agency superiors and had to rely instead on their negotiating skills, their ability to establish trust, and their informal influence as mayoral appointees. They had a status very similar to that of a project manager. By the end of the year, all eight districts were in operation.

That informal influence of district managers, however, probably waned after May 1972, when Comptroller Beame, later to become mayor, released the results of an investigation charging misuses of funds by ONG. Feldstein had bypassed conventional bureaucratic procedures in efforts to get the program underway as expeditiously as possible, and Beame, never sympathetic with the program to begin with and later to wipe it out as mayor, used the powers of his office to cast a cloud of suspicion over it. No evidence, direct or indirect, of corruption was ever produced, but the program immediately became a political liability to the mayor, and he made no serious attempts to rescue it. Indeed, Feldstein soon left and was replaced by his deputy, John Mudd, who, unlike Feldstein, was outside the centers of power in the Lindsay administration. And that change at the top of ONG obviously did not enhance its position vis-à-vis the line agencies it was trying to decentralize.

It soon turned out that the agencies' resistance to decentralization was the biggest obstacle the program faced.[37] The extent of the resistance varied, depending on the agency's structure. In general, old-line agencies, with more homogeneous citywide activities—for example, fire, police, sanitation, parks—and administered through geographically based field operations, were more collaborative than the newer superagencies. The latter, especially the Human Resources Administration, Housing and Development Administration, and Health Services Administration, were organized around functionally based, professional specialties, without territorially decentralized delivery systems. HRA, for example, had several member agencies—social services, manpower training, youth services, addiction services, community development—each of which was an independent entity with its own politically appointed commissioner and specialized professional staff. Even though the HRA administrator at the time, Jule Sugarman, was strongly oriented toward areal administration and administrative decentralization, he didn't have the power within his own agency to implement it there.

The distinction may be made, then, between traditional, old-line agencies with single, homogeneous functions that had a vertical command structure and field operations readily adaptable to decentralization and newer ones with multiple functions that had not yet consolidated internally, let alone decentralized. A classic case of the former was the Police Department whose commissioner, Patrick Murphy, had already moved ahead on decentralization, with outreach, neighborhood police teams, and increased precinct autonomy.

The mayor, while expressing symbolic support for decentralization, was reportedly reluctant to push his administrators far down that path against their will, especially after Comptroller Beame's investigation. That made it very difficult to secure the cooperation of some local service chiefs in the district cabinets, and it clearly hampered the program in its operations.

The key figures in the program, despite their lack of formal authority, were the district managers. They played an integrator and catalyst role. Though there were marked differences in the way the various district managers functioned, ONG did establish broad guidelines. The DMs were not to become community organization advocates or partisan political operators. They were not to become merely community relations buffers for the agencies, essentially funnels for citizen complaints. Rather, they were to encourage more local-level planning and improved service delivery through the service cabinets. And, far from just functioning in a fire-fighting way, reacting to complaints about immediate service programs, they were to lay the groundwork for systemic organizational changes to help prevent problems in the first place.

As it turned out, the early district managers were people with extraordinary political, interpersonal, and management skills.[38] The district manager in Crown Heights, for example, a conflict and problem-ridden district, pitting blacks against Orthodox Jews, was most successful as a political mediator and broker. In Wakefield-Edenwald, in the Bronx, the DM was equally successful in handling the opposition to district service cabinets from political clubs and was also able to bring in more outside funds for district programs. Most of the early DMs went on to high positions in government and business after the program was disbanded.

The programs the DMs initiated through the cabinets were, by and large, *hard* rather than *soft* services. They involved largely environmental issues, like traffic, garbage, street cleaning, safety, and recreation, rather than education, health, and other social services. The issues and programs in hard services were less complex, the outputs were more measurable and attainable in the short term, and the agencies involved, as mentioned above, were more amenable to decentralization.

Unfortunately for the program, no sooner had the eight districts gone into operation and a series of improvement projects gotten underway than the political situation at City Hall changed radically. Mayor Lindsay announced in March 1973 that he would not run for reelection. From then on, the main energies of ONG were devoted to a strategy of implementation through expansion, to solidify the program throughout the city, secure a broader political base, and hopefully prevent its extinction.[39] By the end of August 1973, the number of districts increased from eight to twenty-six, almost half the city. But it was mainly a process of spreading by dilution, as political survival rather than improved service delivery became the goal. The new districts often had neither district managers nor active service cabinets. Commissioners were placed in charge, and to secure more political support, Lindsay issued an executive order in September 1973, calling for the local city council member and the borough president to be members of the cabinet in their areas.

When Beame was elected mayor in November 1973, it was soon apparent that the program was doomed. He had already weakened its support as a result of his earlier investigations and was expected to administer the coup de grace as mayor. This was especially so because of his traditional views: first, government services should be managed hierarchically through established agency bureaucracies and commissioners, functioning on a highly centralized basis, and, second, government programs and services should be adapted to community needs through local party organizations.[40] He correctly saw ONG's district managers and cabinets as a threat to centralized agency heads and local politicians. What happened was that commissioners, invested with strong centralized authority, and local political clubhouse district leaders replaced the decentralized ONG structure. Beame thus politicized the program in the direction of his model of what city government should be. Seeing its strong patronage possibilities, he renamed ONG the Office of Neighborhood Services and political clubhouse presidents, party district leaders, and their relatives began to appear on the payroll in increasing numbers.

Impacts, results

As Barton points out in his summary of the findings of a Columbia University research team that evaluated the ONG experiments, they were a mixed bag. On the positive side, several things emerged. The program made decentralization politically acceptable again in New York City, after the turmoil of the schools struggle. In 1975, a majority of New York City voters were to approve strengthened community boards and district service cabinets. Moreover, more than 80 percent of the local agency staff members who participated in the program found the cabinets useful, and almost all favored continuation and expansion of the district manager–cabinet system of decentralized administration. Also, more than 60 percent of the civic and political leaders interviewed in four communities gave favorable ratings to the program and a higher proportion wanted it continued and strengthened.[41]

Beyond that, a wide range of useful interagency projects was initiated, mostly in the hard services, as already indicated, and at minimal cost. The additional cost for the program was estimated at less than one dollar per capita, including not only the direct expenses of central ONG, the district managers, and their staff and office, but also the time of participating agency officials. Crude estimates of the dollar benefits found that the program almost paid for itself through service improvements, even during its early period, and had the potential to produce greater savings in the long run.

On the negative side, despite the fact that many service delivery improvement projects were undertaken, due largely to the skills of the district managers and their cabinets, two-thirds of the projects experienced long delays or were terminated because the agencies did not cooperate. As the Columbia University evaluators reported, without this service integration mechanism at the local operating level of city government, problems requiring the attention of more than one agency usually were not addressed at all. Even if they were, however, ONG could not compel the agencies to decentralize and grant local service chiefs in the district cabinets the autonomy they needed to carry out the projects. Much stronger mayoral support was required. In brief, the evaluators concluded that the program experienced major implementation problems, perhaps the biggest of which was that the agencies did not delegate sufficient authority to the district service chiefs to enable it to work, and the mayor did not intervene to try to overcome that resistance. Thus, the lack of mayoral support and the resulting non-cooperation of central agency administrators prevented many projects from being implemented.

In addition, competition with rival district level organizations—for example, political clubs, elected councilmen—hurt, as did restrictive union and civil service regulations that some local service chiefs cited to justify their inaction on particular projects. Perhaps as a result of these implementation problems and constraints, no significant overall improvement in service integration was found, nor did community leaders feel more satisfied with city services. Also, an overwhelming majority of the general public never even knew of the local offices that ONG had set up, and thus did not experience any sense of increased access to local government or of increased satisfaction, power, or trust in government.

Overall, the gains were at best incremental, in selectively improving services to citizens in their communities. The district manager cabinets, as a system to coordinate agencies to deal more effectively with complex local service delivery problems, suggested potential, but were untested. As Mudd noted, they indicated an untapped resource among middle-level field managers of city agencies, and demonstrated through the district managers and service cabinets a technique to integrate the activities of an increasingly fragmented non-system of local government. And when administrative decentralization did take place, the field officers often willingly took much initiative in cooperating with one another and with citizen groups to improve service delivery.

Community Boards

The last decentralization initiative assessed in this chapter is the community boards, established in January 1977 and resulting from Charter Revision Commission recommendations and a referendum of November 1975.[42] At that time, the voters of New York City voted yes on six propositions covering a range of reforms, including: (1) newly constituted community boards of up to fifty members, to be selected by borough presidents and city council members from the area; (2) increased advisory powers for the boards in land use, budget, and service delivery; (3) agency coterminality, with common district boundaries for all the main line agencies; (4) geographic budgeting, under which the expense and capital budgets of the city were to be broken out by districts; (5) district managers (and support staff) to be appointed by the boards; (6) district service cabinets, composed of all local service chiefs from the line agencies, presided over by the district managers, with the entire structure to be supported by (7) administrative decentralization of all agencies, though it was left vague as to how this would be done, how fast, and what final form it should take.

It appeared from the Lindsay ONG program of the early 1970s that the public was concerned about services and land use and wanted to participate in decisions on these matters. Participation had taken on a different meaning, however, from what it had been in the school battles in the 1960s. It meant giving advice and being consulted, rather than controlling the operations of government. In that sense, people favored some middle ground between the extremes of the centralized city government that had evolved in the decades preceding the 1960s and full-scale control. People wanted input into land use and service decisions. They wanted a place to go to register complaints and they wanted some response from agency officials whom they could hold accountable for their performance. But they wanted the services to be performed by those responsible.

Beyond this, the local service chiefs and community leaders involved in the Lindsay program had developed positive feelings about the new district manager and cabinet structure as a place from which to get better services and planning. The program indicated the promise of administrative decentralization, even though it was short lived.

The Lindsay program also demonstrated, however, that unless a reform of this nature has a strong political base and, in particular, strong support from the mayor, it will be eliminated. But while Beame was killing off the district manager cabinets after being elected mayor in November 1973, there began a larger debate over the future structure of city government, a debate that he could not control. It was centered in the New York State Charter Revision Commission for New York City, chaired by Republican Senator Roy Goodman. The commission was established by legislation in 1972, with a formal mandate to encourage genuine citizen participation in city government to ensure that city government was responsive to citizen needs and to improve its effectiveness. Informed observers noted that the commission seemed to be serving wider political goals. Wallace Sayre, for example, regarded the commission's decentralization mandate as reflecting Governor Rockefeller's and the state and city Republican party's interest in gaining a foothold in the city, at the Democrats' expense. Others suggested that the commission reflected an ongoing conflict between Rockefeller and Lindsay over the nature and causes of the city's problems and that it was to be Rockefeller's vehicle for highlighting weaknesses in Lindsay's management of the city.

The commission had twelve members, and they could not agree on what position it should take regarding decentralization. One, Edward Costikyan, a Manhattan lawyer and former Tammany Hall leader, argued for a radical shift of authority to neighborhood governments. He was the only advocate, however, for community control. Four members pressed for a return of power to the borough presidents, and a bare majority of seven favored some moderate form of decentralization. The charter revisions already discussed and appearing on the ballot in November 1975, reflected essentially their position.[43]

A big loser in this development was Mayor Beame. By late 1975, he had been weakened politically by his handling of the city's deepening budget crisis and by the state's assuming financial control (through the Municipal Assistance Corporation and the Emergency Financial Control Board) over city affairs. Beame fought hard against the decentralization proposals, but New Yorkers voted yes on them, at the same time rejecting the Costikyan position favoring community control. Decentralization was to be phased in over a period of years, with the new community districts designated by January 1, 1977, and coterminality, supported by decentralized management authority in the agencies, by January 1, 1980.

This new decentralization reform had elements of both its two predecessors, but in watered-down form. There was some administrative decentralization in the provision for district managers and service cabinets, since those features had gained political support from the Lindsay experiments. However, the managers were no longer under the mayor's control. At the same time, there was some political decentralization in that community boards, appointed by the borough president and local city councilperson and having powers themselves to select district managers and establish policy positions for the district, were the centerpiece of the system. Advocates of both previous decentralization reforms found this one an unsatisfactory compromise. Community boards were given advisory powers and were to be heeded by city agencies and private developers, even if not always cheerfully, but they hardly had the powers that district managers had under a mayoral system or that community school boards have, for all their constraints. Costikyan, for example, referred to it as "centralization with a veneer of localism." Adler and Bellush commented, "The current game seems to be more one of centralization than of decentralization."[44]

Under the ONG program, if a district manager wanted a line agency to respond to a local service problem, there was at least some leverage through ONG central and the mayor. Certainly, the manager didn't have line authority, and ONG central and the mayor might choose to be cautious in pressing a top agency official to act, but there was at least a line of access. The manager under the community board system, by contrast, is generally isolated from the line agencies and has little leverage, short of informal networks through the borough president, the mayor's office, or the agencies. Moreover, the district manager is no longer the key figure in the community board system: the board is. It makes policy, and the district manager serves at its pleasure and is accountable to it.

Highlights of implementation: political history

In assessing community boards, it is useful to see them in historical perspective. Their origins date back to 1951 when Robert Wagner, Sr., then borough president of Manhattan, established community planning councils to give citizens a voice in city government.

Some political observers suggest that these councils, in addition to providing a neighborhood voice, enhanced Wagner's political base, thereby helping pave the way for his running for mayor. There were twelve such planning councils at the time, having fifteen to twenty members each. It is interesting to note that Sayre and Kaufman make no mention of these councils in *Governing New York City*.

The next significant development was the amendments to the City Charter in 1963, when Wagner was serving his third term as mayor, establishing sixty-two community planning boards, with five to nine members each. These boards reported to the borough presidents' office and were linked to city government mainly at that level. Then, in the mid- and late-1960s, Mayor Lindsay set up neighborhood city halls and urban action task forces as outreach programs to receive complaints about service delivery problems and act on them. They were also a means of getting commissioners out of their downtown offices and into the communities where they could understand more about the actual implementation problems and impacts of services. And the programs helped in defusing racial tensions, as Lindsay gained a national reputation for having kept New York City cool during summers of ghetto riots and unrest. The district service cabinets of ONG, established a few years later, usually functioned independently of the community planning boards, but some worked in collaboration with the boards as well.

As for the implementation of the community board system since 1977, there is remarkably little objective information available. The public schools and ONG-district service cabinet programs at least had some evaluations, but nothing like that exists for community boards.[45]

One important aspect of implementation was the strong early support from the mayor. Many participants reported that the difference between Koch and Beame in this regard was quite dramatic. Having entered politics as a congressman who had been a leader in an insurgent, anti-Tammany group in Greenwich Village, Koch was sensitive to the concerns of "outsiders," neighborhood constituencies, "fighting City Hall." And his early implementation of the community board program reflected that. Thus, he immediately established a Community Board Assistance Unit (CBAU) to help train board members, district managers, and agency staff perform new roles as mandated in the Charter.[46] He had a Community Liaison Unit (CLU) to deal with policy and political issues in community board–City Hall relations. The Office of Management and Budget had a separate

Office of Community Board Relations (OCBR) that provided much assistance to the boards in improving their budget planning and analysis capability. And the City Planning Commission worked with districts as they conducted land use reviews. Several highly regarded, energetic, and top ranked staff members in the Koch administration were involved in these activities, and they reflected his early commitment to community boards. "He was terrific at the start," explained a top political and civic leader who served on Koch's transition task force. "It is true that he was the most accessible mayor we have had in some time, with his town hall meetings. At first, in 1977, '78, and '79, he always asked prospective commissioners how they felt about community boards and decentralization."[47] This kind of support was critical in providing impetus for the community board system.

Other, nongovernmental agencies also helped. David Grossman, former budget director in the Lindsay administration, provided much technical assistance to the boards through his nonprofit Nova Institute, helping them develop budgetary skills. He also worked closely with the city to help implement geographic budgeting. Still another supporting agency was Interface, a civic watchdog organization formed during the fiscal crisis, which had an extensive training program for board members. David Lebenstein, one of Interface's founders and top executives and a member of Queens, Community Board 7, helped lead this effort; and he was very active as founder and first president of the Citywide Coalition of Community Boards, a group set up to enhance their bargaining power in dealings with city government.

Over time, the neighborhoods did increase their budgetary capability and their power on land use and service problems. It is clear that neighborhoods now have a voice in shaping decisions on these matters. While there are differing views expressed about the ultimate social benefits for the city from that increased neighborhood power, it is a new dimension to the city's politics that clearly did not exist in the New York of Sayre and Kaufman.

Impacts

Perhaps the most direct way to assess the community boards is to review what happened with respect to each of their main functions and with respect to the role of the main players. Their main functions include land use, service coordination, outreach, complaint handling, budget (expense and capital), and coterminality. The main players include the mayor, the borough presidents, councilpersons, staff in the overhead and line agencies, district managers, and community board members.

Land use is the function where community boards have gained the most formal power. The charter established a Uniform Land Use Review Procedure (ULURP) for the boards to participate with the City Planning Commission, the

Board of Estimate, and developers in land use review, and they have played an important role in shaping the direction of development projects. As early as 1980, David Lebenstein noted that this was an area where board members had the most experience.[48] He found that the City Planning Commission supported the recommendations of the local community boards almost 90 percent of the time.[49] Yet, he only gave the boards and the city a grade of C plus on this function. The main weakness, Lebenstein argued, and it was one that Mudd and other critics of the community board system were to make later, was that the boards were primarily reactive and had not taken the initiative in land use planning. Board actions under ULURP are not, by themselves, an effective planning function.[50]

Even if only in a "reactive" role, the boards have had important impacts on developers' plans. As an example, the Zeckendorf Company approached Community Board 4, representing the Clinton and Chelsea neighborhoods of Manhattan, the day after the company acquired the former Madison Square Garden site between Forty-eighth and Forty-ninth Streets and Eighth and Ninth Avenues, according to Edith Fisher, a vice-president. Negotiations that ultimately saw the company agree to provide 162 units of low- and moderate-income housing started soon after. This process has been repeated many times over in recent years, particularly in Manhattan, where developers have been so active. It involves community boards negotiating with developers for changes in projects, often a scaling down to take account of negative environmental impacts (light, air pollution, infrastructure overloading with new populations) and for local amenities. Those who oppose the process, including some top city officials and some developers, refer to it as "blackmail," and it has become the focus of much recent controversy.

To indicate the diversity of perceptions, while the mayor, other top city officials, and some developers see the community boards as having too much power, many board members, by contrast, express deep frustration over their powerlessness and inability to block unwanted projects. Over a relatively short time, local boards had unsuccessfully opposed many developments, including two office and condominium high rises on Columbus Circle, apartment and dormitory towers at Lincoln Center, an expansion of Battery Park City, and the first municipal shelter for the homeless on Staten Island. "I know one board member who says the board's influence is inversely proportional to the importance of the issue before it," said Joseph B. Rose, the chairman of Community Board 5 in Midtown Manhattan.[51]

Other board functions, while important, have evoked less controversy. They often deal with more exclusively local issues. *Outreach* and *complaint handling* are one such function. Many district managers and board members complain that they don't have the resources to inform local residents of their existence and availability to handle complaints about local services. They feel that the city, perhaps through the Community (Board) Assistance Unit, should be helping them more than it does. But their anger at the city administration goes beyond this. They resent the fact that the legitimate complaints that do come in and are passed on to higher levels within the line agencies are not acted upon very expeditiously.

Service delivery is another big disappointment to the managers and community boards for reasons that indicate the most basic weaknesses of the system. Lebenstein gave the city a grade of D and the boards one of B for effort (but not results), indicating the extent of the problem.[52] There are two service delivery issues. One is with regard to particular agencies, considered in isolation. The other and much more important issue is that of service coordination. The main obstacle, with a very few exceptions,[53] has been the city's failure to decentralize its line agencies. As Lebenstein observed:

> Service delivery is an area where the boards are trying valiantly but can get nowhere until local city agency officials are given authority to make decisions. Massive training and reorientation of civil service employees on their roles are required to make this aspect of the charter a success. Otherwise, it's merely a band-aid solution. As long as an agency field person continues to lack authority to make decisions at the community level, the buck will continue to be passed from local to borough to central headquarters.[54]

Though this was written in 1980, the condition has not changed. Indeed, when I testified to the absence of agency decentralization at a 1988 City Charter Revision Commission meeting on community boards, one top borough official who had been involved with the community boards since 1977 explained, "We don't even think about command decentralization any more. That's how much we've given up on it. It has been one of the biggest disappointments of the whole community board operation."

One reason for administrative decentralization's not having taken place relates to the underlying structure of the community board system. As Mudd points out, the district managers who preside over the cabinets are isolated from the line agencies of city government. They try to gain informal influence through developing networks in the city administration, as did their predecessors in the Lindsay program, but they don't have the direct relation to the mayor that their predecessors had through ONG and are thereby reduced in influence.[55]

Budget priorities and review are still another function where community boards play an important role. Overall, estimates are that funding approval for district budget requests is between 30 and 50 percent, with capital budget requests faring better than expense budget requests.[56] But districts vary enormously in the quality of their budget submissions and in their budgetary analysis capability. Beyond that, the budget itself does not have that many discretionary items for the community boards to influence. The city's fiscal crisis and its aftermath led to much retrenchment of programs and to a centralization of decision making. Moreover, many budget decisions are citywide, and boards have often been reduced to the advisory role of reacting to agency requests, rather than participating with agencies in formulating those requests, based on an assessment of neighborhood needs. Lebenstein gave both the boards and the city a grade of C as of 1980 on this function. Though there has been improvement on both sides since then, it has been uneven.[57]

Coterminality has been largely accomplished.[58] The Police Department posed problems, largely because people in the neighborhoods equated any change in the status quo with the shifting or amalgamation of precinct houses, and that evoked much resistance. As coterminality proceeded, there were public protests, some where Mayor Koch was hung in effigy, as people had fears of increasing crime and lowered property values. But by and large, with that one exception, coterminality is a fact of life in New York City. Like other charter-mandated changes, however, it could only be effective if there were administrative decentralization.

A key main player is obviously the mayor. Just as there is a broad consensus that Mayor Koch and his overhead agencies were very supportive in the early years, there is an equally broad one, particularly among borough staff, district managers, and community board members, that he became much less supportive. These people and other, more disinterested observers speculate that his agendas and alliances changed after the late 1970s. "He became closer to the political machines in the outer boroughs," explained one political scientist and citywatcher, "and also to the developers. And both, particularly the developers, were in opposition to the community boards."[59] While all this is speculation, Koch's public statements and behavior give some credence to the perception that he cooled in his support for community boards after the first few years of his long tenure in office.

The mayor's public statements to the press reinforce the negative feelings among board members and managers. In an interview quoted in the *New York Times* (March 15, 1987), he said:

> People are very suspicious of government, and that's understandable, it's historical. People don't want change, truly they don't want it. If what they have is what they like, it's like the last one into the Garden of Eden locks the door. . . . I believe that having their [community boards'] input has improved many projects. But I believe if you give them a veto position, nothing would be built in this town above three stories.

While the statement has some validity and fairness, it is also contentious and interpreted in a context of alienation and distrust. The community boards seize on those parts of the statement that portray the mayor as the "good guy," in favor of development and change, and the community boards as the "bad guys," opposing change. Further, most of them don't expect to be in a veto position and feel that is an unnecessarily aggressive way of characterizing them.

The negative perceptions of the mayor then extend, in a kind of halo effect fashion, to his overhead agencies. The Community Assistance Unit (CAU), the prime liaison agency that provides technical assistance to the boards and agencies and acts as a mediator and broker between the two, is not seen as supportive. It is in a difficult situation where it has to serve the mayor while at the same time assisting the community boards as well. Many participants, on both sides of the fence, see this as a "no win" situation. One top borough staff person, commenting on CAU's performance, summed it up by saying, "How do you (CAU) fight your own boss?" Others are less generous. A Manhattan community board chair explained, "They may claim to represent us with the agencies, but that is not true. The borough president does much more for us than they do. They are all PR, and they drive us around in circles." Another outer borough staff person reported, "They are very passive. They are too little, too late. [The CAU has] no clout now at city hall or with the agencies." Similar views were expressed about the City Planning Commission, which was seen as a prodevelopment agency.[60]

While perceptions often distort what actually takes place, the participants' "definitions of the situation" take on a reality of their own and often shape their behavior. In this instance, several common themes emerge. First, Mayor Koch and his administration were seen as having reversed their early support of community boards. Second, this is seen as related to their constituency pressures and alliances. And third, the borough presidents are increasingly seen as a place for community boards and district managers to go to seek assistance. They are seen as substitutes for CAU, as district managers and board members seek to expand their political networks. There is at the same time an acute awareness that the borough presidents are limited in the leverage they can exert over the line agencies and the mayor. Even when there was a powerful Board of Estimate on which the borough presidents sat, each had only a single vote on that body. That formal role no longer exists. Nevertheless, some, perhaps many, community board members and their managers see the borough presidents as one of the last hopes to increase their neighborhood voice. There is clearly strong competition between them and the mayor for the community boards' allegiance, even though Mayor Koch did not often behave as if that were his perception.

The borough presidents have emerged in that sense, as key lifelines for the community boards. There is a borough district service cabinet and a borough board where all individual district budget projections and other general concerns are aggregated. At least three of the five boroughs have highly professional staff and approaches to managing the community boards. Howard Golden of Brooklyn, for example, has a long history of active involvement in the implementation of the community board concept. Several years ago, he hired Ed Rogowsky, political science professor from Brooklyn College, to be in charge of servicing community boards from the borough office. "He has been a charter implementation stickler," reported one borough staff person. "Golden's role as an activist charter watcher indeed surpasses prior expectation," wrote Robert Greenblatt and Edward Rogowsky.[61] The same deep involvement exists in Queens under the leadership of Claire Shulman, a long-time advocate of neighborhoods, as is her community boards director, Jane Planken, a former district manager under the ONG program. And Manhattan Borough President David Dinkins evoked similar enthusiasm and hope. "He is our advocate with the agencies," reported a Manhattan community board chair.

As of the summer of 1989, there was much controversy regarding the future role of the borough presidents. The Board of Estimate on which they had formerly served and that made major decisions on land use, zoning, and service delivery matters for the boroughs was eliminated that year as in violation of the one-man one-vote principle, and the future status of the borough presidents was unclear. Many community board members and their advocates urged that the borough presidents have more explicit formal authority in relation to the boards, given their strongly supportive relationship with the boards in the past. There remains the issue, however, of their limited power to persuade the line and overhead agencies of city government to be more responsive to community board concerns.

Community board members themselves are obviously important players. Many boards have become very professional and effective, while others have been slower to develop. There are no comprehensive data on the backgrounds of board members, but many come from professional backgrounds. Greenblatt and Rogowsky did collect such data for Brooklyn and found a high proportion of the 900 Brooklyn board members were in professional/managerial occupations.[62] The proportion of such people on Manhattan boards is, if anything, probably even higher. Over the years, board member attendance has been erratic, and several borough directors now do a regular performance appraisal check. "We regularly ask the chair of the board to give us a recommendation on which board members are doing what and who should be reappointed," reported one borough director. "We realize that some of this is just ritual, but it does send out a message to board members that they have to participate if they want to stay." "Three or more absences and I write a letter, asking for reasons," explained another borough director. "Excused absences only are acceptable, and we have had boards down to 30 members."[63]

The other key group is the district managers. While some are primarily reactive, complaint handlers who play a somewhat passive role vis-à-vis their boards, others are involved in planning and policy initiation and are much more proactive. In the early years of community boards (1977–80), the overall quality of district managers was high. "The first round of managers were highly competent," reported Lebenstein. "Some were even better than the ONG people" (despite the fact that ONG district managers had higher salaries and status). He gave them a grade of B plus and characterized them as "a largely professional group of individuals who take their jobs very seriously, work sixty to seventy hours a week and are the most identifiable link between the board and the larger community." Over time, however, there was a large turnover, particularly among the more competent managers. As Lebenstein wrote, "Indeed, a major problem today is the massive turnover of DMs. At least one-third of the original DMs have left (three years later) and the more competent DMs generally get swooped up by entities (both public and private) that can pay them a lot more."[64]

There are signs of significant recent improvements, however. Salaries have gone up in recent years. Many borough community board directors report that the quality now of district managers in their boroughs is quite high, with very few in the not-so-competent category. There is clearly a need to continue to make the position attractive, both in salary terms and in encouraging boards to give managers more policy-making authority.

The other main participant, no longer in existence, was the Citywide Coalition of Community Boards, founded and headed for a while by David Lebenstein. It serviced all the boards to enhance their bargaining power in relation to the city. After a couple of years, there was a revolt from outer borough boards, arguing that this was a Manhattan-dominated group that should not be allowed to continue in leadership. The wife of a Bronx politician soon became the director, though she had few, if any, qualifications for the job, and the coalition disbanded shortly thereafter.

Differences among districts

Some districts have been more effective than others in representing district concerns and prevailing in budgetary decisions. Recent research deals directly with that issue. Political scientist Robert Pecorella has examined the city's response to community board–initiated proposals to the capital budget for fiscal years 1982 through 1985.[65] Specifically, he examined each of the fifty-nine boards' top ten priority proposals for those fiscal years. He found substantial variation among the districts in the proportion of their proposals accepted for inclusion in the city's capital budget and suggested two types of explanations. One dealt with the demographics of the districts, mainly race and social class, the latter measured in terms of median household income. What he found was that white districts did significantly better than minority ones, with high correlations existing, as well, between race and income. As he reported, "Much of the effect of race on community district acceptance rates is contained in median household income." That is, the geographic-based budgeting system as it operated at least in those years favored higher-income white communities at the expense of poor and minority ones.

His second level of explanation dealt with the informal networks of community board members. He was able to distinguish between what he called parochial and cosmopolitan boards. On parochial boards, the board members seek more to establish themselves within their districts, pursuing local alliances. By contrast, cosmopolitan boards seek alliances outside the district, for example, with a councilperson, borough president, mayoral, or agency official. Again, not surprisingly, he found a high correlation between cosmopolitan methods of proposal submission (districts that used extensive outside contacts to enhance their influence) and eventual acceptance by the city. Indeed, the level of cosmopolitanism explained more than any other variable how effective the community board was, with those that were more cosmopolitan having a wider set of networks and generally having their proposals cosponsored with particular city agencies.

In brief, districts need borough and citywide networks to be effective. It is not enough for community boards to just integrate with local constituencies. It turns out that cosmopolitanism is also related to race and social class. The poor minority districts tend to be parochial, are unwilling and/or unable to develop the wider political network needed to get their proposals accepted, and do not fare well.

The other research interpreting why some districts are more effective than others is found in the studies of Robert Rich and Janice Perlman from the Center for Responsive Governance.[66] They also find that poor, minority districts have been less effective than white middle-class ones. Their explanations are that the poverty area districts do not have the technical and political skills on their boards that the white middle-class ones have. Board members must prepare budget documents, testify at hearings, lobby elected officials, do outreach, and write letters. Community board members from middle-class and professional backgrounds have these skills. They also have networks developed over the years from already being part of the political system. As one district manager was quoted in this regard, "One phone call from an influential board member to an agency commissioner is worth more than ten budget consultation meetings or a pile of well-prepared budget forms."[67]

Comparative case studies of districts by this research group yielded one other important finding, namely, that districts with more homogeneous boards in terms of board members' backgrounds are much more effective than those that are more diverse. Homogeneous boards are less factionalized, therefore having more unity, and as a result spending much less time dealing with internal differences and more on developing and using external networks to generate support for positions they have worked out very early. These homogeneous boards are often quite unrepresentative of their districts. Two examples are Districts 14 in the

Midwood-Flatbush section of Brooklyn and District 7 on Manhattan's Upper West Side. Both are regarded as among the most effective boards in the city. The board in Brooklyn has several professionals and civic activists, many having worked in two highly effective development corporations in the area. Board members are extremely well organized, hard working, and competent. Their meetings are well attended, efficiently run, and marked by high consensus and a lack of factions. While they represent only one segment of the community, their effective work on the community board serves the district as a whole quite well.

The central argument is that there is a basic conflict between representativeness and effectiveness. One implication is that it is better to have effective boards that will represent district interests well, even though they are unrepresentative in terms of social background, than to have a community board that is representative of a district's diversity to the point of being too diverse to be able to function effectively.

A more general finding of both studies is that the community board system has differentially favored the white middle-class districts over the poor minority ones. Lebenstein saw this early and he urged the mayor and other top city officials to formulate a policy of differential budgeting that favored the poverty area districts that have the greatest need for technical assistance and staff. As one researcher on community boards had observed in this regard, "It is ironic that the blacks who showed the most militance for community control now get the least out of decentralization."[68] No groundswell support ever developed for this differential budgeting proposal, but one recent development bears on it. Manhattan Borough President David Dinkins developed a program for a technical assistance unit to help community boards that need it. Certainly the poor minority areas that need it the most will benefit.

It is clear that community boards have become institutionalized in New York City. While they are a far cry from community control, they provide an important voice for citizens and neighborhoods in critical land use and service delivery decisions affecting their districts. They draw an increasing range of the public into city government. Recent Manhattan hearings on shelters for the homeless, for example, brought out close to one hundred people to testify, many for the first time in their lives.[69] There was a time, in the early- and mid-1980s, after the initial excitement about the program wore off, when disillusionment and apathy had set in. Many district managers and board members reported a decline in attendance, both by board members and the general public, unless the issue was a highly controversial one that affected people directly.

While that is still the case in some districts, there was, in the late-1980s, a significant upsurge in citizen participation, particularly but not exclusively in Manhattan. This must be attributed in part to the efforts of the city government to site a variety of unappealing facilities throughout the five boroughs—shelters for the homeless, drug treatment centers, halfway houses, prisons, and incinerators.

And there are the massive real estate developments, most of them in Manhattan, but increasingly in the outer boroughs, that community boards and citizens often find alarming. Many are still frustrated at the way decisions seem to get made, and they want to do something about it. "The apathy has now changed," reported a borough staff person. "People want to participate and be informed more. More are lobbying the community boards on their positions. These boards are like a peoples' parliament, and they are increasing in importance."[70]

Taking Stock of Decentralization in New York

As noted in the introduction, decentralization and centralization seem to go in cycles. In the late nineteenth century, New York City government was organized mainly on a decentralized ward basis, with patronage politics determining major decisions. Contracts, appointments, and budgetary decisions were made in a highly particularistic way, by functionaries of the political machine. Starting in the late nineteenth century, the municipal reform movement, led by an upper-middle- and upper-class business and civic elite, began sweeping much of that away and helped create centralized and supposedly "professionalized" bureaucracies. The process reached its peak in the 1950s, having been given much impetus by the Depression and Mayor LaGuardia. Moreover, there was a well-developed ideology associated with this centralization movement that had strong support from academic disciplines—for example, public administration—as well. Centralization, it was argued, would bring with it many benefits—especially better areawide planning, economies of scale, more professionalism, freedom from patronage and parochialism, and more accountability. The community revolution of the 1960s challenged that ideology, and though community control, the main doctrine of that movement, proved unattainable politically, there is strong and increasing support for a neighborhood voice in critical land use and service delivery decisions.

How does one account for these cycles? At least two sets of forces seem to be at work. One that political scientist Robert Pecorella, among others, has documented insightfully, relates to the fiscal status of the city.[71] He suggests that one can characterize urban politics in terms of various historical periods, corresponding to national economic trends. Thus, there are periods of retrenchment and of expansion and a corresponding politics is associated with each. Retrenchment tends to be associated with centralization and expansion with decentralization. Thus, the 1930s under Mayor LaGuardia was a period of much centralization and civil service reform, as the main decisions in the city bureaucracies were increasingly made downtown, at headquarters, where a more professional and citywide planning orientation was assumed to prevail. The City Planning Commission was empowered at the time to create a Master Plan for the city by 1938, and some people are still waiting for it.

The 1960s, in contrast, was a period not only of political activism, reflected in the community revolution, but of expansion and commitment to redistribution programs. And it was a time of decentralization. Then, with the 1970s came retrenchment, associated with the fiscal crisis of 1975, and that led, in turn, to greater centralization to such agencies as the Municipal Assistance Corporation (MAC) and the Emergency Financial Control Board (EFCB). It was also associated with an increased interest in contracting out city services to private sector organizations. At the same time, there has been a continued push, as reflected in the Charter Commission of the early 1970s and the referendum of 1975, for decentralization.

Few evolutionary trends in institutions are a result of just one set of forces, however, and a second seems also to be involved. As Larry Greiner, a professor of management and organizational development at UCLA School of Business, pointed out in a classic article some fifteen years ago, there are patterns of evolution and revolution in organizations that perpetuate a cyclical movement between centralization and decentralization.[72] He argues that as organizations increase in size, scale, and diversity, there is a need for bureaucracy, to make their operations more uniform and standard, and to facilitate more control. Over time, however, the centralized structure that results from this development is seen as stifling the flexibility and responsiveness of local level, geographically dispersed parts of the organization that are themselves quite diverse, serving different markets and not easily manageable from a central headquarters office. So there are then pressures for decentralization. In the business organizations that Greiner writes about, this is often associated with the emergence of various decentralized product divisions that serve different markets. After operating with this type of structure for a while, organizations then find that there is too much fragmentation and not enough central control, as the various geographically decentralized units fail to coordinate or follow common policies that should be followed for the larger institution of which they are a part to thrive. So then the organization recentralizes. Following Greiner, it is likely that New York City government will go through similar swings, as it has in the past.

There is another issue that bears on the relation of centralization to decentralization and that has not been given much systematic attention. It relates to how the two must complement one another for effective planning and service delivery to take place. Viewed in this perspective, it is not an either/or question but one of how they may be managed together. The point gains greater clarity when one reviews what happened to the various decentralization programs in New York City. All illustrate the fact that decentralization can help improve service delivery in a system as large and diverse as New York, but only with an active, coherent, and supportive center. School decentralization, for all its ambiguities and shortcomings, seemed to work reasonably well, but it would have worked better had central taken on more the needed role of standard setter, monitor, and technical assistance provider. As *110 Livingston Street* demonstrated, and later studies and reports confirmed, school headquarters has remained quite fragmented in its structure and operations, and until it gets itself together, there is little likelihood that it can play the kind of monitoring and supporting role for districts and schools that is needed.

Turning to the ONG-Lindsay program and then the community boards, the same pattern holds. There was not the kind of administrative decentralization and line agency support that was needed to make the district service cabinets effective.

Finally, there is a broader issue that the city will have to address, and that relates back directly to the tensions between centralization and decentralization. It is particularly highlighted by what has come to be called the NIMBY ("not in my backyard") phenomenon. During the 1980s, there was an escalation of conflict between City Hall and the community boards. One prevailing definition of the causes of the conflict is that the two sides have such different orientations. The community boards are often seen as more parochial, as uninterested in citywide problems and development, as against areawide (borough and city) planning, and as often functioning as negative veto groups who block the city in its efforts to introduce needed changes—e.g., improved facilities and programs for the needy and major developments to provide more housing and other amenities. The notion is that City Hall sees the large picture, engages in more citywide planning, and is pressing for needed development and service improvements, often in the face of recalcitrant boards.

The community board system is seen from this perspective as having created a "monster," in that much social harm results from their actions, even though they still have only advisory powers. Several negative impacts of community boards are often pointed to, including: (1) they delay action and freeze the policy agenda on important innovative programs and projects; (2) they force the city and developers to throw in many amenities, involving expensive, gold-plated trade-offs; (3) they institute many court suits that further add to the delay and expense; and (4) they push for racist policies, discriminating against minorities and the poor, as they resist drug treatment facilities, shelters for the homeless, or prisons because these will bring the "wrong element" into their neighborhood.

The community boards, on their side, are very angry at what they call the NIMBY myth, which they feel has scapegoated them unfairly for shortcomings of the city itself in its planning process and given them a bad rap. Their advocates argue that if having their input delays projects, that is the price of democracy and it is more than worth paying. If they force the city and developers to give them various amenities in return for their support for projects, so the argument continues, all political decisions of this sort involve trade-offs. Moreover, many of the amenities enhance the quality of life in communities. As for community boards increasing the incidence of court suits, their advocates argue that there will be fewer suits when the city allows for neighborhood input. And, finally, the charge that community boards push for racist policies, discriminating against minorities and the poor, is often unfair, argue their advocates. It is not minorities and the poor they are objecting to, but poor programs and planning by the city.

The more basic issue is how adequately the city in fact plans and develops programs. Many community boards argue that better planning and more humane and efficient programs often result from greater rather than less neighborhood input. "The community boards are asked to be the visionaries when the city does such poor planning and operates always in crisis," explained a community board advocate in one of the borough offices. "The mayor's recent shelter plan for the homeless is a good example of nonplanning and nonconsultation. No wonder it met with so much resistance."[73] From the community boards' perspective, the city's approach to problems typically shows no clear direction, only ad hoc reactions to those crises that gain public attention. Examples cited include city government support for massive developments that are already not in compliance with federal quality standards for air pollution control and that could shut out much light from the surrounding area and contribute to massive traffic and public transportation overloads unless scaled down considerably or accompanied by massive infrastructure improvements.

One city councilman, Abraham Gerges, cites numerous examples of bad-faith dealings of the city with community boards where the end result of some major program decision by the city is much worse than what the community board agreed on. In one instance, CB 1 in Greenpoint in Brooklyn gave the city two locations for homeless shelters only to have HRA come out in the middle of the night, without any consultation, on a sudden, crisis basis with a program that was without the accompanying social services that the board plan involved. In another case, Manhattan CB 6 had worked out a family shelter plan at Bellevue Hospital in collaboration with the City Planning Commission, HRA, the Police and Fire departments, and the Board of Education, only to have HRA, with no consultation and "from out of nowhere" move it to Brooklyn and strip it of its family shelter features. One top city official reported on a meeting with the HRA administrator about this and other projects, where he claimed the administrator finally stated, "We had a tradition of secrecy where we don't tell community groups what we are going to do."[74]

The quality of many programs is often enhanced by getting community input, for example, in Manhattan, community boards forced coordination of the repaving of Second Avenue with sewage construction, after the agencies involved had failed to collaborate. Community Board 14 in Brooklyn was able to get Sanitation Commissioner Steisel to change the time of refuse collection after it was found that the original delivery schedule had resulted in massive traffic tie-ups. The community boards and their district managers, in closer touch than many city agency officials with conditions at the point of service delivery and with consumers of the services, are often able to make significant suggestions for improvement. When they get implemented, they may make a big difference in the quality of life in the city. "It's too bad that there is no press coverage of these successes," bemoaned a top borough official, "because that allows a distorted NIMBY type picture of the role of the boards to prevail."[75]

Unfortunately for the city, the trend in the 1980s was for these two sides, the community boards and City Hall, to become increasingly estranged from one another. Each has fixed negative stereotypes of the other, and each bypasses the other with regularity. Community boards, for example, seek their own outside consultants to do environmental analysis, since they feel they can no longer get much help from the City Planning Commission, even though the commission is mandated to do so in the charter. Indeed, instead of working through such overhead agencies as CAU, the community boards now work through such agencies as the borough president's office. While the latter don't have nearly the same clout with City Hall and the line agencies that CAU and the mayor's other overhead agencies have, any agencies associated with the mayor are automatically defined as the "enemy" and seem to justify that label to the boards by their everyday noncooperativeness.

One temporary solution is to institutionalize a process of increased borough involvement in assisting community boards and in running New York City government, a process already partly underway. The mayor and the downtown offices of his line and overhead agencies are too remote from the neighborhoods. By contrast, the borough level, as a more middle level, is in closer contact with neighborhood problems. Many borough offices have become much more professionalized with regard to their community board functions. And serious thought should be given to increasing their role.

Again, a drawback to this strategy is that the mayor is the top city official closest to the line agencies and ultimately responsible for their performance. And since one important goal of decentralization is to improve management, it makes sense to have the mayor as deeply involved as possible.

In reviewing all three programs for decentralizing New York City government, the design of the ONG-Lindsay one deserves special attention. It was developed pursuant to the diagnosis that two reforms needed to improve service delivery were administrative decentralization and interagency service coordination in the districts. That diagnosis still has much merit. Unfortunately, it still has not been implemented. Mudd maintains that the present community board system provides little incentive for the mayor to get involved in pushing that, since the borough presidents, rather than the mayor, are the key players in the community board system.

Somehow, both these issues have to be dealt with much more effectively than they have been in the past. There remain, both in the school system and in the other line agencies, a series of dysfunctional central bureaucracies that plan poorly, that are themselves riddled internally with turf battles, and that do not relate well in a monitoring or service capacity to the service delivery providers. There also remains a pattern of fragmentation across agencies that hampers effective service delivery. Until both problems are dealt with more effectively, New York City is going to face great difficulty in running an effective local government.

Those are the administrative-managerial issues that must be tended to in the future. But there are political ones as well. Ways must be found to link better the increasingly politicized and agitated neighborhoods with the power elites of the city, to ensure that quality of life considerations are given higher priority in land use and service delivery decisions. As things stand now, the city still follows a style of reactive, top down, and crisis management, that only triggers off a similarly reactive style from the neighborhoods, lessening the chances for the collaborative planning and service delivery that are so essential to the city's future.

Notes

1. As I will discuss in a concluding section, New York and other big cities were very decentralized in the nineteenth century, with the local ward boss often making major decisions on personnel, budget, and the awarding of contracts. Systematic efforts at decentralizing city government as a reform strategy, however, which is the subject of this chapter, are more recent.

2. For a good discussion of the "community revolution" in New York City in the 1960s, see Daniel Bell and Virginia Held, "The Community Revolution," *The Public Interest* 16 (Summer 1969).

3. Analyses of Lindsay's administration, particularly in his first term, appear in David Rogers, *The Management of Big Cities*. New York: Sage, 1970, pp. 39–56; and Nat Hentoff, *A Political Life*. New York: Knopf, 1969.

4. By politics I mean the actions of the main participants in the reform programs analyzed, as they attempt to forward their interests, or at least their perceived interests.

5. Wallace Sayre and Herbert Kaufman, *Governing New York City*. New York: Russell Sage Foundation, 1960; and Norton, 1965. Lyle C. Fitch and Annmarie Hauck Walsh, editors, *Agenda for a City*. Beverly Hills, CA: Sage, 1970, pp. 563–601.

6. Sayre and Kaufman, *Governing New York City*. Chapter 19.

7. *New York Times*, February 6, 1972, Op-ed page.

8. See David Rogers and Norman Chung, *110 Livingston Street Revisited*. New York: New York University Press, 1983, Chapter 1, for a review of some of these developments.

9. Allen H. Barton, et al., editors, *Decentralizing City Government*. Lexington, MA: Lexington, 1977.

10. The discussion to follow is drawn largely from Rogers and Chung, *110 Livingston Street Revisited*, Chapter 1.

11. David S. Seeley, *Education Through Partnership*. Cambridge, MA: Ballinger, 1981, Chapter 13.

12. The following political history comes from interviews with the staff at the Mayor's Office, the Ford Foundation, and the New York Urban Coalition, all of whose organizations supported school decentralization.

13. This was part of a package of restrictions on the activities and practices of foundations that were the price of continued tax exemption. Those other restrictions were in response to real and alleged abuses that had nothing to do with the New York decentralization controversy.

14. One exception was District Council 37, the American Federation of State, County, and Municipal Employees (AFSCME), headed by Victor Gotbaum. Gotbaum took a strong stand against Shanker in the Central Labor Council, supporting some of the goals of the community control advocates. DC 37 backed the decentralization of authority to school boards, though it collaborated with the teachers' union in supporting slates of community school board candidates.

15. The reports include *School Decentralization in New York City*, prepared for the New York State Charter Revision Commission for New York City, June 1974; David Rogers, *The New York City School Headquarters and The Schools: A Policy Paper*, prepared for the Educational Priorities Panel, April 1977; and Nancy Lederman, Jeanne Frankl, and Judith Baum, *Governing The New York City Schools: Roles and Relationships in the Decentralized System*, Public Education Association, February 25, 1987.

16. Reported in *School Decentralization in New York City*, p. 113.

17. This example comes from interviews with the involved executives. It is reported in David Rogers, *Can Business Management Save the Cities?, The Case of New York*. New York: The Free Press, 1978.

18. David Rogers, *Can Business Management Save the Cities?, The Case of New York*, Chapter 4.

19. See Public Education Association, *Governing New York City Schools*, pp. 43ff.

20. These data on reading scores come from the Board of Education's Bureau of Educational Statistics.

21. There is widespread agreement among observers of the city and the public schools on this point. See the Public Education Association's report, *Governing New York City Schools*, p. 8.

22. Office of Educational Statistics, reports on staff ethnic composition, Board of Education, 1986.

23. Office of Community School District Affairs, Board of Education.

24. On the improving quality of community superintendents, see the Public Education Association's report, *Governing New York City Schools*, pp. 13–14.

25. The examples to follow are analyzed in depth in Rogers and Chung, *110 Livingston Street Revisited*, Chapters 2, 3, 6, and 8.

26. Community school board data come from the Office of Community School District Affairs.

27. From interviews done with Public Education Association staff, summarizing the concerns of various interest groups and school officials in relation to decentralization.

28. The legislature enacted this reform in 1988, but it was held unconstitutional by a trial court early in 1989.

29. Discussions of coterminality of the schools with other agencies appear in my foreword to Joseph Cronin's *The Control of Urban Schools*. New York: The Free Press, 1973, pp. xvii ff; and Joseph Viteritti, ''The Urban School District,'' *Urban Education* 21:3 (October 1986): 228–53.

30. As an example, Sandra Feldman, executive director of the United Federation of Teachers, expressed this view. As she stated at a seminar sponsored by the Urban Re-

search Center of New York University: "It had nothing to do with education. . . . It was absolutely not an educational response." *New York Affairs* 8:1 (1983): 103.

31. Some New York City educators have taken this position. Some black leaders have also, arguing that school decentralization focused the political energies of blacks at the local level, thereby deflecting from attempts to develop citywide coalitions that might support black elected officials.

32. The following discussion comes from two histories of this program. One is by Professor Stanley Heginbotham, then of Columbia University, a political scientist, as part of his contribution to the Columbia Bureau of Applied Social Research evaluation of the ONG experiment. It appears in Allen Barton, et al., editors, *Decentralizing City Government*. Lexington, MA: Lexington, 1977, Chapter 2. The second history is John Mudd, *Neighborhood Services*. New Haven, CT: Yale University Press, 1983, Chapters 3–5.

33. See Heginbotham in Barton, *Decentralizing City Government*, p. 32.

34. Mudd, *Neighborhood Services*, p. 70.

35. See Theresa F. Rogers and Nathalie S. Friedman, Chapter 8 in Barton, *Decentralizing City Government*.

36. Mudd, *Neighborhood Services*, pp. 97–98.

37. The discussion to follow comes from several interviews with top staff in the Lindsay administration on how different city agencies responded to pressures for administrative decentralization.

38. Heginbotham, in Barton, *Decentralizing City Government*, pp. 33ff.

39. Ibid., p. 46.

40. Ibid., pp. 47–8; and Mudd, *Neighborhood Services*, p. 152.

41. Barton, *Decentralizing City Government*, pp. 177ff.

42. The historical discussion that follows draws from Mudd, *Neighborhood Services*, pp. 152–56.

43. Ibid., p. 153.

44. Madeline W. Adler and Jewel Bellush, "A Look at the District Managers," *New York Affairs* 6:1 (1980): 52.

45. The main published sources include Richard C. Rich, *Participation and Representation in New York City's Community Board System*, a report from the Center for Responsive Governance, Virginia Polytechnic Institute and State University; Janice Perlman, *Dividing the Big Apple: A Study of Community Boards in New York City*, same auspices; John Mudd, *Neighborhood Services*, Chapter 6; Peter Marcuse, "Neighborhood Policy and The Distribution of Power," unpublished manuscript; and *New York Affairs* 6:1 (1980).

46. CBAU got involved early in several conflicts between community boards and city agencies over coterminality and was reorganized after a couple of years into the Community Assistance Unit (CAU). The latter focused mainly on supporting agency decentralization and on training board members and district staff.

47. David Lebenstein, Staff, Interface, a public research organization, April 17, 1987.

48. David Lebenstein, "A Report Card," *New York Affairs* 6:1 (1980): 11.

49. This number has become common discourse among people who comment on the community boards' power in land use decisions. It is based on informed judgment, rather than hard data.

50. It should be noted that the charter does not give the community boards any formal responsibility for "pro-active" land use planning. Lebenstein and other critics thus are faulting the boards for not having exceeded their statutory responsibilities.

51. *New York Times*, March 15, 1987, Section 4, p. 6.

52. Lebenstein, "A Report Card," p. 12.

53. Parks under Gordon Davis and Sanitation under Steisel are often cited as the exceptions. When they left, however, both agencies were reported as having been recentralized. "It was like a vacuum cleaner," reported a top outer borough staff person, "sucking back authority to the central office when they left."

54. Lebenstein, "A Report Card," p. 12–13.

55. Mudd, *Neighborhood Services*, pp. 190–193.

56. Ibid., p. 199.

57. Lebenstein, "A Report Card," p. 12.

58. Mudd, *Neighborhood Services*, p. 205.

59. Interview, Robert Pecorella, Political Science Department, St. John's University. Interviews for this chapter were conducted between April and July 1987.

60. Interview, Edward Rogowsky, Director, Community Boards, Brooklyn; Interview, Jane Planken, Director, Community Boards, Queens, April–July 1987.

61. Robert Greenblatt and Edward T. Rogowsky, "A Case Study: The Brooklyn Boards," *New York Affairs* 6:1 (1980): 22ff.

62. Ibid., p. 22.

63. Interview, Edward Rogowsky, Director, Community Boards, Brooklyn.

64. Lebenstein, "A Report Card," p. 13.

65. Robert F. Pecorella, "Community Input and the City Budget: Geographically Based Budgeting in New York City," *Journal of Urban Affairs* 8:1 (Winter 1986): 57–70.

66. See Rich, *Participation and Representation in New York City's Community Board System*; and Perlman, *Dividing the Big Apple: A Study of Community Boards in New York City*, p. 45.

67. Interview, Helen Rosenblum, District Manager, Community Board #7, Manhattan.

68. Pecorella, "Community Input and the City Budget: Geographically Based Budgeting in New York City."

69. From interviews with Charter Commission staff attending Charter Commission private sessions concerning community boards and borough presidents, Summer 1988.

70. Interview, Jane Planken, Director, Community Boards, Queens.

71. Robert F. Pecorella, "Coping with Crises: The Politics of Urban Retrenchment," *Polity* 17 (Winter 1984): 298–316.

72. L.E. Greiner, "Evolution and Revolution as Organizations Grow," *Harvard Business Review* (July–August 1972): 37–46.

73. Interview, Edward Rogowsky, Director, Community Boards, Brooklyn.

74. From observation at Charter Commission private sessions concerning community boards and borough presidents, Summer 1988.

75. Ibid.

7

Public Authorities and the Shape of Decision Making

Annmarie Hauck Walsh

With prescience, in 1960 Sayre and Kaufman suggested that "special authorities" might be "teeming" in a few generations. In fact the proliferation occurred in only one generation. Only six of these "strange new creatures" were at work within the borders of New York City then, but uncertainty prevailed on how "to fit this newcomer into the existing governmental framework."[1] Thirty years later special authorities in New York were "teeming," and their place in the governmental framework remained uncertain.

Of the six authorities operating in 1960, only the Port Authority of New York and New Jersey remained an important and independent actor through the 1980s. One—the Brooklyn Sports Center Authority—never actually operated, but is testimony to how issues persist while the skyline changes. It failed to conclude a deal to keep the Brooklyn Dodgers in New York, as the New Jersey Sports Authority failed over twenty-five years later to lure the New York Yankees across the Hudson River. The Planetarium Authority, created in 1933 to sell bonds to the federal Reconstruction Finance Corporation, was administratively absorbed by the Museum of Natural History. The New York City Housing Authority began in 1934 to implement federal public housing law. It manages housing for some half a million people in the city and has utilized city, state, and federal aid in its building program, but its development of new public housing dwindled with the federal housing budget in the 1980s. The Triborough Bridge and Tunnel Authority (TBTA), established in 1946, was the jewel in the crown of Robert Moses' empire and was absorbed into the Metropolitan Transportation Authority (MTA), where it remains a cash cow, contributing revenues from automobile river crossings to help meet deficits of rail mass transit. In 1953, the New York City Transit Authority took over the city-run transit system (earlier a private system) under state legislation requiring it to be self-sustaining, a mandate that proved unrealistic but that has generated continuing pressure for fare increases. The Transit Authority, now a subordinate agency within the MTA, absorbs federal, state, and city tax subsidies, as well as TBTA profits, to meet its deficits.

The Growth of Public Authorities

During the following three decades, the number of government-sponsored corporations operating in the city grew to thirty-six (see Table 7.1), and their capital funds rapidly outstripped those of city government. Despite the small sample of authorities in 1960, Sayre and Kaufman's analysis of the reasons for creating and using them remains generically accurate, although their financial and legal arrangements have become far more complex. The reasons that authorities have thrived and multiplied include financial, political, and management incentives.

The *financial incentives* are dominant. Authorities became more important sources of investment in government-authorized projects than either state or city government. As distinct legal corporations, separate from general government, authorities are not subject to the debt limits or referendum requirements that the state constitution imposes on state and municipal borrowing. Using revenue bonds issued by authorities instead of general obligation bonds issued by the state or city avoids requirements for a popular vote on state borrowing and other state constitutional constraints. Revenue bonds have specific security or revenue flows pledged to support their repayment and interest, such as fares, tolls, rents, or subsidies received by the authority. Authority financing supplements the credit of city government by raising capital directly from the municipal bond market (and in the 1930s by selling bonds to the federal government) without relying on or burdening the city's own credit and ability to borrow.

Authority borrowing in the market for tax-exempt state and local government securities has been a powerful source of public investment funds in New York. The investment community has often shown a preference for investing in authority bonds over general obligation state and municipal bonds. Several specialized authorities can raise more money than a single large authority or city government alone by offering the investment community more variety of bond types and credit backings. Since 1970, the amount of capital raised by authority borrowing in the nation has multiplied much more rapidly than general state and local government borrowing, which rarely kept up with inflation. In New York State, the outstanding long-term bonded debt of authorities (over $40 billion) reached ten times the outstanding debt of the state government. The outstanding debt for authority operations in New York City is approximately half of statewide authority debt and has reached nearly three times the general obligation long-term debt of city government.

The political convenience of using public authorities has often been compelling. Sayre and Kaufman recognized the *political motivations* underlying the authorities. Despite decades of rhetoric about authorities being "nonpolitical and

Table 7.1

Public Authorities Operating in New York City

Authority	Date	Purpose or function	Governing board
Battery Park City Authority	1968	Improvement of Battery Park City Project Area: commercial and residential development via private development contracts on land leased from the city.	3 members appointed by governor; Senate confirmation required.
City University Construction Fund	1966	To provide facilities for CUNY: acquisition, financing, construction management implemented through the Dormitory Authority.	7 members: 2 appointed by governor, 1 by mayor, by temporary president of NYS Senate, 1 by Speaker of NYS Assembly, 2 ex-officio (NYS budget director, chair of CUNY trustees); Senate confirmation required for mayor's and governor's appointees.
Dormitory Authority of the State of NY	1944	To provide financing and construction services for institutions of higher learning, health care facilities, and certain other not-for-profit organizations, and to provide financing for certain student loan programs.	7 members: 4 appointed by governor and confirmed by Senate, 3 ex-officio (NYS comptroller, NYS budget director, NYS commissioner of education).
Facilities Development Authority	1968	Acquires, designs, constructs, rehabilitates, improves facilities for NYS Department of Mental Hygiene.	5 members: 3 appointed by governor and confirmed by Senate, 2 ex-officio (NYS commissioner of health, chairman of NYS Department of Mental Hygiene's Coordinating Council).
Harlem Urban Development Corporation (subsidiary of UDC)	1968	To formulate and implement a comprehensive program of social and economic development for the Harlem community.	29 members: 10 elected officials, 18 selected by current board members, president and CEO appointed by board.

Organization	Year	Purpose	Governance
Long Island Railroad (LIRR) (component of MTA)	1965	The safe, cost-effective, on-time movement of trains for the traveling public; Nassau, Suffolk, New York City.	MTA board members.
Metro-North Commuter Railroad (component of MTA)	1983	Public transportation within the 12 NY counties.	MTA board members.
Metropolitan Suburban Bus Authority (MSBA) (component of MTA)	1973	Provide public bus transportation in Nassau, western Suffolk, and eastern Queens counties.	MTA board members.
Metropolitan Transportation Authority (MTA)	1965	The continuance, development, and improvement of public transportation and related services in 12 counties; financing, planning and oversight of operating components (Metro-North RR, MSBA, LIRR, NYCTA, SIRTA, TBTA).	17 members (14 votes) appointed by governor (11 on recommendation of local officials—4 by NYC mayor); Senate confirmation required.
Municipal Assistance Corporation for NYC (MAC)	1975	To provide capital finance and fiscal oversight for NYC after fiscal crisis.	9 members appointed by governor (4 on recommendation of NYC mayor); Senate confirmation required.
NYC Educational Construction Fund (EFC)	1966	Constructed joint occupancy structures consisting of public schools combined with nonschool commercial facilities.	3 members: president of NYC Board of Education, chancellor of NYC Board of Education, appointee of mayor.
NYC Health and Hospitals Corporation	1969	To promote and deliver comprehensive health care, promote health, welfare, and safety, and join with other health workers and communities in partnership; operates municipal hospitals, affiliation agreements with private hospitals, clinics, and nursing home facilities.	16 members: 10 appointed by mayor (5 are city council designees), 5 ex-officio from mayor's administration, CEO selected by 15 members.

NYC Housing Development Corporation (HDC)	1971	To make mortgage loans through the issuance of HDC bonds or notes to finance construction or rehabilitation of low- and moderate-income multistory housing (subsidiaries include Housing Assistance Corporation to receive MAC funds and Housing NY Corporation to borrow against revenues from Battery Park City Authority).	7 members: 2 appointed by governor, 2 by mayor, 3 ex-officio (NYC commissioner of housing preservation and development, NYC director of OMB, NYC commissioner of finance).
NYC Municipal Water Finance Authority	1984	Issues revenue bonds to finance capital investment in NYC water and sewer system; contract agreements with NYC Water Board and Department of Environmental Protection.	7 members: 1 appointed by governor, 2 by mayor, 4 ex-officio (NYC commissioner of environmental protection, NYS commissioner of environmental conservation, NYC commissioner of finance, NYC director of OMB).
NYC Off-Track Betting Corporation (OTB)	1971	Operates off-track pari-mutuel wagering on horse races in NYC.	5 members appointed by mayor.
NYC Rehabilitation Mortgage Insurance Corporation	1973	Insures institutional mortgages to encourage acquisition and rehabilitation of older residential properties in designated NYC neighborhoods.	7 members: 3 appointed by mayor, 4 ex-officio (NYC commissioner of housing preservation and development, NYC director of OMB, NYC director of city planning, NYC commissioner of finance).
NYC School Construction Authority	1988	Construct public schools and renovate and repair existing buildings.	3 members: 2 appointed by the mayor, 1 ex-officio (NYC schools chancellor).
NYC Transit Authority (NYCTA) (component of MTA)	1953	Provision of safe and efficient public transportation services in NYC; leases and operates city subway and bus services.	MTA board members.
NYC Water Board	1984	Collection of fees for city water and sewerage systems; contracts with Water Finance Authority and Department of Environmental Protection.	7 members appointed by the mayor; 1 must have expertise in science of water resources.

Organization	Year	Description	Membership
NY Convention Center Development Corporation (joint venture of UDC and TBTA)	1979	Construction of Javits Convention Center.	4 members: Urban Development Corporation (UDC) and Triborough Bridge and Tunnel Authority (TBTA) elect 2 members each.
NY Convention Center Operating Corporation	1979	Marketing and management of Javits Convention Center.	13 members: 7 appointed by governor, 2 by temporary president of Senate, 2 by Assembly Speaker, 1 by Senate minority leader, 1 by Assembly minority leader; Senate confirmation required.
NY Job Development Authority (JDA)	1961	Stimulate growth of private sector employment by loaning to companies in the state; loans in NYC through the city-sponsored non-profit Financial Services Corporation.	11 members: 7 appointed by governor, 4 ex-officio (NYS commissioners of commerce, labor, and agriculture, superintendent of banks); Senate confirmation required.
NYS Housing Finance Agency (HFA)	1960	Financing not provided by private capital markets to increase or preserve the supply of socially desirable capital assets, including low- and moderate-income housing, university facilities, civic, cultural, and recreational urban renewal facilities, and medical care facilities.	7 members: 4 appointed by governor, 3 ex-officio (NYS commissioner of housing and community renewal, NYS budget director, NYS commissioner of taxation and finance); Senate confirmation required.
NYS Medical Care Facilities Finance Agency (MCFFA)	1973	Finance construction projects for not-for-profit hospitals, nursing homes, and health maintenance organizations; staffed by HFA.	7 members: 3 appointed by governor, 4 ex-officio (NYS commissioners of taxation and finance and of health, NYS budget director, chairman of NYS Housing Finance Agency); Senate confirmation required.
NYS Project Finance Agency	1975	Special purpose agency established to create long-term financing to UDC from sales of bonds and notes, in order to bail UDC out of defaults and mortgage weaknesses; staffed by HFA.	7 members: 3 appointed by governor, 4 ex-officio (NYS commissioners of taxation and finance and housing and community development, NYS budget director, chairman of NYS Housing Finance Agency); Senate confirmation required.
NYS Thruway Authority	1950	To construct, maintain, and operate thruway system in NYS.	3 members appointed by governor; Senate confirmation required.

NYS Urban Development Corporation (UDC)	1968	To generate industrial, commercial, and civic development in distressed urban areas and to create jobs through retaining existing industries and attracting new industries through the acquisition, construction, and rehabilitation of industrial and manufacturing plants and commercial facilities and by leveraging private development through the use of public funds.	9 members: 7 appointed by governor, 2 ex-officio (superintendent of banks, chairman of Science and Technology Foundation), CEO also appointed by governor; Senate confirmation required (empowered to create subsidiaries).
Port Authority of NY and NJ	1921	To provide transportation, terminal and other facilities of commerce and economic development in the Port of New York District; operates Newark, LaGuardia, and Kennedy Airports, PATH, Port Authority Bus Terminal, World Trade Center, Holland and Lincoln Tunnels, George Washington Bridge, Port Newark-Elizabeth; has joint projects with NYC, including Bathgate Industrial Park and Red Hook Marine Terminal.	12 members: 6 each appointed by governors of NY and NJ; Senate confirmation required.
Power Authority of NYS	1931	Construction and operation of electric generating and transmission facilities; production, sale, purchase, and resale of electricity, including from nuclear power plants.	5 members appointed by governor; Senate confirmation required.
Roosevelt Island Operating Corporation	1984	Management and operation of Roosevelt Island.	9 members: 7 appointed by governor (2 on recommendation of mayor, of which 1 must be island resident, and 2 other island residents), 2 ex-officio (NYS commissioner of housing and community development, NYS budget director); Senate confirmation required.
Staten Island Rapid Transit Operating Authority (SIRTA)	1971	Same as NYCTA, within Staten Island.	MTA board members.

Organization	Year	Purpose	Members
State of NY Mortgage Agency (SONYMA)	1970	To provide secondary money market when there is an inadequate supply of private sector credit for residential loans, oversees the Mortgage Insurance Fund.	9 members: 3 appointed by governor, 1 each by temporary president of the Senate and Speaker of the Assembly, 4 ex-officio (superintendent of banks, NYS comptroller, budget director, commissioner of housing and community renewal); Senate confirmation required.
Triborough Bridge and Tunnel Authority (TBTA became part of MTA in 1968)	1933	Operation and maintenance of toll bridges and tunnels in NYC; ownership, sale of real property.	MTA board members.
United Nations Development Corporation	1968	To provide office space, hotel and other facilities for the UN, foreign missions to the UN and the international community.	15 members: 8 appointed by governor, 5 by mayor, 2 ex-officio (NYC commissioner of housing preservation and development, chairman of NYC Planning Commission).

Source: New York State Assembly Standing Committee on Corporations, Authorities, and Commissions: *Directory of New York State Public Authorities 1985* (Albany, 1986) and annual reports of authorities where available.

Notes: Not public corporations, the Financial Services Corporation (FSC) and Public Development Corporation (PDC) are city-sponsored nonprofit corporations with substantial power over public real estate, commercial and industrial loans, and tax abatements. The Industrial Development Authority is administered by FSC.

autonomous,'' they constitute an integral part of the political process. Sayre and Kaufman wrote that transferring responsibilities to authorities simply changes "the arena in which the political contests over their decisions takes place." Removing agencies from the traditional electoral structure does not end their involvement in the essence of politics, for decisions by their managers affect the stakes of politics: who gains and who loses. And the prizes that authorities distribute are substantial indeed.[2]

That characterization by Sayre and Kaufman remains accurate. Combining public ownership with separate legal status and private investment, corporate authorities have strengthened the power of governors to raise and spend money and to allocate benefits, often enhancing the impact of private participants—bankers, consultants, and developers—in city affairs. The composition of authority boards (see Table 7.1) demonstrates the governor's advantage in appointment power.

Debate continues between those who consider authorities to be management entities that should be as insulated as much as possible from politics (a normative stance), and those who argue that as public instrumentalities authorities are properly part of the democratic political process. The history of authorities in New York City clearly supports the latter view. Public authorities are embedded in the city's political process. In the realm of policy politics, they have dramatic impact on land use and development trends in the city, on transportation and housing costs and quality, and on the availability of open space and recreation. They influence the priorities of public expenditure; in the 1980s the influence was toward private development over public services. Appointments to their boards are concerns of the mayor and governor, with whom their executives must deal, together with legislators, community groups, and the media.

A third set of factors that has stimulated the growth of authorities—the *management incentives*—has a negative thrust: avoidance of the whole complex of administrative rules, laws, practices, and personnel problems that impede quick action and effective project implementation in city government. New York City's unreformed personnel system is one of the major incentives for reliance on public authorities that can be freed from it: in some cases authorities are exempt from civil service altogether, and in others they may establish their own civil service system. In one way or another, most public authorities avoid the services of the city Personnel Department and the detailed tests, rules, job titles, and procedures that it layers over collective bargaining agreements. Some of the key distinctions between city agencies and certain public authorities are that the authorities are permitted—within the parameters of their collective bargaining agreements—to hire staff without taking names off a list of written test results, to promote and dismiss on the basis of performance, and to establish more efficacious human resource and management systems. City agencies that have been converted to public authorities, but are still subject to many of the city's personnel system rules and rights, have struggled for decades to improve internal management with limited results, for example, the Transit Authority and the Health and Hospitals Corporation.

Most public authorities are also exempt from centralized procurement procedures. Some are exempt from the controversial state "Wicks Law," which requires public agencies to utilize three or more prime contractors on every construction project, preventing use of a general contractor responsible for subcontracts. Authorities can contract with consultants more quickly and flexibly than can city agencies. Most are not subject to city budget processes. They may keep and reallocate their earnings through their own budgets without reference to an appropriations process. They can commit resources to project planning and design before or without formal project approvals from the city land use or capital program processes.

Sayre and Kaufman concluded—almost wistfully—that strengthening city taxes and easing restraints from Albany might make authorities less attractive and "increasingly conciliatory." In that, their crystal ball failed. In 1960, the year their first edition was published, the rapid expansion of public authorities throughout New York State began. By the end of the 1980s, the thirty-six special corporations authorized to operate in New York City (see Table 7.1) had major influence on land values and land use, commercial construction, and economic development. They dominated public transportation and controlled most of the automobile routes into Manhattan. They channeled the major portion of public funds being invested in housing (mainly to middle- and above middle-income housing), in health, and in education facilities. For decades, authorities have had considerably more influence over the physical and economic shape of the city than the City Planning Commission, the city council, and the line departments of city government. They can no longer be called "strange new creatures."

The Status of Public Authorities

Public authorities are corporate subsidiaries of government, each established by legislative statute or charter to operate to some extent outside the regular structure of executive departments, usually, but not always, to finance, construct, or operate revenue-producing enterprises. The New York State Constitution requires that all "public benefit corporations" be chartered by individual special acts of the state legislature.

Influenced by the 1921 model of the Port Authority and by the requirements of state law, public authorities operating in the city share a common form. The public benefit corporations (hereafter, "authorities") are distinct corporate entities with powers to spend, borrow, and collect rent or fees. They can enter into contracts, own property, and sue or be sued in their own name. They are internally governed by boards of directors, disparately appointed, some including incumbent government executives. Authorities have no powers to tax or reserve powers to regulate; they are not subject directly to general municipal law. They can exercise only those powers and conduct only those activities authorized in their charter statutes and related laws.

Neither are they "line agencies" of city or state government, like the city police department or the state corrections department. The city and public authorities have contractual relationships. The authorities have a legal identity separate from municipal government, with distinct credit ratings and liabilities. Most are exempt from administrative law that applies to city departments and are not subject to the direct control of city oversight agencies that supervise the finances, personnel management, and procurement activities of ordinary departments. Their powers and structure can usually be changed only by statutory amendment, not by local law or executive order. With a few exceptions, the mayor does not appoint their chief executives. And they are generally permitted "business-type budgets," that is, budgets with less line-item detail and more flexibility for internal change than city agencies.

The hybrid status of the authorities is manifest in overlapping directorates and corporate subsidiaries. The MTA Board is also the governing board of the city-owned Transit Authority, the Staten Island Rapid Transit Operating Authority, the Long Island Rail Road, the Triborough Bridge and Tunnel Authority (TBTA), Metro North Commuter Railroad, and Metropolitan Suburban Bus Authority, each of which retains a distinct corporate status and personnel system. The Urban Development Corporation (UDC) can establish subsidiaries without going back to the legislature; examples include the Roosevelt Island Operating Corporation, the Times Square Development Corporation, and the Harlem Urban Development Corporation. The Jacob Javits Convention Center in Manhattan was constructed by a development corporation jointly owned by UDC and TBTA (itself an affiliate of MTA); the convention center is run by an operating corporation with independent corporate status but with the same president as the development corporation, and no mayoral appointees on its board. The Housing Finance Agency board and executive director also manage four other public benefit corporations.

To implement the city program for affordable housing construction and preservation announced in 1987, two new corporate subsidiaries of the Housing Development Corporation were created to receive funds from three other authorities—the Battery Park City Authority, Municipal Assistance Corporation, and Port Authority. The reader who feels lost at this point is not alone. Mayor Koch stated, "The details of the arrangement [for new housing finance] are not familiar to me or important, as long as we get the money."[3]

Relationships to City and State

Authorities are institutional players with which the mayor must bargain, much as he bargains with private firms involved in development. Table 7.1 includes three types of authority: statewide public benefit corporations with significant operations within the city; public benefit corporations operating exclusively within the city; and local economic development corporations. In the legislative process to establish an authority or to amend its programs, the city has to make compromises with disparate interest groups, unions, and up-state representatives. Support from the governor becomes crucial in this process. Between legislative episodes, the mayor bargains with the authority leaders.

The formal structural ties between the public authorities and city government run the gamut from none, like the UDC, to an authority organized as an internal creature of a city department, like the Financial Services Corporation. The mayor has no powers of appointment or formal veto over some, like UDC, which has a board appointed by the governor. More common is some sharing of the appointment power, with the mayor the weaker partner. For example, the mayor nominates four of the nine directors of the Municipal Assistance Corporation, who are appointed by the governor, and four of the seventeen members of the Metropolitan Transportation Authority. At the other end of the spectrum are the public authorities that have absorbed functions previously carried out by city agencies and remain within the framework of city government, such as the Health and Hospitals Corporation and the Municipal Water Finance Authority.

Authorities Under City Control

The Water Finance Authority is a financing device. A public benefit corporation created by state law, it is governed by a board of four city officials, two private mayoral appointees, and one gubernatorial appointee. Its executive director is also deputy director of the city Office of Management and Budget, and other officers of the corporation are paid as city officials. Its only function is to issue bonds to raise capital for investment in the city's water supply and waste disposal systems. It does not even collect fees from those systems. Fees are collected by another single-function entity—the New York City Water Board, also a legally distinct public benefit corporation. The city Department of Environmental Protection (DEP) continues to operate the water and waste-water disposal systems, linked with the two corporations by way of leases and payment agreements.

Created in 1984, the two new water authorities are totally interdependent. (The Water Authority could not issue bonds and pay debt service without fee revenue collected by the Water Board.) And both are dependent upon DEP for construction management and maintenance of the underlying revenue-producing operations. The two authorities have been combined for auditing and reporting purposes and included in the city's financial statements as component units of "an enterprise fund of the city." They are designed to be self-supporting from water and sewer fees. This complex arrangement is difficult to track from routine public documents.

Why were these public authorities created, if they were to remain an integral part of city government? This question justifies a digression, to demonstrate the complex legal and financial factors that underlie public authority growth. There had been, previously, a Board of Water Supply that was an integral part of city government. Although borrowing for the water supply system was exempt from the constitutional debt limit of the city, the bonds were considered general obligations of the city and therefore part of the city debt in the eyes of the credit markets, affecting the market reception of all city bonds. By creating a legally separate Water Authority that can issue revenue bonds—bonds backed only by revenues from water and sewer fees and not secured by the full faith and credit or tax power of the city—the city government established a mechanism for raising over $8 billion dollars for the ten-year water and sewer systems capital improvement program, without limiting credit available borrowing for other purposes.[4]

But why the second authority—the Water Board? This device avoids a provision of the state constitution that requires a majority vote at general or special elections to approve giving a public corporation both the power to contract indebtedness and the power, within any city, to collect rentals or fees from the owners of real estate for services formerly supplied by the city. That provision prevents state legislation from moving municipal utility services out of local government into public benefit corporations without local referenda. But lawyers concluded that a referendum could be avoided by splitting the two powers—the power to borrow and the power to collect fees—between two public corporate entities and then linking them by financing and rebate agreements.

Consideration was given to moving finance and operations together into a comprehensive operating water and sewer authority. The Department of Environmental Protection's capital projects had lagged badly, but opposition from personnel and from the public employee unions discouraged moving the entire operation to an authority. In the event, the Water Authority plan was a response to the financial incentives, but not to the management incentives, for authority creation.

In contrast, the Health and Hospitals Corporation (HHC) was created in 1969 for the express purpose of improving management of the city's municipal hospital and clinic system. Previously under the Department of Hospitals, the municipal hospital system had been plagued by labor strife, payroll padding, staffing problems, and deteriorating physical conditions. Affiliation agreements with private voluntary hospitals had turned out to be more expensive and more difficult to monitor than anticipated. The corporation was intended to overcome city government procedures that "obstruct and impair efficient operation."[5] Improved management by the new corporation was expected to increase the proportion of costs covered by user charges and third-party insurance (including Medicaid and Medicare).

The corporation did not produce the predicted management improvements. In the process of negotiation and passage of legislation to establish HHC, its original supporters lost on many small issues. The hospital corporation did get new top managers and independent purchase and contracting power, but it has never had adequate middle management and professional staff. Reports over the years have catalogued HHC's problems: inadequate adaptation to changing client populations and lack of strategic planning; chronic vacancies in management and professional positions in the various hospitals; persistently inadequate monitoring of affiliation agreements; weak collection and information systems; poor planning and design of construction projects, ineffective and costly procurement processes, and continued need for subsidies. After seventeen years of turmoil, there was a glimmer of hope as a 1986 report noted significant improvements in both management and finance, and the first balanced budget in the corporation's history.[6]

State Controls

Most formal controls over public authorities are exercised by the state. These include review of the authority's budget review, selective audit of its finances and performance, review of borrowing proposals by the state comptroller and the Public Authorities Control Board for some statewide authorities, and program-related approvals or investigations by the legislature. Committees of both houses of the state legislature have been concerned with the corporations as has a long-standing joint legislative commission. The role of the state comptroller has grown steadily with expanding audit coverage, borrowing approval powers, and issuance of investment guidelines for authorities. The Financial Emergency Act of 1975 required the financial plans of eleven authorities operating in the city to be included in the city's financial plan subject to approval, through 1986, of the state Financial Control Board. Requirements for budget balance were applied to them.

Pressures for more effective state control over all public authorities and for containment of authority proliferation have been felt in Albany and studied by several commissions since the mid-1970s.[7] But proposals for major changes have repeatedly failed.

Authorities remain an alternative most turned to by the governor and the mayor when they want to achieve a particular objective but find themselves blocked by the other players in New York politics and public finance. Authorities are also an organizational alternative that creates ambivalence and suspicion among legislators. One state assemblyman has observed, "Authorities make me nervous. They're chartered by the legislature and commissioned by the governor but they're out of reach of the average citizen or legislator. They seem to be untouchable." Another likened authority leaders to "Roman Emperors."[8]

The Authorities over Time

To understand both the practical appeal of authorities and the ambivalence they foster, one must understand their history. Like most corporations, public authorities are pragmatic structures with flexible functions, adaptable to changing demands and constraints. Each can be tailor made through special legislation to suit the particular set of interests ascendant in its creation. Once established, a special authority can change more easily than can traditional structures of government. Authorities can shift budget and program priorities with less external political and administrative process and tradeoff than executive line agencies. Some can hire and fire and otherwise manage human resources without external approvals. Many have been much more successful than city or state government at recruiting managerial and professional talent. They can plan in quiet and closed circumstances, entering the political arena with fully developed proposals and designs. Because they are pragmatic and flexible, authorities are more a phenomenon in political history than a fixed management form.

Like the prehistory that geologists uncover, authority history in New York manifests some distinct layers, or perhaps they are cycles. Four distinct periods can be identified: 1921 to 1960; 1960 to the early 1970s; the fiscal crisis era of the mid-1970s; and the years since the mid-1970s. From 1921 to 1960, the classic operating authorities built and operated the basic transportation infrastructure of New York City. In theory, their operating revenues were to pay their costs, including debt service. In fact, of the six authorities operating in 1960, only two were and continue to be self-supporting: the Port Authority and the TBTA. But until the 1960s, the concept was clear: authorities built and operated major facilities, and did so without draining tax revenues.

Public Authorities as a Growth Industry : 1960–75

Governor Nelson Rockefeller came to office in 1959 with ambitious goals for housing, higher education, improved health care and transportation facilities, and downtown development in Manhattan. He was quickly frustrated by administrative processes, notably a slow moving and unimaginative Department of Public Works and, within a few years, by voter rejection of proposals for state bond issues.

Rockefeller was publicly committed to both a balanced budget and substantial increases in expenditure. By channeling many expenditures through off-budget authorities, he could generate heavy borrowing for public purposes while maintaining the image of a "pay-as-you-go" state government. The author has written elsewhere that, "Rockefeller could build faster and richer with revenue bonds issued by public authorities, even if those bonds were ultimately backed by the state's credit, indirectly or through subsidization of operating expenses. He could borrow first and make the legislature pay later."[9]

The governor determinedly sought to gain effective control over both the Port Authority and the Triborough Bridge and Tunnel Authority.[10] With his own network of investment bankers, attorneys, and authority managers, he created new public corporations and expanded existing ones. Unlike the earlier authorities, the new ones were established explicitly to implement state policies, particularly those of the executive. They had entrepreneurial leaders who were largely dependent on the governor's support. Several state department heads had ex officio seats on the authority boards—a distinct departure from the Port Authority model.[11]

In addition to gubernatorial leadership, a hallmark of this period was the use of public authorities to finance activities that were not expected to be "self-supporting" from user charges and other operating revenues: mass transportation, low- and moderate-income housing, public higher education, and health care facilities. In partnership, the governor's office and the municipal bond market community—underwriters, rating agencies, bond attorneys and financial advisers—developed credit strategies that fueled the expansion of tax-backed authorities. Several types of indirect tax support were developed and continue to operate in the city's authorities. Authorities were created with start-up state money that was supposed to be repaid, but often was not. Annual, appropriated subsidies for transit became routine. Earmarked taxes are also dedicated to authority revenues or designated as back-up for authority borrowing. For example, the MTA has received the proceeds of a 0.25 percent sales tax supplement levied in the MTA district and also revenue from corporate income taxes and a real estate transfer tax; revenue from the city sales tax is used first for debt service payments on Municipal Assistance Corporation bonds. Leaseback authority debt is issued by authorities, which derive debt service payments from rental income received from government.[12]

Moral obligation bonds and housing

The financial innovation with the most dramatic impact in the 1960s and 1970s was the "moral obligation" bond. In 1960, a prominent bond attorney[13] and a number of investment bankers developed the first "moral obligation" bond for the New York State Housing Finance Agency (HFA), which was to become a model for seventy-nine similar authorities in thirty states by 1975.

Why "moral obligation"? The term had been used in 1938 by a New York constitutional convention committee, warning that the judiciary might hold the state responsible for authority debt (the concern was generated by borrowing by authorities headed by Robert Moses). In 1960, proposed bond issues by authorities that could not operate without subsidies could not be financed unless the state offered special guarantees or specified credit backing. But by terms of the constitution, the state could not directly and legally guarantee the debt of authorities without popular vote on borrowing propositions that were often going down to defeat. "Moral obligation," as incorporated in the legislation for and bond resolutions of the Housing Finance Agency and its authority clones, is a way of avoiding a state legal obligation for debt referendum, nevertheless putting state fiscal resources behind the bonds to the satisfaction of the investment bankers. The moral obligation terms provide that the state legislature will appropriate funds to the authority to bring its reserve funds annually up to a level needed to meet all debt service requirements.

Technically, future elected legislatures cannot be committed to appropriate funds by a current sitting legislature.[14] Hence the enforcement of that language over the thirty-year term of a bond depends on subsequent political decisions, which are not assured. In effect, the arrangement is a practical obligation with negligible relationship to morality. As one investment banker has said, if one of the state corporations defaulted on debt, it would resemble an elephant dying on the state house steps—the government would have to do something about it or suffer from the stench. With state and city government depending on the same players in the financial community for their annual general obligation borrowing, they could ill afford to refuse to bail out a state corporation when and if that were necessary. On this bet, the investment community put its money into housing through the "moral obligation" of the state legislature to back up the authorities.

New York city and state governments had been acting to regulate and supplement private market provision of housing for decades. By the end of the 1950s, there were various tax exemptions and abatements available, and the city and state both had the authority to lend money at low interest rates to limited-profit housing developers. But in the 1960s, the city's regulatory measures seemed to be having a negative effect on the housing supply. The city government intervention in the private housing market was rent control, which, many argued, contributed to abandonment of or disinvestment in privately owned, low-cost housing. A 1968 survey indicated that the city had a three-year net loss of one hundred thousand housing units. Furthermore, the zoning resolution of 1961 had reduced permitted densities for new residential construction in the city. Meanwhile, construction of traditional public housing for low-income people by the Housing Authority was slowing as city costs exceeded federal standards and social and design criticism of large-scale projects mounted. The times seemed ripe for aggressive action by the state government, in the form of ambitious public authority efforts.

The Housing Finance Agency (HFA) became a quick success. It is a bank, not a builder, and it generated a booming banking business, buying secondary mortgages to expand commercial and savings bank lending for middle-income housing. Within fifteen years of its creation, it ranked as one of the nation's largest issuers of tax-exempt securities, accumulating a $15 billion debt. HFA maintained a higher credit rating than the city government. As of 1986, it had $7 billion invested in New York State, over $3 billion of that in New York City.

HFA, like several other large authorities, grew into a public conglomerate. Originally charged with financing limited-profit housing projects through the sale of bonds and purchase of mortgages (such as those for Co-op City in the Bronx), HFA developed into a multipurpose wholesale banking business for a mix of public and private agencies, financing not only housing but hospitals, nursing homes, centers for children and the elderly, and parts of the state university. By 1975 its management was responsible for four other authorities: Medical Care Facilities Finance Agency (MCFFA),[15] Municipal Bond Bank (not operative), the State of New York Mortgage Agency (Sonny Mae), and the Project Finance Agency.

The city government had little direct influence over HFA and the other state authorities during this period, although most of their activity was in the city. The new crop of authority entrepreneurs tried to emulate the giants of the first generation of authority entrepreneurs, Robert Moses and Austin Tobin, by carving out an agenda of economically solid projects and securing managerial independence. Although dependent upon the governor's support and backed by state credit, Paul Belica, the executive director of HFA during this period, maintained, "We are not using public funds; public purpose is not our primary concern and if it were, the state should do the job."[16] In this he echoed statements by Moses, but he spoke too soon, for HFA was soon to be in difficulty that demonstrated its dependence on public funds and its link to public purpose.

Progress on moderate-cost housing was not satisfactory to the governor under HFA's conservative financing policies and the obstacles of local zoning. In 1965 voters rejected, for the fifth time, a low-income housing and slum clearance state borrowing proposal sponsored by the Rockefeller administration. These frustrations led to creation of yet another public authority. The Urban Development Corporation was established in 1968 with powers to override local zoning, with an executive director appointed by the governor, rather than by the board of directors as is typical, with authorization to issue bonds to finance various kinds of development projects, including tax shelter, syndicate-backed housing projects and mixed-income large scale developments, for example, Roosevelt Island. Unlike HFA, UDC manages construction and owns projects as well as participating in development finance. Ninety percent of the housing units it built depended on federal subsidies.

The city government joined the bandwagon in 1971, sponsoring the Housing Development Corporation with financing functions and a board majority appointed by the mayor.

Harnessing the transportation authorities

In addition to creating new authorities, Governor Rockefeller set out to gain control over the Port Authority and other transportation authorities. There was a true crisis in rail transportation in the region in the 1960s: on the suburban railroads, there had been long years of private disinvestment and deferral of maintenance, and there had been no new construction on the subways; the finances of all the rail services were collapsing. A series of state interventions beginning in Rockefeller's first year in office culminated in 1967 in the formation of the Metropolitan Transportation Authority, whose board became the governing body for the state-owned Long Island Rail Road, New York City Transit Authority, and Triborough Bridge and Tunnel Authority.[17] The city and state adopted a planned construction program, preposterously underestimated to cost $1.4 billion, including a major new trunk subway line under Second Avenue, a new rail tunnel under the East River, subway extensions in Queens and Brooklyn, a new crosstown line, interconnections between new and old routes, and various improvements in the Bronx and Staten Island. The Transit Authority was doing the detailed design work in 1969 and estimated completion of the system by 1980. Most of the plan components were incomplete or canceled by 1990.

Other announced regional transportation improvements were to be financed and built by the Port Authority. Under pressure from the governors, the Port Authority implemented legislative authority to purchase the bankrupt Hudson and Manhattan Rail transit lines between New Jersey and Manhattan, renamed PATH.[18] The same 1962 legislation authorized the authority to build the World Trade Center.

Urban development

Another New York City focus of the Rockefeller administration was the development of downtown Manhattan, pioneered by the construction of Chase Manhattan Plaza. David Rockefeller was chairman of Chase Bank and president of the Downtown–Lower Manhattan Association, which developed a plan for downtown including proposals that would later be named the World Trade Center, Battery Park City, Westway, renovation of docks, residential urban renewal, and the Second Avenue Subway. The whole plan was slated for implementation by authorities: MTA, Port Authority, and, when HFA balked at taking on the risky Battery Park proposal, the new Battery Park City Authority. City-owned land and land use decisions would be needed, but the direct involvement of city government was limited.

In this period, the role of public authorities in New York City expanded dramatically, accounting for approximately 75 percent of new public investment. The high publicity and conflict of New York City politics focuses debate over transportation, housing, and health problems on the mayor (see Chapter 3, by David R. Eichenthal, on the role of the mayor). But the capacity to select priorities and implement improvements is scattered. Development planning initiative passed from the private Regional Plan Association and the governmental City Planning Commission to specialized authority entrepreneurs supported by the governor. The governor depended on the authority network both to conduct the planning and to implement it. The authorities in some instances added to the mayor's formal power, for example through some board appointments, but his influence was becoming more difficult to exercise.

The growth of authorities largely escaped the notice of the public and of students of city government.[19] Revenue bonds, moral obligation, and public authority investment priorities are an insiders' game. The authority leaders themselves fended off city leadership. Under the MTA, the Transit Authority resisted attempts by city agencies to participate in design of new routes and the TA provided the Board of Estimate with only information required by law, despite the fact that routes would affect land use and transit operating costs for which the city was providing substantial subsidies. State legislation and court action were required to force the MTA to give local governments information on projected highway and transportation plans and to affirm the right of audit by the state comptroller.

Testing the Limits: 1973–75

Through the authority system, bankers had replaced voters as brakes on growth of public debt. The bankers had been too generous. Neither the Wall Street advisers nor the political leaders foresaw the changes of the early 1970s or recognized the changes as they were occurring. As Rockefeller left for Washington, becoming vice-president in the Gerald Ford administration, his public authority network was on the brink of trouble (the fiscal crisis is discussed in Chapters 2, 11, 9, and 8 by Dick Netzer, Jewel Bellush, H. V. Savitch, and Gerald Benjamin, respectively). Authorities were part of the problem and were to become part of the solution.

In the early 1970s several events converged to change the role of public authorities in New York City. Economic trends changed the context dramatically. Interest rates were rapidly rising, inflating authority costs far beyond estimates. Jobs were decreasing: New York City lost more than 500,000 jobs between 1969 and 1975. Government revenues were not keeping up with government expenditures, especially for the city, but also at the state level.

Political events sharply affected the resources available for authority projects. While the authorities had relieved some pressures on the city to raise capital to invest in infrastructure, mounting imbalances in the city operating budget had been met by borrowing for current needs, a practice that exacerbated fiscal weakness. Federal subsidies for housing programs—crucial leverage for the authority programs—were sharply cut; and federal mass transit assistance fell far short of what the state and city had counted on. A proposed large state transportation bond issue was defeated by the voters. A Supreme Court decision eliminated the Port Authority's part of the rail transportation plan (for example, the rail link to Kennedy airport). Environmental regulations and the array of interest groups and legal methods that backed them up began to slow construction projects, a trend symbolized by the fifteen-year stalemate and ultimate defeat of Westway, the planned highway on the west shore of Manhattan.

Most of the MTA components of the regional transportation plan were halted or delayed, some with great waste, for example, the Second Avenue subway. Maintenance on the transit system continued to be dangerously deferred even as fares rose.

One by one, events also caught up with the housing development authorities. With powers to negotiate tax exemptions, to bypass local zoning and building codes, to condemn property and to begin construction before completing project design, UDC had been financing construction on the "fast track." But within five years of its creation, its revenue projections and debt structure collapsed. The result was a state payout plan to rescue UDC that continued to draw on appropriations through the 1980s. Roosevelt Island development plans were halved. Battery Park City Authority used its first $200 million in bond proceeds for administrative and maintenance costs; it could not get any construction underway and had no operating revenues. Its management was consolidated with that of UDC for the following decade.

Rising interest rates and falling federal housing subsidies hit even the conservative HFA by 1975. As its underlying revenue stream of mortgage loan payments faltered and new projects lost feasibility, it was unable to "roll-over" short-term debt into new long-term bonds. The state and a consortium of banks saved HFA from default, but the authority remains dependent on state appropriations to cover its pre-1975 obligations.[20] HFA continued to require legislative appropriations to replenish debt reserves for housing and health care investment debts.

Authorities Help Weather the Fiscal Crisis

Proving again the pragmatic versatility of the form, new authorities were created to help the other authorities and city government emerge from fiscal crisis. These included the Project Finance Agency (managed by HFA to refinance debt of UDC), the Mortgage Loan Enforcement and Administration Corporation (a UDC subsidiary to handle mortgages in default), and the most successful bailout authority—the Municipal Assistance Corporation for the City of New York (MAC).

A state public benefit corporation with a board appointed by the governor, MAC raised funds from the tax-exempt market during the years of fiscal crisis when the city was shut out of the market and allocated those funds to refinancing city debt and contributing to the city capital budget. City resources were pledged to the state authority's borrowing; in addition to the proceeds of the state sales tax within the city, the stock transfer tax and per capita state aid to the city could have been diverted to MAC for debt service if necessary. In fact, the last two sources were not needed. MAC generated large amounts of cash, from earnings on its debt reserve funds and from refunding operations as interest rates fell in the early 1980s. In the late 1980s, MAC and the state and city governments agreed to use the surplus MAC funds to finance portions of the city's capital program for housing and schools and part of the MTA capital program, thus echoing the earlier era of authority financing of ambitious programs.

The MAC relationship with city government illustrates the complex intergovernmental issues raised by the public authorities. As Mayor Koch described it, MAC funds were city funds but "the MAC board controls the cash register."[21]

The Decade of the Developers: The 1980s

As the city struggled, in the second half of the 1970s, to emerge from the fiscal and economic crisis, priorities shifted toward concern for the "business climate," calling for budget cuts and government action to stimulate business investments in the city. The authorities were among the first institutions to respond to the new opportunities. Authority investment patterns turned sharply away from public infrastructure and housing toward loans, leases, and site development for private business. The complex commingling of private investment, authority money, and state and city resources is represented in Battery Park City (a dramatically different development than had been envisaged by Governor Rockefeller when he sponsored it), the buildings of United Nations Plaza, the Javits Convention Center, Fordham Plaza, UDC-renovated hotels, Port Authority industrial parks and a series of commercial "ports."[22] If the Forty-second Street Development Project is implemented according to UDC plan, public authority developments would dominate the west side of Manhattan almost continuously from the Battery to Times Square.

The World Trade Center became a profit center for the Port Authority; the governors of New York and New Jersey proposed that it be sold to provide funds for infrastructure and housing. But after several years of studies and negotiations, New York State began moving its own offices out of the Trade Center to provide for higher commercial rents to the Port Authority. The Port Authority hailed this arrangement in 1984 as a source of revenues for a Fund for Regional Development that would become the "capital engine" of the region, but this fund did not become a significant source of public investment over the subsequent five years.

Even the Metropolitan Transportation Authority found ways to tap new business-government financial arrangements, for the first time issuing revenue bonds in its own name, backed by state service contracts, tax shelter lease-back partnerships, and new subsidy packages. The ambitious plans of the 1960s for new subway routes, dashed by the fiscal constraints of the 1970s, were replaced with a much needed plan for car purchases, track reconstruction, and rehabilitation of stations, power systems, shops, and yards.

Not-for-profit corporations

The City of New York entered its own corporations into the economic development game (see Chapter 11, by Jewel Bellush, on the developers as an interest group). The mayor's office controls three corporations (run by two management structures) that negotiate and offer loans, land leases, tax abatements, and other benefit packages to commercial enterprises: the Financial Services Corporation (FSC), the Industrial Development Authority (run by FSC management), and the Public Development Corporation (which does not issue bonds but does execute and manage city land and tax abatement deals). These are not "public benefit corporations" with state charters. FSC and PDC are not-for-profit corporations with city sponsorship under general incorporation laws. During the 1980s, the city Financial Services Corporation became the largest single issuer of industrial revenue bonds in the state. These are public bonds, on which the interest paid to the investor is free of federal income taxes, from which the proceeds are lent to private firms.

The Public Development Corporation is governed by a large board of business, labor, and government people, with the majority of appointments determined by the mayor. One of PDC's major advantages is exemption from requirements for competitive bidding for reallocating city land. PDC has had a rocky history of unsuccessful industrial developments and negative management audits, but has been more successful in putting together benefit packages for projects implemented by other authorities or by private developers. Examples include the South Street Seaport and Industrial Design Center in Long Island City. It was a lead agency in downtown Brooklyn development, but drew criticism from business about the timing and effectiveness of its efforts to implement projects there.

Into the 1990s

Another major shift in authority emphasis began after the 1986 federal tax reform, which restricted the use of tax-exempt financing—one of the leading advantages of public authorities over investor-owned companies. Pressure on the authorities shifted to some extent back to the problems of infrastructure, housing, and education. As noted previously, MAC allocated its surplus funds to the city transit system, housing, and schools. A city School Construction Authority was established by state legislation, basically to overcome the administrative obstacles to efficient school construction and rehabilitation embedded in state and city personnel and operating procedures. Battery Park City Corporation, although not planning to build the moderately priced housing envisioned by its original sponsors, agreed with the city to shift some commercial profits into such housing, via the Housing Development Corporation (and its subsidiaries). The Port Authority, under new management, announced a dramatic shift in priorities from the economic development projects, which had some disappointing results, to rehabilitation of the region's transportation infrastructure with a ten-year, $5 billion capital plan.

The Score Card

The cycles in public authority priorities relate to fundamental political and economic trends. In the late 1970s and 1980s, the authorities emphasized "economic development" projects, that sought physical transformation of real estate and competition for business locations. This emphasis reflected the political view that the benefits of increases in real estate values, job expansion, and subsidies to business are essential to the city's well being and will filter down to the city's low-income population. At the end of the 1980s, there was emphasis on direct public authority contributions to low- and moderate-income housing, educational facilities, and public infrastructure, including the transportation network and water and waste disposal systems. This emphasis reflects a political view that public agencies should provide the basic public framework and social services that will attract economic activity in terms of both physical infrastructure and human resources (eschewing direct subsidies to private business). Public authorities are caught up in these contradictions.

The authorities are major players in city affairs, but their flexibility and pragmatism make it difficult to generalize about their effects. Governor Nelson Rockefeller perceived their vulnerability to economic and political shifts, commenting, "We have to build when the boom is on, but we should be ready for the downturns when they come."[23]

Authorities are used to compensate for some of the weaknesses and complex political and administrative constraints on city government. They have been resorted to in perceived crises, from housing or prison shortages, to business job shrinkage and school building deterioration. But their very usefulness in substituting for regular government agencies raises tough questions about why we cannot make government work better without sacrificing political accountability. The financial, managerial, and political claims for using public authorities do not always match actual outcomes.

Financial Impacts of Public Authorities

Money is power, particularly when pressures for public expenditure continue upward while cutbacks in city budgets are needed. Public authorities have clearly succeeded in increasing access to capital for public and selected private projects, particularly during the years between 1960 and 1986, when the total volume of money flowing into the tax-exempt bond markets was increasing rapidly. Often, this access to capital has a downside, in the form of fixed, long-term demands on public appropriations to subsidize operating deficits or debt services. Nonetheless, the ability to borrow has gained supporters for using the authority form for a wide variety of purposes, even among those uncomfortable with the trend toward fragmenting government into multiple corporate actors and with the insulation of particular programs from the give-and-take of annual appropriation politics.

The authority system works effectively for the types of projects that generate returns with the least political uncertainty. Many public authorities in New York that were designed to be self-supporting are in fact dependent on back-up sources of public finance, but because those sources are often specified in contractual arrangements (for example, leases with government agencies, indirect guarantees, or the "moral obligation" promise of appropriations), the authority can become a relatively safe haven for specific programs. Even the financially strong public authorities—like the Port Authority—are not "autonomous"; governors, mayors, and interest groups can influence them with political skill and strategy, but must stay within bounds acceptable to the authority managers and investment advisers.

Authority financial power, like a number of federal grant-in-aid programs, favors capital expenditures over operating expenditures. The areas of authority achievement are oriented toward construction of new hospital wings and nursing homes, not preventative health care, staff salaries, or training; construction of new highways or bridges, not replacement and maintenance; construction of commercial buildings, not rent subsidies or low-cost housing. For example, the public authorities were no help against the neglected maintenance of the New York City subway system in the 1960s and 1970s that was a response to galloping wage and other operating costs.[24] Realism induced by fiscal crisis and evidence of deteriorating transportation infrastructure turned MTA attention to system rehabilitation during the 1980s.

The most direct effect on public finance of authority growth may be the weakening of legislative budget processes, to which other factors also have contributed. In law, public authorities are directly responsible to the state legislature. But authorities escape line item budgets—an important control mechanism of legislative bodies. Legislative appropriations are forced by authority covenants and contracts of earlier years. From MTA service contracts to UDC prison leases, the revenue streams that are pledged to authority bond issues become fixed costs of the future. Moreover, the complex and interdependent relationships among authority expenditures, debt arrangements, credit security, and subsidies have not been well reported to or sorted out by the legislature. Substantial improvements have been made in the reporting of authority finances in the state executive budget and the comptroller's report, but these sources do not cover many of the authorities that operate in the city. Authority leverage in the money markets and their ability to come to the legislature with fully formed projects leave the average legislator little choice between assent and seeming obstructionism.

Authorities are assessed for what they do, not for what they do not. But the question of opportunity cost must be asked even if it cannot be well answered. How might New York City function, for example, if its urban leadership had set out to implement a grand regional plan like that of Paris during the last twenty-five years? Decentralized, heterogeneous, contentious, New York may not be fertile ground for regional planning or broad consensus on priorities. But the urban economy suffers from some of the gaps in the networks created and controlled by the authorities.

For example, in transportation, the lack of a rail freight connection from the South to New England through New York, linking the city's boroughs to long-distance routes, has long been recognized as a serious economic weakness. The original mandate to the Port Authority called for a freight tunnel under the Hudson River, linked to an existing rail loop to the north. The Port Authority throughout its history has found rail freight proposals to be unattractive from a financial standpoint. Yet all of the highways, loans, partnerships, industrial parks, and tax abatements that authorities in the city have funded cannot produce a fraction of the economic advantage that low cost and efficient freight access to the container port facilities and to the interstate lines could have provided for manufacturing in the boroughs of New York City. The freight tunnel was not financially feasible from the perspective of a single authority project analysis. But it might have been economically feasible from the perspective of the city-wide or regional economy. Public costs and public benefits of authority programs aimed at private economic development are not known. The authorities do not keep records that total the costs of tax abatements, interest subsidies, and direct outlays on projects, and thorough analyses of economic impacts are nowhere to be found.

The Management Myth

Textbook rhetoric and authority proponents suggest that public corporations are inherently "businesslike" and therefore well managed. Neither experience nor common sense supports that contention. Businesses of all types run the gamut from well to badly managed, as do public authorities. From time to time, individual authorities operating in New York have been involved in sloppy investment practices, patronage, conflicts of interest, expense account frauds, purchasing kickbacks, excessive dependence on high-priced consultants, lax internal cost controls, and inflated executive salaries.

But it is clear that escape from the administrative procedures and from some of the legal and political constraints on city government has often been a reason for the expansion of authorities. Such escape was the primary purpose for the creation of the School Construction Authority in 1988. It was not given independent borrowing powers and relies on the city's capital budget and state aid as did the Board of Education's Division of School Buildings before it. But facing severe problems with the physical plant of the city school system, the mayor and the governor, on the advice of two special task forces, concluded that it was more feasible to obtain improvements in construction management, leadership, contracting procedures, staff, and design services—in effect a package of changes that could significantly speed school construction and rehabilitation—by creating a new special authority than by inducing change within the existing unit.

This is a two-sided issue. First, it holds some lessons about changes that are needed in city government—particularly in personnel and contracting processes—to make the bureaucracy more effective for carrying out public programs. Second, it indicates that it is not simply the organizational form of the special authority that functionally impacts management, but the particular powers, leadership, and management characteristics of the authority itself; these vary. Authorities like the Health and Hospitals Corporation and the Transit Authority continued, through their transformation from city agencies to public authorities, weak middle management, difficult work rules, obsolete facilities, badly written contracts, and uncoordinated components. They have been struggling with these problems for many years.

Political Impacts

The pluralist model of politics in New York City described in detail by Sayre and Kaufman involves a constant shifting of elements that contributes to systemic stasis, underlying the popular wisdom that it is exceedingly difficult to get anything done in city government. Authorities often do change the arena and the players in the politics of the programs in which they engage. It is activist mayors and governors who use authorities to break through some of the obstacles to action and create specialized pockets of efficacy, even at the expense of giving up some degree of administrative control. "Authorities," said Mayor Koch, "are the path of least resistance."[25] Through appointments to their boards, the mayor has indirect control of some of them. With the more independent state-appointed authorities, the mayor bargains, much as he bargains with private developers.

The authorities have enhanced the power of state government. If the trends of the 1960s through 1980s continue, "home rule" may be limited to services that cannot be spun off or contracted out to corporate satellites. The governor has become a direct and vital player in city affairs through the authorities. Authorities involve the state comptroller (through performance audits, bond approvals, and investment guidelines); the governor's office (through drafting authority charters, appointments, appropriation requests, and budget review); and legislative committees (through statutory action for authority programs, appropriations, investigations, and commission studies).

The business and financial communities of the city become more directly involved in programs through authorities. The financial crises of the 1970s had strengthened this effect, as business leaders, the bond counsel law firms, financial advisers, and private members of the Financial Control Board became active players in city leadership.[26] But the business-banking-bond-counsel group had exercised influence through authorities since the earliest days of the Port Authority. A central strategy of all successful authority leaders has been to cultivate support from its business constituency, drawing on the underwriters, developers, attorneys, consultants, and contractors who benefit from authority business, sit on authority boards, and are partners in authority projects.

The role of the board of directors of authorities raises issues that touch all corporate boards. Board members have been more effective representing the interests of the authorities in the external environment, in the political arena, than in supervising management internally. In many cases governors and mayors have overrelied on the presumption that a prestigious board is the only source of oversight needed. That was certainly the case with the financial collapse of the Urban Development Corporation in the mid-1970s; its mounting difficulties were evident in hindsight, but state and city government had assumed that the board of directors and the lending financial firms could be trusted to provide oversight and to prevent overborrowing. That was not the case.[27]

Board of directors' oversight is limited for several reasons. Board members—including both business and government executives in a part-time position—can pay very limited attention to authority affairs. They are often presented with a great deal of paper and complex decisions at infrequent meetings and in some cases send substitute representatives. They tend to trust management, in some cases to the point of playing the role of rubber stamp. Moreover, practices unacceptable in the public sector may not trigger attention from private board members because the same practices are common in the private sector. Examples are extensive sole source contracting, entertainment of executives by suppliers, and casual expense account procedures.[28]

Without marketing competition, stock prices, and other indicators of performance that are used to judge investor-owned corporations, authorities are less likely to be frequently and effectively assessed. The bottom line is hard to find. Finally, the responsibilities of authority board members have not been clearly delineated by legal sources or by appointing authorities. Experience shows that the board of directors is often limited by information, time and attention, and understanding of its role.

The solution is not a tightly controlling board, which has not proved practical or effective in public, private, or non-profit sectors. State and city governments should develop more explicit program and investment plans to apply to authorities, giving boards and government oversight bodies benchmarks of authority performance and early warning signals of trouble.

In the complex politics of New York, there are losers as well as winners from the authority system. Even with the small sample they had to study, Sayre and Kaufman perceived that the losers would be the bureaucracy, public employee unions, and trade unions involved in city contracts, political party organizations, neighborhood groups, and populist forces, as illustrated in the decrease in voting on borrowing proposals. However, the unions have lost less than they might have, because they have effectively lobbied to keep their interests represented in individual authority charters when legislation is being considered.

The politics of authorities in New York tend to be the politics of policy and personality rather than politics of party. The regular political party organizations have relatively little influence over authorities, which can fend off party patronage with support from business constituencies. Executive-business patronage is more common, with the governor or mayor appointing people to authority boards or encouraging authority projects supported by people who have contributed to campaigns or who represent a constituency of importance to the executive.

Finally, the city's neighborhoods and civic groups—a category that extends to nearly all ethnic groups, minorities, low- and middle-income groups, preservationists and environmentalists—have been often in contention with authorities. Sayre and Kaufman observed in 1960 that

> generally speaking, civic groups line up behind the authorities because they like the authorities' allegedly nonpolitical, businesslike management. The authorities are supported by planning and housing groups, who see them doing much for transportation, transit, housing, and slum clearance that might otherwise not be done. The major newspapers and other media of communication, for similar reasons, tend to treat the authorities favorably.[29]

That observation no longer applies. Dramatic political shifts have taken place in the period since 1960 that put authorities into direct conflict with some communities and civic groups. Some authorities failed to meet expectations of their early supporters. This is certainly the case in low-income housing, mass transportation, and municipal hospitals. The "Straphangers' Campaign," demonstrators against hospital closings, and Queens Citizens' Organization are examples of groups representing users and neighbors, which, with increasing effectiveness, criticized and began to influence the public authorities and their impacts on neighborhoods.

The goals of local interest groups have changed from "slum clearance" to housing and neighborhood preservation; from maximizing physical development to environmental quality; from large project planning to community participation. Neighborhood interests in Staten Island blocked a refuse burning plant planned by the Power Authority, despite crisis level problems in solid waste disposal. Neighborhood and civic group opposition to continued large-scale real estate development, to gentrification, and to commercialization has slowed many other public authority projects. This trend was not welcomed by Mayor Koch, who saw the "not-in-my-backyard" forces growing out of hand. The interest group environment for authorities has become more complex and provides far more public accountability than existed in the days of Robert Moses and Austin Tobin.

The public authorities have utilized several strategies of survival. One has been to move away from original goals and plans, shifting to less challenged activities. They can do this by making skillful use of their major resources— administrative flexibility and finance. Another strategy is to insulate themselves mainly through financial self-sufficiency or concentration on projects with strong business support. Because of their dependence on land, insulation has become difficult for the development authorities. Backers of authorities have tended to view community groups as dysfunctional sources of delay, and to seek exemption from local land use reviews.

Groups who feel that public authorities are runaway horses, inimical to good government or defiant of political control, have for several decades proposed additional formal controls. But adding formal controls has not significantly changed the role of authorities in the past. Authorities are players in a marketplace of financial, managerial, and political forces. Effective leadership influence requires skill in dealing with those factors. Above all, unless state and city government develop stronger mechanisms for coherent planning, establishing investment priorities, and deciding in advance realistic objectives for their corporate subsidiaries, authorities will continue to be practical tools used for varying, not always consistent, purposes with a mixture of accomplishments and failures, and with large leeway for redefining their own priorities. It still remains to be shown whether the special authorities can make significant contributions to service functions that do not pay their way, such as affordable housing, mass transportation, public health, schools, and other services for children.

Notes

1. Wallace S. Sayre and Herbert Kaufman, *Governing New York City: Politics in the Metropolis.* New York: Norton, 1960; 1965 ed., p. 320.

2. Ibid., pp. 324, 325, 337.

3. Interview with the author, Mayor Edward I. Koch, December 21, 1987, New York City, City Hall.

4. The careful reader may raise the question, why could the city not issue revenue bonds itself, without creating an authority? The answer is found in the state constitution, in a provision that does *not* exist in most other states: in New York, ordinary units of government—the state itself, counties, cities, towns, villages and school districts—may

not incur debt without pledging their "full faith and credit"—that is, their tax-raising capacity—to pay interest on and amortize the debt. Bonds backed only by specific types of revenue, like charges for water use, can be issued only by authorities.

5. State of New York, *New York City Health and Hospitals Corporation Act*, dated March 21, 1969.

6. United Hospital Fund of New York. *The State of New York City's Municipal Hospital System, Fiscal Year 1986*. New York: The Fund, 1987.

7. See extensive bibliography in: Annmarie Hauck Walsh, *The Public's Business: The Politics and Practices of Government Corporations*. Cambridge: The MIT Press, 1978. The major recommendations are in New York State Moreland Act Commission on the Urban Development Corporation and Other State Financing Agencies, *Restoring Credit and Confidence: A Reform Program for New York State and Its Public Authorities* (Albany, March 31, 1976). Subsequent developments are summarized in James Leigland, "Issues of Debt and Accountability." *Empire State Report* 12:5 (May 1986): 19–27; Annmarie Walsh and James Leigland, "The Only Planning Game in Town." *Empire State Report* 9:5 (1983): 6–12; Annmarie Walsh and James Leigland, "The Authorities: $24 Billion Debt and Still Growing." *Empire State Report* 9:7 (1983): 33–38; and several unpublished reports by the New York State Legislative Commission on Public Management (formerly the Legislative Commission on Economy and Efficiency in Government).

8. Karen Dewitt, "How Much Power?" in *Empire State Report* (April 1987), quoting Assemblymen Hoyt of Buffalo and Feldman of Brooklyn.

9. Walsh, *The Public's Business*, p. 266.

10. The governor did have considerable formal power to influence the Port Authority, because all actions of the Port Authority board were subject to veto by either of the two state governors (the formal device was approval of the minutes of the board meetings). But the Port Authority's executive director, Austin Tobin, was a formidable battler for PA autonomy, and usually won. The governor's formal powers with respect to TBTA were more indirect, prior to 1968, and the TBTA chairman Robert Moses was an even more formidable adversary until the mid-1960s.

11. The governor's secretary William Ronan had directed a major state study of public authority devices in 1956 (two years before he joined Rockefeller's staff in the latter's first gubernatorial campaign; Ronan was then a dean at New York University): New York State Commission on Coordination of State Activities, *Staff Report on Public Authorities* (March 2, 1956) Albany: Williams Press, 1976. In the 1960s, Ronan oversaw development of the new network from the governor's office. In 1968, he became first chairman of the MTA, and later served as chairman of the Port Authority and on the Power Authority.

12. The authority borrows, builds, and rents the facility to the local or state government, which is then obligated by terms of a lease to make payments to the authority over the life of the debt. This is how the state Department of Corrections planned to fund prisons built by the Urban Development Corporation.

13. John N. Mitchell, later U.S. attorney general, who was convicted for his role in the Watergate affair.

14. Except when necessary to implement a lawful contractual obligation, like payments on bonds approved by the voters in a referendum.

15. MCFFA has been a major source of finance for the private voluntary hospitals and nursing homes in New York City, which through it have had easier access to expansion capital than have the municipal hospitals under the Health and Hospitals Corporation of the city.

16. Interview with the author, Paul Belica, executive director, Housing Finance Agency, quoted in Walsh, *The Public's Business*, p. 135.

17. The MTA had been established in 1965, to operate suburban rail and bus services; the 1967 legislation, which was passed with Mayor Lindsay's support after his own effort in 1966 to gain control of the TBTA failed, extended the MTA's sway to the city subways and the TBTA. The MTA also included the previously created Metropolitan Suburban Bus Authority, the Staten Island Rapid Transit line (acquired from its private railroad owner), the Penn Central commuter rail lines to the north (which became the Metro-North Commuter Railroad), and, prior to 1983, two airports.

18. PATH is the acronym for *Port Authority Trans-Hudson*.

19. For example, none of the fourteen chapter authors of a 1970 volume on issues confronting New York directly discussed the authorities. One chapter pointed out that although the city's financial commitment to transit continued to grow, "Transportation decision making in New York City is today controlled, in large measure, by regional, state, and federal agencies which are beyond the jurisdiction of city government. These agencies, while effective in project development in the past, have often been insensitive to local needs and desires." Joseph McC. Lieper, Clarke R. Rees, and Bernard Joshua Kabak, "Mobility in The City: Transportation Development Issues," in Lyle C. Fitch and Annmarie Hauck Walsh, editors, *Agenda for a City: Issues Confronting New York.* Beverly Hills: Sage Publications, 1970.

20. For example, the country's largest housing development, Co-op City in the Bronx with about 15,000 middle-income apartments, was the scene of a lengthy rent strike shortly after it was first occupied in the early 1970s and quickly went into arrears on its required mortgage payments to HFA. As of the end of the 1980s, the project had never met its annual mortgage obligations.

21. Interview with the author, December 21, 1987.

22. Fishport did not succeed, Teleport is a communications center developed in partnership with private firms, and Xport is a trading company.

23. Interview with the author, Vice-President Nelson A. Rockefeller, Old Executive Office Building, Washington, D.C., January 12, 1976.

24. In fact, the political arrangements for transit that prevailed between the creation of the Transit Authority in 1954 and the fiscal crisis in 1975 virtually guaranteed that maintenance would be neglected. The city, aided with state bond issue funds after 1968 and federal capital grants, retained responsibility for capital expenditures, while the TA was to try to balance the operating budget and minimize the need for operating subsidies. So, the TA spent as little as possible on maintenance—an operating cost—and replaced neglected cars, electrical and mechanical equipment, and the like with new equipment bought with capital funds when the old ones gave out.

25. Interview with the author, December 21, 1987.

26. They influence not only whether or not particular policies will be adopted, but also the details of city action. For example, bond counsel opinions have limited the expenditure of capital budget funds on certain types of school repairs.

27. It should be remembered that a second meaning of the word "oversight" is to ignore or to overlook!

28. Conflict of interest provisions of the City Charter as of 1989 do not appear to apply to either board members or employees of the public authorities. Beginning in 1989, the state Public Officers Law covers only board members who receive compensation other than on a per diem basis on authorities with at least one gubernatorial appointee. Authorities without state appointments may be covered by financial disclosure amendments to the Municipal Government Law, which take effect in 1991. Sixteen of the authorities covered by the Public Authorities Law have conflict of interest provisions in their charters.

29. Sayre and Kaufman, *Governing New York City*, pp. 327–28.

III

The Dependent City

8

The State/City Relationship

Gerald Benjamin

Who's in Charge Here?

Few New York City residents thought it remarkable when their governor, not their mayor, called a "summit conference" to address problems of governance in the city schools in December of 1987. Though such meetings were rare, the educational system of the city was in crisis. High school dropout rates soared while the physical plant of the schools crumbled. The bureaucracy at 110 Livingston Street in Brooklyn seemed incapable of effective action. The Board of Education was increasingly an arena for racial and ethnic conflict as more and more of the children served by the schools were from minority groups.

Despite New York's long tradition of local control in education and the formal separation of educational policy making from the rest of government at both the state and local levels, New York's governor, Mario Cuomo, had earlier announced that education would be the priority policy concern of his second term.[1] The first step toward this goal, Cuomo said, was not the commitment of new resources, but greater accountability of the Regents, at the head of the state education department, to the "people of the state" or, more particularly, to himself, the people's elected representative in the executive chamber. In similar fashion, the governor's initial prescription for educational reform in the city was to place increased power to appoint school board members in the mayor's hands. "The object," Cuomo suggested, "is to give the mayor the capacity and the responsibility for which he will be accountable."[2]

The governor's educational summit, held in his World Trade Center offices, failed to produce agreement on his reorganization plan for the New York City schools. Mayor Edward Koch and Board Chairman Robert F. Wagner, Jr., were supportive. But one of those who attended, Jose Serrano, a leading Latino state Assembly member from the Bronx and chairman of the education committee in his house, called mayoral control a "non-issue" for the coming legislative session. Serrano and many others of the fifty-eight Assembly Democrats from the city regarded Ed Koch as already too powerful in educational decision making in

New York City. More particularly, some black and Latino Assembly members, part of a group that now comprised a quarter of the city delegation in that body in Albany, especially feared lack of responsiveness by the Koch administration to their recommendations on school board appointments, and attempts that might follow reorganization to reduce the powers of local school boards, very important political bases in their local communities.

As important as the views were of those who attended the governor's meeting, however, were the opinions of those who were not present. The Speaker of the Assembly was not there. The president of the teachers' union was not there. And most obviously, neither the chairman of the State Senate Education Committee nor that house's majority leader came to New York City for the day to meet with the governor.

On the Democratic side, Assembly Speaker Mel Miller of Brooklyn expressed skepticism to reporters about whether giving the mayor control of the board would cause "the kids in the schools to see any difference." And Senate Minority Leader Manfred Ohrenstein of Manhattan commented that since he was first elected in 1960, "We've changed the board's structure five or six times and it hasn't done a lot of good."[3]

Then there were the Senate Republicans. The chairman of their education committee, James Donovan from rural Chadwicks in Oneida County, was not invited to the city education summit. The Majority Leader Warren Anderson, of Binghamton, questioned whether "having one person to beat on" (that is, the mayor) was the answer to New York City's educational problems. And the senior of the six Republican Senators from the city, John Marchi of Staten Island, who did attend the meeting, later spoke approvingly of the American "institutional approach" to "keep school systems somewhat at arms length from politics."[4]

Though Governor Cuomo's reorganization plan for the city's schools received a rocky reception at his educational summit, those at the meeting did agree that they needed to take responsibility for school construction from the Board of Education and give it to a new New York City School Construction Corporation, a proposed offshoot of the State Dormitory Authority. This plan was pushed by state Municipal Assistance Corporation (MAC) Chairman Felix G. Rohatyn as a condition of that agency's providing $600 million of its surplus funds for new school construction. Thus, to overcome delays, mismanagement, and corruption in the operation of city government—some due to restrictions placed on the city by state law and regulation—and to get additional resources for the city, reformers now proposed removing another function from local control. School construction was not only to be given to a state-level agency, but to a public authority that was, by design, only indirectly accountable to the governor and legislature. And this in a state that, in its *Local Government Handbook*, described the home rule powers of its local governments as "among the most far-reaching in the nation"![5]

State Involvement in the City

It would be difficult to convince a remote observer viewing these events in New York in December of 1987 that the largest city in the United States, an entity with more people than four-fifths of the states and the fourth largest governmental budget in the nation, was actually self-governing. In a vital area of local policy, the governor, originally from the city but responsive to a statewide constituency, was the primary initiator. State legislators, some from the city but several from outside it, were key actors. Appointees of the governor, not of the mayor, played a major role. Change, not only in policies affecting the city, but in fundamental structures of city government was proposed, not by local action, but by state law. And the only area in which consensus could be found involved taking responsibility for a major subarea of policy making and implementation away from city government and giving it to a new, state-level public authority, the chief virtue of which was not accountability, the governor's stated goal for education in the city, but presumed greater efficiency.

In fact, no understanding of New York City government can be complete without an analysis of the stakes and goals of key actors, both bureaucratic and political, who hammer out their compromises not in New York's City Hall but in the State House in Albany. This brief vignette about the city's troubled educational system only begins to reveal the range and depth of state involvement in the affairs of New York City. Education is not exceptional. Other examples drawn from the headlines of the 1980s—involving mass transit capital financing, programs for the homeless, the construction of a West Side highway, or dealing with AIDS—would reveal a somewhat different mixture of city and state actors. But in virtually every area of policy, the state of New York is intimately involved with governing New York City. Indeed, a look at the index of *McKinney's Consolidated Laws* of New York reveals ninety-one pages dedicated to state statutes solely concerned with New York City, agencies active only in the city, or "Cities of More than 1,000,000," a category that includes (and is meant to include) only New York City.

State involvement in the city takes many forms. Specific state constitutional provisions, apart from those that apply to all New York local governments, constrain the city's taxing and borrowing authority, set out exceptions to these limits, and create a separate city court system. State law may define, or redefine, the city's charter, altering its fundamental institutions for governance and affecting who wins and loses in city politics. State aid provides one of every six dollars in the city's budget, while state mandates, from the executive, the legislature, and the courts, impose added operating costs and policy requirements on the city's managers, limiting their choices. State public authorities—the Battery Park City Authority and the Urban Development Corporation, to cite just two examples—and multistate agencies responsive to the governor—the biggest is the Port of New York Authority—are constantly remaking the physical face of the city. And finally, state elected and appointed officials and the institutions in which they serve oversee the operation of the city government, auditing its books and holding it accountable, even to the point of removing elected officials should their actions warrant this.

The reality of the state role in New York City governance becomes most apparent in moments of high drama. During the fiscal crisis of the mid-1970s for example, strict state oversight of city operations amounted to virtual control of its daily governance. It is not too much to say, as Hugh Carey later did, that as governor during those years he "had to run the city and state at the same time." "For nearly a year," Carey recalled, he, his staff, and private sector advisers,

> labored, with zero margin for error, to take New York City from near rigor mortis in bankruptcy to intensive care. . . . And for the next successive three years, through MAC [the Municipal Assistance Corporation] and its head Felix Rohatyn and a succession of Control Board [Emergency Finance Control Board, later Financial Control Board] members. . . , New York City was carried like a litter case by New York State until it became ambulatory.[6]

The legacy of that crisis is still very much with us. The city now prepares a GAAP (Generally Accepted Accounting Principles) balanced budget and operates under the Integrated Financial Management System adopted in the later 1970s under state supervision. The Office of the Deputy Comptroller for New York City, created during the crisis, continues to monitor city fiscal and management practices. The Municipal Assistance Corporation, as evident from the education case discussed above, plays a major role in city governance. Though the conditions for diminishing the role of the Control Board were met by the city in its tenth anniversary year and though few observers realize it, that board's full powers to reject or approve city budgets, financial plans, contracts, and borrowing will automatically be restored at any time until the year 2008, if the city experiences an operating deficit of more than $100 million, fails to meet its debt service requirements, or loses access to the financial markets.[7]

Another consequence of the fiscal crisis was to alter the distribution of functions between the state and the city. Relieving the city, the state assumed responsibility for (and control of) the City University. It took on much of the cost of the court system, responsibility for supplementary payments under the Supplementary Security Income (SSI) program, and an increased share of other social welfare programs.

Equally important, at least during the 1980s, was the impact of the fiscal crisis on a whole generation of New York state and city leaders. Their priorities, their sense of what was and is possible for government, were significantly altered by the events of the mid-1970s. Even as spending increased in the improved economic climate of the 1980s, state and city leaders constantly invoked the need for prudence and the reality of limits.

Why Is the State Involved?

Historically, contrasting motivations have driven state involvement in New York City. From a vantage outside the city, the appropriate state role vis-à-vis the city has been both defensive and exploitative. Upstate interests (defined here to include the suburban counties) have wanted to limit the impact of New York City's priorities on them, and when the city was rich relative to the rest of the state—the case for almost all its history until recent times—to capture these resources for their own ends. In city politics, the state has been an alternative arena for those who have failed politically in the city. In addition, as in recent years, the city has become poorer relative to its sister counties to the north and east, and as federal largess has diminished, city leaders have increasingly viewed the state as a source for the resources they need to govern. The current state/city relationship presents an apparent paradox: a relatively smaller and poorer city, but one perhaps more consistently influential in defining state priorities than ever before in this century.

The City's Size and Scope of Government

At the high point for this century, just prior to World War II, eleven of every twenty New Yorkers lived in the city. This proportion has since diminished, due to outmigration from the city and faster growth rates in suburban and some rural areas. In the late 1980s, New York City contained just about 40 percent of New York State's population, a far larger proportion than any other big city in the nation relative to its state.

New York City has regularly produced a smaller proportion of the state's votes than the size of its population would indicate, both because of lower participation rates and because many of its residents have been noncitizens. In fact, in recent years the city has been less a factor in gubernatorial elections than at any time since the creation of the greater city in 1898, with the drop off in the ratio of population to voters approaching levels that haven't been seen in half a century (see Table 8.1). Still, the city is the home of about a third of the state's electorate.

The sheer size of the city dictates that anyone who wishes to win statewide elective office be well known there and responsive to it. This is the reason most candidates for governor in both major parties in this century have been recruited downstate. Eight of the sixteen men elected governor since 1898 listed their official homes in the city. Four others, Theodore Roosevelt, Franklin D. Roosevelt, W. Averell Harriman, and Nelson Rockefeller, spent substantial portions of their lives and careers there.

Yet too close an association with the city can be a political liability for a statewide candidate. Perhaps this is why, as political scientist Theodore Lowi

Table 8.1

New York City as a Percent of Statewide Totals, Population and Vote for Governor, Selected Years, 1900–86

Year	Percent of population	Percent of vote for governor	Difference
1900	47.3	39.3	8.0
1910	52.3	40.0	12.3
1920	53.1	42.4	10.7
1930	55.0	44.8	10.2
1940	55.3	47.8 (1942)*	7.5
1950	53.2	49.4	3.8
1960	46.4	41.8 (1962)*	4.6
1970	43.3	38.4	4.9
1980	40.3	31.0 (1982)*	9.3
1985	40.8	28.8 (1986)*	12.0

Sources: Population data from Katherine Trent and Richard Alba, "Demographics," in Benjamin and Brecher (1988) Table 1; election data from various editions of the New York State Bluebook, *The Legislative Manual*. Percentages calculated by the author.
*For the gubernatorial election closest in time to the population figures. The election date is shown in parentheses.

long ago noted, New York City mayors "go nowhere," an observation confirmed most recently in the spectacular failure of Mayor Edward Koch's primary race for the governorship in 1982.[8]

The scope of city government is also enormous. The range of services it provides is unparalleled in the nation, and its payroll far exceeds the state's in size. In 1982, 46 percent of all the local government employees in New York State worked for the city, more than four and a half times the mean for a group of the largest cities in the country examined in one study.[9] The size and scope of the city government virtually assures that the state has to treat it as a special case as the state attempts to devise intergovernmental aid formulas and strategies for service delivery. In the words of Barbara Blum, social service commissioner under Governor Hugh Carey, "New York City is a problem area that needs to be dealt with very differently, both politically and programmatically."[10]

Political Consequences of Social Differences

Unlike the case in other states, even the earliest New Yorkers lacked common roots. By 1644, one traveler reported, eighteen languages were being spoken in the province.[11] About forty years later, Thomas Dongan, during whose governorship New York City received its first charter, reported the diversity in the colony more colorfully. "Here bee not many of the Church of England, few Roman

Catholicks;'' Dongan wrote, "abundance of Quakers preachers men and Women especially; Singing Quakers; Ranting Quakers, Sabbatarians; Antisabbatarians; Some Anabaptists Some Independents; Some Jews; in short of all sorts of opinions there are some and the most part of none at all.''[12]

New York was an exceptional colony in other ways, too. It was the only one that had been ruled for a lengthy period by a power other than Britain and "the only colony whose pattern of settlement did not gradually spread outward from one primary beachhead on the seaboard. The earliest settlements at New York City, Albany, and Eastern Long Island were 150 miles apart, and each developed distinctive cultural and political characteristics.''[13] By the American Revolution, only half of New Yorkers had origins in Great Britain, and the enmity between the English in New York City and the Dutch in Albany was substantial and persistent.

Differences continued into the nineteenth century. Chancellor James Kent speaking at the 1821 constitutional convention predicted, with fear of the "combustible materials that such a city must enclose," that in a century New York City would govern the state.[14] Later immigration of Jews from Eastern Europe, Irish and Italian Catholics, blacks from the South, and Puerto Ricans, all escaping oppression or seeking opportunity, kept the downstate population distinctively different from that of the rest of New York.

This pattern persists. In 1980 New York City was the home of about three-quarters of New York State's blacks and Asians, and seven-eighths of its persons of Puerto Rican descent. By 1990, blacks, Latinos, and Asians comprised a majority of the city's population, and the proportion of that population that is foreign-born was equal to the levels of the early days of this century.[15]

These population changes and the effects of the Federal Voting Rights Act, first applied in the boroughs of Manhattan and Brooklyn in 1974, led to substantial increases in the numbers of minority group members in New York City's delegation in the state legislature, especially the Assembly. In 1967, six black and three Latino Assembly members comprised 13 percent of the city delegation. Twenty years later, thirteen black and four Latino legislators made up 28 percent of that delegation.[16] In fact, with their three colleagues from Buffalo, Rochester, and Nassau County, city members of the Black and Puerto Rican Caucus in the Assembly had sufficient numbers in the Democratic conference in 1987 to deny the Speaker a majority there, that is, they had the potential for the exercise of real power.

As the minority population of New York City increases, the number of minority Assembly members and Senators surely will increase apace. This has implications not only for the future directions of state politics and the city's agenda in Albany, but for the emergence of minority leadership in the city itself.

There has been widespread comment about the failure of minority group leaders to gain political power in New York City to the degree they have in other major cities in the United States.[17] Developments in state politics may help alter this situation in three ways. First, since minority group voters in the city are overwhelmingly Democratic, that party's control of the governorship is likely to lead to high-level appointments for city minority group leaders, who may later build on this base to further political careers in the city. Second, service in the state legislature for blacks and Latinos, as for others before them, is a training ground for higher elective office, both in the state and in the city. Finally, it might prove easier for a minority group leader from the city to rise to real power through the interpersonal politics of the Assembly than by pursuing the elusive wisp of an effective black-Latino-white, liberal, citywide, electoral coalition at home.

Not surprisingly, the different population mix in the city and the rest of the state has important social, as well as political, implications. Minority persons in New York tend to be less educated, poorer, and to suffer more unemployment than whites, and minorities residing in the city tend to be more disadvantaged than those who live elsewhere in the state. More persons in the city live alone, and more households are headed by women. In New York State outside New York City, about three-quarters of the housing units in 1980 were owner occupied and one-quarter rented; within the city, the ratio was reversed. Finally, the city is the locus of more social problems—mental illness, homelessness, drug addiction, and crime—than its proportion of the state's population would seem to indicate.[18]

These facts affect the state/city political relationship in at least two ways. First, the state government is forced or enticed to intervene in what would seem to be the city's own business, like the schools or the administration of rent regulation within the city. Second, some statewide policy areas come to be regarded as "city dominated," or special areas of city concern. This is obvious in higher education, where the City University is separated organizationally from the State University. But it is also true in social services, where more than two-thirds of the local assistance flows to the city, and in corrections, with the overwhelming majority of persons committed to state prisons coming from the city.

Partisan Differences

The base of the Democratic party in New York State has long been in the city, and the base of the Republican party outside the city. For each party, election victory has turned on holding its core and making successful appeals in the opposition's area of strength. Franklin D. Roosevelt did this for the Democrats. Thomas E. Dewey and Nelson A. Rockefeller did it for the Republicans. In 1986, Mario Cuomo's 56 percent marked the first time in modern New York history that a Democrat had gained a majority outside New York City, while the GOP ticket reached new lows in the city (see Tables 8.2 and 8.3).

Table 8.2

Republican Percentage of Party Enrollments, Votes Cast, and Legislative Seats, New York City, 1930–86

Year	Party Enrollments*	Vote for Governor[†]	Number of Assemblymen	Number of Senators
1930	26.6	25.6	3.2	4.2
1934	17.7	22.0	4.8	8.3
1938	19.2	33.6	9.7	8.3
1942	22.1	36.9	12.7	21.7
1946	31.5	45.5	46.3	44.0
1950	23.7	41.4	14.9	12.0
1954	23.2	33.2	13.8	8.0
1958	24.7	42.3	20.9	16.0
1962	25.9	43.4	15.4	8.0
1966	22.2	38.1	16.2	15.4
1970	22.6	44.8	16.2	19.2
1974	20.7	22.9	13.8	23.1
1978	17.1	24.9	10.8	24
1982	16.5	26.1	1.7	25
1986	15.8	16.8	3.4	25

Sources: Gerald Benjamin, "Legal and Political Framework," Tables 2 and 3, and Martin Shefter, "Electoral Framework," Table 2, in Benjamin and Brecher, editors, *The Two New Yorks*. New York: Russell Sage, 1988; data on gubernatorial vote compiled by the author from the New York State Bluebook, *The Legislative Manual*, various years.
*Percentage of major party enrollments only.
[†]Percentages of total votes cast, blanks included.

Already suffering declining enrollments in the city since the early 1960s, Republicans experienced a precipitous drop there in votes for the governorship in 1974, the Watergate year. Further enrollment declines followed. In an essay on regional electoral trends in New York, Martin Shefter comments that "in New York City the Democratic gubernatorial vote declined only modestly during the 24 year period [between 1958 and 1982] . . . but the Republican vote plunged by half between the elections of 1970 and 1974. This transformed the Republicans from narrow losers to the position of hopeless minority in gubernatorial elections in the metropolis." Shefter notes that "the Republican party essentially collapsed as a significant participant in local politics in the mid-1970s."[19] There was no classic fusion coalition after the fiscal crisis similar to the one forged behind Fiorello LaGuardia in 1933, probably because the opportunity was preempted by the state's takeover of the city's affairs.

In the Senate, Republicans were able to hold onto six seats in New York City in 1986, retaining the highest percentage of the city's delegation they had been able to achieve since World War II, as a result of artful apportionment and

Table 8.3

Democratic Percentage of Party Enrollments, Votes Cast, and Legislative Seats, the State Outside New York City, 1930–86

Year	Enrollments*	Vote for Governor†	Number of Assemblymen	Number of Senators
1930	29.8	47.5	22.7	11.1
1934	38.9	47.3	20.4	29.6
1938	33.3	33.6	9.1	7.4
1942	30.7	31.1	5.7	7.4
1946	27.3	27.8	4.8	3.2
1950	30.9	34.2	7.2	3.2
1954	30.7	35.3	4.7	3.0
1958	32.4	33.9	7.2	9.1
1962	33.6	34.6	11.8	6.1
1966	38.3	34.8	28.0	12.9
1970	38.9	32.6	17.1	9.7
1974	41.0	46.6	38.8	20.0
1978	43.9	41.8	37.6	17.1
1982	43.7	41.1	42.2	16.7
1986	45.0	56.4	37.6	19.4

Sources: Gerald Benjamin, "Legal and Political Framework," Tables 2 and 3, and Martin Shefter, "Electoral Framework," Table 2, in Benjamin and Brecher, editors, *The Two New Yorks*. New York: Russell Sage, 1988; data on gubernatorial vote compiled by the author from the New York State Bluebook, *The Legislative Manual*, various years.
*Percentages of major party enrollments only.
†Percentages of total vote cast, blanks included.

incumbency power. A controversial decision by District Council 37 of the American Federation of State, County and Municipal Employees, the largest union of city employees, to back Republican Guy Velella in a special election in 1986 in the Bronx after the death of John Calandra was important in reinforcing GOP Senate strength in the city for a time, though questions remain as to how many of these seats can be held as other incumbents die or resign.

In the Assembly, as in gubernatorial elections, 1974 was a turning point, as Democrats seized firm control of that house by winning large numbers of upstate seats. They held most of these, and Democratic preeminence in the Assembly during the 1980 apportionment, a first in this century, allowed the city's dominant party to eliminate Republican districts that had been protected when that party held the majority. This, in 1982, left the GOP with one Assemblyman from the city. After the 1986 election there were two.

Because of the Republican decline in the city, the Democratic base there is more monolithic, although because of lower turnout it is smaller. The real basis of the Democratic success after the mid-1970s was the inroads the party made in the suburbs, upstate cities, and rural areas. Here, as Shefter demonstrated, the

Republican enrollment advantage has narrowed or, in the case of upstate cities, disappeared entirely.

These trends are evident in all four indicators analyzed here: Democratic enrollment; vote for governor outside the city; Democratic seats in the Assembly from outside New York City; and even Democratic Senate seats from upstate (see Table 8.3). With regard to enrollment, Democrats have rarely been as weak outside the city as Republicans were within it, due largely to Democratic strength in such enclaves as the cities of Albany and Buffalo. Historically, the average Democratic percentage of the upstate vote in gubernatorial elections has been consistently closer to the average Democratic percentage of two-party enrollment than the average Republican percentage of the city vote has been to city GOP enrollment. By the mid-1980s, the Democrats were approaching parity with the GOP in its former areas of dominance. Thus, in 1986, 48 percent of the Democratic enrollments and an enormous 68 percent of the vote on the Democratic line for governor were from outside the city.

Before the mid-1960s, Democrats rarely held more than one in ten legislative seats outside New York City. The congruence between partisanship in that institution and geography was almost perfect. This, and state constitutional provisions that assured Republican dominance of at least one house of the state legislature except in extraordinary political circumstances (more about this below), allowed the use of that institution's power to resist city needs or impose extrinsic priorities on it.

Changes occurred for many reasons: some national in scope, others particular to the state. Prominent among these were national Republican debacles in 1964, the Goldwater year, and 1974, the Watergate year; the reapportionment revolution of the mid-1960s; the loss of the Rockefeller incumbency and coattails, also in 1974; and the outmigration of Democratic partisans from the city to its suburbs and exurbs. By the late 1980s, more than two in five Assembly Democrats and about one in five Senate Democrats represented non–New York City districts.

Upstate Democratic seats are as vulnerable to the loss of incumbents as are Republican seats in the city. But just as, in the past, the congruence of partisanship and geography was highly significant for the state/city relationship, now their diminished congruence in both the Senate and Assembly has the overall effect of making the state legislature more responsive to city needs. In the Assembly, this is helped by the fact that, for decades, successive Democratic Speakers have been from one of New York City's boroughs, Brooklyn, even though Democratic control of the Assembly was achieved by victories in upstate districts. Simultaneously, in the 1970s, Republicans came to be dependent on city seats for their margin of control. This development is not unprecedented, but had not been the case consistently in earlier decades in the state's modern history. It assures that the city will regularly command at least an attentive hearing in that body.

The Constitution as Battleground

By law, the New York State government is sovereign and the city is its creature, "a mere tenant at the will of the legislature."[20] The rules of the game for the state/city relationship are set out in the 1894 state constitution, devised by a Republican majority in part to institutionalize limits on the city's influence in the state and on the city's freedom to govern itself.

Provisions in the constitution dating to the mid-nineteenth century, for example, limit city borrowing for city purposes to ten percent, and the property tax levy for combined city and county purposes (beyond that required to repay debt) to two and a half percent of the average full valuation of taxable real estate. In order to alter or provide exceptions to these major determinants of how the *city* government functions, there must be statewide action to amend the *state* constitution.

Two constitutional provisions that have had a special impact on state/city relations concern the apportionment of the state legislature and the degree of home rule that is afforded the city. On apportionment, the city lost the political battle, but won in the federal courts. On home rule, the city won the political battle, but lost in the state courts. Ironically, both the victory and the loss were far less important than expected. Reapportionment on the basis of one-person, one-vote came too late for the city, by then a smaller proportion of the state, to dominate state-level politics as it might have done earlier, on the basis of size alone. And the failure to gain the full measure of home rule became more and more irrelevant as the city, increasingly poorer than the rest of the state, looked to the government in Albany not as an exploitative force, but as a source of resources and innovative solutions to its burgeoning problems.

Reapportionment[21]

At the 1915 state constitutional convention, Al Smith described New York as "constitutionally Republican." By this he meant that the apportionment plan put into effect twenty years earlier, at the 1894 convention, assured that his party could capture the legislature and especially the Assembly in which he then served as minority leader, only in extraordinary political circumstances. Democrats had a majority in the state Senate for twelve years in the seven decades between 1894 and 1964, while the Assembly was in their hands for only three of these years: 1911, 1913, and 1935.

The provisions Smith criticized, still in the state constitution today, effectively blocked New York City from being represented in the legislature in proportion to its population and therefore from capturing a majority in both houses for the two successive years necessary for passing a constitutional amendment to change these rules. Constitutional requirements notwithstanding, the Republican legislature reapportioned when the governor, who had to sign the redistricting bills, was their copartisan and delayed action when he was not. GOP reapportionments were a subject of regular litigation, but when the Democrats did capture both houses and the governorship simultaneously, in 1935, for example, internal divisions kept them from redressing their grievances.

For a half-century, from roughly 1905 to 1955, the city contained more than half the state's population (see Table 8.1). Throughout this period, New York City had 45 percent or fewer of the members of either house. Change came when the U.S. Supreme Court established the one-person, one-vote rule for all state legislative bodies. Republican scrambling to cope with the decision while retaining control was complicated by Democratic capture of both legislative houses in 1964, the first such outcome in a generation and a half. The federal courts directed that a special election be held in districts designed in accord with the Supreme Court's standard in 1965. A crisis in federalism was precipitated when the New York courts attempted unsuccessfully to block elections under a federal court-approved plan that expanded the size of the Assembly, a clear departure from the state constitution. In the process, the city council's traditional role in reapportionment was lost: the right to design Assembly district boundaries within Senate districts in the city.

New York City emerged with 45 percent of the Assembly seats and 46 percent of those in the Senate in 1965, and its share has declined with every succeeding census. For the city, one-person, one-vote came too late to produce a clear legislative majority; its population no longer justified this outcome. In fact, the city proportion of Senate and Assembly seats is lower today than in the malapportioned legislature of 1964 (though it would be lower still under pre-1964 formulas). There were, however, more Democrats in the city's smaller Assembly delegation in 1987 than in its bigger one in 1964, a reflection of that party's control of reapportionment in that house following the 1980 census. And these Democrats, as noted above, were the core of a solid majority. It is a smaller city, but a more powerful one.

Home Rule

Interestingly, when first incorporated in the seventeenth century and for more than a century thereafter, the city was far more autonomous than it is now. As a municipal corporation, under the feudal concept of the corporation prevalent in British law, New York City was distinct in law from other forms of local government, created by the state for its convenience. The city's charter was inviolable, protected even from state intrusion. Change came in the early nineteenth century, a consequence of two familiar factors, one fiscal, the other political. First, the growing city needed additional resources that only the state could authorize. Second, pressures for increased democratization of municipal government provided an incentive for state action to alter political boundaries and extend the franchise within the city. When the courts acknowledged the state's authority to do so, taking a now familiar role but one that then reversed earlier doctrine, "the singularity and autonomy of the city as a local government" was gone.[22]

Following this assertion of authority, however, the state demonstrated a "scrupulous regard for the city's charter" until the decade of the 1850s.[23] The constitution of 1846 transformed state and city politics, making large numbers of offices elective. In this context, the congruence between partisanship and geography asserted itself, and political corruption in New York City provided a compelling rationale for intervention from the state capitol. At this time, the budget of the city, and the patronage it funded, was far larger than that of the state, an obvious inducement to state intervention.

Republicans seized control through forerunners of modern public authorities, boards for police, fire, health, and excise, the jurisdiction of which reached beyond the city's boundaries to include the then independent entities of Brooklyn, Richmond, Queens, and parts of Westchester (later the Bronx). The outcome of a challenge brought to the Court of Appeals by Mayor Fernando Wood is also familiar to the contemporary observer. The legislature had plenary power, the state's highest court said, to "arrange and distribute the administrative functions for such portions as it may deem suitable to local jurisdictions, retaining other portions to be exercised by officials appointed by a central power, and changing the arrangement from time to time."[24]

Democratic party control of state government in the late 1860s brought a measure of returned autonomy to New York City, under a charter that Boss Charles Marcy Tweed of Tammany Hall was said to have "bought" in the state capitol for $600,000.[25] In the highly competitive and partisan political debates of post–Civil War New York, Democratic governors continued to champion home rule, while Republicans resisted it. Though some leaders were genuine reformers, Samuel Tilden, for example, most in both parties appear in retrospect to have been more interested in patronage than in principle.

Eight separate home rule provisions were offered at the 1894 state constitutional convention. Under pressure from the progressives in their own ranks as well as from Tammany Democrats, the Republicans who controlled the convention did include such a provision in the document, though one that reformers thought did not go far enough. It gave the mayors of big cities a suspensive veto over local laws passed in Albany that affected their jurisdictions and required the legislature to proceed by general law, applying to all cities in a class, when affecting cities' "property, affairs or government."[26] Four years later this "mayor's veto" was used by William Strong, the Fusion mayor of New York and Frederick W. Worter, Republican of Brooklyn, in an attempt to block the creation of the greater city. As we know, they failed, in the face of the influence in the legislature of the Republican "Easy Boss," Thomas Collier Platt.

Platt's was a hoary strategy. He sought to minimize New York City's influence by subsuming the city for governance purposes in a larger geographic entity. His notion that the expanded city would become a Republican bastion, based upon the prevailing voting patterns in Brooklyn and the outlying boroughs, proved wrong. But Platt was correct in seeing that "a uniquely large metropolitan region provided a strong case for state interference in local affairs."[27]

Agitation for additional home rule continued for much of the early twentieth century. Measures continued to be introduced in the legislature annually. Finally, in the 1922 session, the Republican Senate passed a much amended compromise measure, which was approved by the voters the following year. The constitutional amendment included seemingly broad language that retained city government power over local "property, affairs or government," and that allowed cities to "repeal, supersede, or modify" special state laws already passed that affected these.[28] Moreover, to partisans of home rule, the prohibition of state legislation "special or local in terms or effect" except by a two-thirds vote in response to an emergency message from the governor, appeared a secure guarantee. But the Court of Appeals proved them wrong.

Following its previously stated preferences for state power over local autonomy, the court continued to permit statutes that were general in language, though specific in effect. Thus, for example, bills drafted to apply to cities over 1 million in population—a category containing only New York City—are regarded as general and therefore not covered by constitutional restrictions regarding legislative passage of local laws. Moreover, the "substantial state concern" doctrine, devised by Chief Judge Benjamin Cardozo in the landmark case of *Adler* v. *Deegan* in 1929, allowed intervention from Albany in city affairs almost at will. Upholding an admittedly salutary state multiple dwelling law that adopted housing codes for New York City alone, Cardozo wrote for the court that "if the subject be in substantial degree a matter of state concern, the legislature may act, though intermingled with it are concerns of the locality."[29]

Later changes in the constitution did little to mitigate the effect of *Adler* v. *Deegan* because they left unaltered the constitutional language concerning local "property, affairs or government." The consequence, according to a review of the results of litigation by Assistant State Attorney General James Cole, is that home rule in New York remains a "ghost."[30]

In fact, by the mid-1960s, gaining home rule ceased to be a priority for the city. At the 1967 constitutional convention, the first since 1894 controlled by a Democratic majority, it did not press the issue. In the midst of the urban crisis, the city's goal became not to achieve autonomy through constitutional change, but to use the document to mandate full state assumption of such costly functions as community development and public assistance. This attempt failed, however, when the 1967 constitution was rejected at the polls.

What is local "property, affairs or government"? What are "matters of substantial state concern''? If they are what the courts say they are, what will the courts say in specific circumstances? The ambiguities surrounding home rule arising out of how the law has developed in New York are enormously important for the city/state relationship. They allow the avoidance of responsibility at both levels. ''Which government should act?'' remains a perennial prior question to ''What must be done, and how best can we do it?''

The city council seeks to minimize its authority to avoid politically unpopular decisions, while sometimes knowingly exceeding its authority, also for political purposes.[31] Simultaneously, state leaders, especially those from the city, want to get credit but not blame. Whether a home rule message is required or not thus often becomes a matter of political negotiation. One study found that between 1970 and 1973, home rule messages were required for only 16 percent of the bills in which New York City was officially interested. Most were in three categories, two of which were highly politicized: requests for new taxes and pension bills.[32]

Dall Forsythe, when he was the state's first deputy budget director in 1987, commented that New York City was ''the only local government that can throw us off, bring us down, sink us, or otherwise make a mess of things for us.''[33] Thus, the state feels it is necessary to attend to the city's needs. But outside of crisis, the nature of the constitutional relationship assures that this will be on the state's terms, not the city's, a reality that places the city in a lobbying role.

Advancing the City's Interests

The state legislative session is a time of opportunity for New York City, but also a time for danger. Every year, the mayor attempts to evolve a single agenda and a unified approach to the governor and legislature for the city, to maximize the gains and minimize the costs. In fact, the mayor's program has become so extensive that it is second in scope and size only to the governor's.

But the mayor does not control all that happens in Albany that affects the city. The governor, legislative leaders, members of the legislature from within and outside the city, and the departments of state government all have their own priorities. Moreover, others within the city government may disagree with the mayor for political or policy reasons, or a combination of these. The city comptroller may differ with revenue estimates or expenditure projections, making negotiations over the financial package more difficult. The council president may be pressing for particular reforms through state law, uncovered as a result of his or her charter-based ombudsman role. The council majority leader, to assert the independence of the body he or she heads, may decide to go into business for himself or herself in Albany. Individual council members, some of whom have served in the state legislature, have relationships in the executive and legislative branches, and, often, connections with borough political organizations, or what remains of them. Even the mayor's subordinates, commissioners, and their deputies in city departments, have ties with counterparts in state government through which they can quietly affect the agenda of city/state relations.

Then there are the pressures on the legislature from within the city but from outside its government: city employee unions, landlord and tenant groups, business interests, good government organizations, contractors with the city, and so on; the list is endless. But the mayor is the personification of the city, and his or her program is the city's program. He or she develops it annually by seeking recommendations during the summer from people throughout the city government and reviewing unsuccessful proposals from previous years. These are then given priority rankings after review by a coordinating committee including the legislative representative and several other top aides and headed by the first deputy mayor. In addition to selecting about ten key items for special attention, an important objective at this stage is to resolve interagency differences, so that the city government is not perceived as pursuing conflicting goals in the state capitol. Often, draft legislation is prepared, a practice that began just after World War II, during the O'Dwyer administration.

The process of presenting the city program has also become highly institutionalized over the last half century. Prior to the LaGuardia administration, the city's lobbyist reported to the Board of Estimate. LaGuardia's long-time representative in Albany, Reuben Lazarus, was based in the law department. In 1949, under Victor Condello, the lobbying effort was incorporated into the mayor's office, where it has been located since. In 1987, the city representative headed an office with a budget of more than $250,000 and a full- and part-time staff of ten.

The degree to which the lobbying effort should be centralized and the city speak to key state officials with one voice has been an important consideration for mayors. Mayor O'Dwyer required clearance of all correspondence and press releases between the city and state officials on legislative issues. Mayors Wagner and Lindsay issued standard executive orders requiring department representatives called to conferences with state legislators or executive branch officials to inform and get clearance from the legislative representative, though in general one scholar found Wagner more comfortable with autonomous city agency activity in Albany than was Lindsay.[34]

The city's lobbying effort is necessarily colored by the mayor's relationship with the governor, which has a personal, political, and institutional dimension. Partisan differences may at times be overcome, at least behind the scenes, as was the case with Mayor Wagner and Governor Rockefeller, while partisan similarities may produce intraparty rivalries between the two most visible politicians in the state when ambitions clash, as with Rockefeller and Mayor Lindsay or Mayor Koch and Governor Cuomo. These latter two relationships were affected at times, as well, by real personal dislike.

But as the *New York Times* noted in an editorial in 1983, "Even if Governor

Cuomo and Mayor Koch weren't long time rivals, even if they were brothers married to loving sisters, their political offices would drive them apart."[35] This institutional tension is confirmed by an earlier observation by Nelson Rockefeller. "It is always difficult . . . for the Mayor of the City of New York and the Governor of New York State," Rockefeller said. "There is a built in conflict there because the Mayor has got a lot of problems and he's got a constant desire to get more support from Albany."[36]

The mayor's links to key legislative leaders are also consequential for the city's efforts in Albany. Again, party ties are not always helpful. As Wallace Sayre wrote:

> Democratic mayors may find state legislators of their own party determined to press again for claims that they or their allies have earlier lost in city hall, or secure compensatory concessions on new matters from the mayor as the price for their help at Albany. Fusion mayors encounter upstate Republican legislators who doubt the mayor's party loyalty and New York City Democratic legislators who regard him as a city hall interloper.[37]

Surely, Mayor Lindsay's intraparty rivalry with leading city Republican State Senator John Marchi made city/state relations more difficult, while Mayor Koch's cross-party endorsement of Marchi eased these relationships, though it created difficulties for Koch with the Senate Democratic leadership.

In any legislative session, gaining additional aid and avoiding additional costs are two key city concerns. The balance between what the city gives to the state and what it gets back has been an issue since at least the middle of the nineteenth century, when Mayor Fernando Wood suggested secession because of inequitable treatment, a proposal that has arisen intermittently ever since.

Recent research shows, however, that "for at least the past three decades, the city has received improved fiscal treatment from the state. The city's proportion of 'giving' is down and its proportion of 'getting' is up."[38] Moreover, the biggest improvements have been in education aid, the area in which the city has, for a long time, been most disadvantaged. Added help has been provided, too, as noted above, through state assumption of services or costs formerly provided or paid for by the city.

The city, of course, always tries to receive more. For example, in 1987, the appeal was for state money to replace half the funds lost as a result of the termination of the federal revenue-sharing program. In 1988, the target was expansion of unrestricted state revenue-sharing, the amount of which had been frozen for several years. Since the mid-1970s, city objectives each year were cast in terms of a "program to fill the gap" between projected revenues and expenditures. There followed a debate between state and city officials about the accuracy of city projections, and what "counted" toward gap-filling aid.

City estimates of its condition did seem to fluctuate in connection with the state budget cycle. In 1986 and 1987, a massive deficit projected in November, while the state budget was being prepared, turned in May, close to the end of the city fiscal year, to a surplus of between \$600 and \$700 million.[39] These fluctuations were due, in part, to hard-to-predict effects of changes in federal tax law. But the incremental timing of their release and the fact of the city's improved fiscal condition have undermined the "gap-closing" approach. In fact, when offered this argument, Governor Cuomo began to point to the city's surpluses, suggesting that perhaps aid should flow in the other direction.

Instead of aid, the state often prefers to give New York City taxing authority not possessed by other localities. This places the responsibility for unpopular action on local officials and minimizes impacts on citizens outside the city. As a consequence of this approach, the city has the most diverse revenue system of any city in the country and the broadest tax powers of any locality in the state. It must lobby annually in Albany, however, for the renewal of "temporary" taxing authority and sometimes for new taxes. Trade-offs are often necessary, especially in the Republican Senate. In 1986, for example, the majority there rejected Mayor Koch's proposed levies on real estate transfers in favor of a hotel room occupancy tax that exported much of the burden to non-New Yorkers.

In 1922, in a speech before the New York State Conference of Mayors in Buffalo, New York City Mayor John F. Hylan denounced the "perfect Niagara of mandatory legislation, carrying colossal financial burdens" that he said poured out of every session of the state legislature.[40] What Mayor Koch described as the "Mandate Millstone" has been a perennial issue in state/city relations.[41] In 1990, the city estimated that costs imposed by the state unaccompanied by funding total \$4.8 billion.

Avoiding additional mandates caused by new regulations, programs, or benefits given city employees is thus a major goal of the city's defensive lobbying effort. Other lobbying to block action may involve "punitive" welfare legislation or structural changes in government that might diminish mayoral power. A special concern is pension costs added largely as a result of public employee union lobbying efforts in the state legislature. Because of the influence of these unions with individual legislators of both parties—their support of incumbents for reelection is almost universal—the city often has to rely on the governor as its last bastion on pension increases.

City lobbying efforts involve a complex and changing combination of inside and outside strategies. The city attempts, through the media, to create a climate of opinion supportive of city goals. Mayor Wagner's "Christmas Letter" outlining city goals was continued, for a time, by Mayor Lindsay. Later, during his second-term fights for more aid, Lindsay's outside strategy used predictions of cataclysm if the state did not act appropriately. Mayor Beame continued the strategy at the beginning of his tenure. In the 1980s, the city did not take this confrontational approach, although in 1988 Mayor Koch did preemptively announce a slowdown in hiring in fear, he said, of state passage of pension legislation he opposed.[42]

Simultaneously, on the inside track, the city deals with the governor and the legislative leaders and their aides. The mayor's annual travels to Albany are largely symbolic; he or she is brought into negotiations by the staff at a critical stage, when added weight is needed, or a matter is involved that only he or she can decide. The city's lobbyist cultivates relationships with key executive branch officials, and leaders, chairs, and top staff in both legislative houses. Bill sponsors are selected to advance city interests, and decisions made on timing and trade-offs. Some bills are "real," others are symbolic. Some are this year's musts, other are introduced to build a constituency for next year or the year after. When there is a confluence of interests, alliances are formed with others, for example, other cities, counties (the focus most recently has been on suburban counties, rather than cities), or good government groups. But for the city in Albany, as for Richelieu's France in Europe, there are no permanent friends, no permanent enemies, only permanent interests.

By and large, New York City has done well in its relationship with New York State in the years since Sayre and Kaufman wrote. But what of the future? There are two scenarios. One suggests that in the tradition of "progressive pragmatism" that has long prevailed in the Empire State, the state government will continue to respond to the most needy New Yorkers, those least able to provide for themselves. Since these people are disproportionately concentrated in New York City, this means that state government will continue to be as supportive of city government in coming decades as it has clearly been in the recent past.[43]

A second prediction is less sanguine. It suggests that the city has become more powerful in state government, although it has become smaller and less economically dominant in the state, because of a unique combination of political circumstances. As the social and economic trends already in motion continue, however, political power will shift further from city to state. Leaders in Albany will become less likely to be recruited in the city and will have less need to respond to it for their political advancement and survival. The city, this view suggests, is at the peak of its influence and power in the state.

Given the historic record, the second of these predictions seems the most likely. The almost total congruence between partisanship and geography in New York, at least for the Democratic party, is gone, and with it that party's need to identify its interests with a smaller and poorer city. But whatever unfolds, an understanding of the state/city relationship will continue to be essential for an understanding of how the city is governed. That is the enduring reality.

Notes

1. Mario M. Cuomo, *Message to the Legislature*. Albany: Executive Chamber, 1987, p. 7.
2. *New York Times*, December 10, 1987, p. B14.
3. Ibid., p. B14.
4. Ibid., p. B14.

5. New York State Department of State, *Local Government Handbook*. Albany: The Department, 1987, p. 45.

6. Hugh L. Carey, "The Governor," in Gerald Benjamin and T. Norman Hurd, editors, *Making Experience Count: Managing Modern New York in the Carey Era*. Albany: The Rockefeller Institute, 1985, pp. 11, 21; for a comprehensive account of the crisis see Robert W. Bailey, *The Crisis Regime*. Albany: SUNY Press, 1984.

7. Cynthia B. Green and Paul D. Moore, "Fiscal Relationship," in Gerald Benjamin and Charles Brecher, editors, *The Two New Yorks*. New York: Russell Sage Foundation, 1988.

8. "Why Mayors Go Nowhere," *Washington Monthly* (January 1982): 55–59.

9. James Musselwhite, "A Comparative View," in Benjamin and Brecher, editors, *The Two New Yorks*.

10. "Commissioner of Social Services," in Benjamin and Hurd, editors, *Making Experience Count: Managing Modern New York in the Carey Era*, p. 97.

11. Milton M. Klein, "New York in the American Colonies: A New Look," in Jacob Judd and James H. Polishook, editors, *Aspects of New York Society and Politics*. Tarrytown: Sleepy Hollow Restorations, 1974, p. 16.

12. Tom Archdeacon, "The Age of Leisler—NYC, 1689–1710: A Social and Demographic Interpretation," in Judd and Polishook, editors, *Aspects of New York Society and Politics*, pp. 63–64.

13. Patricia U. Bonomi, *A Factious People: Politics and Society in Colonial New York*. New York: Columbia University Press, 1971, p. 54.

14. Quoted in Gerald Benjamin, "Legal and Political Framework," in Benjamin and Brecher, editors, *The Two New Yorks*, p. 108.

15. See Chapter 14, on ethnic factors in city governance, by Shirley Jenkins.

16. Gerald Benjamin, "Legal and Political Framework," in Benjamin and Brecher, editors, *The Two New Yorks*, Tables 6 and 7.

17. See the symposium on "Minority Power in City Politics," Rufus P. Browning and Dale Rogers Marshall, editors, *P.S.* (Summer 1986): 573–640, especially the essay by John Mollenkopf, "New York: The Great Anomaly," pp. 591–97.

18. Trent and Alba, "Population," in Benjamin and Brecher, editors, *The Two New Yorks*, Tables 8 and 10; Emanuel Tobier, "Housing," in Benjamin and Brecher, Table 1; Ester Fuchs, "Criminal Justice," in Benjamin and Brecher, Table 1. Also, see generally the most recent edition of *The New York State Statistical Yearbook*. Albany: The Rockefeller Institute, for current data for the appropriate categories.

19. Martin Shefter, "Electoral Framework," in Benjamin and Brecher, editors, *The Two New Yorks*, pp. 168, 172.

20. This is the celebrated Dillon's Rule, propounded in a 1868 case in Iowa, cited in Advisory Commission on Intergovernmental Relations, *The Question of State Government Capability*. Washington: The Commission, 1985, p. 286.

21. This section is drawn substantially from my essay on "Legal and Political Relationships," in Benjamin and Brecher, *The Two New Yorks*.

22. Henrick Hartog, "Because All the World Was Not New York City: Governance, Property Rights and the State in the Changing Definition of a Corporation, 1730–1860," *Buffalo Law Review* 28 (Winter 1979): 108.

23. Abram C. Bernheim, "The Relations of the City and State of New York," *Political Science Quarterly* 9 (September 1894).

24. *People ex rel. Fernando Wood* v. *Simon Draper et al.*, cited in Bernheim, "The Relations of the City and State of New York," p. 389. See also Edward K. Spann, *The New Metropolis: New York City, 1840–1850*. New York: Columbia University Press, 1981, chapter 14.

25. Seymour Mandelbaum, *Boss Tweed's New York.* New York: John Wiley and Sons, 1965, p. 71.

26. Richard L. McCormack, *From Realignment to Reform: Political Change in New York State.* Ithaca, NY: Cornell University Press, 1981, p. 55.

27. McCormack, *From Realignment to Reform: Political Change in New York State,* p. 92.

28. The home-rule provisions of the state constitution are found in the local governments' article, Article 9.

29. *Adler* v. *Deegan,* 251 N.Y.S. 467 (1929), at 485.

30. James D. Cole, "Constitutional Home Rule in New York: The Ghost of Home Rule," *St. John's Law Review* 59 (Summer 1985): 713–49.

31. Frank Macchiarola, "The State and the City," in Robert H. Connery and Gerald Benjamin, editors, *Governing New York State: The Rockefeller Years.* New York: Academy of Political Science, 1974, p. 109.

32. Elizabeth A. Howe, *Intergovernmental Dependence as a Constraint on Urban Reform: New York City's Relationship with the New York State Legislature During the Second Lindsay Administration.* University of California at Berkeley: Ph.D. Dissertation, 1976, p. 109.

33. Citizens Budget Commission, "New York State and City: How Fares the Relationship," in *CBC Quarterly* 7:1 (Winter 1987): 14–15.

34. Howe, *Intergovernmental Dependence as a Constraint on Urban Reform,* p. 413; Martin Shefter, *City Hall and State House: State Legislative Involvement in the Politics of New York City and Boston.* Harvard University: Ph.D. Dissertation, 1970, pp. 32–34.

35. September 3, 1983.

36. Robert Connery and Gerald Benjamin, *Rockefeller of New York.* Ithaca, NY: Cornell University Press, 1979, p. 256.

37. Wallace Sayre, "The Mayor," in Lyle Fitch and Annmarie Hauck Walsh, editors, *Agenda For a City: Issues Confronting New York.* Beverly Hills, CA: Sage Publications, 1970, pp. 586–87.

38. Green and Moore, "Fiscal Relationship," p. 20.

39. *New York Times,* May 6, 1987, p. 1, and May 31, 1987, p. B7.

40. *New York Times,* January 15, 1922, p. 14.

41. Edward I. Koch, "The Mandate Millstone," *The Public Interest* 61 (Fall 1980): 42–57.

42. Howe, *Intergovernmental Dependence as a Constraint on Urban Reform,* p. 44; *New York Times,* January 5, 1988, p. B3.

43. See the remarks of Evan Davis and Norman Adler in *CBC Quarterly* 7:1 (Winter 1987): 12–13. On "progressive pragmatism," see Donald Roper, "The Governorship in History," in Connery and Benjamin, pp. 16–30.

9

The Federal Impact
on City Politics

H. V. Savitch

When Sayre and Kaufman completed their monumental work on New York's government, federal policy claimed no more than a few pages of attention. The two scholars made some mention of the federal role in road building and urban renewal, and, of course, they compiled a list of grants trickling from the federal spigot—but they said scarcely anything about how Washington shaped the internal politics of New York. Sayre and Kaufman could hardly be expected to foresee the rise of a federal agenda on poverty, revenue sharing, and tax policy. They treated the "feds" as something of a sideshow, rather than as makers of the main arena where issues would be fought, coalitions would be formed, and major actors would win or lose.[1]

The federal role has been anything but a sideshow in the tumultuous years since 1960. Analysis of that role must begin with a few critical generalizations. First, federal policy defines the playing field on which city politics is contested. That is, Washington introduces vital policies into the body politic and, therefore, conditions the actors, groups, and coalitions that form around those policies. Rarely does Washington determine winners or losers, though it has given some players a formidable lead. Mostly, the federal policy agenda provides a structure of political opportunities through which groups coalesce and leaders emerge.

Second, New York's coalitions consist of amalgams of politicians (representing different levels of government and different political parties), established interest groups (for example, banks, labor unions, and developers) independent public corporations (such as antipoverty agencies and public authorities), and loosely strung "people groups" (such as racial or ethnic populations and ad hoc neighborhood organizations).

Third, these diverse and complex coalitions behave in unpredictable ways. They have formed surprising alliances (banks and unions), they have lived in uneasy symbiosis (politicians and antipoverty corporations) and they have sometimes become arch rivals (blacks and Puerto Ricans). So whatever might be said about the potential of the federal policy agenda, coalitions that eventually form are precarious and leaders who emerge from them are vulnerable. Washington may set the turf on which New York politics is played, but it is a high-risk venture and politicians, at all levels, understand the gamble.

Fourth, the political road between New York and Washington works both ways. Much as Washington has an impact on New York, the city may also work its influence on Washington. The relationship between the two, however, is neither always reciprocal nor symmetrical. Where Washington's impact on New York is based on long-term public policy, New York's impact on Washington is short lived and limited to political expediency. Washington's impact is likely to be indirect, persistent, and profound. New York's actions have a tendency toward direct personal entreaties, whose consequences are often sporadic. Nothing better illustrates this contrast than episodes surrounding the War on Poverty. During that era, the federal government infused the city with money and laid down policies on how that money was to be applied and who would spend it. Those policies governed the city's political actions and shaped its political coalitions for more than a decade. Meanwhile, all city politicians could do vis-a-vis Washington was influence key actors to either provide supplemental funds or argue for incremental change on how those funds were to be handled. In effect, Washington could (and did) tell New York to take it or leave it.

Fifth, Washington is a town of diverse institutions, whose policies mount incrementally and sometimes pull in different directions. The White House tugs in one direction, Capitol Hill in another, the Supreme Court in still another and the bureaucracy moves with an altogether different compass. Thus, during the first Nixon administration, the White House pressed for welfare reform, while Capitol Hill was split between those on the left, who felt the reform was too reactionary, and those on the right, who believed it was too liberal. At the same time, the Supreme Court expanded the rights of welfare clients in New York City, while the Department of Health, Education and Welfare sought to constrict welfare roles through stiffer eligibility requirements.[2]

A last introductory point is that there is little chance of New York's escaping from Washington. Our federal system, by nature and by modern necessity, is highly interdependent. Despite the efforts by some to draw boundaries between national and local issues, the last quarter of a century demonstrates that the tie between New York and Washington is highly durable. Like Bre'r Rabbit's tussle with the tar baby, Washington's attempt to rid itself of the city has only enmeshed it in other ways. The 1960s and the War on Poverty brought Washington into New York's neighborhoods, the 1970s brought Washington into New York's treasury, and the 1980s and 1990s bring Washington's influence to bear on New York's real estate market. Each of these periods not only shaped the city's coalitions, but was a precursor for a subsequent era of federal influence.

The War on Poverty Under Wagner and Lindsay

Like his brethren in Chicago, New York's Mayor Robert Wagner saw the War on Poverty as an opportunity to create another program for City Hall. And why not? The War on Poverty was not the first time that New York had received federal aid and the Democrats, now in power in Washington, were of Wagner's political stripe.

Wagner's first approach was to put his trusted ally and President of the City Council, Paul Screvane, in charge of the army waging the poverty war. At the top of the pyramid was a Mayor's Council Against Poverty (CAP), which made overall policy. A second and crucial tier was named the Anti-poverty Operations Board (APOB). The APOB was responsible for translating policy and distributing funds to a broader tier of Community Progress Centers—which were controlled by City Hall and likened to front-line troops.

Screvane occupied command posts at the two uppermost tiers. As vice-chairman of CAP he could influence the basic purposes of the program and as chairman of the APOB he could control its most essential actions. Furthermore, all of APOB's other members were commissioners within the Wagner administration. Screvane's own position as second to the mayor and as Wagner's heir-apparent, put the antipoverty program firmly within City Hall.

There were several reasons for keeping such a tight rein on poverty funding. Obviously, City Hall wanted to claim credit for new services, which were supposed to benefit the neighborhoods. New services also meant additional jobs for City Hall loyalists, and this did not escape Wagner's or Screvane's attention. Both men also might have sensed the possible turmoil and competition which could come by spreading poverty resources too thinly. There was no paucity of opposition to Wagner—not in his own Democratic Party where "regulars," "reformers," conservatives, and radicals had battled each other for decades, not in the ghettos where independent antipoverty corporations such as Haryou-Act, Mobilization for Youth, and Youth in Action had already laid out their own turf, and not in the "establishment," where the Ford Foundation and denominational charities put their own stakes down in the War against Poverty. Finally, as moderate Democrats, Wagner's and especially Screvane's electoral coalition lay with the middle class—the homeowners, white ethnic workers, and small businessmen who resided in the outer boroughs. Making too much of a ruckus about poverty might jeopardize Screvane's mayoral ambitions and taint him with the brush of radicalism.

This tight control was soon challenged. The man who began the assault against City Hall was Adam Clayton Powell, congressman from Harlem and chairman of the committee that oversaw much of the Equal Opportunity Act (the central legislation for the War on Poverty). Powell had built his base out of a local movement for civil rights and a black populism, articulated in the streets and churches of Harlem. Though Wagner and Screvane had good relations with Harlem's leading Democrats, they were poaching on Powell's turf, and the congressman knew how to make things difficult for them. Within months after the passage of the Equal Opportunity Act, Powell had Screvane before his committee, testifying about why more money was not going to noncity agencies and why he was not following the legislative mandate to carry out the program with "maximum feasible participation."[3] Screvane pointed to the centrifugal pressures that threatened to rob City Hall of its authority saying:

> We have been in the process over the last few years of doling out pieces of the City of New York to various groups such as Mobilization for Youth, Haryou-Act, Youth in Action. . . . And after you would delineate the area, fund the organization . . . they would say, "Don't come here with any of your services, don't let anyone impinge on our prerogative, because this is our piece of real estate." What would happen ultimately. . . . We would have a number of little private governments in the City of New York. . . . I am not confident at all that we would be able to solve all the problems we have with this kind of approach.[4]

Screvane's argument hardly impressed Powell. "Private government" was exactly what politicians like Powell wanted. Private government was the politician's arsenal. It provided a rich source of jobs for neighborhood supporters, it gave politicians a forum from which to recruit additional supporters, and it furnished the wherewithal for coalition building. Powell knew this as well as anyone else. His former aide, Livingston Wingate, was the executive director of Haryou-Act.

Powell was not alone. In the Democratic party, a fiery liberal congressman named William Fitts Ryan complained to the Office of Economic Opportunity that New York had violated the principle of "fullest possible participation by the poor." In the Republican party, Congressman John Lindsay urged that the poverty "program must rise from the bottom up," lest the city fall into the trap of "welfare colonialism." In Brooklyn's Bedford Stuyvesant, local leaders protested that City Hall was "trying to put Youth in Action out of business." Youth in Action's board of directors adopted a resolution against the city's Community Progress Centers, claiming that such centers would undermine "indigenous community leadership."[5]

These messages were transmitted to Washington, where they received a sympathetic hearing. The Director of the Office of Economic Opportunity (the lead agency in the War on Poverty), Sargent Shriver, made it clear that City Hall would have to change its approach. Shriver also dragged his heels on New York's request for poverty money, and editorials in the local papers blamed the delay on an inept City Hall.

Wagner and Screvane also had gotten the message and, as pragmatists, they decided to adopt another approach. The Mayor's Council Against Poverty became the New York City Council Against Poverty and eventually was enlarged to include 100 members, with a third of them coming from the poor. Sectarian organizations from the city's Catholic, Jewish, and Protestant charities were also accorded a quota of CAP membership. A new Economic Opportunity Corporation was created to take over key functions of APOB. Wagner and Screvane also downplayed the Community Progress Centers. Independent organizations like Mobilization for Youth and Haryou-Act would continue as the leading neighborhood forces against poverty.

Wagner and Screvane had made their compromises, although they still kept a measure of control. Screvane retained pivotal positions on the new CAP as well as on the Economic Opportunity Council. But the effort to steer the War on Poverty from City Hall had failed. It was the federal agenda on poverty, notably the criticism of City Hall's first plan by Sargent Shriver, that led City Hall to seek a modus vivendi and to institutionalize the role of contending interests.

The state of New York also became a player on the field of antipoverty. Under the Equal Opportunity Act, a state governor could veto a grant from Washington. Just as the debate about the organization of the program within the city came to a close, Governor Nelson Rockefeller hinted that he might exercise his right of refusal. What piqued the governor was the plan for Community Progress Centers. The Governor was concerned that these centers would turn into adjunct clubhouses for the Democratic party. Rockefeller hoped that the city, at long last, might elect a Republican mayor and presented a list of preferred neighborhood groups to be enlisted in the fight against poverty. Rockefeller's political ally, Senator Jacob Javits, went to see Shriver, protesting that Paul Screvane would be hiring neighborhood workers. Javits walked away bitterly convinced that poverty would bring a wealth of voters to the Democrats. There was little Rockefeller or Javits could do. Republicans were in no position to turn down $18 million in federal start-up funding.[6]

By the late spring of 1965, the city was readying itself for another election, which would decide whether or not there was a future in the poverty program. To the surprise of political analysts, Paul Screvane lost the 1965 Democratic mayoral nomination to City Comptroller Abraham Beame. While poverty was just one of several major issues, Screvane did not do as well as expected in black and Latino sections. Screvane also lost to Beame in heavily Jewish areas of Brooklyn, Queens, and the Bronx. The vote showed that Screvane was caught in a no-man's land, failing to attract the white middle classes and also falling short on the minority vote. Beame went on to lose the general election to John Lindsay, who campaigned under the banner of the Republican and Liberal parties.

In keeping with his fresh, no-business-as-usual campaign, Lindsay vowed to completely redo his predecessor's poverty apparatus. Lindsay branded the Wagner-Screvane apparatus a "structural monstrosity" and brought in an experienced poverty administrator, Mitchell Svirdoff, from New Haven. Within a short time, Svirdoff had overhauled the existing bureaucracy.

The strategy established a sleek organization, accountable to a single administrator at the top, yet decentralized at the bottom, so that it could be responsive to the neighborhoods. At the top, Lindsay agreed to a new "superagency," the Human Resources Administration, whose head reported to him. Next, a new CAP was created to make policy. This time however, the CAP consisted of just twenty-four members, drawn from neighborhood antipoverty corporations. The twenty-four CAP members had at their disposal a Community Development Agency (CDA), which served as their working staff. Svirdoff took his post at the apex, as head of the Human Resources Administration.

The new structure for poverty was the modus operandi for Lindsay's two terms in City Hall. That structure served two ends: first, the desire to motivate the poor and bring them into power and second, the hope of building a new coalition of blacks, Latinos, and white liberals. Whatever the rationale, Lindsay's strategy was made possible by President Lyndon Johnson's "Great Society" initiatives, which made the White House sympathetic to the Lindsay approach.

Under Lindsay, City Hall identified in word and in deed with the concept of decentralization. By 1969, twenty-five neighborhoods were designated as poverty areas, and seventeen of these were served by antipoverty corporations. These corporations achieved a remarkable degree of autonomy and actively promoted neighborhood populism. A new awakening pushed for greater community activism in the schools, the assertion of tenant and welfare rights, and the acquisition of political power. Clearly, a new stratum of power was rising in the ghettos of New York City. Traditional groups led by the established black clergyman and the veteran teacher were giving way to the unaffiliated, to the young, and, sometimes, to militant nationalists. Lindsay's emissaries took to the streets, in what were called Urban Action Task Forces, in order to talk with *arriviste* leaders, disgruntled residents, and gangs of youth.

Lindsay's support of neighborhood populism was demonstrated in various ways. When in 1967 Congress adopted the Green Amendment, which was designed to allow the mayor to pack citywide CAPs with public officials, Lindsay refused to do so. Instead he limited the number of public officials serving on CAP to the absolute minimum.[7] Neighborhood populism also seeped into other federally sponsored projects, such as the Model Cities agencies. In the South Bronx, Harlem, and Central Brooklyn, those gaining control of the Model Cities agencies were essentially upstart neighborhood entrepreneurs.[8]

Neighborhood populism worked. By the late 1960s and through the early 1970s, community activists were in full swing. Those seeking to arrive at power pushed, and pushed hard, against those who already had a modicum of it. Black parents fought white teachers for control of the schools; tenants faced off against landlords by waging rent strikes; welfare recipients demanded welfare rights from welfare administrators; and black citizens confronted white police over the issue of brutality. Hardly an issue relating to city services was untouched.[9] New York City was openly polarized, as it had never been before. The turmoil that gripped the city almost cost Lindsay his bid for reelection in 1969. In a three-way race that divided the outer boroughs and scattered the white ethnic vote, Lindsay squeaked through. The coalition of blacks, Latinos, and white liberals (mostly from Manhattan) held for Lindsay at the polls.

Short of a citywide race where vital interests were at stake, the coalition was fractious, self-defeating, and volatile. Blacks and Puerto Ricans struggled with one another for jobs in poverty programs. As Washington began to cut federal spending, the struggles intensified. Leaders of different groups denounced one another. The open rooms and storefronts used for community meetings were cordoned off by barriers of silence, as black and Puerto Rican residents glared at one another.

Such was the mood, that the poor turned against Lindsay. The mayor was accused of perpetuating a conspiracy to "divide and rule." Neighborhood corporations renounced CAP and the CDA as enemies of the people. Meetings and press conferences were laced with hyperbole about the "establishment"—most particularly the "Jewish establishment."

The poverty agenda did bolster the careers of a number of black and Latino leaders. Some of these became borough presidents, or members of the city, state, or national legislatures. Others parlayed the poverty program into public grants-manship. As Lindsay retired from office, the coalition split into still looser assemblages, which still struggle for coherence. Meanwhile, the federal agenda left other, more literal, costs—on ledgers in the city comptroller's office.

The Costs of Coalition

When poverty funds first arrived from Washington in early 1965, most people in the Wagner administration were elated. Money from Washington was a windfall, and $18 million represented a 10 percent increase over the amount Washington had sent New York the previous year. John Lindsay had just announced his candidacy for mayor and was less enthralled with Washington. "New York," he said, "had been dreadfully shortchanged." Eighteen million dollars was "just a drop in the bucket," and he pledged to do better.[10]

A year later, Lindsay sat before a Senate committee, attempting to fulfill his campaign pledge. In a boldly written statement, the mayor declared, "There is no solution in New York. The money must come from federal revenues." The junior Senator from New York, Robert Kennedy, took note of Lindsay's statement, asking him exactly how much money the city needed. Lindsay had a ready answer, "We figure that over and above what the city does now with its own resources and with federal and state contributions, over the next 10 years in the area of $50 billion would be required to make this city thoroughly liveable."[11]

Table 9.1

New York City Expense Budget and Federal Aid, Selected Fiscal Years, 1960–74

Fiscal year	Expense budget (in millions)	Federal aid (in millions)	Federal aid (percent of budget)
(Wagner)			
1960	2,232.2	104.9	4.7
1962	2,603.3	143.7	5.5
1964	3,103.2	180.2	6.0
1966	3,700.2	292.1	7.7
(Lindsay)			
1967	4,497.1	531.6	11.8
1969	6,066.6	895.8	14.8
1971	7,827.6	1,298.0	16.6
1973	9,325.6	1,911.6	20.5
1974	10,248.6	2,021.5	19.7

Source: *Comptroller's Annual Report*, 1959–60 through 1974–75. Office of the Comptroller, The City of New York.
Notes: Fiscal years ending June 30. A newly elected mayor, taking office on January 1, inherits the budget of the previous mayor. Thus, the fiscal 1966 budget was framed during the administration of Robert Wagner, although John Lindsay began his first term in January 1966.

Fifty billion dollars is a hefty sum, even by today's standards. In 1966 it was enormous, amounting to 38 percent of total federal government revenues. In effect, Lindsay was asking for a doubling of his city's budget for each year of the coming decade. Most observers granted the statement as political license. Lindsay could not be serious, and was simply using the figure in order to underscore the severity of New York's problems.

Yet if Lindsay could claim any success, it was the ballooning of New York City's budget and the escalating amounts received from Washington. Table 9.1 portrays this trend for selected years, beginning with part of the Wagner administration in 1960 and going through the Lindsay period.

Lindsay had fallen far short of his fondest wishes, but the amounts he garnered for city expenditures were unprecedented. By the end of his second term, the budget shot up from $4 to $10 billion. Lindsay more than doubled the city's costs, and while he did this, federal funding increased more than fourfold. By Lindsay's last years in office, federal dollars accounted for one-fifth of the city's revenue. Admittedly, this was not all the mayor's doing. Government spending was embedded in the temper of the times, but Lindsay took advantage of those times. Indeed, he led the parade of mayors who exhorted the American people to do more, and he also led them to lobby at the state and national capitals.[12]

These efforts not only brought new dollars from Washington, they also brought new people. Armed with the latest management techniques, young administrators came to New York from Washington, the foundations, the universities, and other cities. They were an altogether different breed of bureaucrat. Fresh, self-assured, and brazen, they rubbed abrasively against their more traditional counterparts.

The new bureaucrats arrived with a belief in radical innovation and with the confidence that they could set things right with better techniques and with more money. Their philosophy was to energize the administrative routines of the city by eliminating old bureaucratic shackles. They would harness this freedom to public purpose by drawing tighter links between policy aims and budget dollars. Program, Planning, and Budget Systems, or PPBS, became a watchword at City Hall.

The change was immediate and the attitude toward experimentation infectious. Within the first year of his tenure, Lindsay and his aides described to a Senate committee the innovations taking place in city government. More than fifty city departments were collapsed into ten "superagencies," a new policy council was organized to implement PPBS, and the city began to enlist groups of welfare recipients to advise social workers. The idea was not just to guide the bureaucracy from on top, but to pressure it from the bottom. As the mayor explained, "Those who receive services must also shape those services."[13]

One proposal to free up the welfare bureaucracy allowed potential recipients to declare eligibility rather than wait until the completion of a lengthy investigative process. The declaration procedure was supposed to do for welfare what the selective audit had accomplished for the Internal Revenue Service—assure enough honesty among those filing so that the city could be relieved of the chore. The mayor's welfare commissioner pointed out at the Senate committee hearing that existing procedure "demeans people's dignity, destroys it, and . . . the welfare worker spends 95 percent of his time checking up rather than helping people."

The shift at City Hall contributed to a ground swell in the welfare rolls. In 1966, the first year of the Lindsay administration, New York had an average monthly case load of a half million. Two years later that number climbed to over three-quarters of a million. By 1970, that number passed the million mark. Before Lindsay left office in 1976, the average monthly case load was 1.2 million.[14] Taken alone, New York's welfare population made it the sixth largest city in America. The costs were substantial. Washington and Albany paid for three-quarters of most welfare payments, while the city picked up the remainder. In the mid-1970s, payments to welfare recipients amounted to over $1 billion annually, consuming more than 15 percent of the city's out-of-pocket expenditures.[15]

Welfare was just one of the types of city spending that fostered the Lindsay coalition and, eventually, the dissolution of that coalition. Every expenditure created a beneficiary, and many beneficiaries joined the mayor's coalition. Moreover, for every claim from a service receiver there was a claim from a service provider. Parents expecting better performance from the schools would be met by teachers striking for higher salaries. Communities wanting comprehensive health care would be trailed by hospital personnel demanding more resources.

The climate of heightened expectations and realized claims—and higher municipal spending—permeated municipal services. The adoption of an open-admissions policy in the City University was followed by a huge building program and salaries for professors, which made them the envy of academe. Nor was it coincidence that the heated debate over a police-civilian review board was succeeded by the most generous labor contract for policemen in the city's history.[16]

Over Lindsay's eight years, claims of this sort fed on one another. Once bona fide members of the coalition institutionalized their claims, nonsupporters filed counterclaims—and surprised themselves by winning. By Lindsay's second term, the coalition of "people groups" from the neighborhoods, minorities, and liberals were joined by nonsupporters, like teacher and police unions, in demanding and receiving favorable treatment. Through the bountiful years, Lindsay managed to find enough money to satisfy these contending interests. But there was often a hitch in federal aid. Because of matching requirements, the dollars from Washington stimulated city expenditures. Sometimes the match was modest, while at other times it was heavy. Aside from welfare, the most severe burdens were attached to medicaid payments. Matching funds, in the range of 20 to 30 percent, were also required for poverty and Model Cities programs as well as for mental health centers—to say nothing about the rebuilding of highways and mass transit.[17]

The lean years, when federal aid was cut, played havoc in the city. Those who came to depend on the poverty program were threatened with layoffs, and they turned to Lindsay. A typical scenario put the mayor in the ungainly position of having to announce the cutback, while denouncing the federal government as the culprit. Even if the poor accepted the mayor's assessment, Washington was too far a distance for them to travel, so they protested to City Hall. Hundreds of demonstrators would mass, carrying placards and disrupting traffic. Clapping to cadence, the demonstrators would shout, "more money, more money." Minor incidents of violence were followed by the ominous plea of "We want to work—not riot." Not wanting to reward the threat, Lindsay would defer action, only to announce a short time later that the city would make up for lost federal funding. By the time the Nixon White House had lopped off large parts of the War on Poverty, the coalition had also become a ward of City Hall.

The profound fiscal implications of these policies were not apparent in the early 1970s. However, there were clues, in the highs both the city and the state had attained in all the wrong categories. The city budget soared higher each year; the share of personal income absorbed by state and local government taxes was higher for residents of New York State than for residents of any other state, by a wide margin; and, by an even wider margin, New York City's municipal indebtedness, however measured, exceeded that of all other cities.[18]

The Fiscal Bubble Breaks on Abe Beame

When Abraham Beame became mayor of New York City in 1974, he inherited an unstable situation. The federal agenda had laid out the playing field, where poor neighborhoods had been succored by City Hall and the municipal unions had achieved recognition and power. Beame stepped onto a field where the players were already lined up, their positions defined and their performance blessed. Had the fiscal crisis never occurred, Beame would have been a maintaining mayor—a man who balanced competing claims on an expanding budget. True to his image as a reliable bookkeeper, the new mayor would have adjusted rather than remade the balance of political interests. When the fiscal crisis did occur, Beame faced those interests on a bloated fiscal bubble, ready to burst. The party stalwart from Brooklyn found himself captured by circumstances.[19] The fiscal crisis broke up existing alignments and ushered in a new coalition, made possible by still another federal policy agenda.

As early as the spring of 1974, New York bankers sounded an alarm about the city's bleak prospects for borrowing. Beame resisted and continued to resist, explaining a year later "that in the real world, all governmental budgets must go up and . . . borrowing will also go up."[20] By the end of 1974, the alarm rang on a genuine crisis. Bankers officially informed City Hall that the financial markets were closed. Beame fought back, accusing the banks of "poisoning our wells," and urged them to "sell the city to the rest of the country."[21]

Denunciations and pleas could not replenish the city's financial stream. Beame turned to Governor Hugh Carey, who, among other things, turned to Washington for help. In an effort to obtain $1.5 billion in aid, both men visited the White House. Their meeting with President Gerald Ford and Vice-President Nelson Rockefeller soon became a grilling session. Ford questioned Beame about excessive expenditures for housing assistance, the cost of transit subsidies, and, finally, about free tuition at the City University. "Mr. President," Beame replied, "if it were not for free tuition, I would not be here today."[22]

Ford's own skepticism and pronouncements by key advisers about New York's profligate ways were not encouraging. New York's call for help was not popular in the rest of the country, least of all in Ford's Republican party. The president was preparing for his party's nomination and he needed the support of conservatives. Still, Beame hung on, and he spoke hopefully about the president's "open mind."[23] The next day Beame received a letter from the

White House. Ford had turned down all the mayor's requests, denying the city advances on medicaid payments, refusing to permit the Treasury to buy city notes, and disallowing the possibility that Washington would furnish any guarantees. Instead, the President counselled fiscal discipline, told the mayor to curtail services, and suggested that the city go to Albany for help.[24]

For the time being, there was little Beame or Carey could do but turn inward. Under prompting from Albany, the city began to tighten its fiscal belt. From the summer of 1975 onward, a wave of cutbacks swept through municipal payrolls. City Hall was forced to change its priorities and, as a result, its supporting coalitions were radically altered. In July, cuts in poverty programs and the announcement of 40,000 layoffs brought the poor and the municipal labor unions onto the streets.[25] The neighborhood poor marched across the city's bridges straight to City Hall. Members of the police and fire forces went on a "job action," slowing down their work or calling in sick. Sanitation workers staged wildcat strikes, and tons of garbage piled up on the sidewalks. The demonstrations were sprinkled with minor acts of violence and petty vandalism, mostly by laid-off workers. The police and firefighters' unions added a special twist to the demonstrations by organizing a "fear city campaign." In an effort to intimidate City Hall, the unions distributed pamphlets whose covers pictured a shrouded skull with the caption, "Welcome to Fear City." Inside pages warned, "By the time you read this, the number of public safety personnel available to protect residents and visitors may have already been further reduced. . . . The best advice we can give you is this: Until things change stay away from New York City."[26]

Though most of the union workers eventually recovered their jobs, this budgetary retreat set the pattern. Welfare payments were frozen, poverty programs slowly disappeared, transit fares increased, and the City University began to charge tuition. New York's welfare state, as critics called it, was discredited and falling apart. And with that, so too was the Lindsay coalition. Yet for all the cuts, the city could not meet its payments and it would continue to slide. Beame and Carey knew this. They also knew they would be back in Washington, asking for help.

Friends in Washington advised that if New York planned to knock once again on the White House door, it had better do so with a plausible case in hand. This required extraordinary measures. Not only must the city make cuts, but it must show a sacrificial readiness to raise additional revenues and curtail the discretion of reckless politicians. In short, City Hall's ability to make coalitions by means of the budgetary dollar must be checked.

Between May and October 1975, a tier of new supervisory agencies had been created. An Emergency Financial Control Board (EFCB) reviewed the city's budget, financial plan, and all contracts. Enforcing the new austerity, a special deputy state comptroller (SDC) audited the city's books and a Municipal Assistance Corporation (MAC) took charge of issuing new securities and held a portion of collected taxes. By the fall of 1975, the city began to replead its case. This time the mayor was shuttled to the background. A new coalition represented the city. Banks and labor unions had joined with key politicians. The names of those who gave testimony before congressional committees bespeak the content of the group—David Rockefeller (Chase Manhattan Bank), Elmore Patterson (Morgan Guaranty), Victor Gotbaum (American Federation of State, County and Municipal Employees), Albert Shanker (American Federation of Teachers), Felix Rohaytn (chairman of MAC), and Governor Hugh Carey.

The coalition came to Washington as both saviors and as culprits. They had been instrumental in putting together the financial arrangements that allowed the city to stay temporarily afloat, yet they were held responsible for having created the fiscal chaos. The bankers were blamed for having fed the city's habit with high-cost loans. The unions were charged with bilking the city through excessive wage agreements. The politicians, whom Carey represented, were accused of covering up these excesses. There they were, in Washington, trying to convince the federal government that the bankers needed to be saved from bearing the losses of a municipal bankruptcy; that the unions ought to have their wage agreements protected; and that the politicians should be shielded from public reprobation.

The mood on both sides of Pennsylvania Avenue was grim. Members of Congress reported that constituents were 30- or 40-to-1 against helping the city. One congressman accused Beame "of buying elections for years and years." Another said that in his area, "when college students want to go to college, they pay tuition. If they cannot afford [it], they work. People pay tolls to travel the highways and bridges."[27] Congress reflected much of the national sentiment, and polls indicated a 49-to-42 percent split against aid for the city.[28]

Elsewhere in Washington, the head of the Federal Reserve, Arthur Burns, continued to oppose aid and warned that federal generosity would encourage other hard-pressed communities to follow New York. Burns anticipated that should New York default, he would make credit available to banks caught in a "liquidity squeeze."[29] Secretary of the Treasury William Simon also prepared for the worst. He argued that the best remedy for the city was a default and the discipline of the financial market.[30] So many people were saying no to New York that it should not have been a great surprise when President Ford announced, in a speech on October 29, 1975, that he would "veto any bill that had, as its purpose, a federal bailout of New York City." The blame was New York's:

> Responsibility for New York City's financial problems is being left on the front doorstep of the federal government—unwanted and abandoned by its real parents.
>
> What I cannot understand—and what nobody should condone is the blatant attempt in some quarters to frighten American people and their representatives

in Congress into panicky support of patently bad policy. The people of this
country will not be stampeded; they will not panic when a few desperate New
York officials and bankers try to scare New York's mortgage payments out of
them.[31]

Most New Yorkers failed to appreciate the president's advice. The headline in
the *Daily News* interpreted Ford's remarks with journalistic bluntness as it read,
"FORD TO CITY: DROP DEAD." Below the boldface type, was a little noticed subhead, which in the same staccato fashion read, "Stocks Skid: Dow
Down 12."[32] While the *Daily News* headline won New York's attention, the
subhead would command national policy. New York City had issued an enormous amount of debt securities, and investors were frightened at the thought of
bankruptcy. The collapse of the nation's largest city might, like a row of domi-
noes, bring down other sectors of the economy. The nation's most prestigious
bankers appeared on Capitol Hill to express worry. Calls from international
investment houses repeated the same theme.[33]

Independent studies confirmed these apprehensions. The Federal Deposit Insurance Corporation revealed that a default would bring "serious consequences"
to 271 banks, spread through 34 states. These banks held New York securities
equal to 20 percent of their net worth. Until November, Burns believed he could
protect these banks from a "liquidity squeeze." By November, he found his
earlier solution had touched the tip of an iceberg. Two-thirds of New York
securities, or some $4.9 billion, were held by scores of insurance companies,
annuity funds, widows, and retirees. According to last-minute surveys, as many
as 160,000 investors held New York paper. This did not include another $3
billion held by commercial banks.[34]

By early November, the White House was speaking more softly. Words like
"stretching out" New York's debt substituted for the opprobrium of a
"bailout." White House spokesmen insisted that Ford's firmness had already
forced New York to take hard steps, and that federal aid to supplement those
decisions would not constitute a "bailout." The change in direction was quickly
transmitted to Congress, and in late November Ford asked that Congress authorize direct Treasury loans to New York City. Even with White House support,
congressional leaders had to struggle. The House voted 213 to 203 in favor of the
legislation. Only 38 Republicans, a third of whom came from New York State,
voted in favor. In the Senate, opponents promptly launched a filibuster, and
leaders had to invoke cloture to stop debate. The measure eventually carried by a
vote of 57 to 30. By the end of 1975 Ford signed the New York City Seasonal
Financing Act, which authorized loans of up to $2.3 billion at any one time, the
loans made in any one fiscal year to be repaid by the last day of that fiscal year
and at an interest rate 1 percent higher than the prevailing Treasury rate; the
lending authority expired on June 30, 1978.

For the time being the fiscal crisis had passed. New York would have to walk the Washington pavement three years later, but 1975 was a crucible. Heaving a sigh of relief, Abe Beame told reporters that 1975 proved New York had "friends in Washington."[35] The year was much more than a test of friendship. It brought in a new coalition on the wings of a budgetary crisis, and it tested the viability of that coalition in the halls of the White House and Capitol Hill. When all the negotiations were completed, the truest test was whether politicians, bankers, and union leaders could meet the conditions of the loan. City politicians had to accept state and federal supervision and close scrutiny; banks and investors had to accept a debt moratorium on short-term notes and a rollover of other securities; the unions came to accept "wage freezes" and were compelled to agree to the investment of substantial portions of the municipal pension funds in city securities.[36]

By the time Beame left office, the new coalition was working smoothly. In 1977, the coalition was institutionalized as the Municipal Union–Financial Leaders group (MUFL). Composed of the chief executives of six large banks, six union leaders, and others, MUFL met regularly to take positions on major decisions confronting the city.[37] MUFL was held together by the cement of mutual interest among big finance, organized labor, and top politicians. Bankers and union leaders recognized the constraints imposed on each other because of the city's vulnerability and agreed to limit claims against New York's political executives.

In obvious ways, New York was at the mercy of Washington's decisions. In still other ways, New York impacted on national politics and shaped policy. Ford's "Drop Dead" statement turned out to be a personal blunder, and Jimmy Carter made the most of it. Shortly afterward, the Democrats put out the word that, "Jimmy Carter would never tell New York to drop dead." In the event, Gerald Ford lost New York State in the 1976 elections, by 275,000 votes out of 6.4 million cast. Had Ford won New York's 41 electoral votes, he would have been back in the White House. By the end of 1975, the city's relationship with Washington had matured into political intimacy. To an extent, New York had become a ward of the federal government, but the "feds" too had become imprisoned by the city. Given the risk that New York's bankruptcy posed to the rest of the nation, Washington had no choice but to bail out the city. During the height of the crisis, Beame and Carey pointedly told Congress that it would be cheaper to help the city than to allow it to collapse. Quoting from other sources, Beame told members of the House that a New York default would increase interest rates by $3 billion. "I believe," said Beame, "it is $14 for every man, woman and child, if the Government fails to act."[38] Carey boosted the cost by mentioning that federal troops might have to be called in to run New York's police, fire, and other services. William Proxmire, who chaired the Senate committee, articulated the discomfort of his colleagues, "What you are telling us is whether the Federal Government provides a guarantee now or not, the Federal

Government is almost certain, in your judgment to have to act to assist New York. It is simply a matter of when and how.''[39]

Koch Amends the Coalition

Nearly three years later, when Congress again held hearings on aid to New York, it had less to worry about. Edward Koch had been a congressman for nine years prior to becoming mayor, and unlike Beame, could appreciate the vantage point from Capitol Hill. While sitting in Congress as mayor-elect, he pledged that once in City Hall he would not countenance fiscal gimmicks, that he would do whatever necessary to balance the city's budget, and that, if all else failed, he would lay off municipal workers and reduce services. Wrote Koch, ''I have said before and I reiterate here, that there will be no bankruptcy for the City of New York. I was not elected as the 105th mayor of this city to turn its government over to a federal judge. Whatever has to be done will be done by this mayor.''[40]

The words and the attitude impressed congressional skeptics. Senator Proxmire spoke in an altogether different tone from his grimmest remarks years earlier. In an approving paraphrase of Koch, Proxmire exclaimed that now New York had a mayor who was ready to shut down the subways and stop municipal building elevators in order to avert collapse. Koch had a ''tough, disciplined attitude,'' explained Proxmire, which the Senator had never sensed in Abe Beame or in Hugh Carey.[41]

Koch's move to City Hall together with Jimmy Carter's ascendancy to the White House made the city's second request for federal aid a good deal easier. By the summer of 1978, Congress had approved new fiscal aid for New York and President Carter had signed the legislation. This time there were no sums given directly to the city in the form of short term or ''seasonal'' help. The new act emphasized indirect assistance through long-term loan guarantees of up to $1.65 billion, which could be committed for as long as fifteen years.[42] Washington was pleased with the city's recovery, but wary about extending its involvement and warned that this was the last time New York (or any other city) could count on special help.

Now it was New York's turn to reciprocate and Ed Koch was unflinching. The new mayor willingly followed through on what his predecessor was forced to begin. Koch held down municipal services and clamped down on the number of welfare recipients through stricter administration. Through the initiative of the state, and with Koch's assent, welfare spending was brought to a standstill. This would have been difficult enough if prices were stable, yet Koch exacted this toll during a time of double-digit inflation. By 1981 the number of welfare recipients had declined to its lowest point in more than a decade.

Again, reading the budget reveals an interesting relationship between city expenditures, federal aid, and political coalitions. Table 9.2 shows budgetary figures for the end of Beame's tenure up through Koch's first term.

Table 9.2

New York City Expense Budget and Federal Aid, Fiscal Years 1976–81

Fiscal year	Expense budget (in millions)	Federal aid (in millions)	Federal aid (percent of budget)
(Beame)			
1976	12,764.0	2,317.2	18.2
1977	13,569.3	2,728.1	20.1
1978	13,998.6	3,291.7	23.5
(Koch)			
1979	13,617.3	2,973.0	21.8
1980	13,210.8	2,623.2	19.9
1981	14,022.4	2,733.3	19.5

Source: *Adopted Budgets: Fiscal Years 1976–1987 (Expense, Revenue and Capital)*, Office of Management and Budget, The City of New York.
Notes: Fiscal years ending June 30. A newly elected mayor, taking office on January 1, inherits the budget of the previous mayor. Thus, the fiscal 1978 budget was framed during the administration of Abraham Beame, although Edward Koch began his first term in January 1978.

We should note that much of Beame's budget was foisted upon him, either directly by the state or by the new fiscal authorities, notably the EFCB. Whatever the source of the constraint, the impact was unmistakable. In contrast to the long period of rapidly rising budgets between 1960 and 1975 (Wagner, and especially the Lindsay and early Beame administrations), by 1976 the expense budget had begun to stabilize. Thereafter, between 1977 and 1980, there was barely movement and one year saw a slight dip in total expenditures. Federal aid also remained stable until 1978, and after that year it began to shrink. The fiscal crisis may have given the initial impetus for political change, but postcrisis budgets converted that change into a durable pattern that devastated the antipoverty coalition.

The disintegration of once powerful constituencies was not just due to budget stringency. Policy decisions also tore at their influence. Upon coming to office, Koch took the poverty bit in his teeth by abolishing all of the city's neighborhood corporations and replacing them with a smaller number of advisory boards. Whatever antipoverty work remained was then parceled out to other agencies. Model Cities was dissolved in much the same way. Its central office was dismantled and its functions scattered. Thus, with a few strokes of the pen, Koch obliterated the bureaucratic apparatus that had once been an element of the antipoverty coalition.

The municipal labor unions were far less tractable. They were well organized, led by tough negotiators, and, because they held a huge amount of New York securities, were at once the city's work force and its creditors. On some issues Koch gave up more than he would have liked. On others, he managed reasonably well. Essentially, the mayor held the municipal wage scale to acceptable limits while winning some concessions through "givebacks" and productivity increases.

The great difference made by Koch occurred in the qualitative relationships between municipal unions and City Hall. The mayor's acerbic style and "go it alone" attitude discouraged any close partnership with organized labor. As labor contracts came due during his first term, Koch would publicly challenge the unions before privately bargaining with them. Koch was especially jealous about protecting what he regarded as mayoral prerogatives. He insisted on broad managerial powers for his commissioners and he rejected union demands for advanced review of his budget.[43]

Koch's behavior created a different political climate, a new set of expectations, and, ultimately, a change in the coalitions that influenced public policy. More than anything, Koch was anxious to show Washington that New York was on a new tack, that it was friendly to business and that it was "a place to create jobs and make a buck."[44] To "make a buck" Koch was determined to give a buck—and more than that. The city embarked on programs that granted hundreds of millions of dollars in tax benefits to encourage development. Commercial and residential investors were given tax abatements to refurbish abandoned space or to build anew. Tax allowances were granted in some of the most congested neighborhoods, adding to the Midtown skyline, as well as in the less sought-after terrain of the West Side. City Hall pumped public and private money for development through an alphabetocracy of agencies such as the Industrial and Commercial Incentive Board (ICIB), which oversaw tax exemptions, the Economic Capital Corporation (ECC), which coordinated loans to private enterprise, and the Office of Economic Development (OED), which recruited venture capital. To top it off, Koch helped establish the New York City Partnership, whose members included the city's corporate elite and whose design was to promote business growth.

It was not that Koch ignored the rest of the city in order to cultivate business. Where money was available, City Hall would plow it into other constituencies. Thus when President Jimmy Carter announced opportunities for the cities, Koch made the most of them. Comprehensive Employment Training Assistance (CETA) and countercyclical revenue sharing were used to pay the salaries of laid-off municipal workers. Community Development Block Grants were used to rehabilitate housing. What counted most, however, were policies that fostered self-sustaining, long-term growth. The strategy was to apply public resources, under favorable market conditions, to leverage substantial amounts of private investment. By this logic all signs pointed to the development of high priced real estate in Manhattan.[45] One of the more attractive programs coming from Washington was the Urban Development Action Grant or UDAG. Between 1977 and

1982, half the UDAG funding was applied to major projects centered in Manhattan. Outer boroughs received only bits and pieces of small projects.[46]

The decision to exploit Manhattan's great lure supplied the rationale for Koch's eventual support of Westway. The massive six-lane, partially depressed highway along the Hudson from the Battery to 42nd Street would have cost an estimated $4 billion, making it the most expensive highway per square inch in the world. As an interstate highway, Washington would have paid for 90 percent of Westway's cost. But Westway was much more than a highway. It was a full-fledged real estate development with housing, commercial, and recreational facilities built above and around it. As it turned out, Westway was defeated, but it furnishes an excellent case of how the potential for federal funds can cement a powerful coalition among politicians, bankers, real estate developers, and organized labor. As Ronald Reagan campaigned for the presidency in 1980, Koch became a more exuberant champion of business and so too, it seemed, of the Republican nominee. Koch invited Reagan to Gracie Mansion and spoke kindly of the Republican while he campaigned for office and after he won the presidency. The mayor's flirtation with Republicanism blossomed into a courtship when Koch accepted its endorsement during the 1981 mayoral race.

Koch's behavior puzzled his supporters and angered his critics. Reagan was set on disposing of federal aid for the cities and did so at his first opportunity. Community development and housing programs were cut to almost nothing, CETA and countercyclical aid were eliminated, revenue sharing fell along with a host of other measures intended for urban residents.

The city's budget provides some interesting clues about what was happening and how Koch was responding to the federal agenda. Table 9.3 shows budgetary amounts for the 1980s up to 1990.

More significantly, this money flowed to the very constituencies that fed the Koch strategy—real estate developers, investment bankers, corporations, and a rising class of "yuppies." As in previous decades, Washington supplied the opportunities for City Hall to shape coalitions. This time, it provided a post-fiscal crisis mandate to curtail social welfare in favor of business growth. As the crisis faded, the mayor took advantage of a surfeit of investor dollars, spurred again by Washington policies, to heat up Manhattan with economic development. It is impossible to know whether this came about by elite design, Ed Koch's prescience, political reflex, guesswork, or a combination of the above. What we surely do know is that during the mayor's three terms he managed to float with the tides of austerity and prosperity. Koch is an arch pragmatist, and he survived in politics by moving with dominant currents—in large part flowing from the Washington agenda—rather than struggling against them. Future mayors, like John Lindsay and Ed Koch in the recent past and Fiorello LaGuardia fifty years ago, will confront Washington-originated changes and currents that are no less powerful.

Table 9.3

New York City Expense Budget and Federal Aid, 1982–90

Fiscal year	Expense budget (in millions)	Federal aid (in millions)	Federal aid (percent of budget)
(Koch)			
1982	15,106.4	2,608.9	17.3
1983	15,673.0	2,445.0	15.6
1984	16,975.0	2,693.7	15.9
1985	18,549.0	2,907.5	15.7
1986	20,427.4	2,998.7	14.7
1987	21,359.8	2,364.4	11.1
1988	22,734.0	2,273.4	10.0
1989	25,396.0	2,704.0	10.6
1990	26,650.0	2,495.0	9.3

Sources: *Adopted Budgets: Fiscal Years 1976–1987 (Expense, Revenue and Capital)*, Office of Management and Budget, The City of New York. Figures for 1988 to 1990 are derived from *The Executive Budget*, Office of Management and Budget, The City of New York, 1988, 1989, 1990.

Notes

1. Out of more than 700 pages of text, Sayre and Kaufman devote less than 30 pages to the role of "other governments" and only a portion of that role is attributed to Washington. See Sayre and Kaufman, *Governing New York City*. New York: Norton, 1960, Chapter 15.

2. For a superb history of this subject see Daniel Moynihan, *The Politics of a Guaranteed Income*. New York: Basic Books, 1973, Chapters 6 and 7.

3. For the evolution, operations, and distortions of the concept of "maximum feasible participation" see Daniel Moynihan, *Maximum Feasible Misunderstanding*. New York: The Free Press, 1969.

4. James Greenstone and Paul Peterson, "Reformers, Machines, and the War on Poverty," in James Q. Wilson, editor, *City Politics and Public Policy*. New York: Wiley and sons, 1968, pp. 286–89.

5. The quotations in this paragraph are from the *New York Times*, various issues in April and May 1965.

6. Nelson Rockefeller was a formidable figure throughout the state and sensitive to federal intrusions and competition from the Democratic party. When the city's plan for its War on Poverty awarded too much discretionary authority to an Equal Opportunity Corporation run by City Hall, Rockefeller balked and refused to endorse the plan. Eventually a compromise was worked out, so that the Equal Opportunity Corporation became the Equal Opportunity Committee. Under that compromise, the Equal Opportunity Committee could receive federal funds, but it could not override state agencies.

7. Lindsay did keep control of the poverty bureaucracy run out of City Hall, most particularly the Community Development Agency (CDA). While Lindsay made the professional resources of the CDA available to neighborhood corporations, he made sure that its administrators were loyal to him. The CDA's first commissioner, George Nicholau,

was replaced by a black who gained experience in the neighborhood poverty movement, Major Owens. Owens soon became a Lindsay stalwart and served as a bridge between poor neighborhoods and City Hall. (Owens later was elected to the U.S. House of Representatives from a Brooklyn district.) For an enlightening case study on the early years of the poverty program in New York see Stephen David, "Welfare: The Community Action Program Controversy" in Jewel Bellush and Stephen David, editors, *Race and Politics in New York City*. New York: Praeger, 1971, pp. 25–58.

8. The Model Cities program was an ambitious effort to improve housing and neighborhood public services, and as committed to popular participation as the neighborhood antipoverty corporations. Model Cities funding often generated still more coalitions of the poor, which staked out claims in the body politic. See Charles Haar, *Between the Idea and the Reality*. Boston, MA: Little, Brown, 1975; and Bernard Frieden and Marshall Kaplan, *The Politics of Neglect*. Cambridge, MA: The MIT Press, 1975.

9. The literature that came out of this period of great controversy in New York City is quite extensive and covers a number of policy areas. For a review of multiple policy areas, consult Bellush and David, *Race and Politics in New York City*; in education, the outstanding study is David Rogers, *110 Livingston Street*. New York: Random House, 1969; for police, see Arthur Niederhoffer, *Behind the Shield*. Garden City, NY: Anchor Books, 1967, and Algernon Black, *The Police and the People*. New York: McGraw-Hill, 1968; for housing, see Michael Lipsky, *Protest in City Politics*. Chicago: Rand McNally, 1970.

10. New York Times, July 7, 1965, p. B2.

11. "Federal Role in Urban Affairs," *Hearings Before the Subcommittee on Executive Reorganization*, Committee on Government Operations, United States Senate, Eighty-ninth Congress, Second Session, August 21 and 23, 1966, Part 3, p. 582. Subsequently referred to as *U.S. Senate Hearings on Urban Affairs: 1966*.

12. Lindsay first led a coalition of mayors from six of New York State's largest cities to lobby in Albany. Soon afterward, in March 1970, he organized another coalition to lobby in Washington, D.C. Lindsay was a strong advocate of a national urban policy and served as co-chairman, along with former U.S. Senator Fred Harris, of the Commission on the Cities in the 1970s. For the commission's findings, consult Commission on the Cities in the 1970s, *The State of the Cities*. New York: Praeger, 1972.

13. *U.S. Senate Hearings on Urban Affairs: 1966*.

14. *Executive Budget—Fiscal Year 1979, Message of the Mayor*, City of New York, Office of Management and Budget, April 26, 1978.

15. "Debt Financing Problems of State and Local Government: The New York City Case," *Hearings Before the Subcommittee on Economic Stabilization*, Committee on Banking, Currency and Housing, House of Representatives, Ninety-fourth Congress, First Session, Part 1, October 20, 1975, p. 899. Subsequently referred to as *House Hearings on New York City's Debt: 1975*. Total expenditures for social services were much higher, costing over $2 billion and consuming 23 percent of the expense budget.

16. This is not to say that the settlement of one controversy followed immediately after another. For example, the controversy over the Police-Civilian Review Board occurred in Lindsay's first term, while police labor contracts were negotiated in Lindsay's second term. City Hall's concessions set a long-term mood for the city, where claims and counterclaims took place over eight years. After the mayor showed himself vulnerable to one group, it took some time before other groups would follow suit. For an analysis of how Lindsay left himself open to labor demands see Raymond Horton, *Municipal Labor Relations in New York City*. New York: Praeger, 1973.

17. See Raymond Horton and Charles Brecher, editors, *Setting Municipal Priorities: 1980*. Montclair, NJ: Allanheld, 1979, Chapter 2; and *House Hearings on New York City's Debt: 1975*, pp. 898–912.

18. *Federal-State-Local Finances: Significant Features of Fiscal Federalism.* 1973–74 Edition, Advisory Commission on Intergovernmental Relations, Washington, D.C. July 1973; *City Financial Emergencies.* Advisory Commission on Intergovernmental Relations, Washington, D.C., July 1973.

19. Beame had been comptroller during Lindsay's last term of office and played a role in fostering the fiscal sleight-of-hand that plagued the city years later. Once he became mayor, Beame's refusal to acknowledge fiscal realities and his foot-dragging over suggested reforms only worsened problems, which were not resolved until Governor Hugh Carey and supervisory bodies controlled by the governor stepped in.

20. *New York Times*, May 25, 1975, p.1.

21. Among the journalistic accounts, see *Time*, June 16, 1975. Also, Fred Ferretti, *The Year the Big Apple Went Bust.* New York: Putnam, 1976; Ken Auletta, *The Streets Were Paved With Gold.* New York: Random House, 1975; and Jack Newfield and Paul DuBrul, *The Abuse of Power.* New York: Viking Press, 1977.

22. *New York Times*, July 2, 1975, p. B4.

23. Ibid., May 14, 1975, p. A1.

24. Lester Sobel et al., editors, *New York and the Urban Dilemma.* New York: Facts on File, 1976, pp.119–20.

25. It is a matter of controversy whether Beame could be relied upon to make the necessary cuts. For a time, Beame would announce cuts that, on further inspection, turned out to be nonexistent, or else he would rehire municipal workers shortly after laying them off. Eventually cuts were made—albeit under threats from the governor, the Emergency Financial Control Board, or the Municipal Assistance Corporation. In September 1975, eight months after the crisis had surfaced, the Office of Management and Budget claimed to have reduced the work force by 31,211 positions by layoffs or by not filling vacancies. See "Reductions in New York City's Full Time Payroll" (New York City Office of Management and Budget, October, 1975), mimeograph. For accounts of how municipal workers responded to these force reductions see the *New York Times*, July 1 and 2, 1975.

26. Sobel et al., editors, *New York and the Urban Dilemma*, p. 123.

27. *House Hearings on New York City's Debt: 1975*, Part 1., p. 18.

28. *New York Times*, November 2, 1975, p.1.

29. *House Hearings on New York City's Debt: 1975*, Part 2, pp. 1651–52.

30. "New York City Financial Crisis," *Hearings Before the Committee on Banking, Housing and Urban Affairs*, United States Senate, Ninety-fourth Congress, First Session, October 9, 10, 18, and 23, 1975, pp. 37–45. Hereafter referred to as *Senate Hearings on New York City's Financial Crisis: 1975.* For a more detailed outline of Burns's and Simon's position see H.V. Savitch, *Urban Policy and the Exterior City.* Elmsford, NY: Pergamon Press, 1979, pp. 176–82.

31. *Vital Speeches*, October 29, 1975.

32. *New York Daily News*, October 30, 1975, p. 1.

33. For the testimony of leading bankers, see *Senate Hearings on New York City's Financial Crisis: 1975*, testimony of Saturday, October 18, 1975.

34. For details, see Savitch, *Urban Policy and the Exterior City*, pp. 176–82; and Sobel et al., editors, *New York and the Urban Dilemma*, p. 33.

35. *New York Times*, December 3, 1975, p. 1.

36. Not all of these conditions were directly and explicitly worked out as a condition of the New York City Seasonal Financing Act of 1975. Some of these (the use of union pension funds for city securities) were agreed to earlier. All of these conditions, in one fashion or another, were a necessary part of federal aid. Also, the debt moratorium was eventually struck down by the courts, although the moratorium served the function of giving the city extra time to sort out its finances.

37. For a discussion of MUFL as well as a general view of the fiscal crisis see Martin Shefter, *Political Crisis/Fiscal Crisis*. New York: Basic Books, 1985, especially pp. 163–66.

38. *House Hearings on New York City's Debt: 1975*, Part I, p. 893.

39. *Senate Hearings on New York City's Financial Crisis: 1975*.

40. "Oversight on the New York Seasonal Financing Act," *Hearings Before the Senate Committee on Banking, Housing and Urban Affairs*, Ninety-fifth Congress, First Session, December 14, 15, and 16, 1977.

41. Ibid.

42. *Congress and the Nation: 1977–1980* #5 (Washington D.C., Congressional Quarterly, 1080), pp. 279–80.

43. For an inside view of how Koch interacted with labor leaders see Ken Auletta, "Profile of Mayor Koch," *New Yorker*, September 10 and 17, 1979.

44. *New York Times*, March 8, 1985, p. B1.

45. For an account of planning strategy in New York which is put in comparative context consult, H. V. Savitch, "Post-Industrial Planning in New York, Paris and London," *The Journal of the American Planning Association* 53 (Winter 1987): 80–90.

46. John Mollenkopf, "Economic Development," in Charles Brecher and Raymond Horton, editors, *Setting Municipal Priorities: 1984*. New York: New York University Press, 1983, p. 141.

IV

Politics

10

The Withering Away of the Party System

Richard C. Wade

"In the government and politics of New York City," asserted Wallace Sayre and Herbert Kaufman in 1960, "it is the county leaders and Assembly District leaders in each party, who have the most to do with governmental decisions."[1] Writing over twenty-five years ago, the authors emphasized the role of parties and particularly their leaders in the governance of the city. It is not as if they did not see the limitations of parties and party leaders, or appreciate the other centers of political influence and power, or, indeed, identify the organizations' continued diminution; rather it is that they could see no other integrating factor in what they called a "multi-centered" political system. Hence parties performed a unique function. The word "parties" or some variation of it appears in the Sayre and Kaufman index far more frequently than any other. Even when they are not central to a decision or agency management, the presence of political parties is always there. Their significance is the subliminal theme of *Governing New York*.

Writing after the LaGuardia era and during the Wagner years, Sayre and Kaufman could have easily traced the formal decline of party power. LaGuardia, though a nominal Republican, owed his electoral success to a fusion of parties and factions, and hence could govern without dependence on any one of them; Robert Wagner, Sr., though cordial to party leaders in the beginning, cast them aside altogether after his first two terms. Moreover, the rise of the American Labor party in the thirties and the Liberal party in the forties attenuated the minority status of the Republicans. A new surge of "reform" in the Democratic ranks further fractionalized the political scene. But, in 1960, it was difficult to tell whether these developments were simply part of a historic ebb and flow in urban politics or a permanent change in the system. Surely the party system of 1960 was less cohesive, less powerful, and less popular than it had been in 1898, the date at which the authors began their survey. And certainly the press still covered politics on the old assumption of the centrality of parties, even as they chronicled their fragmentation.

The authors were not unaware of this paradox. Hence, some of their best chapters are concerned with the "other" players in the game for municipal prizes. Public officials (not all of whom are elected), the organized bureaucracies, state and federal officials, labor and business, nongovernmental groups, and, of course, the electorate occupy some places at the table. Usually, they represent competitive forces, each entering the game to win something, or joining in to preserve what they have. More importantly, they are the permanent players. Elected officials, even those often reelected, are temporary participants. They can hold good cards and sometimes play them skillfully, but even the most accomplished have to make do with weak or indifferent hands. The parties once provided continuity between mayoral administrations; they no longer do. Since 1960, the Robert Wagner, John Lindsay, Abraham Beame, and Edward Koch administrations are more noted for their differences than their similarities. Wagner had sensed their declining power and popularity and discarded the county leaders; Lindsay made them his public enemies; Beame, himself a product of the Democratic party, permitted their return; Koch, as he has written, opened "the front door" to them; and Dinkins, coming out of the Harlem wing of the Democratic party, succeeded without their support. The central fact is that the formal party apparatus has become less important and increasingly an embarrassment to those seeking office.

The Party System in Its Heyday

Perhaps the best gauge of the magnitude of this transformation is the difference between the power of the parties at the turn of the century, when Sayre and Kaufman began their study, and the present system. In 1898 the annexation of the outer boroughs created the municipal boundaries of New York City, and subsequent charters provided it with the structure of governance. In the decades that followed, the influence of political parties was continuous. Though stronger at one time or another, they provided a convenient framework to examine the functioning of municipal government. Indeed, most analyses assumed the permanence of party power and dramatized the internal struggle between "bosses" and "reformers." Writers further assumed that the outcome of each of the battles would result in different policies, programs, and styles of leadership. For the newspapers, especially, following party factionalism and fluctuating personal prominence became a kind of shorthand for reporting on municipal government.

In 1898 there was no doubt about the power of parties in municipal affairs. In New York, dominance rested with the Democratic party, though Republicans were not as anemic as they would be later. The big names were Richard Croker and Charles Murphy, men who never held elected office but wielded more influence than those who did. Administrations came and went, reform succeeded and failed, promising stars shined, then faded. George Washington Plunkitt, the genial Tammany philosopher, noted that reformers were "morning glories," and the organization was a "solid oak." The leaders' power was never as absolute as opponents and newspapers believed, but it insinuated itself into every layer of government and into the affairs of the private sector as well.

County and district leaders carried the organization's wishes throughout the system: from the nomination and election of public officials to the appointment of commissioners, from the highest administrator to the lowest clerk. Contracts for public works and even private construction fell under the attention of party operatives. The criminal justice system from judges to janitors, from clerks to corrections, from police to parole boards, was laced with political considerations. Liquor licenses, franchises, assessments, and easements all stemmed from party connections. Nor were the school and health systems beyond the reach of Tammany's patronage. In short, at the moments of its greatest strength, the Democratic party's hegemony was almost coterminus with municipal governance itself.

The source and persistence of this power alarmed many segments of the city's population. The newspapers saw Tammany as the great obstacle to good government; reformers asserted that its questionable methods corrupted democratic processes; old New Yorkers thought that its immigrant base produced a government, in Thomas Bailey Aldrich's phrase, "of the aliens, by the aliens, for the aliens"; civic groups believed it exploited the poor and smothered self-help and initiative; liberals disliked its cozy relationship with shady business interests; business leaders charged it with inefficiency and high taxes; and socialists claimed it promoted private monopolies that charged high prices for public necessities. No doubt there was some truth in all these charges, but the system would not have lasted if it depended only on bribery, corruption, electoral chicanery, or other illegal tactics. Actually, its roots lay deep in the social and economic conditions occasioned by the great urban explosion of the nineteenth and early twentieth centuries.

Immigration and the "Machine"

Wave after wave of immigrants piling into the inner city and young people streaming in from the American countryside created unprecedented residential congestion. On the Lower East Side the density approached 300,000 people per square mile. No other place in the world—not Naples, not London's East End, not Calcutta—could match these figures. The newcomers, no matter what their origins, faced the same conditions—wretched housing, scarce jobs, inadequate schools, littered streets, erratic services, high crime rates, and endemic disorder.

Indeed, today's problems are not new. The report of the Mayor's Commission on the Year 2000, published in 1987, could have been written a century ago. Jacob Riis coined the phrase "how the other half lives" in a best-selling book in

1890;[2] journalist Joseph M. Rice had already discovered that urban schools did not prepare students for the technology of the twentieth century; Robert Hunter had defined a poverty line and found nearly half of the population fell below it; untreated sewage polluted the river and bays around the city; trains, puffing soft coal, moved into New York from all directions; horse manure dirtied the streets and contaminated the air, and sanitation carts made only irregular garbage pick-ups in the city's neighborhoods; children frolicked in soiled streets and danger-ous lots; the transportation system was a hodgepodge of noisy trolleys, horse-drawn hacks, and overhead railways; and Lincoln Steffens found almost "scientific" corruption in municipal government. Writers have since invested the turn-of-the-century New York with a charming nostalgia, but for most Gothamites life was a tedious low-paying job at one end of the day and a crowded apartment with the barest amenities at the other. At best city govern-ment responded to this broad range of problems with concern and well-meaning programs, but often, too, with neglect, indifference, or even exploitation.

The machine and the boss system grew out of the needs and the vulnerability of people who lived in the most difficult parts of the city. The party organization, nonetheless, was never a charity organization or a social settlement. Indeed, it is not surprising that bossism's methods and objectives were disreputable. It sought exemptions from the law permitting saloons to operate on Sundays, protected gambling and prostitution, and winked at building code violations. On a personal level, it sought leniency for those caught in the web of the law: posted bail for the habitual drunk, attested to the character of a truant student, postponed rent evictions, or reduced the cost of a hospital bill. All of these activities frustrated or skirted the law, but they also aided those unable to manage their own affairs. "The strength of the boss method," wrote reformer Robert A. Woods in 1923,

> lies in the fact that it has to do with supplying tangible benefits to meet keenly felt, unrelenting human needs such as are characteristic of his constituency. He controls some of the best avenues to livelihood; the winning of a job or a license depends on him. A man in need may through him reach the resources of charity. A wrongdoer may through him find immunity from punishment.[3]

Most of all, the party machine acted as a primitive employment agency. Later generations would simply see this function as patronage. But the organization's reach included all employment, even that only marginally connected with public expenditures. And the number of jobs was considerable because Tammany reached its apex between 1880 and 1930 as New York built what is now called its "infrastructure." This included streets, sewers, bridges, tunnels, and water and electrical systems, as well as innumerable schools, parks, and transit sys-tems. Private construction matched public building, and nearly all of it was done manually, which required only tough hands and strong backs. Employers, want-ing franchises and lax enforcement of building codes and ordinances, had to indulge, if not co-opt, political power. They needed labor; the machine provided it. The neighborhood desperately sought jobs; the political system gave it access to them.

Tammany generally supported the idea of an ever growing New York; indeed, if the price was right, its spokesmen could be the city's greatest boosters. Of course, leaders, and even those down the line, took their cut at every chance. They contributed handsomely to the rampant corruption of the political process, participated in boodle and bribery, continually raised taxes, indulged special business interests, and protected prostitution and gambling. And men who held only modest jobs suddenly became rich. Reformers and newspapers harped on the sordid aspects of the regular organization, but neighborhood residents accepted machine shenanigans as a matter of course. After all, if your own politicians would not protect and provide the most elementary services, who would? Machine corruption and a ballot cast on election day seemed a small price to pay for the benefits received.

Tammany's dominance was contested both within the Democratic party and by shifting forces outside. The most prominent and enduring opponents were the Republicans. They drew their strength from the new areas of development, where the middle classes moved to improve their housing and escape the old neighborhoods. Manhattan and Brooklyn alike had "silk stocking" enclaves where the GOP stood for success and traditional values. The Irish ascendancy in the Democratic party also prompted other, newer groups to seek recognition under the Republican banner. But its importance rested on the statewide following where the names Charles Evans Hughes and Theodore Roosevelt represented social solidity and electoral victories. Even though a minority within the city, the Republican party too had its regular and reform wings.

Cosmopolitan Gotham was not, of course, without its minority parties. Many represented single issues, and their success fluctuated with public interest in their special concerns. Others were ideological and hence more permanent, and some became adept at magnifying their importance in close elections, especially for lower offices. Still others drew on ethnic cohesion and organized for protection or recognition within the Democratic system. The long paper ballots of the time resonated with names and parties that reflected the rich diversity of the Imperial City.

But the Democratic party was the center of this somewhat fragmented political universe. The crucial struggle took place between regulars and reformers. Usually the contests were between slates in mayoral elections, though they could take place over other offices. Especially heated were contests involving charter revision where reformers sought to tame Tammany with structural reorganizations that were designed to contain the worst abuses of party rule. These charter fights stemmed in part from the fact of the consolidation that created the five-county city and the need for an appropriate governing instrument.

The Center Versus the Periphery

Beyond the issue of a strong or weak mayor, the power of the Board of Estimate, the composition of the city council, and such problems of civil service and electoral processes lay a fundamental political question: who was to shape the future of the city? Would the center, with its large numbers and many newcomers, use City Hall to protect and enhance its interests, or would the balance move to more dynamic areas beyond the line of development, where an increasing population could translate its wealth and success into political hegemony? The "organization" was a political expression of life at the center; reform was just as much the political expression of the growing numbers of residential neighborhoods on the city's periphery. The tension between the two was the permanent condition of political struggle, though constant urban development continuously expanded the physical size of the battlefield. The outer areas had both a residential stake in their communities and an economic stake, either in property or employment, downtown. The machine's aim was to attenuate the conditions in its dense and vulnerable neighborhoods and receive a larger share of the fruits of the booming metropolis.

This contest characterized American urban politics as well as New York's for the half century before the Great Depression of the 1930s. Each side had its share of successes. In the process, the machine tempered its grossest practices, and reformers softened many of their moral judgments of the people who lived in congested downtown neighborhoods. This adjustment was accelerated by the exodus of second and third generation inner-city dwellers who moved to the pleasant residential areas previously occupied by older inhabitants. In New York the accommodation was most strikingly illustrated by the extraordinary skill of Alfred E. Smith who built a successful career on bringing together the warring factions. He was equally at home with Tammany and reformers, or with "Big Tim" Sullivan and Frances Perkins. Though the twenties was a period of national Republican supremacy, Smith was reelected governor time and time again on the awkward alliance of old antagonists.[4] Roosevelt later used the same technique as governor, then as president.

The year 1928 was the high noon of the power of the Democratic party in New York City. Its favorite son, Alfred E. Smith, headed the national ticket; a friend and neighbor, Franklin D. Roosevelt, was about to become the state's governor, and Tammany's grip on City Hall had never seemed more secure. The stock market boomed on Wall Street, skyscrapers rose majestically toward the sky, and at Yankee Stadium the Bronx Bombers symbolized the effortless superiority of the city. The voices of reform were overwhelmed by the sheer success of the system; only a few skeptics mumbled about the consequences of this sybaritic indulgence.

Actually, beneath the surface the ground was trembling. The real estate building cycle moved downward in 1927 and 1928; the stock exchange behaved erratically. In the fall of 1929, the whole gilded economic edifice of the nation collapsed. The city had known hard times before, and initially it was assumed that the decline, even if sharp, would be but a temporary halt in the nation's and the city's inevitable progress upward. But this depression was different from its predecessors. The economy hit bottom but, instead of bouncing up, it stuck. The year 1930 gave way to 1931 and then to 1932, and there were still no signs of recovery. As politicians and the public awaited a return, widespread suffering moved across the country. In the cities, the old reliance on makeshift relief, a combination of charity and municipal handouts, was quickly exhausted; states soon reached their borrowing limits; and a bewildered president clung to the old expectations of a resilient economy. It was the nation's first urban depression,[5] and it would permanently alter the governance of cities and with it the party system on which this governing rested.

The Depression as Political Watershed

The depression was as much a watershed for the history of New York as the rest of the country. For more than two centuries the city had managed its own affairs. It had tunneled under rivers and thrown bridges over them; it reached miles upstate for its fresh water; it constructed an immense subway and elevated transit complex; it erected the world's most extensive and elaborate school and hospital systems. And it did this without a penny from Albany and Washington; indeed it had enough money left over to send some to each. The Great Depression marked the end of this urban self-sufficiency; in the modern period New York would become increasingly dependent on state and federal funds. As a result, much of the development and many of the services once provided by local institutions gradually drifted to the national government.

After 1933, Franklin Roosevelt and his New Deal, propelled by persistent unemployment, widening poverty, and desperation, began to provide national programs for urban dwellers that municipal government could only provide sporadically and inadequately. Whatever jobs were available emanated from Washington through the Works Progress Administration (WPA), the Public Works Administration (PWA), and from countless local public projects. Moreover, there was now unemployment insurance for those who were temporarily without work. The Social Security Act provided help to the elderly; school-work programs and conservation projects kept young people busy; and public housing and the Federal Housing Administration (FHA) furnished shelter for the homeless and security for homeowners. In addition, Washington supported the federal theater, art programs, and countless musical groups designed to preserve the creativity of unemployed artists. In short, what city government had provided on a primitive level was now furnished more generously by the national government. More importantly, these services were now provided as a matter of right, not political patronage. Thus, the essential rationale for the old boss system slowly slipped away.

This fact was concealed for some time because Democratic bosses supported Roosevelt and his new policies. City governments were initially the only local agencies available to administer relief and new programs; across the country machines seemed to prosper and saw their power enhanced. In Chicago, Boston, Memphis, and Jersey City, to cite notorious examples, prominent bosses loomed larger than ever and flaunted their relations with F.D.R. Yet even in the 1930s, as the locus of authority shifted to Washington, the most durable leaders were those who were the most effective in extracting money from the nation's capital.

Washington's power slowly eroded the foundations and autonomy of local political organizations, but the New Deal's sponsorship of unions also undermined a large portion of the patronage historically available to the machine. Now the unions found the jobs, exercised discipline in the workplace, protected employed workers, and, along with the federal government, took care of them during slack times. The union hall replaced the old political clubhouse for many members. Here were the bar, the meeting room, pool tables, bowling lanes, and even facilities for family recreation. At the union bank, workers cashed checks, saved for vacations, and, later, paid their medical bills. New York City seemed to embody the change: the central piece of labor reform bore the name of Senator Robert F. Wagner; Sidney Hillman of the Amalgamated Clothing Workers became the symbol of trade union political power; when at the Democratic convention of 1940, the password among the New Deal faithful was "clear it with Sidney"; and an independent Republican, Fiorello LaGuardia, overwhelmed Tammany three times at the polls.

Indeed, the rise of LaGuardia, a liberal congressman in the twenties and a defeated mayoral candidate in 1929, perhaps best embodied the sudden fall of the organization from its giddy heights. His initial victory over a scandal-ridden Tammany City Hall fit the usual pattern of the mutiny of voters against inordinate plunder, but his continuance in office for twelve years was a measure of the sea of change created by the new politics of the dependent city. The "Little Flower" instinctively understood that New York could no longer provide expected urban services, much less renewed expansion, with self-generated revenue, but would have to look more and more to Washington. No mayor was better situated. The president was from New York, and no longer had to fear reprisals from Tammany; the mayor was popular and aggressive but, in a Democratic city, he still needed F.D.R.'s support. The arrangement was mutually satisfactory.

Indeed, no one understood the new axis of power between the cities and Washington better than LaGuardia. His unique entree to the president and his cordial relationship with the New Deal insiders, especially the reformers, meant that New York would receive more than its share of federal funds. The U.S.

Conference of Mayors had been established in the last year of the Hoover administration by Frank Murphy of Detroit and James Curley of Boston to appeal for federal help for the distressed big cities. LaGuardia later became president of the organization, a position he held for ten years. In fact, although it was not widely known, he spent half his time in Washington during his last term. New Yorkers need only walk around a bit to see the tangible results of the unlikely alliance between a patrician Democrat and the city's first Italian-American chief magistrate. In tracing the end of the self-sufficient city and the beginning of the dependent one, Fiorello LaGuardia can be seen as the first of the modern mayors.

His long ascendancy exposed the cleavages within the Democratic party. The control of the regulars suffered since the city's most visible figures—Roosevelt, Governor Herbert Lehman, Senator Wagner, and LaGuardia—were independents. Often LaGuardia would observe during elections that not a single county chairman of either party favored his candidacy. In addition, a Democratic weakness spawned smaller parties with strategic influence if not great numbers. In 1936, the anti-Tammany feeling was so widespread that even James Farley, the machine Democrat from the city who had become Democratic national chairman, countenanced the establishment of the American Labor party to give a non-Democratic line for the disaffected party members to vote for Roosevelt. It soon had a life of its own, institutionalizing the fragmentation of the majority party.[6] By the end of World War II, the old bonds of loyalty had been greatly weakened, even if they had not entirely snapped.

Reform New Style

Some analysts believed that these years of depression and war were aberrations in the historic tradition of Tammany hegemony and, as soon as the commanding figures had left the scene and the country returned to normalcy, the old political system would reassert itself. The emergence of Carmine DeSapio as the "New Boss" seemed to suggest that the tiger once again strode the ramparts of party power. A cover story in *Time* magazine seemed to put the issue beyond doubt by observing that the new leaders placed winning ahead of old-fashioned ruthlessness. Yet the abyss between regulars and reformers could not be bridged. The sons of Roosevelt and Wagner rose quickly; Eleanor Roosevelt and Herbert Lehman gave legitimacy to a younger wave of independents; a whole generation found plentiful, well-paying jobs in the marketplace instead of on the public payroll. Yet Kaufman and Sayre were not alone in believing New York politics in 1960 could best be understood in familiar party terms.

But new forces were undermining the old structure and shaping a new system. There had been many harbingers, but the clearest was the mayoral election of 1961. Robert Wagner, Jr., had served two terms as a Democrat in his father's mold—though independent, he was acceptable to the organization.

Unlike the Senator, however, he was in City Hall, not in Washington, and the fragile accommodation broke down in the face of daily contact. He decided to seek a third term on an antiboss platform promising that he would replace all five county chairmen if elected. When charged with "running against himself," he cheerfully replied, "I could find no better opponent." He brought down what was left of Tammany, including DeSapio himself. In a final gesture, the next party leader closed the clubhouse doors on Thirty-eighth Street and sold the building.

Three years later, the contest for the U.S. Senate revealed how little was left of the old. Robert Kennedy had been born and raised in New York but lived most of his life in Massachusetts and Washington. After his brother's assassination he decided to make the race in New York. In the end the Kennedy name counterbalanced the "carpetbagger" label, but it was significant that he had no fixed ties to the old organization and only tenuous ones to the reform wing. But the general disarray of the Democratic party made it possible for someone who could not even vote in New York to walk away with one of the state's highest offices. It wasn't long before he lined up with independent candidates against the regulars in a contest for judge of the surrogate court, one of the last bulwarks of the Manhattan machine.[7]

If the 1961 mayoral election suggested the embarrassing decline of the power of the Democratic organization, the next contest glaringly exposed its feebleness. John V. Lindsay, a Republican congressman from the East Side of Manhattan, defeated the regular Democrat, running as a liberal Republican with strong support from the incumbent Republican governor, Nelson Rockefeller. He also had the nomination of the Liberals, and of a revived old City Fusion party. Lindsay's was not a victory, however, for his own party, but a measure of the disaffection of Democratic voters and clear evidence of their increasing independence.

His first term was rocky, and despite a favorable press and some national notoriety, his popularity sagged. In 1969, he was denied even his own party's nomination and was forced to run on the Liberal line against both major parties. Even with commercials that began detailing endless small mistakes on his watch only to magnify presumed successes, he managed to contrive a second term. Yet a few years later, to prepare for a quixotic run for the presidency, he changed his registration to a Democrat without any sense of betrayal to anybody. It was now possible to sail the independent sea with all sail and no party ballast at all.

More illustrative still was the Democratic presidential primary in 1972. The selection of delegates to the national convention is, after all, the one remaining function that unreservedly belongs to major political parties. Historically, it had been the convenient battleground of reformers against the organization. Kennedy and McCarthy had divided the independents in 1968, and new national Democratic regulations opened the process to even more public participation. George McGovern, virtually unknown in New York, entered the primary. Endorsed by only two well-known Democrats, the borough president of the Bronx and the Queens chairman, opposed by 60 out of the 62 state county chairmen, and spending less than a quarter of a million dollars, the South Dakota Senator won 240 out of 249 elected delegates. Tammany Hall in its heyday had never done that; reformers, in their wildest dreams, had never imagined it.

A Momentary Victory for the Machine

The next mayoral election, in 1973, gave some credence to the notion that McGovern's campaign might be a mere aberration, especially since he was so badly beaten in November. Abraham Beame had been the comptroller for two terms,[8] had always sturdily supported the Brooklyn Democratic organization, and was preeminently a regular. He ultimately won. Yet he was forced into a runoff since he had less than a majority in the primary and faced two serious candidates in the general election. For a brief moment the past returned to City Hall and patronage flowed back into traditional channels. In less than a year, however, the fiscal crisis overwhelmed the city, and the power, briefly enjoyed by the party leaders, moved even more decisively to Albany and Washington.

Beame was soon mayor in name only. The budget was ultimately placed under the Municipal Assistance Corporation (MAC), a state agency; financing for traditional city functions, such as the City University, and funding of portions of the court and prison systems were transferred to Albany. The city tried to shed as much as possible of its health, welfare, and educational costs, which were traditionally borne by municipal revenue.[9] The Imperial City of a generation earlier was increasingly a mendicant seeking succor wherever it could find it. Meanwhile, areas of party patronage shrunk substantially as decisions moved away from City Hall.

The election of 1977 saw the remnants of the Democratic party at bay again. Beame sought vindication in an electoral victory, but the political vacuum occasioned by the fiscal crisis brought in five serious and independent candidates. Edward Koch, a reform congressman from the Village; Mario Cuomo, handpicked by Governor Hugh Carey; Bella Abzug, a left-liberal congresswoman; Percy Sutton, a leader in the black community; and Herman Badillo, the most prominent Latino in public life, all reached for the brass ring. What was significant was that the organization could get only 17 percent of the total vote for an incumbent mayor; put another way, more than four out of every five votes went to the irregulars.

Yet the county chairmen were not stripped of all their resourcefulness. In his anxiety to defeat Cuomo in the runoff, Koch courted the support of the battered leaders by promising consideration in City Hall in return for whatever the troops might bring him on election day. The new mayor would ultimately discover that what he thought to be somewhat old wine was, in fact, hemlock. Even so, he had to face a stubborn Cuomo, now running on the Liberal line alone, who attracted over 40 percent of the votes in the November election.

Over the next four years, the Village reformer became more conservative. Abandoning his liberal past, Koch felt more and more comfortable in the white neighborhoods of the outer boroughs. "I love the middle class," he trumpeted with the air of discovery. When he came up for reelection in 1981, he played for the grand slam—nomination by all parties—and succeeded in getting the Republican and Conservative endorsements, as well as that of the Democrats. The only jarring note was his failure to win the nod from the Liberals, who noted his hasty retreat from the positions that had earned him their support when he was in Congress. Perhaps even more arresting was the fact that an unknown assemblyman from Brooklyn received 37 percent of the vote in the Democratic primary, although he was hopelessly outspent. Yet all seemed serene and *New York* magazine ran an article that asked the question, "Why is Ed Koch, next to Ronald Reagan, the most popular politician in America?"[10]

Riding the crest of his popularity as mayor, Koch inexplicably decided to run for governor only a few months after the election. His opponent was his 1977 foe, Mario Cuomo, then the Lieutenant Governor. Dutifully, party leaders fell in line; the state committee voted its endorsement; the money rolled in. While the press assumed a Koch victory, it failed to take into account the decisive power of independents in New York state Democratic primaries. The record was very clear: McGovern had defeated Humphrey in 1972; Hugh Carey had disposed of the party's nominee, Howard Samuels, in 1974; Senator Edward Kennedy had routed an incumbent president, Jimmy Carter, in 1980. Cuomo's victory, far from being an upset, was simply another episode in the decline of party organization. Pundits groped for an ethnic explanation. Yet a majority of Jews had voted for Cuomo, and Koch had divided the "Italian vote." Indeed, Koch barely carried the city that had given him a huge majority only months before.

Koch, stunned by defeat and especially Cuomo's large margin, sought vindication in reelection in 1985. His principal opponent, City Council President Carol Bellamy, provided a convenient foil for his restoration. She held an unimportant office, had quarreled from time to time with Koch, and was something of a symbol of New York's feminist movement. But she had already endorsed Koch over Cuomo in 1982, declaring him to be a "good" and "effective" mayor. Once again, party leaders fell in line with enthusiasm; contributions, especially from grateful developers, produced the largest war chest in the city's history, and the press was more enthusiastic than before. Missing were the endorsements of the Republican and Conservative parties, which had had enough of Koch's ecumenical politics and reverted to their historically assigned minority roles. Bellamy was no Cuomo; she accepted the inevitable primary results and only went through the motions on the Liberal line in the general election.

Scandals Old Style

It had been a personal victory for Koch. The only Democratic figure at his private swearing in on New Year's Eve was Stanley Friedman, the "boss" of the Bronx. Within months the euphoria of victory was replaced by unfolding scandals that spread throughout the administration and reached into the inner rooms of City Hall. The press was soon comparing the administration to the dark days of Jimmy Walker and Boss Tweed. The irony was that the disclosures began with the very party leaders that Koch had wooed in 1977, and the hanky-panky centered in what pockets of patronage had been left in the system. Soon it involved at least two boroughs, Queens and Brooklyn, where the vestiges of the organization seemed to have survived. Manhattan, the historic source of spectacular corruption, was so disorganized that it was immune from the disease. Yet, as the *Washington Post* observed in the summer of 1987, "a score of officials—from some of the most powerful elected office holders in the city, to several of Mayor Edward I. Koch's closest associates and department heads, to judges, and a state legislator—have been indicted, convicted, or forced out under a cloud in the last 20 months. More are under investigation."[11]

Donald Manes, the Democratic county leader and borough president, had built an apparently formidable Democratic party in Queens, next to Staten Island the most conservative and Republican of the outer boroughs. His predecessor, Matthew Troy, had reveled in its growing influence in the city, only to stumble in a private matter and wind up with a short stint in jail. But Manes had accumulated the old-fashioned power. "In Queens, you had one-stop service," New York State Attorney General, Robert Abrams, observed. "If you wanted a city contract, you went to Donald Manes. If you wanted a judgeship, you went to Donald Manes. If you wanted a job in government, if you wanted a cable franchise, you went to Donald Manes."[12]

The occasion of his fall was a scheme concocted by a friend in the Parking Violations Bureau to funnel money, some through bribes, to a small ring of officials in return for an exclusive city contract. Oddly enough, it was not uncovered by the Koch administration or any New York law enforcement officer, but rather in Chicago where the ring had begun to operate. Manes's complicity was clear, but before any legal action could begin he committed suicide on the second try. After the first attempt, the mayor had gone to the bedside and kissed him on the forehead and told the press he was "my friend." A few weeks later, he announced that his strongest supporter in Queens was a "crook." Then, a Queens assemblywoman was forced to resign her position in Albany because of having assistants on the state payroll to work for Richard Rubin, Manes's second in command in the Queens Democratic party; later, Rubin, found guilty on other irregularities, was sent to prison.

Since Manes had combined his leadership of the party with his elected office as borough president, his demise decapitated the regular organization. But the epicenter of corruption was the Bronx. Here Stanley Friedman had built the strongest party machine in postwar New York. He controlled the borough president's office, had comfortable alliances with two powerful congressmen, Mario Biaggi and Robert Garcia, and had accommodated the changing demography of the Bronx by placing black and Latino leaders within his patronage orbit. He even tamed the reform movement by feeding it a share of judgeships. He had been a deputy mayor under Beame and had mastered the intricate mysteries of the city bureaucracy. The iron fist had never had much of a velvet glove, but now it was found to be in the public till. A company he had established had invented a hand-held computer to be used by the Parking Violations Bureau through a no-bid contract. The U.S. attorney discovered that the company had liberally distributed stock, money, and favoritism to create a monopoly. Friedman was found guilty on several charges and sentenced to prison. The mayor once again went through the ritual of proclaiming his friendship to Friedman at the beginning of the exposé and then publicly denouncing him after the indictment.

The Bronx Democratic party, now leaderless, was dealt still another blow when the federal investigator uncovered a criminal conspiracy in the activities of Wedtech, a military supply company in the Bronx. Created ostensibly as a minority-owned enterprise, it lived on no-bid Defense Department contracts. As the probe widened, it was clear that the corporate officers were bribing everyone remotely involved in the federal process, including congressmen Biaggi and Garcia, and reaching all the way to the White House. As the indictments came down, one after another party figure fell under a cloud. The borough president resigned. Politically, the Bronx Democratic organization, once the city's most powerful, had become a wasteland.

Another pillar of the party crumbled in the wake of the corruption. The hegemony of the Brooklyn machine antedated the consolidation of 1898, and for decades it had managed to flourish under organization mayors and survive under reform ones. It was not, however, immune from the attrition of parties that characterized the postwar years. Yet, even after McGovern had elected every Brooklyn delegate to the national convention in 1972, its leader, Meade Esposito, managed to create the illusion of sturdy power despite his modest performance. Indeed, he was the cover story of the *New York Times Magazine* in 1973, as evidence of the durability and utility of the old-fashioned boss system.[13] In 1977, Koch made a secret trip to his home seeking support against Cuomo. Once tendered, the mayor honored the assistance by appointing Anthony Ameruso, an Esposito protege, to the head of the Transportation Department even though his own screening panel found him unqualified. He later resigned under investigation, though Koch insisted on praising him as he grabbed his pension and ran. Esposito himself was indicted for improperly attempting to get federal contracts for a Brooklyn Navy Yard firm with which he had an insurance connection.[14]

The most celebrated case of the corruption in the Koch administration involved Bess Myerson, the commissioner of cultural affairs and a close personal friend of the mayor. She had been the centerpiece of his election in 1977 when a whispering campaign alleged the candidate was homosexual. His manager, David Garth, quickly responded by pairing Myerson and Koch at public appearances and even hinting that an "announcement" might follow. The episode turned out to be a "clean trick," but the public had every right to consider the relationship very close. When Koch had trouble replacing a succession of cultural commissioners, he turned to his old friend. It later developed, however, that Myerson had been dating a contractor who was involved in city contracts as well as a troublesome separation from his previous wife. In the middle of the divorce proceedings, she hired the judge's daughter in what a grand jury considered to be an attempt to get favorable treatment for her paramour. After his customary defense of his friend, Koch forced her resignation. Anthony Capasso ultimately went to prison, but Ms. Myerson was acquitted of the bribery charge. The mayor had previously tried to distance himself from the corruption in his administration. It was now more difficult.

The final scandal was the most embarrassing of all. The Feerick Commission, appointed by Governor Cuomo to explore statewide political corruption, finally came to the city in 1989. Among other ethical transgressions, the commission discovered a patronage mill operating in the basement of City Hall. An agency whose announced purpose was to send out minority candidates for the positions in the administration was, in fact, putting people on the payroll at the request of party leaders and personal supporters of the mayor. Worse still, when about to be discovered, the operatives destroyed documents and then lied, under oath, to the commission. In response, Koch permitted the agency head to retire with a large pension, demote his deputy, and plead innocence because he could not be expected to "see through the floor of his office" to the basement. The scandals had indeed come home, and would be an issue in his attempt to win reelection.

Actually, the dereliction of Democratic organizations comprised only a part of the oozing blot of corruption at City Hall, but Koch had so identified himself with the regular party that the public could scarcely distinguish between them. The mayor had proudly asserted that he had invited the leaders "in the front door" of Gracie Mansion; he cut his reform ties; and he called opponents "wackos" and "elitists." He let it be known that certain Democratic candidates "were not my kind of Democrat."[15] Hence, when nonparty-sponsored members of his administration got caught in the web of scandals, regular organizations suffered some guilt by association. The number of forced resignations, quick exits, indictments, and prison sentences portrayed an ethical disarray in the very center of the administration, which involved not only dedicated party stalwarts but the mayor's personal friends as well.

The most vivid illustration of the withering away of the parties was the election of 1989. The numbers are evidence alone. Democrats outnumber Republicans five to one; the GOP candidate received almost 49 percent of the vote. Moreover, that candidate, Rudolph Giuliani, had never run for office before, had once been a Democrat, and had sought both the Liberal and Conservative party nominations. In addition, though appointed U.S. Attorney by Ronald Reagan, he considered the charge of having been a "Reagan Republican" a mischievous slur, hinting that he was more akin to Fiorello LaGuardia, New York's quintessential independent. He even tried to exhume the old City Fusion party to escape his party identity. When it was all over, however, he received only 54,000 votes on the Liberal party line where Lindsay and Cuomo had once prospered. Clearly, registered Democrats had no inhibitions about abandoning their habitual party preference.

The Democratic party organizations were also irrelevant in the contest. Borough leaders divided their formal endorsements among Koch, Dinkins, and Ravitch. But everywhere, district leaders followed their own inclinations. After Dinkins had vanquished Koch in the primary, white Democrats began to desert to Giuliani. In the last two weeks, the Dinkins campaign brought in a dozen national Democratic figures to stem the drift away from the party's nominee. Each implored voters to stay with the party of their fathers and their own registration. But the habitual ties no longer bound; the old loyalties no longer held; party no longer counted.

Indeed, throughout the last twenty-five years, the increasing weakness of political parties forced mayoral candidates to create coalitions outside the old structure. Lindsay, Koch, Dinkins, and Cuomo all appealed to voters over the heads of party leaders and contrived ad hoc alliances apt to their own purposes without regard to the long-range interests of their party. Indeed, political activists regarded "coalition building" among assorted interests more important than seeking the sanction of the old established parties.

Functionless Parties

Nor was this decline hard to explain. The Depression and the New Deal had fundamentally altered the context that had given birth and meaning to the old party structure. In addition, the post–World War II media explosion removed its last significant functions. Traditionally, one of the party's crucial roles was as mediator between the candidate and the voter. Its platform established general positions on issues; its gatherings furnished a podium; its district leaders and club members distributed literature and conducted canvasses. For candidates seeking smaller offices, the party was almost the only contact with the electorate. Nearly as important, it played a large role in raising campaign funds. But, by the 1970s, these party functions had been replaced by a new system created by the electronic revolution of the past three decades.

New York City is the special locus of this revolution. It is the television center of the nation; the network news broadcasts from midtown; TV celebrities live here; its slickest and most expensive advertisements are dubbed "Madison Avenue." It is not by chance that David Garth, the new politics' most accomplished practitioner, came to national attention by his handling of campaigns for New York mayors Lindsay and Koch. The Big Apple, in short, is the country's media capital, and the corrosive effects of the new techniques on the old political system are perhaps more readily apparent here than elsewhere in the country.

The most visible illustration of this change is the emergence of the political consultant as the center of the campaign organization. He or she replaces party leaders as the locus of activity. He or she devises the themes, writes the scripts, produces the television commercials, handles the press, contracts the polls, creates the schedules, and even dictates the clothes and haircut of the aspirant. Reporters find an interview with the consultant as important as meeting with the principal. Indeed, the press gauges the seriousness of a campaign on the basis of whether one of the top consultants is willing to take on the candidate as a client.

In the 1989 election, the scrambling for nationally known media advisers occupied the press for months. Garth, of course, would stick with Koch; Dinkins finally settled on Doak and Schrum from Washington; Richard Ravitch reached to California to get Tony Podesta. On the Republican side, both Rudolph Giuliani and Ronald Lauder sought Roger Ailes, who had run President George Bush's 1988 campaign. Ailes first chose Lauder, then switched to Giuliani. To the media these decisions were at least as important as subsequent political endorsements.

But the most significant fact is that the consultants have no relationship to the party at all. In fact, they are often nonpartisan, contracting out to regulars or reformers of either party. Some, in rare gestures of conviction, declare they will only take on certain kinds of campaigns. Yet they have no roots or loyalty to the traditional party structure. And after one effort, win or lose, it's on to the next election. They are the new professional politicians, just as the bosses were before them. Their careers and incomes are in politics; their clubhouse is the computer room; they build their own media alliances; they celebrate their victories and conveniently forget their defeats; and they pride themselves on the cold professionalism of their work, eschewing any sentimental attachment to clients or political ideology.

Moreover, in this process the parties also lost their recruiting function. Formerly, the ambitious sought political office after a period of party service, often at lowly stations. Now the young head directly toward elective offices with a party registration card as their only evidence of fealty. In fact, many consider a close affiliation with the day-to-day affairs of the party to be the mark of a hack; a fresh, nonpartisan face appeals more to the electorate than a veteran standard bearer. The spread of primaries in place of conventions or caucuses opened the way to further end-runs around the organization. It has become the general wisdom that a prudent distance from the party is an asset for those seeking elective office.

The new media campaign managers care little for old-time canvassing, where party workers went door-to-door to discover preferences, deliver literature, and argue the candidate's case. Those foot soldiers were, after all, untrained in modern interviewing techniques; they worked at odd hours; they often returned with useless material; and even good campaigns could not provide full voter coverage. Large banks of telephones are more reliable. Paid operators call scientifically selected numbers; the message is uniform; computers swallow the responses and spit out the printouts. The new system is expensive, and there is no way of knowing if it is effective, but every campaign for important office finds all its components necessary.

Polling, too, is an indispensable part of the media campaign. Previously, campaigns relied on reports from the districts, the judgment of trusted advisers, and the instincts of the old hands in the business, but now all candidates use polls. Indeed, despite their frequent and sometimes flagrant errors, the press and the media treat the results as news stories; columnists scatter ratings throughout their interpretations; analysts worry that their wide use has almost become a surrogate election, even affecting the actual outcome. And one poll won't do. Anxious managers and candidates can hardly get enough of them, especially in the climactic weeks of the campaign. What is important is that the survey is bought and sold outside the party organization altogether.

The 1989 mayoral election perhaps best illustrates this obsession of the media with polling. Each major newspaper arranged with a network television station to do its own polling. The purpose was essentially to make news, not to do serious surveys. The results appeared on the front pages and dominated the evening news. Since everyone was doing it, the election was one long horse race. The candidates' standing in the polls transcended anything they might say about issues—even as the press decried an "issueless campaign." When the polls declared the Democratic primary a two-man race between Koch and Dinkins, the media treated it as a two-man race. In all this, the parties were merely ineffectual bystanders.

The Media as Substitutes for Parties

The media campaign is all business. There is none of the genial chaos that characterized traditional politics. At headquarters, a few people mill about numberless machines. Everything is computerized. Paid employees run the terminals; paid telephoners call the numbers from purchased printouts; rented machines slap labels on direct-mail envelopes. Mercenaries grind out "position papers," and press releases are quickly dispatched to a computerized "key" list of newspapers, television and radio stations, and columnists and commentators. The old political clubs meet irregularly, at best, where their modest memberships hear the candidates, or, more often, their surrogates. Faded photographs hang on the wall as wistful reminders of an importance long gone, and reporters only occasionally drop by looking for a little local color.

At the center of the new system is the paid television commercial, though its radio equivalent is still useful in limited markets. It is the modern substitute for conventional campaigning. The candidate is not seen live; the message, in fact, is often delivered by a professional voice. The purpose is to project the candidate who is like the viewer, but better. The commercial does not seek truth but plausibility. It confines itself to a handful of "issues" that are the candidate's long suit and are reiterated until the viewer is convinced that they are the issues of paramount importance to others even if they are not to him.

More recently, media managers have decided to portray the opponent as well as the candidate, thus usurping another traditional party function. Formerly the organization assumed the role of adversary, leaving the nonpartisan high road to the nominee. Now the candidate's own commercials attack the opponent. Euphemistically called "negative campaigning," it brings successful TV advertising techniques into politics. In thirty seconds, voice-over pictures transform an opponent into an enemy, question his integrity, impugn his judgment, and warn the public of the consequences of his possible victory. Though widely derided by analysts and commentators, these commercials have become a continuing, if not elevating, part of electronic politics.

The central fact about commercials is their cost. For maximum advantage they are presented in prime time, in conjunction with programs with large voting audiences. Since most advertisers head for the same viewers, the price is necessarily high. And the financial risks attendant on a media campaign are borne solely by the candidate, not by the media managers. Booking for commercial spots has to be made far in advance and money paid on the barrelhead. In the past, suppliers of campaign materials—literature, telephones, and office expenses—were more tolerant. Some creditors had to wait years for their money and then had to settle for a percentage of the original bill. Now the candidate is on a "pay as you go" basis.

Historically, the party had funded candidates or facilitated their ability to raise contributions. In the era of electronic politics, the burden of financing has shifted to the individual. Local parties avoid debts by annual dinners or courting a few donors to keep even ritualistic activity alive. Candidates, meanwhile, devise their own strategy for attracting the contributions necessary for the escalating costs of campaigning. This requires elaborate fund-raising schemes sponsored by the aspirant's own finance committee. It also means that the candidate must spend endless hours on the phone or attending small lunches, hoping to reach what the press considers a serious threshold of contributions.

Many people can afford political giving, but few do it. The result is a hectic and often unseemly courtship of a handful of wealthy people. Though some potential donors have only a dilettante's concern in politics, most have interests more directly related to government. They expect what the trade euphemistically calls "access" to the winner, a reward formerly bestowed by the party. The result is that the power of money is larger now than it ever was in the old system. In the 1985 mayoral election, the winner spent more than all his predecessors combined since 1960. Two candidates for city council president spent more than the usual cost of a senatorial election in most states. The process had become so gross that it stimulated a nationwide movement for financial reform. In New York, the new regulations restricted the total amount of money a candidate could spend, and established a ceiling of $3,000 for individual contributions. It is instructive that the restrictions were directed toward individual campaigns where the action is, not at party fund-raising, where it used to be.

Deprived of its historical functions, the party has clung to what is left. The most significant is the selection of judges. To be sure, the patronage is largely confined to lawyers who are elected or appointed to the bench and a few thousand clerks, court reporters, and guards. Yet the money is so substantial that Carmine DeSapio could observe at the Democratic convention in Buffalo in 1958, "Let the reformers have the Senate [nomination], I'll take the Surrogate [Judge]." But the good government cry of "get the clubhouse out of the court house" has resulted in screening committees that temper the worst abuses of the old process. Yet, like Banquo's ghost, party leaders hover over judicial conventions hoping for one last deal, one last arrangement.

The No-Party System

The end of parties does not, of course, mean the end of politics, but rather the beginning of a no-party system dominated by an independent electorate. Across the country, ticket splitting has become commonplace. Republicans have won the presidency in five of the six elections between 1968 and 1988, but have seldom managed a majority in Congress. The solid Democratic South has begun to elect GOP governors and senators; Republican strongholds, like Maine and Vermont, repeatedly break from their customary allegiances. Paid commercials minimize the party affiliations of candidates; increasingly they eliminate them altogether. Pollsters trace the dilution of loyalties. Voters who call themselves "independents" usually equal those who identify themselves with the major parties; when the labels "Independent Democrat" and "Independent Republican" are also offered by pollsters, two out of every three opt for independence.

The independence virus is not only general but specific. Blacks had historically been the most reliable members of the Democratic coalition. As early as the twenties, Tammany had begun a policy of incorporation, assuming that blacks were just the most recent immigrants to the city who, like the Irish, Germans,

Italians, and Jews before them, would find the party a useful vehicle to enter the political mainstream. Successive leaders followed the same technique, and blacks increasingly found their spokesmen on the Democratic ticket from lower offices to borough president and Congress. The center of their activity was, of course, Harlem and Manhattan, but they also got a modest cut of the citywide patronage pie, such as one of the three members of the Civil Service Commission. Yet, as late as 1960, Sayre and Kaufman thought them such an insignificant part of governing New York that there are only four entries in the index, and the most prominent black, Adam Clayton Powell, is mentioned only because his reelection was opposed by the district leaders.

In the past twenty years, the old black political cohesion has begun to come apart, suggesting that the Powell episode was not an aberration but a harbinger. The first division was generational. The familiar names, like Basil Paterson (former state and city official and candidate for statewide office), Percy Sutton (former Manhattan borough president and candidate for mayor in 1977), and Charles Rangel (long-time member of the U.S. House of Representatives), are increasingly pushed aside by younger, more impatient figures. The second division was geographical, as the growing black population spilled out of Harlem into the Bronx, Queens, and Brooklyn. While some organizations accommodated themselves to the newcomers, others were not nimble enough to ward off the disaffected dissidents who increasingly won primary battles with regular Democrats, black or white. The other division was internal, between political leaders and ministers of large churches, which alone in the black community command large audiences. Their disagreements usually concerned community issues, but they quickly developed a political dimension.

The 1989 mayoral election brought a sudden unity to the conflicting factions. The success of Jesse Jackson's presidential primaries of 1984 and 1988 suggested the fruits of unity, just as Farrell's defeat in 1985 had demonstrated the consequences of disunity.[16] David Dinkins was the most prominent elected Democrat in city government. He had nurtured white support for a quarter century, and his relaxed style had an appeal that went beyond race. His candidacy transcended, at least for a time, the divisions that had crippled previous black efforts. And in Mayor Koch he had an opponent whose early minority support had almost entirely evaporated, and whose assault on Jesse Jackson in 1988 had alienated what little was left. The candidacy was further buoyed by union endorsements and the support of assorted liberals. It was significant that only one of the party leaders joined his campaign, and he was black and from Manhattan. Dinkins's victory provides the black community at least some respite from the vigorous competition that has characterized the last two decades.

New York Latinos show the same restlessness. Many have resented being lumped with blacks under the term "minority." Nor do they fit the usual immigrant stereotype, since the Puerto Ricans are Americans by birth. Moreover, the new migrants are from all over the Caribbean and South America. But their total numbers will soon equal the black population. Indeed, together the two groups probably comprise half of the city's total. Yet Latinos are not mentioned at all in Sayre and Kaufman's index on New York's governing process. They have never been an integral part of the Democratic party, hence their increasing independence is not so surprising. Koch attempted to wean them away from their uneasy alliance with the blacks, with some early success. But by 1989 his vote dropped below one-third, as a new generation began to assert itself politically. While Herman Badillo endorsed Mayor Koch in the primary, Bronx Borough President Fernando Ferrer and Assemblyman Jose Serrano backed Dinkins. Observers freely predict that Serrano will replace the convicted Robert Garcia in Congress, and Ferrer is likely to be the first Latino to occupy Gracie Mansion. The newcomers owe nothing to the Democratic party, are comfortable with independent voters, and grew up in the age of electronic politics and its kleig lights.

The Democratic party has also had trouble retaining the allegiance of the city's organized workers. The clothing unions, in fact, had already launched competing parties with their commanding role in the founding of the American Labor party and the Liberal party, and their differences with Tammany had deep historical roots. The more recent organization of municipal workers heightened the political interests of the unions even as it presented them with an awkward strategic dilemma: how to bargain with an employer they might have helped get elected, or how to handle a mayor who had just defeated them at the polls.

In addition, the older organizations suffered the inevitable generation gap. Younger members inherited unions, they did not build them, and while accepting their elected officials' views on contracts, they became notoriously independent in their political choices. Nothing illustrated this better than the 1984 election when, nationwide, half the members of organized labor voted for Ronald Reagan in the face of nearly unanimous support for Walter Mondale by virtually every local and national labor leader. Moreover, better-paid unionists moved easily to the suburbs where they identified with their communities rather than their organizations, thus diluting their importance in municipal politics. Candidates still found labor endorsements useful, but scarcely critical. Worse still for labor's influence in the Democratic party, New York's changing economy attracted white-collar workers or service employees, both of whom are hard to organize and impossible to influence politically.

The Democratic party's traditional roots were in the Irish, Jewish, and, to some degree, Italian communities. As time went on and as each successive ethnic generation rose economically and socially, they moved out of the old areas into the pleasant residential neighborhoods in the outer reaches of the city where old ties weakened and old habits faded. Soon they, too, joined the independent ranks, voting for candidates rather than party. The Irish, particularly, opted for the suburbs, but the others soon followed. Their voting patterns, once somewhat predictable, now ranged across party lines and ignored the old attachments to either regulars or reformers. The result, in the 1980s, was the election and reelection of Mario Cuomo, a liberal Democratic governor; Alfonse D'Amato, a conservative Republican U.S. Senator; Daniel Patrick Moynihan, a liberal Democratic Senator; and Edward Koch, a former reformer, as a maverick mayor. This independent electorate continually upset conventional analysis and scrambled ethnic and racial expectations, but it is unlikely to return ever again to party moorings.

To complicate traditional party allegiances further, a new college-educated generation grew up with a different perception of politics. They entered an economy that knew no depression but only prosperity. They found their jobs in the private sector and never had to rely on patronage or political favoritism (unless they sought to become judges). The New Deal had provided a floor of security for them in their old age as well as in the periods of unemployment. Medicare and Medicaid later lifted the burden of the care of their parents from their shoulders. In short, they didn't need politics in the conventional sense. Yet their numbers made them the object of political attention.

The corrosive effect of the welfare state and the electronic revolution on the party system is best embodied in the new generation. Their independence is rooted in the education benefits included in the "G.I. Bill" passed in 1944. Its impact on politics was not foreseen at the time nor fully noted by commentators since. It is not mentioned by Sayre and Kaufman, yet it has had a profound effect on American society and the breakup of the old party structure. Passed quickly and almost without debate, it opened up higher education to a whole generation whose families never had the opportunity to go to college and most of whom believed it beyond their reach.[17] Before World War II fewer than 14 percent of young people went to college; by the 1980s, more than 60 percent did so.

The Decline in Participation

These voters grew up without any permanent party ties or partisan loyalties. They might be moved by an issue, or sometimes divided by one, and they move easily across party lines, split tickets, and often do not participate at all. They and their children are increasingly the center of the no-party system. Marinated for years in the television and media innovations, they seem to the older generation rootless and, indeed, fickle. They prefer personalities to party, social action to political participation, and a greater interest in the future than a longing for the past. Whatever ethnic and religious political loyalties they inherited have already faded and are certainly no longer compelling.

In the past, the party had been the mediator in disputes between various factions within its ranks. Patronage was the most effective glue, but symbolic nominations often provided a gesture of recognition of newly arrived and otherwise neglected groups. When Tim Sullivan was in Albany, he persuaded his colleagues to make Columbus Day a state holiday as a bow to Italian-Americans who had moved into his ward in large numbers. The loyalty of blacks was rewarded with the borough presidency of Manhattan, and the adoption of Martin Luther King's birthday as a city observance. Regulars and reformers alike believed in the "balanced ticket" and, even when they clashed, they were careful not to slight any powerful ethnic or racial constituency.

The spread of the primary system to every level of elected office destroyed this old representational system. Now candidates went directly to the voters who had only a modest stake in a balanced outcome. Indeed, in 1962, the state Democratic party fielded a slate of four Jews and one black—all from the metropolitan area. The 1985 city election left New York with three Jewish white males as the only officers elected at-large. The year before there was not one black or Latino member of the Board of Estimate, and a court pronounced the city council so gerrymandered as to have virtually disenfranchised the minority population. Party slatemaking had always tried to prevent this malapportioned result; yet the new politics has no capacity to assure even some modest representation.

The new no-party system, however, was accompanied by an alarming decrease in voting participation. As the grassroots of traditional campaigning withered, the electorate increasingly became spectators with no personal connection with the political process. The decline was national, with just over 50 percent of the voters turning out to elect Ronald Reagan. In the city, the slide was more precipitous; fewer than 20 percent of the eligible voters gave a "mandate" to Mayor Koch in his reelection "landslide." The irony is unmistakable: the society that once invented free elections now has the lowest participation rate of any democracy in the world.

Nor is there any indication that this dismal record will be reversed. The old party system disintegrated because its functions are provided in other ways. Government programs created a welfare state that better serves the public and does so without political obligations; the media brings the candidates and issues directly to the voters without the mediation of the party apparatus. While the old practitioners, regulars and reformers, bewail the general electoral untidiness and electronic impersonality of the new system, the public accepts it with resignation if not much enthusiasm.

Nostalgia for "the good old days" has become almost a cottage industry among political experts and academic commentators. They invest the old party structure with attributes it never had and excuse abuses it certainly contained. James Reston, who has written about American politics for half a century, said he wanted to spend his retirement years trying "to bring back the smoke filled rooms so that the next presidential candidates will be chosen by people who know something about them."[18] But this is like trying to glue autumn leaves onto barren branches. The voter sits in the living room, unmolested by party canvassers or calls from party headquarters, looking at the evanescent events on the television screen and deciding whom to vote for, or whether to vote at all.

Notes

1. Wallace S. Sayre and Herbert Kaufman, *Governing New York City: Politics in the Metropolis.* New York: Norton, 1960, p. 452.

2. Jacob Riis, *How the Other Half Lives: Studies Among the Tenements of New York.* New York: Scribner and Sons, 1902.

3. Robert A. Woods, *The Neighborhood in Nation-Building: The Running Comment of Thirty Years at the South End House.* Boston, MA: Riverside Press, 1923, p. 69.

4. Until 1939 the governor was elected for a two-year term.

5. The census of 1920 revealed that, for the first time, more Americans lived in cities than in the country. Earlier depressions had been briefer and dominated by rural issues and distress.

6. In 1944, the American Labor party (ALP) split; its right wing became the more permanent Liberal party. The ALP moved to the left, became identified with pro-Soviet causes and did not survive the early years of the Cold War.

7. The Democratic nomination for elected judicial positions (the mayor appoints some lower court judges, but most state judges are elected by district or countywide, under party labels, with Democrats almost always the winners) remains the one important plum that the party organization can bestow, but the Manhattan Surrogates have usually been independents, since the Kennedy intervention.

8. The two terms were 1962–65 and 1970–73. He was out of office from 1966 through 1969, having won the Democratic nomination for mayor in 1965 but lost the election to Lindsay.

9. See Chapter 8 by Gerald Benjamin for further discussion of the changing relationship of the city and state governments.

10. Norman Podhoretz, "Why Reagan and Koch Are the Most Popular Politicians in America," *New York Magazine* 14 (April 6, 1981): 30–32.

11. Howard Kurtz, "Biaggi Influence-Peddling Trial to Open," The *Washington Post,* August 24, 1987, p. A9.

12. Ibid.

13. Hendrick Hertzberg, "Hi, Boss, Said the Judge to Meade Esposito," *New York Times Magazine,* December 10, 1972.

14. The Democratic party organization in Brooklyn did not entirely evaporate after Esposito's fall. Rather, political power and influence devolved to the members of the borough's delegation to the state legislature, which remains the largest in the Assembly and still includes the Speaker.

15. "Interview with Edward I. Koch," *Playboy* 29:4 (April 1982): 98; see also Edward I. Koch, with William Rauch, *Mayor.* New York: Simon & Schuster, 1984, pp. 183–85, 309.

16. In 1985 a black and Latino committee attempted to bring forth a candidate to run against Koch. After great public squabbling it came up with Dennis Farrell, the Democratic leader of Manhattan, who was badly beaten.

17. The "G.I. Bill" covered tuition, books, and stipends to returning veterans for periods tied to the length of their military service; extensions offered similar benefits to veterans of the Korean and Vietnam wars. To accommodate the demand by veterans after 1945, the states enormously expanded the capacity of the publicly supported higher education institutions (and created many new ones), so that even when the numbers of veterans shrunk substantially during the late 1950s, enrollments continued to grow. The "G.I. Bill" fundamentally altered expectations, converting higher education into something to which all were entitled.

18. James Reston, *New York Times,* February 6, 1989, p. A15.

11

Clusters of Power: Interest Groups

Jewel Bellush

This chapter spotlights the role of pressure groups, their influence on the political process, and the impact, in turn, of the political system on them. The theoretical underpinning for this analysis draws heavily on the framework of the pluralist model evolved by Wallace Sayre and Herbert Kaufman and their colleagues Robert Dahl and Edward Banfield, among others. Their theory provides a useful launching pad for reformulating some key propositions concerning groups—the roles they play and the influence they exert.

Although Sayre and Kaufman suggest that groups and their relationships vary from one policy area to another, the underlying theme of this chapter is that, while these relationships are not fixed permanently, they are structured rather than fluid. The structure and relations of groups are linked to the social and economic fabric of New York City, and these groups' interactions provide an ongoing and yet changing context in which decision making occurs and policy evolves. The system is much less open and responsive than Sayre and Kaufman contend, particularly where race is involved. Indeed, the omission of race from the Sayre and Kaufman analysis demonstrates one of the major limitations to the pluralist theory.[1]

A rich and expanding variety of pressure groups operates in the ever-changing environment of New York. But this does not mean that everyone in the city has more or less equal access to government. Instead, there are distinct and important clusters of power: power congeals. The result is that the rewards and punishments allocated by governmental officials vary substantially among the sectors of the city's population.

This chapter is divided into three major sections, each dealing with a radically different period in the city's recent history: the community revolution of the 1960s; the fiscal crisis of 1975–76; and the postcrisis era from 1977 to the 1980s.

Civil Life: Tradition and Change

Within a few short years after the publication of Sayre and Kaufman's paperback edition, the traditional civic organizations were confronted with a new challenging phenomenon—the emergence of groups sparked by the civil rights, antiwar, and student protest movements that swept across the nation. In this section, we examine some of the civic organizations familiar to the New York scene, the new groupings that emerged during the 1960s, their impact on civic life, and the legacy they left.

Classic Civic Groups

During the first half of the twentieth century, civic life in New York was organized primarily around five types of organizations: good government, tax-conscious, planning/housing oriented, neighborhood preservation, and social service providers for the low income population.

Good government associations, often dubbed the "goo-goos," included the Citizens Union, the League of Women Voters, the City Club, and the Bar Association of New York, among others—those pledged to an honest, impartial, and efficient municipality. Their major focus has been largely on structural reform directed toward improving governmental performance and producing a more informed and educated voter. Their specific proposals usually included strengthening executive authority, eliminating patronage through civil service reform, introducing primary elections, and improving the budget process. Some of the strategies they pursued encompassed charter reform, lobbying, coalitions, and political education of the voting public.

Among the traditional means of political education was the widespread distribution of pamphlets and brochures such as the "Facts for Voters" and the "Voters Directory." Infrequent, but influential, political coalitions usually focused around an issue of major import, generally framed in a neutral, nonpartisan style. The leaders and activists in these groups were predominantly volunteers drawn largely from the city's middle class. Generally, they were highly educated, committed individuals with an intense interest in responsible government. It was Edward Banfield who articulated the expansive, philosophical outlook of these participants when he wrote:

> The ideal of "good government" was a class ideal, of course. . . . The lower class thinks of "goodness" in terms of some advantage for the individual or the family, whereas the middle-class thinks of it in terms of the community or some larger abstract public.[2]

A second group of civic organizations was animated by concern about the level and mix of local taxes, for example, the Citizens Budget Commission (CBC), the chambers of commerce in Manhattan and the outer boroughs, and the real estate boards. These groups often joined the good government forces seeking structural reform or heightened civil service standards. Their special focus, however, remained financial, attentive to policies affecting taxation and govern-

mental expenditures. They have been the perennial watchdogs of the city's budget—reminding, cajoling, and even threatening officials with dire consequences
if they did not spend less, keep taxes low, and manage the bureaucracy more
efficiently.

Over the years and certainly on into the 1960s, the CBC has been one of the
most vigorous organizations concerned with fiscal issues—lobbying for balanced
budgets and publishing reports and studies that were inevitably critical of the
ever-increasing city debts. Unlike most other civic groups, which depend on a
voluntary corps of determined activists, CBC and the chambers of commerce
have usually been supported with substantial funds contributed by their membership, drawn largely from business and commercial interests. This has tended to
ensure stable, ongoing staffs providing expertise and information. Many a city
administration has solicited the CBC's views on troubling fiscal issues, even
calling on the organization to conduct inquiries.

Sayre and Kaufman viewed CBC as

> the most active, the most specialized and one of the most effective representa-
> tives of the business community in the city's political process. Its primary
> function is to guard the most important taxpaying groups in the city against all
> avoidable increases in their tax bills, a function the CBC has performed with
> energy and skill for a quarter century.[3]

Another assortment of civic organizations devoted itself to the city's housing
and planning needs and to the preservation of historic buildings and areas. The
Regional Plan Association, for example, has labored for years to spotlight many
of the economic and social needs of the metropolitan region, proposing vitally
needed improvements. Its famous Regional Plan of New York and its Environs
(the first regional plan, 1929) laid out the regional network of highways, park-
ways, bridges, tunnels, and major parks. It became the primary influence in
bringing to the city the concept of the super-block planning scheme, best exemplified at Rockefeller Center.

The major concerns of the Citizens Housing and Planning Council
(CHPC) have been to ensure continued construction of low- and middle-
income housing and to improve city planning. Founded in the 1930s, it was a
vital element in support of public housing during the New Deal and subsequent administrations and provided a much needed voice to balance local,
more parochial opposition.

Until recent years, the Municipal Art Society was viewed as an elitist group
concerned primarily, if not exclusively, with making the city beautiful. With its
origins going back to the beaux-arts era, it sought to focus attention on the city's
aesthetic aspects and on the preservation of landmarks and parks.

Another old-style civic organization was the neighborhood group formed for
a wide variety of purposes—individual homeowners guarding their property val-

ues and tax assessments, small shopkeepers demanding better public services, and tenants complaining of rent increases or poor maintenance. Because of the city's immense size and geographical spread, the expansive territorial divide between Manhattan and the four outer boroughs motivated many business interests in dispersed retail areas to create their own associations.

A fifth category of civic groups was concerned with the ever-present, growing social problems of the low income and the poor of a burgeoning city, for example, the settlement houses, the Community Service Society, the Citizens Committee for Children, the Urban League, the Community Council of Greater New York, and various sectarian associations intimately involved in the daily work of social agencies, Catholic Charities, the Jewish Federation, and the Protestant Council. These communal organizations were private, voluntary groups, sustained by individual contributions and by those with wealth and status sufficient to give the respective association recognition, political visibility and clout. Without exception, volunteers were motivated by a social conscience, reaping satisfaction in "doing good."

The New Civics

One of the most serious drawbacks in the structure of old civic organizations was the distance from the city's growing minority populations, the blacks and the Latinos, and sometimes their lack of interest in, or sensitivity to, vital social, economic, and housing needs of the minority poor. While the social service organizations articulated the pressing problems of the poor and provided desperately needed services to the minorities, they were managed mostly by whites, often affluent women, driven by a sense of duty to help the homeless, but who, at the same time, were to some extent out of touch with the clients they were serving. (See Chapter 13 by Charles Hamilton on patron-client relationships.) It was no surprise to knowledgeable observers that by the 1960s, these civic units would be pushed from the center of the political stage by a new, more dynamic and militant breed of civic life.

We describe them as "the new civics," ushered in by the community revolution. Three major forces came together, at about the same time, to spark the emergence of this new interest group formation: the civil rights movement, a body of radical thought, and government-sponsored pluralism.

The civil rights movement helped catalyze other social eruptions—student rebellions and peace protests in New York and throughout the nation. These developments, in turn, contributed not only to the emergence of new groupings but to a degree of activism that reminded many of the militant union movements of the 1930s. There was a sudden, startling change in the political climate that helped foster a very high degree of civic awareness, personal involvement, and a rare optimistic spirit, particularly among many city blacks. Of overriding importance was a developing belief that through such direct, personal involvement as sit-ins, freedom rides, boycotts, picketing, and other manifestations of militancy, their deplorable conditions could be changed and life improved dramatically.

In the South, the legal barriers to integration in transportation, hotel accommodations, lunch counters, and schools were crumbling.[4] New groups emerged in the city's neighborhoods, centering many of their activities around rent strikes and improving local schools, all part of the flourishing of involved community organizations. This new militant mood and intensified civic participation by increased numbers of the urban poor and blacks contrasted dramatically with the acquiescence of preceding decades. Not long before, most academic and journalistic observers of the urban scene, including Gunnar Myrdal, had described the city's minorities as listless, powerless, and apathetic. Sayre and Kaufman had paid little or no attention to the racial dimensions of city politics. In fact, they assumed, as did many pluralists at the time, that inactivity was a sign of satisfaction with the status quo.

Coincidental with the civil rights movement sweeping the country, a number of radical professionals were expressing challenging and dissenting viewpoints in the fields of urban planning, social welfare, health, and education. They conveyed deep dissatisfaction, indeed disdain, with the pluralists' defense of traditionally democratic institutions affording adequate channels for achieving access to the system by the diverse groups in American society. These radicals, mostly academics, insisted that the nation's poor and minority populations were alienated from the institutions of our society and could only be linked to the institutional mainstream when they themselves felt accepted. These radicals conjectured that only active involvement in community affairs would improve the competence of poor minorities to deal with their manifold problems. By learning new skills and developing a more positive perspective, they would evince more productive behavior. Furthermore, active participation in the planning and implementation of programs to end poverty would not only provide job training, but also open new opportunities for the unskilled and poorly educated. By involving the poor, they felt that a new constituency would be created which, once politicized, would ultimately be capable of managing its own struggles with city officialdom and effectively pressuring for improvement of service delivery to their communities. Daniel Moynihan noted that "community action with citizen participation was a coherent and powerful idea working its way into national policy, albeit little noticed or understood at the time."[5]

Among the many proposals projected by these radical writers were advocacy planning, community control, black power, neighborhood government, and a plethora of suggestions for citizen participation in specific programs dealing with education, mental health, welfare, housing, and community planning. The rhetoric flowing from these radical doctrines was inspired by two basic assumptions: if people were organized at the neighborhood level and if they were empowered with authority over their own local institutions, they would end paternalism and dependency, dramatically improve the quality of community services, achieve a more equitable distribution of the city's resources, and, ultimately, receive more conscientious and responsible treatment from city government and its agencies.[6]

Both the social upheavals of the period and the popularity of the broad-ranging radical ideas helped stimulate new public policies in Washington and New York, which we designate "sponsored pluralism." These were pioneering governmental programs devised to open the political process to a far wider constituency, particularly those who had not previously participated in the traditional political process. An integral part of the antipoverty program included the basic assumption that, if the poor could be involved from the start in seeking solutions to their problems, a more enlightened and extensive program would emerge because of their intimate understanding of their own situation. Thus, the Community Action Program (CAP) was established in communities where large concentrations of the poor resided, empowering them, through "maximum feasible participation," to design their own programs. Since these CAPs were authorized to distribute funds, proponents believed that the urban poor would demonstrate a deep commitment, in fact, a zealot's missionary spirit, to organize and actively participate in the decision-making process.

It was casually assumed that, once organized, the poor would master the necessary political skills, identify the points of access, and select the targets for applying pressure. With these achievements, the poor would become politically self-sufficient. A key element of the radical doctrine was that the new process would enable the poor to break out of the vicious cycle of poverty. Thus, the antipoverty program evolved as a new form through which to channel the energies of the civil rights movement.

At the same time, these radical tenets impacted on a number of important developments in New York City, particularly during the mayoralty of John V. Lindsay (1965–73). A former Republican congressman, Lindsay became mayor after having brought together a rather loose, comparatively weak coalition of Republicans, independent Democrats, the tattered remnants of Fiorello LaGuardia's Fusion movement, and other reform groups. Seeking to broaden his constituency, Lindsay sought consciously to build bridges to the black and lower-income communities. The changing climate provided by movement politics and the radical ideology under discussion, proved uniquely attractive to him. As one of Lindsay's associates subsequently put it:

> The civil rights movement was central to John Lindsay's career. It was one of the great political movements in American History, and it is almost impossible to overestimate its impact on American Government, North and South. The driving force of the movement was a sense of moral outrage at the racist character of American society, an outrage fed by the brutal response of Southern authorities to early civil rights organizing and gradual exposure of the subtle, more hypocritical white resistance to black progress in the North.[7]

Lindsay criticized "distant," "impersonal power," and the "faceless bureaucrats" who did not understand, or indeed care, about what the people they served wanted. Attacking poor quality and unresponsive planning, he urged that "we cannot plan for the citizenry unless we plan with them, unless we are willing to give to individuals, to neighborhoods, and to communities the power to be heard and the power to challenge, the power most of all to actually decide as much as is possible what their communities will look like and how they will work."[8]

Charles Morris, a Lindsay aide, suggested that the mayor was attracted to ideas propagated by the radicals: "massive government interventions to solve ghetto problems, participatory democracy for blacks and Puerto Ricans, community control of anti-poverty programs and schools, and a view that civil disorders were more a reflection of white failings than of black indiscipline."[9]

As mayor, Lindsay launched a series of neighborhood-based experiments throughout the city, seeking to give voice to these formerly silent elements by opening new channels to City Hall. He embraced the radical rhetoric, anticipating that involvement of the poor would foster significant improvements in municipal services. Some of the city's leading private foundations, but particularly the well-endowed Ford Foundation, were attracted to these new doctrines, having been increasingly sensitized by the moving rhetoric and goals of Rev. Martin Luther King, Jr., and the civil rights movement. Making government more responsive to the burgeoning needs of the urban minorities and the poor became a top priority in determining the allocation of many foundation resources. Encouraged by Lindsay's style and sympathetic sentiments, the Ford Foundation provided the money, staff, and support that launched one of the most controversial experiments in sponsored pluralism—school decentralization. Its impact for good and for bad on the city is still being felt to this very day. (See Chapter 6 by David Rogers and Chapter 13 by Charles V. Hamilton.)

New Politics, Racial Dimensions

During the Lindsay years, black politics took many forms and manifestations. In particular, there was the emergence of a new civic style by black leaders—the utilization of militant tactics that included direct confrontations with the city's bureaucracy. Traditionally, black politics in New York had been moderate in style and substance. Politicians like Hulan Jack and Adam Clayton Powell, Percy Sutton and Shirley Chisholm, among others, had pursued the customary practice of party politics. Likewise, such a pressure group as the National Association for the Advancement of Colored People had pursued the conventional functions of lobbying and legal presentations before the judiciary in the process of battling to extend civil rights. The Urban League operated in a most restrained manner in the city's economic life, preparing blacks for jobs through skills training and educational programs. Both groups were relatively weak and poorly funded, with comparatively little involvement of the black community to be helped.

In the early 1960s, the civil rights movement suddenly sparked dramatic changes in the political life of many blacks, encouraging militancy and inducing a new commitment. As this crusade evolved, militant elements emerged. New leaders were urging immediate and formidable confrontations with established institutions and with clenched fists, shouted, "black power." Adherents of this sharp, resounding thrust believed that to develop confidence and pride among blacks, a more assertive form of race consciousness was required. To achieve a sense of self-worth, the new leaders pursued a strategy of separatism from white society. Activist Stokely Carmichael and academician Charles Hamilton expressed the popular version of this concept in their work, *Black Power*, in which they insisted that

> the goal of black people must NOT be to assimilate into middle class America, for that class-as-a-whole is without a viable consciousness as regards humanity. . . . The values of that class ultimately support cloistered little closed societies, tucked away neatly in tree-lined suburbia.[10]

Attacking institutional racism, the authors vehemently criticized the dilapidated housing of the nation's Harlems and vigorously attacked forced ghettoization and blatant discrimination by merchants and real estate brokers. They urged blacks to organize independently into their own social and economic groups, nurture their political capacities, and, only then, take on the white institutions obstructing their way to opportunity and social justice. Only after securing black solidarity and skills should blacks consider joining alliances with others. "Enter coalitions," urged the authors, "only after you are able to stand on your own."[11] At that time, the rationale of black power, the furious battles over school decentralization, recurring rent strikes, and increasing sit-ins at welfare offices across the city engendered a pervading sense of unease, indeed fear among most whites.

Community Politics: Achievements

Community-based politics of the 1960s exposed the searing ills of race and poverty in new and dramatic ways. The traditional channels of party and pressure group politics had proven unresponsive to the many needs of those who had long suffered outside the system.[12] The new politics, inspired by President Lyndon Johnson's Great Society programs and Mayor Lindsay's extensive neighborhood outreach, designed specifically for the poor ghetto communities, provided new path-breaking channels for pioneering interest group formations. The antipoverty and model cities programs made jobs and services available to many who had long been on the outside. Jill Joness writes that "the poverty programs opened up a whole new world of jobs that offered good pay, prestige within the community, and the prospect of participating in the Great Society."[13]

Mayor Lindsay's outreach to these disaffected constituencies helped ensure that many newcomers would enter the political arena, with a significant impact on their communities. Human services were enlarged and extended to many more city dwellers than ever before, money was channeled through nonestablishment agencies in the ghettos—Head Start centers, family planning programs, neighborhood law offices, comprehensive health centers, day care centers, and summer job programs for ghetto teenagers. The most extensive community participatory effort in the nation took place in New York City. A host of community-based systems was created and placed alongside traditional institutions, for example, planning boards, school boards, community corporations, health districts, Urban Action Task Forces, neighborhood city halls, and local welfare centers.[14]

Appointments to the city's bureaucracy included unusual numbers of responsive and sympathetic administrators. The Human Resources Administration (HRA) was created to address ghetto population needs; HRA sought to radically improve the delivery of social services and to broaden employment opportunities for minorities within the agency itself. Following some traditional patterns where, for example, the police department had provided opportunities for the Irish, the sanitation agency for the Italians, and the educational system had facilitated a substantial number from the Jewish community, large numbers of blacks and Latinos were encouraged to move into HRA. It was reported that, of the 14,000 individuals employed by the city's antipoverty program, about 80 percent of those who worked in the poor communities were local residents. HRA Director Mitchell Ginsberg proudly noted that these local programs were being "run by grassroots, nontraditional social agencies." He defended this strategy by insisting that "inasmuch as one of the primary goals of the community action program is to give community people the opportunity to learn the ways of organized effort and to thus enter the mainstream of society, they must be allowed to learn by doing."[15]

The city's civil service system recruited large numbers of minority caseworkers, other professionals, hospital workers, school paraprofessionals, and black clerical workers. By the latter part of the 1960s, these black workers also benefited from unionization of the public service, winning increased wages and a variety of much needed benefits, including health and pensions. But most important, they were accorded a sense of human dignity. Through these means, thousands upon thousands of blacks were being linked to the city's economic, social, and political establishments.[16]

By identifying his administration with the city's minorities, Lindsay was able to avoid some of the more destructive demonstrations, riots, and looting that occurred elsewhere in the nation. He had put in place a number of devices that helped facilitate speedy communication of imminent trouble spots to sensitively oriented aides. During this period, increasing numbers of blacks and Latinos were initiated into the political socialization process through new participatory channels that provided training grounds for leadership development.

With the creation of these innovative institutional forms at the neighborhood level, new opportunities were provided for broadened participation, particularly among the poor, the minorities, and the other disaffected. Finally, the Lindsay administration provided much needed recognition, status, and patronage for these new activists. At the same time, the mayor sought to use the emerging, indigenous leadership as a base for his own political constituency, bypassing the established groups traditionally associated with the Democratic party organization.

Community Politics: Limitations

For all their success, the militant newcomers for the most part did not forge permanent ongoing relationships with the rest of the community. The new participants, operating primarily at the grassroots level, were absorbed within their own bailiwicks. As a result, they were inattentive to or, more accurately perhaps, distracted from the larger and more lucrative game of power politics played out in the citywide arena, where the prizes were far more substantial. Charles Hamilton underscored this point in his criticism of Lindsay's decentralization strategies that, he felt, diverted the main energies of blacks from the scene of big stakes. Furthermore, most New York City neighborhoods are large, with variegated populations. Thus conflicts emerged on a number of fronts between blacks and Latinos, between blacks and Hasidic Jews, among blacks themselves, and among Latinos as well.

In addition, putting new actors in the ghetto communities did not automatically invite cooperation from established bureaucracies. Tensions frequently surfaced between black participants and civil servants downtown. The latter included many experienced professionals who felt that the newcomers on the pressure group scene did not understand the problems and complexities of the bureaucracies. Furthermore, they were viewed as too strident. Finally, a goodly number of administrators and their associates were simply unwilling to share their authority, which often was quite limited to begin with.[17]

Another Lindsay strategy to ensure minority support was the scattered-site public housing program. This plan sought to integrate segments of the low-income populations within middle-class, white areas of the city. Prior to the Lindsay administration, New York City had a vast public housing program, consisting of a relatively small number of very large projects, with these projects concentrated within a small number of neighborhoods. Thus, only a small number of middle-class New Yorkers were affected by public housing location decisions. Quietly, and with a minimum of public fanfare, earlier boards of estimate would cut deals with their own members, the five borough presidents, each of whom agreed to take a share of the proposed public housing.

The Lindsay plan, designed to overcome the racial separation and other negative attributes of traditional public housing, called for much smaller projects on scattered sites outside the ghettos, thus making the issue a noisy public one. "A definite shift in political style was instituted: from negotiation marked by extensive bargaining and compromise within a private, if not secret, context, to a politics of open struggle, intense conflict, and public confrontation."[18] The confrontation was worst over a proposal for a project to be located in Forest Hills, Queens, a relatively affluent community of expensive owner-occupied houses and new apartment houses. The controversy rocked the city for months. The divisive battle was well documented by a bright young lawyer, Mario Cuomo, who was brought onto the scene as an arbitrator in search of a solution that would allay tensions between the city administration and the middle-class, white residents. New York City was not as safe from open racial conflict as the early successes of the Lindsay community politics had suggested.[19]

The most serious community conflict sparked by the Lindsay administration—whose local reverberations were soon felt nationally—was generated by the mayor's effort to decentralize the school system. As one of his more perceptive aides put it subsequently, "If Lindsay's sensitive handling of urban disorders earned him national prominence in the spring of 1968, his handling of the racially charged school strikes that occurred only a half-year later . . . nearly ended his political career."[20]

In retrospect, even the mayor recognized his strategic error in limiting the initial experiment to black and Latino districts. The shrill ensuing confrontations between, on the one hand, black parents and militant cadres and, on the other, mostly white teachers and administrators—to a large extent, between blacks and Jewish teachers—continued for months, poisoning not only the workings of the school system, but also city government in general. To this day, the school imbroglio of 1968–69 has had a discordant impact on interracial relations.

The tragic school conflict did not end Lindsay's encounter with community politics. An increase in publicized charges of police brutality in ghetto areas led to a rising demand that more civilians be placed on the police review board. When the city council, responding to police pressure, voted down the mayor's request that a majority of the review board be composed of civilians, he incorporated his proposal in the form of an executive order. A fireball of protest, inspired by an angered Patrolmen's Benevolent Association (PBA), eventually resulted in the issue being placed on the November ballot as a referendum item. Once more, racial tensions were exacerbated, with an angry response from the city's white ethnic groups. Attracted by the "law and order" defense enunciated by police officers and their union, they campaigned vigorously and emotionally against the mayor's proposal. This issue further divided the city, for many fearful white middle-class voters sided with the police.

For the first time in years, a majority of the city's electorate opposed a liberal referendum item on the ballot. While the blacks voted overwhelmingly for a civilian-run review board, Irish and Italian Catholics opposed it by a decisive majority. Jewish voters were divided on the issue. The authors of a study of this referendum, concluded that "many of the progressive values that underlie the call for urban reform and aid to blacks and other minority groups still hold the allegiance of city voters. Nonetheless, a more narrowly defined 'politics of interest' has come to have an influence greater than the traditional politics of liberal values."[21]

Sayre and Kaufman's optimistic view of pluralism was based on a politics of reason and calmness. Groups would organize, coalitions would form, and conflicts would be resolved by accommodation, bargaining, and negotiation. Racial issues simply did not conform to this paradigm of conflict resolution.

Admittedly, during the initial phase of the civil rights revolution there had been substantial public support, if not enthusiasm, for eliminating the legal barriers to integration. With changes in the character of civil rights issues and particularly when a number of these controversial issues surfaced at the neighborhood level in New York City, such as school decentralization, the police review board, and integrated housing, the enthusiasm for civil rights receded and was replaced by heightened tensions and divisiveness.

As Lindsay's community-based experiments were put in place, they fostered and reflected increasing intergroup hostility. To increasing numbers of whites, black militancy appeared aggressive and threatening. Other whites felt that by devoting as much attention as it did to black needs, the Lindsay administration was neglecting existing problems in white communities, particularly those of the lower and middle class. Jill Joness noted the paradox when she observed that the initial success of the civil rights movement had "inspired more effort and more recruits, but the greater the success of the movement, the greater the public resentment. There was little sympathy for the unruly tactics, especially when they resulted in more and more families on the dole." Along similar lines, Charles Morris found that "black development was a more complex problem than was often admitted, and not one that would be solved only by removing discriminatory barriers and providing compensatory programs."[22]

By the early 1970s, the after-effects of these divisive battles were having their impact throughout the city. Somewhat typical was the behavior of many residents in Canarsie, Brooklyn. After the local school board approved the transfer of a few dozen black children, many of the local citizenry reached a stage of near-hysteria. Various objections were offered, but they were reduced to the fact that many of the white parents just did not want black students brought into their school. According to a study of this controversy, the white middle-class folk of

Canarsie saw themselves "as victims of forces that were disrupting life across New York City. . . . Discontent stiffened their resolve to regain control."[23]

Godfrey Hodgson, a British journalist who watched the civil rights movement unfold, wrote that "the schism went deeper than mere political disagreement. It was as if, from 1967 on, for several years, two different tribes of Americans experienced the same outward events but experienced them as two quite different realities."[24]

The new civics of the 1960s, representing a host of community-based groups, were a cluster of power sparked by the civil rights movement. Because they were supported by government, the programs that stimulated their emergence can be called "sponsored pluralism." Thus, the city's political system and channels were opened to new voices and forces that had not previously been taken seriously by the pluralist theorists.

The older civics had been almost exclusively white, middle-class groups concerned primarily with structural reform of governmental systems. Their restrained strategies focused mainly on traditional methods. In sharp contrast, these newcomers to city politics represented a profoundly different clientele who resorted to a series of radical strategies. Mostly blacks, Latinos, and representatives of the city's poor, their agenda centered on the social and economic issues that were relevant and timely to them, if not to the better-off majority.

The Fiscal Crisis: A New Cluster of Power

By the middle of the 1970s, most of the offshoots of the community revolution had been seriously weakened and were pushed from center stage by the city's fiscal crisis. The city's brush with bankruptcy between 1975 and 1977 created the environment for the emergence of a new cluster of power of unlikely and unexpected collaborators—bankers/investors and public service unions. We now review the background of the crisis, trace the evolution of this new group formation, and assess its impact on city politics.

New York City has not been a stranger to fiscal crises. Most of them have usually involved the closing of credit markets to the city, the imposition of a bailout plan, and the implementation of a retrenchment program. Martin Shefter, an observer of this most recent fiscal crisis, has written that

> the events of 1975 . . . were only the most recent of a series of fiscal crises that for well over a century have erupted periodically in New York: in 1856, 1871, 1907, 1914, 1932–33, and 1975. . . . Indeed, these episodes occur with sufficient regularity that fiscal crises should be regarded not as aberrations, but as an integral part of American urban politics.[25]

The key decision makers who played a predominant role in the 1930s crisis, however, constituted a single elite, a consortium of bankers. In addition, New

York State Governor Herbert Lehman, a prominent member of the financial community, facilitated the final Bankers Agreement, which was written in his office.[26] In contrast, the 1975 experience enlarged the circle of involved economic notables because the municipal employee unions were intimately engaged in the key decision making. Again, as in 1934, the state's governor intervened and played an important role. Unlike his predecessor, however, who was a respected member of the financial elite and deeply knowledgeable in fiscal matters, Governor Hugh Carey had to utilize the expertise of others, including former federal judge Simon Rifkind (senior partner in one of the city's most prominent law firms), former Mayor Robert Wagner and Felix Rohatyn, a prominent member of the financial community. In both crises, the mayor was, to all extent and purposes, a mere bystander.

Actors and Their Stakes

Bankers and investors

By the end of 1974, most banks had drastically reduced their holdings of New York securities. What ensued was an increasingly depressed market for the city's notes and bonds. Legal advisers, meanwhile, warned the financial community that if the city could not meet its debt service obligations, the underwriters of its notes confronted the possibility of losing substantial sums.

Charles Morris, a financial aide to Lindsay, noted that an ongoing public dispute between the mayor and Comptroller Harrison Goldin, over the size of the deficit, "was disquieting" since their respective figures differed by as much as $200 million. "Beame," he wrote, "repeatedly announced austere fiscal measures that had a way of dissolving upon close examination."[27]

In March 1975, the bond market was closed to the city. At the same time, however, the financial community did not want to entertain the possibility of bankruptcy. In the first place, if the city were declared in default and therefore bankrupt, the value of their New York securities would drop precipitously. Secondly, bankers realized that their reputations were at stake, for it was they who these many years had knowingly permitted the city to pursue its flawed fiscal policies and poor accounting practices. If the municipal notes, underwritten by the banks, were not redeemed at full value when due, the banks feared that investors might deem them liable for these losses. As the world financial center, New York's fiscal collapse might spark serious repercussions in the national and international banking systems.

In addition, bankruptcy would require involvement by elements of the federal court system and, inevitably, judicial control over the city's finances. The bankers feared, as a result, that the city would eventually be absolved from some of its outstanding fiscal obligations. At the same time, the financial elite could not envision the courts' ordering drastic reductions in the city's operating expenditures. Finally, it would be difficult, if not impossible, for a bankrupt city to obtain, from the federal government and from other sources, loans necessary to enable it to function from day to day.

Public employee unions

Confronted with the same crisis, the leadership of the city's public employee unions came to similar conclusions—bankruptcy had to be avoided at all costs. But fruitful collaboration among these unions was another matter. Over the years, ideological and tactical differences had motivated the civil service unions to pursue their own agendas. In fact, relationships between some of them had been particularly hostile, marked by years of bitter jurisdictional disputes. In addition, each jealously guarded its respective bargaining arrangements, hoping to edge out the others in attaining special concessions from the city. The more traditional union leaders, typified by Albert Shanker of the teachers union, tended to follow a more conservative approach to political and social issues. In contrast, Victor Gotbaum and the District Council #37 (DC 37) of the American Federation of State, County and Municipal Employees (AFSCME) tended to be more concerned with broader community-oriented issues and more outspoken about national and international issues.[28]

Nevertheless, in the final analysis, the stakes for labor proved far too critical for them to reject cooperation. As Barry Feinstein, head of Teamsters Local 237, put it, "We all decided New York simply could not go bankrupt, that it would be worse than the sacrifices we had to make. . . . We were just scared to death of all the questions default and bankruptcy evoked. No one had the slightest idea what this would actually mean for our pensions, the possibility of large unchallenged layoffs, and the impact on our retirees."[29]

The unbridled and increasing attacks on municipal labor's "fat" pensions and "soaring" wage scales had pushed the unions into a defensive posture. Jack Bigel, pension expert and wage negotiations consultant to several of these unions, warned labor leaders that, this time around, the financial crisis confronting the city was real and extremely dangerous. Bigel's contacts with city and state budget administrators provided him with invaluable access to fiscal facts and figures. Highly skillful as well in his role as a broker, he did a masterful job in weaving together these suspicious union leaders. It was Albert Shanker who gave Bigel the credit for his negotiating activities and for "connecting the key actors to each other and fashioning the compromises."[30]

Once the unions finally decided to march to the same drummer, it was apparent that Victor Gotbaum, executive director of DC 37, would serve as their spokesman and key strategist. Heading the largest municipal union, whose disciplined membership afforded him a stable organizational base, and widely respected for his forceful negotiating skills and consummate handling of the media, he was the unquestioned choice. Gotbaum feared placing the city under the control of a federal bankruptcy judge, worried that it would create an entirely new ball game. Not only would union and city officials be excluded from the bargaining and negotiating processes, but a federal referee would determine all financial and employment decisions and cut the work force, alter the city's contributions to pension and health funds, and possibly undermine other gains won in years of collective bargaining. "I won't roll the dice," warned Gotbaum, "with some federal appointee over the lives of our members—there are human beings who would suffer, not statistics." In the aftermath of the crisis, it was Felix Rohatyn who suggested that it was Gotbaum's strategy and leadership that saved thousands upon thousands of municipal jobs.[31]

As the situation worsened and layoffs proved inevitable, the municipal unions first agreed that an acceptable form of work force shrinkage would be through attrition, beginning with provisionals. Others would be encouraged to take early retirement. And the unions promised to join city officials to pressure the state and federal governments for additional assistance.

Enter Governor Hugh Carey

As the city's situation continued to deteriorate, the mayor oscillated between threatening new layoffs and reassuring the public that the city was not in as bad a shape as others claimed. With the cutoff of the city's cash flow, however, his prestige plummeted. It was at this point that Governor Carey intervened and, in a succession of steps, took command. The governor and his aides were fully aware that a city bankruptcy would put the credit of the state government (and of other local governments in New York State) in serious jeopardy, and probably further undermine the already declining state economy. Furthermore, bankruptcy probably would make it impossible for the city to borrow funds for a very long time. Finally, he concluded that there would be little help, if any, from the federal government, certainly not before the city was able to put its financial house in order again. To deal with the immediate cash needs, the state advanced the city $800 million in May. But this proved to be too little to avert what appeared to be the inevitable disaster.

Class conflict muffled

With the banks refusing to lend money to New York City, the federal government opposing loans to the beleaguered municipality, the public attacking the civil service unions and "expensive" contracts, and the spreading fear of imminent default, the union leadership came to a very disheartening decision. They would be willing to surrender some of the gains they had achieved after many years of struggle, including reductions of city contributions into welfare and pension funds for new workers, elimination of reduced work hours in the summer, and permission to transfer employees among departments, but even these concessions quickly proved inadequate.

At the same time, union heads began to show annoyance with the bankers, who gave the appearance of quietly sitting on the sidelines, waiting for the city to surrender to their terms. Teamster leader Barry Feinstein attacked them for pursuing a selfish agenda, charging "complete subservience of the city to the banking community." He worried that the bankers "would even name the accounts, tell the city how to operate its administration, and, indeed, who would do what. There was no disguise in what they wanted—they would run the city as a bankers' government."[32]

Fearing that the unions were trapped, Gotbaum decided to force the bankers into a more public posture by leading some 10,000 city workers into the financial caverns of the Wall Street area to picket the headquarters of the First National City Bank. Signs and shouted slogans attacked huge banking profits while public workers suffered setbacks. Gotbaum warned, "Jobs and services are a hell of a lot more important than profits." And then with characteristic dramatic flare, he announced the withdrawal of $15 million in union funds from the bank.[33]

The governor, too, felt it was time to act decisively. Guided by his recently appointed group of financial advisers, he entered the contentious scene. From Wall Street, he selected Felix Rohatyn of Lazard Frères, an investment specialist known for his articulate and skillful business acumen. As one of the governor's consultants, he served as emissary to both the financial community and the public employee unions. It became his responsibility to win their support for the tough decisions that were made later that summer and fall. In the process of putting new institutional arrangements in place, Rohatyn navigated among his investment and banking associates, the union leadership, and city and state officials. He won the confidence of the key players, enabling him to pull the antagonists into a collaborative effort of intricate mutual dependence, which eventually succeeded in avoiding bankruptcy.

The first formal step toward state assumption of full control over the city's finances was the creation, in June 1975, of the Municipal Assistance Corporation for the City of New York (MAC), a state government agency with a board dominated by the governor's appointees. MAC was directed to issue its own long-term bonds on behalf of the city, to pay off the city's short-term debt. The bonds were backed by diverting certain city revenues to MAC to service the MAC bonds, including the city's 4 percent sales tax and its stock transfer tax. The city was required to achieve a balanced budget within a specified period, to end the practice of issuing long-term bonds to finance current operations, and to reform various other financial practices. MAC was given responsibility for overseeing these reforms.

MAC was authorized to borrow a total of $3 billion during the summer, in the expectation that this amount would sustain the city until October, when the city would be able to reenter the bond market on its own. This expectation turned out to be far too optimistic. In part this was because the city's short-term debt that had to be refinanced turned out to be far higher than the $3 billion authorized for MAC debt; it was nearly $6 billion including interest. But even more important, MAC was unable to successfully market even the first $1 billion bond issue in early July, because of widespread skepticism about the city's capacity to manage its finances.[34]

Once MAC acknowledged its inability to sell the bonds required, additional layoffs appeared imminent. An emergency session of the key actors convened at the Americana Hotel in July with a series of round-the-clock meetings stretching over an entire week. MAC pushed city officials and the unions to accept a far more stringent arrangement, with the understanding that money would then be forthcoming from the bankers. The package provided for the deferment of wage increases won in the previous contract, postponement to 1976 of a cost-of-living adjustment agreed to in 1974, and the surrender of reduced summer hours by those in air-conditioned offices. The city was told to eliminate or consolidate select agencies, delete certain expense items from the capital budget, increase transit fares, cut expenditures for transit and higher education, and introduce specified management and productivity reforms. MAC agreed to press for transfer of the costs of several city-provided services to the state, for example, courts and correction departments.

At first, the teachers and police unions refused to go along with these changes. Although they finally agreed to the wage deferral, it seriously strained the union coalition. Gotbaum was convinced from the start that to avoid layoffs, the unions had few other options. But police and firefighter leaders were confronted with internal stresses as rank and filers threatened to challenge their control. At one point in the tense negotiations, Albert Shanker and Gotbaum almost came to physical blows.

Toward the end of the summer, it was evident that the measures had proven inadequate. The city was forced to accept greater cutbacks in personnel and services. MAC board members Dick Netzer and Donna Shalala and State Budget Director Peter Goldmark urged Governor Carey to push for new state legislation that placed the city's finances under the firm control of a new state institution. The governor called a special session of the legislature to convene just after Labor Day 1975, and the Financial Emergency Act was then passed. Thus the Emergency Financial Control Board (EFCB) was established and given detailed powers over city finances including review of the city's newly required financial plan, with the power to make modifications of that plan; approval of all contracts and expenditures; approval of revenue estimates; and approval of borrowings. The act required the city to develop a three-year financial plan and produce a balanced budget by fiscal 1978. Overall, the city was required to reform dramatically its budgeting and financial practices, as well as further reducing expenditures.

Membership on the EFCB comprised the governor, state and city comptrollers, the mayor, and three public representatives—people from the private sector—appointed by the governor. The business community was thus accorded a formal role in the most important decision-making body to handle the fiscal crisis. Not only were they leaders in the private banking world and directly affected by the city's financial policies, but their appointments gave them responsibility inside a powerful state authority. Obviously, the financial elite had to be reassured that its investments in the city were protected. Neither the unions nor the general public was represented. Mayor Beame, meanwhile, had but one vote, his own. He was literally left on the sidelines, with home rule temporarily suspended.

Initially, the municipal unions felt uneasy with their exclusion from the EFCB. But Gotbaum nudged his colleagues to accept the new legislation. Governor Carey signalled the municipal unions that he was aware of and sensitive to their anxieties. And to allay their fears, he invited the key labor leaders to his chambers to sit in on the crucial meeting during which the framework for the new authority was created. As Barry Feinstein recalls it, "We were actually surprised to be at this high-level gathering. As we quietly looked around the room of state and city officials we realized that we were the only outsiders privileged to be present." Carey had thus made clear his recognition of labor's vital role as a partner in future negotiations.[35]

At the same time, labor's confidence in the integrity and openness of Rohatyn had grown during the trying summer months. Gotbaum and Bigel, in particular, had developed close working relations with him and were impressed with his knowledge and skill in handling complex negotiations. Gotbaum also found Rohatyn was a caring individual, sensitive to the social needs of the city and of its public workers. During the critical weeks and months, he and Gotbaum developed a warm, personal respect for each other, which helped smooth relationships between the governor, the bankers/investors, and labor's representatives.

In addition, labor had won an important concession in the writing of the EFCB legislation—the integrity of collective bargaining was explicitly preserved. On the other hand, although the unions had pressed to make attrition the primary, or even sole, strategy for cutting the work force, they won no such guarantee and there were mass layoffs.

Despite the creation of the EFCB, MAC had limited success in selling bonds in the early fall. The city's financial position continued to worsen. The state's commitment, meanwhile, was so heavy that its note issues also became risky. New and unconventional sources of financing were necessary. One possibility that had been suggested early in the summer was the investment of municipal pension funds, jointly governed by the unions and the city, in MAC bonds. By early fall, Gotbaum and Bigel decided to recommend this step to pull the city back from bankruptcy.

This decision sparked one of the most heated debates of the fiscal crisis within and among the municipal unions. Each leader, in turn, had to be convinced that the use of his[36] union's pension funds was the only alternative left to save the city. Legal experts warned that cooperating unions could be sued for loaning portions of their pension funds, especially when the city was in such serious trouble. Technically, the funds belonged to present and future retirees—the union members. Board members of the various funds were worried about their fiduciary responsibilities. Bigel played an important role in facilitating this use of pension funds, arguing that eventually labor would accrue a profit, rather than losses, from the deal. Although he was proven correct, at the time the risks seemed considerable.

Initially, Shanker stood firm against the entire proposal. Later he agreed to it provided that the EFCB would formally recognize the recently negotiated teacher contract. He underscored that it was the teachers who had suffered most from the cutbacks since more than 15,000 had been dismissed in one year. Class size had increased and supporting services had been cut drastically, especially discouraging in the face of a changing student population. Pressure from two influential friends, Richard Ravitch and former Mayor Robert Wagner, finally converted Shanker. At that point, the $8.5 billion in pension fund holdings became the basis for the borrowing of $4 billion from the banks. With this infusion of new capital, MAC bonds were purchased, making it unnecessary for the city or MAC to float public offerings of notes or bonds.

The pension fund arrangements were a key to other measures that, in combination, brought the immediate crisis to an end by the end of the year 1975. Bankers and other investors agreed to exchange their maturing short-term notes for MAC bonds and to provide some new credit. The union and banker participations were a prerequisite for federal help, in the form of legislation providing for seasonal loans (that is, loans paid off within the same fiscal year) over the next three years, of up to $2.3 billion.

The coalition had miraculously held together. Rohatyn had skillfully woven the private and public players into an interdependent network, making it increasingly difficult for any of them to withdraw from the intricate web of agreements. Together they faced the crisis and made some very tough decisions, with the governor taking the political heat—and credit—for the solutions.

Impact, Financial and Political

Before the crisis receded, leaders of the municipal unions and of the city's financial world institutionalized a regular series of meetings into what became known as the Municipal Union–Financial Leaders Group (MUFL).[37] On a num-

ber of economic and political issues, each side modified its positions to accommodate the other. The bankers, for example, came to appreciate the union rationale for an agency shop and withdrew their long-standing opposition. They also
withheld attacking the wage levels and fringe benefits of public service workers,
recognizing that the compensation levels of New York's employees were comparable to those in many other cities.

For their part, the unions reappraised their stands on issues of importance to
the financiers: they agreed to support their requests for higher interest rates on
mortgages and for the construction of the West Side convention center. Both
sides agreed that the social service programs were a national responsibility and
jointly urged the federal government to assume larger percentages of the cost of
aid to families with dependent children and Medicaid, to lighten the city's tax
burden. While the stolid meetings of MUFL may not have produced much
drama, in the long run they did help create a calmer climate for exchanging
views and some changes in attitudes and legislative priorities.

Another major thrust of the new power cluster was change in the city's
governmental structure. Dr. Robert Bailey has depicted the years 1975–78 as
"the crisis regime."[38] During these years, home rule was in effect suspended
and the city council, long considered a weak reed, was further debilitated. The
Board of Estimate was seriously constrained by the limit placed on expenditures,
and Mayor Beame was subject to quite specific directives from the state's overseers. The extent of the state's intervention was illustrated by an embarrassing
"demand" that a number of the mayor's key administrators be replaced, and by
insistence that the mayor reduce the number of positions exempt from civil
service, support the imposition of tuition fees on City University students, and
agree to fare hikes on the city's subways and buses. Services were seriously cut
and much needed capital improvements postponed. For a number of years, state
controls helped constrain group demands, including those from organized labor.
The state's control of city finances was not lifted until ten years after "the crisis
regime," long after the city itself had regained access to the credit markets and
operated with annual budget surpluses.

Tower Power

Following the election of Edward Koch as mayor in 1977, the city government
began to move in new directions. The power cluster formed during the fiscal
crisis was replaced by a new set of players—the city's chief executive and the
big real estate developers who together remade the famed Manhattan skyline. In
this last section, we review the mayor's urban development policy, the rationale
behind it and the manner in which his administration encouraged its implementation. In addition, we identify those who constituted the real estate elite—their
resources and strategies—and their impact on the city.

Having assumed office just as the city was emerging from a near-catastrophic fiscal crisis and a massive eight-year economic decline, the mayor had to give top priority to the city's economic health and financial viability. The immediate concern was meeting the stringent requirement, set in place by state authorities, for balancing the budget. As with the Great Depression, the trauma of the fiscal crisis had left a deep imprint on city officials. "Default fears," suggested one of them, were "seared into the mayor's mind."[39] Despite deep cuts and a constrained budget, the Moody bond ratings had not yet reflected a city fully recovered. It meant, among other things, that the mayor remained on the defensive for years. Koch's rationale for his austere budgets was that he had no alternative. It took more political courage, he insisted, to stand up against all those complaining about job security of city workers and the needs of the poor than to appropriate nonexistent funds. Reporter Andy Logan sought to explain the mayor's strategy. "From the point of view of the true interests of the city, he undoubtedly feels, it will not be counted against him in the long run if his mind is on the demands of Moody's Investors Service."[40]

Entering his second election campaign, the mayor continued to worry that the city was not yet out of the fiscal woods and that more drastic reductions would be required. In his typically sardonic manner, he posed the dilemma as one in which "the fiscal '82 budget was a peculiarly simple one. It fell between hard times and hard times."[41] Besides the pervading pall of the fiscal crisis, the city administration was confronted with extensive new cutbacks in federal programs. Mayor Koch benefited, to an extent, from the fact that decisions involving the deepest cuts had been made prior to his election. When confronted with civic groups demanding increased allocations or criticizing his cutbacks, he would often fall back on the excuse that he was constrained by state-imposed regulations. Bound by the requirement to balance the city's budget by 1982, he persistently underscored the limitations in which he was forced to operate, "I am attacked for cutting too much by every group in this city when the cut affects them. We are trying to keep the balance. But to cut just to show our resolve, to curry favor with the fiscal savants, is not intelligent."[42]

Another concern weighing heavily on the mayor was the changing character of the city's economy. Most threatening was the steady decline of its industrial sector, which meant a serious loss of revenue and job opportunities for blue-collar workers. Between 1958 and the mid-seventies more than four hundred thousand manufacturing jobs left the city, a decline of some 40 percent overall, and representing over $3.5 billion in lost wages. Between 1980 and 1985, the loss of city jobs to the outlying metropolitan region reached some eight thousand annually. In addition, the mayor had to deal with repeated threats of large corporations, such as Mobil Oil, J.C. Penney, AT&T, and the Dreyfus Corporation, to move their central office activities from the city. These actual and threatened economic losses to the suburbs and to other parts of the nation added to the mayor's pressures.[43]

There was, however, a hopeful sign in this dismal economic picture and that was the emerging strength and steady growth of the city's service sector. Long recognized as the world's financial capital, New York was sustained by an expansion of its finance, insurance, real estate, and other business services. The almost frenetic activity of the financial and legal businesses in easing the way for corporate mergers and acquisitions and the ability to move funds in moments by electronic transfers helped brace the city's economy during its postfiscal crisis period. The great bulk of the five hundred thousand increase in jobs between 1977 and 1988 was in finance and business services.[44]

New York also began to attract corporate enterprise as the city's economy became increasingly internationalized. Some 60 percent of foreign corporations located their American headquarters in the city, spinning off other economic activities to service corporations, for example, banking, law, accounting, marketing, advertising, and public relations. As one writer put it, "Blossoming like a jungle in springtime," the service sector expansion gave the city fresh momentum. Office building construction proliferated throughout the business district with increasing rapidity, carving a new skyline for residents and tourists. Downtown development evolved into a spectacular revival. The mayor quickly sensed that this new enterprise provided an attractive opportunity for stimulating the economy and would be an indispensable source of city revenue. By upgrading deteriorating districts and encouraging new office construction, he believed that the city's prestigious central business district (CBD) would be vitalized and the service sector energized, taking up the slack left by declining industrial enterprises. In addition, new construction included hotels for a growing tourist trade and luxury condominiums in, and around, Manhattan's CBD for increasing numbers of highly paid managers and executives who opted for city living.[45]

As many have claimed, real estate was to New York what oil was to Texas. While only ten office buildings were constructed in Manhattan during the five-year period of 1976–80, forty-seven new structures were completed during the following five years, with the boom continuing through the late 1980s. Development not only provided new sources of municipal revenue, it served, in a very concrete and visual way, to symbolize New York's fiscal recovery and renewed vitality. As the shining, glass-enclosed steel structures soared to new heights in various parts of Manhattan, they evoked a positive sense of growth and progress. A goodly number of these projects had been approved prior to Koch's assumption of the mayoralty (but few were actually started in the 1974–77 period of economic and fiscal crisis). Since they were completed after Koch entered City Hall, the credit accrued to him, reinforcing the upbeat image he was determined to project. The new towers often replaced unattractive, if not blighted blots on the cityscape. Koch put it succinctly when he said, "The city of New York can never become static, can never lose the change and growth, because that's what makes it the city of New York."[46]

Mayor Koch also encouraged Manhattan development because of his personal conviction that the work of economic affairs was best performed by the private sector. Leaving behind his earlier reputation as a New Deal liberal, he publicly embraced, with evident satisfaction, indeed eagerness, a new more conservative orientation sweeping across the country. Soon after taking office, he underscored that "the main job of municipal government is to create a climate in which private business can expand in the city to provide jobs and profit. It's not the function of government to create jobs on the public payroll."[47]

To grow and build the city-physical became the centerpiece of the mayor's program. What, specifically, did the mayor bring to his budding alliance with the developers? How did his administration respond to their many needs?

Public Entrepreneur

Mayor Koch quickly assumed the role of public entrepreneur by successfully linking the political and economic sectors through masterful utilization of his political skills and managerial resources.[48] In his political capacity, Koch was able to deliver a large, stable constituency that helped sustain support for extensive real estate development. Except for the black community, he became one of the most popular mayors since Fiorello LaGuardia. His conscious outreach to old, white ethnic groups attracted enthusiastic support from the white middle class and blue collar workers. He touched, favorably, large numbers of whites who felt that the restless decade of the sixties had not treated them well. While his manner and speech tended to distance him even further from alienated minority groups, he successfully courted the favor of most others. Koch emerged as the dominant leader of what remained of a once powerful Democratic party. He enhanced his position by cooperating with those party officials who retained an influential role in their respective bailiwicks. Through patronage, contracts, and skill in negotiating votes among borough presidents, he usually persuaded a majority on the Board of Estimate to support development proposals.

In addition, his distinctive, ebullient style served well the spirit of development and growth. His upbeat outlook, burning optimism, and buoyant mood became infectious and helped dramatize the hope and expectations of a thriving enterprising city. His wit, flavored with sarcasm, sparked admiration and popular support. Although inheriting a city still suffering from the fiscal crisis, he careened about with self-satisfaction and a self-confidence that exuded a spiritual uplift. Equally talented in public relations, the mayor skillfully used the media to enhance public support for development. His robust flamboyance was of special appeal to reporters and editors who gave him front page billing and prime time on television. From City Hall's Blue Room, while standing alongside developers with pictorial displays and models, he would proudly announce a new project.

Managerial leadership

At the height of the fiscal crisis, the state government left Mayor Beame standing helplessly at the sidelines, while all but suspending home rule. Once Mayor Koch made it clear that he intended to run a tight ship by pruning city expenses and putting a firm limit on civic and union demands, Governor Hugh Carey signalled the various state overseers that it was time to begin the process of returning the city's authority.[49]

Paradoxically, in light of the treatment of Mayor Beame, the office of the mayor had been strengthened by the reforms instituted by the new state agencies. To ensure more effective control over budget making, purchasing, accounting, and financial reporting, the legislation provided for greater centralization of the city's financial affairs. In his monograph on the fiscal crisis, Professor Robert Bailey put it succinctly: "The financial crisis brought it a new Taylorist mood, a new wave of reformism. Efficiency, scientific management, increased productivity, and financial expertise were constant themes among critics of New York's fiscal performance."[50]

The mayor was required to prepare a financial plan detailing expenditures and indicating specifically that adequate revenues were provided. He was likewise charged with additional authority in overseeing city operations. Administrators had to be more detailed in their reports to the mayor, particularly when seeking increases in expenditures. Quasi-independent agencies, such as the municipal hospital system and the Board of Education, were brought under closer supervision by the requirement that their budgets be included in the mayor's financial plan. This all added up to the mayor having important new authority for imposing fiscal discipline on the city's far-flung bureaucracy. As a result, the mayor was able to increase significantly his input into managerial affairs. Koch was prepared, indeed anxious, to take advantage of this enhanced authority. Determined to reestablish New York's traditional, strong executive style of governance, he stood ready at center stage of the policy-making system. He set his sights clearly and with assurance and communicated his goals in unambiguous terms. He put in place an administrative staff equally enthusiastic and supportive of his program. As the city's central figure, the mayor utilized his political skills and managerial resources to create the setting attractive to the real estate elite.

The Real Estate Goodies

"The city presents a rich variety of goals, stakes, rewards and prizes," according to Sayre and Kaufman, "all offered by and serving as strong incentives for participation in its political and governmental system."[51] Along similar lines, political scientist Theodore Lowi has suggested that the "patronage state" was not built only on job patronage, but on "the policies which produced resources that could be distributed to a variety of interests and claimants." It was obvious to developers that, to construct their towers, they had to deal with the city's officialdom. As one of them noted, "If you're going to build in New York you have to see government as a partner." Having a friend at City Hall would indeed be helpful.[52]

Mayor Koch positioned his administration as a willing partner with developers in three ways: through financial assistance, supportive land use policies, and special administrative arrangements. The city's financial policies have a direct and significant impact on real estate development, for example, allocations for capital improvements, assessments, property taxes, subsidy and loan programs, and tax abatements. Mayor Koch was certain to utilize them all.

Budget allocations supportive of development were accorded top billing, according to Raymond Horton and Charles Brecher; they found that, between 1978 and 1983, development functions went from "least-favored to most-favored status" in the city's budget. Current operating expenditures that served to facilitate development increased 72 percent, as compared to an overall increase of 33 percent. Capital expenditures for infrastructure, a major contribution to the development process, more than doubled during the same period, from $407 million to $866 million. At the same time, social expenditures were being severely constrained.[53]

Tax abatements constituted another major inducement to developers. The Industrial and Commercial Incentives Board (ICIB), launched in the Beame administration and continued by Mayor Koch, was authorized to make such awards. Over the years, the board had been generally responsive to developers' requests for substantial tax relief, particularly for projects within the Manhattan central business district, which was experiencing a healthy comeback. Some of the largest abatements were those given to two developer groups, the Fisher Park Avenue Company and the Tishman-Speyer-Silverstein group, and to two major corporations, AT&T and the New York Telephone Company. In addition, controversial exemptions were granted for the construction of hotels, health and racquet clubs, and television studios.[54]

Land Use Policies

Large-scale projects must move through a labyrinth of agencies regulated by detailed zoning rules, further complicated by the variances granted over the years. Over 700 pages in length, the zoning law (which deals with the size, height, bulk, density, and setbacks of structures, among many other items) has been amended so many times that the additional modifications are longer than the original zoning resolution itself. While developers must confront many limitations and constraints, a number of techniques governing land use have been devised to provide them with greater flexibility. Some observers have dubbed the process as "zoning by negotiation."

One device utilized extensively is the special permit which enables the City Planning Commission and the developer to negotiate specific exceptions to the zoning law, such as modification of land coverage and setbacks of buildings. Another technique that entails negotiation between the city and developers has been the incentive bonus. Under this arrangement, a builder was permitted up to a 20 percent increase in the size of a project, provided the developer offered certain amenities that benefited the general public, such as new public spaces, interior arcades, gallerias, plazas, open outdoor areas, landscaped terracing, subway station renovations, and retail space.

Reportedly, it had been suggested that developers were making money out of air. The air space above a building zoned for higher utilization could be sold and added to an adjacent building or lot. The air rights above a landmarked building might be sold for a new structure being built across the street or diagonal to it. The sale of air rights enables higher and wider structures than zoning regulations normally permit. To illustrate the process: an owner of a four-story brownstone, who could theoretically construct a sixteen-story building on the same lot, is permitted to sell the twelve stories of vacant air, called "undeveloped air rights," to a next-door neighbor who owns a vacant lot.

A number of conflicts concerning air rights transfers have surfaced over landmarked houses of worship, in particular St. Bartholomew's on Park Avenue at 50th Street and St. Paul's Chapel in the Wall Street area of lower Manhattan. Claiming financial hardship, both churches anticipated that the sale of their air space would provide much needed revenues. At St. Bartholomew, the developer originally proposed a fifty-nine–story office tower adjacent to the church. This was reduced to forty-seven stories following stiff opposition within the congregation. In return for its air rights, St. Paul's anticipated a $4 to $5 million endowment for its charitable activities from developer Peter Kalikow, who planned an addition to a building he owns across the street.

One of the leading lawyers behind air rights transfer, Samuel Lindenbaum, simplifies the idea in this manner:

> The zoning resolution assigns to every parcel a bundle of development rights, many of which are undeveloped. The resolution simply provides a mechanism by which an owner can sell transfer development rights to an adjacent property. All you've done is move the checkers around.[55]

At times, a developer combines these various devices in construction plans to enlarge a project to new heights, beyond the familiar New York skyline. Perhaps one of the most "creative packages" was arranged by developer Bruce Eichner for his seventy-two–story City spire on West 56th Street. Under the zoning law, a thirty-four–story structure was permitted. Eichner agreed to renovate the City

Center Theater at a cost of $5.5 million in exchange for a twelve-story bonus. In addition, an air rights transfer from the theater to his lot was acquired by contributing $3 million to the New York City Opera and another $3 million to the New York City Ballet, permitting another twenty-six stories. Thus Cityspire became a slender high rise chiseled into a narrow street, double the size provided by the zoning law.

"For Sale"

Another opportunity seized upon by developers has been in connection with the sale of city-owned land. Albert Scardino, a *New York Times* real estate reporter, has suggested that this is the way that the city sets the criteria for the bidding process and thus puts "the government into partnership with the builders in the biggest new real estate game in town."[56]

One of the largest and most valuable land sales offered by the city was the Coliseum site, at the edge of Central Park and Columbus Circle. City officials decided that the Coliseum had proven inadequate and had outlived its usefulness. As a result, they prepared the way for construction of a replacement project, equal in size to the Empire State Building, which would provide more space for leasing and thus produce more revenue. Endorsing the proposal of the Metropolitan Transit Authority (MTA) for renovations of a nearby subway station, the City Planning Commission literally required bidders to utilize the full 20 percent bonus to insure adequate income to cover these costs. Developer Mortimer Zuckerman won the bid for his twin towers of fifty-eight and sixty-eight stories. City officials were ecstatic, claiming that the project would produce hundreds of millions of dollars for the mass transit improvements and some $100 million annually in general revenues. Deputy Mayor for Economic Affairs, Alair Townsend, welcomed the bid for going beyond all expectations. The mayor's finance commissioner was quoted as saying that "this was one of the most unusual sites in terms of development potential and revenue potential, and not to use it to its potential would have been a crime."[57]

Another valuable site that the city offered for sale was at South Ferry, the dramatic entrance to the magnificent harbor. The administration decided to take bids privately, hoping that this would stimulate participation of more developers. According to reporter Albert Scardino, the city behaved like a private entrepreneur by keeping the bidding process confidential and by permitting the developer, Richard Kahan, to offer two separate bids, both identical in financial aspects, but differing in their designs. Eventually, he won the prize, with a plan to clear the old Ferry site and construct a sixty-story office building.[58]

The city also made available a number of other attractive sites, such as the Kips Bay waterfront, adjacent to the United Nations and fronting on the East River, specifying that the land be used for luxury housing, and land in the Times

Square area designated for high-rise offices. Another large site, the Hudson River Center project, bordered the Javits Convention Center and extended some twenty-five acres over the water. The city's requirements for this area included provisions for a marina, esplanade, luxury apartments, hotel, retail stores, a restaurant, the city car pound, health club, and exhibit space.

Enlisting the State Government

Yet another technique aiding Manhattan development has been the city's use of public authorities. The Koch administration supported the state's Urban Development Corporation (UDC) in undertaking a mammoth restructuring of the world famed Times Square area. The plan, evolved by a group of developers but catalyzed by city officials, projected fundamental alterations in the entertainment district. Their objectives included clearance of the area's sleazy qualities—the pornographic shops, the street-side drug sales, and prostitution—to be replaced by construction of four huge office towers, a merchandise mart and hotel, conversion of old movie houses into legitimate theaters, and the creation of new retail space. To encourage developers and to hasten its completion, the mayor and governor agreed that the UDC would manage the project.

The UDC is a state agency, originally designed by Governor Nelson Rockefeller to facilitate the construction of subsidized housing throughout the state by circumventing municipal and county governments and any of their restrictive legislation. It is somewhat ironic that, during his administration, Mayor Lindsay viewed UDC as threatening his authority and thus strongly opposed its utilization. (See Chapter 7 by Annemarie Hauck Walsh on public authorities.) Mayor Koch, on the other hand, warmly embraced this state intervention in the Times Square plan. Why?

In the first place, by involving UDC, the mayor was able to secure additional state funding. Secondly, this device bypassed those city officials who might otherwise obstruct or delay the implementation of the project, for example, the members of the Board of Estimate. Generally, city involvement tended to delay projects by its detailed rules and regulations. For example, by circumventing the city government, land condemnation was speeded up and negotiations with developers made more flexible. Furthermore, Koch was often impatient with the delays normally resulting from community involvement in the decision-making process. The UDC was able to bypass the local boards. Thus, UDC appeared to provide a less intrusive governmental process, enabling a smoother collaborative effort between the private and public sectors.

By improving the appearance of Times Square, and by attracting developers to clear the squalor about it, Koch sought to open new large adjacent areas for development. The Times Square project served as a clear signal to developers that new space was being created for them, and they scrambled to buy up older buildings just north of the area, between West 45th and 49th Streets. Several developers quickly put projects on the drawing boards: new hotels, theaters, a retail arcade, luxury apartments, and, inevitably in Manhattan, new tall office buildings.

In evident appreciation, the real estate interests rallied behind Koch as another election approached. At his 60th birthday party, in preparation for his third run for mayor, he was surrounded by the top developers who had come to pay him homage and who helped fill his campaign chest to overflowing.

"We'll Take Manhattan" . . . *and They Did*

Sayre and Kaufman explain that pressure groups vary in the scope of their interests and in the degree of persistence with which they pursue these interests. Those with a single functional interest generally manifest a high persistence of political activity within relatively narrow segments of the political process. Sayre and Kaufman suggest that these groups may have, within their special area of competence, greater influence than others. However, they claim that this is circumscribed, contending that

> the most significant fact for the city's politics, perhaps, is that there are few enduring alliances uniting any substantial number of these groups. They are incurably pluralistic, competitive, specialized in their interests, jealous of their separate identities.[59]

Although no single elite may run New York City, as Sayre and Kaufman contend, nevertheless some group or groups can and do dominate the process within a given policy area. For a period, it is possible for one group to become a dominating force, highly successful in winning some grand prizes, indeed huge profits.

By the end of the 1970s and on into the next decade, the real estate interests reemerged to take command of Manhattan's central business district. They etched a new dramatic skyline by constructing mammoth office towers, corporate spires, high-rise luxury condominiums, a "new town" at Battery Park, and a financial cluster nearby. And on they went with plans for a new Madison Square Garden, a new Union Square, twin towers to replace the Coliseum, and Donald Trump's dream Television City.

However, not all of these projects were initiated or embraced enthusiastically by developers. Some of the biggest undertakings were initiated by public agencies. For example, the convention center was developed by a state public authority and substantially financed by the state government. For well over a dozen years, the Battery Park City Authority was unable to attract private participation in that massive project, although private developers eventually became enthusiastic partners. Times Square redevelopment was also conceived by public agencies, as were the plans for the Coliseum site and for South Ferry. Thus, the city and the state governments have been vigorous entrepreneurs, rather than merely responding to private developer initiatives, but the public agency initiatives have proven advantageous to the developers. A collateral advantage of public agency initiation of large-scale development projects is the blessing of many of the projects by traditional civic groups like the Regional Plan Association.

Real estate in New York has long been a family affair, with successive generations of the same families ceaselessly assembling land and building apartment houses and commercial structures. The dominance of the older families was challenged during the postcrisis boom by newcomers, some of them New Yorkers but more from other parts of the United States—Houston, Atlanta, and Boston, for example—abroad, including Canada, London, and Argentina. The new, independent developers have been catalysts for upgrading marginal and deteriorating streets and neighborhoods. They have made a vital contribution in reviving the hotel industry, which, in turn, feeds into the growing tourist trade. Changes in retailing practices have enabled the conversion of former department store sites like Best and Company and Bonwit Teller on Fifth Avenue to new, high-rise offices.

Assembling sites is an extraordinary challenge, since much of the attractive land is highly utilized and well developed. After identifying prime spots, developers often find owners and tenants refusing to leave. As a result, "gathering" bits and pieces of acreage has proven tricky, demanding an insider's expertise and unusual mastery of this unique craft. One developer remarked, pointedly, that "brain surgery is easier than site assemblage today."[60] Since these real estate ventures require immense, intricate fiscal arrangements, many entrepreneurs have become financial wizards, moving easily among bankers, mortgage brokers, insurance company executives, and other investors in designing enormous deals. Besides coping with immense financial complexities, these developers had to create, coordinate, and direct organizations encompassing professional staffs drawn from urban planning, construction, engineering, architecture, law, management, and marketing. Being an intensely competitive business, timing is of the essence.

But the ability to achieve governmental approvals and financial support is also of the essence. What accounts for the ability of developers to achieve a high level of access to governmental officialdom? In the first place, they held a distinct advantage during the Koch years because the city administration enthusiastically encouraged their efforts, giving their projects high priority. Secondly, the appeal of the "build and grow" image of construction activity attracted broad support.[61] Thirdly, the developers displayed consummate skill in playing the political game. Those from older family operations inherited political networks that had been laboriously built by their fathers with local and citywide political parties, politicians, and elected officials. As for the newcomers, they either quickly mastered the paths to influence or paid those with skills to do so. Important connections were made permanent and productive through personal relationships, social contacts, attending the right fund-raising events and celebrations, and contributing to the coffers of the Democratic party and to candidates for political office.

Political money

In a study of campaign contributions to members of the city's Board of Estimate, it was disclosed that real estate "biggies" were among the top donors. As noted in Chapter 4 by David Eichenthal, the board was—before 1990—the key decision-making body (other than the mayor) with respect to zoning variances, tax abatements, leases of city property, the city's own building plans, and the city budget.

Of $6.2 million donated in one mayoralty campaign, about half came from real estate contributors, and another $1.2 million from financial interests, many involved in real estate development. In 1985, among the five largest contributors, three who gave $100,000 or more were in real estate: the J & D Real Estate Corporation, Glick Development Associates, and Hartz Mountain Development. The largest contributions were to Mayor Koch, Borough President Andrew Stein of Manhattan, and Comptroller Harrison Goldin, in that order. Times Square developers gave members of the Board of Estimate in excess of $170,000. The list of big contributors ($10,000 or over), read like a Who's Who of major Manhattan developers. Another sizeable source of money came from big law firms with a substantial real estate practice.[62]

The Real Estate Board of New York (REBNY)

In addition to political contributions, developers are extremely well serviced by their trade association, one of the most effective of its kind in the city. REBNY has grown steadily to over 5,700 members, having doubled in five years, during the 1980s. Included among its membership are brokers, bankers, lawyers, and property managers, which helps enlarge the network of developers within the business community. Although constituting only 15 percent of the membership, developers hold a predominant influence over the organization and are deeply involved in its major activities and extensive committee system. "We do have an extremely active membership," former research director Arthur Margon emphasized, "There is much expertise in the individuals as well as inside their respective organizations with which we are affiliated."[63]

Well-financed, and having a stable organizational structure, REBNY attracts an extremely well-qualified professional staff, including experts in real estate economics, public policy analysts, and specialists in the city's political process.

Key staff members have often been drawn directly from public service and know their way around the maze of agencies, indeed, are familiar with the personnel. As a result, they are able to closely monitor the bureaucracy and analyze policies for their impact on the industry. Three presidents of REBNY—Kenneth Patton, Richard Rosan, and Steven Spinola—held top posts within city government. With community boards having an advisory but important role in reviewing proposed projects in their respective districts, REBNY staff constantly monitor their activities. "Uniform Land Use Review Procedure (ULURP) Watch," an attractive newsletter for members, covers the latest information available on landmarks, environmental issues, and board hearings. Frequent seminars are organized for district managers, chairs of community boards, and their land use committees, in order to facilitate an ongoing exchange of views with representatives of real estate.[64]

Friends

Over the years, developers have built close ties with bankers, investors, insurance companies, construction firms, and large architectural outfits. On occasion, these "friends" have become partners in a venture. Another group of business colleagues, who share a common agenda in support of physical development, lower property taxes, less governmental regulation, and reduced electric rates, includes the Chamber of Commerce and Industry, the Economic Council, the Lower Manhattan Downtown Association, the Associated Builders, the Rent Stabilization Association, and, since 1979, the New York Partnership.[65]

Strategies

Strengthened by these valuable resources—their own skills, lucrative incomes, extensive networks, and supportive business associations—developers pursued a number of effective strategies that helped ensure government support for their bold ventures: the use of "process brokers," former city officials, and a public-spirited civic outreach.

Access to government has been vital to the industry's successful takeover. *New York Times* reporter Sam Roberts calls those who have mastered this game of access "the process brokers."[66] Highly skilled and experienced technicians, these individuals serve in the largest and most prestigious public relations and law firms. Their proficiency and resourcefulness in managing the intricacies of government are finely tuned. While the judicial process itself is the province of lawyers, working the other parts of government requires knowledgeable assistance from both public relations and the law profession. Sandy Lindenbaum, an attorney and well-connected process broker, has been a master in negotiating with the city on behalf of developers for offering public amenities in exchange for higher and bigger buildings. Explaining the key to his success he noted that "in dealing with the agencies that I've been dealing with, there tends to be continuity. Chairpersons and chairmen come and go. But there's an institutional memory. Staff stays on for a long time."[67]

An unquestioned kingpin of public relations in the city has been Howard Rubenstein. Rubenstein serves both sides of the street—as counselor and adviser to top governmental officials, as well as to big real estate developers. His far-flung operation covers a diverse group of interests, growing within a decade from seventy to two hundred important clients. A highly professional staff brings skills to the firm's activities, and Rubenstein himself is a master at image-making. His detailed, in-depth knowledge of the city's media is widely acclaimed. Intimately acquainted with real estate and business reporters, he supplies the stories that interest them most.

Carefully planned breakfast seminars include his extensive network of prestigious individuals. An invitation to the *New York Post* breakfast signifies that one has made it into the right circle. Leaving nothing to chance, he plans the seating himself, to make certain that individuals with common pursuits are placed alongside each other. Breakfast meetings held for the Association for a Better New York, headed by real estate developer Lewis Rudin but invented by Rubenstein, are well attended. Seating usually includes a good mix of real estate magnates and public officials.

At least a dozen major players in the real estate industry are typically on Rubenstein's list of clients.[68] In addition, the Rubenstein firm represents hospitals, universities, foundations, museums, and a number of labor unions, among others. These prove useful when an outreach to a broader community is sought. With such extensive, broad-based networks, Rubenstein's advice constitutes an important strategic resource.

The various facets of the economy related directly or indirectly to the real estate industry attract many of the best and brightest in the city. Law firms engaged in Manhattan real estate recruit the more politically astute, well-connected lawyers who have had some governmental experience. Exofficials without law degrees are generally attracted to public relations firms or move directly into the real estate industry. We call these individuals "the graduates." Other writers have described this recruitment process as the "revolving door." The graduates bring with them detailed knowledge of laws and regulations and helpful information on the bureaucratic structure and the right individual or agency to call. Among the graduates are former mayors and top administrators of key agencies.

"Social grease"

In his works of art, Hans Haacke has sharply ridiculed the civic-minded activities of wealthy business interests. With deep penetrating sarcasm, he has depicted their philanthropic behavior as "social grease." And while this indictment appears severe, it is undeniable that "doing good" often serves to enhance the public image of private enterprise. "In their own way," explained research director Margon at REBNY, "developers are concerned about New York. They are a very philanthropic group."[69] Those developers who were descendants of older real estate families included many of Jewish ancestry. Sharing an ancient tradition of charity, called "Zedecha," they have been extremely active in philanthropic causes, usually being among the biggest donors to a host of Jewish institutions, communal, and civic organizations. They also serve on boards of hospitals, universities, and cultural and civic institutions, giving much of their time, money, and expertise. They also encourage staff members to assist the city's not-for-profit groups.

Perhaps with mixed motives of civic pride and good business sense, some developers have sought out architects with an international reputation. Among these notables have been I. M. Pei, Alexander Cooper, Philip Johnson, Edward Larrabee Barnes, John Burgee, Cesar Pelli, and Helmut Jahn. Some of their attractively designed structures have won special awards from the Municipal Art Society for the high quality of "public art."

Through skillful use of the process brokers, invaluable assistance from the graduates, and their own public-spirited outreach, developers have been able to network the governmental arena and provide Manhattan with a new facial, if not spiritual, uplift.

Impact of Tower Power

The towering new Manhattan structures built after the fiscal crisis demonstrated the unusual success of collaborative efforts between real estate developers and the Koch administration. In his classic, *Who Governs?* Robert Dahl suggests that "rapid, comprehensive change in the physical pattern of a city is a minor revolution."[70] In many ways, this holds true for Manhattan during this period. Dramatic development not only gave the city a new look and vitality, but it enhanced its position as the world's leading renowned financial and business service center. The changing skyline evoked a message of confidence in the present and optimism in the city's future. With evident pride and enthusiasm, developers and public officials defended the spectacular growth of new highrise office and luxury condominiums, underscoring the stimulation of many new enterprises, expanded job opportunities, increased city revenues, and reclaimed property in deteriorated areas. This development policy, they maintained, had averted economic flight and attracted new headquarter operations.

However, development had some serious drawbacks. As early as 1982, *New York Times* architectural reporter Paul Goldberger sought to alert the public when he warned that the city is not likely to collapse this year or this decade, if 10 new skyscrapers are built, or 100. New York is remarkably resilient, and its total strangulation is not the issue. What is likely to happen is not collapse, but something far less dramatic—a slow, steady increase in noise and the tension and the crowding and the shadows. Such changes are impossible to quantify, impossible to measure in absolute terms.[71]

Within four years, the city's poor air quality had become an issue of serious concern to City Hall and Washington. Under the standards set by the federal Environmental Protection Administration (EPA), the city's carbon monoxide and ozone concentrates, along with other pollutants, had reached such a dangerous level that drastic improvements were required. The threat of federal sanctions in 1986 endangered the city's plans for garbage-burning resource recovery plants and highway construction. Relenting somewhat, the EPA extended the date for meeting its mandate.[72]

It was becoming increasingly clear that the broader implications of development had been neglected, illustrating a basic lack of city planning or direction. A former vice-chairman of the City Planning Commission, Martin Gallent, oftentimes a lone dissenter, urged the administration to analyze the impact of these new high-rise projects on heavily developed parts of the city. Warning that increased density was producing heightened human discomfort in the financial district, he underscored the blockage of air and light in its narrow, canyon-molded streets. The vital transportation network, he pointed out, was also suffering from increasing pressure. In one of his many dissents on the commission, Gallent noted that

> perceptions, yours and mine included, can often tell you more about a situation than engineering statistics. While the total subway system may be able to carry more people, the perception of this subway rider is that rush hour traffic in this lower Manhattan area is close to the threshold of my tolerance. Many people have opted out of the subway, and are using other private or public transportation.[73]

It was increasingly evident that the megatowers were creating greater intensity on city sidewalks and worsening a deteriorating traffic situation. More and more city streets were being darkened by longer shadows. Critics noted, and with good reason, the danger of the city becoming monocultures of high-rise offices and housing residences. Planning Professor Richard Schaffer of Columbia University, warned that "just because this isn't Paris doesn't mean we can't be a little better than we are. There are civic concerns beyond private profit."[74]

The steady decline of affordable housing for middle- and low-income populations was among these serious civic concerns. Mayor Koch finally recognized this problem when he stated in his "Address on the State of the City," in January 1987:

> Today, I'm pleased to announce a new policy governing the sale of city-owned
> land for residential development. Our previous objective was to sell the land
> for the highest price. . . . But the housing crisis has convinced me that this
> valuable resource must now be devoted to the production of low and moderate-
> income housing.

The administration had shown little concern with the extraordinary heights of
buildings or their location in heavily congested areas. Precious landmarks and
unique sights were being overwhelmed by towering spires, for example, the new
Coliseum site buildings, Cityspire, and projects planned on the sites at St.
Bartholomew's, the Metropolitan Club, the Whitney and Guggenheim museums,
and the sixty-story behemoth at the entrance of the city's harbor.

Furthermore, property tax abatements came under increasing criticism.
Highly questionable were those extended to developers in the midtown area,
where real estate values were skyrocketing. How and why, asked the critics,
should abatements be granted for luxury and supra-luxury apartment house condominiums and for health and racquet clubs? Urban economist George Sternlieb,
of Rutgers University, claimed that tax abatement contributed, along with other
factors, to a rise in land values. Ford Foundation housing specialist, Louis
Winnick, found that "every subsidy gets capitalized—tax abatements, deprecia-
tion allowances—you can't avoid some capitalization, but too much subsidy was
given too capriciously."[75] A *Daily News* editorial scored these big developers
for projects "that didn't need a government subsidy."[76] City Comptroller Harrison Goldin, happy to join the critics of the Koch administration, underscored the
city's haphazardness in making many of these awards. He insisted that City Hall
lacked "any discernable policy or criteria for granting exemptions." Any company, he suggested, "with the sophistication, resources, and persistence to utilize
the process," could win an abatement.[77]

AT&T stunned city administrators when it suddenly and unexpectedly announced plans to move the staff of its new midtown headquarters out of the city.
Real estate prices had reached such a high level in the area as to make it more
lucrative for the company to take its operations to a less expensive community,
and lease out the unneeded space in its building. Since AT&T had received a
substantial tax abatement, Koch hit the roof, threatening to sue. Shortly thereafter, a settlement was reached and the tension subsided.

Another serious problem sparked by these mammoth projects was steady
encroachment into stable neighborhoods and a rising threat to the housing of
diverse economic and ethnic populations. For example, many residents of the
Clinton community (to the west of the theater district) believed that they were
menaced by the complex on the site of the old Madison Square Garden and even
more by the Times Square redevelopment project. Pressures on rents and prices
of apartments were felt, as buildings were acquired in the process of assembling
sites for future construction.

Fears of invasion were also manifest in the Upper West Side of Manhattan, where developers accelerated construction of high-rise luxury apartment buildings. Known as an attractive diversified community, the West Side had provided a mix of decent housing for moderate income and working class residents and diverse ethnic groups. Complaining bitterly that her community was "under siege," city council member Ruth Messinger sparked a vigorous campaign against these new developments. Opposing the forced departure of long-time, lower-income residents and small shopkeepers from the neighborhood, she carried her message throughout the district. She charged that developers had benefited tremendously from administration policies that ensured lucrative zoning awards. Messinger was also involved in a battle at the southern rim of her district where the new Coliseum project was located. Three affected community boards joined her in urging that the building's height be cut, but to no avail. Comptroller Goldin, who had originally voted for the project, conceded that the district's critics had good cause to complain. He recommended to the head of the City Planning Commission that "we should no longer study each proposed new project in a vacuum" and on "an individual basis" but that the Commission should formulate guidelines for "a comprehensive environmental and community impact analysis of the future of the entire West Side."[78]

The mammoth undertaking at Times Square also evoked criticism. The project, it was feared, would duplicate the recent development pattern of east midtown, resulting in avenues of high-rise office buildings bereft of amenities on a human scale. The Clinton community and theater-related establishments feared inroads into their moderate rentals. There was some concern that the remnants of the garment center would be eliminated. The Municipal Art Society led a campaign defending the character of Times Square as colorful, alive, and attractive for tourists and theater goers. In his study of the Times Square project, Princeton Professor Robert Ponte complained that the primary goal was to benefit the real estate interests. He concluded that "a practical orientation was adopted, focussing less on solving fundamental social problems than on finding how to make real estate development possible in the core."[79] Finally, the city's utilization of the UDC for Times Square meant that the city administration had abrogated its responsibilities. It would not review the plan in detail and would avoid neighborhood input, bypassing the community's ULURP process.

In the 1977 election, Mayor Koch successfully mobilized a broad, new coalition that enthusiastically acclaimed his type of confident, aggressive leadership and generally supported his program, including development. When development took off in the late 1970s and early 1980s, there was much enthusiasm for it. Indeed, the big projects seemed a hopeful beginning for the city's economic comeback and stimulant for vitalization of the business center. As the city showed major improvements—a new physical appearance, financial stability and an economic boom—the enthusiasm and general consensus for development began to wane. At first, the opposition that did exist was weak and defensive. Critics were overwhelmed by the excitement generated by the build-and-grow enthusiasts. But by the end of the 1980s, although the critics had not achieved political dominance, they did dominate the media and had won many adherents in the civic community. The build-and-grow coalition could no longer automatically carry the day.

Conclusion

Pluralists contend that a changing cast of active participants influences the power game. Sayre and Kaufman underscored this view for New York, indicating that a wide assortment of groups organize, press their claims, win some prizes, but lose others. Depicting the political scene as one of ever shifting, dispersed, and specialized groups and alliances, the authors conclude that the city's power game is kaleidoscopic, lacking a structure.

Looking at New York's pressure groups only within the pluralist framework discounts, indeed neglects, the findings in this chapter. Obviously, there are at least two patterns of power—the Sayre and Kaufman pluralistic model—and another that emerges in these case studies—"clusters of power." One cluster, the community revolution of the sixties, opened up the urban system to new groups. While unanticipated by the pluralists, it actually expanded pluralism, although for a short time. During the fiscal crisis, another cluster emerged, this one dominated by the investors/bankers and the municipal unions, both in close collaboration with the state government represented by the governor. In the postcrisis period and well into the eighties, still another cluster surfaced. It brought on stage a new alliance of real estate developers and their colleagues (bankers, builders, and insurance executives) and the city administration, with the mayor as key governmental actor.

Thus, the pluralist model requires modification in important respects. First, the model must allow for the formation of groups comprised of newcomers with relatively little experience or tradition for mastering the power game: the playing field is not really all that level and the game not that open. Second, groups may achieve what appears to be success, only to find that their influence is short lived and limited, as was the case with community politics in the 1960s. Third, some divisions among groups, in particular the racial dimension of politics, do not respond readily to accommodation and compromise; serious tensions can continue for years. Fourth, certain groups control substantial resources and possess the necessary skills for repeatedly winning substantial prizes provided by the political system. The outcome of the urban political process is not necessarily a little something for all the players, but a very unequal distribution of the prizes.

Notes

1. Jewel Bellush and Stephen David, editors, *Race and Politics in New York City*. New York: Praeger, 1971, Introduction.

2. Edward Banfield, editor, *Urban Government*. New York: The Free Press of Glencoe, 1961, p. 209.

3. Wallace Sayre and Herbert Kaufman, *Governing New York City: Politics in the Metropolis*. New York: Norton, 1965, pp. 507, 508.

4. What most New York black groups, and those in Northern cities, did not realize at the time, was the dramatic difference between removing legal barriers and removing the socioeconomic obstacles to fuller opportunity and greater equality. See Bayard Rustin, "From Protest to Politics," in Irving Howe, editor, *The Radical Papers*. Garden City, NY: Doubleday, 1966, pp. 335–49.

5. As quoted in Daniel Bell and Virginia Held, "The Community Revolution," *The Public Interest* 16 (Summer 1969): 149.

6. Frances Piven and Richard Cloward, *Regulating the Poor*. New York: Random House, Pantheon Books, 1971; Paul Davidoff, "Advocacy and Pluralism in Planning," *Journal of American Institute of Planners* 31 (December 1965): 331–38; Marilyn Gittell, *Participants and Participation: A Study of School Policy in New York City*. New York: Praeger, 1967.

7. Charles Morris, *The Cost of Good Intentions*. New York: Norton, 1980, p. 57.

8. John Lindsay, *The City*. New York: Norton, 1969, pp. 120–23.

9. Morris, *The Cost of Good Intentions*, p. 60.

10. Charles Hamilton and Stokely Carmichael, *Black Power*. New York: Random House, 1967, p. 40.

11. Ibid., p. 81.

12. Bellush and David, *Race and Politics in New York City*. For other criticisms, see Charles Hamilton, "The Patron-Recipient Relationship and Minority Politics in NYC," *Political Science Quarterly* (Summer 1979): 211–28.

13. Jill Joness, *We're Still Here*. New York: The Atlantic Monthly Press, 1986, p. 152.

14. Morris, *The Cost of Good Intentions*, p. 65; John Mudd, "Beyond Community Control: A Neighborhood Strategy for City Government," *Publius* 6:4 (Fall 1976): 113–36.

15. As quoted in Bell and Held, "The Community Revolution," p. 161.

16. Jewel Bellush and Bernard Bellush, *Union Power and New York*. New York: Praeger, 1984, Chapters 14 and 15.

17. Joness, *We're Still Here*, pp. 178ff., 188ff. See also Diana Gordon, *City Limits*. New York: Charterhouse, 1973.

18. Jewel Bellush, "Housing: Scatter-Site Controversy," in Bellush and David, *Race and Politics in New York City*, p. 115, Chapter 4.

19. Ibid., pp. 98–133; Mario Cuomo, *Forest Hills Diary: The Crisis of Low Income Housing*. New York: Random House, 1974.

20. Morris, *The Cost of Good Intentions*, p. 78.

21. Edward Rogowsky, Louis Gold, and David Abbott, "Police: The Civilian Review Board Controversy," in Bellush and David, *Race and Politics in New York City*, p. 95.

22. Joness, *We're Still Here*, p. 179; Morris, *The Cost of Good Intentions*, p. 78.

23. Jonathan Rieder, *Canarsie*. Cambridge, MA: Harvard University Press, 1985, p. 171.

24. Godfrey Hodgson, *America in Our Time*. Garden City, NY: Doubleday, 1976, p. 363.

25. Martin Shefter, *Political Crisis/Fiscal Crisis: The Collapse and Revival of New York City.* New York: Basic Books, xii–xiii.

26. Jewel Bellush, *Herbert Lehman as Governor of New York.* Ph.D. thesis, Columbia University, 1955; Ken Auletta, *The Streets Were Paved with Gold.* New York: Random House, 1979, pp. 33–34.

27. Shefter, *Political Crisis/Fiscal Crisis*, p. 230; Morris, *The Cost of Good Intentions*, pp. 223, 229ff., 225.

28. Bellush and Bellush, *Union Power and New York*, Chapters 6 and 18. DC 37 represents the bulk of municipal workers, aside from the uniformed forces (police, fire, and sanitation), teachers, and transit workers. Although DC 37 includes many professionals, most of its members are in the lower-paid civil service jobs and many are minority group members. Thus, social consciousness comes naturally to DC 37.

29. Ibid., p. 387.

30. Interview with Albert Shanker, President, American Federation of Teachers, December 13, 1982.

31. Interview with Victor Gotbaum, Executive Director, District Council #37, AFSCME, September 16, 1980; Bellush and Bellush, *Union Power and New York*, p. 387.

32. Interview, Gotbaum; Bellush and Bellush, *Union Power and New York*, p. 393.

33. Fred Ferretti, *The Year the Big Apple Went Bust.* New York: Putnam, 1976, pp. 192–93. The bank's name was subsequently changed to Citibank.

34. Interview with Dick Netzer and Donna Shalala, president of Hunter College, formerly treasurer of Municipal Assistance Corporation, February 16, 1982; Morris, *The Cost of Good Intentions*, p. 233; for more details see Auletta, *The Streets Were Paved with Gold*; Robert Bailey, *The Crisis Regime.* Albany, NY: State University Press, 1985; Shefter, *Political Crisis/Fiscal Crisis.*

35. Interview, Barry Feinstein, President, Teamsters Local 237, May 6, 1981.

36. Until Sandra Feldman became head of the United Federation of Teachers in the 1980s, none of the major players on the union side was a woman.

37. Bellush and Bellush, *Union Power and New York*, pp. 413–15.

38. Bailey, *The Crisis Regime.*

39. Interview, Martin Gallent, former vice-chair, City Planning Commission, October 28, 1986.

40. *The New Yorker*, June 4, 1979, p. 95.

41. Edward Koch, *Mayor.* New York: Simon and Schuster, 1984.

42. As quoted in the *New York Times*, October 22, 1979, p. B4.

43. Koch, *Mayor.* See various volumes, Charles Brecher and Raymond Horton, editors, *Setting Municipal Priorities.* Montclair, NJ: Allanheld, 1981; New York: New York University Press, 1984, 1985, 1986, 1987.

44. There had been a decline of about 600,000 jobs between 1969 and 1977. Data from unpublished tabulations prepared for the Metropolitan Transportation Authority by the Regional Plan Association, 1989.

45. *New York Magazine*, July 23, 1979, p. 32; Emanuel Tobier, "Manhattan Emerges as 'World City.' " *Real Estate Review* 14:1 (Spring 1984): 47–52.

46. As quoted in the *New York Times*, March 15, 1987, section 4, p. 6.

47. As quoted in Shefter, *Political Crisis/Fiscal Crisis*, p. 175.

48. Jewel Bellush and Murray Hausknecht, *Urban Renewal: People, Politics and Planning.* Garden City, NY: Doubleday, 1967, p. 223.

49. Interview, Professor Dick Netzer, New York University, December 2, 1986.

50. Bailey, *The Crisis Regime*, p. 140.

51. Sayre and Kaufman, *Governing New York City*, p. 39.

52. Sayre and Kaufman, *Governing New York City*, p. 39; Theodore Lowi, *The Per-*

sonal President. Ithaca: Cornell University Press, 1985, p. 30.; *New York Magazine,* February 24, 1986, p. 38.

53. Charles Brecher and Raymond Horton, "Expenditures," in Brecher and Horton, *Setting Municipal Priorities, 1984.* New York: New York University Press, 1983, pp. 86, 74; Roberta Gratz, "Save the Helen Hayes," *New York Magazine,* November 19, 1979, pp. 74–75; "Invasion of the Monster Buildings," *New York Magazine,* June 11, 1979, p. 40.

54. Harrison Goldin, City Comptroller, "Performance Audit of the Industrial and Commercial Incentive Board," March 12, 1979, p. 18. Requests for abatements ranged between $285,000 for the New York Health and Racquet Club to $10.5 million for the New York Telephone Company office building at 1166 Avenue of the Americas.

55. *Daily News,* October 26, 1986, p. 26.

56. Albert Scardino, *New York Times,* December 7, 1986, part 2, pp. 35ff.

57. Martin Gallent, "Mortgaging Light and Air," *Newsday,* November 17, 1986; *New York Times,* December 7, 1986, part 2, pp. 35–37, 112, 114, 116.

58. *New York Times,* December 7, 1986, part 2, pp. 35–37, 112, 114, 116.

59. Sayre and Kaufman, *Governing New York City,* pp. 78–80.

60. *New York Times,* May 11, 1986, section 8, p. 24.

61. Real Estate Board of New York (REBNY), "A Survey of Poll Results: Public Attitudes Toward Development and Property Ownership in New York City," 1985, 12 East 41st Street, NY, NY 10017.

62. Data drawn from State Senator Franz Leichter, "News from Leichter," Release to Press, November 26, 1985, with report, "Leichter Documents Close Relationships Between Campaign Contributions and Board of Estimate Votes." See Koch, *Mayor,* pp. 288–89.

63. Interview, Arthur Margon, Research Director of REBNY, November 6, 1986; materials cited as well as background on REBNY at offices, on file, 12 East 41st Street, NY, NY 10017.

64. Ibid.

65. Interview, James Gifford, vice-president, New York City Partnership, April 28, 1986; NY Chamber of Commerce and Industry, "New York Chamber Advocacy Agenda for 1986," 22 pp.

66. Sam Roberts, "Who Runs New York Now?" *New York Times Magazine,* April 28, 1985, p. 27.

67. As quoted by Peter Wilkinson, *Manhattan, Inc.,* January 1988, p. 58.

68. In the first quarter of 1985, he had fifteen real estate clients who paid the firm roughly $100,000 in quarterly fees, according to information on file with the Office of the City Clerk, "Legislative Advocates for the Quarter, January–March, 1985."

69. Interview with Arthur Margon, November 6, 1986.

70. Robert Dahl, *Who Governs?* New Haven, CT: Yale University Press, 1961. See Chapter 10, which details urban redevelopment.

71. Paul Goldberger, "The Limits of Urban Growth," *New York Times Magazine,* November 14, 1982.

72. Stephen Kass and Michael Gerrard, "Clean Air Sanctions—City's Development in Peril?" *New York Law Journal* (October 10, 1986): 1, 28.

73. Martin Gallent, Dissent, May 13, 1985, City Planning Commission, Case: 60 Wall St., Ca;/No. 1 c850321 ZSM. Files, City Planning Commission.

74. H. Alan Hoglund in *New York Times,* November 24, 1986, p. A15, written as a letter to the editor; *New York Magazine,* May 13, 1985, p. 47.

75. *New York Times,* March 29, 1987, section 8, p. 21, and *Daily News,* November 4, 1980, editorial.

76. Ibid.

77. Harrison Goldin, "Performance Audit," March 12, 1979, pp. 17–18.

78. Letter from Harrison Goldin to Herbert Sturz, Chair, City Planning Commission, October 14, 1986.

79. Robert Ponte, "Manhattan's Real Estate Boom," *New York Affairs* 8:4 (1985): 18–31. See also Bellush and Hausknecht, *Urban Renewal*; Norman Fainstein and Susan Fainstein, "The Politics of Urban Development," *City Almanac* 17:6 (April 1984). Published by J.M. Kaplan Center for NYC Affairs of the New School for Social Research.

12

The Media in the
Game of Politics

Edwin Diamond and Piera Paine

One morning in the fall of 1987, as the New York City Board of Estimate meeting moved through its agenda, a bright light appeared in the rear of the room. One of the surrogates on the board announced, "May I introduce the acting borough president of the Bronx, Cecil Joseph?" The light in the rear moved forward: a television crew from Channel 31, the municipally owned station in New York, was recording Joseph's first day at the board. The new borough president sat down, voted "yes" on two routine resolutions as the camera whirred away and then left, followed by the TV crew. Next, the board worked on some more substantive business. Manhattan Borough President, David Dinkins, rose to discuss the question of building new jails, a lively and important issue in a city that has been driven to use floating barges for some of its inmate population. But the camera by then had gone to "black," and Channel 31's audience was similarly in the dark. Dinkins' comments did not rate mention on television that night.

Channel 31 at least had sent a crew to the meeting. The commercial stations ignored the board entirely. It was nothing extraordinary: only television's normal manner of treating governmental business in New York City. "Covering the Board or the City Council is pretty dull stuff," a news director at one of the commercial stations explained. "We want people to watch our newscasts, and people tend to watch interesting things." Queens Borough President Claire Shulman was sympathetic to the demands on TV news, "You can't tell camera crews to come down at 2 P.M. and when they get here tell them the item doesn't come up until 4 or 5." Television, it seems, has other priorities in the news.[1]

The media, it is often said, mirror society. Sometimes, such truisms are correct, and any analysis of contemporary news coverage in America must start from here. Almost immediately, however, the story becomes more complex—especially when the media under analysis are New York City's newspapers and broadcast outlets, and especially when the society being considered is New York City's municipal government and politics in the years since 1963. This has been a time of tumultuous dislocations in the city and in the city's media, changes that are still being felt today. Both the New York media and New York society, mirror and reality, were transformed in important ways during this period. Seven daily newspapers were being published within the city limits when the decade of the 1960s began; by the end of that decade, four of these papers were gone, and television had risen to become a major source of public news for hundreds of thousands of new New Yorkers (who, in earlier times, might have joined the ranks of the news reading audience).

Yet some things remained unaltered amid all the change. "New York is the greatest city in the world—and everything is wrong with it," the beginning of a newspaper series declared. The articles went on to list the evidence of the city's "crisis": one in every five New Yorkers living in poverty, a welfare roll bigger than the total combined populations of five U.S. states, substandard public schools, courts so jammed that it took some cases up to four years to come to trial, thousands of jobs lost because of high taxes and the price of doing business in the city. And, above all, the stark contrasts between the New York of the wealthy and the city's seemingly permanent underclass. The series could have appeared yesterday in a New York paper. In fact, the first article ran on January 25, 1965, in the pages of the *New York Herald Tribune*. Today, the city's "crisis" remains, while the *Herald Tribune*, once on everybody's list of the three or four best newspapers in the United States, has long since disappeared, a victim of the same forces that killed three other New York City newspapers in the 1960s.

The apparently unyielding nature of the city's problems and the demonstrably fragile nature of a significant part of its media form a major theme of this chapter. Any effort to judge the way that the media have reported on municipal affairs over the past three decades must take into account both the city's bedrock problems and its distracted, if not vulnerable, media. Such an exercise must also factor in another reflection of weakness—the essentially reactive roles played by print and electronic news organizations in the public life of New York City. When it comes to the public life of the city, New York media do not view their primary function as adversarial or investigative, or even as reportorial: no "record" of the public business is kept.

The (Overly) Celebrated "Power of the Press"

Many otherwise well-informed men and women find this theme of media passivity hard to comprehend. Intellectuals, academics, and civil servants, by and large, are all convinced of the "power of the press." But this conviction grows out of the confusion of celebrity-making with policy formation; those who believe in press power are making the mistake of confusing the presentation of popular or entertaining materials with the systematic airing of public issues.

In theory, newspapers and television stations are supposed to have the ability to set agendas, to elevate some events at the expense of others. Walter Lippmann, the premier philosopher of the press, seven decades ago offered a vivid image of the agenda-setting tradition: the press-as-light, darting onto the darkened stage of public affairs and illuminating events, bringing to life the news, calling attention to the triumphs—or more likely, shortcomings—of city employees and political leaders alike. But this classic model of the press has been true, at best, as metaphor. The reality is quite different. The hands on the media spotlight are those of the journalists; but the director usually is, in that apt contemporary term, "the newsmaker." Mayor Edward Koch, during most of his period in office, was perhaps the most effective news-making personality in the city since the days of Fiorello LaGuardia. He became the consummate director, the true agenda-maker. As the Koch years showed, even when the media do control the movement of the spotlight, they often focus on the fringe, rather than the core, issues of New York government and politics.

Media Power: Separating Fact from Fantasy

To argue that the New York City media have been reactive to events rather than active in covering municipal affairs is not to deny them the power in the city that they do possess. But we must be clear in defining what that power is and is not. First of all, the media analyzed here wield what might be called "reach power." New Yorkers are heavy consumers of media, more so than most other Americans. Many New York City residents, for example, are likely to read two or more newspapers daily. In 1985, some 20 percent of the readers of the *New York Times* also looked at the *New York Post*, while 30 percent of *Post* readers also read the *Daily News*.[2] When we add to these reading habits the fact that New Yorkers on average also watch more than two hours of television daily—about the national norm—it is clear why the impression of media power is so widespread. Television newspeople, for example, are among the most widely recognized New Yorkers at any social gathering. Indeed, their presence at a news event, say a press conference or political rally, often distracts from the "on-stage" proceedings. But media pervasiveness is not the same as media persuasiveness.

The second aspect of media influence might be called "intensity power." The concentration of news outlets in New York can turn the city into an auditorium of deafening noise, as if everyone were carrying giant soundboxes on the streets. The city's blasters can make every New Yorker aware overnight of a name or an event. In the classic formulation, journalists may not be able to tell their audiences what to think—circumstances of family, class, community, race, religion, peers, occupation, income, and education all play influential roles in the formation of attitudes and beliefs. But journalists, by dint of repetition and volume, can tell their audiences what to think about: pupil achievement scores, Central Park violence, a racial episode in Queens, a "crumbling" bridge structure, or a prospective rise in tunnel tolls.

Third, the media also wield considerable "emotional power." Television especially is good at dramatizing the materials of the news, by presenting the general in the particular and by touching what the market researchers call the "hot buttons" of personal response. Thus, the Bernhard Goetz "subway vigilante" case in 1985 set off the wider alarms about violence, race, and class in the city; thus, too, the killing of Lisa Steinberg focused attention on child abuse and the overall inadequacy of the city's social services and welfare systems. Each week, three or four New York children suffer serious injuries or are killed by abusive adults, without "making news." Television's power to give a specific human face to these statistics, however, can create "big news."

The final aspect of media power is economic. The city's media are high-volume businesses. As of the end of 1989, four daily newspapers were being published in the city: the *Daily News*, *New York Newsday*, the *New York Post*, and the *New York Times*.[3] Among the city's broadcast outlets, no fewer than six television stations have large news-gathering staffs of twenty or more people: the three stations owned and operated by the Big Three networks, ABC, CBS, and NBC (Channels 7, 2 and 4, respectively); and the three stations owned by independent chains and corporations, Fox Broadcasting's Channel 5, Tribune Company's Channel 11, and the Music Corporation of America's Channel 9. In addition, two New York City radio stations, WCBS and WINS, have significant news-gathering operations, while a dozen other area radio stations have more modest news staffs.

All this represents only the daily English language news. In addition, there are: *El Diario/La Prensa*, a Spanish-language paper published six times a week and owned by the Gannett Corporation; the *New York Amsterdam News*, selling about 65,000 copies weekly in the black community; the *Village Voice*, with a weekly circulation of 150,000, and the *New York Observer*, a weekly started in the summer of 1987, as well as more than two dozen smaller weekly and neighborhood papers in Manhattan and the other boroughs.

These smaller outlets are important to New York precisely because they are so resolutely "local," right down to their statistics of precinct crime and news of the neighborhood schools. The *Village Voice* in particular occupies a special category in the media life of the city, midway between the "uptown" dailies and the neighborhood weeklies. The *Voice* has done some of the most persistent and aggressive reporting on municipal government of all the New York media over the past two decades. But in any assessment of what most New Yorkers are told most of the time about their city government, the media that count are the mainstream news organizations: the four major dailies, the six TV stations and the radio outlets that offer sustained informational service.

The Owners: Mostly Remote, Invariably Rich

These news organizations usually are owned by extremely profitable corporations. In the case of ABC, CBS, and NBC, of course, the status of the parent corporation is well known. General Electric, the owner of NBC, was ranked number three on the *Business Week* list of the 1,000 "most valuable companies" of 1987. Even the less visible companies boast enormous wealth. The Tribune Company, based in Chicago, owns both the *Daily News* and Channel 11, as well as the *Chicago Tribune* and newspapers and radio and television stations in Florida, the Midwest, and California. Rupert Murdoch's News America Corporation controlled the *New York Post* until February 1988 as well as Channel 5 and newspapers and television stations in Boston, Washington, Los Angeles, and San Antonio—and that does not count Murdoch's extensive media holdings in Australia and England. *New York Newsday* and its sister publication, *Long Island Newsday*, are owned by the Times Mirror Corporation of Los Angeles (newspapers, TV stations, cable systems, and magazines—number 108 on *Business Week's* most valuable list). Some of the smaller New York weeklies are also part of this chain of affluence: the *Village Voice* is owned by Leonard Stern of Hartz Mountain (pet food and real estate). Gannett, *El Diario's* owner, is the largest newspaper group in the United States, publishers of *USA Today* and ninety-six other dailies and weeklies (as of January 1, 1988). The *New York Observer* was founded by Arthur Carter, a Wall Street investor and centimillionaire.

Paradoxically, though, the profitability of the parent corporations is not always reflected in their New York properties. The city's television broadcast outlets, without exception, are money makers. NBC's Channel 4 has been called for a number of years "the world's richest TV station"—the station with the highest rated programs, and therefore the most valuable advertising time, in the largest commercial television market anywhere. The economic health of the New York newspapers, as distinct from their parent corporations, is another story. The city's newspapers, like some patient with a debilitating form of flu, are both flushed with feverish business activity and numbed by the chill of prospective financial failure. The threat of further newspaper closings, before the new decade of the 1990s, hangs over the industry. The *Daily News*, *New York Newsday*, and the *Post* all lost money in the mid- and late-1980s, by some estimates as much as $10 million each in the year 1987 alone. In 1988, the *Daily News* moved closer to profitability and the *Post*, under new owner Peter Kalikow, cut its losses to "only" $5 million for the year.

Only the *New York Times*, of the four major New York dailies, is consistently profitable. In 1986, for example, the parent New York Times company reported over $1.68 billion in revenues, most of it earned by the *Times* newspaper, though other company properties also were profitable. These profit centers include the Times' five TV stations, its thirty-five regional papers, principally in the Southeast and Far West, its ten periodicals, including *Golf Digest* and *Family Circle*, and the Canadian newsprint operations. The *Times* newspaper alone in the mid-1980s regularly achieved net earnings of well over $100 million annually—the precise bottom line is unknown, because the corporation does not break out individual figures. However, as recently as the mid-1970s, during the New York fiscal crisis, the *Times* newspaper's profit margins were no more than $2.5 million a year, according to executives then present. And going back another decade, to the mid-1960s when there were no extensive Times Company holdings, the *Times* newspaper itself actually lost money one year.

These financial numbers, for the *Times*, and for the other news outlets, are essential for understanding the relative degrees of power and weakness of New York City's media, and through that, to understand the strengths and shortcomings of the news coverage of city affairs since 1960. The balance of this chapter is devoted to an analysis of the last three decades of media coverage of New York City municipal affairs, organized around three "case studies." They are: first, the "city in crisis" of the mid-1960s that led to the election of John V. Lindsay as mayor; second, the fiscal bankruptcy drama of the mid-1970s during the administration of Mayor Abraham Beame; and third, the municipal corruption scandals of the mid-1980s during the third term of Mayor Edward I. Koch.[4] These three cases lead to our conclusion that Lippmann's metaphorical spotlight has been as often as not in the service of New York's established political and social institutions, including its incumbent political figures.

The 1960s and Early 1970s: "Crisis" and Contraction

Most contemporary accounts of the decline of the New York City media start by dealing with the big strike of 1962–63, which shut down 7 dailies for a total of 114 days. Television news expanded its coverage of the city and resourceful New Yorkers got their hands on out-of-town papers; but neither the surface coverage (still) of the former, nor the sketchy stories of the latter, could help the attentive public find out what was going on in their city. Decisions were made, managers managed, teachers taught (or tried to), the city ran—all in a news vacuum. When the strike was over, Hearst's morning tabloid, the *Daily Mirror*, had ceased publication, and the *Herald Tribune*, a paper whose roots went back to 1835, was in deep financial trouble, its revenue losses from the strike reaching $110 million. Moreover, the fundamental issue facing the New York newspaper industry, the antiquated technology that made newspaper production so costly and inefficient, had not been addressed in the 1963 settlement to any significant degree by either management or the unions involved. As a later generation would learn to say, all that pain and no gain.

In the 1960s, labor-saving technologies such as teletypesetting, photocomposition—and much later, computer editing systems—were desperately needed by

New York's newspapers. But modern equipment and lower operating costs would not be enough. The fortunes of the newspapers were closely related to what was happening in the city itself. New York's economy and its population had grown little during the 1950s. As in other large American cities, middle-class families were departing for the suburbs; manufacturing jobs also were departing, some to the suburbs and some to other parts of the country; the cargo and passenger business of the Port of New York had begun what turned out to be a precipitous decline.

New York City shared in the national economic exuberance of the 1960s, with a growing white-collar work force and service employment and a strong boom in office and apartment construction. Yet, the economic and social strains that began in the previous decade remained, and their effects could be seen in increasing budgetary difficulties for the municipal government. Unhappily, this was hardly the subject to which the media spotlight was directed.

Typically, the media's interests and energies in this period were directed at the mayoral elections. The high visibility and high excitement—in news terms—of the quadrennial electoral "drama" invariably attracts greater attention than the drabber business of how the city is being managed from day to day. "Politics" was a fight, sketched in bold strokes, and journalists liked being at ringside to report it. "Government," with its bureaus and boards, paper trails, and swollen files, took place in dustier, less glamorous venues. If government had more appeal than politics for journalists, then they might have become civil servants in the first place. American journalism has always been better at paying attention to politics rather than to government.

The owners and publishers, too, prefer to get involved in campaigns rather than civic administration. Midway through Robert Wagner's third term, the Republican *Herald Tribune*, owned by the patrician sportsman-investor John Hay "Jock" Whitney, concluded that the city might be ready for a Fusion candidate once again.[5] The *Herald Tribune* decided that the reform movement had found its candidate in the person of John V. Lindsay, a liberal Republican congressman from the Seventeenth "silk stocking" District of Manhattan.[6] Jock Whitney made two key contributions to the Lindsay candidacy. Together with his associate, Walter Thayer, Whitney raised an initial campaign war chest of $500,000 for Lindsay. And, more to the point, their paper gave Lindsay a platform for his campaign—the *Herald Tribune's* "City in Crisis" series. Lindsay would later acknowledge that the newspaper provided "a raison d'être for me to run."

Beginning on January 25, 1965, and for the four months that followed, the *Herald Tribune* published articles under the "City in Crisis" headline almost daily.[7] The articles were zealous in tone. The paper involved itself in what today we would call "interactive communicating." It set up twenty-four-hour special phone lines to receive reaction to the articles as well as complaints and comments about city government. The *Herald Tribune* was on a grand mission, and, when battles were won, the paper did not balk at self-congratulation. On February 25, for example, the paper published two articles about its own series. One noted that the City Club of New York presented an award to the *Herald Tribune* for the "City in Crisis." The other credited the pressure of earlier articles for the appointment of twenty-six new housing inspectors after a year-long delay.

The series, in its breadth, depth, and steady appearance, made for powerful journalism. Taken individually, stories were antithetical to the traditional news coverage of city government as exemplified, for example, in the *Herald Tribune's* major rival, the *New York Times*. The "Crisis" series, though it said a great deal about the administration of the city, was more about the lives of individual people. City officials were less likely to be heard than were New York's residents and businesspeople. The mayor, Wagner, was in the position of having to respond to the quotes of such people and to the problems they cited in the "Crisis" articles. In the past, the mayor's official statements at press conferences or public and political meetings had been the occasions for the news.

The *Times* would publish an article with the headline "Borough Presidents Defend Their Offices" and the article would show the presidents were necessary liaisons for the citizenry. But the *Herald Tribune* approach was less kind: "Borough Prez—Big Title Little Job." Mayor Wagner did get his day in the stories— "The Mayor's View: A Town of 'Throbbing Vitality' " (January 27, 1965). But the authors of the series more typically granted authority to citizens at the expense of the mayor. Thus, a news story on February 24, "At a crowded public hearing on the 1965–66 executive capital budget yesterday, Mayor Wagner accused a civic leader of being misinformed only to learn shortly thereafter that it was he, and not the civic leader, who was misinformed."

Such treatment of the city administration continued well beyond the series and into the political campaign. Wagner himself was out of the picture before the primary; he chose not to seek a fourth term. The Democratic nominee, Abraham Beame, felt the heat that Wagner might have received from the *Herald Tribune*. Lindsay had started at least ten points behind Beame in the polls, and the *Herald Tribune's* front pages charted each upward tick in the Lindsay ratings, creating the sense of Republican-Fusion "momentum." This favorable treatment continued right up to election day, when the *Herald Tribune* ran a front-page editorial stating that a Lindsay victory would make possible the beginning of the end of "wallowing misrule." When Lindsay won by three percentage points, Walter Thayer was heard to exult in the *Tribune's* city room that night, "Well, we did it!"

New York City's newspapers mirrored the city's travails not just in their pages, but in their own financial affairs as well. Quite simply, the newspapers of the city were not very well run. (Television, though economically healthy from the start, was not a major journalistic force until a decade later and contributed very little to the coverage of either politics or government in the 1960s.) One remarkable characteristic of the city's newspapers in the 1960s was the "visitors" status of their proprietors: four of the seven were owned by corporations whose major interests lay elsewhere than the city. The afternoon *Journal American* and the morning *Mirror* were part of the Hearst empire of California, and the *World Telegram* belonged to Scripps Howard of Ohio. Jock Whitney, though a newcomer to journalism, was at least a New Yorker. He had acquired the *Herald Tribune* in the 1950s from the tired, and warring, factions of the Reid family. The *Times*, while most resolutely the property of the heirs of Adolf Ochs, had gone through its own managerial turmoil. In 1961, Arthur Ochs Sulzberger, Jr., the linear descendant of the founder, had been passed over as publisher. The family had judged his brother-in-law, Orville Dryfoos, the more experienced man. But Dryfoos died after just two years in the publisher's post. The junior Sulzberger was known as "Punch"—for his "sunny disposition and wandering attention," as the author Richard Kluger put it. Sulzberger became publisher in June 1963. He was then thirty-seven years old.

Dryfoos died before his fifty-first birthday, a victim of a heart attack and, in a way, a casualty of the infamous 114-day newspaper strike. Dryfoos had been involved as the managements of the New York City papers tried to maintain a united front in their negotiations with the so-called Big Six union, Local No. 6 of the International Typographical Union, the printing work force in the city. The strike was a waste for all; its divisive issues required at least another decade to settle. In the years since the 1960s, photocomposition techniques, automation, and electronic production have replaced the antiquated "hot type" machinery of nineteenth-century technology at New York's newspaper plants. But because the 1963 settlement had involved wages in the main, it had left largely untouched the need of the city's newspaper industry to enter, two-thirds of the way through, the twentieth century. Later, when the new technology finally arrived, it was too late to benefit the majority of the city's papers. The *Mirror* had ceased publication, despite the fact that it was, after the *Daily News*, the largest selling newspaper in the United States, but one with a very small share of newspaper advertising revenues.

The *Herald Tribune*, the *World Telegram* and the *Journal American* tried, briefly, to combine their disparate styles and audiences into a hybrid called the *World Journal Tribune*.[8] On the day the new paper was supposed to come out, the American Newspaper Guild struck the new company. The paper finally appeared on newsstands nearly five months later, and for a time struggled, and survived. At one point, the paper had a circulation of 700,000 daily, making it the fourth largest evening newspaper in the country. But it was too costly to sustain, given its antiquated equipment, anemic advertising base, and top-heavy staff—the Guild strike had been settled only after the paper agreed to keep hundreds of employees it didn't want, creating a payroll it couldn't meet. In May 1967, when the Big Six asked for more wage increases in a new contract, the owners gave up. They had published for eight months.

In theory, as the decade of the sixties wound down, the three remaining New York City newspapers should have been able to strengthen their positions and audience shares, each serving distinct constituencies and profiting handsomely. But the market did not work out in that textbook way, for a variety of reasons.

Five and a half million New Yorkers were regular newspaper readers in the early 1960s. After each prolonged strike or folding of a paper, these readers did not redistribute themselves among the survivor papers in some neat mathematical way. Some readers moved out of New York and began sampling the papers that surrounded the city. Some of those who continued to commute to work in the city continued to read its papers. But just as some new suburbanites changed their political affiliations, so too did some of them change their newspaper habits, "voting" their new suburban choices, such as *Newsday* on Long Island, or the Bergen County *Record* in New Jersey. Other members of the potential audience—principally, the newer New Yorkers migrating to the city—simply never became newspaper readers. Television became their major source of news and information; among other things, it was readily available, entertaining, free, and required a minimal facility in the English language.

Thus, the city's media more and more stratified into distinct social and economic groupings, or bluntly, into social-economic classes. The *Times* claimed the highest "demographics," to use the newly fashionable market researchers' word: the better educated, higher income readers. Indeed, the *Times* became less and less a New York City newspaper appealing to a local audience and more and more a national paper for the "top people" wherever they lived. The *Times* readership eventually divided roughly into one-third New York City–based readers, one-third New York suburban area readers, and one-third national (beyond fifty miles of the city). And even within New York City, *Times* readers clustered in the borough of Manhattan.

At the opposite, or poor, end of the market, demographically speaking, was local television, with its audience of the newly arrived and the low-income, less-educated nonreaders or light readers. This sorting out of media choices by class left the middle market for the *Daily News* and the *Post*. As long as the city's middle class was numerous, the two papers were strong. They were believed to have distinctive constituencies. The *Daily News* had a largely middle-class Irish and Italian Catholic readership, and the *Post* a largely middle-class Jewish audience.

As a rule of civic thumb, police, fire, and sanitation workers read the *News*; school teachers and other civil servants, the *Post*. The papers' editors believed this, and so did the city's political leaders.

The mid-market papers suffered from changes in the residences, job locations, and commuting patterns among these ethnic and class groups. More of these people moved to the suburbs, more worked outside the Manhattan central business district, and fewer of them commuted to work by public transportation (and did not buy the papers to read on the way to or from work). So, from a circulation of 3 million in the 1960s, the *News* had declined to half that by the 1980s. The changed demographics of the city affected not only circulation, but also how the newspapers covered the city and consequently what information was made available to its citizens.

The *Times* could boast the largest foreign staff of any U.S. newspaper, as well as comprehensive coverage of Washington by a bureau of three dozen reporters and editors. The *Times* also dominated coverage of the arts, culture, and social life of the city—or, to be more precise, of Manhattan. Its chronicles of the life of Brooklyn, the Bronx, Queens, and Staten Island were somewhat less than complete. At the same time, the *Daily News* and the *Post*, the papers that in an earlier era would have been paying close attention to the outer boroughs, were becoming preoccupied with their own survival. Eventually both papers would be faced with the prospects of finding new owners, with deep pockets, or of shutting down altogether. (The *Post*, in fact, was sold to the real estate developer Peter J. Kalikow in early 1988.) Their coverage of city affairs suffered in these uncertain times. Meanwhile, local television, the new mass medium of the most numerous class in the city, could not, by its structure and values, sustain serious coverage of municipal affairs. Local television attention to the city became stylized in the formula, "news (meaning fires, crime, and accidents), weather, and sports."

The gaps in media attention became glaringly obvious during the great fiscal crisis of the mid-1970s.

The Big Surprise: The Bankruptcy Story

Great events often go unattended. So it was with New York's close brush with municipal bankruptcy in 1975. The record shows that the city's newspapers and broadcast outlets missed the opening stages of New York's plunge toward fiscal disaster. To be sure, there were the usual year-end stories about the prospective shortfalls in the city's budgets. But these had become routine announcements, and they received treatment in passing—that is, one or two days of modest attention in the middle of the daily flow of news and then consignment to the category of "old news."

The reasons why such stories receive "routine" attention have already been indicated. Budgetary reporting in particular suffered both from media overdependence on official news sources and from media fixation with politics at the expense of attention to governance. What's more, the general-interest media—as late as the 1970s—had not yet developed reporters and editors with expertise in such civic topics as capital budgets, accounting practices, and the administration of pension funds. Those specialized talents came to journalism later, as editors belatedly began to realize the importance of these relatively "dull" topics. In fact, one of the good consequences of the New York City fiscal crisis was that news organizations realized their need for specialist reporters who knew how to read financial documents and who could keep track of sophisticated economic activities.

Professor Dick Netzer, in Chapter 2 of this book, has traced how even the political actors were slow to realize the seriousness of the fiscal situation. In some cases, these insiders never did comprehend the significance of their actions. The writer and columnist Ken Auletta has described how a casual decision reached as part of the settlement package for the 1966 Transit Workers strike had cost the city millions of dollars—but did not become public knowledge until it was "discovered" by the *Daily News* in 1971. And then, when reporter Dick Oliver, who had been digging through the transit negotiation records on assignment from the *News*, found the 1966 materials and confronted Robert Price, the decision maker involved, Price expressed his surprise. "If [you say] I did it, I did it," he told Oliver. "I'm amazed I had such authority. . . . Where was the mayor?"[9]

The reelection of John Lindsay in 1969, with the near-unanimous support of the city's media, coincided with the end of the economic boom of the 1960s, in New York City as in the nation. But neither the economic turnaround nor the warnings of expert observers made much impact or gained much media attention. A few months before the 1969 elections, the Citizens Budget Commission issued a study, "The Financial Outlook for New York City," that pointed out that New York City faced "choices between what is wanted and what can be afforded."[10] But the timing was wrong; the report came out on July 20, when New Yorkers—as well as millions of other Americans—had their heads in the clouds: The U.S. Apollo astronauts had just landed on the moon. To New Yorkers, 1969 became known as the year of the "moon, the Mets and the mayor." After the Apollo triumph, the New York Mets baseball club, perennial doormats of the National League, won the world series in October, and Lindsay defeated challengers John Marchi and Mario Proccacino. It seemed to be an era of miracles, not of budget mismanagement. Lindsay, triumphant, extended his vision beyond the city; he campaigned for the Democratic nomination for president of the United States in late 1971 and early 1972.

The city's newspapers, in their own way, reflected the outlook of the Lindsay administration. They, too, were looking beyond the city. By the 1970s, the sharp population shifts of the middle class from the city to the suburbs were evident to all concerned. The surviving papers suffered and particularly, as we have seen, the *Daily News* and the *Post*. But even the upper-end *Times* was not immune. Between 1970 and 1975, the average daily circulation of the *Times* dropped from 908,000 to 828,000, and its Sunday circulation declined from 1,468,900 to 1,440,000. Both advertising and profits suffered. The *Times* responded to its own fiscal crisis in a number of ways, including a major editorial reorganization of the paper that unified the previously separate daily and Sunday papers.

The new single command of the *Times* had two immediate effects on how the paper covered New York City municipal affairs. First of all, the consolidation made A. M. Rosenthal the single most important *Times* editorial power. And although Abe Rosenthal had attended the City College of New York and had started working for the *Times* in New York City, he had made his journalistic reputation covering the United Nations and, later, as a foreign correspondent assigned to Warsaw, New Delhi, and Tokyo. He finally resettled in New York, became *Times* managing editor in 1969, and executive editor in 1977. By training, Rosenthal was inclined to look outward to the wider world and to seek to enhance the role of the *Times* as the newspaper with the best, and largest, national and foreign staff of any news organization in the world.

On the other hand, Rosenthal was an extremely competitive and dedicated *Times* man, who took fierce pride in every aspect of the paper. He was aware of the paper's broader orientation and its elevation of national and international news over "mere" metropolitan stories. He resolved to have the *Times* do a superior job covering the city itself. But his definition of "local news" represented a break from traditional policies. In the period of his editorship, the *Times* started its special interest reporting of such topics as food, restaurants, fashion, design, and "life style." This became known as the "sectional revolution" that created four special Sunday sections targeted for suburban readers in New Jersey, Connecticut, Long Island, and Westchester county, as well as three new daily sections—"Living" on Wednesdays, "Home" on Thursdays, and "Weekend" on Fridays. Later came "Science Times" on Tuesday and "Sports Extra" on Mondays.

These new sections were seen as vehicles to attract both younger, more affluent readers and the advertisers who wanted to reach them. "Science Times," for example, was able to sell pages of ads for computers and related high-technology equipment. More to the point of municipal coverage, the special-interest sections changed the content of the *Times*' news columns. So-called soft or featurized subjects claimed more space: the hottest new restaurants, the latest in loft redecorating, the changing relations between men and women, new advances in family nutrition or health. With the arrival of the new sections, *Times* circulation and advertising revenues began climbing again. By the end of 1987, the *Times* was able to report a daily circulation of 1.1 million, an all-time record. No one could really argue that "soft" meant "not newsworthy." Coverage of how people live, love, and bring up children are certainly as important as any article about the shortfall in municipal budgets or the work rules for the city sanitation department, but the elevation of one set of topics inevitably meant relatively less attention to other topics.

Or so some *Times* men and women thought. Sydney Schanberg was one of them. Schanberg had been one of the *Times*' journalistic stars, winner of the

Pulitzer Prize for his coverage of the fall of Cambodia (his eyewitness accounts were retold in the motion picture, *The Killing Fields*). When Schanberg returned to New York from Southeast Asia, he served as editor of the *Times* Metropolitan section for a time and then became a *Times* columnist, writing mainly about local and municipal matters. His column on the *Times* Op-ed page tended to stand out: of the *Times'* six regular Op-ed columnists, only Schanberg wrote about New York City politics and municipal matters. The others concentrated on the bigger political pictures in Washington and abroad.

Both Schanberg's metro pages during his editing days and his column were the stuff of conflict and confrontation. Schanberg was an advocate of more coverage of what he called the "Un-Beautiful City"—the New York of welfare hotels, AIDS and drug addicts, mean streets, and indifferent bureaucracies. His insistence on attention to these stories—some would say his "twisted" coverage of them—brought him into conflict with city officials and specialists in municipal affairs. He also clashed with *Times* senior managers who conceived of the city in different, and far rosier, hues—the sparkling, affluent New York of the *Times'* special-interest sections. In 1985, Schanberg lost his column after a dispute with his editors; subsequently he left the paper to begin a column on city affairs for *New York Newsday*.

The *Times*, of course, had more than a passing interest in the "Beautiful City." Indeed, the *Times'* news pages and its coverage of the city's cultural amenities and "life styles" was one of the major merits of city living—the great city had a great newspaper as its chronicler. And so, though the *Times* may have been slow to awaken to the city's fiscal crisis, when the paper did respond—toward the end of the second Lindsay administration in 1973—the metropolitan desk gave it full, often front-page coverage. By 1974, reporter Steven Weisman was filing several comprehensive, well-informed stories each week. Also the *Times'* editorial board spoke firmly and decisively. It loved New York, and so the great city must be saved, even if this meant that sacrifices had to be exacted out of the "other" New York.

Two examples of *Times* coverage during the fiscal crisis were emblematic of this approach to sacrifice.[11] The first, an editorial entitled "Civic Teamwork," appeared on March 11, 1975. "Hope of solving New York City's staggering economic problems," the editorial began, "rests to a considerable degree on unionized civil service workers' willingness to improve performance quality and productivity to bring down payroll costs."

The second example, a *Times* news story less than a month later, illustrated the *Times'* wish to reassure its readership—and perhaps itself—about the city's future. On April 3, 1975, Standard & Poor's, the credit rating agency, suspended New York City's "A" rating. The *Times* headlines and approach suggested that the move "may be temporary." A subheadline read, "Beame Assails Action: 'We Have Never Defaulted,' the Mayor Says, Promising to Balance the Budget." The next day, a second credit agency, Moody's, kept the city's rating at

"A." The *Times* story on page one quoted Jackson Phillips, senior vice-president of Moody's, who said, "We're prepared for the wind to blow." The *Times* added in the second paragraph of the story, "[Phillips] was summarizing—with the kind of simple metaphor that taps into the intuitive mentality of the investor—the assertion that the city would weather its latest cash crisis." It was, as it turned out, a storm that fell on some New Yorkers more than others. Within two years, the municipal labor force had been reduced by more than 20 percent, and there were substantial, very uneven reductions in city services.

The 1980s: Koch, Corruption and Consciousness Raising

In the spring of 1975, media awareness of the New York City fiscal crisis crested. Former Mayor Beame now remembers the period as among his finest hours. "I set up meetings with every conceivable group," he recalled in a 1987 interview with Peter Blauner of *New York* magazine. "I talked to newspaper reporters, newspaper editors, civic groups, governmental groups like the Board of Estimate, and the City Council. I discussed the whole question and set up a program to overcome it within two years."

Other participants would remember a different cast of heroes who "saved" New York City: the financier Felix Rohatyn, Governor Hugh Carey, the Municipal Assistance Corporation, Victor Gotbaum and other municipal union leaders, among others. In fact, the decisions on retrenchment and debt refinancing had been made in the first two years.[12] Inflation and, later, the long-running bull market on Wall Street, probably helped the subsequent fiscal recovery as much as any local or state political entity. The Reaganesque good times of the 1980s—good for the well-off—helped bring to the city higher tax receipts, a Manhattan building boom, increases in the number of jobs in the financial district, and a host of new business ventures. One immediate beneficiary of New York's economic resurgence was Edward I. Koch, who was first elected mayor in 1977, and then reelected in 1981 and 1985.

If Mayor Beame recalls learning how to deal with New York City's media retroactively—calling in reporters and editors after the bad news was out—then Mayor Koch proved to be a master of prospective news management. Indeed, examination of the media's treatment of the mayor during Koch's first two terms discloses a "cult of Koch."[13] The mayor was a best-selling author who has appeared in the movies (*The Muppets Take Manhattan*) and has been the subject of a Broadway play, *Mayor!*, based on his 1984 autobiography. Koch was a celebrity, appearing on "Saturday Night Live," "Gimme a Break," MTV, the Johnny Carson show, quiz shows, television movies, and the soap opera "All My Children." Koch once had to beg for publicity at the start of his political career as a liberal reformer in the 1960s. Now, as mayor, nearly everything that emerged from Koch's mouth was deemed news.

Naturally, he benefited from the city's recovery from the fiscal crisis of the

1970s. He was seen on television lobbying in Albany for state aid and in Washington for federal loan guarantees. During his administration, the city balanced its budget, restored the city's work force to nearly its precrisis size, and began a major capital program to reverse the deterioration in the city's infrastructure. Initially, too, reporters liked him. "Everything about him was New York," wrote the newspapermen-authors of *I, Koch*. "He had a mouth like ten opinionated cabbies rolled into one. But his mouth had a bunch of microphones to talk into."[14] Koch made for good copy. He was affable and open, often stopping by the press room at City Hall to drop tasty tidbits on hungry reporters.

Koch's relationship with the press was calculated and, as such, it had its limits. According to Lee Dembart of the *New York Times*, Koch's "openness" only succeeded in moving "the wall" further back. Reporters were seeing the Koch that Koch wanted them to see. No matter: the *Daily News*, the *Times* and the *Post* endorsed Koch for governor in 1982 (he lost, anyway) and for reelection as mayor in 1981 and 1985. Koch insisted in his own writings that New Yorkers returned him to office because they perceived his integrity and trusted his word. The image of a fiery mayor not afraid to speak his mind—an image constantly presented in his brief radio and television "sound bites"—reinforced the perception of the mayor as an honest man. The inference was that a man who "speaks his mind" is prima facie honest.

But "perception" and "image" are qualities independent of issues. Concentrating as it did on the personal qualities of Mayor Koch, the media coverage lost sight of some of the complexities of the issues themselves. Thus polls prior to the 1985 mayoral election showed that while Koch had a high approval rating, most of the respondents could not correlate their positive responses with specific mayoral accomplishments. Nevertheless, the mayor's public image served him well, muting criticism over the inadequacy of many city services. When the mayor declared that services must be limited for budgetary reasons—because Albany and Washington were pursuing "ludicrous policies"—he was believed.

Eventually, the mayor's carefully constructed image became vulnerable to the onslaught of realities. On September 4, 1985, the *Times* endorsed Koch for reelection with these words: "He has hired first-rate officials, provided honest government and greatly improved municipal management." (Four years later, the ardor of the *Times* had cooled; its warmest words, as the 1989 mayoral primaries approached, were for challenger Richard Ravitch.)

Just as Reagan had his Iran-Contra scandal, Koch had his municipal corruption scandal. Both the mayor and the president had invested a great effort in manufacturing their public personas and in the management of the media. Poised above the fray, Reagan and Koch pictured themselves as betrayed by subordinates. As their scandals unfolded, the stories of unaccountable leadership and out-of-control bureaucracy undercut both leaders' carefully cultivated images. Press confidence in their leadership began to flag and with it their popularity ratings. While the personal honesty of Reagan and Koch remained unquestioned by the majority, many voters concluded that the two were incapable of controlling their administrations. Yet the voters continued to laud the men, if not the results. No one believed that Koch, for example, had ever personally profited from a penny of graft.

Conclusions: The Mirror and the Reality

During Mayor Koch's third term, his relations with the media deteriorated. There were widespread defections from the "cult of Koch." Yet the day-to-day news coverage of city government showed no marked changes. Political writer Jack Newfield of the *Village Voice* declared that "no daily newspaper [was doing] the kind of tough investigative reporting" that the *Herald Tribune* had done in the 1960s. Yet the situation was beginning to change, especially thanks to the municipal coverage of *New York Newsday*, which had begun publishing a daily edition in 1985.

New York Newsday, the city cousin of the successful Long Island edition, went beyond reporting of scandals to dig deep into the un-beautiful City for stories about waste disposal, police relations with minorities, and the welfare system. In addition, the *Times*, the *Daily News*, and the *Post*, began to make up for earlier episodes of municipal myopia. The *Daily News* especially became reinvigorated under the direction of a new publisher, James Hoge. He renegotiated labor contracts, moved the paper's printing operations out of Manhattan to save money and speed production, and increased coverage of city affairs. Even the august *Times* unbent and opened news bureaus in the Bronx and Queens. Only television news seemed unable to break out of its quick-take, superficial approach to the city's news. Television's audience, however, continued to patronize the city's newscasts with their tired formulas of "slash and trash" coverage of violent crime, smoky fires, and traffic mishaps.

Because the city's media reflect the city's society, the metro news pages of New York's newspapers and the local coverage of the New York broadcast outlets too often aim no higher than the audiences they serve. Fred Dicker of the *New York Post* described this "unique period" in contemporary New York, "when the public at large does not care about the political system." The Bronx Democratic party organization, Dicker said by way of elaboration, "consists of 50 people in a borough of 1.2 million." Of course, even the most alienated or apathetic New Yorker in the Bronx or the other boroughs, eventually learns about an approaching mayoral election by watching television news or by catching the TV political spots of one or another of the candidates. But, as this chapter has argued, there is that other world of civic activity involving the day-to-day operations of the city administration. This is "politics" too. In this largely hidden world, most New York reporters and editors would acknowledge that, in the words of Michael Oreskes of the *New York Times*, "Newspapers and television have no presence or significance at all."[15]

Until enough readers, viewers, and critics raise their voices clearly and persistently about this state of affairs, New York City's government will continue to run—and, we fear, run down—largely in secret.

Notes

1. These two paragraphs are based on interviews conducted by Bradley Finklestein, a member of the News Study Group in the New York University Journalism Department.

2. According to studies conducted in 1985 by Christine D. Urban of Urban and Associates, a market research and consulting group.

3. A fifth daily, the *Wall Street Journal*, is more properly classified as a national newspaper—written and edited in New York but transmitted by satellite to eighteen printing plants throughout the country. Just over 5 percent of the *Journal's* 1.9 million circulation, or 110,000 readers, live in the New York region.

4. The analysis reported here was done by the members of the News Study Group at New York University.

5. "Fusion" in New York City politics traditionally has meant a coalition, for the purposes of electing a mayor, of antiorganization Democrats, independents, and Republicans. Fiorello LaGuardia, who was a Republican on the far left of his party when a member of the U.S. House of Representatives, is the most successful Fusion politician in New York history, having been elected to three terms during which he totally dominated New York City politics and government. As LaGuardia said of himself at the end of his tenure in 1945, he could have been elected on *any* ticket, including a laundry ticket.

6. So called because of the unusually high income levels in the district, whose boundaries were drawn (by the state legislature) to permit the election of at least one Republican from Democratic Manhattan. By the 1950s, only a liberal Republican could be elected in the district, no matter how gerrymandered.

7. Marcy Lefkovitz of our News Study Group reexamined the "City in Crisis" series and compared it with representative stories in the *New York Times* for the same period.

8. Journalists called it "The Widget" and news vendors referred to it as "The Telegram," their name for the old *World Telegram*.

9. Ken Auletta, *The Streets Were Paved With Gold*. New York: Random House, 1979, pp. 61–62. Price was Mayor John Lindsay's first deputy mayor; the transit strike occurred during the first few days of the first Lindsay administration.

10. Quoted by Auletta, *The Streets Were Paved With Gold*, p. 74. This was hardly the first such warning. The Citizens Budget Commission had been making them throughout the 1960s and a Temporary Commission on City Finances that had been appointed in 1964 during the Wagner administration and reported just after Lindsay's election offered a pessimistic long-term outlook on the city's economy and finances. This "news" was treated as just another "report."

11. These examples were suggested by Kira Jahn of our News Study Group.

12. That is, between May 1975 and June 1977. By the latter date, the debt refinancing program was largely under way (if not accomplished) and, in June 1977, the last serious effort by the city government to repeat the bad old habits, a proposed operating budget that expanded city employment despite the deficit, was rebuffed by the state's controllers of the city's finances.

13. This is the term used by John Fox of our News Study Group after making this analysis.

14. Arthur Browne, Dan Collins and Michael Goodwin, *I, Koch*. New York: Dodd, Meade, 1985, p. 172.

15. Dicker and Oreskes were speaking at a roundtable conference held by the Nova Institute in New York City. The proceedings were published by the Institute in March 1982.

V

Demography as Politics

13

Needed, More Foxes: The Black Experience

Charles V. Hamilton

On a summer evening, on June 20, 1960, a black political leader from Harlem, J. Raymond Jones (affectionately known for his political astuteness as "The Fox"), gave a speech to the Lexington Democratic Club of New York City. The title of the talk was "The Negro in New York Politics."[1] The club was a prominent group of "reform" Democrats on Manhattan's East Side. In their political orientation, they were "liberals" who generally eschewed the patronage-orientation of old-line machine politics, as well as the emphasis on race and ethnicity as organizational criteria for mobilizing voters.[2]

Nineteen-sixty was an important dynamic political and racial time in the country and city. The civil rights movement, which was largely focused on the South, was hitting its stride. The Supreme Court six years earlier had declared racially segregated schools unconstitutional, and Southern politicians had signed a "Southern Manifesto" calling for resistance to that decision through interposition and nullification. They were championing states' rights. The famous Montgomery bus boycott had, five years earlier, given prominence to a new, young national leader, Rev. Martin Luther King, Jr., and a new organization, the Southern Christian Leadership Conference. Just four months before Jones's speech, black students in Greensboro, North Carolina, had begun the massive student sit-in movement, challenging segregated facilities of public accommodations.

Nationally, an eight-year Eisenhower presidency was drawing to a close. Locally, the Democratic Party was split between "regulars" and "reformers," and Mayor Robert Wagner was getting ready to run for reelection in 1961 as a "reformer," challenging his previous party-regular supporters. Both sides, given the predicted closeness of the race, would need all the votes they could get. In addition, the Manhattan Democratic party, Tammany Hall, had been involved in a continuing battle with Congressman Adam Clayton Powell from Harlem. And Powell and Jones, in one of their off-again, on-again political alliances, had formed the United Democratic Leadership Team to attempt more effective mobilization of black voters.

J. Raymond Jones talked about all these things that June evening in 1960. But he said more. He put his remarks in a historical context, discussing the relationship of blacks to the national and local parties going back to the New York State Constitution of 1777. He told why blacks supported the Federalists against the Saint Tammany Society. And he brought his story up to the 1930s:

> The economic plateau established by the Roosevelt administration, and reinforced by that of Harry Truman, provided the base from which the Negro was then able to launch his concerted drive for full civil rights. . . . Moreover, the support which New York Negroes gave to the administrations of Harriman, LaGuardia, O'Dwyer and Wagner, was translated into effective and far reaching local legislation of prime importance to Negroes in the field of civil rights and in the economic sphere of his [sic] existence.

Whatever else J. Raymond Jones was, he was a crafty politician. He understood votes and counting, and he had no illusions about the necessity to bargain and compromise. Likewise, he was not apologetic about the use of patronage as a means not only of gaining party loyalty but as a means, an important one, for laying a "base" for further economic development.

Jones knew that many of the reformers to whom he was speaking that evening looked askance at patronage politics. He stated bluntly:

> In touching on these matters, I have, no doubt, wounded some reformers in terms of their positions on ethnic representation and political patronage. So be it. We understand their position, though we cannot share it. We are not rich enough, if you will, to be idealistic about political jobs. We have many able young people whom you will not hire in your private enterprises. No one should prevent them from serving, and serving ably, in analogous capacities in the government. Your present high socioeconomic status is derived, in part, from the fact that your grandparents and parents used the political structures and services of the city, state and nation to advance themselves and, necessarily, you. You may have forgotten this simple political and economic fact. We have not, and will not, until we have also enjoyed this advantage, especially because so many other private economic structures are effectively closed to us. If political power and place corrupt—and we do not think that necessarily the case—we have the historical right, like your forebears, to be corrupted. Our sons and grandsons—once they reach your position—may condemn us for our frantic drive for upward mobility. You ought not to. In short, it is not fair to change the rules in the middle of the game, especially when it is, for us, not a game but a grim struggle.

And so Jones talked that night three decades ago on Manhattan's East Side about politics—national and local. He talked about issues: civil rights and economic policies. And he defended the United Democratic Leadership Team, which to some seemed like an emphasis on "racial politics." But Jones was no "black nationalist," as that term was used then or now.[3] Jones said:

Two aspects of this leadership group (U.D.L.T.) appear to excite the sensibilities of both reformers and regulars alike. One has to do with the theory that, by working together and voting together, we somehow, now, constitute a dangerous racial bloc. In answer to such a charge, let me say that we are doing neither more nor less than any other ethnic or racial group has done in the history of New York politics. The white Protestants of Northern Europe ancestry began it, and they were followed by those of German, Irish, Jewish and Italian extraction—emerging as voting blocs. They used this very device to integrate themselves into the full spectrum of our American culture. Are we to be condemned for following a precedent for being slow in learning from previous groups? Whatever you think, you must note, in all objectivity, that the Negro's social-economic and political mobility has been and still is restricted by America's mores as they apply to color, and this makes it all the more necessary that we, as minority citizens, follow this historic avenue toward group achievement.

And so I begin this chapter on the black political experience by focusing on J. Raymond Jones's little-noted speech before a reform Democratic club one evening in June 1960. Three decades have passed. What has been that experience? Jones admonished that "it is not fair to change the rules in the middle of the game. . . ." but many things *have* changed. These were not, to be sure, rule-changes calculated to defeat the laudable inclusionary goals articulated by Harlem's preeminent politician. They were, however, fundamentally significant systemic changes that affected the fate of blacks in New York City politics and continue to do so.

This chapter will chart those changes and comment on the consequences. The reader is entitled to know, however, that to the extent that this chapter has a particular ideological tone and value-bias (and, hopefully, it does), these have their roots in the sentiments and sensibilities expressed by "The Fox" on that summer evening.

Political Change

Four phenomena must be considered when talking about the black political experience in New York City over the last three decades: the relative decline of the political party as a major patronage-based and voter mobilization entity; the rise of public service unions as important politicizing instruments; the use and decline of antipoverty politics in several black communities; and the city fiscal crisis of the mid-1970s.

More than a few observers have commented on the decline of the "party-in-the-electorate," notably Richard Wade in Chapter 10 of this book. New York City remains a Democratic party city, but the role of the party as a major entity for mobilizing voters and dispensing patronage has declined. Political clubs are still useful for circulating petitions for potential candidates and slating candidates for particular offices. But they have fallen prey to the often-cited influences of mass communication, growing importance of civil service, and the impact of financing. Individuals capable of amassing a personal following and fortune (this, of course, is a national development, not peculiar to New York City) can ignore the party structure. Voters, likewise, feel less loyalty to the party, further encouraging primary challenges, as well as demonstrating increasing tendencies to engage in split-ticket voting, switching during the general election, and registering as independents. Factions within the party have proliferated, leaving Tammany Hall and the Brooklyn (Kings county) party structures only shadows of their former selves.

Martin Shefter has studied this development, concluding:

> After Mayor LaGuardia left office, the machine was no longer the central institution through which disparate interests were articulated and aggregated. . . . First a large number of social forces organized as generally independent interest groups. The Liberal Party stands out as an example of this point. . . . Because most of the city's interest groups were independently organized, they were in a position to express their dissatisfaction through independent action in the city's electoral arena.[4]

This general development put a premium on the capacity of individuals or particularized interest groups to build and sustain a personal following distinct from the formal party apparatus. Those with a maximum of resources including money, access to influential sources such as the media, and a loyal constituency would be in a preferred position to compete in the newly unfolding political terrain.

Coinciding with this party decline was the rise, beginning especially in the early 1960s, of the power of public service unions in New York City.[5] Employment in city, county, and state governments increased steadily, even as that in the federal government remained rather constant since the 1940s. These new employees were organized into effective bargaining agencies, and they also proceeded to perform several other functions previously performed by the local political party. For example, the various union locals mobilized their members to support sympathetic candidates. The unions lobbied local, state, and national policy makers. The locals monitored the performances of decision makers and kept their constituencies informed. In addition, union members were introduced to campaign techniques and taught the political strategies for holding elected officials accountable. The most efficient unions provided social as well as economic services to their members in much the way that earlier local party precinct organizations had. Thus, the unions came to represent important political training mechanisms for union and political leadership for the rank-and-file members.

In New York City, black union members benefited from these experiences. They attended the legislative workshops conducted by the unions. They learned the mechanisms of preparing informative newsletters and of forming political coalitions, and they learned the importance of delivering specific, tangible benefits. This is not an insignificant development in understanding the process of politicization in New York City during the period of the last two decades. The incorporating, aggregating, and socializing functions performed by the earlier political machines vis-à-vis newly arrived European immigrants were, in part, taken over by the newly developing public service unions. To be sure, they were not political parties per se, but the focus here is on their "politicizing" roles, and those roles were important. They served, to an extent, to fill the vacuum left by the decline of the local party structures.

The advent of the Great Society programs in the mid-1960s provided yet another development to take into account (this is the subject of the next section). When the "War on Poverty" began to channel resources into the local communities and cities, it influenced the way individuals and groups organized themselves politically.[6] There was heated disagreement from the beginning on exactly what the various Great Society programs ought to attempt. Even the many framers of the programs debated among themselves.[7] It is reasonably clear, however, that the major piece of legislation, the Economic Opportunity Act of 1964, (creating the Office of Economic Opportunity) envisioned generally a two-pronged attack: a "war" against economic deprivation and, at least in the minds of some, an effort to enhance "political empowerment." There was to be not only an equitable distribution of goods and services, but also, some hoped, an equitable distribution of decision-making power. Thus, local communities began to see new structures develop—not political parties and not public service unions—that ostensibly would be composed of the local people served ("maximum feasible participation"). But this development was to have serious consequences for the political and politicizing experiences of some black New York constituencies.

If the Great Society programs represented a period of heightened organizational activity and relative financial affluence, just ten years later the fiscal crisis of New York City presented a stark reversal. The city was close to bankruptcy. A "crisis" was at hand (see Chapter 2 by Dick Netzer). As is so often the case in crises, there is little pretense that the "normal processes" of political decision making will prevail. Hastily improvised structures of "elite-mobilization politics" are devised to meet the crisis situation. Such structures are composed of those "elites" who are recognized—formally and informally—as the most resourceful for solving the immediate crisis. In a sense, the normal pluralist process of inclusion and bargaining is suspended (see Chapter 11 by Jewel Bellush). There was no denying that many New Yorkers would suffer as a result of the fiscal crisis. Neither was there a denial that blacks would be adversely affected. Cuts and layoffs had to be made, and the most recently hired—often blacks—and the most recently expanded programs—typically aimed at poor people—were cut disproportionately.

The New Patron-Recipient Relationship

Exactly what had taken place in the years between J. Raymond Jones's speech and the fiscal crisis? How did it happen that there was no reasonably viable political apparatus in place in 1975 to protect blacks from suffering unduly from the fiscal crisis? Even allowing for the hyperbole that normally accompanies political speeches, why could political observers of the New York scene conclude that blacks in that city demonstrated little of the promise evidenced in Jones's speech?

An interesting development occurred in the 1960s. The federal government enacted legislation designed to alleviate poverty. Resources were directed to state, city, and local community groups aimed at addressing a number of problems, from a deficient early childhood education to various forms of employment training for the unskilled to several kinds of services for the elderly poor. Throughout the country, local groups geared up to become the agencies to deliver such services. Sometimes they were coordinated by and worked with the local, city-established political authorities. Sometimes they were in direct contention with those authorities. The important point here is that in New York City, where various organizations had formed in the early 1960s, there developed a dynamic process centered around getting federal funds and delivering services.

The organizations included community corporations established by state charter, delegate agencies that received money from those community corporations: churches, block associations, tenants councils, and civil rights groups. In another place, this author recorded, for New York City:

> In 1978, the anti-poverty programs had 26 community corporations and 276 delegate agencies throughout the city. There were 115 Head Start centers. The community action programs received approximately $39 million in city and federal funds, and $13 million for the city's Head Start program. The federal government's jobs program, the Comprehensive Employment Training Act (CETA), had approximately $171.9 million, and the Model Cities program had a budget of $34.6 million. One source in the mayor's office reported that there were more than 400 individual anti-poverty projects throughout New York City.[8]

Although some of these organizations had been involved in political activities, in the new programs political considerations were theoretically, and in many cases actually, eschewed. The government programs were not to be used in a partisan manner. Voter registration could be conducted as a legitimate civic educational activity, but not as a partisan political activity.

But a different kind of antipoverty politics did develop. Local people ran for positions on the community boards. They presumably mobilized and attempted to get out votes in their favor. These elections were highly contested in some areas. And, indeed, some observers even attempted to show a connection between the politicization process of the antipoverty elections and the predicted carryover into the larger electoral arena. For example:

> Participation in the Community Corporation electoral process makes real the promise of community organization, demonstrably assisting community residents to come together—to organize around their own interests and issues and to prepare for participation in the larger electorate.[9]

Still another enthusiastic prediction follows:

> The Community Corporation elections of July, 1972 represent a shattering of apathy within New York City's twenty-six poverty areas. The sixty-five thousand voters who participated in the election constituted a force slightly larger than the turnout for the two preceding Democratic mayoral primaries in those same communities. What was set in motion in July, 1972 continued to gain momentum in the June, 1973 mayoral primary. . . . All observers now recognize that there is a new awakened mass, a new political force in New York City. . . . The old apathy is dead.[10]

What, precisely, was the nature of the relationship that antipoverty politics fostered, that I have called a "patron-recipient" relationship? The benefit structure was pyramidal. There was a broad base of needy people to be serviced, at the bottom. A few agencies in the community received funds from a few sources: government (federal, state, local) and private foundations. These were the patrons. Thus, as the grant money came in to the servicing agencies, recipients lined up. The only criterion for receiving benefits was to be a member of the "target" population. There was no requirement to register and to vote. Unlike with the traditional party-machine patron-client relationship, there was no viable exchange, no quid pro quo, no exchange of services for votes.

In addition, such a benefit relationship—unilateral in nature—created vertical structures of fragmented influence. Intermediary servicing agencies gained legitimacy to the extent that they could get "funded" and, at times, demonstrate that they were able to service a recipient class. This legitimacy came not from the recipients but from the patrons. Thus, a plethora of community agencies cultivated good relations with foundation officers and government grant-making sources. A new cottage industry—"grantsmanship"—developed. Individual and organizational credibility was based on the capacity to capture and control grants, not on the ability to mobilize voters to capture and control local institutional budgets. That is, attention was focused substantially on "getting funded" to deliver individualized services, not on capturing established public positions of decision making. The only "patronage" such a relationship had to offer was "good services."

In addition to not encouraging the horizontal building of a sustained political base, the relationship more frequently than not stressed benefits to individuals, not to collectivized groups. In the language of political science, emphasis was placed on the delivery of "divisible" benefits, not "indivisible" benefits.[11] This is also important in assessing the politicizing influence of this patron-recipient relationship. Recipients received benefits in their individual capacities as needy. Hopefully, if the particular program is successful, recipients eventually will no longer need the services. They will have improved lives, and they will move on—to be replaced by other needy recipients.

The traditional machine patron-client relationship provided both divisible and indivisible benefits, and so could sustain loyalties even as people's lives changed. In this new relationship, neither were loyalties sustained, nor were they intended to be sustained, and a continuing mass constituency could not be developed. Thus, a combination of the vertical structures of fragmented influence and the shifting-flowing constituency base worked against building a viable organizational base. At bottom, the patron-recipient relationship depended on the flow of grants from the patron. And this, in turn, depended not only on the existence of a steady needy class. More importantly, it depended on decisions made by those external to the local communities and by those subject to many other pressures—economic and electoral—outside the effective purview of the dependent recipient class. Thus, the patron-recipient process was "depoliticizing" precisely because it failed to take into account the very important fact that it was the elective political offices that ultimately controlled the fate of those programs.

It is understandable that some observers would miss this at the time. After all, more than a few community activists did, in fact, cut their political teeth on the antipoverty politics of that era. Some did move on to the larger electoral arena. But this has to be seen more as a process of elite politicization than one of a mass phenomenon. While some activist elites were learning particular political skills, the masses were not being politicized into understanding the utility of the vote for purposes of extracting indivisible benefits.

The Antipoverty Activists

It is worth taking a brief look at the social characteristics of selected community antipoverty activists, to shed some light on the oft-asserted notion that many of the activists were newly politicized by the various programs. Who were some of these community activists in one specific locale, Harlem? J. Raymond Jones and his colleagues had put together a rather extensive cadre of people in the 1950s and early 1960s. They carried petitions, attended Monday and Thursday evening political club meetings, took requests from voters, and delivered patronage-type services, and they urged their constituents to vote. Such people were election-district captains in the mode of the traditional party patron-client relationship.

With the advent of antipoverty politics in that community, we began to see, if not entirely new people, certainly different functions being performed. In 1972–73, a survey revealed that active participants in the various delegate agencies were enacting the roles previously played by the bottom-level party officials, the "captains" of election districts, a small geographic unit with five hundred to one thousand voters.[12] It appears that most were either involved civically or politically prior to the poverty programs or had an inclination in that direction. They appeared to live in family environments that supported such involvement. A rather small number seemed to have deliberately given up their precious overt partisan political activity, but in open discussion, several indicated that they did not have as much time to devote to "politics." This was stated at times in a regretful tone, but always as a development that had to be accepted. Even those who carried petitions or attended political club meetings felt that these activities were secondary to their roles with the various service delivery agencies. The interviewees generally focused the discussions on the nature of their programs, the quality of services they delivered, and the vast needs of the constituents they serviced. Occasionally, there would be reference to the need to get more people to understand the value of "participation." At times, this referred to voter registration and voting. More often than not, however, it meant mobilizing in a protest mode to lobby for more government funds or to avoid cuts in budgets.

It was clear that several had become involved for reasons that related to their personal lives, some when their children began to attend school and the inadequacies of the educational system became apparent to them, others from contact with city officials resulting in less-than-satisfactory responses regarding community services. While many stated that they engaged in partisan political activity, the fact is that only twelve were registered voters in 1972; nineteen, however, considered themselves Democrats. Several indicated a feeling of distrust for "politicians," and believed that such persons were less interested in "helping people" and more concerned about "getting elected." Essentially, this attitude came down to a feeling that protest action was a much better way to get politicians to respond than voting.

A final point on this particular subject is worth noting. One was able to discern, from attending innumerable community meetings and talking to these community activists, the development of an important new role. Whether it was a policy committee meeting of the East Harlem Model Cities or a local block association, invariably there was one person in the group who was quite knowledgeable about the many programs that offered funds for various services. In addition, this "resource person" knew the details about grantmaking, recent guideline changes, eligibility requirements, and the like. Such a person was highly respected as a source of information and technical advice.

A good illustration of this point was a meeting of the East Harlem Model Cities Policy Committee.[13] The committee members agreed to hear from a visiting group of men known as the 126th Street Block Association. The group stated that most of its members were "ex-cons and ex-drug users" and wanted to help "straighten out" younger people "because we know this neighborhood and can do it." The group wanted "technical assistance" from the policy committee in preparing a proposal to establish a drug detoxification and job referral program. The men brought pictures of their work sweeping the streets and cleaning the neighborhood. The group was at the time occupying a city-owned building, and paying the city $100 per month. The building had been abandoned by the owner, who owed $15,000 in overdue property taxes. One member of the committee informed the group that there were "ex-offender funds" the group could apply for. In addition, she talked about a new program called "hostel-house." After further discussion, the committee voted to "put a hold on the building and to make sure that no demolition or sale of the building takes place, with the purpose being to save the building for a drug detoxification program and other programs of the 126th Street Block Association." The chairperson asked the group to meet with the resource person immediately after the meeting to set a date when they could get together to draft a proposal. The group left quite satisfied.

In a real sense, the new antipoverty structures had replaced the party apparatus as a place to turn to for help. At no time, however, during the discussion of the group's interests and needs was there mention of voting or mobilizing persons in the community for electoral purposes. The emphasis as ethos was entirely on fitting needs to potentially available funded programs.

The point of this brief vignette is that this kind of experience was beginning to pervade the thinking of many who thought about connecting process and product in the governmental system. A differently politicized atmosphere was setting in that gradually reinforced the patron-recipient relationship. Voting as a mode of bringing pressure was not seen as a particularly effective means of achieving desired ends.

This post-hoc analysis—one that concludes that the new relationship was basically "depoliticizing"—should not be understood as concluding that that result was in any way intended. Many, if not most, of the community activists and higher decision makers assumed that there would, in fact, be positive consequences for the electoral process. Some antipoverty participants did believe that the various activities would lead to a "new awakening." They believed that as masses of people became involved—albeit as recipients—"apathy" would be overcome, and there would be positive results in the form of increased voter registration and electoral participation in the larger political arena. Did this happen? We turn now to some electoral data to get a fuller picture of the black political experience in New York City.

Electoral Behavior: 1961–68

When J. Raymond Jones gave his speech to the Lexington Democratic Club in 1960, an intraparty battle was looming between the "regulars" and the "reformers.'' Mayor Wagner was beginning to cast his lot with the latter, and Jones and the black voters obviously would be important in the next year's mayoral race. Jones was signaling the kinds of demands his constituents would make.

In a heated two-way primary contest, State Comptroller Arthur Levitt lost to Mayor Wagner. Two Harlem Assembly districts were especially courted by both candidates. In one, there were 20,296 registered Democrats and a little over 44 percent (9,026) turned out, which is an impressive rate of participation. Wagner carried the district with 5,199 votes—a respectable majority of 57.5 percent. In the other, Wagner received 10,285 votes out of 16,327 cast—62.9 percent—with a 42 percent turn-out. Grateful for Jones's support, Wagner appointed Jones as a political secretary through whom he would deal with all the city Democratic party organizations.[14] Two predominantly black assembly districts in Brooklyn supported Wagner by almost two to one, but with lower turnout rates than in Harlem. In the early 1960s, there was general recognition that the pinnacle of black astute political leadership and organization resided in Harlem under the tutelage of Jones.

The rest of the 1960s was one of the most highly politicized periods in modern American history. The civil rights movement reached its zenith, spreading its demands beyond the South into all sections of the country. Protest politics became a regular phenomenon. Political assassinations—of President John F. Kennedy in 1963 and Martin Luther King, Jr., and Robert Kennedy in 1968—created an atmosphere of severe trauma, unlike anything that most living Americans had experienced. Lyndon Johnson and the national Democratic party soundly trounced a decidedly conservative Barry Goldwater and the Republicans in 1964, electing a Congress with a liberal stamp. But the climate of liberalism was short lived—by the end of the decade, it began to dissipate, torn apart by the Vietnam War and rising protests from angry, impatient urban ghetto residents. And, as noted, the antipoverty programs were creating different structures and expectations from many people. It was not a time of politics as usual, and, understandably, many came to question the efficacy of a supposedly pluralist system that had its own guidelines about how political agendas should be presented and dealt with.

By the end of the decade, J. Raymond Jones had retired to his native St. Thomas. Congressman Adam Clayton Powell was, after a time, an effective chairman of the important House of Representatives Committee on Education and Labor, reeling from years of New York legal battles and fights to avoid congressional censure and exclusion for financial improprieties. In 1970, he was rejected by the voters of Harlem. New political faces were appearing on the New York black political scene. In Brooklyn, the first black woman, Shirley Chisholm, was elected to congress in 1968. And in Harlem, younger blacks were running for citywide office.

The 1969 Municipal Elections[15]

The 1969 local elections are interesting, from the standpoint of this chapter, in several respects. The city's political climate reflected the national scene. Racial issues were rife. Overt rhetoric as well as code words influenced political debates. Liberals favored expansion of antipoverty programs, meaning more funds from the federal government and greater involvement of "grass-roots" people. Conservatives called for "law and order." Mayor John Lindsay lost his Republican party's nomination for reelection, having been defeated in the primary by an influential, highly respected, and conservative state senator, John Marchi, and chose to run on the Liberal party ticket. The Democrats nominated a perceived "law and order" candidate, Mario Procaccino. To win, Lindsay needed the support of as strong a coalition of liberal whites and blacks as he could mobilize. This would require many Democrats, including blacks, to pull another party lever. And they did. Lindsay won.

In two of Harlem's assembly districts, blacks gave Lindsay 73.8 percent and 78.3 percent of their votes, respectively, with turn-outs in the 30 percent range.[16] Blacks clearly were not constrained by party labels, but demonstrated their preference for the candidate perceived to be the more sympathetic to their needs and aspirations. They also strongly supported, in the Democratic primary, the minority candidates for citywide office. In the Democratic primary that year, one black, Charles Rangel, ran for president of the city council against five opponents, and the leading Puerto Rican politician in the city, Herman Badillo, ran for mayor against four opponents. The results for the two districts in these races appear in Table 13.1.

In the race for council president, Rangel carried these black assembly districts by a wide margin, based on turn-outs of 27 and 22 percent, respectively—low, but normal for New York City primary elections. Rangel did not win the nomination, but has become a senior and influential member of the U.S. House of Representatives. Badillo's support in these two districts in the race for mayor was substantial—close to 50 percent, despite the presence in that contest of former Mayor Wagner who had been popular among black voters. Despite the presence of a black candidate in the race for council president and no black candidate in the race for mayor, the total number of votes cast for mayor was considerably higher. This is a common experience: as voters go down the ballot from the top offices to those deemed less important, the total number of votes cast trails off.

As noted, blacks switched their traditional party allegiance in the general mayoral election, supporting Lindsay overwhelmingly on the Liberal party line. At the same time, Percy E. Sutton, a prominent black Harlem politician, ran successfully for borough president of Manhattan, with both the Democratic and Liberal party nominations. He received substantial black support on the Liberal

Table 13.1

Voting Results in the 1969 Democratic Primary in Two Harlem Assembly Districts

	Assembly districts	
	72nd	74th
President of the city council		
Charles B. Rangel	3,634 (68.6%)	3,624 (45.6%)
Hugh Carey	593	973
Jimmy Breslin	252	562
Francis X. Smith	236	493
Elinor C. Guggenheimer	280	482
Robert A. Low	302	502
Total	5,297	6,636
Mayor		
Herman Badillo	3,238 (47.9%)	4,083 (49.3%)
Mario Procaccino	844	868
James H. Scheuer	268	171
Norman Mailer	458	528
Robert F. Wagner	1,939	2,630
Total	6,747	8,280

line. When blacks switched for Lindsay, they pulled the Liberal lever for Sutton. In fact, in these two districts, the vote for Sutton on the two lines was almost as high as the vote for Lindsay (on his lines, Liberal and Independent), despite the fact that thousands of voters in these districts who voted for mayor did not vote for council president.

The 1973 Election

By 1973, there had been more than a small amount of talk in black political circles about electing a black mayor of New York. Other cities were beginning to have such "firsts": Gary, Indiana; Newark, New Jersey; Cleveland, Ohio; Los Angeles, California. The increasing number of black elected officials became a new focus of interest and commentary in the South and North. But in 1973 in New York City, the mantle fell to the Puerto Rican, Herman Badillo. He entered the mayoral primary against three opponents. His support among black voters was considerable, although not overwhelming.

As Table 13.2 shows, in the initial four-person primary,[17] Badillo won about half the vote in the two Harlem districts. This first primary was followed a few weeks later by a runoff between Badillo and Beame, which the latter won; he

Table 13.2

Voting Results in the 1973 Democratic Primary in Two Harlem and Three Brooklyn Assembly Districts

| | Harlem assembly districts | | Brooklyn assembly districts | | |
	72nd	74th	54th	55th	56th
Mayoral primary					
Abraham Beame	2,717	3,544	851	1,070	1,612
Mario Biaggi	1,030	714	307	262	288
Albert Blumenthal	1,346	1,095	268	437	371
Herman Badillo	5,671 (52.6%)	4,807 (47.3%)	2,472 (63.4%)	2,937 (62.4%)	2,510 (52.4%)
Total	10,764	10,160	3,898	4,706	4,781
Mayoral runoff					
Herman Badillo	8,477 (69.0%)	7,355 (62.6%)	4,354 (78%)	5,592 (80.8%)	5,119 (72.8%)
Abraham Beame	3,803	4,387	1,224	1,325	1,910
Total	12,280	11,742	5,578	6,917	7,029

went on to become the city's first Jewish mayor. Badillo won about two-thirds of the votes in the Harlem districts in this contest. In Brooklyn, however, Badillo's support among blacks was substantially higher (in percentage terms), in both the initial primary and in the runoff election. Turn-out in Brooklyn was even lower than it was in Harlem, dipping as low as 16.4 percent in the first election, with only a little improvement in the runoff.

The 1977 Election

By 1977, many black leaders believed that the time was ripe for a serious black candidate for mayor. Incumbent Mayor Beame was seeking reelection, but he had been badly tarnished by the city's fiscal crisis of two years earlier, the impact of which was very evident in 1977. Beame had not only been conspicuously inept at the peak of the crisis in 1975, but he had also served as comptroller during the budget juggling and fiscal gimmickry of the early 1970s. The general consensus was that Beame would run badly in the primary,[18] and that encouraged a large field of candidates. Under the election law, if no candidate received more than 40 percent of the vote in the primary, the two top vote-getters compete in a runoff election. With a large number of candidates, it is possible for any one candidate with a solid base of support in a portion of the voting population to come in first or second, thus making it to the runoff—as Badillo had done in 1973.

Thus, a minority candidate stood a reasonable chance. Some blacks felt that, in Percy Sutton, they had a strong candidate. Sutton had a long record as an effective Manhattan borough president and loyal Democratic party participant and he had a presence that could attract white, as well as black, votes. Seven persons ran in the primary, with several candidates appealing for the support of each of the traditional constituencies. Badillo ran again and appealed, with Sutton, for the minority vote. Three candidates with reputations as liberal Democratic members of Congress— Herman Badillo, Edward Koch, and Bella Abzug—appealed to liberal-leaning voters. Most of the candidates promised fiscal rectitude and offered themselves as reformers, notably including Koch, Badillo, Joel Harnett, who had been a leader of the old-time civic group, the City Club, and Mario Cuomo, who was vigorously supported by Governor Hugh Carey.

In the end, Sutton finished a disappointing fifth in the primary. He ran poorly outside the predominantly black districts. Moreover, his Harlem political base did not provide him the substantial support a home-grown candidate would expect.

While Sutton carried the Harlem assembly districts, it was not an impressive showing, averaging only about 50 percent of the total vote. Neither was the turn-out large, especially when compared to the experience of black candidates running for mayor in other cities, where black voters were turning out in the 70–80 percent range and giving the black candidate as much as 90 or 95 percent of their vote. Such high turn-outs and percentages of the vote cast not only reflect racial preference or ethnic identity, but also can happen when a local candidate is expected to do exceptionally well against "outsiders." Sutton generally received better support from black districts in Brooklyn, close to 60 percent of the vote, than from his Harlem home base. Another prominent Harlem politician emerged in 1977, David Dinkins, who bid for Sutton's vacated position of Manhattan borough president. A black had held that position, serving thereby on the important Board of Estimate, since 1953. Dinkins faced three opponents and finished a respectable second, losing to Andrew Stein by 3,698 votes out of a total 188,310 cast.

After the 1977 losses, there was a good deal of local political commentary on the waning fortunes of black New York City politics. While elsewhere black candidates were successfully competing for office, this was not happening in New York City, except for legislative seats. No black or Latino occupied a high local elective position. Blacks of various ideological outlooks searched for the causes of apparent black political impotence in the city. The most frequent explanation placed the blame on factionalism among black political groups and individuals.[19] Persistent rivalries between black and Puerto Rican political factions also were evident.

These feuds were exacerbated by the geographical divisions of the city into the five boroughs, with formally distinct political structures and some borough-based offices at stake in the political struggle, like the borough presidencies and judgeships. Thus, within each of the boroughs, there were political prizes to be gained. The pursuit of these prizes was not necessarily aided by enlisting in a citywide effort or alliance. In fact, an individual with political ambitions from a Brooklyn or Queens home base might find that an alliance with forces in Manhattan or the Bronx would make it harder to pull together the needed support close to home.

The 1981 Election

As the 1981 city elections came closer, black leaders searched for strategies to alleviate the bleak political picture. Ad hoc groups talked of finding a desirable candidate who could make a successful bid for mayor against Edward Koch, who was sure to run for reelection for a second term. Koch as a mayor was seen by many blacks as insensitive and racially polarizing. Koch's deliberate and friendly outreach to white ethnics and middle-class communities signalled a coolness to black voters. His rhetoric, like his focus on "law and order" and denunciation of "poverty pimps," seemed full of code words for hostility toward blacks and black aspirations. Specific Koch administration actions, like the revamping of the antipoverty community structures and the closing of Sydenham Hospital in Harlem, were perceived as hostile acts against the black community. Blacks began to discuss ways to form alliances with Puerto Ricans and liberal whites in order to field a viable candidate.

The preferred candidate was Basil Patterson, who had been active in state government as a legislator, candidate for statewide office, and cabinet member and was one of Harlem's most prominent black lawyer-politicians. Ultimately, his candidacy did not materialize, but the interest in winning other positions—notably, Manhattan borough president—remained. Because that position had been held by a black for so long, its occupancy by a white politician, Andrew Stein, was looked upon as a clear barometer of the decline of black political fortunes. David Dinkins made no secret of his continuing interest in capturing the office from Stein. Dinkins's respectable showing in 1977 was further cause for optimism. Black political attention focused on the upcoming Stein-Dinkins primary. The mayoral challenge to Koch fell to a liberal white state legislator from Brooklyn, Frank I. Barbaro.

In a sense, the 1981 primary could be seen as a "turning point" election. While Dinkins did not defeat Stein, there were two interesting features about the race. Blacks voted in larger numbers for the less visible position of borough president than for mayor, contrary to the "trail-off" voting pattern in previous elections. Secondly, the local black candidate began to receive the kind of home-base support black candidates had been getting in other cities, averaging over 72 percent in Harlem districts. Dinkins had substantially improved his performance over 1977, in both turnout and percentage of the vote cast.

In the mayoral primary, Barbaro, although white, was seen as sympathetic to blacks—in marked contrast to Koch. Thus, for the first time since 1969, there was an incentive for black voters to vote *against* a specific candidate. In 1969, as noted earlier, Procaccino was considered less sympathetic to black citizens, and blacks responded by switching to Lindsay on the Liberal line. In 1981, there was a parallel with Koch and Barbaro. Consequently, the white Barbaro did considerably better in the black districts in 1981 than the black Sutton did in those same districts in 1977, when there was no front-runner who was perceived an anti-black. In 1981, Barbaro won by large percentages in the Harlem districts, taking between 61 and 70 percent of the vote cast. In black districts in Brooklyn, Barbaro's support was about 10 percentage points lower. In Brooklyn, there was no prominent black on the ticket for a borough position, as Dinkins was in Manhattan. The comparable results suggest that Dinkins's candidacy was an added incentive to turn-out. In this sense, there might have been a black "coat-tail" effect in Manhattan.[20]

Elections in 1984 and 1985

Something else happened in 1981 that was important for understanding the black political experience—the beginning of the Reagan administration. If there were episodic negative incentives to politicizing blacks on the local scene, it is safe to say that the advent of the Reagan presidency served to infuse many black communities with a sense of political embattlement. Budget cuts, which impacted negatively on large numbers of blacks and a decidedly different national administration stance on enforcement of civil rights (for example, the reversal of affirmative action policies) contributed to an atmosphere that led many blacks throughout the country to realize that they confronted a national political climate drastically different from the 1960s. This culminated in the highly charged candidacy of the Reverend Jesse Jackson for president in 1984. Through a series of rallies and events throughout the country, his candidacy burst on the scene leaving few black communities untouched. On the heels of the rallying cry, "Our time has come," many black politicians around the country began to calculate the impact of this new phenomenon on their own political fortunes. Black New York politics did not escape the ferment. Some activists saw in the Jackson campaign an opportunity to increase voter registration rolls and affect local contests. This was, indeed, one of the announced goals of the Jackson national campaign strategists. Jackson often expressed the hope that the rising interest in his candidacy would spill over and stimulate local liberal and minority efforts around the country.

Thus, some New Yorkers saw a mutually beneficial relationship between Jackson's presidential effort and their own local fate, although this was not a uniform view. Congressman Charles B. Rangel from Harlem chose to support the former Vice-President, Walter Mondale, while David Dinkins cast his lot with Jesse Jackson. Concerted voter registration drives were conducted. In Manhattan, Jesse Jackson came in a respectable second out of a field of seven. He did exceptionally well in Harlem assembly districts, as expected, taking over 70 percent of the vote cast.

There is no question that the Jackson presidential candidacy fueled black political aspirations in various sections of the country. As a result of the enthusiasm generated, black politicians began to search for ways to build their own local bases. As the 1985 mayoral election approached, talk revived about a black challenge to Mayor Koch, who was widely expected to win a third term with ease. Factional rivalries emerged and no agreement could be reached on a candidate. A black state legislator, Herman D. Farrell, Jr., ran against five other candidates, including the incumbent Koch. Koch won handily, and Farrell was soundly defeated.

Farrell's performance in the black districts was nowhere near that of Jackson's the previous year and even below that of Barbaro, the white liberal candidate four years earlier. In the two Harlem black districts, Farrell barely surpassed Koch and got less than 45 percent of the vote cast, although one of the districts was the one Farrell represented in the state legislature. The anti-Koch vote in Harlem was split between Farrell and a white liberal, Carol Bellamy, who was city council president.

From another perspective, however, 1985 marked the black return to the Board of Estimate. David Dinkins, in his third try for the office of borough president, defeated State Assemblyman Jerrold L. Nadler in the primary by a wide margin, 97,183 to 52,171. Black voters clearly distinguished between this contest and the mayoral race. Dinkins received over 90 percent of the vote in the black districts in Harlem and did almost as well in the adjacent East Harlem district that was heavily Puerto Rican. Dinkins's percentage of the vote in those districts was the highest achieved by a black candidate since the peak periods of Adam Clayton Powell's popularity in Harlem years earlier.

In Brooklyn, a black candidate, State Assemblyman Albert Vann, placed a distant second out of a field of four for borough president. Vann had been a strong Jesse Jackson supporter, but more importantly, he had favored Herman Badillo over Farrell for the 1985 mayoral race. This decision created tension within the Brooklyn black political leadership ranks. Vann outpolled Farrell, in their respective races, in black Brooklyn districts, by very wide margins. In fact, Farrell got less than one-third of the votes cast in these districts. Neither Vann nor Farrell drew votes at all comparable to those received by Jackson in 1984 or by Dinkins in Manhattan in the same year. Thus, the various races in 1985 reflected all the intragroup and leadership rivalries between blacks and Puerto Ricans and the usual tensions between Manhattan and Brooklyn black leaders. The factionalism has been difficult to reconcile.

Elections in 1988 and 1989

Jesse Jackson ran for the Democratic nomination for president again in 1988. As in 1984, his campaign mobilized blacks in substantial numbers. In 1988, he was able to broaden his base to include Latinos and liberal whites, and this time all black leaders supported Jackson. The result was that Jackson narrowly won a plurality of the votes cast in New York City and many of the delegates to the national convention. The black districts gave Jackson 90 percent or more of their votes, and the turnout in the primary in the black districts was higher than in the general election in November 1988.

Despite the success in coalition-building, the Jackson candidacy did involve considerable racial polarization. Mayor Koch fiercely opposed Jackson, stressing Jackson's involvement in the Israeli-Palestinian conflict on the side of the Palestinians. Blacks tended to see this as yet another indication of Koch's enmity. But another voice, that of the now-retired Harlem Fox, J. Raymond Jones, saw the racial aspects as a concomitant of not working at the grass roots and building political organizations at the community level, in the old-fashioned way, "There is no better way than by starting low and climbing the ladder. Jesse Jackson's campaign for the Presidency is a classic case of an attempt of an imposition on the party from the top, and the danger of an overemphasis on race."[21]

By late 1988, the polls were showing Mayor Koch to be very unpopular. His third term had been marked by scandals and trials of political associates, and his administration was widely viewed as tired. His strong support among Latinos had seemingly evaporated, and whites as well as blacks and Latinos were telling pollsters that they considered Koch to be unnecessarily divisive. The early polls suggested that David Dinkins, now the incumbent Manhattan borough president, could beat Koch in the primary, although it appeared that Rudolph Giuliani, former U.S. Attorney in Manhattan and the likely Republican nominee, could beat either of them in the general election.

Black leaders, most labor unions, and white liberals rallied to Dinkins's candidacy. Dinkins won the primary by a wide margin, and went on to defeat Giuliani by a narrow margin in the general election, becoming New York's first black mayor on January 1, 1990.

The Decade of the Eighties: A Perspective for the Nineties[22]

The black political experience in New York during the decade of the 1980s was shaped by both negative and positive developments. On the negative side, blacks may have been especially disadvantaged by the general breakdown of traditional political life, particularly the declining party system. In addition, general voter participation in primaries and regular elections dipped, by the mid-1980s, to so low a level that the vitality of democracy on the local scene became of grave concern to scholars and civic leaders. Furthermore, the "Reagan Revolution" and the turn to the conservative right seemed to remove the immediate economic and social concerns of blacks and the poor from the national political agenda.

As mayor, Edward Koch likewise contributed to a sense of alienation and to increasing the distance of blacks from politics. At first, he appeared to incorporate black participation in his administration, appointing a black deputy mayor, responsible for municipal labor relations in a city whose labor force was made up increasingly of blacks. He also recruited more blacks for professional and managerial posts. A Latino, thought to be an ally of blacks, became his deputy mayor for policy. But, then, a decided change in strategy and style occurred. The mayor neglected to clear appointments with established black political leaders and they clearly became offended. He exacerbated the situation when, during reorganization of antipoverty programs, he failed to consult with them. Mayor Koch's decision to close several municipal hospital facilities in black districts, where health care was considered by many to be inadequate, evoked angry responses. The mayor's style of shooting from the hip, particularly his loquaciousness, increased his difficulties with the black community. Martin Shefter put it pointedly: "The mayor's rhetoric during his first term was especially feisty on racial issues, contributing to his popularity among the city's white ethnic groups and causing strains in his relationship with New York racial minorities."[23]

The black political response to the perceived adverse climate in Washington and at City Hall was marked by internal disarray among community groups, contentiousness, and factionalism. With the rewards of politics declining precipitously, competition for the remaining spoils heightened significantly.

The increasing ethnic differentiation of the city's population, white, black, and Latino, complicated politics for black leaders. For example, there was an increase in the variety of white ethnics living in the city, and distinctions among them with respect to needs and aspirations have been sharper, as noted in Chapter 14 by Shirley Jenkins; they compete with blacks for a place in the sun. Within the black community itself, there are very important differences. While blacks constitute some 30 percent of the city's population, about one-third are from the Caribbean area, contributing to greater diversity than uniformity in thinking and behavior.[24]

When Herman Farrell, a black leader—he was Democratic county leader and a member of the state Assembly—ran for mayor against Koch in 1985 as part of the Coalition for a Just New York, he received only 40 percent of the black vote and 28 percent of the Latino vote. Admittedly, he was a very weak candidate. He not only lacked the skills to enhance a major candidacy but he had little outreach beyond his immediate Manhattan circle of organizational support. Years of feuding between the black leadership in Brooklyn and Manhattan and between black politicos and Latinos had continued unabated during the Farrell candidacy. By the mid-1980s, only 56 percent of the blacks in New York City were registered to vote, compared to Chicago's 70 percent.

For most of the 1980s (except for the Jackson presidential campaigns), these weaknesses and handicaps made for political quiescence in black neighborhoods. This was heightened by the continuing sense of disappointment that the high hopes and promises of the 1960s and early 1970s—of the Kennedy and Johnson national administrations and the Lindsay city administration—remained unfulfilled. Furthermore, a number of emotionally laden events, most of them involving violent interracial physical confrontations, heightened frustration and anger among many blacks. A number of non-mainstream black figures attempted to use each of these events as the basis for a mass protest movement comparable to the 1960s. The black community did not respond to the calls for demonstrations and marches, and the would-be leaders remained isolated figures.

More positively, the candidacy of Jesse Jackson for president in 1984 and 1988 resulted in very sizeable black turnouts. The numbers of registered blacks increased dramatically and they voted almost unanimously for this magnetic black spokesman, who, with a well-organized campaign, captured New York City in the 1988 presidential primaries. The Jackson phenomenon, however, depended primarily on his charismatic character and flamboyant rhetoric. His was more a personal success, for it did not dig deeply into the economic or political organizational base on which blacks could build for the future. As David Jones, executive director of the Community Service Society of New York put it:

> And that's what we didn't realize, that you need to have some sort of institutional power base even if you aren't personally connected to it. I still have trouble convincing people of this. Many young lawyers listen to me like I'm from Mars.

> I think a black professional leadership group is essential, though not the whole
> story. Jesse Jackson reaches the grassroots population that I can't even come
> near. . . . But ultimately you also have to have a group that can exercise some
> control, not only in the political sector but also in the economy of the city.[25]

There have been a number of bright spots for black New Yorkers on the
electoral front. With 25 percent of the city's voting population, blacks are gaining in their proportion of elected representatives. As of 1989, blacks numbered
thirteen of the city's sixty members of the state Assembly (21 percent), while in
the state Senate, four of twenty-five members of the city delegation (16 percent)
were black. In Congress, blacks comprised four out of the city's fourteen representatives (27 percent), and in the city council seven of thirty-five (20 percent).
David Dinkins served as Manhattan borough president, bolstered by his place of
importance on the Board of Estimate. Each of these elected officials is tied to
considerable political activity at the grass-roots level in Queens, Brooklyn, Manhattan, and the Bronx. With Republicans seemingly unwilling or unable to extend a welcome mat to the city's blacks, what is left of the Democratic party has
been their only game in town.

The 1989 campaign for mayor was a success for blacks in both the ultimate
triumph of David Dinkins and in the nature of his victory in the Democratic
primary. In the primary, Dinkins decisively defeated incumbent Koch as well as
two other able contestants. The other candidates were Harrison Goldin, who had
been an articulate city comptroller since 1974, and Richard Ravitch, builder,
lawyer, and civic activist who, at critical times, had headed a number of state
agencies, including the Metropolitan Transportation Authority.

During the 1989 mayoral primaries, relations between blacks and whites
seemed tense, if not fragile. Perhaps it was the gentle, comforting personality of
Dinkins that helped many white New Yorkers overcome some of their anxieties
about a black mayor in City Hall. At any rate, about 30 percent of white Democratic voters chose Dinkins, along with nearly all black voters; the black primary
turn-out was much above the turn-out in previous municipal primaries. Dinkins
won a majority of all votes cast in the primary, and had a wide margin over
Koch, much wider than the last pre-election polls had forecast.

This was a stunning success. Professor Martin Kilson of Harvard has written
about the "transethnic imperative." He contends that, for black politicians to be
successful, they "must appeal across ethnic boundaries as a matter of course."
He admits that this sometimes requires the most tactful crossing of extremely
sensitive, if not hostile, ethnic and religious boundaries.[26] Dinkins had to reach
out again and again, with particular sensitivity, to what he thought were representative groups that made up the many Jewish communities. To great numbers
of Jewish voters, the black politics of the 1980s had become characterized by the
anti-Semitic utterances of Louis Farrakan and tactless remarks by Jesse Jackson,
who became symbols of fear, if not hate.

Other white ethnic groups were even more difficult to attract to Dinkins. But this candidate's coolness and quiet, reassuring style contrasted sharply with Koch's sniping and sarcastic manner. Dinkins also received vital, almost unanimous support from labor leaders and their organizations, even those with predominantly white memberships. The excitement generated by his candidacy among black unionists insured large numbers of telephone canvassers and doorbell ringers. The unions created a sizeable and well-organized field operation which did a remarkable job in getting out the vote. And then there were the political activists who Joe Klein of *New York Magazine* dubbed the "Upper Left Side liberals"—white liberals, usually Manhattan residents, who often are moved only by ideology and stand well to the left of most Democratic voters— who also rallied to the black candidate.[27]

Dinkins was able to attract much more in campaign contributions than any other candidate, as a number of prominent business figures, led by investment banker Felix Rohatyn, rallied to the Dinkins cause. Dinkins was able to recreate the old New Deal coalition, bringing together labor, liberals, reformers, regular politicians, blacks, and, among the largest white ethnic groups, many of the Jews.

Traveling the political mainstream, Dinkins managed, initially, to calm many of those who feared voting for a black candidate. Underscoring the need for unity, he promised to bring people together. After his decisive primary victory, he squeezed to victory in the general election, defeating Republican Rudolph Giuliani, 50 to 48 percent. Race did not play an overt role in the general election campaign, but probably explains the narrowness of the margin in the voting. Also, Giuliani vigorously attacked Dinkins for past indiscretions and sloppiness in personal financial matters.

So, Dinkins was spectacularly successful in 1989, after a decade of disappointments in the black political experience. One clue to why it was that David Dinkins became the first black mayor of New York is in his political upbringing. As a young man and political neophyte, he had been schooled in the Carver Democratic Club in Harlem under the tutelage of "The Fox," J. Raymond Jones. Jones had been attracted to him because of his unique ability to get along with people. Similarly, many young black business and political leaders had received their training under "The Fox," assigned to lowly tasks while waiting their turns to rise up the political ladder. Jones wrote recently:

> The objective behind all this was to develop in the individual a sense of responsibility to the party and its constituency, and with it to provide public exposure.[28]

Conclusions

Three decades have passed since J. Raymond Jones visited the Lexington Democratic Club and delivered his talk. There have been many speeches and much action since, and one is tempted—as the lawyers say—to file a "demurrer." But that is, perhaps, too simplistic. To be sure, there was an accusatory tone, almost one of polite protest, about Jones's address. He seemed to be both imploring and threatening. But Jones was, indeed, a political "fox." He knew that whatever he said, his words would mean little in his world of politics if he could not get his constituents to vote. He understood political organization, never confusing rhetoric and reality. That such confusion has at times crept into black New York politics cannot be denied.

For some time, much black political action has been, understandably, heavily characterized by mobilization for protest action. No one familiar with the history of black Americans would suggest that such action has not been necessary or functional. At the same time it is accurate to say that protest in its various functional forms cannot substitute for sustained, often invisible, organizational effort. Jones and his supporters worked toward this end, but much of what they sought and accomplished often has seemed lost or forgotten.

The patron-recipient relationship concentrated on perfecting a service delivery and benefit structure that did not, rhetoric notwithstanding, emphasize electoral mobilization. And where it did, it concentrated on capturing and controlling grants and ephemeral program funds. It did not focus on mobilizing masses of constituents for the task of learning the intricacies of capturing and controlling political positions of institutional power. It cultivated a perpetual cadre of "demand makers" and focused its efforts on becoming "decision makers" over grant-funded goods and services—but not decision makers with respect to the power to tax and spend, that is, political office and the ordinary structure of government. This was, on balance, an unfortunate period of politicization for many blacks in New York City. Not for all, by any means. Some labor unions did not make that mistake. Indeed, some local politicians and small political organizations have always understood the significance of the ballot, but their efforts were not sufficient.

Too few black New Yorkers have seen serious utility in the electoral franchise as a means of achieving goals. Thus, that tool remains underutilized. However, the excitement generated by Dinkins's candidacy may encourage black political activists to devote concentrated efforts to building the necessary grassroots electoral organizations around the city, that is, conscious, deliberate attention to partisan mobilization and activity. There is an abundance of civic action in the black communities—all the way from externally funded social services to viable local self-help groups. It is difficult not to find a "cause" with some actual or potential "funded program" about to attack it. These span the range from worthy to worthless. But it *is* difficult to find the same level of attention paid to partisan political goals—organizing masses not only in response to overt crises or periodic "villains," but to the long-term efficacy of voting regularly and cohesively and doing so in such a way that those who are the beneficiaries of those votes would ignore them at their peril.

This is the true patron-client relationship. It does not work each time but, properly utilized, it has been known to work over time. When the patrons need the clients, then a viable reciprocal relationship exists. It is interdependent.

And this process does not necessarily begin with the highest or most visible office. In fact, it seldom does with minorities—any minorities. It begins with capturing and controlling those strategic positions of institutional power nearest at hand and then moving from that base. It involves building seniority in collegial bodies like the state legislature and Congress. Along these lines, another bright spot for black New Yorkers is the Albany legislative scene, where important benefits are dispensed, even more than in the past as city government responsibilities have shifted to the state. The black and Latino caucus, largely composed of legislators from New York City, is well organized and taken seriously by the leadership. Clusters of political activists have gathered around the elected legislators, an emerging building block for local partisan politics.

Successful politics requires the development of similar building blocks in other institutional settings, like the newly more powerful city council. It involves reaching agreements to support others in return for support. But always it involves reciprocity and the ability to reward and punish. Which means one must have something others want or need. In the political system, that means for most ordinary folk their ability not only to vote—but to exercise a mass, mobilized vote.

This is the lesson not yet sufficiently taught or learned in the New York black political experience. "The Fox" understood this. The formula is not especially complex, but it does call, most assuredly, for more "foxes."

Notes

1. J. Raymond Jones, "The Negro in New York Politics," June 20, 1960 (unpublished).

2. James Q. Wilson, *The Amateur Democrat*. Chicago, IL: University of Chicago Press, 1962.

3. There is a long political tradition of black nationalism in various forms, going back to the nineteenth century. The common theme has been that blacks can live decently only under a political structure of their own, with substantial or complete political autonomy. When Jones spoke, the leading nationalist, or separatist, was Malcolm X, who was drawing large and attentive crowds on the street corners of Harlem.

4. Martin Shefter, *Political Crisis/Fiscal Crisis, The Collapse and Revival of New York City*. New York: Basic Books, 1985, pp. 34–37.

5. Jewel Bellush and Bernard Bellush, *Union Power and New York, Victor Gotbaum and District Council 37*. New York: Praeger, 1984.

6. See J. David Greenstone and Paul Peterson, *Race and Authority in Urban Politics, Community Participation and The War on Poverty*. New York: Russell Sage Foundation, 1973.

7. See Daniel P. Moynihan, *Maximum Feasible Misunderstanding*. New York: Free Press, 1969; and John Donovan, *The Politics of Poverty*. New York: Pegasus, 1967.

8. Charles Hamilton, "The Patron-Recipient Relationship and Minority Politics in

New York City," *Political Science Quarterly* 94:2 (Summer 1979): 211–27, 216.

9. James E. Greenridge, *Community Corporation Elections 1972: A History and Analysis.* New York: Community Development Agency, Fall 1973, p. 1.

10. The statement was made by Major R. Owens; the quote appears in Hamilton, "The Patron-Recipient Relationship," p. 217.

11. See Robert A. Dahl, *Who Governs?* New Haven, CT: Yale University Press, 1961.

12. This research was conducted from October 1972 to June 1973 by the author while he was a scholar-in-residence at the Russell Sage Foundation. Unpublished data in the files of the author, Columbia University.

13. This meeting, on October 25, 1972, was attended by the author as a representative of city council member, Charles Taylor. Minutes and notes taken by the author in files, Columbia University.

14. Nathan Glazer and Daniel Patrick Moynihan, *Beyond the Melting Pot.* Cambridge, MA: The MIT Press, 1963, p. 300.

15. All the election data in this article are from the annual reports of the Board of Elections in the City of New York, and the official canvasses and records of the Board of Elections, New York City. The annual reports up to 1969 are at the Municipal Reference Library.

16. The districts were the Seventy-second and Seventy-fourth assembly districts (A.D.s).

17. The four candidates' positions at the time were: Beame was city comptroller (which he had been in 1962–65 and again since 1970); Biaggi was a U.S. Representative from the Bronx; Blumenthal was a member of the state Assembly from Manhattan; and Badillo was also a member of the U.S. House of Representatives and had been borough president of the Bronx.

18. Beame received only a little over 20 percent of the votes in the primary.

19. See John Mollenkopf, "New York: The Great Anomaly," *PS* 19:3 (Summer 1986).

20. It is also possible that Barbaro did less well in the Brooklyn districts because blacks were aware that Barbaro had represented a mainly white ethnic district in Brooklyn viewed as virulently antiblack.

21. Quoted by Sam Roberts in a column headed "The Harlem Fox," in the *New York Times*, March 20, 1989.

22. Editors' note: Between preparation of the chapters for this book and its actual printing, very recent developments have required some updating. We feel additional comments are in order concerning the latest on the status of black politics in New York City.

23. Shefter, *Political Crisis/Fiscal Crisis*, p. 178.

24. Philip Kasinitz, "The Minority Within . . . ," *New York Affairs* 10:1 (Winter 1987): 44–58.

25. Interview, as quoted in *Dissent* (Fall 1987), p. 534.

26. Martin Kilson, *Dissent* (Fall 1989), pp. 528–29.

27. Joe Klein, "The Lion in Summer: Koch on the Comeback Trail," *New York Magazine*, 22:35 (September 4, 1989): 38.

28. J. Raymond Jones, *The Harlem Fox.* Albany, NY: State University of New York Press, 1989.

14

New Immigrants: Ethnic Factors in Governance and Politics

Shirley Jenkins

The ethnic factor has been conspicuous in New York City politics for genera-tions. Many, perhaps most, New Yorkers identify with ethnic groups and claim common racial, religious, national, and/or cultural backgrounds. Together, their votes affect the political prospects of any candidate and the ways in which the electoral process operates. The balanced ticket has a long history, although which specific ethnic groups are needed to constitute "balance" has changed over the years. There was a time when mayors of New York visited countries known as the "three Is"—Ireland, Italy, and Israel; Mayor Koch added China and Nicaragua to the list.

The ethnic factor in New York City political life is not confined to the ballot box. Since the late 1960s, racial and ethnic conflict at the community level or about specific services or decisions has been the rule, not the exception. The raised political consciousness and political participation of minority groups pro-duced major changes throughout the nation: the politics of accommodation gave way to the politics of confrontation and even of conflict. New York City had its share of both.

The aspect of ethnicity that has received the least attention in the literature and is the principal focus of this chapter is the responsiveness of local government to special ethnic needs in the normal execution of government functions. The education and care of children, for example, the health of residents, and the acculturation of newcomers could hardly be accomplished without ethnic-sensitive programs. Thus, the ethnic factor is essential to everyday public management and decision making.

The Demographic Imperative

Ethnic diversity is indigenous to New York City, the major port of entry for the settlement of the United States. But the newspaper headline, "City Minorities

Table 14.1

Total Population and Foreign Born Population, New York City: 1970–80

	1970	1980	Change, 1970–80	
			Number	Percent
Total population	7,894,798	7,071,639	− 823,159	−10.4
Foreign born	1,437,058	1,670,199	+233,141	+16.2
Percent of total	18.2	23.6		

Sources: U.S. Census of Population: 1970. Final report PC(1)–C34, NY, Table 81. *U.S. Census of Population: 1980.* Final report PC80–1–C34, NY, Table 116.

May Now Be Majority,'' did not refer to the ethnic succession of European immigrants—first Dutch, British, German, Irish, then Italian, Russian, Polish, Greek, and other Southern and Eastern Europeans.[1] What made the headlines was that blacks, Asians, and Latinos in New York by 1986 were estimated to be 54 percent of the city's population. Some are old residents, some are migrants from the South and Puerto Rico, many are recent immigrants, refugees, and entrants from the Caribbean area and Asia.

To document the dimensions of ethnicity in New York, three sets of data are particularly useful. The first is the changing ethnic composition of the city population since 1970. Between 1970 and 1980, the total city population declined about 800,000 (more than 10 percent), as the traditional majority white population fell by 1.3 million, from 63 percent of the total to 52 percent, and the black, Latino, and Asian populations increased by 500,000. Between 1980 and 1987 (according to Regional Plan Association estimates made for the Metropolitan Transportation Authority), the total population increased by nearly 300,000. There was a continued decline in the white population, but at a much slower rate than during the 1970s, to 46 percent of the total, a small rise in the black population, and large increases in the Latino and Asian populations.

A second set of data documents the substantial immigration to the city. As shown in Table 14.1, the number of new entrants rose as the total city population declined.

In 1980 there were at least 1.67 million persons of foreign birth in New York, probably an undercount that includes few of the undocumented people. Nearly one in every four census-recorded New Yorkers was foreign born. Moreover, the percent of foreign born in New York from Europe declined from 56.1 in 1970, to 34.6 in 1980. The percent from the West Indies rose over that decade from 15.8 percent to 26.2 percent. These trends persisted through the 1980s.

Implications of the growth in the Latino and black population in New York, both indigenous and foreign born, are highlighted by a third set of data, reflecting

Table 14.2

Median Family Income and Poverty Rates by Race/Ethnicity,
New York City, 1984

Race/Ethnicity	Income	Poverty rate*
Non-Latino white	$31,000	9.0
Non-Latino black	17,544	31.9
Latino	13,280	42.9
Entire population	21,714	23.5

Source: March 1985 Current Population Survey tape files, adapted from Emanuel Tobier, *Poverty in New York City: 1980–85*. New York: Community Service Society of New York, 1987, pp. 3–7.
*Percent of group with income below the officially defined poverty line.

unevenness in income distribution. Economically, there has been a steady bifurcation of income and class in New York, with the poor losing ground in access to resources, services, and housing, with many of the middle class in retreat to the outer suburbs, and with the city primarily a place for the rich and the poor. This income split correlates highly along ethnic lines, as shown in Table 14.2.

Large numbers, many newly arrived, many who are poor, mean that ethnic populations predominate not only in size, but among those in need. Thus not just ethnicity, but ethnic poverty, create issues in the governing of New York.

This chapter deals with ethnic issues as they are played out in the various aspects of New York City government. It does not address the social problems of the groups under discussion, but explores how ethnic factors affect the structure and function of city operations.

The New Ethnicity

Ethnic issues, as already noted, are not new in the governing of the city. They began with the use of wampum for the purchase of Manhattan Island and contin- ued with the change of the name from New Amsterdam to New York. As the city grew and the franchise expanded, they were important in vote-getting, patronage, and delivering city services. The issues persisted, although the form of expres- sion changed over time and under different administrations, and were given varied attention by political scientists. In Roy Peel's study of clubhouse politics in New York in 1929, he identified 750 special national clubs in New York City, mainly Italian, then German and Slavic, as well as 32 racial clubs, black, Chinese and Filipino.[2] Over the years the nationality groups, the "white ethnics" re- tained their cultural identity, but tended to move into mainstream politics. By 1975, when Norman Adler and Blanche Blank reviewed the role of the political club, however, clubs were no longer as prominent, and they analyzed the issue in terms of the black-white differential.[3] They reported 80 percent of club membership to be white, 18 percent black, and 1 percent Asian. Sayre and Kaufman, in 1960, did not point to ethnicity or race as an independent factor in the governing of New York. Their book index made only two references to "ethnic groups," one to "race relations," four to "Negroes," and one to "immigrants."[4]

Although the New York City population was always an amalgam of many ethnic groups, a result of both immigration and migration, the prevailing ideology of the first half of the twentieth century was that of the "melting pot," based on the theory that modernization, through the twin factors of industrialization at the workplace and public education, would result in a fusion of ethnic cultures and the production of a homogenized, Americanized New Yorker. This did not happen, however, and although manifestations of ethnicity changed over generations, ethnic factors persisted beyond earlier expectations.

Differences were kept alive through continuing immigration, worldwide conflict intensifying national loyalties, and use of ethnic and social identity to fan political and social demands. By the second part of this century, the ideology of cultural pluralism had emerged as a more viable explanation of urban ethnic relations than the melting pot. The expectation was that, although assimilation would continue, there would also be different groups living side by side with both accommodation and conflict. Under the Lindsay administration, there was a new emphasis on helping minority groups, particularly blacks and Latinos, with federal support under the poverty programs. This was tempered, however, by a special effort to provide access to services to organizations of "white ethnics," in particular, Polish, Greek, Italian, and Jewish associations.

The increasing importance of ethnicity as an independent variable in the governing of New York during the 1970s and 1980s can be traced to:

1. New national immigration legislation, notably the Immigration Reform Act of 1965 and the Refugee Act of 1980, resulting in substantially increased numbers of Latinos, Asians, and blacks arriving in the city from abroad.

2. Economic and technological changes that resulted in increased demand for a highly skilled work force and the loss of entry jobs, thus widening the gap between the trained and untrained labor forces.

3. The poverty programs of the late 1960s and early 1970s, which encouraged community participation in the political process and raised expectations of the poor and the minority populations.

4. Affirmative action concepts that gave legal sanction to minority goals and opened new opportunities for education and professional employment to a sector of formerly excluded minority persons.

5. A resurgence of activity by "white ethnics" designed to secure special services targeted for their own groups, in part the celebrated "backlash" in response to black activism and gains.

6. The shift in ideology from the melting pot to concepts of cultural pluralism, where retention of cultural differences was accepted, and even valued.

These factors shaped the new ethnicity of the 1980s: a pluralistic, participatory phenomenon. To what extent has this been reflected in the governing of New York? How has the city government responded to claims on its attention and services and to the growing need for mediation among ethnic groups?

Line Agencies and Ethnic Policies

There are at least four ways in which the line agencies of municipal government may be involved in ethnic issues.[5] One is in response to advocacy by ethnic groups in the city who may claim they are inadequately served. A second is in response to demands of their own minority staff, who claim they are inadequately represented, whether in numbers or in positions of power. An example is the Fire Department, which has had to deal with both kinds of criticism. A major fire in Harlem brought an accusation, denied by the department, of slow response to minority areas; at the same time the proportion of firefighters in the department who are black has been under recurring legal challenge.

A third way city agencies deal with ethnicity is when they are assigned to implement specific ethnic programs. Translation services, bilingual educational programs, equal opportunity offices, and human rights activities are all areas where sensitive ethnic issues are involved.

The fourth, and the most far-reaching way ethnicity is involved is in the day-to-day provision of services, which can suffer badly if ethnic factors are not recognized. One example is in the operation of the emergency rooms in city hospitals. This is a service that has had to change because of the demographic changes in people served, requiring ethnic responsiveness to the customs, cultures, and languages of patients coming for care. This accommodation of programs to ethnic needs is new in the administration of services and is often not apparent to traditional administrators schooled in the ethnic-blind, color-blind civil service tradition.

Health and Hospitals

Over the years many hospitals in New York City have operated within an implicit, if not explicit, ethnic context. This has been the case for municipal health facilities serving areas that are racially or ethnically segregated neighborhoods. It also was true in the past of religiously affiliated voluntary hospitals and nursing homes that were focused on the needs of their sponsoring community.

Harlem Hospital in Manhattan was not designed to serve blacks, Lincoln Hospital in the Bronx was not mandated to serve Latinos, and Elmhurst Hospital in Queens was not conceived to serve Asians, but they each have large numbers of minority patients because of their locations in neighborhoods with recognizable racial and ethnic concentrations. And hospitals with sectarian sponsorship have often faced conflicts between their ideological commitments and patient choices. This applies to dietary restrictions for Jewish institutions and to issues of family planning clinics and abortion for Catholic hospitals.

Ethnic factors affect patient compliance with medications and diet regimens, patient cooperation in test procedures, such as drawing of blood samples, patient misuse of emergency room facilities for general out-patient care, patient adherence to scheduled appointments, patient acceptance of the need for prenatal care, and patient acceptance of Western concepts of mental illness and diagnoses and willingness to cooperate in psychiatric treatment. Language differences are part but not all of the problem: custom, culture, conflicts with traditional native medicine and native healers are also involved. Not the least of the problems in health delivery is the large number of uninsured patients and the policy questions on entitlements, which particularly affect newcomers and undocumented aliens.

Another type of ethnic difficulty in the health care settings is interethnic conflict within staffs, where black and Latino workers, often at different rungs in the hospital hierarchy, compete for jobs and status. Another problem common in nursing home settings is interethnic conflict between overworked minority staff members and feeble elderly white residents. All of these factors have driven the city health managers to try to develop an active, ethnic-sensitive program, rather than just reacting to trouble when it arises.

One change in ethnic management was the establishment in the early 1980s of two ethnic clinics in Gouverneur Hospital, a Latino clinic and an Asian clinic. Each is bilingual and bicultural, with an ethnic staff from each respective group at all professional levels. Patients of each group can enter the clinics and receive services in their own languages, relating to medical personnel from their own or related cultures. These clinics have been very successful, and there are plans to replicate this work in other hospitals. This is a model that might have been rejected as segregationist twenty years earlier. Today it succeeds because it is recognized as meeting ethnic needs and is offered as an option and not as a mandate.

There are numerous specific programs for outreach to ethnic groups. The Department of Mental Health, Mental Retardation and Alcoholism Services, for example, encourages provider agencies to develop culturally relevant services. The Health and Hospitals Corporation, from the Office of Vice-President of Mental Hygiene, sponsors a Mental Health Interpreter Training Project for hospital employees who are nonclinical bilingual staff and for volunteers, who serve as interpreters for non-English speaking patients. Recruitment and training of bilingual professional staff are high priorities, but are difficult to sustain in part because of the limited pool and competition with the private sector.

In addition to broad-based efforts, there are specific program initiatives designed to meet special needs. For example, the Refugee Health Program of the New York City Department of Health conducted a screening of Indochinese women of child-bearing age for Hepatitis B. To reach this group, home visits were conducted by two health department employees, one Vietnamese and one Cambodian. At job and language training centers for refugees, they conducted slide and tape presentations in Lao, Khmer, Vietnamese and H'mong, as well as English. Vaccinations were undertaken for women found to be susceptible, and all children under five years of age were screened.

Education

With approximately 80 percent of the children in the city public schools being from one or another minority group, it is not difficult to understand the need for ethnic components in education. These arise most critically around issues of language, and the Board of Education has bilingual teachers in Spanish, Chinese, Vietnamese, Creole, Arabic, and a number of other languages and does in fact give instruction in dozens of languages and dialects. Two levels of work are given: immigrant children with no history of formal schooling in their own country can get basic education in their native language to achieve literacy, and children who have had schooling before they immigrated can get subject teaching in their native language while learning English. But ethnic issues go beyond language and are involved in the serious dropout rate for minority children in the city's schools, which is both an educational and a social problem.

Staffing and administration of the school system are riddled with ethnic issues and conflicts. There has been recruitment of bilingual teachers from Spanish-speaking countries, but questions have been raised about their capacity on the English side. Indeed, the whole bilingual program has become increasingly controversial. One position is that it has been inadequately implemented, and it seems apparent that large numbers of Latino students have been poorly educated in either Spanish or English. The opposing position is that bilingualism is wrong as such; allegedly, it delays students' entry into the mainstream of the economy and culture. Those holding this position urge intensive instruction of newcomers in English as a foreign language, with little or no other bilingual instruction.

The most conspicuous ethnic tensions in the New York City school system have been in the struggles for political and administrative control of the system, which are discussed at length in Chapter 6 by David Rogers on decentralization. However, even had there been no interethnic rivalries at this level, the school system would have great difficulty in coping with the varied ethnic needs, given its difficulties in responding to the educational needs of children of any group.

Human Resources Administration

Ethnic advocacy is a major issue in the delivery of welfare services, which is not unexpected because of the heavy utilization of foster care by black and Latino clients. In June 1984, for example, 60.3 percent of all foster children were black, 14.5 percent were Puerto Rican, 7.3 percent were other Latino, 2.6 percent were Asian, and 2.3 percent were interracial. Thus minority children were 87 percent of the foster care population.[6] Bilingual workers and bilingual information programs have been mandated so that clients can have access to information on entitlements. In income maintenance, a separate office has been established to serve Indochinese refugees, and another office receives applications from Cubans and Haitians who have special "entrant" status, and non-Indochinese refugees. An innovative program for foster care for unaccompanied refugee minors has been implemented. City workers have been assigned to ethnic associations and other outreach programs have been undertaken, with materials in different languages.

The Human Resources Administration has expressed its readiness to work with ethnic associations and community groups and has sought information on the needs of newcomers, which go beyond the basics of food and shelter. For example, it has supported a Community Council of Greater New York study of health practices and family patterns among Haitians, Cambodians, and Dominicans.[7] The extent to which research findings affect practice is not clear, but the need for knowledge of ethnic differences has been recognized.

Ethnic issues in social services go beyond program development and staff organization and even beyond advocacy. There are unanswered ethnic questions that are controversial and touch the essence of social work practice. In child welfare, for example, where family matters are involved, the issue of "mixing or matching" is crucial.[8] Among the relevant questions are whether interracial foster placements and adoptions should be arranged, whether clients should be able to choose therapists of their own group, and whether there should be a prescribed mix in residential settings for adolescents. These are issues of social work practice which public social service workers, either by omission or commission, are involved with on a day-to-day, case-by-case basis.

Other City Agencies

Most city agencies are affected by ethnic issues and have made efforts to improve their human relations. But, often, the minor or superficial operational changes have done little to relieve the ethnic tensions for that agency. This is not surprising, given the depth and intransigence of the racial issues.

One example of such an administrative effort is the establishment in the New York City Police Department of a New Immigrant Unit to address the needs of newcomers, try to give them a positive image of the police, and intervene for better reception of immigrants in the community. As part of that program, the department has sent police officers into selected schools for classroom contacts with immigrant children, to seek to dispel their fears of authority figures. Officers have met with hundreds of community groups and visited centers to inform immigrants of their rights. The department has run public service announcements in foreign language newspapers. In addition, the department has employed Korean, Cambodian, and Russian-speaking receptionists in several precincts, tried to recruit more minority officers, and introduced ethnic issues into its training programs. On the other hand, in October 1987, several hundred demonstrators under the sponsorship of the coalition group Koreans Against Anti-Asian Violence, protested alleged police brutality against a member of their group.[9]

Ethnic Staff and Administration

The presence of ethnic staff and ethnic administrators is an important component of implementing ethnic policies and programs, since this implies a heightened sensitivity to needs and a lower level of discrimination and prejudice. There are also usually a different community perception of enforcement and a greater potential for communication when those in authority are of the same ethnic group. This is not true for every individual or every case, but the potential exists for improved relationships where the ethnic diversity of the population is reflected in the ethnic diversity of those who administer programs, whether they are the political appointees who are the top managers, permanent civil service staff members or provisional employees.[10]

Table 14.3 indicates the ethnic distribution of positions at the senior management level in city government agencies under the direct jurisdiction of the mayor as of 1986. Obviously, the nonwhite groups were underrepresented relative to their shares of the city's population. It is less clear whether they were underrepresented relative to their shares of the pool of qualified candidates. But, of course, that pool reflects a history that includes disadvantages of various kinds, not just recent occupational and educational choices.

There is strong ethnic pressure for the appointment of increased numbers of senior minority officials. Minority groups are not of a single mind, however, and coalitions around candidates are difficult to achieve. A minority commissioner is not even assured of the full support of his or her own community, and may even, as in the case of a black police commissioner, become a target for attack by a sector of his own group. One problem is the perception sectors of the minority community have of the role of the minority commissioner. When a black social worker was appointed as commissioner of welfare, a prominent black newspaper greeted him as a black commissioner for Harlem. The appointee quickly responded during a television interview that his race did not limit his responsibility

Table 14.3

**Commissioners and Deputy Commissioners in Mayoral Agencies,
New York City, March 31, 1986**

	Number	Percent of total
White	120	78.4
Black	20	13.1
Latino	11	7.2
Other	2	1.3
Total	153	100.0

Source: City of New York, *Report of the Mayor's Commission on Hispanic Concerns*, December 10, 1986, p. 105.

to blacks: his responsibility was for policy and service to all the residents of New York. He went on to say, however, that inasmuch as blacks and Latinos represented the majority of the population in need of the services of his department, he expected to be keenly sensitive to the needs of those groups.

In some situations, it has been suggested that the urgent need for effective leadership should override ethnic choices. Following the resignation of a Latino school chancellor, a newly appointed black member of the Board of Education commented, "I don't care what a person's gender or color is, we need someone who understands poor kids." She went on to say, "It would be wonderful if we could find a minority or find a woman but at this point that is not the issue."[11] Others felt the issue was less "understanding" than administrative skills. As that search developed, and it became clear that a black chancellor would be appointed, the names of four eligible candidates emerged. The issue shifted from pressure to appoint a black educator, to which one to appoint. This is a good example of how ethnic issues will change with the increase in the pool of potential candidates, and how factors other than race, such as qualifications and political stance, will modify decision making on the single factor of racial or ethnic background.

The untimely death of the black chancellor after a brief time in office resulted in an outpouring of grief and support from a broad sector of minority teachers, children, and parents. Many in the city realized for the first time the impact on the minority community of the role model afforded by a highly respected minority administrator.

What about the ethnic composition of the city government work force below the top management level? Table 14.4 compares the ethnic distribution of the population of the city, all people in the labor force living in the city, and the holders of the more than 1,100 different job titles in New York City government.[12]

Table 14.4

Percent Distribution of New York City Population, Civilian Labor Force, and Municipal Employees, by Ethnic Group

	White	Black	Latino	Other[a]
Population[b]	52.4	24.0	19.9	3.8
Civilian labor force[b]	57.4	21.9	16.4	4.2
Municipal employees[c]	57.7	31.7	9.0	1.0

Source: City of New York, *Report of the Mayor's Commission on Hispanic Affairs*, December 10, 1986, p. 92.
   a. Includes Asians and Native Americans.
   b. 1980 Census.
   c. As of June 30, 1985.

These data show the city to be a heavy employer of blacks, whereas Latinos and "others" (Asians and Native American) are underrepresented in the civil service. Lack of facility in English is part of this problem, as is date of migration to New York.

Another voice that raises ethnic issues in city government is that of ethnically defined organizations of city employees. In both the police and fire departments there are separate organizations for the black staff, which often take independent stands on issues relevant to their own members. In August 1987, for example, the black firefighters association, the Vulcan Society, filed a broad racial discrimination suit against the city. It charged that black firefighters have been discriminated against in the "testing, hiring, training, and other conditions of employment," and that blacks constitute only 4.4 percent of the total firefighting force, although they constitute 29 percent of the city's population.[13] Black police officers also meet in their own organizations to deal with issues and conflicts that arise from what has been called being "black in blue." The National Black Police Association is one example of an organization concerned with sensitivity training to racial issues in police departments and recognizing the special ties of black police officers to the black community. "We know if we take off our uniforms," said their information director, "whites would treat us the same way as they do other blacks. . . ."[14]

Historically, ethnic specialization has dominated the city job market, in part due to more or less benign reasons connected with the immigration and assimilation process (skills brought from the old country; family and friend networks that provide information about certain occupations and industries; the greater comfort of working with one's own group; and the use of *padrone* systems of recruiting for jobs) and in part due to outright discrimination against outsiders.[15] Civil service examinations and labor contracts, initiated to protect city workers through the merit system, tend to support the status quo. Successful implementation of affirmative action under equal opportunity requirements can only be accomplished by making changes in these protective systems. So ethnic equity in the distribution of municipal jobs, both on a managerial and line level, remains a central issue for city government.

Programs and Instruments Across Agency Lines

Special Programs

Often, city programs on ethnicity cut across the specific responsibilities of the line agencies, requiring the creation of new administrative machinery.

Human rights

The New York City Human Rights Commission is an example; its mission is to combat discrimination and to promote amicable intergroup relations. The commission grew out of the Committee on Unity, established in 1944 in the La Guardia administration to encourage racial and religious harmony. Since 1955 (in its current form), the commission has investigated complaints and enforced the city's antidiscrimination laws. The commission has not been a model of administrative efficiency; a year-long study concluded in February 1988 found that the commission had a backlog of more than 1,000 cases, extending back into the 1970s.

Immigration

In July 1984, an Office of Immigrant Affairs was created and located in the Department of City Planning, to coordinate programming to deal with immigration issues. The office functions as a central clearing house, dealing with city agency activities, state and federal government offices, and private groups.

Adult literacy

Another program that has special relevance for ethnicity is the New York City Adult Literacy Initiative. This program underwent major expansion in 1985, when earlier federally funded adult education services were substantially buttressed by a cooperative effort of the state and city, supported in part by Municipal Assistance Corporation funds. In 1987, the Initiative served 45,000 students in the city, 50.8 percent in programs of English as a second language, 3.2 percent in basic education in their native language, 45.1 percent in basic education in English, and 0.9 percent in mathematics. Of the students in the program in 1987, 90 percent were nonwhite: 49.4 percent were Latino, 29.2 percent were black,

11.1 percent were Asian, and 0.3 percent were Native American. The Initiative avoided the controversies in the school system about bilingual education; the less controversial goal of producing literate job holders is the basis for the program.[16]

Investigatory Commissions

An investigatory commission is often appointed when an issue is controversial and the policy implications unpopular. Sometimes, it serves to diffuse attention and avoid action. In the area of ethnic relations, however, this can backfire, if a strong advocacy group seizes the opportunity provided by the investigation to dramatize its needs. This was the case in the report of the Mayor's Commission on Hispanic Concerns, submitted in December 1986, which opened by frankly linking ethnic efforts with political rewards. It states, "On the night of the Mayor's victory in the September 1985 Democratic primary, he thanked the Hispanic community for its overwhelming support of his candidacy and stated that he wanted to be measured by what he did for Hispanics over the next four years." Shortly thereafter on October 4, 1985, he announced the appointment of sixteen members of the Hispanic community to serve on the Mayor's Commission on Hispanic Concerns.[17] The charge was to report on specific steps to improve the conditions of the Latino community, including improvements in the delivery of municipal services.

The commission was well staffed and funded, and its report gives a comprehensive and hard-hitting analysis of Latino needs. Dozens of specific recommendations are made on education, economic development, housing, employment, health, justice, and language services.

One theme running through the many commission recommendations is a strong call for ethnic identification. The recommendation on dropouts, for example, is "that the City's dropout rate be tabulated according to race, ethnic origin and language spoken at home, in order to provide the Board of Education with sufficient information to tailor dropout prevention programs to the specific needs of Latino students."[18] This recommendation represents a new posture for a minority group and a major change from the position of civil rights advocates taken in an earlier period.

Antidiscrimination groups in New York in the late 1940s and 1950s sought suppression of ethnic identity data in order to prevent ethnic discrimination. For example, photos were not to be attached to applications so employers or admissions personnel could not see if applicants were black or white. There were public drives against identification of ethnic or religious background when reporting news, especially when the story referred to criminal behavior. This color-blind and ethnic-blind position obviously is incompatible with affirmative action programs that seek to open new opportunities for designated ethnic groups, by identifying individuals or members of the group who should have special attention. The report of the Hispanic Commission goes even further in pressing for the use of ethnic identification as a basis for program development and the allocation of funds.

Three months after the Commission's report, an official rejoinder was published.[19] City Hall accepted recommendations concerning the extension and improvement of existing ethnic programs, bilingual efforts, and ethnic outreach for Latino development. On the other hand, the administration rejected proposed measures that would conflict with the civil service merit system or where the expansion of goals for Latinos could be at the expense of other groups. For example, the recommendation that the city sponsor preparation courses for Latino candidates who wish to take city examinations, to help them with both substance and fear of failure, was rejected, in part because such courses "could not be limited to Latinos but would have to be open to all candidates." One outcome was agreement to publish an annual report on Hispanic concerns.

A Mayor's Commission on Black New Yorkers was appointed in January 1986, three months after the appointment of the Commission on Hispanic Concerns. The report of the black group was not submitted until November 14, 1988, just short of three years later.[20] According to the document, Mayor Koch acknowledged "an unacceptable disparity between the economic status of blacks and the white population" and said his goal was to reduce this disparity.[21] The commission defined its goals as developing recommendations in the areas of support for black business, education, job training, and employment. The report leans heavily on demographic data and other statistics, much of it based on the 1980 Census and government reports. Aside from the section on education, the report focuses on economic issues. Even the conclusions in the education section have an economic focus, stating, "our children are entitled to a twelfth-grade education; the city's economy requires it."[22]

In the section on "Black Employment in City Government," the commission found that one-third of the city's labor force is black, but the level of employment varies, with blacks being over 60 percent of the city's office and clerical workers, 20 percent of managers, but only 10 percent senior managers, with no black senior managers in almost half of city agencies. Further analysis by city departments was done, based on 1986 and 1987 data from the City Commission on Human Rights. The distribution of black employees in city government varied greatly. The three departments with the highest percent levels were Juvenile Justice (71.9), Social Services/HRA (60.5), and Corrections (55.2). Senior management positions held by blacks in these three departments were 40 percent, 27 percent, and 17 percent respectively. Departments with the lowest distribution of black employees were Uniform Police (10.7), Collective Bargaining, and Landmarks (15.0 each). At the time these data were reported, no information was available on several departments, including fire, transportation, and personnel.[23]

Overall, the tone of the document was expressed in its Executive Summary, which stated, "While the impact of the legacy of discrimination, including the denial of educational and economic opportunity, can scarcely be remedied overnight, there are reasonable solutions, well within the scope of city government, to many of the problems identified in this report."[24]

During the Koch administration, there was also a Task Force on Asian-American Affairs within the mayor's office. The task force report was not published, but most of the recommendations reportedly had been implemented by August 1989.[25] Those recommendations deal with improvements in communications, language services, economic development activities, and mental health services for the rapidly growing Asian communities.

Ethnic Advisers

In addition to creating special programs and investigatory commissions, elected officials in New York have appointed "advisers" on ethnic affairs at both the mayoral and borough president levels. These are political appointees, who do not necessarily have a strong power base in the minority communities. But the existence of such advisers represents recognition of the incipient problems and the need to monitor ethnic relations.

An Ethnic Advisory Council was established in the mayor's Office at City Hall in 1978, with the inauguration of the new Koch administration. Chaired by the mayor's special assistant for ethnic affairs, this group was informally constituted, without an official mandate. Its members were appointed on recommendation of community leaders. By 1989, there were four offices to deal with various groups, one for Latinos, one for Asians, one for blacks, and one for white ethnics. None had much visibility outside their respective communities.

There have been three main functions for the Ethnic Advisory Council, according to its chairman. The first is to recognize early warning signals of ethnic conflict and head off potential crises. The other two tasks are to inform the communities of government policies on ethnic issues and to try to develop an informed electorate on ethnic relations. Conferences and meetings are held to these ends. For example, an all-day teach-in was held at John Jay College at which senior staff of various government offices made presentations on their department's services to the community.

One illustration of crisis intervention in the early 1980s was the response to Indian-Latino strains in Queens. Here the council's staff worked to get greater community understanding of the culture and customs of the new Indian arrivals, as well as to have the latter group be more open with neighborhood groups about their cultural practices. A small but useful outcome was that a plaque was placed on an Indian temple identifying it as a house of worship, and people were invited to attend the services. Being open to the public gave the temple credibility and more acceptance. Another example was the council's attention to Korean-black differences on 125th Street in Harlem, where economic competition for business has exacerbated interracial and interethnic tensions.

There have been examples of crisis intervention in ethnic matters elsewhere in City Hall. For example, there was substantial media attention to the case of the "Park Avenue Deli," a store rented in December 1983 by two Korean immigrants, much to the chagrin and hostility of some residents of this exclusive neighborhood and in presumed conflict with regulations promulgated by the Department of Buildings and the Landmarks Preservation Commission. Political considerations brought the matter to the attention of the comptroller's office where astute intervention resulted in a compromise solution. An anti-Asian episode was averted, and the deli, with a modified design and plan for operations, was able to open for business. Although a small episode, this was a marker case for the ethnic community, which managed to assert its interests and maneuver through the political conflicts of the established bureaucracies.

Ethnic advisers function actively at the borough president level. In Brooklyn, there has been an assistant to the borough president for ethnic affairs for several years, with a multiethnic staff that includes representatives of the major ethnic communities in the borough. Inevitably, conflict mediation in the neighborhoods is an important activity. An example of crisis intervention was the involvement of the Brooklyn borough president in the conflicts in Williamsburgh between Hasidic Jews and Latinos. In that crowded neighborhood, conflicts of culture and custom were inevitable, and they were exacerbated by mutual ethnic mistrust, discrimination, and racism. The role of the borough president was to mediate between leaders of both groups. Verbal conciliation does not solve underlying problems, but it averts violence and buys time for more basic program intervention.

One example of a negotiated agreement on an ethnic issue occurred in December 1988 in Brooklyn, between the Bedford Stuyvesant Community and the Nostrand/Fulton Korean American Merchants Association. A negotiating team, chaired by the New York state assemblyman from the Fifty-sixth District, Albert Vann, conducted a lengthy series of sessions between black representatives and Korean merchants around conflictual issues in the neighborhood. A series of community demands were met, and in a signed agreement the Korean merchants agreed to publicly apologize to the black community for misunderstandings, facilitate the sale of his business by an offending merchant, have forty-three businesses transfer their accounts into local banks, establish a not-for-profit Bedford-Stuyvesant Community Trust Fund, open their bulk purchasing structure to other local entrepreneurs, help train local youth for business, and, finally, participate in courses where both black and Korean history and culture are presented.

This agreement addresses a long-standing grievance of black communities: alleged exploitation by retail establishments run by other ethnic groups. Political leadership from a local state assemblyman and technical assistance from both the

New York State and New York City Divisions of Human Rights facilitated the agreement.

Each borough functions differently in structuring its response to ethnic issues, in part because each faces different problems. In Queens, the position of director of the Office of Immigration Services was initiated with the inauguration of a new borough president in August 1986. The impetus was the ethnic diversity of newcomers to that borough and the range of their needs. The main task of the new office has been outreach. The outreach has been to ethnic leadership, rather than community residents, but there is an effort to orient newcomers, primarily Asians, to city services.

Ethnic Factors at the Local Level

The two neighborhood-government networks have important minority representation: the thirty-two elected community school boards and the fifty-nine appointed community boards. These organizations are discussed more fully in Chapter 6 by David Rogers, dealing with decentralization. At this point, our concern is with their ethnic diversity.

The school boards are elected by a small fraction of eligible voters, who include both neighborhood residents and parents. In the May 1989 election, only 7.2 percent of those eligible voted.[26] Numbers of blacks and Latinos on these boards increased in the decades between 1973 and 1983 from 37 percent to 45 percent of the total, a fairly high ethnic representation. Within the 45 percent, blacks were 63 percent and Latinos 37 percent.[27] By 1989, minority representation had risen to nearly 48 percent. There are numerous operational problems, however. The boards have been widely criticized as not speaking for their total electorate, being embroiled in political issues rather than the educational needs of the children, and in some cases being involved in corruption and fraud. However, as Rogers says, "Effective decentralization cannot exist without a strong center, and that is yet to develop."

The community boards serve to provide a link between New York City's neighborhoods and the central bureaucracy. Board members, appointed by borough presidents and the city council, are unpaid, usually people active in local civic and business organizations. Each board has a district manager and a modest budget. They make recommendations on land-use issues and local needs and priorities for services. Since they operate at the neighborhood level, they can be close to ethnic issues and, since they involve community groups, they tend to have significant ethnic representation. This representation, however, is not proportional to population.

With fifty-nine community boards in the city and a wide range of needs and performances, it is difficult to generalize about them. One study analyzed the degree to which the community board system facilitates effective representation

Table 14.5

Percent Distribution of Residents, Actives, and Community Board Members in Eight Community Districts in New York City, 1981, by Ethnicity, Income Level, and Education

	Residents	Actives	Members
Ethnicity:			
Black	23	14	16
White	50	74	70
Latino	20	6	12
Other	7	6	3
All groups	100	100	100
Income:			
Less than $15,000	45	33	17
$15,000–$40,000	49	48	54
More than $40,000	6	19	29
All groups	100	100	100
Education:			
Elementary	20	5	1
High school graduate	38	24	9
Some college	15	18	23
College graduate	26	52	67
All groups	100	100	100

Source: Based on data in Richard C. Rich, *Participation and Representation in New York City's Community Board System*, Washington, DC: Center for Responsive Governance.

of residents. Sponsored by the Center for Responsive Governance, and undertaken with the assistance of the Community Service Society of New York City, this project took eight communities as its base, selected for their representativeness on various criteria, two each in the Bronx, Brooklyn, and Manhattan, and one each in Queens and Staten Island. Three samples were used in each of these eight communities: a random telephone interview of residents, interviews with "actives" in each, defined as the persons who attended community board meetings, and the members of the boards themselves.[28]

The characteristics of the membership of these eight boards, and of the population in the neighborhood and the actives who come to meetings, are shown in Table 14.5.

Although these data refer to only eight boards and a single year, they give useful insights into the ethnic composition. For the communities studied, minorities were 50 percent of the population, and 30 percent of the board members.

Income and education data give further information and highlight the low representation of Latino and Asian residents. The data contrast with higher ethnic representation on the school boards, which are elected rather than appointed.

In general, the study found that few in the neighborhoods were aware of the work of the community boards, but those who were involved were very concerned. The contributions of the community boards are particularly relevant where there is a mix of ethnic groups and a mediating function is undertaken, and where there is a newcomer group whose needs have been unrecognized and advocacy on the local level is initiated.

An example of a mixed neighborhood is Board 7 in Flushing, Queens. This was a settled, middle-class, primarily white community, where there has been a substantial influx of Asian immigrants, including Chinese, Koreans, and Indians. The board has been concerned with issues of language, acculturation, and service for the Asian newcomers, but it also worries about established, primarily white, business and development interests; a black community concerned with gentrification and underrepresentation; an orthodox Jewish community protesting the decline of small shops serving them; and the service needs that local schools and hospitals are supposed to meet.[29] Mediation, selection of priorities, and coalition building are all board functions.

In Washington Heights, Manhattan, the domain of Community Board 12, a different ethnic situation has emerged. This has been a neighborhood dominated by Latino interests since the 1970s, but the predominant Latino population has shifted from Puerto Rican to Cuban to Dominican. The large Dominican population, including many undocumented newcomers, has substantial needs for housing, health care, education, job training, and social services. The community board is a channel for the expression of these varied needs. Expressing the needs, however, does not mean that they will be met. As Rogers points out, there may be a conflict for the boards between representativeness and effectiveness, with neighborhoods represented by white middle-class boards doing better in securing results than districts with poor and minority representatives.

Ethnic Associations

Ethnic associations are a special form of organization and ethnic grouping. They are voluntary mutual-aid groups whose membership is confined to a specific ethnic minority. Those associations that are involved in meeting social service needs fill an important gap between the family, the primary group for mutual aid, and the large human resources bureaucracy, either voluntary or public. The number of ethnic associations has increased sharply since the 1965 and 1980 legislation liberalizing the admission of immigrants and refugees.[30]

Ethnic associations can provide a bridge between city agencies and ethnic clients who are entitled to services. Outreach workers from the Human Resources Administration use the ethnic associations in this way. Also, classes in English as a second language are often sponsored by the associations. Leaders of the ethnic associations serve as spokespersons for their groups on community boards and other advisory bodies.

Some ethnic associations serving immigrants operate as multifunction social agencies, with substantial government funding. Others provide a narrower band of services to newcomers. Refugee groups have organized Mutual Assistance Associations, which have been the direct recipients of federal-, state-, or city-based funding, to provide, among other things, youth services and employment training.[31] A further role for the ethnic associations is as advocate in the political and policy aspects of ethnic aspirations. For example, the Chinatown Planning Council successfully protested the size of a projected detention center in Chinatown and worked with other groups to secure the building of housing in the community for elderly Chinese. A Korean association has been active in intervening with police with regard to neighborhood restrictions on local Korean groceries. The associations act as watchdogs on application of restrictive legislation and on protection of their members, and thus are a part of the ethnic presence in the city.

Most ethnic associations concern themselves only with the needs of their own ethnic group. Coalitions tend to be single-issue based—sometimes a piece of legislation such as the 1986 Immigration Reform and Control Act, with its impact on the undocumented, will arouse interethnic interest, but usually only for the affected groups. Sometimes a neighborhood situation of intergroup geographical contiguity will force intergroup cooperation or at least compromise. But broad interethnic coalitions are slow to develop. One effort to establish a format for relating to the needs of different groups was the Network of Ethnic Associations, sponsored by the Community Council of Greater New York. With private foundation funding from the Revson Foundation, the council brought together leaders of ethnic associations, for the purposes of communication, cooperation, and collaboration. The leaders sought to participate in programs of technical assistance and to gain visibility in the formal social agency establishment. Some tentative alliances were made among groups, but the dissolution of the sponsoring agency, and the end of the funding, set this innovative program adrift.

Ethnicity in the Political Process

The elemental demographic trends in New York—the growth of the black, Latino, and Asian populations, in part from overseas immigration—assure that ethnic and racial considerations will be important in the governing of New York. But population numbers alone are not a sufficient condition to assure full political recognition. For that, the members of any group need to acquire citizenship, they must register to vote, and they must actually vote. Minority voting has been lower, proportionate to population numbers, than white voting, generally attributed to apathy, frustration, and the sense that a vote will not make a difference. This can change, however, with a strong minority candidate, as happened in the 1988 presidential primaries, when the candidacy of Jesse Jackson brought high minority voting participation.

For immigrants, the first step to full political participation is citizenship. Until the 1986 immigration legislation providing an amnesty to illegal entrants, the thousands of undocumented aliens were out of the voting stream, whether or not they wished for citizenship. But there seem to be major differences among the various national groups with respect to attitudes toward naturalization. Nationwide census data show that, in 1980, 50.5 percent of all immigrants were naturalized citizens. The percent naturalized varied from 72.3 percent for European immigrants to 29.0 percent for Latin Americans. Among the latter group, only 25.5 percent of immigrants from the Dominican Republic had become naturalized citizens.[32] These variations in part reflect recency of entry—the most recent entrants have not had the time needed to acquire citizenship—but also attitudinal differences.

The low percentage of naturalization for Dominicans is of special interest for New York City, where the Dominicans represent the single largest group of newcomers. In interviews, refugees and immigrants point out some disadvantages that come with U.S. citizenship. For example, Indochinese refugees believe that it is easier to have relatives brought over if refugee status is maintained; certain preferences for relatives are said to be lost once citizenship has been achieved. Many newcomers from Latin America are reluctant to renounce citizenship in their country of origin. Many wish to travel home freely and to buy property and invest money in home countries. These rights could be jeopardized if they became American citizens. Also, people who do travel back and forth—or hope to—are likely to retain a strong emotional identification with the old country (unlike refugees) and will become naturalized without a strong reason to do so. But the political influence of ethnics without citizenship with candidates for public office, both before and after election, is likely to be very limited.

Blacks and Latinos, both native-born and naturalized, represent a potential force at the ballot box, but numerous analyses show that the minority vote in the city has traditionally been low. Table 14.6 compares electoral participation in 1982 and 1984 for the main ethnic groups.

As can be seen, registration and turnout were not high for either electoral year. But for each year there was a lower rate for minorities than for whites, on both counts.

The experience of the 1988 Democratic presidential primary in New York City may introduce a new chapter in analysis of minority voting potential. The presence of a strong black candidate with a well-managed national campaign apparatus and a vigorous attention to domestic issues resulted in his receiving a

Table 14.6

Voter Registration and Voter Turnout, by Ethnic Group, New York City, 1982–84

	Latinos		Blacks		Whites		Total	
	1982	1984	1982	1984	1982	1984	1982	1984
Registration rate (%)	35.1	51.8	39.4	56.1	48.7	60.2	44.7	57.8
Voter turnout rate (%)	66.3	69.6	64.2	70.0	71.8	81.7	69.8	77.6

Source: Angelo Falcon, *Black and Latino Politics in New York City: Race and Ethnicity in a Changing Urban Context*. New York: Institute for Puerto Rican Policy, October 1985. Calculated from data from the New York City Board of Elections, New York State Legislative Task Force on Reapportionment, and the U.S. Census Bureau.

plurality of the votes in New York City. It also resulted in some of the highest voting turnout rates in the state. Although the vote for Jesse Jackson was highest in predominantly black communities, he drew very well in the Latino communities, as well.

As Charles V. Hamilton points out in Chapter 13, numerous factors mitigate against the development of a strong minority coalition in New York. Among them are the lack of a single minority group of dominant size, inter- and intra-ethnic conflicts, and the absence of a structure for dialogue. Thus, there have been few minority people in the top political positions in the city. One small example of this was noted when the minor illness of the mayor in 1987 focused interest on the mayoralty succession. The deputy mayor and the two other officials elected citywide, the president of the city council (the designated successor), and the comptroller, were all of the same group as the mayor: white, male, and Jewish. The strong run of a black candidate in the 1989 mayoral election may indicate changes in the attitudes of the city's electorate.

The failure of coalition, both within and among the ethnic minorities in New York, however, does not mean that ethnicity is not a factor in the broader political process. The problem is that separate ethnic allegiances may cause divisiveness in situations where common economic and social needs would be expected instead to forge coalition. Black leaders take positions separate from whites, from Latinos, and from other blacks on borough lines, as well as on the basis of place of origin, for example, southern U.S. versus West Indian origin. The victory of David Dinkins in 1989 showed that coalition is possible in New York, given favorable circumstances such as an unpopular incumbent and a nonthreatening minority candidate. Dinkins's success heralds a new chapter in the future of ethnic politics in New York City.

For their part, Latinos in New York are becoming more vocal and more ready to assert their special needs. Many Latinos resist being grouped together, preferring to be identified in terms of places of origin, like Dominicans, Colombians, Cubans, or Puerto Ricans. But despite this preference, the situation of Latinos—the economic and social conditions—is tending to produce a "group identity and consciousness [that] is appropriate for social action and mobilization."[33]

Conclusion

Ethnicity is a pervasive consideration in city politics, in advocacy, and in service delivery. But ethnic needs and interests are often not articulated effectively, let alone acted on. Sometimes this is because the interests of different ethnic groups diverge; in cases where interests coincide, coalitions are hard to forge and even harder to sustain; in other cases, deeply rooted racism blocks the minority group from taking its place in the historic ethnic succession.

At the neighborhood level, the opportunities for ethnic involvement in local governance are more frequent than in citywide offices. Both the elected school boards and the appointed community boards have minority members. Political and public interest activities are generated around neighborhood issues, and heads of ethnic organizations in certain neighborhoods assume positions of community leadership. This activity presumably trains newcomers to participate in political affairs, but it may have an unforeseen cost. With so much organizational effort on the part of ethnic leaders going into local issues, there may be little energy left for the larger problems of city, state, and national government.

Whether this cost is worth bearing depends on how much activity at the neighborhood level impacts on the lives of the people affected, on the one hand, and how much activity by the government (until now the domain of the white political establishment) impacts on their lives, on the other hand. It also depends on the extent to which ethnic leaders in the neighborhoods move into more powerful elective and appointive posts over time, and the extent to which involvement of ordinary people in neighborhood activities increases their participation in broader issues and causes.

Perhaps the greatest advance in recognizing ethnic concerns has been in the incorporation of ethnic factors in the management of city social and health services. Special ethnic needs have been recognized, and programs have been put in place to meet them, which would not have been even considered possible in 1960 when the Sayre and Kaufman book was published. Some of these programs have been discussed in this chapter. Not all are functioning in an optimal way and, even if they were, they would not meet all the needs. But the concept has been accepted, and the ideology of ethnic-related services has become part of the culture in many aspects of city operations. This is not a matter of largess or buying off minority groups; rather, it is the only way to be effective in delivering the city services that touch the lives of most New Yorkers.

Notes

1. The headline was on the front page of the *New York Times*, October 24, 1986.
2. Roy V. Peel, *The Political Clubs of New York*. New York: Ira S. Friedman, revised edition, 1968.
3. Norman M. Adler and Blanche Davis Blank, *Political Clubs in New York*. New York: Praeger, 1975.
4. Wallace Sayre and Herbert Kaufman. *Governing New York*. New York: Russell Sage, 1960.
5. Line agencies are the direct providers of services to the public, in contrast to staff agencies that oversee and provide overhead services to the line agencies, services like budget, personnel, and real property management.
6. Synia Yam-Wong, *Characteristics of Children in New York City's Foster Care System*. New York: Community Service Society of New York, 1987.
7. Roy Leavitt and Mary Lutz, *Three Immigrant Groups in New York City in the Human Services: Dominicans, Haitians, Cambodians*. New York: The Community Council of Greater New York, 1988.
8. Shirley Jenkins and Elaine Norman, *Filial Deprivation and Foster Care*. New York: Columbia University Press, 1972.
9. *New York Times*, October 19, 1987, p. B4.
10. Shirley Jenkins, *The Ethnic Dilemma in Social Services*. New York: Free Press, 1981.
11. *New York Times*, August 15, 1987, p. 31.
12. Only about 10 percent of the resident labor force is employed by the city government. Thus, this is mostly a measure of the ethnic composition of private sector jobs held by city residents.
13. *New York Times*, August 23, 1987, p. 37.
14. *New York Times*, February 14, 1988, p. 26.
15. "Padrone" is an Italian word meaning, in this connection, "boss"; the padrone is a person from an ethnic group who takes on the task of recruiting and supervising people of his or her group.
16. New York City Adult Literacy Initiative: Summary Final Report for Fiscal Year 1987, New York: Literacy Assistance Center, 1987.
17. City of New York, December 10, 1986. *Report of the Mayor's Commission on Hispanic Concerns*, Edgardo N. Vasquez, Chairman.
18. *Commission on Hispanic Concerns*, p. 53.
19. City of New York, March 9, 1987. *City Response to the Report of the Mayor's Commission on Hispanic Concerns*, Edward I. Koch, Mayor.
20. City of New York, November 14, 1988. *The Report of the Mayor's Commission on Black New Yorkers*, William H. Howard, Chairman.
21. *Commission on Black New Yorkers*, p. i.
22. *Commission on Black New Yorkers*, p. 201.
23. *Commission on Black New Yorkers*, pp. 93, 95.
24. *Commission on Black New Yorkers*, p. iii.
25. According to a communication to the author, August 7, 1989.
26. *New York Times*, June 11, 1989, p. 40.
27. Angelo Falcon, *Black and Latino Politics in New York City: Race and Ethnicity in a Changing Urban Context*. New York: Institute for Puerto Rican Policy, Inc., October 1985.
28. Richard C. Rich, *Participation and Representation in New York City's Community Board System*. Washington, DC: Center for Responsive Governance.

29. *New York Times*, November 9, 1986, p. 56.

30. Shirley Jenkins, editor, *Ethnic Associations and the Welfare State: Services to Immigrants in Five Countries*. New York: Columbia University Press, 1988.

31. Shirley Jenkins and Mignon Sauber, "Ethnic Associations in New York and Services to Immigrants," in Jenkins, editor, *Ethnic Associations and the Welfare State*, pp. 21–105.

32. U.S. Bureau of the Census, October 1984, *Statistical Profile of the Foreign Born: 1980 Census of Population*. Washington, DC: Government Printing Office.

33. Felix M. Padilla, "On the Nature of Latino Ethnicity," *Social Science Quarterly* 65:2 (June 1984): 651–64.

VI

Epilogue

15

The New Charter: Will It
Make a Difference?

Joseph P. Viteritti

In November 1986, U.S. District Court Judge Edward R. Neaher ruled that the Board of Estimate, New York City's most powerful governmental body, was unconstitutional. He found that the system of voting which allocates equal representation to boroughs regardless of population size violates the one-person, one-vote standard protected by the Fourteenth Amendment of the Constitution.[1] Within one month Mayor Edward Koch, acting under the authority granted to him through New York State's Municipal Home Rule Law, appointed a fifteen-member Charter Revision Commission, chaired by Richard Ravitch to evaluate the governmental system and to recommend changes.[2] Simultaneously, the mayor, joined by the borough presidents, vowed to appeal the decision to a higher court.

In October 1987, the district court decision was upheld by a unanimous three-person panel of the Court of Appeals. In an attempt to save the Board of Estimate from the imposition of legal remedies that could eventually result in its annihilation, Mayor Koch instructed his corporation counsel to take the case to the U.S. Supreme Court. City Council Majority Leader Peter Vallone, recognizing that his legislative body would be the direct beneficiary of any actions taken to jeopardize the power or existence of the Board of Estimate, filed papers with the court supporting the earlier decisions. In the meantime the Charter Revision Commission set into motion a process of review and discussion that would result in the most profound restructuring of the municipal government in a century.

The Board of Estimate and the Municipal Government

Most New Yorkers concerned with municipal affairs mistakenly believe that the Board of Estimate was created as part of a grand scheme of municipal government, cast in the image of the federal Constitution, that would provide the boroughs with a representative forum to counterbalance a local legislative body chosen on the basis of population, much as the U.S. Senate does in relation to the

House of Representatives. Although that constitutional model might have influenced the thinking of some reformers at a particular point in time, the history of the Board of Estimate is more complex.

The truth is that the body, originally known as the Board of Estimate and Apportionment, has had three institutional lives in its 125-year history: once as an instrument of state control over local affairs, then as an arm of mayoral power within the city government, and finally in the form most recently known through which it would balance citywide interests with those of the boroughs. While the history of the institution is intrinsically interesting, charting the functions and composition of the Board of Estimate over time also serves as a reliable barometer of the changing structure of power in city government throughout the last century.[3]

The Board of Estimate and Apportionment was created by the state legislature in 1864 for the specific purpose of assessing the expenses of the Metropolitan Police District that encompassed New York, Brooklyn, Westchester, and Richmond. It was composed of the police commissioners from the metropolitan district, all of whom were appointees of the governor, and the comptrollers from the cities of New York and Brooklyn, who were then popularly elected within their respective jurisdictions. The board was part of a larger state apparatus through which Republican politicians in Albany intervened in the affairs of Democratically controlled New York City.[4] As early as 1857, the state legislature enacted wide-ranging legislation in which the legislature took the power to appoint the heads of administrative departments in the city as part of a reformist campaign against municipal corruption. Although the Board of Estimate and Apportionment created in 1864 was unabashedly and unambiguously constituted as a state agency, it retained the authority to assess taxes from local jurisdictions to support the functioning of the special police district.

In 1870 the state legislature returned the power over administrative appointments to the municipality, where it was exercised by the mayor subject to the approval of the council. The Metropolitan Police District was abolished as well as the state-dominated Board of Estimate and Apportionment. A city charter approved in 1873 created a new board by the same name, but with broader responsibility to manage the city finances and a different composition. It included the mayor, the president of the Board of Taxes and Assessment, who was an appointee of the mayor, the comptroller, and the president of the Board of Aldermen. Although the latter two members were not chosen by the mayor, the creation of the new board and the conspicuous presence of the mayor and his appointee on it represented an important step in shifting the budgetary power of the city legislature to another local institution. In 1884 the pattern advanced further when the president of the Board of Aldermen, who was previously chosen by the local legislature, became popularly elected. In 1893 the corporation counsel, another appointee of the mayor, was added to the board, giving the chief executive decisive sway over three of its five votes. (Both the corporation counsel and the president of the Board of Taxes and Assessments had terms that exceeded the mayor's.)

The Greater City, 1898

The document drafted by the Charter Revision Commission of 1897 had two major impacts on the structure of New York. First and foremost, it led to the consolidation of the "Greater City" through the annexation of Brooklyn, western Queens, and Richmond (what was then the Bronx was already part of New York County).[5] Beyond that, it perpetuated and accelerated a form of governance characterized by an exceptionally strong mayor. Under the plan that took effect in 1898, the mayor continued to strongly influence three of five votes on the Board of Estimate and Apportionment, which prepared the budget for approval by a two-house Municipal Assembly. The local legislature had no power to add to the budget, and the board exercised final approval over expenditures. The board also had final discretion over franchises, debts, taxes, and assessments. It took a full five-sixths majority of both legislative houses to override a mayoral veto. The mayor was also the dominant member of the Board of Public Improvements, which approved all major public works projects in the city. In addition to his own seat, he appointed eight of its fifteen members. The other six members included the comptroller, who was popularly elected, and the five borough presidents, who were only permitted to vote on matters concerning their own boroughs.

For all practical purposes, the structure of the newly consolidated city did not provide an institutional mechanism for the representation of borough interests. While members of the Municipal Assembly could conceivably align their votes by borough, the large cumbersome legislature was ineffectual, and it was easily overshadowed by the mayor and the Board of Estimate and Apportionment that he controlled. The role of the borough presidents within this arrangement was minuscule. In addition to sitting on the Board of Public Improvements, the borough presidents chaired local boards that would consider proposals for public works within twenty-two neighborhood districts. A primitive form of community government, these bodies, composed of municipal legislators from their respective districts, were authorized to make recommendations to the Board of Public Improvements.

In 1900 Governor Theodore Roosevelt, urged by a coalition of fellow Republicans and Brooklyn Democrats to take action against the rampant corruption that had resulted from Tammany's control over city government, appointed a new charter commission. Within a year, a plan was devised that significantly reduced the power of the mayor and restructured the Board of Estimate and Apportionment to reflect borough constituencies. Removed from the board were the corporation counsel and the president of the Department of Taxes and Assessments, both appointees of the mayor. Remaining on the board were the mayor, the comptroller, and the president of the Board of Aldermen, all of whom were elected independently. Added to the board were the five borough presidents. A system of weighted voting allocated three votes to each of the citywide officials, two votes each to the borough presidents of Manhattan and Brooklyn, and one vote each to the presidents of the smaller boroughs of Queens, Richmond, and the Bronx.

In addition to providing the borough presidents with membership on the Board of Estimate and Apportionment, the charter enacted in 1901 granted these officials significant administrative authority over the construction and maintenance of public works within their respective boroughs. They continued to chair local boards whose role in the initiation of public projects grew with the abolition of the Board of Public Improvements. Final authority on public improvements was shared between the Board of Estimate and Apportionment and a unicameral Board of Aldermen.

In 1905, the Board of Estimate and Apportionment was given discretion over city franchises that was previously held by the mayor. In 1916, the board was granted the power to regulate zoning, thus instituting a significant role in the planning process for the board as a whole and its individual members. In 1924, an amendment to the Municipal Home Rule Law was enacted in Albany declaring the Board of Estimate and Apportionment the upper house of a bicameral Municipal Assembly composed of itself and the Board of Aldermen.

In 1935, a charter commission appointed by Mayor Fiorello LaGuardia and chaired by Judge Thomas Thatcher once again recast the shape of the municipality, this time swinging the pendulum back somewhat in the direction of mayoral power. Under the Thatcher Charter, preparation of the expense budget was transferred from the Board of Estimate to the mayor. The mayor also appointed six of the seven members of a new City Planning Commission that had initial jurisdiction over zoning changes and the preparation of the capital budget. The renamed Board of Estimate retained authority to override zoning changes and modify capital budget items. While the board was no longer considered a legislative body, it would still share authority to approve the expense budget with a city council. It also retained absolute jurisdiction over franchises.

In 1958, the original weighted voting scheme of the board was amended. All the borough presidents were given an equal number of votes (two), while the citywide officials were given four votes each.[6] In 1961, a charter commission appointed by Mayor Robert Wagner recommended the creation of two at-large council seats per borough in order to provide electoral opportunities for minority parties.[7] At Mayor Wagner's urging, the commission recommended the shift of the executive power the borough presidents had over public works to the mayor's office. The borough presidents assumed new responsibilities in the area of community government, appointing members to community planning boards. These latter reforms gave birth to a system of community government that came into full bloom in 1975 when community boards and borough boards assumed an advisory role in land use, budgeting, and service monitoring.[8]

The system of government that prevailed in New York during the 1980s was an anomaly among American municipalities, a clear reflection of the city's unique political history and culture. It allowed for three distinct levels of representation. First, there was a citywide perspective represented by the mayor, city council president, and comptroller. Then there was a borough dimension reflected by the borough presidents. And most recently there was a neighborhood perspective most clearly identified in the fifty-eight community boards. New York's was not a mayor-council form of government in the real sense of the term, for the balance traditionally struck between the executive and legislative branches had been disrupted by the existence of a powerful third body that functioned as a kind of board of directors. Composed of the city's chief executive, five borough executives, the city's chief financial officer, and the formally designated presiding officer of the city legislature (who is not chosen by the legislature, but by the voters), the Board of Estimate, in Sayre and Kaufman's words, "occupies the center of gravity in the city's political process."[9] At least it did until very recently.

One-Person, One-Vote

While the federal court decision handed down in November of 1986 shook the structure of New York government at its very foundations, it should have come as no surprise to city attorneys. Five years earlier, a federal district court ruled that the election of two at-large council members from boroughs with vastly different populations was in violation of the one-person, one-vote standard and thereby unconstitutional.[10] The decision was subsequently affirmed by a circuit Court of Appeals and the Supreme Court. In 1982, Mayor Koch appointed a charter commission chaired by Michael Sovern, the president of Columbia University, whose recommendations led to the elimination of the at-large council seats.

Given the unequivocal mandate issued by the federal judiciary on the topic of equal representation among the boroughs, it was only a matter of time until the Board of Estimate would be subject to a legal challenge. The population of Brooklyn is six times that of Staten Island, nevertheless each had an equal vote on the Board of Estimate. Since the population of Brooklyn is predominantly black and Latino (51 percent) and that of Staten Island is predominantly white (85 percent), the lawsuit initiated by the New York Civil Liberties Union on behalf of residents from the larger borough had serious racial implications.

There were some diehard supporters of the Board of Estimate, among whom the borough presidents were the most vocal, who actually convinced themselves that the Supreme Court would override the lower court decisions allowing the institution to remain intact. They had argued that since the board was not a legislative body, it would not be held to the same standard of representation as the council had been. For all practical purposes, the argument was irrelevant. No matter how the Board of Estimate was classified by the existing charter, it was an important policy-making body, and one that performed functions that were undeniably legislative. The legal realities of the situation motivated others in the board's camp to explore alternatives that would allow the Charter Commission to comply with the constitutional mandates but preserve the institution in another form.

The proposal that received most serious discussion in the early days of the Charter Commission's deliberations was weighted voting. According to this plan, the existing membership of the Board of Estimate would remain unchanged, but the votes of the borough presidents would be weighted by population.[11] This approach, however, presented another set of problems. Legal experts advising the commission warned that a weighted voting scheme might violate the provisions of the federal Voting Rights Act.[12] Consequently, there was a serious risk that such a proposal would not receive preclearance from the U.S. Department of Justice; even if the plan were adopted it would most surely generate another court challenge.

The Voting Rights Act requires that all American citizens be provided with "fair and effective representations." This is interpreted to mean that all racial and language minorities must enjoy an equal opportunity to participate in elections and to choose representatives of their choice. Attorneys for the commission identified two particular problems with regard to weighted voting that would dilute the effectiveness of minority voters: officials elected citywide (the mayor, city council president, and comptroller) would continue to control a majority of votes on the board, and each borough president would again serve as a single representative of a large and diverse district. These criticisms seemed to point the commission toward an alternative that would focus on the creation of a larger legislative body for which representatives would be chosen from smaller, more homogeneous districts.

Charter Revision, Phase I

The New York State Municipal Home Rule Law requires that, regardless of the specific reasons for its appointment, a Charter Commission should prepare proposals that reflect a general review of the entire charter. In this case, it would have been difficult to do otherwise, for tampering with the structure and powers of the Board of Estimate would have a practical impact on every other organ of government. It would not be an exaggeration to claim that, in February of 1987, the Ravitch Commission initiated the most comprehensive assessment of New York City government ever to have occurred. The commission recruited a staff of forty-three people and engaged outside consultants from universities and research organizations who prepared numerous reports on the institutions and processes of city government. Many of these documents included detailed discussions of policy options for consideration by the commission members. In April and May, the commission held six public hearings where it heard testimony from approximately 350 people, including present and former city officials, community representatives, spokespersons from organized interest groups, and private citizens.

By the end of February 1988, Ravitch had prepared a set of tentative proposals for consideration by the members that would redistribute the budgeting, contracting, and land use powers of the Board of Estimate to the mayor, city council, borough presidents, and comptroller. On April 4, he presented a plan to enlarge and restructure the city council. That same day, the U.S. Supreme Court agreed to consider an appeal submitted by the city to overturn the lower court rulings. At that point the entire strategy of the commission changed.

State law required the commission to place a set of propositions on the November 1988 ballot, when its mandate for operation would expire. In anticipation of a Supreme Court ruling on the legal viability of the Board of Estimate, the commission decided on April 14 to postpone developing any proposals on the board's functions and composition. Instead it would recommend to the voters amendments that did not change the structure of government. These larger issues of governance were left for a second charter commission appointed after November that hopefully would have the benefit of a final judicial decision before rewriting the charter.

The scaled-down agenda of the Ravitch Commission appeared on a November 1988 ballot in the form of five propositions concerning conflicts of interests of city officials, infrastructure maintenance planning by city agencies, administrative procedures in city government, mayoral incapacity and the filling of vacancies in elected offices, and campaign finance and voter assistance. On November 8, the day of the presidential election, the voters of New York City overwhelmingly approved the five propositions put before them.[13]

Phase II, A New Government

On December 14, 1988, one week after the U.S. Supreme Court began hearing oral arguments on the appeal of the *Morris* case, Mayor Koch appointed his former corporation counsel, Frederick A. O. Schwarz, Jr., to chair a new charter commission. Eleven individuals who had served with the Ravitch Commission were reappointed and joined by three new members.[14] The staff of the original commission, which had already conducted voluminous research, was left in place. There was a real irony to the situation: as city attorneys were defending the constitutionality of the Board of Estimate in the nation's highest court, the former head of the Law Department was developing a plan to replace this powerful body that had become a cornerstone of the municipal government.

Since all other tangential charter issues had been resolved by the outcome of the November referendum, the primary agenda of the Schwarz Commission was to determine how the powers of the Board of Estimate could be redistributed if the Supreme Court confirmed the lower court decisions. These powers were in four significant areas: promulgation and approval of the budget, planning and land use, awarding of contracts, and granting of franchises. The institutional changes had to be accomplished in such a way as to avoid any further constitutional conflicts or violations of the Federal Voting Rights Act. And, of course, the members of the Charter Commission had to confront the fundamental dilemma of governance faced by all those who have taken on the responsibility of writing a constitution in a free society: to design an effective system of checks and balances among the various branches of government without creating insurmountable impediments to the efficient operation of public business.[15]

On March 22, 1989, the Supreme Court ruled that the voting structure of the Board of Estimate violated the one-person, one-vote standard protected by the Fourteenth Amendment.[16] A month later, Schwarz presented a set of preliminary proposals to the commission that called for the elimination of the Board of Estimate and substantially restructured the municipal government. Over the next several months, the commission held ten public hearings and two public forums. It spent in excess of 200 hours listening to commentary from more than 800 people. The public discussions of proposals and counterproposals among commission members were often characterized by heated debate and conducted under the watchful eye of the news media. On June 27, the commission voted to revise the initial recommendations of the chairman; it approved a final set of proposals on August 2.

Incorporated within the final package were two significant strategic decisions. First, it was decided that, rather than delay the referendum until the 1990 election, which was legally permissible, the propositions would be put before the voters in November of 1989. This would coincide with the citywide municipal elections. The chairman and a majority of the commissioners were of the opinion that sufficient time and energy had been given to discussion and deliberation since the Ravitch Commission began to work in January of 1987. Moreover, they believed that a relatively large turnout expected for a highly competitive mayoral contest would assure maximum public participation on the charter referendum.

It was also determined that a predominant share of the powers held by the Board of Estimate would be transferred to an enlarged city council. This point went to the heart of the constitutional issue of equal representation and was designed to maximize the political efficacy of racial and language minorities throughout the city. Consistent with a substantial body of political science research, it was assumed that the creation of a larger legislative body with members chosen from smaller homogeneous districts would result in a city council containing a higher percentage of minority members.[17] This more representative body, it was hoped, would serve as a viable counterweight to a strong mayor who was elected by the majority of voters on an at-large basis.

The plan was to elect the council in 1989 for only a two-year term, rather than the usual four. Another council election would be held in 1991 after a redistricting commission had an opportunity to redraw district lines utilizing data from the 1990 census. At that time the size of the council would be expanded from thirty-five to fifty-one members elected from smaller districts. A preliminary analysis by the commission staff projected that approximately twenty seats (about 40 percent) would be won by minority legislators.

The recommendations developed by the Schwarz Commission were put to the voters on November 7, 1989, in the form of two propositions. The first proposal (Question 2) concerned the larger issues of governance: abolishing the Board of Estimate, enlarging the city council and enhancing its powers, redefining the roles of the borough presidents and council president, and establishing new procedures for awarding city contracts and monitoring equal employment practices. The second proposal (Question 3) focused on new processes relating to landmarks preservation: establishing an independent panel to hear appeals of decisions by the Landmarks Preservation Commission (LPC) transferring powers of the Board of Estimate to the city council regarding the approval or disapproval of the LPC's designations, making the LPC independent of the Parks Department, and requiring the City Planning Commission to hold public hearings on the designation of historic districts. A closely contested mayoral race between David Dinkins and Rudolph Giuliani led to one of the largest voting turnouts in recent history. While both propositions on the charter changes were approved by a majority of the electorate, the level of affirmation was significantly lower than that attained by the Ravitch Commission proposals a year earlier.[18]

The last step needed before the restructuring provided by the new charter could begin on January 1, 1990, was certification by the U.S. Department of Justice that the new structure was in conformance with the Voting Rights Act. That approval came quickly, in December 1989, only five weeks after the electoral success of the charter proposal.[19]

The Reallocation of Power

With the elimination of the Board of Estimate, the new design of the municipality is cast in the classic mold of executive-legislative balance or, as it is defined at the local level, a mayor-council form of government. Thus, while the mayor has authority to propose the city budget to the council and to veto its actions, the council can override a veto with a two-thirds majority and has the sole power to approve or modify the budget.

Under the new charter, the council assumes the land use powers formerly held by the Board of Estimate, allowing it to review all zoning decisions made by the City Planning Commission and functioning as the final decision maker on such questions. The former seven-member City Planning Commission has been replaced by a thirteen-person body. Seven members of this new commission, including the chair, are appointed by the mayor, five by the borough presidents (one per borough), and one by the president of the city council. All zoning changes, housing plans, urban renewal projects, urban development proposals, and most dispositions of city-owned property approved by the City Planning Commission are automatically reviewed by the city council. The council also may review commission actions on city capital projects, special zoning permits, map changes, and dispositions of city-owned nonresidential property if either the affected borough president and community board object to the action, or if a majority of the council members vote to do so. The council's power over city capital projects is further enhanced by its ability to reject items in the capital budget. The mayor may veto any action taken by the council regarding land use, but this veto can be overturned by a two-thirds majority.

The city council determines the kinds of franchises to be solicited by the city, as well as the terms, conditions, and procedural requirements to be followed. The administrative task of selecting franchises and negotiating contracts is now assigned to the department responsible for that policy area.[20] All franchise agreements are subject to final review and approval by the mayor and a Franchise and Concession Review Committee. The panel is composed of one representative each of the corporation counsel and the director of the Office of Management and Budget, two representatives of the mayor, the comptroller, and the affected borough president or presidents. Under its legislative power, the council is authorized to approve a new and detailed contract budget for procurement. Thereafter, city agencies are permitted to implement contracts in accordance with rules promulgated by a new Procurement Policy Board. Three appointees of the mayor and two appointees of the comptroller sit on the board.

Given the far-reaching reallocation of power under the new charter, the obvious questions on the minds of most observers are those that define the fundamental stakes of the political process: Who won? Who lost? From an institutional perspective, the clear winner is the city council. For the first time in more than a century, the council does not share its important budget-making functions with the Board of Estimate. It serves in an unambiguous and uncompromised way as the legislative body of the city. The council also has powers over land use previously held by the Board of Estimate, that will allow it to review and reverse actions taken by the City Planning Commission. The city council enjoys new prerogatives with regard to franchises and contracts. While the administrative details of these processes are delegated to executive agencies, the council has the opportunity to set policy, establish standards, and define the process through which franchises and contracts are awarded.

In attempting to determine who the losers are in this vast restructuring of the municipal government, the instinctive response is to look to those public officials who once sat on the Board of Estimate. For the most part that is correct, except that not all members suffered the same degree of political damage. The greatest losses were suffered by the borough presidents, whose traditional base of power in the political process was their membership on the Board of Estimate. For this significant loss, the new charter gave them very little in return. Under the new plan, the borough presidents collectively appoint five members of a thirteen-member City Planning Commission, they may introduce legislation in the council, and they can allocate 5 percent of the capital budget and 5 percent of the nonmandated increases in the expense budget. All in all, it is a poor exchange from the perspective of borough hall.

Next on the list of casualties, but in very different respects, are the comptroller and the city council president. Although the comptroller lost significant prerogatives enjoyed as a member of the Board of Estimate, she, unlike the borough presidents and council president, still retains a meaningful role in the government. As the chief fiscal officer of the city, the comptroller has the responsibility to conduct financial and performance audits, prepares reports on the city's economy and finances, and is empowered to stop agencies from entering into contracts if there is reason to believe that corrupt practices were involved in the award process. The comptroller also sits on the committee that awards city franchises and is a member of the Procurement Policy Board that establishes contracting standards for agencies.

The outcome with regard to the council president is another matter. The only new role of any importance he assumes under the charter is to appoint one member of the City Planning Commission. His loss of membership on the Board of Estimate leaves the council president with little to do that is of significance within the new governmental system. It is a position of official incapacity, which leads one to wonder why its existence was preserved in the new charter. Its preservation is particularly perplexing within a plan of government designed to increase the power of the local legislature, which ordinarily should be entitled to choose its own presiding officer.

It is too soon to assess how the mayor will fare under the new charter. True, he is no longer a member of the powerful Board of Estimate. However, the board has not been his to control for some time, and it very often served as a check on his substantial power as the city's chief executive. In the new government, the mayor appoints a mere majority (seven of thirteen) of the City Planning Commission, rather than its full membership as previously. And the power of that body is greatly weakened by the fact that the city council can override its actions.

In the final analysis, the key determinant of mayoral power in New York will be the way the council chooses to respond to its newly defined constitutional role. Historical precedents do not favor the prospects of a strong legislative body in New York. However, this pattern can be largely explained by the existence of a powerful Board of Estimate with which the council was required to share responsibility. If the council is to emerge as a real center of power in the city, then it must develop a strong leadership structure that exercises its recently gained prerogatives in a meaningful way. Only then will it be able to serve as an effective rival to a highly visible chief executive, who controls the daily machinery of city government and is the chosen leader of a majority of voters. That all remains to be seen.

Conclusion: The Charter, A Matter of Style

There is little doubt that the monumental task the Ravitch and Schwarz commissions set out to accomplish was carried out with great diligence. Few other American cities have ever been placed under such comprehensive and probing scrutiny. The entire drama was played in broad daylight with widespread citizen participation, healthy dialogue, and uncommon intelligence. One never got the impression that the desire to maximize public involvement had succumbed to the ordinary political hazards of parochial self-interest. The immediate goal, dismantling an institution found to be inconsistent with the principles of democratic statehood, was achieved. The peculiar three-headed government that was once New York's has been replaced by a municipality conceived in the classic mayor-council form.

As Montesquieu taught us more than two centuries ago, a constitution is more than the legal anatomy of a government. It represents the "spirit" of a people and should reflect the history, traditions, and values of those it is to govern. New York has a very rich political culture. Unfortunately, it is not entirely captured in the new charter. Nobody committed to the principles of democracy takes issue with the concept of one-person, one-vote as an underlying governmental ideal. However, there are a variety of institutional mechanisms through which that ideal can be achieved. The unique political character of New York requires a complex institutional framework that allows for three levels of representation: citywide, borough, and community. New Yorkers identify themselves as citizens of a city, residents of a borough, and members of a community. All are important, and each defines a distinct political constituency.

The citywide perspective is epitomized in the office of the mayor, that most visible of public figures, elected by a majority of voters, who, more than anyone else, serves as spokesperson for the municipality. The role is important because a government needs an institutional mechanism to overcome parochial interests that sometimes stand in the way of the common good. In no arena of local government policy making is this dilemma of representative government so disturbing as in land use, where the NIMBY ("not in my backyard!") phenomenon has often prevented programs with merit from reaching fruition. One significant problem with the new charter is that it considerably weakens the influence of the mayor on land use, and places unlimited power in the hands of the city council where a system of reciprocal parochialism is likely to rule the day. Will it ever be possible to find an acceptable site for a jail, drug treatment center, or garbage disposal facility in New York again?

This is not to suggest that the mayoralty is a weak office under the new charter. The mayor still appoints department heads, drafts the executive budget, and, perhaps more than before, makes important decisions with regard to franchises and contracts. This is as it should be, because it is the mayor, as chief executive, who is responsible for the daily workings of the multibillion dollar corporation that delivers essential services to millions of people throughout the five boroughs. As all managers of large organizations, he must be given adequate discretion to get the job done efficiently and effectively.

Since the mayor is a creature of majoritarian politics, sometimes he does not adequately represent the will of certain minorities. It is for this reason that the legislative branch plays such a crucial role in a democratic system. While collectively the legislature expresses a majority perspective, its stance is tempered by compromise, since the legislative body has the greatest capacity among democratic institutions to serve as a forum for diverse minority constituents. For this reason, the inclination of the charter commission to bolster the council was sound, the decision to increase its size constructive. But the final structure arrived at after all the discussion is severely inadequate.

The inadequacy concerns the important role that a local legislative body can play, as a mechanism through which the representatives of distinct communities can influence the policy-making process. One of the more striking features of the "community revolution" that swept New York and other cities during the 1960s is that its advocates, in New York at least, failed to recognize the historical connection between neighborhood government and councilmanic politics. There are reasonable explanations for this failure. To begin with, the community government movement grew out of a fundamental mistrust of traditional institutions, and the council was certainly a product of conventional political accommodations. Moreover, with a strong mayor and a powerful Board of Estimate, there was not much at stake in councilmanic politics, and thus not much to attract the 1960s activists in search of structural reforms.

If the intentions of the charter commission are borne out, the stakes in councilmanic politics will be much higher in the 1990s. Neighborhood government in the form of community boards has already become an important aspect of the local political process. The system that emerged from the 1975 charter granted community boards important advisory and consultative powers in budgeting, land use, and service monitoring. However, the boundaries of service districts do not coincide with those of the council. One of the fundamental goals of community government is to create a microcosm of the larger system at the neighborhood level, so that services can be coordinated and citizens will achieve greater efficacy in dealing with small self-sufficient units. Given an opportunity to develop service and capital budgets on a district level, community government is supposed to provide a channel through which neighborhood activists make their needs known to decision makers.

In reality, New York has three structures of neighborhood government, one defined by community service districts, one defined by local school districts, and one defined by councilmanic districts, none of which are coterminous. The managerial outcome is the existence of two separate service delivery systems, one municipal, the other educational, that are difficult, if not impossible to integrate and coordinate.[21] The political consequence is that service districts lack a single representative who can advocate their interests in the council. The charter commission chose not to tamper with this tripartite network of neighborhood institutions, and thus missed an important opportunity to develop a more effective system of community government.

The most significant flaw in the government created by the new charter concerns borough representation. The new structure simply does not provide an effective vehicle through which borough constituencies can articulate their interests. Preoccupied with rectifying the constitutional foibles of the Board of Estimate, the new charter reduces the borough presidents to mere figureheads, but puts nothing in their place to fill the vacuum. By focusing its attention on what to do with the borough presidents, the commission gave insufficient consideration to alternative mechanisms for borough representation that would comply with constitutional standards. One possibility, dismissed without serious consideration during the Schwarz Commission deliberations, is a bicameral legislature, with a second, smaller house whose members were elected on a district, rather than an at-large basis (to comply with the Voting Rights Act).[22] As nonvoting members of the smaller house, borough presidents could have led borough delegations apportioned on the basis of population, remaining in full compliance with constitutional standards. While bicameralism is not a standard feature of contemporary local government in the United States, it has a longstanding tradition within New York's unique political setting.

The attorneys who represented the plaintiffs in the constitutional challenge to the Board of Estimate presumed that there were no real or legitimate boroughwide constituencies. Charter commission members apparently agreed. This position ignores nearly a century of local political history, beginning with consolidation, in which the outer boroughs had to struggle to get their fair share of the governmental and economic pie. Commission members did not appreciate the traditional, historical, and political significance New Yorkers, particularly those living outside of Manhattan, attach to the borough. It is that kind of custom that gives New York a unique political culture, that gives meaning to the phrase "New York Style." And some of those deep-seated political values are missing in the new charter.

Notes

1. *Morris* v. *Board of Estimate* (647 F. Supp. 1463), 1986.
2. In addition to Mr. Ravitch, other members of the commission were Harriet Michel, vice-chair; Nathan Leventhal, secretary; Aida Alvarez; Amalia V. Betanzos; Fred W. Friendly; Judah Gribetz; Frank J. Macchiarola; Therese M. Molloy; Patrick J. Murphy; Archibald R. Murray; John A. O'Hare; W. Bernard Richland; David G. Trager; and Robert F. Wagner.
3. For a more detailed analysis of this history see Joseph P. Viteritti, "The Tradition of Municipal Reform: Charter Revision in Historical Context," in Frank Mauro and Gerald Benjamin, editors, *Restructuring The New York City Government*. New York: Academy of Political Science, 1989. For a history of the Board of Estimate and New York City's other financial institutions see Edward Dana Durand, *The Finances of New York City*. New York: Macmillan, 1898.
4. For an analysis of the role and significance of the Metropolitan Police District, see James F. Richardson, *The New York Police: Colonial Times to 1901*. New York: Oxford University Press, 1970, pp. 82–164. For a historical discussion of state-city relations, see Chapter 8 in this volume and Gerald Benjamin, "The Political Relationship," in Gerald Benjamin and Charles Brecher, editors, *The Two New Yorks*. New York: Russell Sage Foundation, 1988.
5. For an account of the consolidation debate see David C. Hammack, *Power and Society: Greater New York at the Turn of the Century*. New York: Russell Sage Foundation, 1982, pp. 185–229.
6. This system would be revised again in 1978, when each citywide official was given two votes and each borough president one.
7. Each party was prohibited from nominating more than one at-large council candidate per borough.
8. For an analysis and evaluation of the evolution of community government in New York City see Joseph P. Viteritti and Robert F. Pecorella, "Community Government and the Decentralization of Services." Report prepared for the New York City Charter Revision Commission, Urban Research Center of New York University, 1988.
9. Wallace S. Sayre and Herbert Kaufman, *Governing New York City*. New York: Russell Sage Foundation, 1960, p. 262.
10. *Andrews* v. *Koch* (528 F Supp. 246), 1981.
11. Based on the relative populations of each borough, votes would have been allocated as follows: Brooklyn, six; Queens, five; Manhattan, four; the Bronx, three; Staten Island, one.
12. See M. David Gelfand and Terry E. Allbritton, "Voting Rights and the Board of Estimate," in Frank Mauro and Gerald Benjamin, editors, *Restructuring the New York City Government*.
13. The range of positive responses ran from 79.8 to 88.9 percent.
14. Simon P. Gourdine, Mario J. Paredes, and Joseph M. Sullivan replaced Frank J. Macchiarola, Joseph O' Hare, and Robert F. Wagner.
15. See Joseph P. Viteritti and Louis Koenig, "Adapting the Federal Model: The

428 JOSEPH P. VITERITTI

Application of Separation of Powers and Checks and Balances to Local Government."
Report prepared for the New York City Charter Commission, Urban Research Center of
New York University, 1988.

16. *Morris* v. *Board of Estimate*, 109 S. Ct. 1433 (1989).

17. See Susan Welch and Timothy Bledsoe, *Urban Reform and its Consequences*.
Chicago: University of Chicago Press, 1988; Timothy Bledsoe, "A Research Note on the
Impact of District/At-Large Elections on Black Political Efficacy," *Urban Affairs Quarterly* 22 (1986): 166–74; Richard Engstrom and Michael D. McDonald, "The Election of
Blacks to City Councils: Clarifying the Impact of Electoral Arrangements on the
Seats/Population Relationships," *American Political Science Review* 75 (1981): 344–54.

18. Question 2 was approved by 54.6 percent of the voters, and Question 3 by 54.2
percent.

19. *New York Times*, December 14, 1989, p. A1.

20. Previously these functions were handled by a Bureau of Franchises that was an
arm of the Board of Estimate.

21. See Joseph P. Viteritti, *Across the River: Politics and Education in the City*. New
York: Holmes and Meier, 1983, pp. 307–27.

22. See Joseph P. Viteritti, Jewel Bellush, and Dick Netzer, "The Washington Square
Proposal: A Bicameral Legislature for New York City." Urban Research Center of New
York University, April 10, 1989.

A Thirty-Year Chronology
of Events

In the chapters of this book, the key political, social, intellectual, and economic events of the years from the late 1950s through 1989—which are the setting for the analysis of New York City politics and government—are mentioned and sometimes described at length. For the reader's convenience, the following chronology is provided, organized under three headings: events in national politics and nationwide changes and movements; events at the state government level; and events that were specific to New York City.

National Events

The decade of the 1960s	Blacks, other minorities, and women campaign vigorously for civil rights and economic advancement. College students are active in those campaigns, and in the movement against the Vietnam War.
	Congress greatly broadens the scope of civil rights laws and creates major new antipoverty and other social programs.
February 1960	Four young black students from North Carolina Agricultural and Technical College, Greensboro, North Carolina, begin a sit-in movement at Woolworth's lunch counter, to demand that blacks be served.
November 1960	Massachusetts Senator John F. Kennedy elected President.
1961	SNCC campaign to register blacks is begun in Mississippi. Campaign workers are jailed.
Spring 1961	Founding of Student Nonviolent Coordinating Committee (SNCC), students' own organization for black civil rights.

Summer 1961	Freedom Riders—black and white students test the Supreme Court decision that was to end segregated bus terminals—confrontations with southern mobs, violence, jailings.

Fall 1961   Albany, Georgia—SNCC leaders press for integrating the bus station and other public places. "We Shall Overcome" becomes the movement's anthem. Jailings.

1962   James Meredith, black applicant, denied admission to the University of Mississippi by Governor Ross Barnett. President Kennedy sends federal marshals—confrontation, violence. Two die, but Meredith is registered.

Publication of Michael Harrington's *The Other America*, a dramatic portrait of the nation's poor, made invisible by affluence and suburbanization.

The Kennedy administration is pressed by massive demonstrations of civil rights groups, in Washington and in other cities.

March 1962   *Baker* v. *Carr*—Supreme Court decision, requiring that state and local legislative bodies be districted so that there is "one person, one vote."

June 1962   Students for a Democratic Society (SDS) founded.

1963   Publication of *Beyond the Melting Pot*, by Glazer and Moynihan, which highlighted the limits to ethnic and racial assimilation in American urban life.

Riots, beatings by whites and police, maltreatment by officials mark civil rights demonstration in Birmingham, Alabama. Arrest of the Rev. Martin Luther King, Jr. President Kennedy calls out 3,000 troops. Birmingham police chief "Bull" Connor's police dogs and fire hoses galvanize the national mood—including the White House. June 1963 radio address by the president.

Publication of Betty Friedan's *The Feminine Mystique*, helps stimulate the feminist movement.

Medgar Evers, state desegregation leader, is shot in Jackson, Mississippi.

August 1963	Washington—250,000 "Freedom Marchers" (blacks and whites) descend on the city to demonstrate. Rev. King's "I have a dream . . ." speech.
November 1963	President Kennedy is assassinated in Dallas, Texas.
1964	The first of the major pieces of social legislation of the 1960s passes, the Economic Opportunity Act, providing programs designed to attack the causes of poverty, like illiteracy, unemployment, and inadequate public services.
	Civil rights marches and protests continue in South. Rev. King is awarded the Nobel Peace Prize.
July 1964	Civil Rights Act is signed by President Lyndon B. Johnson. The act outlaws discrimination in public accommodation facilities, including schools, and in employment; and broadens the guarantee of voting rights.
October 1964	The beginning of the era of student unrest, with the birth of the Free Speech Movement at the University of California in Berkeley.
November 1964	In a landslide, the voters reelect President Johnson and a Democratic-controlled Congress.
1965	Selma, Alabama—outbreaks of violence; Rev. King heads a procession of 4,000 civil rights demonstrators from Selma to the state capital at Montgomery to deliver petition. The Ku Klux Klan shoots at marchers.
August 1965	Severe race riots in Watts district of Los Angeles result in 35 dead, 4,000 arrested and $40 million in property damage.
1965–68	Years of racial riots in ghettos of large cities: Los Angeles, Chicago, Newark, Detroit, and others.
	President Johnson's ambitious domestic legislative program is adopted by Congress, including new federal aid to elementary and secondary education; creation of the Medicare and Medicaid programs; the Model Cities program to help cities plan and execute coordinated physical and social programs in slum and blighted areas; broad new housing programs; the Voting Rights Act of 1968; new forms of federal assistance to higher education; basic reform of the immigration laws; new water and air quality laws; and the Omnibus Crime Control and Safe Streets Act of 1968.

1965–68	Vietnam War dissenters demonstrate around the country, often led by the Rev. Martin Luther King and other civil rights leaders. For example, in April 1967, 250,000 assemble in Central Park and march to the United Nations to hear Rev. King, Dr. Spock, and Stokely Carmichael, new head of SNCC. Other large demonstrations in 1967 occur at the Pentagon and the Lincoln Memorial, and in New York and San Francisco.
1966	Under Stokely Carmichael's leadership, the SNCC and other civil rights organizations adopt "Black Power" as their new rallying cry, indicating a shift away from the traditional white-black alliance for civil rights.
1967	Riots in the black ghettos of Cleveland, Newark, and Detroit.
March 1968	Publication of the report of the National Advisory Commission on Civil Disorders (known as the Kerner Commission), warning of the division of the country into two societies, one the poor blacks and other minorities in the central cities.
	Senator Robert F. Kennedy declares his candidacy for the Democratic nomination for president, on an anti-war platform.
	President Johnson announces that he will not run for reelection.
April 1968	Rev. Martin Luther King, Jr., is assassinated in Memphis, Tennessee.
April–May 1968	Columbia University demonstration and sit-in, with three issues joined—civil rights, protest over the war, and student power.
June 1968	Senator Robert Kennedy is assassinated in Los Angeles after winning the California Democratic primary, over Senator Eugene McCarthy.
August 1968	Democratic National Convention in Chicago, marked by demonstration, riots, and police brutality outside the convention hall. Vice-President Hubert Humphrey wins the nomination.

November 1968	Former Vice-President (1953–61) Richard Nixon elected president.
1969	Hundreds of thousands in several U.S. cities demonstrate against the war in Vietnam.
The decade of the 1970s	Although the country has conservative presidents, most of the social programs begun in the 1960s continue to expand, and new programs are enacted. Federal aid to cities grows very rapidly, until 1979, under both Republican and Democratic administrations.
Spring 1970	The war escalates, with U.S. ground forces invading Cambodia. Widespread student and other protests. At Kent State University in Ohio, four students are killed by the National Guard. This triggers a new nationwide wave of protests and student occupations of buildings.
1971	The Supreme Court unanimously decides that school busing may be ordered for racial desegregation.
	Nixon orders ninety-day freeze on wages and prices to curb inflation.
	The 26th Amendment to the U.S. Constitution, giving 18-year-olds the right to vote, is ratified.
1972	Active U.S. participation in the Vietnam War declines. At year's end, fewer than 24,000 U.S. troops remain in Vietnam and, by January 1973, the active U.S. role ends.
	During the election campaign, Washington, D.C. police arrest five persons breaking into the headquarters of the Democratic National Committee in the Watergate complex. Thus begins the affair known to history as "Watergate."
February 1972	President Nixon goes to China, opening relations with mainland China for the first time since 1949.
November 1972	Nixon is reelected in a near-record landslide. The Democrats win control of both houses of Congress.
1972–73	Vice-President Agnew resigns, after scandals connected with his days as governor in Maryland unfold. Gerald Ford, the Republican leader in the House of Representatives, is named by Nixon to replace Agnew.

1973   The Supreme Court decides the landmark case of *Roe* v.
                    Wade, limiting the power of the states to restrict abortions.

Late 1973   In the wake of war in the Middle East, the Arab oil-
                    producing states declare an embargo on oil exports to the
                    United States. The Organization of Petroleum Exporting
                    Countries (OPEC) announces a fivefold increase in oil
                    prices, thus beginning an era of concern about energy
                    supplies and costs. The oil price increase triggers the
                    worst recession in the United States since 1937, begin-
                    ning in late 1974.

1973–74   Congressional investigations of the Watergate affair are
                    launched and culminate with the House of Representatives
                    beginning the process of impeaching the president.

August 1974   President Nixon resigns. Vice-President Gerald Ford suc-
                    ceeds him, and appoints former New York Governor Nel-
                    son Rockefeller as Vice-President.

1975–76   New York City fiscal crisis. In Washington, there is ini-
                    tial opposition to any federal government intervention in
                    the White House, the Treasury Department, and on Capi-
                    tol Hill. In November 1975, President Ford changes his
                    position, and in December Congress authorizes a pro-
                    gram of seasonal loans to New York City over the next
                    three years.

November 1976   Jimmy Carter, a former governor of Georgia but outsider to
                    the Washington establishment, narrowly defeats President
                    Ford in the general election, after having swept to the Dem-
                    ocratic nomination easily.

1977   Tom Bradley, a black Democrat, is elected mayor of Los
                    Angeles.

June 1978   California voters, in a referendum, approve Proposition 13
                    which amends the state constitution to reduce property
                    taxes by more than 60 percent. This was followed by more
                    tax-cutting referenda in California and in other states, be-
                    coming known as the "taxpayers' revolt," and indicating a
                    more conservative mood in the country generally.

1979	The Shah is overthrown in Iran; U.S. citizens are held hostage in the American Embassy in Teheran until January 1981. Iran's oil exports fall, providing OPEC with a pretext for doubling oil prices. Gasoline shortages and long lines at gas stations in the United States, and acceleration of worldwide inflation.
The decade of the 1980s	The Reagan years: A conservative period dominated by efforts to reduce the size and scope of domestic government, by privatizing the provision of public services, deregulating private industry, reducing taxes, and cutting government spending for domestic programs (while increasing defense outlays sharply).
November 1980	Ronald Reagan, former governor of California, easily defeats Jimmy Carter for the presidency.
1981	Reagan's first budget is a smashing political success. In a single bill, Congress agrees to eliminate numerous programs and heavily cut many others, with especially heavy cuts in aid to state and local governments, cuts that continue throughout the Reagan years. A companion bill provides for very large cuts in income tax rates.
August 1981	Federal air traffic controllers go on strike and President Reagan fires all the strikers, setting a new hard tone in labor relations for both the public and private sectors.
1981–82	The Federal Reserve's successful effort to end inflation by monetary stringency leads to an even more severe recession than in 1974–75. This time, unlike earlier recessions, the federal government takes no explicit action to counter the recession.
Mid-1980s	The large federal tax cuts have led to record federal budget deficits and record deficits in the balance of international trade. The United States becomes a debtor nation, for the first time in this century.
1986	President Reagan proposes and the Congress enacts a radical reform of the federal income tax, in which hundreds of special "tax preferences" are eliminated, to yield lower tax rates and a less complex structure. This reform is widely emulated at the state and local government level.

Late 1980s The longest unbroken economic upsurge on record (from the recession of 1982) is accompanied by increasing concern about the loss of U.S. competitiveness in the world economy and about increasingly dramatic domestic social problems, including drugs and crime, homelessness, AIDS, and poor educational attainment. The huge budget deficits, which the president and Congress seem unable to reduce significantly, handicap efforts to deal with both the social and economic problems.

1987 The conservative political mood abates. The Senate refuses to confirm the president's nomination of Robert Bork, a brilliant and outspokenly conservative legal scholar, to the Supreme Court. Increasing concern about the deterioration of the nation's infrastructure leads to increased appropriations for this purpose, with one of the major bills vetoed by Reagan. The veto was easily overridden, for the first time in the Reagan years.

October 1987 Huge drop in stock prices on Wall Street on "Black Monday," a steeper decline than in the great crash of 1929. No immediate economic repercussions, but over the next two years there are increasing signs of weakness in the nation's financial institutions.

November 1988 Vice President George Bush elected president, defeating the Democratic nominee, Governor Michael Dukakis of Massachusetts.

1988–89 Sweeping movement toward democracy and away from socialist economies in the Soviet Union and elsewhere in Eastern Europe indicates the end of the 40-year-old Cold War, and the possibility of major changes in U.S. budget and policy priorities in the 1990s.

State Events

November 1958 Nelson A. Rockefeller is elected governor. On taking office, Rockefeller begins a succession of major new policy initiatives, that included—in his first term—major new agencies to finance private housing construction, expansion of the State University, development of a nuclear industry in New York, creation of the New York State Council on the Arts, state intervention to rescue the faltering commuter railroads, and (by agreement with the governor of New Jersey) new roles for the Port Authority of New York and New Jersey, including construction of the World Trade Center.

The decade of the 1960s	The state government under Rockefeller's leadership continues to undertake new roles. The state budget grows rapidly, and state taxes increase virtually every year.
1962	The Conservative party is organized to oppose the "liberalism" of the state's Republican party.
November 1962	Rockefeller is reelected governor.
1963–66	Major initiatives of Rockefeller's second term include the construction of monumental state buildings in the South Mall Complex in Albany, the launching of a Pure Waters Program under which the state paid for most of the nonfederal costs of water pollution control projects, and the adoption of a comprehensive anti-drugs program.
November 1966	Rockefeller is reelected governor.
1967	The state government's role in the financing, operation and control of transportation in the state is radically transformed. A state Department of Transportation is established, assuming functions previously scattered among several agencies. In the downstate metropolitan region, the Metropolitan Transportation Authority is created, combining separate rail, bus, and highway agencies in a single unit under state control. A $2.5 billion bond issue—the first of several—to finance major improvements in transportation facilities throughout the state is approved by the voters.
	Passage of the Taylor Law which governs public employee labor relations in the public sector in New York State. The law establishes procedures for union representation and collective bargaining, and provides for neutral administration. Public service strikes are illegal, with heavy penalties.
	Rockefeller outlines an expanded health program. The following year, hospitals and nursing homes are given access to state agency bond financing. In the fifteen years of Rockefeller's administration (January 1959–December 1973), the state financed twenty-three new state mental health facilities and construction and expansion of 109 voluntary and municipal hospitals and nursing homes. Per capita state and local government expenditures for health were far higher than in any other state.

1968   The legislature enacts a program of aid (known as Bundy aid) to private colleges and universities.

                        Creation of the Urban Development Corporation to plan, finance, and construct housing and community facilities, new towns, and business facilities, using borrowed money backed by federal and state subsidies and largely free from local land use controls.

November 1970   Rockefeller is elected to a fourth term as governor.

1971–73   Protection of the environment becomes a major focus for the Rockefeller administration. State environmental agencies are reorganized and given additional powers and duties. A series of bills protecting the Adirondacks is enacted.

                        Crime and the criminal justice system are another major focus. In September 1971, a riot at the state prison at Attica is put down with considerable loss of life. Rockefeller establishes the McKay Commission to study the causes and actions; other temporary commissions and task forces are set up to study the state court system and other aspects of the crime and criminal justice problems. A new Narcotic Addiction Control Program providing severe penalties is enacted.

                        Rockefeller initiatives are made in other areas, including welfare reform and urban redevelopment, including the creation of the Battery Park City Authority.

December 1973   Governor Rockefeller resigns to head a Commission on Critical Choices. He is succeeded by Lt. Governor Malcolm Wilson.

November 1974   U.S. Representative Hugh Carey is elected governor, defeating Malcolm Wilson.

Late 1974   A national credit crunch, deepening recession (especially in the Northeast) and New York City's increasingly obvious fiscal problems combine to threaten the credit standing of various state financing agencies. The Urban Development Corporation is on the edge of defaulting on its debt obligations.

1975	Governor Carey takes the initiative in rescuing New York City from bankruptcy. In June, the Municipal Assistance Corporation is created; in September, the state takes formal control over city finances with the passage of the Financial Emergency Act and creation of the Emergency Financial Control Board and the Office of the Special Deputy Comptroller for New York City. State financing agencies, especially the Urban Development Corporation, are reorganized. The state takes financial responsibility for the senior colleges of the City University and for other functions, from the city.
1976	After years of increasing taxes, the first of a series of major reductions in state personal and corporate income taxes is begun.
1978	Carey is reelected governor, with Mario Cuomo as Lt. Governor.
1979–82	The state continues to closely monitor the finances of the city. Improving economic conditions and revenues permit expansion of state services in numerous directions, after the cutbacks of the previous years.
November 1982	Mario Cuomo is elected governor after defeating Mayor Edward Koch in the Democratic primary.
1983–86	Cuomo's first term begins in the face of a large state budget deficit, in part a result of a national economic recession. With economic recovery, the state is able to finance substantial improvements in health and social services and major investments in infrastructure and the environment.
November 1986	Cuomo is reelected governor.
1987	In the wake of scandals in New York City government and in the state legislature, Governor Cuomo creates a statewide panel with subpoena powers to probe unethical acts by public officials.
January 1987	Cuomo, in his State of the State address, calls for a slower growth rate in spending and a large tax cut. In the course of the 1987 legislative session, one of the most contentious in years, a major tax cut, the third since 1976, is enacted (largely following the design proposed by the Assembly leadership, rather than the governor); but substantial increases in spending for welfare and school aid are also approved.

1987–88   The state government continues to launch new initiatives in various areas, including economic development, the war on drugs, and health care, with rising spending, despite a slower rate of growth of the state economy and the reduction in revenues related to the 1987 tax cut.

1989   Balancing the state budget becomes a major preoccupation, with considerable debate about postponing the last stage of the 1987 tax cut.

New York City Events

1961   Robert F. Wagner is elected to a third term as mayor, after a campaign in which Wagner had been opposed by the Democratic county leaders and the popular Democratic state comptroller in the primary and the popular Republican state attorney general in the general election.

Early 1960s   Increase of unionization of municipal employees, under a mayor in favor of collective bargaining and generally sympathetic to unions.

1964   Birth of the "welfare rights" movement in New York City, with activists campaigning and taking legal action to expand the entitlements of actual or potential welfare recipients. By 1965, more than 500,000 people are on welfare in New York.

June 1964   Responding to civic concerns about frequent tax increases and the increasing use of what became known as "fiscal gimmicks" to balance the budget, the mayor and council create a blue-ribbon Temporary Commission on City Finances. In a series of reports over the next two years, the commission highlights the city's fiscal problems, predicts that they will worsen, and prescribes some major reforms; a number of the most important ones are enacted in 1966 and 1967.

1964 and 1965   Despite a buoyant local and national economy and increasing state and federal aid to New York, permitting the expansion of programs, dissension and unease about racial and other social problems and about fiscal issues increases. In July 1964, race riots occur in Harlem and, in February 1965, Malcolm X, charismatic Black Muslim leader and founder of the Organization of Afro-American Unity, is assassinated.

1965   Welfare caseworkers and supervisors win a strike, leading a change in collective bargaining rules. Bargaining is extended beyond wages and hours, to cover conditions of work and other personnel matters.

District Council 37, American Federation of State, County and Municipal Employees, wins a representation election for the municipal hospital system, giving it a majority of all city employees. A new militancy results.

The *Herald Tribune*, one of the city's three morning newspapers, runs a heavily advertised series on the "City in Crisis," dramatizing the problems confronting New York and contributing to the sense that a new face in city government is needed.

November 1965   The city's vulnerability is shown by a major power failure that blacked out the entire northeastern United States for twenty-four hours or more, the first time in history that New York City experienced a citywide blackout.

U.S. Representative John V. Lindsay is elected mayor, on the Republican and Liberal Party lines.

January 1966   As Mayor Lindsay takes office, the subways and buses are shut down by a strike by transit workers, the first since the system came under public auspices. This is Lindsay's first confrontation with the unions, and his first failure in those confrontations.

1966   When Mayor Lindsay takes office, the civil rights movement is at its zenith and there is a sense of "crisis" in race relations. In 1966, Lindsay establishes an Urban Action Task Force in response to first disturbances he encountered, and walked the streets in that and succeeding summers; unlike other cities, there are no major race riots in New York. To deal with charges of police brutality, Lindsay proposes the establishment of a civilian review board; in a referendum placed on the ballot after a campaign by the police union, the proposal is defeated overwhelmingly.

1966–67   Mayor Lindsay proposes substantial reorganization of the structure of city government, and major tax reforms. Most of them are implemented, although some that require state legislation are defeated by a combination of lack of support from the governor and active opposition in the state legislature and city council.

1967–68

Mayor Lindsay's program to deal with the problems of minorities and the ghettos includes the creation of three school districts to experiment with decentralization and community control; aggressive use of federal funds for housing and renewal, especially under the Model Cities program that focussed on three "target" neighborhoods; expansion of minority enrollment at the City University under the "open enrollment" program; and acquiescence in many of the demands of the welfare rights movement. Lindsay gains national attention as an advocate for urban minorities as Vice-Chairman of the National Advisory Commission on Civil Disorders.

1968

Ocean Hill school district decentralization controversy: in the fall, the teachers strike over the firing of individual teachers by the Ocean Hill board. The controversy inflames relations between blacks and Jews, with a major and continuing impact on city politics.

In an accidental breakdown of negotiations, the sanitation workers go on strike; Lindsay reacts sharply and the conflict escalates. Eventually, Lindsay asks Governor Rockefeller to call out the National Guard; Rockefeller refuses and sides with the union, making the rift between the mayor and governor open.

February 1969

A heavy and unexpected Sunday snow blankets the northeast and catches the city government unprepared. Much of Queens is snowbound for days. Both Lindsay and the Sanitation Department are blamed and the incident is taken to show how the city government is indifferent to the needs of ordinary middle-class neighborhoods, while favoring the ghettos.

November 1969

Lindsay reelected mayor as Liberal party nominee, after losing the Republican primary. After the 1968 strikes, Lindsay set about repairing relations with the municipal unions and, by the election, received the endorsement of key unions, including the sanitation workers.

Fall 1969

The nation goes into an economic recession after eight years of prosperity, and the city's economy goes into a decline that does not end until 1977.

| 1970 | In response to a *New York Times* expose of major and wide-spread corruption in the Police Department, Lindsay appoints an investigating commission. Numerous indictments and reforms result. |

1970–75   City expenditures continue to climb steeply, despite the economic decline, in response to inflation, generous labor contract settlements, rising welfare rolls, and court decisions. Federal and state aid increases and there are city tax increases, but large deficits occur in most years, lightly disguised by various "gimmicks" authorized by the state legislature.

August 1971   Lindsay converts from Republican to Democrat and early the next year enters the race for the Democratic nomination for president, as "the candidate of the cities." After doing poorly in the early primaries, he withdraws.

1971–72   The city's program of placing small public housing projects on scattered sites outside the ghetto areas erupts in controversy in Forest Hills, an affluent community in Queens. Mario Cuomo, a Queens lawyer, adroitly negotiates a compromise and gains public prominence.

November 1973   Voters return to the Democratic fold as City Comptroller Abraham Beame is elected mayor.

1974–76   The years of the great fiscal crisis. The city has huge operating budget deficits and increasing short-term debt. There is increasing difficulty in selling city notes after the fall of 1974, and by the spring, the city has no access to the credit markets. The state government in a series of steps takes control of the city's finances, establishing the Municipal Assistance Corporation to borrow money on behalf of the city and the Emergency Financial Control Board to supervise the city's budget. There are large cutbacks in city staffing, deferment of scheduled pay increases, and many types of service reductions. By late 1976, the worst of the cutbacks have occurred and the city's finances have stabilized. Some city functions are assumed by the state government.

July 1977

A power failure in Westchester causes another citywide blackout, continuing longer than the 1965 blackout. In contrast to 1965, this time there is much looting and little action to stop it. The blackout comes to symbolize both the ineffectiveness of the city administration and the poor state of race relations.

November 1977

U.S. Representative Edward I. Koch is elected mayor, after a Democratic primary in which the incumbent mayor does poorly, and a runoff and general election in which Koch defeats Mario Cuomo, then a member of Governor Carey's cabinet.

1978–81

Assisted by a strong economic recovery and under the close scrutiny of state monitoring agencies, the Koch administration achieves a balanced budget ahead of schedule and begins to restore city services. An office construction boom, that continues until 1990, begins in Manhattan.

1981

Koch is reelected mayor by a huge majority, with both the Democratic and Republican party nominations.

1982–85

The local economy is booming, with the boom extending beyond Manhattan to the other boroughs, encouraged by tax abatements and other municipal incentives. The city's budget has a surplus. City services are enhanced. The city begins ambitious efforts to rebuild its infrastructure and launches a major housing development program.

1985

Koch is reelected mayor by a wide margin.

1986–88

The city budget continues to show surpluses, despite substantial increases in city outlays for infrastructure, housing, schools, and pressing social problems. In 1987, the city's bond rating is increased to its highest level since 1975. In June 1987, the report of the New York City Commission on the Year 2000 (the commission was appointed by Koch and chaired by Robert F. Wagner, Jr.), *New York Ascendant*, is released, an optimistic view of the future of the city that sees its problems as soluble, even with limited resources.

1986–89   The city government is rocked by a series of scandals in-
               volving party leaders and elected officials in Queens, the
               Bronx and Brooklyn. Racial and ethnic tensions grow, with
               a variety of incidents and criminal trials—Howard Beach,
               Bernhard Goetz, Bensonhurst. The problems of homeless-
               ness, poverty, drugs, and AIDS, common to other large
               American cities, appear to overwhelm New York, despite
               the continuing economic prosperity.

1989   Economic growth in the city appears to have stopped and
               large budget gaps are in prospect as the mayoral election
               approaches. By the end of the year, budget retrenchment
               has begun.

November 1989 David Dinkins is elected mayor.

Index

1966 Transit Workers Strike and, 350
readership of, 348–49
New York Herald Tribune, 33, 74
"City in Crisis" series in, 340, 344–46
financial troubles of, 344
merger of, 347–48
New York Journal American, 347
New York Mirror, 347
New York Newsday, 342, 343, 352, 355
New York Observer, 342
New York Post, 74, 341–43, 348–50, 354, 355
Koch and, 354
municipal coverage of, 355
readership of, 348–49
New York Sierra Club, 25*n. 14*
New York State. *See* State government, New York
New York Times, 239–40, 330, 341–44, 346–55
decline in circulation of, 350–51
fiscal crisis and, 45, 352–53
focus of, 348, 351–53
Koch and, 354
management of, 347
municipal coverage of, 351–52, 355
profitability of, 343–44
New York Urban Coalition, 151
New York World Journal Tribune, 347–48
New York World Telegram, 347
NIMBY (not in my backyard) phenomenon, 75–76, 181–83, 217, 425
Nixon, Richard, 246, 254
Nova Institute, 170

OCB. *See* Office of Collective Bargaining
OCBR. *See* Office of Community Board Relations
O'Connor, Frank, 95, 102
O'Dwyer, Paul, 83*n. 5*, 102, 239
OED. *See* Office of Economic Development
Office building construction, 39, 318
Office of Collective Bargaining (OCB), 118–19
Office of Community Board Relations (OCBR), 170
Office of Economic Development (OED), 262
Office of Economic Opportunity, 248

Office of Immigrant Affairs, 396
Office of Legislative Oversight and Analysis, 98
Office of Management and Budget (OMB), 129, 169–70
Office of Municipal Labor Relations (OMLR), 119
Office of Neighborhood Government (ONG), 144, 160–64, 167, 181
Beame and, 163–65, 167
city agencies and, 163, 166
district managers and, 168
Ohrenstein, Manfred, 224
Oil crisis, 40
Oliver, Dick, 350
OMB. *See* Office of Management and Budget
OMLR. *See* Office of Municipal Labor Relations
110 Livingston Street (Rogers), 155, 181
ONG. *See* Office of Neighborhood Government
Oreskes, Michael, 355
Oversight powers, 95–98, 103–4
Owens, Major, 265*n. 7*

Paine, Piera, 33, 45
Parks, Department of, 118, 120
Party system, 18, 20. *See also specific parties*
blacks and, 290–91, 361–62, 378
boss and machine, 272–78, 283–86
Cuomo and, 282–83
decline of, 271–94
G.I. Bill and, 293, 295*n. 17*
Great Depression and, 277–78
media and, 75, 76, 78, 80–81, 286–90
primary system and, 294
scandals and, 283–86
decline in voter participation and, 293–94
elites and, 12
functions of, 273–76, 286
fusion, 356*n. 5*
fusion candidacies and, 75–78
heyday of, 272–73
immigrants and, 273–76
Latinos and, 291–92
mayor and, 63, 64, 75–76
minority parties and, 275
1989 mayoral election and, 286
no-party system, 290–93

Contributors

JEWEL BELLUSH is Professor Emeritus of Political Science at Hunter College of the City University of New York. She is the former staff director for the Commission on State/City Relations under Mayor John Lindsay of New York and is coauthor of *Union Power and New York: Victor Gotbaum and District Council 37* and *Race and Politics in New York City.*

GERALD BENJAMIN is Professor of Political Science at the State University of New York at New Paltz and Majority Leader of the Ulster County Legislature. He is author or editor of many books on New York politics, most recently (with Charles Brecher) *The Two New Yorks.*

BLANCHE BLANK is Professor of Political Science at Yeshiva University and a member of the Commission for the Higher Education of the Middle States Association of Colleges. She served as director of Mayor John Lindsay's Task Force on Personnel for the city of New York in 1966 and is author of *American Government and Politics*; *Political Clubs in New York* (in collaboration); and articles on local politics and public administration in the *Nation*, *New York Affairs*, *Journal of Comparative Administration*, and other periodicals. She is currently at work on a study of the federal grand jury system.

EDWIN DIAMOND is Professor of Journalism at New York University and has written many books on the media. His most recent book, now in the second edition, is *The Spot: The Rise of Political Advertising on Television*, published by The MIT Press. He is the media columnist for *New York Magazine* and is currently working on a book on New York City newspapers, to be published by Doubleday and Company.

DAVID R. EICHENTHAL is a graduate of the University of Chicago and New York University School of Law. In 1989, he was a candidate for the Democratic nomination for a city council seat in Brooklyn. He currently serves as New York City Comptroller Elizabeth Holtzman's representative to the Board of Estimate.

CHARLES V. HAMILTON is Wallace S. Sayre Professor of Government at Columbia University. He is author of *The Black Experience in American Politics, The Bench and the Ballot,* and other books and articles on race and urban politics. His current research involves social policies of civil rights organizations.

SHIRLEY JENKINS is Professor Emeritus at Columbia University, Research Scholar at its School of Social Work, and Director of the Center for the Study of Social Work Practice. She has done research at the United Nations; Community Council of Greater New York; Graduate Center of the City University of New York; and Baerwald School of Social Work, Hebrew University, Jerusalem. Her publications include over fifty articles and chapters and ten books, most recently *The Ethnic Dilemma in Social Services* and *Ethnicity and the Welfare State.*

DICK NETZER is Senior Fellow at the New York University Urban Research Center and Professor of Economics and Public Administration at the university's Robert F. Wagner Graduate School of Public Service. He is a former dean of the school and was the founding director of the Urban Research Center. He has been a member of the board of directors of the Municipal Assistance Corporation since the onset of the New York City fiscal crisis. For more than thirty years he has written and advised on the finances of New York City and State and on the region's economy.

PIERA PAINE collaborated with Professor Edwin Diamond on their chapter while she was a graduate student in the Department of Journalism at New York University. She is now a graduate of that program.

DAVID ROGERS is Professor of Management and Sociology at the Stern School of Business at New York University. He has done many studies on managing the politics of change in big cities. His books include *110 Livingston Street, The Management of Big Cities, Improving the Quality of Urban Management* (edited with Willis Hawley), *Can Business Management Save the Cities,* and *110 Livingston Street Revisited* (with Norman Chung). He is now completing a book on how four big New York City banks are repositioning themselves in the context of major changes in the environment of financial services.

H. V. SAVITCH is Professor at the School of Urban Policy, College of Urban and Public Affairs, University of Louisville. He has written for a number of professional journals and has authored *Urban Policy and the Exterior City* and recently completed *Post Industrial Cities.* Professor Savitch served as a consultant for David Dinkins, who is now mayor of the city of New York.

JOSEPH P. VITERITTI is Senior Research Scientist and Associate Research Professor at New York University's Robert F. Wagner Graduate School of Public Service. He is the author of three books and more than forty articles and professional papers on urban government. He has directed several blue-ribbon panels on government operations and served as a consultant to numerous city agencies and task forces including the recent Charter Revision Commission.

RICHARD C. WADE is Distinguished Professor of Urban History at the Graduate Center, City University of New York. He is the author of *The Urban Frontier*, *Slavery in the Cities*, and other books on American cities. He was also a consultant to the McGovern Commission on the Reform of the Democratic Party in 1968–1969 and a Commissioner of Housing in Chicago during 1969–1971.

ANNMARIE HAUCK WALSH is Luther Gulick Scholar in Residence at the Institute of Public Administration, where she was president during 1982–1988. She has been a consultant to the New York City Mayor's Office on contracting, a member of the Capital Task Force for the New York City School Board, and consultant to numerous government agencies in the United States and abroad. Dr. Walsh is author of *The Public's Business: The Politics and Practices of Government Corporations*, and other books and articles in comparative government and public management. She has been named the first Belle Zeller Distinguished Visiting Professor in Public Policy and Administration at Brooklyn College.